English Literature for Boys and Girls

ENGLISH LITERATURE
FOR BOYS AND GIRLS

NOTE

THE lists of books given at the end of some chapters do not claim to be either final or complete, but are the best for the purpose, obtainable at a moderate price, which have come under the writer's notice, and it is hoped that they may be of some little assistance to those who choose books for young readers to read in connection with the *Literature*. Where several editions of one book are given, the most simple version is always placed first. Occasionally where no good simplified version is obtainable an ordinary inexpensive edition is mentioned.

ENGLISH LITERATURE
FOR BOYS AND GIRLS

BY H. E. MARSHALL

AUTHOR OF "AN ISLAND STORY," "SCOTLAND'S
STORY," "AN EMPIRE STORY"

Illustrated with 20 Drawings in Color

BY JOHN R. SKELTON

NEW YORK
FREDERICK A. STOKES COMPANY
PUBLISHERS

TO

ELIZABETH DOROTHEA PRIAULX TAUDEVIN

HELEN GERTRUDE BAKER

AND

JOHN RAYMOND KEEN

TO BOYS AND GIRLS—AN APOLOGY

DEAR BOYS AND GIRLS,—This is not the book you asked for—it is not the book that any of you have asked for, and I hope that you will not be very much disappointed. But in case you should be I will tell you how this book came to be written, and that may make you feel less disappointed.

Long, long ago I said, "If ever I have two brass farthings to rub one against the other I know what I shall do—I shall write an English Literature for Boys and Girls." But the days and months and years went on, and I never saw even one brass farthing. I wonder if ever any one did. Did you?

Still I kept the hope and kept the wish ready. And at last one day a Magician came. I can't stop to tell you what he was like, but he wasn't a bit like any Magician I ever read about. He put two golden pennies into my hand and said in a very solemn voice, "Rub them one against the other and the first wish you wish shall be granted to you. Be careful. Remember, only one wish. So choose with thought." Then he vanished. But of course I could not choose with thought, for the wish I had kept ready all the time just slipped off my tongue, and as I rubbed my golden pennies together I said quickly, "I wish to write an English Literature for Boys and Girls."

So I had my wish and have done my part. It is for you to do the rest. You know in fairy tales when people get their wishes they often find that instead of

being made happy they are made unhappy by the fulfillment. But if you like my book, then I can truly say that
my wish has brought only happiness in its fulfillment. And
if you like my book, which is now yours, and if you say
so, and if your kind Fathers and Mothers and Uncles and
Aunts buy it for you, who knows but one day the Magician
will come again with two more golden pennies, and let me
wish another wish. Then I shall wish to write the history
of —— the country you asked for. Meantime I am, as
always, your slave and friend,

H. E. MARSHALL.

OXFORD, 1909.

TO "THE OLYMPIANS"—AN EXPLANATION

THIS preface, let me begin by stating, is not meant for my proper audience of Boys and Girls, but for the "Olympians," those semi-fairy godmothers and godfathers whose purses ought to be bottomless as their kindness is limitless. Having thus freed my pen let me proceed with my preface, in the happy consciousness that I may with impunity use five-syllabled words should I so desire.

My preface is an explanation, and an apology. For every one who writes a literature for young people begins with an apology for writing it, and with an explanation of why they wrote it. We explain that in spite of the many excellent literatures published none exactly suits our purpose and, while apologizing for adding to the number, we proceed to write one to please ourselves. My position is the same as that of all those who have gone before me, and I have no more original explanation to offer for adding yet another Literature to the many already published.

None of the Literatures which it has been my fortune to come across suits my purpose, for they are all written for use in schools, while my desire has been to produce a book which a boy or girl will read, not as a task, but as a pleasure. It is my belief that this is the first attempt of the kind that has been made, and whether I have succeeded or failed my young readers must decide.

The object with which I write being to amuse and interest rather than to teach, a great deal has been left out which must of necessity have been included in a book meant for school use. No attempt has been made to include even all the great names. Such an attempt could result, in the space at my disposal, in little more than a catalogue of names and dates. A selection therefore has been made of the most representative writers in the various periods treated, and any one who loves our literature will at once realize how difficult such selection was. I have chosen for the most part those men and works which seemed best to illustrate the widening and deepening of our literature, but occasionally I have chosen to tell of some work chiefly because of its appeal to young people, while others for obvious reasons have been passed over in silence. In treating of a great man it is not always his greatest work that I have emphasized, but rather that which most easily comes within the grasp of young minds. I have of set purpose treated the early portions of our literature at much greater length than is usual, it being my belief that what was attractive to a youthful nation will be most attractive to the young of that nation. Lastly, I have, especially in the earlier portions, tried to keep literature in touch with history, and to show how the political development of our country influenced, and in its turn was influenced by, the literary development.

In writing such a book my indebtedness to those who have gone before me is extreme, but to make acknowledgments to all who have helped me to produce it would be wellnigh impossible, for it would be to catalogue the reading of a lifetime. The list would make a brave show; too brave a show for such a small result. The great among the dead I trust know my gratitude. Should the great among the living chance to cast an eye upon my poor book, I pray them to take it as an evidence equally of my indebtedness and my gratitude. My direct borrowings I have never failed, I hope, to acknowledge throughout the text by quotation marks and notes. While expressing my gratitude to others I must add one word of thanks to Mr. J. R. Skelton, whose excellent portrait-pictures have helped not a little to illuminate the text and lighten the task of explanation.

In concluding, it seems to me I can do little better than add to my already frequent borrowings by quoting a few lines from John Colet, that stern-seeming but tender-hearted man who, four hundred years ago, wrought so much for young folks, and tried to smooth for them the thorny path of learning.

"I have made this lytle boke, not thynkynge that I coude say ony thynge beter than hath be sayd before, but I toke this besynes, hauynge grete pleasure to shewe the testymony of my good mynde onto the schole. In whiche lytel warke yf ony newe thynges be of me, it is alonely that I have put these partes in a more clere ordre, and have made them a lytel more easy to yonge wyttes than (me thynketh) they were before. Judgying that no thynghe may be to softe nor to famlyer for lytel chyldren, specyally lernynge a tongue onto them al straunge. In whiche lytel boke I have lefte many thynges out of purpose, consyderyng the tendernes and small capacyte of lytel myndes. . . . I praye God all may be to his honour, and to the erudicyon and profyt of chyldren my countre men, Londoners especyally, whome dygestynge this lytel warke I had alwaye before myn eyen, consyderynge more what was for them than to shewe ony grete connyge, wyllyng to speke the thynges often before spoken in suche maner as gladli yonge begynners and tender wyttes myght take and conceyve. Wherefore I praye you, al lytel babys, al lytel chyldren, lerne gladly this lytel treatyse, and commende it dylygently onto your memoryes. Trusting of this begynnynge that ye shal procede and growe to parfyt literature, and come at the last to be gret clarkes. And lyfte up your lytel whyte handes for me, whiche prayeth for you to God. To Whom be al honour and imperyal maieste and glory. Amen."

H. E. MARSHALL.

OXFORD, 1909.

CONTENTS

CONTENTS

LIST OF ILLUSTRATIONS

ENGLISH LITERATURE
FOR BOYS AND GIRLS

CHAPTER I

IN THE LISTENING TIME

Has there ever been a time when no stories were told? Has there ever been a people who did not care to listen? I think not.

When we were little, before we could read for ourselves, did we not gather eagerly round father or mother, friend or nurse, at the promise of a story? When we grew older, what happy hours did we not spend with our books. How the printed words made us forget the world in which we live, and carried us away to a wonderland,

> "Where waters gushed and fruit trees grew
> And flowers put forth a fairer hue,
> And everything was strange and new;
> The sparrows were brighter than peacocks here,
> And their dogs outran our fallow deer,
> And honey bees had lost their stings,
> And horses were born with eagles' wings." [1]

And as it is with us, so it is with a nation, with a people.

In the dim, far-off times when our forefathers were wild, naked savages, they had no books. Like ourselves, when we were tiny, they could neither read nor write. But do you think that they had no stories? Oh, yes! We may be sure that when the day's work was done, when the fight

[1] Robert Browning.

or the chase was over, they gathered round the wood fire and listened to the tales of the story-teller.

These stories were all of war. They told of terrible combats with men or with fierce strange beasts, they told of passion, of revenge. In them there was no beauty, no tenderness, no love. For the life of man in those far-off days was wild and rough; it was one long struggle against foes, a struggle which left little room for what was beautiful or tender.

But as time went on, as life became more easy, in one way or another the savage learned to become less savage. Then as he changed, the tales he listened to changed too. They were no longer all of war, of revenge; they told of love also. And later, when the story of Christ had come to soften men's hearts and brighten men's lives, the stories told of faith and purity and gentleness.

At last a time came when minstrels wandered from town to town, from castle to castle, singing their lays. And the minstrel who had a good tale to tell was ever sure of a welcome, and for his pains he was rewarded with money, jewels, and even land. That was the true listening time of the world.

It was no easy thing to be a minstrel, and a man often spent ten or twelve years in learning to be one. There were certain tales which all minstrels had to know, and the best among them could tell three hundred and fifty. Of these stories the minstrels used to learn only the outline, and each told the story in his own way, filling it in according to his own fancy. So as time went on these well-known tales came to be told in many different ways, changing as the times changed.

At length, after many years had passed, men began to write down these tales, so that they might not be forgotten. These first books we call Manuscripts, from the Latin words *manus,* a hand, and *scribere,* to write, for they were all written by hand. Even after they were written down there were many changes made in the tales, for those who wrote or copied them would sometimes miss lines or alter others. Yet they were less changed than they had been when told only by word of mouth.

These stories then form the beginnings of what is called our Literature. Literature really means letters, for it comes from a Latin word *littera,* meaning a letter of the alphabet. Words are made by letters of the alphabet being set together, and our literature again by words being set together; hence the name.

As on and on time went, every year more stories were told and sung and written down. The first stories which our forefathers told in the days long, long ago, and which were never written down, are lost forever. Even many of those stories which were written are lost too, but a few still remain, and from them we can learn much of the life and the history of the people who lived in our land ten and twelve hundred years ago, or more.

For a long time books were all written by hand. They were very scarce and dear, and only the wealthy could afford to have them, and few could read them. Even great knights and nobles could not read, for they spent all their time in fighting and hunting, and had little time in which to learn. So it came about that the monks who lived a quiet and peaceful life became the learned men. In the monasteries it was that books were written and copied. There too they were kept, and the monasteries became not only the schools, but the libraries of the country.

As a nation grows and changes, its literature grows and changes with it. At first it asks only for stories, then it asks for history for its own sake, and for poetry for its own sake; history, I mean, for the knowledge it gives us of the past; poetry for joy in the beautiful words, and not merely for the stories they tell. Then, as a nation's needs and knowledge grow, it demands ever more and more books on all kinds of subjects.

And we ourselves grow and change just as a nation does. When we are very young, there are many books which seem to us dull and stupid. But as we grow older and learn more, we begin to like more and more kinds of books. We may still love the stories that we loved as children, but we love others too. And at last, perhaps, there comes a time when those books which seemed to us most dull and stupid delight us most.

At first, too, we care only for the story itself. We do not mind very much in what words it is told so long as it is a story. But later we begin to care very much indeed what words the story-teller uses, and how he uses them. It is only, perhaps, when we have learned to hear with our eyes that we know the true joy of books. Yes, hear with our eyes, for it is joy in the sound of the words that makes our breath come fast, which brings smiles to our lips or tears to our eyes. Yet we do not need to read the words aloud, the sight of the black letters on the white page is enough.

In this book I am going to tell you about a few of our greatest story-tellers and their books. Many of these books you will not care to read for yourselves for a long time to come. You must be content to be told about them. You must be content to know that there are rooms in the fairy palace of our Literature into which you cannot enter yet. But every year, as your knowledge grows, you will find that new keys have been put into your hands with which you may unlock the doors which are now closed. And with every door that you unlock, you will become aware of others and still others that are yet shut fast, until at last you learn, with something of pain, that the great palace of our Literature is so vast that you can never hope to open all the doors even to peep inside.

CHAPTER II

THE STORY OF THE CATTLE RAID OF COOLEY

OUR earliest literature was history and poetry. Indeed, we might say poetry only, for in those far-off times history was always poetry, it being only through the songs of the bards and minstrels that history was known. And when I say history I do not mean history as we know it. It was then merely the gallant tale of some hero's deeds listened to because it was a gallant tale.

Now the people who lived in the British Isles long ago were not English. It will be simplest for us to call them all Celts and to divide them into two families, the Gaels and the Cymry. The Gaels lived in Ireland and in Scotland, and the Cymry in England and Wales.

It is to Ireland that we must go for the very beginnings of our Literature, for the Roman conquest did not touch Ireland, and the English, who later conquered and took possession of Britain, hardly troubled the Green Isle. So for centuries the Gaels of Ireland told their tales and handed them on from father to son undisturbed, and in Ireland a great many old writings have been kept which tell of far-off times. These old Irish manuscripts are perhaps none of them older than the eleventh century, but the stories are far, far older. They were, we may believe, passed on by word of mouth for many generations before they were written down, and they have kept the feeling of those far-off times.

It was from Ireland that the Scots came to Scotland, and when they came they brought with them many tales. So it comes about that in old Scottish and in old Irish manuscripts we find the same stories.

Many of the manuscripts which are kept in Ireland have never been translated out of the old Irish in which they were written, so they are closed books to all but a few scholars, and we need not talk about them. But of one of the great treasures of old Irish literature we will talk. This is the *Leabhar Na h-Uidhre,* or *Book of the Dun Cow.* It is called so because the stories in it were first written down by St. Ciaran in a book made from the skin of a favorite cow of a dun color. That book has long been lost, and this copy of it was made in the eleventh century.

The name of this old book helps us to remember that long ago there was no paper, and that books were written on vellum made from calf-skin and upon parchment made from sheep-skin. It was not until the twelfth century that paper began to be made in some parts of Europe, and it was not until the fifteenth century that paper books became common in England.

In the *Book of the Dun Cow,* and in another old book called the *Book of Leinster,* there is written the great Irish legend called the *Tain Bo Chuailgne* or the *Cattle Raid of Cooley.*

This is a very old tale of the time soon after the birth of Christ. In the book we are told how this story had been written down long, long ago in a book called the *Great Book Written on Skins.* But a learned man carried away that book to the East. Then, when many years had passed, people began to forget the story of the Cattle Raid. So the chief minstrel called all the other minstrels together to ask if any of them knew the tale. But none of them could remember more than a few verses of it. Therefore the chief minstrel asked all his pupils to travel into far countries to search for the rest which was lost.

What followed is told differently in different books, but all agree in this, that a great chief called Fergus came back from the dead in order to tell the tale, which was again written down.

The story is one of the beautiful Queen Meav of Connaught. For many years she had lived happily with her husband and her children. But one day the Queen and her husband began to argue as to which of them was the richer. As they could not agree, they ordered all their treasures to be brought before them that they might be compared.

So first all their wooden and metal vessels were brought. But they were both alike.

Then all their jewels, their rings and bracelets, necklets and crowns were brought, but they, too, were equal.

Then all their robes were brought, crimson and blue, green, yellow, checked and striped, black and white. They, too, were equal.

Next from the fields and pastures great herds of sheep were brought. They, too, were equal.

Then from the green plains fleet horses, champing steeds came. Great herds of swine from forest and glen were brought. They, too, were equal.

Lastly, droves and droves of cattle were brought. In the King's herd there was a young bull named Whitehorned. When a calf, he had belonged to Meav's herd, but being very proud, and thinking it little honor to be under the rule of a woman, he had left Meav's herd and joined himself to the King's. This bull was very beautiful. His head and horns and hoofs were white, and all the rest of him was red. He was so great and splendid that in all the Queen's herd there was none to match him.

Then Meav's sorrow was bitter, and calling a messenger, she asked if he knew where might be found a young bull to match with White-horned.

The messenger replied that he knew of a much finer bull called Donn Chuailgne, or Brown Bull of Cooley, which belonged to Dawra, the chief of Ulster.

"Go, then," said Meav, "and ask Dawra to lend me the Bull for a year. Tell him that he shall be well repaid, that he shall receive fifty heifers and Brown Bull back again at the end of that time. And if Dawra should seem unwilling to lend Brown Bull, tell him that he may come with it himself, and that he shall receive here land equal to his own, a chariot worth thirty-six cows, and he shall have my friendship ever after."

So taking with him nine others, the messenger set out and soon arrived at Cooley. And when Dawra heard why the messengers had come, he received them kindly, and said at once that they should have Brown Bull.

Then the messengers began to speak and boast among themselves. "It was well," said one, "that Dawra granted us the Bull willingly, otherwise we had taken it by force."

As he spoke, a servant of Dawra came with food and drink for the strangers, and hearing how they spoke among themselves, he hastily and in wrath dashed the food upon the table, and returning to his master repeated to him the words of the messenger.

Then was Dawra very wrathful. And when, in the morning, the messengers came before him asking that he should fulfill his promise, he refused them.

So, empty-handed, the messengers returned to Queen Meav. And she, full of anger, decided to make good the boastful words of her messenger and take Brown Bull by force.

Then began a mighty war between the men of Ulster and the men of Connaught. And after many fights there was a great battle in which Meav was defeated. Yet was she triumphant, for she had gained possession of the Brown Bull.

But the Queen had little cause for triumph, for when Brown Bull and White-horned met there was a fearful combat between them. The whole land echoed with their bellowing. The earth shook beneath their feet and the sky grew dark with flying sods of earth and with flecks of foam. After long fighting Brown Bull conquered, and goring White-horned to death, ran off with him impaled upon his horns, shaking his shattered body to pieces as he ran.

But Brown Bull, too, was wounded to death. Mad with pain and wounds, he turned to his own land, and there

> "He lay down
> Against the hill, and his great heart broke there,
> And sent a stream of blood down all the slope,
> And thus, when all the war and Tain had ended,
> In his own land, 'midst his own hills, he died." [1]

The Cattle Raid of Cooley is a strange wild tale, yet from it we can learn a great deal about the life of these old, far-away times. We can learn from it something of what the people did and thought, and how they lived, and even of what they wore. Here is a description of a driver and his war chariot, translated, of course, into English prose. "It is then that the charioteer arose, and he put on his hero's dress of charioteering. This was the hero's dress of charioteering that he put on: his soft tunic of skin, light and airy, well tanned, made of skin, sewn, of deer skin, so that it did not restrain the movement of his hands outside. He put on his black upper cloak over it outside. . . . The charioteer took first then his helm, ridged like a board, four-cornered. . . . This was well measured to him, and it was not an over weight. His hand

[1] *The Tain*, by Mary A. Hutton.

brought the circlet of red-yellow, as though it were a plate of red gold, of refined gold smelted over the edge of the anvil, to his brow as a sign of his charioteering, as a distinction to his master.

"He took the goads to his horses, and his whip inlaid in his right hand. He took the reins to hold back his horses in his left hand. Then he put the iron inlaid breast-plate on his horses, so that they were covered from forehead to fore-foot with spears, and points, and lances, and hard points, so that every motion in this chariot was war-near, so that every corner, and every point, and every end, and every front of this chariot was a way of tearing." [1]

We can almost see that wild charioteer and his horses, sheathed in bristling armor with "every front a way of tearing," as they dash amid the foe. And all through we come on lines like these full of color and detail, which tell us of the life of those folk of long ago.

[1] *The Cattle Raid of Cualngé,* by L W. Faraday.

CHAPTER III

ONE OF THE SORROWS OF STORY-TELLING

The Tain gives us vivid pictures of people and things, but it is not full of beauty and of tender imagination like many of the Gaelic stories. Among the most beautiful and best known of these are perhaps the *Three Sorrows of Story-Telling*. These three stories are called: *The Tragedy of the Children of Lir; The Tragedy of the Children of Tuireann;* and *Deirdre and the Sons of Usnach*. Of the three the last is perhaps the most interesting, because the story happened partly in Scotland and partly in Ireland, and it is found both in old Irish and in old Scottish manuscripts.

The story is told in many old books, and in many ways both in prose and in verse. The oldest and shortest version is in the *Book of Leinster,* the same book in which is found *The Tain.*

The tale goes that one day King Conor and his nobles feasted at the house of Felim, his chief story-teller. And while they feasted a daughter was born to Felim the story-teller. Then Cathbad the Druid, who was also at the feast, became exceeding sad. He foretold that great sorrow and evil should come upon the land because of this child, and so he called her Deirdre, which means trouble or alarm.

When the nobles heard that, they wished to slay the new-born babe. But Conor spoke.

"Let it not be so done," he said. "It were an ill thing

11

to shed the blood of an innocent child. I myself shall care for her. She shall be housed in a safe place so that none may come nigh to her, and when she is grown she shall be my one true wife."

So it was done as King Conor said. Deirdre was placed in a safe and lonely castle, where she was seen of none save her tutor and her nurse, Lavarcam. There, as the years passed, she grew tall and fair as a slender lily, and more beautiful than sunshine.

Now when fourteen years had passed, it happened one snowy day that Deirdre's tutor killed a calf to provide food for their little company. And as the calf's blood was spilled upon the snow, a raven came to drink of it. When Deirdre saw that, she sighed and said, "Would that I had a husband whose hair was as the color of the raven, his cheeks as blood, and his skin as snow."

"There is such an one," said Lavarcam, "he is Naisi the son of Usnach."

After that there was no rest for Deirdre until she had seen Naisi. And when they met they loved each other, so that Naisi took her and fled with her to Scotland far from Conor the King. For they knew that when the King learned that fair Deirdre had been stolen from him, he would be exceeding wrathful.

There, in Scotland, Deirdre and Naisi lived for many years happily. With them were Ainle and Ardan, Naisi's two brothers, who also loved their sister Deirdre well.

But Conor never forgot his anger at the escape of Deirdre. He longed still to have her as his Queen, and at last he sent a messenger to lure the fair lady and the three brave brothers back to Ireland.

"Naisi and Deirdre were seated together one day, and between them Conor's chess board, they playing upon it.

"Naisi heard a cry and said, 'I hear the call of a man of Erin.'

" 'That was not the call of a man of Erin,' says Deirdre, 'but the call of a man of Alba.'

"Deirdre knew the first cry of Fergus, but she concealed it. Fergus uttered the second cry.

" 'That is the cry of a man of Erin,' says Naisi.

" 'It is not indeed,' says Deirdre, 'and let us play on.'

"Fergus sent forth the third cry, and the sons of Usnach knew it was Fergus that sent forth the cry. And Naisi ordered Ardan to go to meet Fergus. Then Deirdre declared she knew the first call sent forth by Fergus.

" 'Why didst thou conceal it, then, my Queen?' says Naisi.

" 'A vision I saw last night,' says Deirdre, 'namely that three birds came unto us having three sups of honey in their beaks, and that they left them with us, and that they took three sups of our blood with them.'

" 'What determination hast thou of that, O Princess?' says Naisi.

" 'It is,' says Deirdre, 'that Fergus comes unto us with a message of peace from Conor, for more sweet is not honey than the message of peace of the false man.'

" 'Let that be,' says Naisi. 'Fergus is long in the port; and go, Ardan, to meet him and bring him with thee.' " [1]

And when Fergus came there were kindly greetings between the friends who had been long parted. Then Fergus told the three brothers that Conor had forgiven them, and that he longed to see them back again in the land of Erin.

So although the heart of Deirdre was sad and heavy with foreboding of evil, they set sail for the land of Erin.

[1] Theophilus O'Flanagan

But Deirdre looked behind her as the shore faded from sight and sang a mournful song:—

> "O eastern land I leave, I loved you well,
> Home of my heart, I loved and love you well,
> I ne'er had left you had not Naisi left." [1]

And so they fared on their journey and came at last to Conor's palace. And the story tells how the boding sorrow that Deirdre felt fulfilled itself, and how they were betrayed, and how the brothers fought and died, and how Deirdre mourned until

> "Her heart-strings snapt,
> And death had overmastered her. She fell
> Into the grave where Naisi lay and slept.
> There at his side the child of Felim fell,
> The fair-haired daughter of a hundred smiles
> Men piled their grave and reared their stone on high,
> And wrote their names in Ogham [2] So they lay
> All four united in the dream of death " [3]

Such in a few words is the story of Deirdre. But you must read the tale itself to find out how beautiful it is. That you can easily do, for it has been translated many times out of the old Gaelic in which it was first written, and it has been told so simply that even those of you who are quite young can read it for yourselves.

In both *The Tain* and in *Deirdre* we find the love of fighting, the brave joy of the strong man when he finds a gallant foe. *The Tain* is such history as those far-off times afforded, but it is history touched with fancy, wrought with poetry. In the *Three Sorrows* we have Romance. They are what we might call the novels of the time. It is in stories like these that we find the keen sense of what is beautiful in nature, the sense of "man's brotherhood with bird and beast, star and flower," which has become the

[1] Douglas Hyde   [2] Ancient Gaelic writing   [3] Douglas Hyde

mark of "Celtic" literature. We cannot put it into words, perhaps, for it is something mystic and strange, something that takes us nearer fairyland and makes us see that land of dreams with clearer eyes.

BOOKS TO READ

The Celtic Wonder World, by C L Thomson   *The Enchanted Land* (for version of *Deirdre*), by L Chisholm. *Three Sorrows* (verse), by Douglas Hyde.

CHAPTER IV

THE STORY OF A LITERARY LIE

WHO wrote the stories which are found in the old Gaelic manuscripts we do not know, yet the names of some of the old Gaelic poets have come down to us. The best known of all is perhaps that of Ossian. But as Ossian, if he ever lived, lived in the third century, as it is not probable that his poems were written down at the time, and as the oldest books that we have containing any of his poetry were written in the twelfth century, it is very difficult to be sure that he really made the poems called by his name.

Ossian was a warrior and chief as well as a poet, and as a poet he is claimed both by Scotland and by Ireland. But perhaps his name has become more nearly linked to Scotland because of the story that I am going to tell you now. It belongs really to a time much later than that of which we have been speaking, but because it has to do with this old Gaelic poet Ossian, I think you will like to hear it now.

In a lonely Highland village more than a hundred and fifty years ago there lived a little boy called James Macpherson. His father and mother were poor farmer people, and James ran about barefooted and wild among the hills and glens. When he was about seven years old the quiet of his Highland home was broken by the sounds of war, for the Highland folk had risen in rebellion against King George II., and were fighting for Prince Charlie,

16

hoping to have a Stewart king once more. This was the rebellion called the '45, for it was fought in 1745.

Now little James watched the red coats of the southern soldiers as, with bayonets gleaming in the sun, they wound through the glens. He heard the Highland battle-cry and the clash of steel on steel, for fighting came near his home, and his own people joined the standard of the Pretender. Little James never forgot these things, and long afterwards, when he grew to be a man and wrote poetry, it was full of the sounds of battle, full, too, of love for mountain and glen and their rolling mists.

The Macphersons were poor, but they saw that their son was clever, and they determined that he should be well taught. So when he left school they sent him to college, first to Aberdeen and then to Edinburgh.

Before he was twenty James had left college and become master of the school in his own native village. He did not, however, like that very much, and soon gave it up to become tutor in a family.

By this time James Macpherson had begun to write poetry. He had also gathered together some pieces of old Gaelic poetry which he had found among the Highland folk. These he showed to some other poets and writers whom he met, and they thought them so beautiful that he published them in a book.

The book was a great success. All who read it were delighted with the poems, and said that if there was any more such poetry in the Highlands, it should be gathered together and printed before it was lost and forgotten for ever. For since the '45 the English had done everything to make the Highlanders forget their old language and customs. They were forbidden to wear the kilt or the tartan, and everything was done to make them speak English and forget Gaelic.

So now people begged Macpherson to travel through

the Highlands and gather together as much of the old poetry of the people as he could. Macpherson was at first unwilling to go. For one thing, he quite frankly owned that he was not a good Gaelic scholar. But at length he consented and set out.

For four months Macpherson wandered about the Highlands and Islands of Scotland, listening to the tales of the people and writing them down. Sometimes, too, he came across old manuscripts with ancient tales in them. When he had gathered all he could, he returned to Edinburgh and set to work to translate the stories into English.

When this new book of Gaelic poetry came out, it again was a great success. It was greeted with delight by the greatest poets of France, Germany, and Italy, and was soon translated into many languages. Macpherson was no longer a poor Highland laddie, but a man of world-wide fame. Yet it was not because of his own poetry that he was famous, but because he had found (so he said) some poems of a man who lived fifteen hundred years before, and translated them into English. And although Macpherson's book is called *The Poems of Ossian,* it is written in prose. But it is a prose which is often far more beautiful and poetical than much that is called poetry.

Although at first Macpherson's book was received with great delight, soon people began to doubt about it. The Irish first of all were jealous, for they said that Ossian was an Irish poet, that the heroes of the poems were Irish, and that Macpherson was stealing their national heroes from them.

Then in England people began to say that there never had been an Ossian at all, and that Macpherson had invented both the poems and all the people that they were about. For the English knew little of the Highlanders and their customs. Even after the '15 and the '45 people in the south knew little about the north and those who lived there. They thought of it as a land of wild mountains and glens, a land of mists and cloud, a land where wild chieftains ruled over still wilder clans, who, in their lonely valleys and sea-girt islands, were for ever warring against each other. How could such a people, they asked, a people of savages, make beautiful poetry?

Dr. Samuel Johnson, a great writer of whom we shall hear more later, was the man of his day whose opinion about books was most thought of. He hated Scotland and the Scottish folk, and did not believe that any good thing could come from them He read the poems and said that they were rubbish, such as any child could write, and that Macpherson had made them all up.

So a quarrel, which has become famous, began between the two men. And as Dr. Johnson was far better known than Macpherson, most people agreed with him and believed that Macpherson had told a "literary lie," and that he had made up all the stories.

There is no harm in making up stories. Nearly every one who writes does that. But it is wrong to make up stories and then pretend that they were written by some one else more famous than yourself.

Dr. Johnson and Macpherson were very angry with and very rude to each other. Still that did not settle the question as to who had written the stories; indeed it has never been settled. And what most men believe now is that Macpherson did really gather from among the people of the Highlands many scraps of ancient poetry and tales, but that he added to them and put them together in such a way as to make them beautiful and touching. To do even that, however, a true poet was needed, so people have, for the most part, given up arguing about whether Macpherson wrote Ossian or not, and are glad that such a beautiful book has been written by some one.

I do not think that you will want to read Ossian for

yourself for a long time to come, for the stories are not always easy to follow. They are, too, often clumsy, wandering, and badly put together. But in spite of that there is much beauty in them, and some day I hope you will read them.

In the next chapter you will find one of the stories of Ossian called Fingal. Fingal was a great warrior and the father of Ossian, and the story takes place in Ireland. It is told partly in Macpherson's words.

CHAPTER V

THE STORY OF FINGAL

"CATHULLIN sat by TURA's wall, by the tree of the rustling sound. His spear leaned against a rock. His shield lay on grass, by his side. And as he thus sat deep in thought a scout came running in all haste and cried, 'Arise! Cathullin, arise! I see the ships of the north. Many, chief of men, are the foe! Many the heroes of the sea-born Swaran!'

"Then to the scout the blue-eyed chief replied, 'Thou ever tremblest. Thy fears have increased the foe. It is Fingal King of deserts who comes with aid to green Erin of streams.'

"'Nay, I beheld their chief,' replied the scout, 'tall as a glittering rock. His spear is a blasted pine. His shield the rising moon. He bade me say to thee, "Let dark Cathullin yield."'

"'No,' replied the blue-eyed chief, 'I never yield to mortal man. Dark Cathullin shall be great or dead.'"

Then Cathullin bade the scout summon his warriors to council. And when they were gathered there was much talk, for some would give battle at once and some delay until Fingal, the King of Morven, should come to aid them. But Cathullin himself was eager to fight, so forward they marched to meet the foe. And the sound of their going was "as the rushing of a stream of foam when the thunder is traveling above, and dark-brown night sits on half the hill." To the camp of Swaran was the sound carried, so that he sent a messenger to view the foe.

21

"He went. He trembling, swift returned. His eyes rolled wildly round. His heart beat high against his side. His words were faltering, broken, slow. 'Arise, son of ocean! arise, chief of the dark brown shields! I see the dark, the mountain stream of battle. Fly, King of ocean! Fly!'

"'When did I fly?' replied the King. 'When fled Swaran from the battle of spears? When did I shrink from danger, chief of the little soul? Shall Swaran fly from a hero? Were Fingal himself before me my soul should not darken in fear. Arise, to battle my thousands! pour round me like the echoing main. Gather round the bright steel of your King, strong as the rocks of my land, that meet the storm with joy, and stretch their dark pines to the wind.'

"Like autumn's dark storms, pouring from two echoing hills, towards each other approached the heroes. Like two deep streams from high rocks meeting, mixing, roaring on the plain; loud, rough and dark in battle meet Lochlin and Innis-fail. Chief mixes his strokes with chief, and man with man; steel clanging sounds on steel. Helmets are cleft on high. Blood bursts and smokes around. Strings murmur on the polished yews. Darts rush along the sky, spears fall like the circles of light which gild the face of night. As the noise of the troubled ocean when roll the waves on high, as the last peal of thunder in heaven, such is the din of war. Though Cormac's hundred bards were there to give the fight to song, feeble was the voice of a hundred bards to send the deaths to future times. For many were the deaths of heroes; wide poured the blood of the brave."

Then above the clang and clamor of dreadful battle we hear the mournful dirge of minstrels wailing o'er the dead.

"Mourn, ye sons of song, mourn! Weep on the rocks

of roaring winds, O maid of Inistore! Bend thy fair
head over the waves, thou lovelier than the ghost of the
hills, when it moves, in a sunbeam at noon, over the
silence of Morven. He is fallen! thy youth is low! pale
beneath the sword of Cathullin. No more shall valor
raise thy love to match the blood of kings. His gray
dogs are howling at home, they see his passing ghost.
His bow is in the hall unstrung. No sound is on the hill
of his hinds."

Then once again, the louder for the mourning pause, we
hear the din of battle.

"As roll a thousand waves to the rocks, so Swaran's
host came on. As meets a rock a thousand waves, so
Erin met Swaran of spears. Death raises all his voices
around, and mixes with the sounds of shields. Each hero
is a pillar of darkness; the sword a beam of fire in his hand.
The field echoes from wing to wing, as a hundred hammers
that rise by turn, on the red son of the furnace."

But now the day is waning. To the noise and horror
of battle the mystery of darkness is added. Friend and
foe are wrapped in the dimness of twilight.

But the fight was not ended, for neither Cathullin nor
Swaran had gained the victory, and ere gray morning
broke the battle was renewed.

And in this second day's fight Swaran was the victor,
but while the battle still raged white-sailed ships appeared
upon the sea. It was Fingal who came, and Swaran had
to fight a second foe.

"Now from the gray mists of the ocean, the white-sailed
ships of Fingal appeared. High is the grove of their masts,
as they nod by turns on the rolling wave."

Swaran saw them from the hill on which he fought, and
turning from the pursuit of the men of Erin, he marched
to meet Fingal. But Cathullin, beaten and ashamed,
fled to hide himself: "bending, weeping, sad and slow, and

dragging his long spear behind, Cathullin sank in Cromla's wood, and mourned his fallen friends. He feared the face of Fingal, who was wont to greet him from the fields of renown."

But although Cathullin fled, between Fingal and Swaran battle was renewed till darkness fell. A second day dawned, and again and again the hosts closed in deadly combat until at length Fingal and Swaran met face to face.

"There was a clang of arms! their every blow like the hundred hammers of the furnace. Terrible is the battle of the kings; dreadful the look of their eyes. Their dark brown shields are cleft in twain. Their steel flies, broken from their helms.

"They fling their weapons down. Each rushes to his hero's grasp. Their sinewy arms bend round each other: they turn from side to side, and strain and stretch their large spreading limbs below. But when the pride of their strength arose they shook the hills with their heels. Rocks tumble from their places on high; the green-headed bushes are overturned. At length the strength of Swaran fell; the king of the groves is bound."

The warriors of Swaran fled then, pursued by the sons of Fingal, till the hero bade the fighting cease, and darkness once more fell over the dreadful field.

"The clouds of night come rolling down. Darkness rests on the steeps of Cromla. The stars of the north arise over the rolling of Erin's waves: they shew their heads of fire, through the flying mist of heaven. A distant wind roars in the wood. Silent and dark is the plain of death."

Then through the darkness is heard the sad song of minstrels mourning for the dead. But soon the scene changes and mourning is forgotten.

"The heroes gathered to the feast. A thousand aged oaks are burning to the wind. The souls of warriors brighten with joy. But the king of Lochlin (Swaran) is silent. Sorrow reddens in his eyes of pride. He remembered that he fell.

"Fingal leaned on the shield of his fathers. His gray locks slowly waved on the wind, and glittered to the beam of night. He saw the grief of Swaran, and spoke to the first of bards.

"'Raise, Ullin, raise the song of peace. O soothe my soul from war. Let mine ear forget in the sound the dismal noise of arms. Let a hundred harps be near to gladden the king of Lochlin. He must depart from us with joy. None ever went sad from Fingal. The lightening of my sword is against the strong in fight. Peaceful it lies by my side when warriors yield in war.'"

So at the bidding of Fingal the minstrel sang, and soothed the grief of Swaran. And when the music ceased Fingal spoke once more:—

"'King of Lochlin, let thy face brighten with gladness, and thine ear delight in the harp. Dreadful as the storm of thine ocean thou hast poured thy valor forth; thy voice has been like the voice of thousands when they engage in war.

"'Raise, to-morrow, raise thy white sails to the wind. Or dost thou choose the fight? that thou mayest depart renowned like the sun setting in the west.'"

Then Swaran chose to depart in peace. He had no more will to fight against Fingal, so the two heroes swore friendship together. Then once again Fingal called for the song of minstrels.

"A hundred voices at once arose, a hundred harps were strung. They sang of other times; the mighty chiefs of other years." And so the night passed till "morning trembles with the beam of the east; it glimmers on Cromla's side. Over Lena is heard the horn of Swaran. The sons of the ocean gather around. Silent and sad they rise on the wave. The blast of Erin is behind their sails. White as the mist of Morven they float along the sea."

Thus Swaran and his warriors departed, and Fingal, calling his men together, set forth to hunt. And as he hunted far in the woods he met Cathullin, still hiding, sad and ashamed. But Fingal comforted the beaten hero, reminding him of past victories. Together they returned to Fingal's camp, and there the heroes sang and feasted until "the soul of Cathullin rose. The strength of his arm returned. Gladness brightened along his face. Thus the night passed away in song. We brought back the morning with joy.

"Fingal arose on the heath and shook his glittering spear. He moved first towards the plain of Lena. We followed in all our arms.

" 'Spread the sail,' said the King, 'seize the winds as they pour from Lena.'

"We rose on the wave with songs. We rushed with joy through the foam of the deep."

Thus the hero returned to his own land.

NOTE—There is no book of Ossian specially edited for children. Later they may like to read the Century Edition of Macpherson's *Ossian* edited by William Sharpe. Stories about Ossian will be found among the many books of Celtic tales now published.

CHAPTER VI

ABOUT SOME OLD WELSH STORIES AND STORY-TELLERS

You remember that the Celtic family was divided into two branches, the Gaelic and the Cymric. So far we have only spoken about the Gaels, but the Cymry had their poets and historians too. The Cymry, however, do not claim such great age for their first known poets as do the Gaels. Ossian, you remember, was supposed to live in the third century, but the oldest Cymric poets whose names we know were supposed to live in the sixth century. As, however, the oldest Welsh manuscripts are of the twelfth century, it is again very difficult to prove that any of the poems were really written by those old poets.

But this is very certain, that the Cymry, like the Gaels, had their bards and minstrels who sang of the famous deeds of heroes in the halls of the chieftains, or in the market-places for the people.

From the time that the Romans left Britain to the time when the Saxons or English were at length firmly settled in the land, many fierce struggles, many stirring events must have taken place. That time must have been full of brave deeds such as the minstrels loved to sing. But that part of our history is very dark. Much that is written of it is little more than a fairy tale, for it was not until long afterwards that anything about this time was written down.

The great hero of the struggle between the Britons and the Saxons was King Arthur, but it was not until many many years after the time in which he lived that all the

27

splendid stories of his knights, of his Round Table, and of his great conquests began to take the form in which we know them. Indeed, in the earliest Welsh tales the name of Arthur is hardly known at all. When he is mentioned it is merely as a warrior among other warriors equally great, and not as the mighty emperor that we know. The Arthur that we love is the Arthur of literature, not the Arthur of history. And I think you may like to follow the story of the Arthur of literature, and see how, from very little, it has grown so great that now it is known all the world over. I should like you to remember, too, that the Arthur story is not the only one which repeats itself again and again throughout our Literature. There are others which have caught the fancy of great masters and have been told by them in varying ways throughout the ages. But of them all, the Arthur story is perhaps the best example.

Of the old Welsh poets it may, perhaps, be interesting to remember two. These are Taliesin, or "Shining Fore-head," and Merlin.

Merlin is interesting because he is Arthur's great bard and magician. Taliesin is interesting because in a book called *The Mabinogion,* which is a translation of some of the oldest Welsh stories, we have the tale of his wonderful birth and life.

Mabinogion really means tales for the young. Except the History of Taliesin, all the stories in this book are translated from a very old manuscript called the *Red Book of Hergest.* This Red Book belongs to the four-teenth century, but many of the stories are far far older, having, it is thought, been told in some form or other for hundreds of years before they were written down at all. Unlike many old tales, too, they are written in prose, not in poetry.

One of the stories in *The Mabinogion,* the story of

King Ludd, takes us back a long way. King Ludd was a king in Britain, and in another book we learn that he was a brother of Cassevelaunis, who fought against Julius Cæsar, so from that we can judge of the time in which he reigned.

"King Ludd," we are told in *The Mabinogion,* "ruled prosperously and rebuilt the walls of London, and encompassed it about with numberless towers. And after that he bade the citizens build houses therein, such as no houses in the kingdom could equal. And, moreover, he was a mighty warrior, and generous and liberal in giving meat and drink to all that sought them. And though he had many castles and cities, this one loved he more than any. And he dwelt therein most part of the year, and therefore was it called Caer Ludd, and at last Caer London. And after the strange race came there, it was called London." It is interesting to remember that there is still a street in London called Ludgate. Caer is the Celtic word for Castle, and is still to be found in many Welsh names, such as Carnarvon, Caerleon, and so on.

Now, although Ludd was such a wise king, three plagues fell upon the island of Britain. "The first was a certain race that came and was called Coranians, and so great was their knowledge that there was no discourse upon the face of the island, however low it might be spoken, but what, if the wind met it, it was known to them.

"The second plague was a shriek which came on every May-eve over every hearth in the island of Britain. And this went through peoples' hearts and frightened them out of their senses.

"The third plague was, however much of provision and food might be prepared in the king's courts, were there even so much as a year's provision of meat and drink, none of it could ever be found, except what was consumed upon the first night."

The story goes on to tell how good King Ludd freed the island of Britain from all three plagues and lived in peace all the days of his life.

In five of the stories of *The Mabinogion,* King Arthur appears. And, although these were all written in Welsh, it has been thought that some may have been brought to Wales from France.

This seems strange, but it comes about in this way. Part of France is called Brittany, as you know. Now, long long ago, before the Romans came to Britain, some of the people who lived in that part of France sailed across the sea and settled in Britain. These may have been the ancient Britons whom Cæsar fought when he first came to our shore.

Later, when the Romans left our island and the Picts and Scots oppressed the Britons, many of them fled back over the sea to Brittany or Armorica, as it used to be called. Later still, when the Saxons came, the Britons were driven by degrees into the mountains of Wales and the wilds of Cornwall, while others fled again across the sea to Brittany. These took with them the stories which their minstrels told, and told them in their new home. So it came about that the stories which were told in Wales and in Cornwall were told in Brittany also.

And how were these stories brought back again to England?

Another part of France is called Normandy. The Normans and the Bretons were very different peoples, as different as the Britons and the English. But the Normans conquered part of Brittany, and a close relationship grew up between the two peoples. Conan, Duke of Brittany, and William, Duke of Normandy, were related to each other, and in a manner the Bretons owned the Duke of Normandy as overlord.

Now you know that in 1066 the great Duke William

came sailing over the sea to conquer England, and with him
came more soldiers from Brittany than from any other
land. Perhaps the songs of the minstrels had kept alive
in the hearts of the Bretons a memory of their island home.
Perhaps that made them glad to come to help to drive out
the hated Saxons. At any rate come they did, and brought
with them their minstrel tales.

And soon through all the land the Norman power
spread. And whether they first heard them in Armorica
or in wild Wales, the Norman minstrels took the old Welsh
stories and made them their own. And the best of all the
tales were told of Arthur and his knights.

Doubtless the Normans added much to these stories.
For although they were not good at inventing anything,
they were very good at taking what others had invented
and making it better. And the English, too, as Norman
power grew, clung more and more to the memory of the
past. They forgot the difference between British and
English, and in their thoughts Arthur grew to be a national
hero, a hero who had loved his country, and who was not
Norman.

The Normans, then, brought tales of Arthur with them
when they came to England. They heard there still other
tales and improved them, and Arthur thus began to grow
into a great hero. I will now go on to show how he became still greater.

In the reign of Henry I. (the third Norman king who
ruled our land) there lived a monk called Geoffrey of
Monmouth. He was filled with the love of his land, and
he made up his mind to write a history of the kings of
Britain.

Geoffrey wrote his book in Latin, because at this time
it was the language which most people could understand.
For a long time after the Normans came to England, they
spoke Norman French. The English still spoke English,

and the British Welsh or Cymric. But every one almost
who could read at all could read Latin. So Geoffrey chose
to write in Latin. He said he translated all that he wrote
from an old British book which had been brought from
Brittany and given to him. But that old British book
has never been seen by any one, and it is generally thought
that Geoffrey took old Welsh tales and fables for a foundation, invented a good deal more, and so made his history,
and that the "old British Book" never existed at all. His
book may not be very good history—indeed, other historians were very angry and said that Geoffrey "lied
saucily and shamelessly"—but it is very delightful to
read.

Geoffrey's chief hero is Arthur, and we may say that
it is from this time that Arthur became a great hero of
Romance. For Geoffrey told his stories so well that they
soon became famous, and they were read not only in
England, but all over the Continent. Soon story-tellers
and poets in other lands began to write stories about
Arthur too, and from then till now there has never been a
time when they have not been read. So to the Welsh
must be given the honor of having sown a seed from
which has grown the wide-spreading tree we call the
Arthurian Legend.

Geoffrey begins his story long before the time of Arthur.
He begins with the coming of Brutus, the ancient hero
who conquered Albion and changed its name to Britain,
and he continues to about two hundred years after the
death of Arthur. But Arthur is his real hero, so he tells
the story in very few words after his death.

Geoffrey tells of many battles and of how the British
fought, not only with the Saxons, but among themselves.
And at last he says: "As barbarism crept in they were no
longer called Britons, but Welsh, a word derived either
from Gualo, one of their dukes, or from Guales, their

Queen, or else from their being barbarians. But the Saxons did wiselier, kept peace and concord amongst themselves, tilling their fields and building anew their cities and castles. . . . But the Welsh degenerating from the nobility of the Britons, never after recovered the sovereignty of the island, but on the contrary quarreling at one time amongst themselves, and at another with the Saxons, never ceased to have bloodshed on hand either in public or private feud."

Geoffrey then says that he hands over the matter of writing about the later Welsh and Saxon kings to others, "Whom I bid be silent as to the kings of the Britons, seeing that they have not that book in the British speech which Walter, Archdeacon of Oxford, did convey hither out of Brittany, the which I have in this wise been at the pains of translating into the Latin speech."

BOOKS TO READ

The Mabinogion, translated by Lady Charlotte Guest Everyman's Library.
Geoffrey of Monmouth's *Histories,* translated by Sebastian Evans

CHAPTER VII

HOW THE STORY OF ARTHUR WAS WRITTEN IN ENGLISH

GEOFFREY OF MONMOUTH had written his stories so well, that although he warned people not to write about the British kings, they paid no heed to his warning. Soon many more people began to write about them, and especially about Arthur.

In 1155 Geoffrey died, and that year a Frenchman, or Jerseyman rather, named Robert Wace, finished a long poem which he called *Li Romans de Brut* or the *Romances of Brutus*. This poem was founded upon Geoffrey's history and tells much the same story, to which Wace has added something of his own. Besides Wace, many writers told the tale in French. For French, you must remember, was still the language of the rulers of our land. It is to these French writers, and chiefly to Walter Map, perhaps, that we owe something new which was now added to the Arthur story.

Walter Map, like so many of the writers of this early time, was a priest. He was chaplain to Henry II., and was still alive when John, the bad king, sat upon the throne.

The first writers of the Arthur story had made a great deal of manly strength: it was often little more than a tale of hard knocks given and taken. Later it became softened by the thought of courtesy, with the idea that knights might give and take these hard knocks for the sake of the lady they loved, and in the cause of all women.

34

Now something full of mystery was added to the tale. This was the Quest of the Holy Grail.

The Holy Grail was said to be a dish used by Christ at the Last Supper. It was also said to have been used to hold the sacred blood which, when Christ hung upon the cross, flowed from his wounds. The Holy Grail came into the possession of Joseph of Arimathea, and by him was brought to Britain. But after a time the vessel was lost, and the story of it even forgotten, or only remembered in some dim way.

And this is the story which the poet-priest, Walter Map, used to give new life and new glory to the tales of Arthur. He makes the knights of the round table set forth to search for the Grail. They ride far away over hill and dale, through dim forests and dark waters. They fight with men and fiends, alone and in tournaments. They help fair ladies in distress, they are tempted to sin, they struggle and repent, for only the pure in heart may find the holy vessel.

It is a wonderful and beautiful story, and these old story-tellers meant it to be something more than a fairy tale. They saw around them many wicked things. They saw men fighting for the mere love of fighting. They saw men following pleasure for the mere love of pleasure. They saw men who were strong oppress the weak and grind down the poor, and so they told the story of the Quest of the Holy Grail to try to make them a little better.

With every new writer the story of Arthur grew. It seemed to draw all the beauty and wonder of the time to itself, and many stories which at first had been told apart from it came to be joined to it. We have seen how it has been told in Welsh, in Latin, and in French, and, last of all, we have it in English.

The first great English writer of the stories of Arthur

was named Layamon. He, too, was a priest, and, like Wace, he wrote in verse.

Like Wace, Layamon called his book the *Brut,* because it is the story of the Britons, who took their name from Brutus, and of Arthur the great British hero. This book is known, therefore, as Layamon's *Brut.* Layamon took Wace's book for a foundation, but he added a great deal to it, and there are many stories in Layamon not to be found in Wace. It is probable that Layamon did not make up these stories, but that many of them are old tales he heard from the people among whom he lived.

Layamon finished his book towards the end of the twelfth century or the beginning of the thirteenth. Perhaps he sat quietly writing it in his cell when the angry barons were forcing King John to sign the Magna Charta. At least he wrote it when all England was stirring to new life again. The fact that he wrote in English shows that, for Layamon's *Brut* is the first book written in English after the Conquest. This book proves how little hold the French language had upon the English people, for although our land had been ruled by Frenchmen for a hundred and fifty years, there are very few words in Layamon that are French or that are even made from French.

But although Layamon wrote his book in English, it was not the English that we speak to-day. It was what is called Early English or even sometimes Semi-Saxon. If you opened a book of Layamon's *Brut* you would, I fear, not be able to read it.

We know very little of Layamon; all that we do know he tells us himself in the beginning of his poem. "A priest was in the land," he says:

> "Layamon was he called
> He was Leouenathe's son,   the Lord to him be gracious.
> He lived at Ernleye   at a noble church
> Upon Severn's bank.   Good there to him it seemed

Fast by Radestone, where he books read.
It came to him in mind, and in his first thoughts,
That he would of England the noble deeds tell,
What they were named and whence they came,
The English land who first possessed
After the flood which from the Lord came.

Layamon began to journey, far he went over the land
And won the noble books, which he for pattern took.
He told the English book that Saint Beda made
Another he took in Latin which Saint Albin made,
And the fair Austin who baptism brought hither.
Book the third he took laid it in the midst
That the French clerk made. Wace he was called,
He well could write
                .   .   .   .   .
Layamon laid these books down and the leaves turned
He them lovingly beheld. the Lord to him be merciful!
Pen he took in fingers and wrote upon a book skin,
And the true words set together,
And the three books pressed to one "

That, in words such as we use now, is how Layamon
begins his poem. But this is how the words looked as
Layamon wrote them:—

        "An preost wes on leoden   lazamon wes ihoten
         he wes Leouenaðes sone   liðe him beo drihtě "

You can see that it would not be very easy to read
that kind of English. Nor does it seem very like poetry
in either the old words or the modern. But you must
remember that old English poetry was not like ours. It
did not have rhyming words at the end of the lines.

Anglo-Saxon poetry depended for its pleasantness to
the ear, not on rhyme as does ours, but on accent and
alliteration. Alliteration means the repeating of a letter.
Accent means that you rest longer on some syllables, and
say them louder than others. For instance, if you take
the line "the way was long, the wind was cold," way, long,

wind, and cold are accented. So there are four accents in that line.

Now, in Anglo-Saxon poetry the lines were divided into two half-lines. And in each half there had to be two or more accented syllables. But there might also be as many unaccented syllables as the poet liked. So in this way the lines were often very unequal, some being quite short and others long. Three of the accented syllables, generally two in the first half and one in the second half of the line, were alliterative. That is, they began with the same letter. In translating, of course, the alliteration is very often lost. But sometimes the Semi-Saxon words and the English words are very like each other, and the alliteration can be kept. So that even in translation we can get a little idea of what the poetry sounded like. For instance, the line "*wat heo ihoten weoren: and wonenc heo comen*," the alliteration is on w, and may be translated, "*what they called were, and whence they came*," still keeping the alliteration.

Upon these rules of accent and alliteration the strict form of Anglo-Saxon verse was based. But when the Normans came they brought a new form of poetry, and gradually rhymes began to take the place of alliteration. Layamon wrote his *Brut* more than a hundred years after the coming of the Normans, and although his poem is in the main alliterative, sometimes he has rhyming lines such as, "*mochel dal heo iwesten: mid harmen þen mesten*," that is:—

> "Great part they laid waste
> With harm the most."

Sometimes even in translation the rhyme may be kept, as:—

> "And faer forh nu to niht
> In to Norewaieze forh riht."

which can be translated:—

> "And fare forth now to-night
> Into Norway forth right."

At times, too, Layamon has neither rhyme nor alliteration in his lines, sometimes he has both, so that his poem is a link between the old poetry and the new.

I hope that you are not tired with this long explanation, for I think if you take the trouble to understand it, it may make the rest of this chapter more interesting. Now I will tell you a little more of the poem itself.

Layamon tells many wonderful stories of Arthur, from the time he was born to his last great battle in which he was killed, fighting against the rebel Modred.

This is how Layamon tells the story of Arthur's death, or rather of his "passing":

> "Arthur went to Cornwall with a great army
> Modred heard that and he against him came
> With unnumbered folk. There were many of them fated.
> Upon the Tambre they came together,
> The place was called Camelford, evermore has that name lasted
> And at Camelford were gathered sixty thousand
> And more thousands thereto Modred was their chief.
> Then hitherward gan ride Arthur the mighty
> With numberless folk fated though they were.
> Upon the Tambre they came together,
> Drew their long swords, smote on the helmets,
> So that fire sprang forth. Spears were splintered,
> Shields gan shatter, shafts to break.
> They fought all together folk unnumbered.
> Tambre was in flood with unmeasured blood.
> No man in the fight might any warrior know,
> Nor who did worse nor who did better so was the conflict mingled,
> For each slew downright were he swain were he knight.
> There was Modred slain and robbed of his life day.
>   In the fight
> There were slain all the brave
> Arthur's warriors noble.
> And the Britons all of Arthur's board,

And all his lieges   of many a kingdom.
And Arthur sore wounded   with war spear broad.
Fifteen he had   fearful wounds
One might in the least   two gloves thrust.
Then was there no more   in the fight on life
Of two hundred thousand men   that there lay hewed in pieces
But Arthur the king alone,   and of his knights twain.
But Arthur was sore wounded   wonderously much
Then to him came a knave   who was of his kindred
He was Cador's son   the earl of Cornwall.
Constantine hight the knave.   He was to the king dear.
Arthur him looked on   where he lay on the field,
And these words said   with sorrowful heart.
Constantine thou art welcome   thou wert Cador's son,
I give thee here   my kingdom.
Guard thou my Britons   so long as thou livest,
And hold them all the laws   that have in my days stood.
And all the good laws   that in Uther's days stood
And I will fare to Avelon   to the fairest of all maidens
To Argente their Queen,   an elf very fair,
And she shall my wounds   make all sound
All whole me make   with healing draughts,
And afterwards I will come again   to my kingdom
And dwell with the Britons   with mickle joy
Even with the words   that came upon the sea
A short boat sailing,   moving amid the waves
And two women were therein   wounderously clad
And they took Arthur anon   and bare him quickly
And softly him adown laid   and to glide forth gan they.
Then was it come   what Merlin said whilom
That unmeasured sorrow should be   at Arthur's forth faring.
Britons believe yet   that he is still in life
And dwelleth in Avelon   with the fairest of all elves,
And every Briton looketh still   when Arthur shall return.
Was never the man born   nor never the lady chosen
Who knoweth of the sooth   of Arthur to say more.
But erstwhile there was a wizard   Merlin called
He boded with words   the which were sooth
That an Arthur should yet   come the English to help."

You see by this last line that Layamon has forgotten
the difference between Briton and English.   He has

forgotten that in his lifetime Arthur fought against the English. To him Arthur has become an English hero And perhaps he wrote these last words with the hope in his heart that some day some one would arise who would deliver his dear land from the rule of the stranger Normans. This, we know, happened. Not, indeed, by the might of one man, but by the might of the English spirit, the strong spirit which had never died, and which Layamon himself showed was still alive when he wrote his book in English.

CHAPTER VIII

THE BEGINNING OF THE READING TIME

WE are now going on two hundred years to speak of another book about Arthur. This is *Morte d'Arthur,* by Sir Thomas Malory.

Up to this time all books had to be written by hand. But in the fifteenth century printing was discovered. This was one of the greatest things which ever happened for literature, for books then became much more plentiful and were not nearly so dear as they had been, and so many more people could afford to buy them. And thus learning spread.

It is not quite known who first discovered the art of printing, but William Caxton was the first man who set up a printing-press in England. He was an English wool merchant who had gone to live in Bruges, but he was very fond of books, and after a time he gave up his wool business, came back to England, and began to write and print books. One of the first books he printed was Malory's *Morte d'Arthur.*

In the preface Caxton tells us how, after he had printed some other books, many gentlemen came to him to ask him why he did not print a history of King Arthur, "which ought most to be remembered among us Englishmen afore all the Christian kings; to whom I answered that divers men hold opinion that there was no such Arthur, and all such books as be made of him be but famed matters and fables."

But the gentlemen persuaded Caxton until at last he undertook to "imprint a book of the noble histories of the said King Arthur and of certaine of his knights, after a copy unto me delivered, which copy Sir Thomas Malory tooke out of certaine bookes in the Frenche, and reduced it into English."

It is a book, Caxton says, "wherein ye shall find many joyous and pleasant histories, and noble and renowned acts. . . . Doe after the good and leave the ill, and it shall bring you unto good fame and renowne. And for to pass the time this booke shall be pleasant to read in."

In 1485, when *Morte d'Arthur* was first printed, people indeed found it a book "pleasant to read in," and we find it so still. It is written in English not unlike the English of to-day, and although it has a quaint, old-world sound, we can readily understand it.

Morte d'Arthur really means the death of Arthur, but the book tells not only of his death, but of his birth and life, and of the wonderful deeds of many of his knights. This is how Malory tells of the manner in which Arthur came to be king.

But first let me tell you that Uther Pendragon, the King, had died, and although Arthur was his son and should succeed to him, men knew it not. For after Arthur was born he was given to the wizard Merlin, who took the little baby to Sir Ector, a gallant knight, and charged him to care for him. And Sir Ector, knowing nothing of the child, brought him up as his own son.

Thus, after the death of the King, "the realm stood in great jeopardy a long while, for every lord that was mighty of men made him strong, and many weened to have been King.

"Then Merlin went to the Archbishop of Canterbury and counselled him for to send for all the lords of the realm, and all the gentlemen of arms, that they should come to

London afore Christmas upon pain of cursing, and for this cause, that as Jesus was born on that night, that he would of his great mercy show some miracle, as he was come to be king of all mankind, for to show some miracle who should be right wise king of this realm.   So the Archbishop by the advice of Merlin, sent for all the lords and gentlemen of arms that they should come by Christmas even unto London. . . . So in the greatest church of London, whether it were Pauls or not the French book maketh no mention, all the estates were long or [1] day in the church for to pray.   And when matins and the first mass were done, there was seen in the churchyard, against the high altar, a great stone foursquare, like unto a marble stone, and in the midst thereof was like an anvil of steel a foot on high, and therein stuck a fair sword naked by the point, and letters there were written in gold about the sword that said thus:—"Whoso pulleth out this sword of the stone and anvil is rightwise king born of all England."

"Then the people marvelled and told it to the Archbishop. . . . So when all masses were done, all the lords went to behold the stone and the sword.   And when they saw the scripture, some essayed; such as would have been king   But none might stir the sword nor move it.

"'He is not here,' said the Archbishop, 'that shall achieve the sword, but doubt not God will make him known.   But this is my counsel,' said the Archbishop, 'that we let purvey ten knights, men of good fame, and they to keep the sword.'

"So it was ordained, and then there was made a cry, that every man should essay that would, for to win the sword. . . .

"Now upon New Year's Day, when the service was done, the barons rode unto the field, some to joust, and some to tourney, and so it happened that Sir Ector rode unto the

[1] Before

jousts, and with him rode Sir Kay his son, and young Arthur that was his nourished brother. So as they rode to the jousts-ward, Sir Kay had lost his sword, for he had left it at his father's lodging, and so he prayed young Arthur for to ride for his sword.

" 'I will well,' said Arthur, and rode fast after the sword, and when he came home, the lady and all were out to see the jousting. Then was Arthur wroth and said to himself, "I will ride to the churchyard, and take the sword with me that sticketh in the stone, for my brother Sir Kay shall not be without a sword this day." So when he came to the churchyard Sir Arthur alit and tied his horse to the stile, and so he went to the tent and found no knights there, for they were at the jousting, and so he handled the sword by the handles, and lightly and fiercely pulled it out of the stone, and took his horse and rode his way until he came to his brother Sir Kay, and delivered him the sword.

"And as soon as Sir Kay saw the sword he wist well it was the sword of the stone, and he rode to his father Sir Ector and said: 'Sir, lo here is the sword of the stone, wherefore I must be king of this land.'

"When Sir Ector beheld the sword he returned again and came to the church, and there they alit all three, and went into the church. And anon he made Sir Kay to swear upon a book how he came to that sword.

" 'Sir,' said Sir Kay, 'by my brother Arthur, for he brought it to me.'

" 'How got ye this sword?' said Sir Ector to Arthur.

" 'Sir, I will tell you. When I came home for my brother's sword, I found no body at home to deliver me his sword, and so I thought my brother Sir Kay should not go swordless, and so I came hither eagerly and pulled it out of the stone without any pain.'

" 'Found ye any knights about the sword?' said Sir Ector.

" 'Nay,' said Arthur.

" 'Now,' said Sir Ector to Arthur, 'I understand ye must be king of this land.'

" 'Wherefore I,' said Arthur, 'and for what cause?'

" 'Sir,' said Ector, 'for God will have it so, for there should never man have drawn out this sword, but he that should be rightwise king of this land. Now let me see if ye can put the sword there as it was and pull it out again.'

" 'That is no mastery,' said Arthur. And so he put it in the stone. Therewithall Sir Ector essayed to pull out the sword and failed.

" 'Now essay,' said Sir Ector unto Sir Kay. And anon he pulled at the sword with all his might, but it would not be.

" 'Now shall ye essay," said Sir Ector unto Arthur.

" 'I will well,' said Arthur, and pulled it out easily.

"And therewithall Sir Ector knelt down to the earth, and Sir Kay."

And so Arthur was acknowledged king. "And so anon was the coronation made," Malory goes on to tell us, "and there was Arthur sworn unto his lords and to the commons for to be a true king, to stand with true justice from henceforth the days of his life."

For the rest of all the wonderful stories of King Arthur and his knights you must go to *Morte d'Arthur* itself. For the language is so simple and clear that it is a book that you can easily read, though there are some parts that you will not understand or like and which you need not read yet.

But of all the books of which we have spoken this is the first which you could read in the very words in which it was written down I do not mean that you could read it as it was first printed, for the oldest kind of printing was not unlike the writing used in manuscripts, and so seems hard to read now. Besides which, although nearly all the words Malory uses are words we still use, the spelling is a little different, and that makes it more difficult to read.

The old lettering looked like this:—

"𝔚ith that 𝔖ir 𝔄rthur turned with his knights, and smote behind and before, and ever 𝔖ir 𝔄rthur was in the foremost press till his horse was slain under him."

That looks difficult. But here it is again in our own lettering:—

"With that Sir Arthur turned with his knights, and smote behind and before, and ever Sir Arthur was in the foremost press till his horse was slain under him."

That is quite easy to read, and there is not a word in it that you cannot understand. For since printing came our language has changed very much less than it did before. And when printing came, the listening time of the world was done and the reading time had begun. As books increased, less and less did people gather to hear others read aloud or tell tales, and more and more people learned to read for themselves, until now there is hardly a boy or girl in all the land who cannot read a little.

It is perhaps because *Morte d'Arthur* is easily read that it has become a storehouse, a treasure-book, to which other writers have gone, and from which they have taken stories and woven them afresh and given them new life. Since Caxton's time *Morte d'Arthur* has been printed many times, and it is through it perhaps, more than through the earlier books, that the stories of Arthur still live for us. Yet it is not perfect—it has indeed been called "a most pleasant jumble." [1] Malory made up none of the stories; as he himself tells us, he took them from French books, and in some of these French books the stories are told much better. But what we have to re-

[1] J Furnivell

member and thank Malory for is that he kept alive the stories of Arthur. He did this more than any other writer in that he wrote in English such as all English-speaking people must love to read.

BOOKS TO READ

Stories of King Arthur's Knights, by Mary Macgregor *Stories from Morte d'Arthur*, by C. L Thomson *Morte d'Arthur*, Globe Edition.

CHAPTER IX

"THE PASSING OF ARTHUR"

FOUR hundred years after Malory wrote his book, another English writer told the tales of Arthur anew. This was the poet Alfred, Lord Tennyson. He told them in poetry.

Tennyson calls his poems the *Idylls of the King.* Idyll means a short poem about some simple and beautiful subject. The king that Tennyson sings of is the great King Arthur.

Tennyson wrote many other poems besides the *Idylls of the King.* Of these we will speak later, just now it is only the Arthur story that we are following.

Tennyson takes his stories, some from *The Mabinogion,* some from Malory, some from other books. He has told them in very beautiful English, and it is the English such as we speak to-day. He has smoothed away much that strikes us as rough and coarse in the old stories, and his poems are as different from the old stories as a polished diamond is different from the stone newly brought out of the mine. Yet we miss something of strength and vigor. The Arthur of the *Idylls* is not the Arthur of *The Mabinogion* nor of Malory. Indeed, Tennyson makes him "almost too good to be true": he is "Ideal manhood closed in real man, rather than that gray king" of old.

And now I will give you part of the last of the Arthur poems, *The Passing of Arthur,* so that you may read it along with Layamon's account of the hero's death, and

49

see for yourselves the difference between the two. *The Passing of Arthur* is written in blank verse, that is verse which does not rhyme, and which depends like the old English verse on the accent. Yet they are not like.

> "So all day long the noise of battle roll'd
> Among the mountains by the winter sea;
> Until King Arthur's Table, man by man,
> Had fall'n in Lyonnesse about their lord,
> King Arthur. Then, because his wound was deep,
> The bold Sir Bedivere uplifted him,
> And bore him to a chapel nigh the field,
> A broken chancel by a broken cross,
> That stood in a dark strait of barren land:
> On one side lay the Ocean, and on one
> Lay a great water, and the moon was full "

Then the King bids Sir Bedivere take his sword Excalibur,

> "And fling him far into the middle mere
> Watch what thou seest, and lightly bring me word.

Sir Bedivere takes the sword, and,

> "From the ruin'd shrine he stept
> And in the moon athwart the place of tombs,
> Where lay the mighty bones of ancient men,
> Old knights, and over them the sea-wind sang
> Shrill, chill, with flakes of foam. He, stepping down
> By zigzag paths, and juts of pointed rock,
> Came on the shining levels of the lake "

But when Sir Bedivere drew Excalibur and saw the jewels of the hilt shine in the wintry moonlight, he could not find it in his heart to cast anything so beautiful and precious from him. So, hiding it among the reeds by the water's edge, he returned to his master.

> "Then spake King Arthur to Sir Bedivere:
> 'Hast thou perform'd my mission which I gave?
> What is it thou hast seen? or what hast heard?'

> And answer made the bold Sir Bedivere.
> 'I heard the ripple washing in the reeds,
> And the wild water lapping on the crag.' "

But King Arthur well knew that Sir Bedivere had not obeyed him. "This is a shameful thing for men to lie," he said, and once more sent the knight to do his bidding.

Again Sir Bedivere went, but again he could not make up his mind to cast away the sword. "The King is sick, and knows not what he does," he said to himself. So a second time he hid the sword and returned.

> "Then spoke King Arthur, breathing heavily·
> 'What is it thou hast seen? or what hast heard?'
>
> And answer made the bold Sir Bedivere.
> 'I heard the water lapping on the crag,
> And the long ripple washing in the reeds.'
>
> To whom replied King Arthur, much in wrath:
> 'Ah, miserable and unkind, untrue,
> Unknightly, traitor-hearted! Woe is me!
> Authority forgets a dying king.' "

Then, sorrowful and abashed before the anger of the dying King, Sir Bedivere turned, and running quickly lest his courage should fail him, he reached the water's edge and flung the sword far into the lake.

> "But ere he dipt the surface, rose an arm
> Clothed in white samite, mystic, wonderful,
> And caught him by the hilt, and brandish'd him
> Three times, and drew him under in the mere "

Then Sir Bedivere, in wonder, returned to the King, who, when he saw him come, cried:—

> " 'Now see I by thine eyes that this is done.
> Speak out what is it thou hast heard, or seen?' "

So Sir Bedivere told the King how truly this time he had cast away the sword, and how an arm "clothed in white samite, mystic, wonderful," had caught it and drawn it under the mere. Then at the King's bidding Sir Bedivere raised Arthur and bore him to the water's edge.

> "Then saw they how there hove a dusky barge,
> Dark as a funeral scarf from stem to stern,
> Beneath them; and descending they were ware
> That all the decks were dense with stately forms,
> Black-stoled, black-hooded, like a dream—by these
> Three Queens with crowns of gold and from them rose
> A cry that shiver'd to the tingling stars,
> And, as it were one voice, an agony
> Of lamentation, like a wind that shrills
> All night in a waste land, where no one comes,
> Or hath come, since the making of the world.
>
> Then, murmur'd Arthur, 'Place me in the barge'
> So to the barge they came. There those three Queens
> Put forth their hands, and took the King, and wept"

Then slowly from the shore the barge moved. And Sir Bedivere, as he saw his master go, was filled with grief and loneliness, for he only of all the brave King's knights was left. And so he cried in mourning:—

> "'Ah! my Lord Arthur, whither shall I go?
> Where shall I hide my forehead and my eyes?
> For now I see the true old times are dead
>
> .   .   .   .   .
>
> And I, the last, go forth companionless,
> And the days darken round me, and the years,
> Among new men, strange faces, other minds"

Mournfully from the barge Arthur answered and bade him pray, for "More things are wrought by prayer than the world dreams of," and so he said farewell,

> "and the barge with oar and sail
> Moved from the brink, like some full-breasted swan"

Long stood Sir Bedivere thinking of all that had come

and gone, watching the barge as it glided silently away, and listening to the wailing voices,

> "till the hull
> Look'd one black dot against the verge of dawn,
> And on the mere the wailing died away "

Sir Bedivere turned then and climbed,

> "Ev'n to the highest he could climb, and saw,
> Straining his eyes beneath an arch of hand,
> Or thought he saw, the speck that bore the King,
> Down that long water opening on the deep
> Somewhere far off, pass on and on, and go
> From less to less and vanish into light.
> And the new sun rose bringing the new year "

The poem moves along with mournful stately measures, yet it closes, like Layamon's farewell to Arthur, on a note of hope. Layamon recalls Merlin's words, "the which were sooth, that an Arthur should yet come the English to help." The hope of Tennyson is different, not that the old will return, but that the new will take its place, for "the old order changeth yielding place to new, and God fulfils himself in many ways." The old sorrows vanish "into light," and the new sun ever rises bringing in the new year.

BOOK TO READ

Idylls of the King, by Alfred, Lord Tennyson, price 2s. 6d. (Macmillan).

CHAPTER X

THE ADVENTURES OF AN OLD ENGLISH BOOK

THE story of Arthur has led us a long way. We have almost forgotten that it began with the old Cymric stories, the stories of the people who lived in Britain before the coming of the Romans. We have followed it down through many forms: Welsh, in the stories of *The Mabinogion;* Latin, in the stories of Geoffrey of Monmouth; French, in the stories of Wace and Map; Semi-Saxon, in the stories of Layamon; Middle English, in the stories of Malory; and at last English as we now speak it, in the stories of Tennyson. Now we must go back and see why it is that our Literature is English, and why it is that we speak English, and not Gaelic, or Cymric, or Latin, or French. And then from its beginnings we will follow our English Literature through the ages.

Since historical times the land we now call England has been conquered three times, for we need hardly count the Danish Invasion. It was conquered by the Romans, it was conquered by the English, and it was conquered by the Normans. It was only England that felt the full weight of these conquests. Scotland, Ireland, and, in part, Wales were left almost untouched. And of the three it was only the English conquest that had lasting effects.

In 55 B.C. the Romans landed in Britain, and for nearly four hundred years after that they kept coming and going. All South Britain became a Roman province, and the people paid tribute or taxes to the Roman Emperor. But

54

they did not become Romans. They still kept their own language, their own customs and religions.

It will help you to understand the state of Britain in those old days if you think of India to-day. India forms part of the British Empire, but the people who live there are not British. They are still Indians who speak their own languages, and have their own customs and religions. The rulers only are British.

It was in much the same way that Britain was a Roman province. And so our literature was never Latin. There was, indeed, a time when nearly all our books were written in Latin. But that was later, and not because Latin was the language of the people, but because it was the language of the learned and of the monks, who were the chief people who wrote books.

When, then, after nearly four hundred years the Romans went away, the people of Britain were still British. But soon another people came. These were the Anglo-Saxons, the English, who came from over the sea. And little by little they took possession of Britain. They drove the old dwellers out until it was only in the north, in Wales and in Cornwall, that they were to be found. Then Britain became Angleland or England, and the language was no longer Celtic, but English. And although there are a few words in our language which can be traced to the old Celtic, these are very few. It is thus from Anglo-Saxon, and not from Gaelic or Cymric, that the language we speak to-day comes.

Yet our Celtic forefathers have given something to our literature which perhaps we could never have had from English alone. The Celtic literature is full of wonder, it is full of a tender magic and makes us feel the fairy charm of nature, although it has not the strength, the down-rightness, we might say, of the English. It has been said that every poet has somewhere in him a Celtic strain.

That is, perhaps, too much to believe. But it is, perhaps, the Celtic love of beauty, together with the Saxon love of strength and right, to which we owe much of our great literature. The Celtic languages are dying out, but they have left us something which will last so long as our literature lasts.

And now, having talked in the beginning of this book of the stories which we owe to our Celtic forefathers, let us see what the Saxons brought us from over the sea.

Almost the oldest Anglo-Saxon book that we have is called *Beowulf*. Wise men tell us that, like the tales of Arthur, like the tales of Ossian, this book was not at first the work of one man, but that it has been gradually put together out of many minstrel songs. That may be so, but what is sure is that these tales are very old, and that they were sung and told for many years in the old homes of the English across the sea before they came to Britain and named it Angleland.

Yet, as with the old Gaelic and Cymric tales, we have no very old copy of this tale. But unlike these old tales, we do not find *Beowulf* told in different ways in different manuscripts. There is only one copy of *Beowulf*, and that was probably written in the tenth or eleventh century, long years after the English were firmly settled in the land.

As *Beowulf* is one of our great book treasures, you may like to hear something of its story.

Long ago, in the time when Queen Elizabeth, James i., and Charles i. sat upon the throne, there lived a learned gentleman called Sir Robert Bruce Cotton. He was an antiquary. That is, he loved old things, and he gathered together old books, coins, manuscripts and other articles, which are of interest because they help to make us understand the history of bygone days.

Sir Robert Cotton loved books especially, and like

many other book lovers, he was greedy of them. It was said, indeed, that he often found it hard to return books which had been lent to him, and that, among others, he had books which really ought to have belonged to the King.

Sir Robert's library soon became famous, and many scholars came to read there, for Sir Robert was very kind in allowing other people to use his books. But twice his library was taken from him, because it was said that it contained things which were dangerous for people to know, and that he allowed the enemies of the King to use it. That was in the days of Charles I., and those were troublous times.

The second time that his library was taken from him, Sir Robert died, but it was given back to his son, and many years later his great-great-grandson gave it to the nation.

In 1731 the house in which the library was took fire, and more than a hundred books were burned, some being partly and some quite destroyed. Among those that were partly destroyed was *Beowulf*. But no one cared very much, for no one had read the book or knew anything about it.

Where Sir Robert found *Beowulf,* or what he thought about it, we shall never know. Very likely it had remained in some quiet monastery library for hundreds of years until Henry VIII. scattered the monks and their books. Many books were then lost, but some were saved, and after many adventures found safe resting-places. Among those was *Beowulf*.

Some years after the fire the Cotton Library, as it is now called, was removed to the British Museum, where it now remains. And there a Danish gentleman who was looking for books about his own land found *Beowulf,* and made a copy of it. Its adventures, however, were not over. Just when the printed copies were ready to be published, the British bombarded Copenhagen. The house in which the copies were was set on fire and they were all burned. The Danish gentleman, however, was not daunted. He set to work again, and at last *Beowulf* was published.

Even after it was published in Denmark, no Englishman thought of making a translation of the book, and it was not until fifty years more had come and gone that an English translation appeared.

When the Danish gentleman made his copy of *Beowulf*, he found the edges of the book so charred by fire that they broke away with the slightest touch. No one thought of mending the leaves, and as years went on they fell to pieces more and more. But at last some one woke up to the fact that this half-burned book was a great treasure. Then it was carefully mended, and thus kept from wasting more.

So now, after all its adventures, having been found, we shall never know where, by a gentleman in the days of Queen Elizabeth, having lain on his bookshelves unknown and unread for a hundred years and more, having been nearly destroyed by fire, having been still further destroyed by neglect, *Beowulf* at last came to its own, and is now carefully treasured in a glass case in the British Museum, where any one who cares about it may go to look at it.

And although it is perhaps not much to look at, it is a very great treasure. For it is not only the oldest epic poem in the Anglo-Saxon language, it is history too. By that I do not mean that the story is all true, but that by reading it carefully we can find out much about the daily lives of our forefathers in their homes across the seas. And besides this, some of the people mentioned in the poem are mentioned in history too, and it is thought that Beowulf, the hero himself, really lived.

And now, having spoken about the book and its adventures, let us in the next chaper speak about the story. As usual, I will give part of it in the words of the original, translated, of course, into modern English. You can always tell what is from the original by the quotation marks, if by nothing else.

CHAPTER XI

THE STORY OF BEOWULF

HROTHGAR, King of the Spear Danes, was a mighty man in war, and when he had fought and conquered much, he bethought him that he would build a great and splendid hall, wherein he might feast and be glad with his people.

And so it was done. And when the hall was built, there night by night the thanes gathered and rejoiced with their King; and there, when the feast was over, they lay them down to sleep.

Within the hall all was gladness, but without on the lone moorland there stalked a grim monster, named Grendel, whose dark heart was filled with anger and hate. To him the sound of song and laughter was deep pain, and he was fain to end it.

"He, the Grendel, set off then after night was come to seek the lofty house, to see how the Ring Danes had ordered it after the service of beer. He found them therein, a troup of nobles sleeping after the feast. They knew not sorrow, the wretchedness of men, they knew not aught of misfortune.

"The grim and greedy one was soon prepared, savage and fierce, and in sleep he seized upon thirty of the thanes, and thence he again departed exulting in his prey, to go home with the carcases of the slain, to reach his own dwelling.

"Then was in the morning twilight, at the breaking of day, Grendel's war-craft revealed to men. Then was lamentation upraised after the feast, a great noise in the morning.

"The mighty prince, a noble of old goodness, sat unblithe; the strong in armies suffered, the thanes endured sorrow, after they beheld the track of the hated one, the accursed spirit."

But in spite of all their grief and horror, when night came the thanes again lay down to rest in the great hall. And there again the monster returned and slew yet more thanes, so that in horror all forsook the hall, and for twelve long years none abode in it after the setting of the sun.

And now far across the sea a brave man of the Goths, Beowulf by name, heard of the doings of Grendel, and he made up his mind to come to aid King Hrothgar.

"He commanded to make ready for him a good ship; quoth he, he would seek the war-king over the swan's path; the renowned prince since he had need of men.

"The good chieftain had chosen warriors of the Geátish people, the bravest of those who he could find. With fifteen men he sought the sea-wood. A warrior, a man crafty in lakes, pointed out the boundaries of the land.

"The time passed on, the ship was on the waves, the boat beneath a mountain, the ready warriors stept upon the prow. The men bore into the bosom of the bark bright ornaments, their ready warlike appointments.

"The men shoved forth the bounden wood, the men upon the journey they desired.

"Then likest to a bird the foam-necked ship, propelled by the wind, started over the deep waves of the sea, till that about one hour of the second day, the wreathed prowed ship had sailed over, so that the traveller saw the land.

"Then quickly the people of the Westerns stepped upon the plain. They tied the sea-wood, they let down their shirts of mail, their war-weeds. They thanked God because that the waves had been easy to them."

And now these new-come warriors were led to King Hrothgar. He greeted them with joy, and after feasting and song the Danes and their King departed and left the Goths to guard the hall. Quietly they lay down to rest, knowing that ere morning stern battle would be theirs.

"Then under veils of mist came Grendel from the moor; he bare God's anger. The criminal meant to entrap some one of the race of men in the high hall. He went under the welkin, until he saw most clearly the wine hall, the treasure house of men, variegated with vessels. That was not the first time that he had sought Hrothgar's home. Never he, in all his life before or since, found bolder men keepers of the hall.

"Angry of mood he went, from his eyes, likest to fire, stood out a hideous light. He saw within the house many a warrior sleeping, a peaceful band together. Then his mood laughed. The foul wretch meant to divide, ere day came, the life of each from his body."

Quickly then he seized a warrior and as quickly devoured him. But as he stretched forth his hand to seize another, Beowulf gripped him in his awful grasp.

Then began a terrible combat. The hall echoed with cries and sounds of clashing steel. The Goths awoke, joining in the fight, but all their swords were of no avail against the ogre. With his bare hands alone Beowulf fought, and thought to kill the monster. But Grendel escaped, though wounded to death indeed, and leaving his hand, arm, and shoulder behind in Beowulf's grip.

When morning came there was much rejoicing. Hrothgar made a great feast, at which he gave rich gifts to Beowulf and his friends. The evening passed in song and laughter, and when darkness fell the Danes lay down to rest in the hall as of old.

But the evil was not over. Grendel indeed was slain, but his mother, an ogre almost as fierce as he, was ready to avenge him. So when night fell she hastened to the hall, and carried off Hrothgar's best loved thane.

"Then was there a cry in Heorot. Then was the prudent king, the hoary warrior, sad of mood, when he learned that his princely thane, the dearest to him, no longer lived. Quickly was Beowulf fetched to the bower, the man happy in victory, at break of day."

And when Beowulf heard the mournful tale he comforted the King with brave and kindly words, and quickly he set forth to the dreadful mere, the dwelling of the water-witch, Grendel's mother. And here he plunged in ready to fight.

"Soon did she, who thirsting for gore, grim and greedy, for a hundred years had held the circuit of the waves, discover that some one of men, some strange being, was trying from above the land. She grappled then towards him, she seized the warrior in her foul claws."

Then beneath the waves was there a fierce struggle, but Beowulf in the end conquered. The water-witch was slain, and rejoicing, the hero returned to Hrothgar.

Now indeed had peace come to the Danes, and loaded with thanks and rewards, Beowulf returned homeward.

Many years passed. Beowulf himself became king in his own land, and for fifty years he ruled well, and kept his folk in peace. Then it fell that a fearful Fire-Dragon wasted all the land, and Beowulf, mindful of his deeds of old, set forth to slay him.

Yet ere he fought, he bade farewell to all his thanes, for he knew well that this should be his last fight.

"Then greeted he every one of the men, the bold helm bearer greeted his dear comrades for the last time. I would not bear sword or weapon against the worm if I knew how else I might proudly grapple with the wretch, as I of old with Grendel did. But I ween this war fire is hot, fierce and poisonous; therefore have I on me shield and byrnie. . . . Then did the famous warrior arise beside his shield, hard under helmet he bare the sword-shirt, under the cliffs of stone, he trusted in the strength of one man; nor is such an expedition for a coward."

Fiercely then did the battle rage between hero and dragon. But Beowulf's sword failed him in his need, and it was like to go ill with him. Then, when his thanes who watched saw that, fear fell upon them, and they fled. One only, Wiglaf was his name, would not forsake his liege lord. Seizing his shield and drawing his sword, he cried, "Come, let us go to him, let us help our chieftain, although the grim terror of fire be hot."

But none would follow him, so alone he went: "through the fatal smoke he bare his war helmet to the assistance of his lord."

Fierce was the fight and long. But at length the dragon lay dead. Beowulf had conquered, but in conquering he had received his death wound. And there, by the wild seashore, he died. And there a sorrowing people buried him.

"For him, then, did the people of the Geáts prepare upon the earth a funeral pile, strong, hung round with helmets, with war boards and bright byrnies as he had requested. Weeping, the heroes laid down in the midst their dear lord.

"Then began the warriors to awake upon the hill the mightiest of bale-fires. The wood smoke rose aloft, dark from the foe of wood. Noisily it went mingled with weeping. . . .

"The people of the Westerns wrought then a mound over the sea: it was high and broad, easy to behold by the sailors over the waves, and during ten days they built up the beacon of the war-renowned, the mightiest of fires.

. . . Then round the mound rode a troupe of beasts of war, of nobles, twelve in all. They would speak about their King, they would call him to mind. They praised his valor, and his deeds of bravery they judged with praise, even as it is fitting that a man should extol his friendly lord, should love him in his soul, when he must depart from the body to become of naught.

"Thus the people of the Geáts, his hearth comrades, mourned their dear lord. They said that he was of the kings of the world, the mildest and gentlest of men, the most gracious to his people, and the most jealous of glory."

BOOKS TO READ

Stories of Beowulf, by H L Marshall. *Beowulf,* translated by W. Huyshe.

CHAPTER XII

THE FATHER OF ENGLISH SONG

ALTHOUGH there are lines in *Beowulf* which seem to show that the writer of the poem was a Christian, they must have been added by some one who copied or retold the story long after the Saxons had come to Britain, for the poet who first told the tale must have been a heathen, as all the Saxons were.

The Britons were Christian, for they had learned the story of Christ from the Romans. But when the Saxons conquered the land they robbed and ruined the churches, the Christian priests were slain or driven forth, and once more the land became heathen.

Then, after many years had passed, the story of Christ was again brought to England. This time it came from Ireland. It was brought from there by St. Columba, who built a church and founded a monastery on the island of Iona. And from there his eager, wandering priests carried the story far and wide, northward to the fortress of the Pictish kings, and southward to the wild Saxons who dwelt amid the hills and uplands of Northumbria.

To this story of love and gentleness the wild heathen listened in wonder. To help the weak, to love and forgive their enemies, was something unthought of by these fierce sea-rovers. Yet they listened and believed. Once again churches were built, priests came to live among the people, and the sound of Christian prayer and praise rose night and morning from castle and from hut.

For thirty years and more St. Columba, the passionate and tender, taught and labored. Many monasteries were founded which became, as it were, the lighthouses of learning and religion. There the monks and priests lived, and from them as centers they traveled out in all directions teaching the heathen. And when at last St. Columba closed his tired eyes and folded his weary hands, there were many more to carry on his work.

Then, also, from Rome, as once before, the story of Christ was brought. In 597, the year in which St. Columba died, St. Augustine landed with his forty followers. They, too, in time reached Northumbria; so, side by side, Roman and Celt spoke the message of peace on earth, goodwill toward men.

The wild Saxon listened to this message, it is true. He took Christianity for his religion, but it was rather as if he had put on an outer dress. His new religion made little difference to his life. He still loved fighting and war, and his songs were still all of war He worshiped Christ as he had worshiped Woden, and looked upon Him as a hero, only a little more powerful than the heroes of whom the minstrels sang. It was difficult to teach the Saxons the Bible lessons which we know so well, for in those far-off days there were no Bibles. There were indeed few books of any kind, and these few belonged to the monks and priests. They were in Latin, and in some of them parts of the Bible had been translated into Latin. But hardly any of the men and women of England could read or understand these books. Indeed, few people could read at all, for it was still the listening time. They learned the history of their country from the songs of the minstrels, and it was in this way, too, that they came to learn the Bible stories, for these stories were made into poetry. And it was among the rugged hills of Northumbria, by the rocky shore where the sounding waves beat and beat all day long, that the first Christian songs in English were sung. For here it was that Caedmon, the "Father of English Song," lived and died.

At Whitby there was a monastery ruled over by the Abbess Hilda. This was a post of great importance, for, as you know, the monasteries were the schools and libraries of the country, and they were the inns too, so all the true life of the land ebbed and flowed through the monasteries. Here priest and soldier, student and minstrel, prince and beggar came and went. Here in the great hall, when work was done and the evening meal over, were gathered all the monks and their guests. Here, too, would gather the simple folk of the countryside, the fishermen and farmers, the lay brothers and helpers who shared the work of the monastery. When the meal was done the minstrels sang, while proud and humble alike listened eagerly. Or perhaps "it was agreed for the sake of mirth that all present should sing in their turn."

But when, at the monastery of Whitby, it was agreed that all should sing in turn, there was one among the circle around the fire who silently left his place and crept away, hanging his head in shame.

This man was called Caedmon. He could not sing, and although he loved to listen to the songs of others, "whenever he saw the harp come near him," we are told, "he arose out of shame from the feast and went home to his house." Away from the bright firelight out into the lonely dark he crept with bent head and lagging steps Perhaps he would stand a moment outside the door beneath the starlight and listen to the thunder of the waves and the shriek of the winds. And as he felt in his heart all the beauty and wonder of the world, the glory and the might of the sea and sky, he would ask in dumb pain why, when he could feel it touch his heart, he could not also sing of the beauty and wonder, glory and might.

One night Caedmon crept away as usual, and went "out of the house where the entertainment was, to the stable, where he had to take care of the horses that night. He there composed himself to rest. A person appeared to him then in a dream and, calling him by name, said, 'Caedmon, sing some song to me.'

"He answered, 'I cannot sing; for that was the reason why I left the entertainment and retired to this place, because I cannot sing.'

"The other who talked to him replied, 'However, you shall sing.'

"'What shall I sing?' rejoined he.

"'Sing the beginning of created things,' said the other.

"Whereupon he presently began to sing verses to the praise of God, which he had never heard, the purport whereof was thus:—

> 'Now must we praise the guardian of heaven's kingdom,
> The creator's might and his mind's thought;
> Glorious father of men! as of every wonder he,
> Lord eternal, formed the beginning.
> He first framed for the children of earth
> The heaven as a roof, holy Creator!
> Then mid-earth, the Guardian of mankind,
> The eternal Lord, afterwards produced,
> The earth for men, Lord almighty.'

"This," says the old historian, who tells the story in Latin, "is the sense, but not the words in order as he sang them in his sleep. For verses, though never so well composed, cannot be literally (that is word for word) translated out of one language into another without losing much of their beauty and loftiness." [1]

Awakening from his sleep, Caedmon remembered all that he had sung in his dream. And the dream did not fade away as most dreams do. For he found that not

[1] Bede, *Ecclesiastical History*

only could he sing these verses, but he who had before been dumb and ashamed when the harp was put into his hand, could now make and sing more beautifully than could others. And all that he sang was to God's glory.

In the morning, full of his wonderful new gift, Caedmon went to the steward who was set over him, and told him of the vision that he had had during the night. And the steward, greatly marveling, led Caedmon to the Abbess.

The Abbess listened to the strange tale. Then she commanded Caedmon, "in the presence of many learned men, to tell his dream and repeat the verses that they might all give their judgment what it was and whence his verse came."

So the simple farm laborer, who had no learning of any kind, sang while the learned and grave men listened. And he who was wont to creep away in dumb shame, fearing the laughter of his fellows, sang now with such beauty and sweetness that they were all of one mind, saying that the Lord Himself had, of His heavenly grace, given to Caedmon this new power.

Then these learned men repeated to Caedmon some part of the Bible, explained the meaning of it, and asked him to tell it again in poetry. This Caedmon undertook to do, and when he fully understood the words, he went away. Next morning he returned and repeated all that he had been told, but now it was in beautiful poetry.

Then the Abbess saw that, indeed, the grace of God had come upon the man. She made him at once give up the life of a servant which he had been leading, and bade him become a monk. Caedmon gladly did her bidding, and when he had been received among them, his brother monks taught to him all the Bible stories.

But Caedmon could neither read nor write, nor is it at all likely that he ever learned to do either even after he became a monk, for we are told that "he was well advanced

in years" before his great gift of song came to him. It is quite certain that he could not read Latin, so that all that he put into verse had to be taught to him by some more learned brother. And some one, too, must have written down the verses which Caedmon sang.

We can imagine the pious, humble monk listening while another read and translated to him out of some Latin missal. He would sit with clasped hands and earnest eyes, intent on understanding. Then, when he had filled his mind with the sacred story, he would go away by himself and weave it into song. Perhaps he would walk about beneath the glowing stars or by the sounding sea, and thank God that he was no longer dumb, and that at last he could say forth all that before had been shut within his heart in an agony of silence. "And," we are told, "his songs and his verse were so winsome to hear, that his teachers themselves wrote and learned from his mouth."

"Thus Caedmon, keeping in mind all he heard, and, as it were, chewing the cud, converted the same into most harmonious verse; and sweetly repeating the same, made his masters in their turn his hearers.

"He sang the creation of the world, the origin of man, and all the history of Genesis; and made many verses on the departure of the children of Israel out of Egypt, and their entering into the land of promise, with many other histories from holy writ."

As has been said, there are lines in *Beowulf* which seem to have been written by a Christian   But all that is Christian in it is merely of the outside; it could easily be taken away, and the poem would remain perfect. The whole feeling of the poem is not Christian, but pagan. So it would seem that what is Christian in it has been added long after the poem was first made, yet added before the people had forgotten their pagan ways.

For very long after they became Christian the Saxons kept their old pagan ways of thought, and Caedmon, when he came to sing of holy things, sang as a minstrel might. To him Abraham and Moses, and all the holy men of old, were like the warrior chieftains whom he knew and of whom the minstrels sang. And God to him was but the greatest of these warriors. He is "Heaven's Chief," "the Great Prince." The clash and clang of sword on shield sound throughout the poem. Banners flutter and trumpet calls are heard "amid the grim clash of helms." War filled the greatest half of life. All history, all poetry were bound up in it. Caedmon sang of what he saw, of what he knew. He was Christian, he had learned the lesson of peace on earth, but he lived amid the clash of arms and sang of them.

CHAPTER XIII

HOW CAEDMON SANG, AND HOW HE FELL ONCE MORE ON SILENCE

ONE of Caedmon's poems is called *The Genesis.* In this the poet begins by telling of how Satan, in his pride, rebelled against God, and of how he was cast forth from heaven with all those who had joined with him in rebelling.

This story of the war in heaven and of the angels' fall is not in the Bible. It is not to be found either in any of the Latin books which the monks of Whitby may have had. The story did not come from Rome, but from the East. How, then, did Caedmon hear it?

Whitby, we must remember, was founded by Celtic, and not by Roman monks. It was founded by monks who came from Ireland to Iona, and from thence to Northumbria. To them the teaching of Christ had come from Jerusalem and the East rather than from Rome. So here again, perhaps, we can see the effect of the Celts on our literature. It was from Celtic monks that Caedmon heard the story of the war in heaven.

After telling of this war, Caedmon goes on to relate how the wicked angels "into darkness urged them their darksome way."

> "They might not loudly laugh,
> But they in hell-torments,
> Dwelt accursed
> And woe they knew
> Pain and sorrow,

73

> Torment endured
> With darkness decked,
> Hard retribution,
> For that they had devised
> Against God to war."

Then after all the fierce clash of battle come a few lines which seem like peace after war, quiet after storm.

> "Then was after as before
> Peace in heaven,
> Fair-loving thanes,
> The Lord dear to all"

Then God grieved at the empty spaces in heaven from whence the wicked angels had been driven forth. And that they might at last be filled again, he made the world and placed a man and woman there. This to the chief of the fallen angels was grief and pain, and his heart boiled within him in anger.

"Heaven is lost to us," he cried; "but now that we may not have it, let us so act that it shall be lost to them also. Let us make them disobey God,

> "Then with them will he be wroth of mind,
> Will cast them from his favor,
> Then shall they seek this hell
> And these grim depths,
> Then may we have them to ourselves as vassals,
> The children of men in this fast durance"

Then Satan asks who will help him to tempt mankind to do wrong. "If to any followers I princely treasure gave of old while we in that good realm happy sate," let him my gift repay, let him now aid me.

So one of Satan's followers made himself ready. "On his head the chief his helmet set," and he, "wheeled up from thence, departed through the doors of hell lionlike in air, in hostile mood, dashed the fire aside, with a fiend's power."

Caedmon next tells how the fiend tempted first the man and then the woman with guileful lies to eat of the fruit which had been forbidden to them, and how Eve yielded to him. And having eaten of the forbidden fruit, Eve urged Adam too to eat, for it seemed to her that a fair new life was open to her. "I see God's angels," she said,

> "Encompass him
> With feathery wings
> Of all folk greatest,
> Of bands most joyous.
> I can hear from far
> And so widely see,
> Through the whole world,
> Over the broad creation.
> I can the joy of the firmament
> Hear in heaven.
> It became light to me in mind
> From without and within
> After the fruit I tasted."

And thus, urged by Eve, Adam too ate of the forbidden fruit, and the man and woman were driven out of the Happy Garden, and the curse fell upon them because of their disobedience.

So they went forth "into a narrower life." Yet there was left to them "the roof adorned with holy stars, and earth to them her ample riches gave."

In many places this poem is only a paraphrase of the Bible. A paraphrase means the same thing said in other words. But in other places the poet seems to forget his model and sings out of his own heart. Then his song is best. Perhaps some of the most beautiful lines are those which tell of the dove that Noah sent forth from the ark.

> "Then after seven nights
> He from the ark let forth
> A pallid dove
> To fly after the swart raven,

Over the deep water,
To quest whether the foaming sea
Had of the green earth
Yet any part laid bare.
Wide she flew seeking her own will,
Far she flew yet found no rest
Because of the flood
With her feet she might not perch on land,
Nor on the tree leaves light
For the steep mountain tops
Were whelmed in waters.
Then the wild bird went
At eventide the ark to seek.
Over the darkling wave she flew
Weary, to sink hungry
To the hands of the holy man."

A second time the dove is sent forth, and this is how the poet tells of it:—

"Far and wide she flew
Glad in flying free, till she found a place
Fair, where she might rest   With her feet she stept
On a gentle tree   Gay of mood she was and glad
Since she sorely tired, now could settle down,
On the branches of the tree, on its beamy mast.
Then she fluttered feathers, went a flying off again,
With her booty flew, brought it to the sailor,
From an olive tree a twig, right into his hands
Brought the blade of green.

"Then the chief of seamen knew that gladness was at hand, and he sent forth after three weeks the wild dove who came not back again; for she saw the land of the greening trees. The happy creature, all rejoicing, would no longer of the ark, for she needed it no more." [1]

Besides *Genesis* many other poems were thought at one time to have been made by Caedmon. The chief of these are *Exodus* and *Daniel*. They are all in an old book, called the *Junian MS.*, from the name of the man,

[1] Stopford Brooke.

Francis Dujon, who first published them. The MS. was found among some other old books in Trinity College, Dublin, and given to Francis Dujon. He published the poems in 1655, and it is from that time that we date our knowledge of Caedmon.

Wise men tell us that Caedmon could not have made any of these poems, not even the *Genesis* of which you have been reading. But if Caedmon did not make these very poems, he made others like them which have been lost. It was he who first showed the way, and other poets followed.

We need not wonder, perhaps, that our poetry is a splendor of the world when we remember that it is rooted in these grand old tales, and that it awoke to life through the singing of a strong son of the soil, a herdsman and a poet. We know very little of this first of English poets, but what we do know makes us love him. He must have been a gentle, humble, kindly man, tender of heart and pure of mind. Of his birth we know nothing; of his life little except the story which has been told. And when death came to him, he met it cheerfully as he had lived.

For some days he had been ill, but able still to walk and talk. But one night, feeling that the end of life for him was near, he asked the brothers to give to him for the last time the Eucharist, or sacrament of the Lord's Supper.

"They answered, 'What need of the Eucharist? for you are not likely to die, since you talk so merrily with us, as if you were in perfect health.'

"'However,' said he, 'bring me the Eucharist.'

"Having received the same into his hand, he asked whether they were all in charity with him, and without any enmity or rancour.

"They answered that they were all in perfect charity

and free from anger; and in their turn asked him whether he was in the same mind towards them.

"He answered, 'I am in charity, my children, with all the servants of God.'

"Then, strengthening himself with the heavenly viaticum,[1] he prepared for the entrance into another life, and asked how near the time was when the brothers were to be awakened to sing the nocturnal praises of our Lord.

"They answered, 'It is not far off.'

"Then he said, 'Well, let us wait that hour.' And signing himself with the sign of the cross, he laid his head on the pillow, and falling into a slumber ended his life so in silence."

Thus his life, which had been begun in silence, ended also in silence, with just a few singing years between.

"Thus it came to pass, that as he had served God with a simple and pure mind, and undisturbed devotion, so he now departed to His presence, leaving the world by a quiet death. And that tongue which had composed so many holy words in praise of the Creator, uttered its last words while he was in the act of signing himself with a cross, and recommending himself into His hands."[2]

At Whitby still the ruins of a monastery stand. It is not the monastery over which the Abbess Hilda ruled or in which Caedmon sang, for in the ninth century that was plundered and destroyed by the fierce hordes of Danes who swept our shores. But in the twelfth century the house was rebuilt, and parts of that building are still to be seen.

[1] The Eucharist given to the dying.
[2] Bede, *Ecclesiastical History.*

CHAPTER XIV

THE FATHER OF ENGLISH HISTORY

WHILE Caedmon was still singing at Whitby, in another Northumbrian village named Jarrow a boy was born. This boy we know as Bede, and when he was seven years old his friends gave him into the keeping of the Abbot of Wearmouth. Under this Abbot there were two monasteries, the one at Jarrow and the other at Wearmouth, a few miles distant. And in these two monasteries Bede spent all the rest of his life.

When Bede was eight years old Caedmon died. And although the little boy had never met the great, but humble poet, he must have heard of him, and it is from Bede's history that we learn all that we know of Caedmon.

There is almost as little to tell of Bede's life as of Caedmon's. He passed it peacefully, reading, writing, and teaching within the walls of his beloved monastery. But without the walls wars often raged, for England was at this time still divided into several kingdoms, whose kings often fought against each other.

Bede loved to learn even when he was a boy. We know this, for long afterward another learned man told his pupils to take Bede for an example, and not spend their time "digging out foxes and coursing hares."[1] And when he became a man he was one of the most learned of his time, and wrote books on nearly every subject that was then thought worth writing about.

[1] C. Plummer.

Once, when Bede was still a boy, a fearful plague swept the land, "killing and destroying a great multitude of men." In the monastery of Jarrow all who could read, or preach, or sing were killed by it. Only the Abbot himself and a little lad were left. The Abbot loved the services and the praises of the church. His heart was heavy with grief and mourning for the loss of his friends; it was heavy, too, with the thought that the services of his church could no longer be made beautiful with song.

For a few days the Abbot read the services all alone, but at the end of a week he could no longer bear the lack of singing, so calling the little lad he bade him to help him and to chant the responses.

The story calls up to us a strange picture. There stands the great monastery, all its rooms empty. Along its stone-flagged passages the footsteps of the man and boy echo strangely. They reach the chapel vast and dim, and there, before the great altar with its gleaming lights, the Abbot in his robes chants the services, but where the voices of choir and people were wont to join, there sounds only the clear high voice of one little boy.

That little boy was Bede.

And thus night and morning the sound of prayer and praise rose from the deserted chapel until the force of the plague had spent itself, and it was once more possible to find men to take the places of those singers who had died.

So the years passed on until, when Bede was thirty years of age, he became a priest. He might have been made an abbot had he wished. But he refused to be taken away from his beloved books. "The office," he said, "demands household care, and household care brings with it distraction of mind, hindering the pursuit of learning." [1]

Bede wrote many books, but it is by his *Ecclesiastical*

[1] H Morley, *English Writers*

History (that is Church history) that we remember him best. As Caedmon is called the Father of English Poetry, Bede is called the Father of English History. But it is well to remember that Caedmon wrote in Anglo-Saxon and Bede in Latin.

There were others who wrote history before Bede, but he was perhaps the first who wrote history in the right spirit. He did not write in order to make a good minstrel's tale. He tried to tell the truth. He was careful as to where he got his facts, and careful how he used them. So those who came after him could trust him. Bede's *History,* you remember, was one of the books which Layamon used when he wrote his *Brut,* and in it we find many of the stories of early British history which have grown familiar to us.

It is in this book that we find the story of how Gregory saw the pretty children in the Roman slave market, and of how, for love of their fair faces, he sent Augustine to teach the heathen Saxons about Christ. There are, too, many stories in it of how the Saxons became Christian. One of the most interesting, perhaps, is about Edwin, King of Northumbria. Edwin had married a Christian princess, Ethelberga, sister of Eadbald, King of Kent. Eadbald was, at first, unwilling that his sister should marry a pagan king. But Edwin promised that he would not try to turn her from her religion, and that she and all who came with her should be allowed to worship what god they chose.

So the Princess Ethelberga came to be Queen of Northumbria, and with her she brought Paulinus, "a man beloved of God," as priest. He came to help her to keep faithful among a heathen people, and in the hope, too, that he might be able to turn the pagan king and his folk to the true faith.

And in this hope he was not disappointed. By

degrees King Edwin began to think much about the Christian faith. He gave up worshiping idols, and although he did not at once become Christian, "he often sat alone with silent lips, while in his inmost heart he argued much with himself, considering what was best to do and what religion he should hold to." At last the King decided to call a council of his wise men, and to ask each one what he thought of this new teaching. And when they were all gathered Coifi, the chief priest, spoke.

" 'O King,' he said, 'consider what this is which is now preached to us; for I verily declare to you, that the religion which we have hitherto professed has, as far as I can learn, no virtue in it. For none of your people has applied himself more diligently to the worship of our gods than I. And yet there are many who receive greater favors from you, and are more preferred than I, and are more prosperous in their undertakings. Now if the gods were good for anything, they would rather forward me, who have been more careful to serve them. It remains, therefore, that if upon examination you find those new doctrines, which are now preached to us, better and more efficacious, we immediately receive them without delay.'

"Another of the King's chief men, approving of his words and exhortations, presently added: 'The present life of man, O King, seems to me, in comparison of that time which is unknown to us, like to the swift flight of a sparrow through the room wherein you sit at supper in winter, with your commanders and ministers, and a good fire in the midst, while the storms of rain and snow prevail abroad. The sparrow, I say, flying in at one door and immediately out at another, whilst he is within is safe from the wintry storm; but after a short space of fair weather, he immediately vanishes out of your sight into the dark winter from whence he had emerged. So this life of man appears for a short space, but of what went before, or what is to follow, we are utterly ignorant. If, therefore, this new doctrine contains something more certain, it seems justly to deserve to be followed.' "

Others of the King's wise men and counselors spoke, and they all spoke to the same end. Coifi then said that he would hear yet more of what Paulinus had to tell. So Paulinus rose from his place and told the people more of the story of Christ. And after listening attentively for some time Coifi again cried out, " 'I advise, O King, that we instantly abjure and set fire to those temples and altars which we have consecrated without reaping any benefit from them.'

"In short, the King publicly gave his license to Paulinus to preach the Gospel, and renouncing idolatry, declared that he received the faith of Christ. And when he inquired of the high priest who should first profane the altars and temples of their idols with the enclosures that were about them, Coifi answered, 'I; for who can more properly than myself destroy those things which I worshiped through ignorance, for an example to all others through the wisdom which has been given me by the true God?'

"Then immediately, in contempt of his former superstitions, he desired the King to furnish him with arms and a stallion. And mounting the same he set out to destroy the idols. For it was not lawful before for the high priest either to carry arms or to ride upon any but a mare.

"Having, therefore, girt a sword about him, with a spear in his hand, he mounted the King's stallion and proceeded to the idols. The multitude, beholding it, concluded he was distracted. But he lost no time, for as soon as he drew near the temple he profaned the same, casting into it the spear which he held. And rejoicing in the knowledge of the worship of the true God, he com-

manded his companions to destroy the temple, with all
its enclosures, by fire." [1]

One reason why I have chosen this story out of Bede's
History is because it contains the picture of the sparrow
flitting through the firelit room. Out of the dark and cold
it comes into the light and warmth for a moment, and
then vanishes into the dark and cold once more.

The Saxon who more than thirteen hundred years
ago made that word-picture was a poet. He did not
know it, perhaps, he was only speaking of what he had
often seen, telling in simple words of something that
happened almost every day, and yet he has given us a
picture which we cannot forget, and has made our literature by so much the richer. He has told us of something,
too, which helps us to realize the rough life our forefathers
lived. Even in the king's palace the windows were without glass, the doors stood open to let out the smoke from
"the good fire in the midst," for there were no chimneys,
or at best but a hole in the roof to serve as one. The
doors stood open, even though "the storms of snow and
rain prevailed abroad," and in spite of the good fire, it
must have been comfortless enough. Yet many a stray
bird might well be drawn thither by the light and warmth.

Bede lived a peaceful, busy life, and when he came to
die his end was peaceful too, and his work ceased only
with his death. One of his pupils, writing to a friend,
tells of these last hours. [2]

For some weeks in the bright springtime of 735 Bede
had been ill, yet "cheerful and rejoicing, giving thanks
to almighty God every day and night. yea every hour."
Daily, too, he continued to give lessons to his pupils, and
the rest of the time he spent in singing psalms. "I can

[1] Dr Giles's translation of *Ecclesiastical History*
[2] Extracts are from letter of Cuthbert, afterwards Abbot of Wearmouth and
Jarrow, to his friend Cuthwin.

with truth declare that I never saw with my eyes, or heard with my ears, any one return thanks so unceasingly to the living God," says the letter. "During these days he labored to compose two works well worthy to be remembered besides the lessons we had from him, and singing of psalms: that is, he translated the Gospel of St. John as far as the words, 'But what are these among so many,' into our own tongue for the benefit of the church, and some collections out of the *Book of Notes* of Bishop Isidor.

"When the Tuesday before the Ascension of our Lord came, he began to suffer still more in his health. But he passed all that day and dictated cheerfully, and now and then among other things said, 'Go on quickly; I know not how long I shall hold out, and whether my maker will not soon take me away.'

"But to us he seemed very well to know the time of his departure. And so he spent the night awake in thanksgiving. And when the morning appeared, that is Wednesday, he ordered us to write with all speed what he had begun. . . .

"There was one of us with him who said to him, 'Most dear Master, there is still one chapter wanting. Do you think it troublesome to be asked any more questions?'

"He answered, 'It is no trouble. Take your pen and make ready and write fast. . . .'

"Then the same boy said once more, 'Dear Master, there is yet one sentence not written.'

"And he said, 'Well, then write it.'

"And after a little space the boy said, 'Now it is finished.'

"And he answered, 'Well, thou hast spoken truth, it is finished. Receive my head into your hands, for it is a great satisfaction to me to sit facing my holy place, where I was wont to pray, that I may also, sitting, call upon my Father.'"

And sitting upon the pavement of his little cell, he sang, "Glory be to the Father and to the Son, and to the Holy Ghost." "When he had named the Holy Ghost he breathed his last, and departed to the heavenly kingdom."

So died Bede, surnamed the Venerable.

We have come to think of Venerable as meaning very old. But Bede was only sixty-two when he died, and Venerable here means rather "Greatly to be honored."

There are two or three stories about how Bede came to be given his surname. One tells how a young monk was set to write some lines of poetry to be put upon the tomb where his master was buried. He tried hard, but the verse would not come right. He could not get the proper number of syllables in his lines.

"In this grave lie the bones of　　　　　　Bede,"

he wrote. But he could not find an adjective that would make the line the right length, try how he might. At last, wearied out, he fell asleep over his task.

Then, as he slept, an angel bent down, and taking the pen from the monk's tired fingers, wrote the words, "the Venerable," so that the line ran, "In this grave lie the bones of the Venerable Bede." And thus, for all time, our first great historian is known as The Venerable Bede.

BOOK TO READ

The Ecclesiastical History of the English Nation, by Bede, translated by Dr Giles.

CHAPTER XV

HOW ALFRED THE GREAT FOUGHT WITH HIS PEN

WHILE Caedmon sang his English lays and Bede wrote his Latin books, Northumbria had grown into a center, not only of English learning, but of learning for western Europe. The abbots of Jarrow and Wearmouth made journeys to Rome and· brought back with them precious MSS. for the monastery libraries. Scholars from all parts of Europe came to visit the Northumbrian monasteries, or sent thither for teachers.

But before many years had passed all that was changed. Times of war and trouble were not yet over for England. Once again heathen hordes fell upon our shores. The Danes, fierce and lawless, carrying sword and firebrand wherever they passed, leaving death and ruin in their tiack, surged over the land. The monasteries were ruined, the scholars were scattered. A life of peaceful study was no longer possible, the learning of two hundred years was swept away, the lamp of knowledge lit by the monks grew dim and flickered out.

But when sixty years or more had passed, a king arose who crushed the Danish power, and who once more lit that lamp. This king was Alfred the Great.

History tells us how he fought the Danes, how he despaired, and how he took heart again, and how he at last conquered his enemies and brought peace to his people.

Alfred was great in war. He was no less great in peace.

As he fought the Danes with the sword, so he fought
ignorance with his pen. He loved books, and he longed
to bring back to England something of the learning which
had been lost. Nor did he want to keep learning for a
few only. He wanted all his people to get the good of it.
And so, as most good books were written in Latin, which
only a few could read, he began to translate some of them
into English.

In the beginning of one of them Alfred says, "There
are only a few on this side of the Humber who can understand the Divine Service, or even explain a Latin epistle
in English, and I believe not many on the other side of
the Humber either. But they are so few that indeed I
cannot remember one south of the Thames when I began
to reign."

By "this side of the Humber" Alfred means the south
side, for now the center of learning was no longer Northumbria, but Wessex.

Alfred translated many books. He translated books
of geography, history and religion, and it is from Alfred
that our English prose dates, just as English poetry dates
from Caedmon. For you must remember that although
we call Bede the Father of English History, he wrote in
Latin for the most part, and what he wrote in English has
been lost.

Besides writing himself, Alfred encouraged his people
to write. He also caused a national Chronicle to be
written.

A chronicle is the simplest form of history. The old
chronicles did not weave their history into stories, they
simply put down a date and something that happened on
that date. They gave no reasons for things, they expressed no feelings, no thoughts. So the chronicles can
hardly be called literature. They were not meant to be
looked upon as literature. The writers of them used

them rather as keys to memory. They kept all the stories in their memories, and the sight of the name of a king or of a battle was enough to unlock their store of words. And as they told their tales, if they forgot a part they made something up, just as the minstrels did.

Alfred caused the *Chronicle* to be written up from such books and records as he had from the coming of the Romans until the time in which he himself reigned. And from then onwards to the time of the death of King Stephen the *Saxon Chronicle* was kept. It is now one of the most useful books from which we can learn the history of those times.

Sometimes, especially at the beginning, the record is very scant. As a rule, there is not more than one short sentence for a year, sometimes not even that, but merely a date. It is like this:—

"Year 189. In this year Severus succeeded to the empire and reigned seventeen winters. He begirt Britain with a dike from sea to sea.

"Year 190.

"Year 199.

"Year 200. In this year was found the Holy Rood."

And so on it goes, and every now and again, among entries which seem to us of little or no importance, we learn something that throws great light on our past history. And when we come to the time of Alfred's reign the entries are much more full. From the *Chronicle* we learn a great deal about his wars with the Danes, and of how he fought them both by land and by sea.

The *Saxon Chronicle,* as it extended over many hundred years, was of course written by many different people, and so parts of it are written much better than other parts. Sometimes we find a writer who does more than merely set down facts, who seems to have a feeling for how he tells his story, and who tries to make the thing he writes about living. Sometimes a writer even breaks into song.

Besides causing the *Chronicle* to be written, Alfred translated Bede's *History* into English. And so that all might learn the history of their land, he rebuilt the ruined monasteries and opened schools in them once more. There he ordered that "Every free-born youth in the Kingdom, who has the means, shall attend to his book, so long as he have no other business, till he can read English perfectly." [1]

Alfred died after having reigned for nearly thirty years. Much that he had done seemed to die with him, for once again the Danes descended upon our coasts. Once again they conquered, and Canute the Dane became King of England. But the English spirit was strong, and the Danish invasion has left scarcely a trace upon our language. Nor did the Danish power last long, for in 1042 we had in Edward the Confessor an English king once more. But he was English only in name. In truth he was more than half French, and under him French forces began already to work on our literature. A few years later that French force became overwhelming, for in 1066 William of Normandy came to our shores, and with his coming it seemed for a time as if the life of English literature was to be crushed out forever. Only by the *Chronicle* were both prose and poetry kept alive in the English tongue. And it is to Alfred the Great that we owe this slender thread which binds our English literature of to-day with the literature of a thousand years ago.

[1] Preface of Bœthius' *Pastoral Care,* translated into English by Alfred.

CHAPTER XVI

WHEN ENGLISH SLEPT

"William came o'er the sea,
With bloody sword came he.
Cold heart and bloody sword hand
Now rule the English land."

The Heimskringla.

WILLIAM THE NORMAN ruled England. Norman knights and nobles filled all the posts of honor at court, all the great places in the land. Norman bishops and abbots ruled in church and monastery. The Norman tongue was alone the speech in court and hall, Latin alone was the speech of the learned. Only among the lowly, the unlearned, and the poor was English heard.

It seemed as if the English tongue was doomed to vanish before the conquering Norman, even as the ancient British tongue had vanished before the conquering English. And, in truth, for two hundred years it might have been thought that English prose was dead, "put to sleep by the sword." But it was not so. It slept, indeed, but to awake again. For England conquered the conqueror. And when English Literature awoke once more, it was the richer through the gifts which the Norman had brought.

One thing the Normans had brought was a liking for history, and soon there sprang up a whole race of chroniclers. They, like Bede, were monks and priests. They lived in monasteries, and wrote in Latin. One after another they wrote, and when one laid down his pen, another took it up. Some of these chroniclers were mere painstaking men who noted facts and dates with care. But others were true writers of literature, who told their tales in vivid, stirring words, so that they make these times live again for us. The names of some of the best of these chroniclers are Eadmer, Orderic Vitalis, and William of Malmesbury.

By degrees these Norman or Anglo-Norman monks became filled with the spirit of England. They wrote of England as of their home, they were proud to call themselves English, and they began to desire that England should stand high among the nations. It is, you remember, from one of these chroniclers, Geoffrey of Monmouth (see chapter vi), that we date the reawakening of story-telling in England.

As a writer of history Geoffrey is bad. Another chronicler [1] says of him, "Therefore as in all things we trust Bede, whose wisdom and truth are not to be doubted: so that fabler with his fables shall be forthwith spat out by us all."

But if Geoffrey was bad as a writer of history, he was good as "a fabler," and, as we have seen in chapter vii., it was to his book that we owe the first long poem written in English after the Conquest.

The Norman came with sword in hand, bringing in his train the Latin-writing chroniclers. But he did not bring these alone. He brought minstrels also. Besides the quiet monks who sat in their little cells, or in the pleasant cloisters, writing the history of the times, there were the light-hearted minstrels who roamed the land with harp and song.

The man who struck the first blow at Hastings was a minstrel who, as he rode against the English, sang. And

[1] William of Newbury.

the song he sang was of Roland, the great champion of Charlemagne. The Roland story is to France what the Arthur story is to us. And it shows, perhaps, the strength of English patriotic spirit that that story never took hold of English minds. Some few tales there are told of Roland in English, but they are few indeed, in comparison with the many that are told of Arthur.

The Norman, however, who did not readily invent new tales, was very good at taking and making his own the tales of others. So, even as he conquered England by the sword, he conquered our literature too. For the stories of Arthur were told in French before they came back to us in English. It was the same with other tales, and many of our old stories have come down to us, not through their English originals, but through the French. For the years after the Conquest are the poorest in English Literature.

From the Conquest until Layamon wrote his *Brut,* there was no English literature worthy of the name. Had we not already spoken of Layamon out of true order in following the story of Arthur, it is here that we should speak of him and of his book, *The Brut.* So, perhaps, it would be well to go back and read chapter vii., and then we must go on to the Metrical Romances.

The three hundred years from 1200 to 1500 were the years of the Metrical Romances. Metrical means written in verse. Romance meant at first the languages made from the Latin tongue, such as French or Spanish. After a time the word Romance was used to mean a story told in any Romance language. But now we use it to mean any story of strange and wonderful adventures, especially when the most thrilling adventures happen to the hero and heroine.

The Norman minstrels, then, took English tales and made them into romances. But when the English began once more to write, they turned these romances back again into English. We still call them romances, although they are now written in English.

Some of these tales came to us, no doubt, from the Danes. They were brought from over the sea by the fierce Northmen, who were, after all, akin to the Normans. The Normans made them into French stories, and the English turned them back into English.

Perhaps one of the most interesting of these Metrical Romances is that of *Havelok the Dane.*

The poem begins with a few lines which seem meant to call the people together to listen:—

> "Hearken to me, good men,
> Wives, maidens, and all men,
> To a tale that I will tell to
> Who so will hear and list thereto."

We can imagine the minstrel as he stands in some market-place, or in some firelit hall, touching his harp lightly as he sings the words. With a quick movement he throws back his long green cloak, and shows his gay dress beneath. Upon his head he wears a jaunty cap, and his hair is long and curled. He sings the opening lines perhaps more than once, in order to gather the people round him. Then, when the eager crowd sit or stand about him, he begins his lay. It is most probably in a market-place that the minstrel stands and sings. For *Havelok the Dane* was written for the people and not for the great folk, who still spoke only French.

> "There was a king in byegone days
> That in his time wrought good laws,
> He did them make and full well hold,
> Him loved young, him loved old,
> Earl and baron, strong man and thane,
> Knight, bondman and swain,
> Widows, maidens, priests and clerks
> And all for his good works."

If you will compare this poetry with that of Layamon, you will see that there is something in it quite different from his. This no longer rests, as that does, upon accent and alliteration, but upon rhyme. The English, too, in which it is written, is much more like the English of to-day. For *Havelok* was written perhaps a hundred years after Layamon's *Brut*. These are the first lines as they are in the MS.:—

> "Herknet to me gode men
> Wiues maydnes and alle men
> Of a tale þat ich you wile telle
> Wo so it wile here and yerto dwelle."

That, you see, except for curious spelling, is not very unlike our English of to-day, although it is fair to tell you that all the lines are not so easy to understand as these are.

CHAPTER XVII

THE STORY OF HAVELOK THE DANE

The good king of whom we read in the last chapter was called Athelwold, and the poet tells us that there were happy days in England while he reigned. But at length he became sick unto death. Then was he sore grieved, because he had no child to sit upon the throne after him save a maiden very fair. But so young was she that she could neither "go on foot nor speak with mouth." So, in this grief and trouble, the King wrote to all his nobles, "from Roxburgh all unto Dover," bidding them come to him.

And all who had the writings came to the King, where he lay at Winchester. Then, when they were all come, Athelwold prayed them to be faithful to the young Princess, and to choose one of themselves to guard her until she was of age to rule.

So Godrich, Earl of Cornwall, was chosen to guard the Princess. For he was a true man, wise in council, wise in deed, and he swore to protet his lady until she was of such age as no longer to have need of him. Then he would wed her, he swore, to the best man in all the land.

So, happy in the thought that his daughter should reign after him in peace, the King died, and there was great sorrow and mourning throughout the land. But the people remained at peace, for the Earl ruled well and wisely.

> "From Dover to Roxburgh
> All England of him stood in awe,
> All England was of him adread."

Meanwhile the Princess Goldboru grew daily more and more fair. And when Earl Godrich saw how fair and noble she became, he sighed and asked himself:—

> "Whether she should be
> Queen and lady over me.
> Whether she should all England,
> And me, and mine, have in her hand
> Nay, he said,
> 'I have a son, a full fair knave,
> He shall England all have,
> He shall be king, he shall be sire.' "

Then, full of his evil purpose, Godrich thought no more of his oath to the dead king, but cast Goldboru into a darksome prison, where she was poorly clad and ill-fed.

Now it befell that at this time there was a right good king in Denmark. He had a son named Havelok and two fair daughters. And feeling death come upon him, he left his children in the care of his dear friend Godard, and so died.

But no sooner was the King in his grave than the false Godard took Havelok and his two sisters and thrust them into a dungeon.

> "And in the castle did he them do
> Where no man might come them to,
> Of their kin   There they prison'd were,
> There they wept oft sort,
> Both for hunger and for cold,
> Ere they were three winters old
> Scantily he gave them clothes,
> And cared not a nut for his oaths,
> He them nor clothed right, nor fed,
> Nor them richly gave to bed.
> Thane Godard was most sickerly
> Under God the most traitorly
> That ever in earth shapen was
> Except the wicked Judas."

After a time the traitor went to the tower where the children were, and there he slew the two little girls. But the boy Havelok he spared.

"For the lad that little was,
He kneeled before that Judas
And said, 'Lord, mercy now!
Homage, Lord, to you I vow!
All Denmark I to you will give
If that now you let me live' "

So the wicked Earl spared the lad for the time. But he did not mean that he should live. Anon he called a fisherman to him and said:—

"Grim, thou wist thou art my thral,
Wilt thou do my will all
That I will bid thee?
To-morrow I shall make thee free,
And give thee goods, and rich thee make,
If that thou wilt this child take
And lead him with thee, to-night,
When thou seest it is moonlight,
Unto the sea, and do him in!
And I will take on me the sin."

Grim, the fisherman, rejoiced at the thought of being free and rich. So he took the boy, and wound him in an old cloth, and stuffed an old coat into his mouth, so that he might not cry aloud. Then he thrust him into a sack, and thus carried him home to his cottage.

But when the moon rose, and Grim made ready to drown the child, his wife saw a great light come from the sack. And opening it, they found therein the prince. Then they resolved, instead of drowning him, to save and nourish him as their own child. But they resolved also to hide the truth from the Earl.

At break of day, therefore, Grim set forth to tell Godard that his will was done. But instead of the thanks and reward promised to him, he got only evil words. So, speeding homeward from that traitor, he made ready his boat, and with his wife and three sons and two daughters and Havelok, they set sail upon the high sea, fleeing for their lives.

Presently a great wind arose which blew them to the coast of England. And when they were safely come to land, Grim drew up his boat upon the shore, and there he built him a hut, and there he lived, and to this day men call the place Grimsby.

Years passed. Havelok lived with the fisherman, and grew great and fair and strong. And as Grim was poor, the Prince thought it no dishonor to work for his living, and he became in time a cook's scullion.

Havelok had to work hard. But although he worked hard he was always cheerful and merry. He was so strong that at running, jumping, or throwing a stone no one could beat him. Yet he was so gentle that all the children of the place loved him and played with him.

> "Him loved all, quiet or bold,
> Knights, children, young and old,
> All him loved that him saw,
> Both high men and low,
> Of him full wide the word sprang
> How he was meek, how he was strong."

At last even the wicked Godrich in his palace heard of Havelok in the kitchen. "Now truly this is the best man in England," he said, with a sneer. And thinking to bring shame on Goldboru, and wed her with a kitchen knave, he sent for Havelok.

"Master, wilt wed?" he asked, when the scullion was brought before him.

"Nay," quoth Havelok, "by my life what should I do with a wife? I could not feed her, nor clothe her, nor shoe her. Whither should I bring a woman? I have no

cot, I have no stick nor twig. I have neither bread nor
sauce, and no clothes but one old oat. These clothes
even that I wear are the cook's, and 1 am his knave."

At that Godrich shook with wrath. Up he sprang
and began to beat Havelok without mercy.

> "And said, 'Unless thou her take,
> That I well ween thee to make,
> I shall hangen thee full high
> Or I shall thrusten out thine eye.'"

Then seeing that there was no help for it, and that he
must either be wedded or hanged, Havelok consented to
marry Goldboru. So the Princess was brought, "the
fairest woman under the moon." And she, sore afraid at
the anger and threats of Godrich, durst not do aught to
oppose the wedding. So were they "espoused fair and
well" by the Archbishop of York, and Havelok took his
bride home to Grimsby.

You may be sure that Havelok, who was so strong and
yet so gentle, was kind to his beautiful young wife. But
Goldboru was unhappy, for she could not forget the disgrace that had come upon her. She could not forget
that she was a princess, and that she had been forced to
wed a low-born kitchen knave. But one night, as she
lay in bed weeping, an angel appeared to her and bade
her sorrow no more, for it was no scullion that she had
wed, but a king's son. So Goldboru was comforted.

And of all that afterward befell Havelok and Goldboru,
of how they went to Denmark and overcame the traitor
there, and received the kingdom; and of how they returned again to England, and of how Godrich was punished, you must read for yourselves in the book of *Havelok the Dane*. But this one thing more I will tell
you, that Havelok and Goldboru lived happily together
until they died. They loved each other so tenderly that

they were never angry with each other. They had fifteen children, and all the sons became kings and all the daughters became queens.

I should like to tell you many more of these early English metrical romances. I should like to tell you of Guy of Warwick, of King Horn, of William and the Werewolf, and of many others. But, indeed, if I told all the stories I should like to tell this book would have no end. So we must leave them and pass on.

BOOKS TO READ

The Story of Havelok the Dane, rendered into later English by Emily Hickey
The Lay of Havelok the Dane, edited by W. W. Skeat in the original English.

CHAPTER XVIII

ABOUT SOME SONG STORIES

BESIDES the metrical romances, we may date another kind of story from this time. I mean the ballads.

Ballad was an old French word spelt balade. It really means a dance-song. For ballads were at first written to be sung to dances—slow, shuffling, balancing dances such as one may still see in out-of-the-way places in Brittany.

These ballads often had a chorus or refrain in which every one joined. But by degrees the refrain was dropped and the dancing too. Now we think of a ballad as a simple story told in verse. Sometimes it is merry, but more often it is sad.

The ballads were not made for grand folk. They were not made to be sung in courts and halls. They were made for the common people, and sometimes at least they were made by them. They were meant to be sung, and sung out of doors. For in those days the houses of all but the great were very comfortless. They were small and dark and full of smoke. It was little wonder, then, that people lived out of doors as much as they could, and that all their amusements were out of doors. And so it comes about that many of the ballads have an out-of-door feeling about them.

A ballad is much shorter than a romance, and therefore much more easily learned and remembered. So many people learned and repeated the ballads, and for three hundred years they were the chief literature of the people. In those days men sang far more and read and thought far less than nowadays. Now, if we read poetry, some of us like to be quietly by ourselves. Then all poetry was made to be read or sung aloud, and that in company.

I do not mean you to think that we have any ballads remaining to us as old as the thirteenth or the beginning of the fourteenth century, which was the time in which *Havelok* was written. But what I want you to understand is that the ballad-making days went on for hundreds of years. The people for whom the ballads were made could not read and could not write; so it was of little use to write them down, and for a long time they were not written down. "They were made for singing, an' no for reading," said an old lady to Sir Walter Scott, who in his day made a collection of ballads. "They were made for singing an' no for reading; but ye hae broken the charm now, an' they'll never be sung mair."

And so true is this, that ballads which have never been written down, but which are heard only in out-of-the-way places, sung or said by people who have never learned to read, have really more of the old-time feeling about them than many of those which we find in books.

We cannot say who made the ballads. Nowadays a poet makes a poem, and it is printed with his name upon the title-page. The poem belongs to him, and is known by his name. We say, for instance, Gray's *Elegy*, or Shakespeare's *Sonnets*. But many people helped to make the ballads. I do not mean that twenty or thirty people sat down together and said, "Let us make a ballad." That would not have been possible. But, perhaps, one man heard a story and put it into verse. Another then heard it and added something to it. Still another and another heard, repeated, added to, or altered it in one way or another. Sometimes the story was made better by the process, sometimes it was spoiled. But who those men were who made and altered the ballads, we do not know. They were simply "the people."

One whole group of ballads tells of the wonderful deeds of Robin Hood. Who Robin Hood was we do not certainly know, nor does it matter much. Legend has made him a man of gentle birth who had lost his lands and money, and who had fled to the woods as an outlaw. Stories gradually gathered round his name as they had gathered round the name of Arthur, and he came to be looked upon as the champion of the people against the Norman tyrants.

Robin was a robber, but a robber as courtly as any knight. His enemies were the rich and great, his friends were the poor and oppressed.

> "For I never yet hurt any man
>   That honest is and true;
> But those that give their minds to live
>   Upon other men's due.
>
> I never hurt the husbandmen
>   That used to till the ground;
> Nor spill their blood that range the wood
>   To follow hawk or hound.
>
> My chiefest spite to clergy is
>   Who in those days bear a great sway;
> With friars and monks with their fine sprunks
>   I make my chiefest prey "

The last time we heard of monks and priests they were the friends of the people, doing their best to teach them and make them happy. Now we find that they are looked upon as enemies. And the monasteries, which at the beginning had been like lamps of light set in a dark country, had themselves become centers of darkness and idleness.

But although Robin fought against the clergy, the friars, and monks who did wrong, he did not fight against religion.

> "A good manner then had Robin,
>   In land where that he were,
> Every day ere he would dine,
>   Three masses would he hear.
>
> The one in worship of the Father,
>   And another of the Holy Ghost,
> The third of Our Dear Lady,
>   That he loved all the most.
>
> Robin loved Our Dear Lady,
>   For doubt of deadly sin,
> Would he never do company harm
>   That any woman was in "

And Robin himself tells his followers:—

> "But look ye do no husbandman harm
>   That tilleth with his plough
>
> No more ye shall no good yeoman
>   That walketh by green wood shaw,
> Nor no knight nor no squire
>   That will be good fellow.
>
> These bishops and these archbishops,
>   Ye shall them beat and bind,
> The high sheriff of Nottingham,
>   Him hold ye in your mind."

The great idea of the Robin Hood ballads is the victory of the poor and oppressed over the rich and powerful, the triumph of the lawless over the law-givers. Because of this, and because we like Robin much better than the Sheriff of Nottingham, his chief enemy, we are not to think that the poor were always right and the rulers always wrong. There were many good men among the despised monks and friars, bishops and archbishops.

But there were, too, many evils in the land, and some of the laws pressed sorely on the people. Yet they were never without a voice.

The Robin Hood ballads are full of humor; they are full, too, of English outdoor life, of hunting and fighting.

Of quite another style is the ballad of Sir Patrick Spens. That takes us away from the green, leafy woods and dells of England to the wild, rocky coast of Scotland. It takes us from the singing of birds to the roar of the waves. The story goes that the King wanted a good sailor to sail across the sea. Then an old knight says to him that the best sailor that ever sailed the sea is Sir Patrick Spens.

So the King writes a letter bidding Sir Patrik make ready. At first he is pleased to get a letter from the King, but when he has read what is in it his face grows sad and angry too.

"Who has done me this evil deed?" he cries, "to send me out to sea in such weather?"

Sir Patrick is very unwilling to go. But the King has commanded, so he and his men set forth. A great storm comes upon them and the ship is wrecked. All the men are drowned, and the ladies who sit at home waiting their husbands' return wait in vain.

There are many versions of this ballad, but I give you here one of the shortest and perhaps the most beautiful.

> "The king sits in Dumferling toune
>   Drinking the blude reid wine:
> 'O whar will I get a guid sailor,
>   To sail this schip of mine?'
>
> Up and spak an eldern knicht,
>   Sat at the king's richt kne·
> 'Sir Patrick Spence is the best sailor
>   That sails upon the se'

The king has written a braid letter,
    And signed it wi his hand,
And sent it to Sir Patrick Spence,
    Was walking on the sand.

The first line that Sir Patrick red,
    A loud lauch lauched he,
The next line that Sir Patrick red,
    The teir blinded his ee.

'O wha is this has done this deed,
    This ill deed don to me,
To send me out this time o' the yeir,
    To sail upon the se?

'Mak hast, mak hast, my merry men all,
    Our guid schip sails the morne'
'Oh, say na sae, my master deir,
    For I feir a deadlie storme.

'Late, late yestreen I saw the new moone,
    Wi the auld moone in her arme,
And I feir, I feir, my deir master,
    That we will cum to harme'

O, our Scots nobles wer richt laith
    To weet their cork-heild schoone;
Bot lang owre a' the play wer played
    Thair hats they swam aboone.

O lang, lang, may their ladies sit,
    Wi their fans into their hand,
Or eir they see Sir Patrick Spence
    Cum sailing to the land

O lang, lang, may the ladies stand,
    Wi their gold kaims in their hair,
Waiting for their ain deir lords,
    For they'll see them na mair.

Haf ower, haf ower to Aberdour,
    It's fiftie fadom deip,
And thair lies guid Sir Patrick Spence.
    Wi the Scots lords at his feit."

And now, just to end this chapter, let me give you one more poem. It is the earliest English song that is known. It is a spring song, and it is so full of the sunny green of fresh young leaves, and of all the sights and sounds of early summer, that I think you will like it.

> "Summer is a-coming in,
> Loud sing cuckoo;
> Groweth seed and bloweth mead,
> And springeth the wood new,
>   Sing cuckoo!
>
> Ewe bleateth after lamb,
> Loweth after calf the cow;
> Bullock starteth, buck verteth,[1]
>   Merry sing cuckoo
>
> Cuckoo, cuckoo, well singeth thou cuckoo,
> Thou art never silent now
> Sing cuckoo, now, sing cuckoo,
>   Sing cuckoo, sing cuckoo, now!'"

Is that not pretty? Can you not hear the cuckoo call, even though the lamps may be lit and the winter wind be shrill without?

But I think it is prettier still in its thirteenth-century English. Perhaps you may be able to read it in that, so here it is:—

> "Sumer is ycumen in,
> Lhude sing cuccu;
> Groweth sed, and bloweth med,
> And springth the wde nu,
>   Sing cuccu!
>
> Awe bleteth after lomb,
> Lhouth after calve cu;
> Bulluc sterteth, bucke verteth,
>   Murie sing cuccu

---

[1] Turns to the green fern or "vert" *Vert* is French for "green."

Cuccu, cuccu, well singes thu cuccu,
Ne swike thu naver nu.
Sing cuccu, nu, sing cuccu,
    Sing cuccu, sing cuccu, nu!" [1]

BOOKS TO READ

Stories of Robin Hood, by H. E Marshall   *Stories of the Ballads,* by Mary Macgregor   *A Book of Ballads,* by C L Thomson.   *Percy's Reliques of Ancient English Poetry* (Everyman's Library)

[1] Ritson's *Ancient Songs.*

CHAPTER XIX

"PIERS THE PLOUGHMAN"

DURING the long years after the Norman Conquest when English was a despised language, it became broken up into many dialects. But as time went on and English became once more the language of the educated as well as of the uneducated, there arose a cultured English, which became the language which we speak to-day.

In the time of Edward III. England was England again, and the rulers were English both in heart and in name. But England was no longer a country apart, she was no longer a lonely sea-girt island, but had taken her place among the great countries of Europe. For the reign of Edward III. was a brilliant one. The knightly, chivalrous King set his country high among the countries of Europe. Men made songs and sang of his victories, of Crecy and of Calais, and France bowed the knee to England. But the wars and triumphs of the King pressed hardly on the people of England, and ere his reign was over misery, pestilence, and famine filled the land.

So many men had been killed in Edward's French and Scottish wars that there were too few left to till the land. Then came a terrible disease called the Black Death, slaying young and old, rich and poor, until nearly half the people in the land were dead.

Then fewer still were left to do the work of the farms. Cattle and sheep strayed where they would, for there were none to tend them. Corn ripened and rotted in the fields,

for there were none to gather it. Food grew dear as
workers grew scarce. Then the field laborers who were
left began to demand larger wages. Many of these laborers were little more than slaves, and their masters
refused to pay them better. Then some left their homes
and went away to seek new masters who would be willing
to pay more, while others took to a life of wandering
beggary.

The owners of the land had thought that they should
be ruined did they pay the great wages demanded of them.
Now they saw that they should be ruined quite as much
if they could find no one at all to do the work. So laws
were made forcing men to work for the same wages they
had received before the plague, and forbidding them to
leave the towns and villages in which they had been used
to live. If they disobeyed they were imprisoned and punished.

Yet these new laws were broken again and again,
because bread had now become so dear that it was impossible for men to live on as little as they had done before.
Still many masters tried to enforce the law, and the land
was soon filled not only with hunger and misery, but with
a fierce class hatred between master and man. It was the
beginning of a long and bitter struggle, and as the cry of
the poor grew louder and louder, the hatred and spirit of
revolt grew fiercer.

But the great of the land seemed little touched by the
sorrows of the people. While they starved and died, the
King, surrounded by a glittering court, gave splendid
feasts and tournaments. He built fair palaces and chapels,
founded a new round table, and thought to make the
glorious days of Arthur live again.

And the great among the clergy cared as little for the
poor as did the great among the nobles. Many of them
had become selfish and worldly, some of them wicked,

though of course there were many good men left among them too.

The Church was wealthy, but the powerful priests kept that wealth in their own hands, and many of the country clergy were almost as miserably poor as the people whom they taught   And it was through one of these poor priests, named William Langland, that the sorrows of the people found a voice.

We know very little about Langland. So little do we know that we are not sure if his name was really William or not. But in his poem called *The Vision of Piers the Ploughman* he says, "I have lived in the land, quoth I, my name is long Will." It is chiefly from his poem that we learn to know the man. When we have read it, we seem to see him, tall and thin, with lean earnest face, out of which shine great eyes, the eyes that see visions. His head is shaven like a monk's; he wears a shabby long gown which flaps in the breeze as he strides along.

Langland was born in the country, perhaps in Oxfordshire, perhaps in Shropshire, and he went to school at Great Malvern. He loved school, for he says:—

> "For if heaven be on earth, and ease to any soul,
> It is in cloister or in school. Be many reasons I find
> For in the cloister cometh no man, to chide nor to fight,
> But all is obedience here and books, to read and to learn."

Perhaps Langland's friends saw that he was clever, and hoped that he might become one of the great ones in the Church. In those days (the Middle Ages they were called) there was no sharp line dividing the priests from the people. The one shaded off into the other, as it were. There were many who wore long gowns and shaved their heads, who yet were not priests. They were called clerks, and for a sum of money, often very small, they helped to sing masses for the souls of the dead, and performed other offices in connection with the services of the Church. They were bound by no vows and were allowed to marry, but of course could never hope to be powerful. Such was Langland; he married and always remained a poor "clerk."

But if Langland did not rise high in the Church, he made himself famous in another way, for he wrote *Piers the Ploughman*. This is a great book. There is no other written during the fourteenth century, in which we see so clearly the life of the people of the time.

There are several versions of *Piers,* and it is thought by some that Langland himself wrote and re-wrote his poem, trying always to make it better. But others think that some one else wrote the later versions.

The poem is divided into parts. The first part is *The Vision of Piers the Ploughman,* the second is *The Vision Concerning Do Well, Do Bet, Do Best.*

In the beginning of *Piers the Ploughman* Langland tells us how

> "In a summer season when soft was the sun,
> I wrapped myself in a cloak as if I were a shepherd
> In the habit of a hermit unholy of works,
> Abroad I wandered in this world wonders to hear
> But on a May morning on Malvern Hills
> Me befell a wonder, a strange thing   Methought,
> I was weary of wandering, and went me to rest
> Under a broad bank by a burn side
> And as I lay, and leaned, and looked on the waters
> I slumbered in a sleeping it sounded so merry."

If you will look back you will see that this poetry is very much more like Layamon's than like the poetry of *Havelok the Dane.* Although people had, for many years, been writing rhyming verse, Langland has, you see, gone back to the old alliterative poetry. Perhaps it was that, living far away in the country, Langland had

written his poem before he had heard of the new kind of
rhyming verses, for news traveled slowly in those days.

Two hundred years later, when *The Vision of Piers
the Ploughman* was first printed, the printer in his preface
explained alliterative verse very well. "Langland wrote
altogether in metre," he says, "but not after the manner
of our rimers that write nowadays (for his verses end not
alike), but the nature of his metres is to have three words,
at the least, in every verse which begin with some one
letter. As for example the first two verses of the book
run upon 's,' as thus:

> 'In a *s*omer *s*eason whan *s*ette was the *s*unne
> I *s*hope me into *s*hrobbes as I a *s*hepe were.'

The next runneth upon 'H,' as thus:

> 'In *h*abite as an *H*ermite un*h*oly of workes.'

This thing being noted, the metre shall be very pleasant to
read. The English is according to the time it was written
in, and the sense somewhat dark, but not so hard but that
it may be understood of such as will not stick to break the
shell of the nut for the kernel's sake."

This printer also says in his preface that the book was
first written in the time of King Edward III., "In whose
time it pleased God to open the eyes of many to see his
truth, giving them boldness of heart to open their mouths
and cry out against the works of darkness. . . . There
is no manner of vice that reigneth in any estate of man
which this writer hath not godly, learnedly, and wittily
rebuked." [1]

I hope that you will be among those who will not "stick
to break the shell of the nut for the kernel's sake," and
that although the "sense be somewhat dark" you will
some day read the book for yourselves. Meantime in the
next chapter I will tell you a little more about it.

[1] R. Crowley in his preface to *Piers Ploughman*, printed in 1550.

CHAPTER XX

WHEN Langland fell asleep upon the Malvern Hills he dreamed a wondrous dream. He thought that he saw a "fair field full of folk," where was gathered "all the wealth of the world and the woe both."

> "Working and wondering as the world asketh,
> Some put them to the plough and played them full seldom,
> In careing and sowing laboured full hard."

But some are gluttons and others think only of fine clothes. Some pray and others jest. There are rogues and knaves here, friars and priests, barons and burgesses, bakers and butchers, tailors and tanners, masons and miners, and folk of many other crafts. Indeed, the field is the world. It lies between a tower and a dungeon. The tower is God, the dungeon is the dwelling of the Evil One.

Then, as Langland looked on all this, he saw

> "A lady lovely in face, in linnen i-clothed,
> Come adown from the cliff and spake me fair,
> And said, 'Son, sleepest thou? Seest thou this people
> All how busy they be about the maze?' "

Langland was "afeard of her face though she was fair." But the lovely lady, who is Holy Church, speaks gently to the dreamer. She tells him that the tower is the dwelling of Truth, who is the lord of all and who gives to each as he hath need. The dungeon is the castle of Care.

> "Therein liveth a wight that Wrong is called,
> The Father of Falseness"

Love alone, said the lady, leads to Heaven,

"Therefore I warn ye, the rich, have ruth on the poor.
'hough ye be mighty in councils, be meek in your works,
For the same measure ye meet, amiss or otherwise,
Ye shall be weighed therewith when ye wend hence "

"Truth is best in all things," she said at length. "I have told thee now what Truth is, and may no longer linger." And so she made ready to go. But the dreamer kneeled on his knees and prayed her stay yet a while to teach him to know Falsehood also, as well as Truth. And the lady answered:—

" 'Look on thy left hand and see where he standeth,
Both False and Flattery and all his train.'
I looked on the left hand as the Lady me taught.
Then was I ware of a woman wondrously clothéd,
Purfled with fur, the richest on earth.
Crowned with a crown. The King hath no better
All her five fingers were fretted with rings
Of the most precious stones that a prince ever wore;
In red scarlet she rode, beribboned with gold,
There is no queen alive that is more adorned."

This was Lady Meed or Bribery. "To-morrow," said Holy Church, "she shall wed with False." And so the lovely Lady departed.

Left alone the dreamer watched the preparations for the wedding. The Earldom of Envy, the Kingdom of Covetousness, the Isle of Usury were granted as marriage gifts to the pair. But Theology was angry. He would not permit the wedding to take place. "Ere this wedding be wrought, woe betide thee," he cried. "Meed is wealthy; I know it. God grant us to give her unto whom Truth wills. But thou hast bound her fast to Falseness. Meed is gently born. Lead her therefore to London, and there see if the law allows this wedding."

So, listening to the advice of Theology, all the company rode off to London, Guile leading the way.

But Soothness pricked on his palfrey and passed them all and came to the King's court, where he told Conscience all about the matter, and Conscience told the King.

Then quoth the King, "If I might catch False and Flattery or any of their masters, I would avenge me on the wretches that work so ill, and would hang them by the neck and all that them abet."

So he told the Constable to seize False and to cut off Guile's head, "and let not Liar escape." But Dread was at the door and heard the doom. He warned the others, so that they all fled away save Meed the maiden.

> "Save Meed the maiden no man durst abide,
> And truly to tell she trembled for fear,
> And she wept and wrung her hands when she was taken."

But the King called a Clerk and told him to comfort Meed. So Justice soon hurried to her bower to comfort her kindly, and many others followed him. Meed thanked them all and "gave them cups of clean gold and pieces of silver, rings with rubies and riches enough." And pretending to be sorry for all that she had done amiss, Meed confessed her sins and was forgiven.

The King then, believing that she was really sorry, wished to marry her to Conscience. But Conscience would not have her, for he knew that she was wicked. He tells of all the evil things she does, by which Langland means to show what wicked things men will do if tempted by bribery and the hope of gain.

"Then mourned Meed and plained her to the King." If men did great and noble deeds, she said, they deserved praise and thanks and rewards.

> " 'Nay,' quoth Conscience to the King, and kneeled to the ground,
> 'There be *two* manner of Meeds, my Lord, by thy life,
> That one the good God giveth by His grace, giveth in His bliss
> To them that will work while that they are here.' "

What a laborer received, he said, was not Meed but just Wages. Bribery, on the other hand, was ever wicked, and he would have none of her.

In spite of all the talk, however, no one could settle the question. So at length Conscience set forth to bring Reason to decide.

When Reason heard that he was wanted, he saddled his horse Suffer-till-I-see-my-time and came to court with Wit and Wisdom in his train.

The King received him kindly, and they talked together. But while they talked Peace came complaining that Wrong had stolen his goods and ill-treated him in many ways.

Wrong well knew that the complaint was just, but with the help of Meed he won Wit and Wisdom to his side. But Reason stood out against him.

> " 'Counsel me not,' quoth Reason, 'ruth to have
>   Till lords and ladies all love truth
>   And their sumptuous garments be put into chests,
>   Till spoiled children be chastened with rods,
>   Till clerks and knights be courteous with their tongues,
>   Till priests themselves practise their preaching
>   And their deeds be such as may draw us to goodness.' "

The King acknowledged that Reason was right, and begged him to stay with him always and help him to rule. "I am ready," quoth Reason, "to rest with thee ever so that Conscience be our counsellor."

To that the King agreed, and he and his courtiers all went to church. Here suddenly the dream ends. Langland cries:—

> "Then waked I of my sleep   I was woe withal
>   That I had not slept more soundly and seen much more."

The dreamer arose and continued his wandering. But he had only gone a few steps when once again he sank upon the grass, and fell asleep and dreamed. Again he saw the field full of folk, and to them now Conscience was preaching, and at his words many began to repent them of their evil deeds. Pride, Envy, Sloth and others confessed their sins and received forgiveness.

Then all these penitent folk set forth in search of Saint Truth, some riding, some walking. "But there were few there so wise as to know the way thither, and they went all amiss." No man could tell them where Saint Truth lived. And now appears at last Piers Plowman, who gives his name to the whole poem.

> "Quoth a ploughman and put forth his head,
> I know him as well as a clerk knows his books
> Clear Conscience and Wit showed me his place
> And did engage me since to serve him ever.
> Both in sowing and setting, which I labour,
> I have been his man this fifteen winters"

Piers described to the pilgrims all the long way that they must go in order to find Truth. He told them that they must go through Meekness; that they must cross the ford Honor-your-father and turn aside from the brook Bear-no-false-witness, and so on and on until they come at last to Saint Truth.

"It were a hard road unless we had a guide that might go with us afoot until we got there," said the pilgrims. So Piers offered, if they would wait until he had plowed his field, to go with them and show them the way.

"That would be a long time to wait," said a lady. "What could we women do meantime?"

And Piers answered:—

> "Some should sew sacks to hold wheat.
> And you who have wool weave it fast,
> Spin it speedily, spare not your fingers
> Unless it be a holy day or holy eve
> Look out your linen and work on it quickly,
> The needy and the naked take care how they live,
> And cast on them clothes for the cold, for so Truth desires."

Then many of the pilgrims began to help Piers with his work. Each man did what he could, "and some to please Piers picked up the weeds."

> "But some of them sat and sang at ale
> And helped him to plough with 'Hy-trolly-lolly.'"

To these idle ones Piers went in anger. "If ye do not run quickly to your work," he cried, "you will receive no wage; and if ye die of hunger, who will care."

Then these idle ones began to pretend that they were blind or lame and could not work. They made great moan, but Piers took no heed and called for Hunger. Then Hunger seized the idle ones and beat and buffeted them until they were glad to work.

At last Truth heard of Piers and of all the good that he was doing among the pilgrims, and sent him a pardon for all his sins. In those days people who had done wrong used to pay money to a priest and think that they were forgiven by God. Against that belief Langland preaches, and his pardon is something different. It is only

> "Do well and have well, and God shall have thy soul.
> And do evil and have evil, hope none other
> That after thy death day thou shalt turn to the Evil One."

And over this pardon a priest and Piers began so loudly to dispute that the dreamer awoke,

> "And saw the sun that time towards the south,
> And I meatless and moneyless upon the Malvern Hills."

That is a little of the story of the first part of *Piers Ploughman*. It is an allegory, and in writing it Langland wished to hold up to scorn all the wickedness that he saw around him, and sharply to point out many causes of misery. There is laughter in his poem, but it is the terrible and harsh laughter of contempt. His most bitter words, perhaps, are for the idle rich, but the idle poor do not escape. Those who beg without shame, who cheat and steal, who are greedy and drunken have a share of his wrath. Yet Langland is not all harshness. His great word is Duty, but he speaks of Love too. "Learn to love, quoth Kind, and leave off all other." The poem is rambling and disconnected. Characters come on the scene and vanish again without cause. Stories begin and do not end. It is all wild and improbable like a dream, yet it is full of interest.

But perhaps the chief interest and value of *Piers Ploughman* is that it is history. It tells us much of what the people thought and of how they lived in those days. It shows us the first mutterings of the storm that was to rend the world. This was the storm of the Reformation which was to divide the world into Protestant and Catholic. But Langland himself was not a Protestant. Although he speaks bitter words against the evil deeds of priest and monk, he does not attack the Church. To him she is still Holy Church, a radiant and lovely lady.

BOOK TO READ

The Vision of Piers Ploughman, by W. Langland, done into modern English by Professor Skeat.

CHAPTER XXI

HOW THE BIBLE CAME TO THE PEOPLE

In all the land there is perhaps no book so common as the Bible. In homes where there are no other books we find at least a Bible, and the Bible stories are almost the first that we learn to know.

But in the fourteenth century there were no English Bibles. The priests and clergy and a few great people perhaps had Latin Bibles. And although Caedmon's songs had long been forgotten, at different times some parts of the Bible had been translated into English, so that the common people sometimes heard a Bible story. But an English Bible as a whole did not exist; and if to-day it is the commonest and cheapest book in all the land, it is to John Wyclif in the first place that we owe it.

John Wyclif was born, it is thought, about 1324 in a little Yorkshire village. Not much is known of his early days except that he went to school and to Oxford University. In time he became one of the most learned men of his day, and was made Head, or Master, of Balliol College.

This is the first time in this book that we have heard of a university. The monasteries had, until now, been the centers of learning. But now the two great universities of Oxford and Cambridge were taking their place. Men no longer went to the monasteries to learn, but to the universities; and this was one reason, perhaps, why the land had become filled with so many idle monks. Their

122

profession of teaching had been taken from them, and they had found nothing else with which to fill their time.

But at first the universities were very like monasteries. The clerks, as the students were called, often took some kind of vow,—they wore a gown and shaved their heads in some fashion or other. The colleges, too, were built very much after the style of monasteries, as may be seen in some of the old college buildings of Oxford or Cambridge to this day. The life in every way was like the life in a monastery. It was only by slow degrees that the life and the teaching grew away from the old model.

While Wyclif grew to be a man, England had fallen on troublous times. Edward III., worn out by his French wars, had become old and feeble, and the power was in the hands of his son, John of Gaunt. The French wars and the Black Death had slain many of the people, and those who remained were miserably poor. Yet poor though they were, much money was gathered from them every year and sent to the Pope, who at that time still ruled the Church in England as elsewhere.

But now the people of England became very unwilling to pay so much money to the Pope, especially as at this time he was a Frenchman ruling, not from Rome, but from Avignon. It was folly, Englishmen said, to pay money into the hands of a Frenchman, the enemy of their country, who would use it against their country. And while many people were feeling like this, the Pope claimed still more. He now claimed a tribute which King John had promised long before, but which had not for more than thirty years been paid.

John of Gaunt made up his mind to resist this claim, and John Wyclif, who had already begun to preach against the power of the Pope, helped him. They were strange companions, and while John of Gaunt fought only for more power, Wyclif fought for freedom both in religion and in life. God alone was lord of all the world, he said, and to God alone each man must answer for his soul, and to no man beside. The money belonging to the Church of England belonged to God and to the people of England, and ought to be used for the good of the people, and not be sent abroad to the Pope. In those days it needed a bold man to use such words, and Wyclif was soon called upon to answer for his boldness before the Archbishop of Canterbury and all his bishops.

The council was held in St. Paul's Cathedral in London. Wyclif was fearless, and he obeyed the Archbishop's command. But as he walked up the long aisle to the chapel where the bishops were gathered, John of Gaunt marched by his side, and Lord Percy, Earl Marshal of England, cleared a way for him through the throng of people that filled the church. The press was great, and Earl Percy drove a way through the crowd with so much haughtiness and violence that the Bishop of London cried out at him in wrath.

"Had I known what masteries you would use in my church," he said, "I had kept you from coming there."

"At which words the Duke, disdaining not a little, answered the Bishop and said that he would keep such mastery there though he said 'Nay.' " [1] Thus, after much struggling, Wyclif and his companions arrived at the chapel. There Wyclif stood humbly enough before his Bishop. But Earl Percy bade him be seated, for as he had much to answer he had need of a soft seat.

Thereat the Bishop of London was angry again, and cried out saying that it was not the custom for those who had come to answer for their misdeeds to sit.

"Upon these words a fire began to heat and kindle between them; insomuch that they began to rate and

[1] Foxe, *Acts and Monuments*

revile one the other, that the whole multitude therewith disquieted began to be set on a hurry." [1]

The Duke, too, joined in, threatening at last to drag the Bishop out of the church by the hair of his head. But the Londoners, when they heard that, were very wrathful, for they hated the Duke. They cried out they would not suffer their Bishop to be ill-used, and the uproar became so great that the council broke up without there being any trial at all.

But soon after this no fewer than five Bulls, or letters from the Pope, were sent against Wyclif. In one the University of Oxford was ordered to imprison him; in others Wyclif was ordered to appear before the Pope; in still another the English bishops were ordered to arrest him and try him themselves. But little was done, for the English would not imprison an English subject at the bidding of a French Pope, lest they should seem to give him royal power in England.

At length, however, Wyclif was once more brought before a court of bishops in London. By this time Edward III. had died, and Richard, the young son of the Black Prince, had come to the throne. His mother, the Princess of Wales, was Wyclif's friend, and she now sent a message to the bishops bidding them let him alone. This time, too, the people of London were on his side; they had learned to understand that he was their friend. So they burst into the council-room eager to defend the man whose only crime was that of trying to protect England from being robbed. And thus the second trial came to an end as the first had done.

Wyclif now began to preach more boldly than before He preached many things that were very different from the teaching of the Church of Rome, and as he was one of the most learned men of his time, people crowded to

[1] Foxe, *Acts and Monuments.*

Oxford to hear him. John of Gaunt, now no longer his friend, ordered him to be silent. But Wyclif still spoke. The University was ordered to crush the heretic. But the University stood by him until the King added his orders to those of the Archbishop of Canterbury. Then Wyclif was expelled from the University, but still not silenced, for he went into the country and there wrote and taught.

Soon his followers grew in numbers. They were called Poor Priests, and clad in long brown robes they wandered on foot through the towns and villages teaching and preaching. Wyclif trusted that they would do all the good that the old friars had done, and that they would be kept from falling into the evil ways of the later friars. But Churchmen were angry, and called his followers Lollards or idle babblers.

Wyclif, however, cared no longer for the great, he trusted no more in them. It was to the people now that he appealed. He wrote many books, and at first he wrote in Latin. But by degrees he saw that if he wanted to reach the hearts of the people, he must preach and teach in English. And so he began to write English books. But above all the things that he wrote we remember him chiefly for his translation of the Bible. He himself translated the New Testament, and others helped him with the Old Testament, and so for the first time the people of England had the whole Bible in their own tongue. They had it, too, in fine scholarly language, and this was a great service to our literature. For naturally the Bible was a book which every one wished to know, and the people of England, through it, became accustomed to use fine stately language.

To his life's end Wyclif went on teaching and writing, although many attempts were made to silence him. At last in 1384 the Pope summoned him to Rome. Wyclif did not obey, for he answered another call. One day, as

'EXPELLED FROM THE UNIVERSITY, WYCLIF WENT INTO THE COUNTRY AND
THERE WROTE AND TAUGHT.'

he heard mass in his own church, he fell forward speechless. He never spoke again, but died three days later.

After Wyclif's death his followers were gradually crushed out, and the Lollards disappear from our history. But his teaching never quite died, for by giving the English people the Bible Wyclif left a lasting mark on England; and although the Reformation did not come until two hundred years later, he may be looked upon as its forerunner.

It is hard to explain all that William Langland and John Wyclif stand for in English literature and in English history. It was the evil that they saw around them that made them write and speak as they did, and it was their speaking and writing, perhaps, that gave the people courage to rise against oppression. Thus their teaching and writing mark the beginning of new life to the great mass of the people of England. For in June, 1381, while John Wyclif still lived and wrote, Wat Tyler led his men to Blackheath in a rebellion which proved to be the beginning of freedom for the workers of England. And although at first sight there seems to be no connection between the two, it was the same spirit working in John Wyclif and Wat Tyler that made the one speak and the other fight as he did.

CHAPTER XXII

CHAUCER—BREAD AND MILK FOR CHILDREN

To-day, as we walk about the streets and watch the people hurry to and fro, we cannot tell from the dress they wear to what class they belong. We cannot tell among the men who pass us, all clad alike in dull, sad-colored clothes, who is a knight and who a merchant, who a shoemaker and who a baker. If we see them in their shops we can still tell, perhaps, for we know that a butcher always wears a blue apron, and a baker a white hat. These are but the remains of a time long ago when every one dressed according to his calling, whether at work or not. It was easy then to tell by the cut and texture of his clothes to what rank in life a man belonged, for each dressed accordingly, and only the great might wear silk and velvet and golden ornaments.

And in the time of which we have been reading, in the England where Edward III. and Richard II. ruled, where Langland sadly dreamed and Wyclif boldly wrote and preached, there lived a man who has left for us a clear and truthful picture of those times. He has left a picture so vivid that as we read his words the people of England of the fourteenth century still seem to us to live. This man was Geoffrey Chaucer. Chaucer was a poet, and is generally looked upon as the first great English poet. Like Caedmon he is called the "Father of English Poetry," and each has a right to the name. For if Caedmon was the first great poet of the English people in their new home of England, the language he used was Anglo-Saxon. The language which Chaucer used was English, though still not quite the English which we use to-day.

But although Chaucer was a great poet, we know very little about his life. What we do know has nothing to do with his poems or of how he wrote them. For in those days, and for long after, a writer was not expected to live by his writing; but in return for giving to the world beautiful thoughts, beautiful songs, the King or some great noble would reward him by giving him a post at court. About this public life of Chaucer we have a few facts. But it is difficult at times to fit the man of camp, and court, and counting-house to the poet and story-teller who possessed a wealth of words and a knowledge of how to use them greater than any Englishman who had lived before him. And it is rather through his works than through the scanty facts of his life that we learn to know the real man, full of shrewd knowledge of the world, of humor, kindliness, and cheerful courage.

Chaucer was a man of the middle class. His father, John Chaucer, was a London wine merchant. The family very likely came at first from France, and the name may mean shoemaker, from an old Norman word *chaucier* or *chaussier,* a shoemaker. And although the French word for shoemaker is different now, there is still a slang word *chausseur,* meaning a cobbler.

We know nothing at all of Chaucer as a boy, nothing of where he went to school, nor do we know if he ever went to college. The first thing we hear of him is that he was a page in the house of the Princess Elizabeth, the wife of Prince Lionel, who was the third son of Edward III. So, although Chaucer belonged to the middle class, he must have had some powerful friend able to get him a place in a great household.

In those days a boy became a page in a great household

very much as he might now become an office-boy in a large merchant's office. A page had many duties. He had to wait at table, hold candles, go messages, and do many other little household services. Such a post seems strange to us now, yet it was perhaps quite as interesting as sitting all day long on an office stool. In time of war it was certainly more exciting, for a page had often to follow his master to the battlefield. And as a war with France was begun in 1359, Geoffrey went across the Channel with his prince.

Of what befell Chaucer in France we know nothing, except that he was taken prisoner, and that the King, Edward III., himself gave £16 towards his ransom. That sounds a small sum, but it meant as much as £240 would now. So it would seem that, boy though he was, Geoffrey Chaucer had already become important. Perhaps he was already known as a poet and a good story-teller whom the King was loth to lose. But again for seven years after this we hear nothing more about him. And when next we do hear of him, he is *valet de chambre* in the household of Edward III. Then a few years later he married one of Queen Philippa's maids-in-waiting.

Of Chaucer's life with his wife and family again we know nothing, except that he had at least one son, named Lewis. We know this because he wrote a book, called *A Treatise on the Astrolabe,* for this little son. An astrolabe was an instrument used in astronomy to find out the distance of stars from the earth, the position of the sun and moon, the length of days, and many other things about the heavens and their bodies.

Chaucer calls his book *A Treatise on the Astrolabe, Bread and Milk for Children.* "Little Lewis, my son," he says in the beginning, "I have perceived well by certain evidences thine ability to learn science touching numbers and proportions; and as well consider I thy busy prayer in special to learn the treatise of the astrolabe." But although there were many books written on the subject, some were unknown in England, and some were not to be trusted. "And some of them be too hard to thy tender age of ten years. This treatise then will I show thee under few light rules and naked words in English; for Latin canst thou yet but small, my little son. . . .

"Now will I pray meekly every discreet person that readeth or heareth this little treatise, to have my rude inditing for excused, and my superfluity of words, for two causes. The first cause is for that curious inditing and hard sentence is full heavy at one and the same time for a child to learn. And the second cause is this, that soothly me seemeth better to write unto a child twice a good sentence than he forget it once. And Lewis, if so be I shew you in my easy English as true conclusions as be shewn in Latin, grant me the more thank, and pray God save the King, who is lord of this English."

So we see from this that more than five hundred years ago a kindly father saw the need of making simple books on difficult subjects for children. You may never want to read this book itself, indeed few people read it now, but I think that we should all be sorry to lose the preface, although it has in it some long words which perhaps a boy of ten in our day would still find "full heavy."

It is interesting, too, to notice in this preface that here Chaucer calls his King "Lord of this English." We now often speak of the "King's English," so once again we see how an everyday phrase links us with the past.

CHAPTER XXIII

CHAUCER—"THE CANTERBURY TALES"

CHAUCER rose in the King's service. He became an esquire, and was sent on business for the King to France and to Italy. To Italy he went at least twice, and it is well to remember this, as it had an effect on his most famous poems. He must have done his business well, for we find him receiving now a pension for life worth about £200 in our money, now a grant of a daily pitcher of wine besides a salary of "7½d. a day and two robes yearly."

Chaucer's wife, too, had a pension, so the poet was well off. He had powerful friends also, among them John of Gaunt. And when the Duke's wife died Chaucer wrote a lament which is called the *Dethe of Blaunche the Duchess,* or sometimes the *Book of the Duchess.* This is one of the earliest known poems of Chaucer, and although it is not so good as some which are later, there are many beautiful lines in it.

The poet led a busy life. He was a good business man, and soon we find him in the civil service, as we would call it now. He was made Comptroller of Customs, and in this post he had to work hard, for one of the conditions was that he must write out the accounts with his own hand, and always be in the office himself. If we may take some lines he wrote to be about himself, he was so busy all day long that he had not time to hear what was happening abroad, or even what was happening among his friends and neighbors.

132

"Not only from far countree,
That there no tidings cometh to thee;
Not of thy very neighbours,
That dwellen almost at thy doors,
Thou hearest neither that nor this "

Yet after his hard office work was done he loved nothing better than to go back to his books, for he goes on to say:

"For when thy labour done all is
And hast y-made thy reckonings,
Instead of rest and newe things
Thou goest home to thy house anon,
And all so dumb as any stone,
Thou sittest at another book,
Till fully dazéd is thy look,
And livest thus as a hermite
Although thine abstinence is light."

But if Chaucer loved books he loved people too, and we may believe that he readily made friends, for there was a kindly humor about him that must have drawn people to him. And that he knew men and their ways we learn from his poetry, for it is full of knowledge of men and women.

For many years Chaucer was well off and comfortable. But he did not always remain so. There came a time when his friend and patron, John of Gaunt, fell from power, and Chaucer lost his appointments. Soon after that his wife died, and with her life her pension ceased. So for a year or two the poet knew something of poverty—poverty at least compared to what he had been used to. But if he lost his money he did not lose his sunny temper, and in all his writings we find little that is bitter.

After a time John of Gaunt returned to power, and again Chaucer had a post given to him. And so until he died he suffered ups and downs. Born when Edward III. was in his highest glory, Chaucer lived to see him hated by his people. He lived through the reign of Edward's grandson,

Richard II., and knew him from the time when as a gallant yellow-haired boy he had faced Wat Tyler and his rioters, till as a worn and broken prisoner he yielded the crown to Henry of Lancaster, the son of John of Gaunt. But before the broken King died in his darksome prison Chaucer lay taking his last rest in St. Benet's Chapel in Westminster. He was the first great poet to be laid there, but since then there have gathered round him so many bearing the greatest names in English literature that we call it now the "Poets' Corner."

But although Chaucer lived in stirring times, although he was a soldier and a courtier, he does not, in the book by which we know him best, write of battles and of pomp, of kings and of princes. In this book we find plain, every-day people, people of the great middle class of merchants and tradesmen and others of like calling, to which Chaucer himself belonged. It was a class which year by year had been growing more and more strong in England, and which year by year had been making its strength more and more felt. But it was a class which no one had thought of writing about in plain fashion. And it is in the *Canterbury Tales* that we have, for the first time in the English language, pictures of real men, and what is more wonderful, of real women. They are not giants or dwarfs, they are not fairy princes or knights in shining armor. They do no wondrous deeds of strength or skill. They are not queens of marvelous beauty or enchanted princesses. They are simply plain, middle-class English people, and yet they are very interesting.

In Chaucer's time, books, although still copied by hand, had become more plentiful than ever before. And as more and more people learned to read, the singing time began to draw to a close. Stories were now not all written in rhyme, and poetry was not all written to be sung. Yet the listening time was not quite over, for these were still the days of talk and story-telling. Life went at leisure pace. There was no hurry, there was no machinery. All sewing was done by hand, so when the ladies of a great household gathered to their handiwork, it was no unusual thing for one among them to lighten the long hours with tales read or told. Houses were badly lighted, and there was little to do indoors in the long winter evenings, so the men gathered together and listened while one among them told of love and battle. Indeed, through all the life of the Middle Ages there was room for story-telling.

So now, although Chaucer meant his tales to be read, he made believe that they were told by a company of people on a journey from London to Canterbury. He thus made a framework for them of the life he knew, and gave a reason for them all being told in one book.

But a reason had to be given for the journey, for in those days people did not travel about from place to place for the mere pleasure of seeing another town, as we do now. Few people thought of going for a change of air, nobody perhaps ever thought about going to the seaside for the summer. In short, people always had a special object in taking a journey.

One reason for this was that traveling was slow and often dangerous. The roads were bad, and people nearly all traveled on horseback and in company. For robbers lurked by the way ready to attack and kill, for the sake of their money, any who rode alone and unprotected. So when a man had to travel he tried to arrange to go in company with others.

In olden days the most usual reason for a journey, next to business, was a pilgrimage. Sometimes this was simply an act of religion or devotion. Clad in a simple gown, and perhaps with bare feet, the pilgrim set out. Carrying a staff in his hand, and begging for food and shelter by the road, he took his way to the shrine of some

saint. There he knelt and prayed and felt himself blessed
in the deed. Sometimes it was an act of penance for some
great sin done; sometimes of thanksgiving for some great
good received, some great danger passed.

But as time went on these pilgrimages lost their old
meaning. People no longer trudged along barefoot,
wearing a pilgrim's grab. They began to look upon a
pilgrimage more as a summer outing, and dressed in their
best they rode comfortably on horseback. And it is a
company of pilgrims such as this that Chaucer paints for us.
He describes himself as being of the company, and it is
quite likely that Chaucer really did at one time go upon
this pilgrimage from London to Canterbury, for it was a
very favorite one. Not only was the shrine of St.
Thomas at Canterbury very beautiful in those days,
but it was also within easy distance of London. Neither
costing much nor lasting long, it was a journey which
well-to-do merchantmen and others like them could well
afford.

Chaucer tells us that it was when the first sunshiny
days of April came that people began to think of such
pilgrimages:—

> "When that April with his showers sweet,
> The drought of March hath pierced to the root,"

when the soft wind "with his sweet breath inspired hath
in every holt and heath the tender crops"; when the little
birds make new songs, then "longen folk to go on pilgrimages, and palmers for to seeken strange lands, and especially from every shire's end of England, to Canterbury they
wend."

So one day in April a company of pilgrims gathered at
the Tabard Inn on the south side of the Thames, not far
from London Bridge. A tabard, or coat without sleeves,
was the sign of the inn; hence its name. In those days

such a coat would often be worn by workmen for ease in working, but it has come down to us only as the gayly colored coat worn by heralds.

At the Tabard Inn twenty-nine "of sundry folk," besides Chaucer himself, were gathered. They were all strangers to each other, but they were all bound on the same errand. Every one was willing to be friendly with his neighbor, and Chaucer in his cheery way had soon made friends with them all.

> "And shortly when the sun was to rest,
> So had I spoke with them every one."

And having made their acquaintance, Chaucer begins to describe them all so that we may know them too. He describes them so well that he makes them all living to us. Some we grow to love; some we smile upon and have a kindly feeling for, for although they are not fine folk, they are so very human we cannot help but like them, and some we do not like at all, for they are rude and rough, as the poet meant them to be.

CHAPTER XXIV

CHAUCER—AT THE TABARD INN

CHAUCER begins his description of the people who were gathered at the Tabard Inn with the knight, who was the highest in rank among them.

> "A knight there was, and that a worthy man,
>
> . . . . . .
>
> And though he was worthy he was wise,
> And of his port as meek as any maid.
> He never yet no villainy ne'er said
> In all his life unto no manner wight;
> He was a very perfect, gentle knight."

Yet he was no knight of romance or fairy tale, but a good honest English gentleman who had fought for his King. His coat was of fustian and was stained with rust from his armor, for he had just come back from fighting, and was still clad in his war-worn clothes. "His horse was good, but he ne was gay."

With the knight was his son, a young squire of twenty years. He was gay and handsome, with curling hair and comely face. His clothes were in the latest fashion, gayly embroidered. He sat his horse well and guided it with ease. He was merry and careless and clever too, for he could joust and dance, sing and play, read and write, and indeed do everything as a young squire should. Yet with it all "courteous he was, lowly and serviceable."

With these two came their servant, a yeoman, clad in hood of green, and carrying besides many other weapons a "mighty bow."

As was natural in a gathering such as this, monks and

138

friars and their like figured largely. There was a monk, a worldly man, fond of dress, fond of hunting, fond of a good dinner; and a friar even more worldly and pleasure-loving There was a pardoner, a man who sold pardons to those who had done wrong, and a sumpnour or summoner, who was so ugly and vile that children were afraid of him. A summoner was a person who went to summon or call people to appear before the Church courts when they had done wrong. He was a much-hated person, and both he and the pardoner were great rogues and cheats and had no love for each other. There was also a poor parson.

All these, except the poor parson, Chaucer holds up to scorn because he had met many such in real life who, under the pretense of religion, lived bad lives. But that it was not the Church that he scorned or any who were truly good he shows by his picture of the poor parson. He was poor in worldly goods:—

> "But rich he was in holy thought and work,
> He was also a learned man, a clerk
> That Christ's gospel truly would preach,
> His parishioners devoutly would he teach;
> Benign he was and wonder diligent,
> And in adversity full patient
>
> .   .   .   .   .   .
>
> Wide was his parish, and houses far asunder,
> But he left naught for rain nor thunder
> In sickness nor in mischief to visit
> The farthest of his parish, great or lite [1]
> Upon his feet, and in his hand a staff.
> The noble ensample to his sheep he gave,
> That first he wrought, and afterward he taught "

There was no better parson anywhere. He taught his people to walk in Christ's way. But first he followed it himself.

[1] Little

Chaucer gives this good man a brother who is a plow-man.

> "A true worker and a good was he,
> Living in peace and perfect charity."

He could dig, and he could thresh, and everything to which he put his hand he did with a will.

Besides all the other religious folk there were a prioress and a nun. In those days the convents were the only schools for fine ladies, and the prioress perhaps spent her days teaching them. Chaucer makes her very prim and precise.

> "At meat well taught was she withal,
> She let no morsel from her lips fall,
> Nor wet her fingers in her sauce deep
> Well could she carry a morsel, and well keep
> That no drop might fall upon her breast.[1]
>
> In courtesy was set full mickle her lest.[2]
> Her over lip wiped she so clean,
> That in her cup there was no morsel seen
> Of grease, when she drunken had her draught"

And she was so tender hearted! She would cry if she saw a mouse caught in a trap, and she fed her little dog on the best of everything. In her dress she was very dainty and particular. And yet with all her fine ways we feel that she was no true lady, and that ever so gently Chaucer is making fun of her.

Besides the prioress and the nun there was only one other woman in the company. This was the vulgar, bouncing Wife of Bath. She dressed in rich and gaudy clothes, she liked to go about to see and be seen and have a good time. She had been married five times, and though she was getting old and rather deaf, she was quite ready to marry again, if the husband she had should die before her.

---

[1] It should be remembered that in those days forks were unknown, and people used their fingers.　　　　[2] Pleasure.

Chaucer describes nearly every one in the company, and last of all he pictures for us the host of the Tabard Inn.

> "A seemly man our host was withal
> For to have been a marshal in a hall.
> A large man he was with eyen stepe,[1]
> A fairer burgesse was there none in Chepe,[2]
> Bold was his speech, and wise and well y-taught,
> And of manhood him lacked right naught,
> Eke thereto he was right a merry man."

The host's name was Harry Baily, a big man and jolly fellow who dearly loved a joke. After supper was over he spoke to all the company gathered there. He told them how glad he was to see them, and that he had not had so merry a company that year. Then he told them that he had thought of something to amuse them on the long way to Canterbury. It was this:—

> "That each of you to shorten of your way
> In this voyage shall tell tales tway [3]—
> To Canterbury-ward I mean it so,
> And homeward ye shall tellen other two;—
> Of adventures which whilom have befallen.
> And which of you the beareth you best of all,
> That is to say, that telleth in this case
> Tales of best sentence, and most solace,
> Shall have a supper at all our cost,
> Here in this place, sitting at this post,
> When that we come again fro Canterbury.
> And for to make you the more merry
> I will myself gladly with you ride,
> Right at mine own cost, and be your guide."

To this every one willingly agreed, and next morning they waked very early and set off. And having ridden a little way they cast lots as to who should tell the first tale. The lot fell upon the knight, who accordingly began.

[1] Bright   [2] Cheapside, a street in London
[3] Twain.

All that I have told you so far forms the first part of the book and is called the prologue, which means really "before word" or explanation. It is perhaps the most interesting part of the book, for it is entirely Chaucer's own and it is truly English.

It is said that Chaucer borrowed the form of his famous tales from a book called *The Decameron,* written by an Italian poet named Boccaccio. Decameron comes from two Greek words *deka,* ten, and *hemera,* a day, the book being so called because the stories in it were supposed to be told in ten days. During a time of plague in Florence seven ladies and three gentlemen fled and took refuge in a house surrounded by a garden far from the town. There they remained for ten days, and to amuse themselves each told a tale every day, so that there are a hundred tales in all in *The Decameron.*

It is very likely that in one of his journeys to Italy Chaucer saw this book. Perhaps he even met Boccaccio, and it is more than likely that he met Petrarch, another great Italian poet who also retold one of the tales of *The Decameron.* Several of the tales which Chaucer makes his people tell are founded on these tales. Indeed, nearly all his poems are founded on old French, Italian, or Latin tales. But although Chaucer takes his material from others, he tells the stories in his own way, and so makes them his own; and he never wrote anything more truly English in spirit than the prologue to the *Canterbury Tales.*

Some of these stories you will like to read, but others are too coarse and rude to give you any pleasure. Even the roughness of these tales, however, helps us to picture the England of those far-off days. We see from them how hard and rough the life must have been when people found humor and fun in jokes in which we can feel only disgust.

But even in Chaucer's day there were those who found such stories coarse. "Precious folk," Chaucer calls them.

He himself perhaps did not care for them, indeed he explains in the tales why he tells them. Here is a company of common, everyday people, he said, and if I am to make you see these people, if they are to be living and real to you, I must make them act and speak as such common people would act and speak. They are churls, and they must speak like churls and not like fine folk, and if you don't like the tale, turn over the leaf and choose another.

"What should I more say but this miller
He would his words for no man forbear,
But told his churls tale in his manner.
Me thinketh that I shall rehearse it here;
And therefore every gently wight I pray,
For Goddes love deem not that I say
Of evil intent, but for I might rehearse
Their tales all, be they better or worse,
Or else falsen some of my matter:
And therefore, who so listeth it not to hear,
Turn over the leaf and choose another tale,
For he shall find enow, both great and small,
In storial thing that toucheth gentlesse,
And eke morality and holiness,—
Blame not me if that ye choose amiss.
This miller is a churl ye know well,
So was the Reeve, and many more,
And wickedness they tolden both two.
Advise you, put me out of blame;
And eke men shall not make earnest of game."

If Chaucer had written all the tales that he meant to write, there would have been one hundred and twenty-four in all. But the poet died long before his work was done, and as it is there are only twenty-four. Two of these are not finished; one, indeed, is only begun. Thus, you see, many of the pilgrims tell no story at all, and we do not know who got the prize, nor do we hear anything of the grand supper at the end of the journey.

Chaucer is the first of our poets who had a perfect sense

of sound. He delights us not only with his stories, but with the beauty of the words he uses. We lose a great deal of that beauty when his poetry is put into modern English, as are all the quotations which I have given you. It is only when we can read the poems in the quaint English of Chaucer's time that we can see truly how fine it is. So, although you may begin to love Chaucer now, you must look forward to a time when you will be able to read his stories as he wrote them. Then you will love them much more.

Chaucer wrote many other books beside the *Canterbury Tales,* although not so many as was at one time thought. But the *Canterbury Tales* are the most famous, and I will not trouble you with the names even of the others. But when the grown-up time comes, I hope that you will want to read some of his other books as well as the *Canterbury Tales.*

And now, just to end this long chapter, I will give you a little poem by Chaucer, written as he wrote it, with modern English words underneath so that you may see the difference.

This poem was written when Chaucer was very poor. It was sent to King Henry IV., who had just taken the throne from Richard II. Henry's answer was a pension of twenty marks, so that once more Chaucer lived in comfort. He died, however, a year later.

THE COMPLAYNT OF CHAUCER TO HYS PURSE

To yow my purse, and to noon other wight
To you my purse, and to no   other wight
Complayne I, for ye by my lady dere;
 Complain I, for ye be my lady dear,
I am so sorry now that ye been lyght,
I am so sorry now that ye be   light,
For certes, but yf ye make me hevy chere
For certainly, but if ye make me heavy cheer
Me were as leef be layde upon my bere;
 I would as soon be laid   upon my bier;

For which unto your mercy thus I erye,
For which unto your mercy thus I cry,
Beeth hevy ageyne, or elles mote I dye.
Be   heavy again, or else   must I die

Now voucheth-sauf this day or hyt be nyght
Now   vouchsafe   this day before it be night
That I of you the blisful sovne may here,
That I of you the blissful sound may hear,
Or see your colour lyke the sonne bryght,
Or see your colour like   the   sun   bright,
That of yelownesse hadde neuer pere
That of yellowness   had   never peer
Ye be my lyfe, ye be myn hertys stere,
Ye be my life, ye be my   heart's guide,
Quene of comfort, and of good companye,
Queen of comfort, and of good   company,
Beth heuy ageyne, or elles moote I dye
Be   heavy again, or else   must I die

Now purse that ben to me my lyves lyght
Now purse that art to me my life's light
And saveour as down in this worlde here,
And saviour as down in this world here,
Oute of this towne helpe me thrugh your myght,
Out of this town   help me through your might,
Syn that ye wole nat bene my tresorere,
Since that ye will not   be   my treasurer,
For I am shave as nye as is a ffrere;
For I am shaven as close as is a friar,
But yet I pray vnto your curtesye,
But yet I pray unto your courtesy,
Bethe hevy agen or elles moote I dye.
Be   heavy again or else   must I die

L'ENVOY [1] DE CHAUCER

O conquerour of Brutes albyon,
O   conqueror of Brutus' Albion,
Whiche that by lygne and free eleccion
Who   that by line and free election
Been verray kynge, this song to yow I sende;
Art   very   king, this song to you I send,

---

[1] This is from a French word, meaning "to send," and is still often used for the last verse of a poem. It is, as it were, a "sending off."

And ye that mowen alle myn harme amende,
And ye that ait able all my harm amend,
Haue mynde vpon my supplicacion.
Have mind upon my supplication

In reading this you must sound the final "e" in each word except when the next word begins with an "h" or with another vowel. You will then find it read easily and smoothly.

BOOKS TO READ

Stories from Chaucer (prose), by J. H Kelman   *Tales from Chaucer* (prose), by C L Thomson   *Prologue to the Canterbury Tales and Minor Poems* (poetry), done into Modern English by W W Skeat   *Canterbury Tales* (poetry), edited by A. W. Pollard (in Chaucer's English, suitable only for grown-up readers)

NOTE.—As there are so many books now published containing stories from Chauncer's *Canterbury Tales*, I feel it unnecessary to give any here in outline.

CHAPTER XXV

THE FIRST ENGLISH GUIDE-BOOK

AND now, lest you should say, "What, still more poetry!" I shall give you next a chapter about a great story-teller who wrote in prose. We use story-teller in two senses, and when we speak of Sir John Mandeville we use it in both. He was a great story-teller.

But before saying anything about his stories, I must first tell you that after having been believed in as a real person for five hundred years and more, Sir John has at last been found out. He never lived at all, and the travels about which he tells us so finely never took place.

"Sir John," too, used to be called the "Father of English Prose," but even that honor cannot be left to him, for his travels were not written first in English, but in French, and were afterwards translated into English.

But although we know Sir John Mandeville was not English, that he never saw the places he describes, that indeed he never lived at all, we will still call him by that name. For we must call him something, and as no one really knows who wrote the book which is known as *The Voyages and Travels of Sir John Mandeville,* we may as well call the author by the name he chose as by another.

Sir John, then, tells us that he was born in St. Albans, that he was a knight, and that in 1322 he set out on his travels. He traveled about for more than twenty years, but at last, although in the course of them he had drunk of the well of everlasting youth, he became so crippled with gout that he could travel no longer. He settled down, therefore, at Liége in Belgium. There he wrote his book, and there he died and was buried. At any rate, many years afterwards his tomb was shown there. It was also shown at St. Albans, where the people were very proud of it.

Sir John's great book was a guide-book. In those days, as we know, it was a very common thing for people to go on pilgrimages. And among the long pilgrimages the one to the Holy Land was the most common. So Sir John wrote his book to help people on their way, just as Mr. Baedeker and Mr. Murray do now.

It is perhaps the earliest, and certainly one of the most delightful, guide-books ever written, although really it was chiefly made up of bits out of books by other people.

Sir John tells of many different ways of getting to Palestine, and relates wonderful stories about the places to be passed through. He wrote in French. "I know that I ought to write in Latin," he says, "but because more people understand French I have written in French, so that every one may understand it." Afterwards it was translated into Latin, later into English, and still later into almost every European language, so much did people like the stories.

When these stories appeared it was something quite new in Literature, for until this time stories were always written in poetry. It was only great and learned books, or books that were meant to teach something, that were written in prose.

Here is one of Sir John Mandeville's tales.

After telling about the tomb of St John at Ephesus, Sir John goes on: "And then men pass through the isles of Cophos and Lango, of the which isles Ipocras was lord. And some say that in the isle of Lango is Ipocras's daughter

in form of a Dragon. It is a hundred foot long, so men say.
But I have not seen it. And they say the people of the
isles call her the lady of the country, and she lieth in an old
castle and sheweth herself thrice a year. And she doeth
no man harm. And she is thus changed from a lady to a
Dragon through a goddess whom men call Diana.

"And men say that she shall dwell so until the time
that a knight come that is so hardy as to go to her and kiss
her mouth. And then shall she turn again to her own
kind and be a woman. And after that she shall not live
long.

"And it is not long since a knight of the island of
Rhodes that was hardy and valiant said that he would kiss
her. But when the Dragon began to lift up her head, and
he saw it was so hideous, he fled away. Then the Dragon
in her anger bare the knight to a rock and cast him into the
sea, and so he was lost.

"Also a young man that wist not of the Dragon went
out of a ship and went through the isle till he came to a
castle. Then came he into the cave and went on till he
found a chamber. And there he saw a lady combing her
hair, and looking in a mirror. And she had much treasure
about her. He bowed to the lady, and the lady saw the
shadow of him in the mirror. Then she turned towards
him and asked him what he would. And he answered he
would be her lover.

"Then she asked him if he were a knight, and he said
'Nay.' She said then he might not be her lover. But
she bade him go again to his fellows and make him knight,
and come again on the morrow. Then she would come out
of the cave and he should kiss her on the mouth. And she
bade him have no dread, for she would do him no harm.
Although she seemed hideous to him she said it was done
by enchantment, for, she said, she was really such as he
saw her then. She said, too, that if he kissed her he should

have all the treasure, and be her lord, and lord of all these isles.

"Then he departed from her and went to his fellows in the ship, and made him knight, and came again on the morrow for to kiss the damsel. But when he saw her come out of the cave in the form of a Dragon, he had so great dread that he fled to the ship. She followed him, and when she saw that he turned not again she began to cry as a thing that had much sorrow, and turned back again.

"Soon after the knight died, and since, hitherto, might no knight see her but he died anon. But when a knight cometh that is so hardy to kiss her, he shall not die, but he shall turn that damsel into her right shape and shall be lord of the country aforesaid."

When Sir John reaches Palestine he has very much to say of the wonders to be seen there. At Bethlehem he tells a story of how roses first came into the world. Here it is:

"Bethlehem is but a little city, long and narrow, and well walled and enclosed with a great ditch, and it was wont to be called Ephrata, as Holy Writ sayeth, 'Lo, we heard it at Ephrata.' And toward the end of the city toward the East, is a right fair church and a gracious. And it hath many towers, pinnacles and turrets full strongly made. And within that church are forty-four great pillars of marble, and between the church the Field Flowered as ye shall hear.

"The cause is, for as much as a fair maiden was blamed with wrong, for the which cause she was deemed to die, and to be burnt in that place, to the which she was led.

"And as the wood began to burn about her, she made her prayer to our Lord as she was not guilty of that thing, that He would help her that her innocence might be known to all men.

"And when she had this said she entered the fire. And

anon the fire went out, and those branches that were burning became red roses, and those branches that were not kindled became white roses. And those were the first roses and rose-trees that any man saw. And so was the maiden saved through the grace of God, and therefore is that field called the Field of God Flowered, for it was full of roses."

Although Sir John begins his book as a guide to Palestine, he tells of many other lands also, and of the wonders there. Of Ethiopia he tells us: "On the other side of Chaldea toward the South is Ethiopia, a great land. In this land in the South are the people right black. In that side is a well that in the day the water is so cold that no man may drink thereof, and in the night it is so hot that no man may suffer to put his hand in it. In this land the rivers and all the waters are troublous, and some deal salt, for the great heat. And men of that land are easily made drunken and have little appetite for meat. They have commonly great illness of body and live not long. In Ethiopia are such men as have one foot, and they walk so fast that it is a great marvel. And that is a large foot that the shadow thereof covereth the body from sun and rain when they lie upon their backs."

Sir John tells us, too, of a wonderful group of islands, "and in one of these isles are men that have one eye, and that in the midst of their forehead. And they eat not flesh or fish all raw.

"And in another isle dwell men that have no heads, and their eyes are in their shoulders and their mouths is in their breast. . . .

"And in another isle are men that have flat faces without nose and without eyes, but they have two small round holes instead of eyes and they have a flat mouth without lips. . . .

"And in another isle are men that have the lips about

their mouth so great that when they sleep in the sun they cover all their face with the lip."

But I must not tell all the "lying wonders of our English knight,"[1] for you must read the book for yourselves. And when you do you will find that it is written with such an easy air of truth that you will half believe in Sir John's marvels. Every now and again, too, he puts in a bit of real information which helps to make his marvels seem true, so that sometimes we cannot be sure what is truth and what is fable.

Sir John wandered far and long, but at last his journeyings ended. "1 have passed through many lands and isles and countries," he says, "and now am come to rest against my will." And so to find comfort in his "wretched rest" he wrote his book. "But," he says, "there are many other divers counties, and many other marvels beyond that 1 have not seen. Also in countries where I have been are many marvels that I speak not of, for it were too long a tale." And also, he thought, it was as well to leave something untold "so that other men that go thither may find enough for to say that I have not told," which was very kind of him.

Sir John tells us then how he took his book to the holy father the Pope, and how he caused it to be read, and "the Pope hath ratified and affirmed my book in all points. And I pray to all those that read this book, that they will pray for me, and I shall pray for them."

BOOK TO READ

The Voyages and Travels of Sir John Mandeville, edited by A. W Pollard

---

[1] Colonel Sir Henry Yule, *The Book of Sir Marco Polo*.

CHAPTER XXVI

BARBOUR—"THE BRUCE," THE BEGINNINGS OF A STRUGGLE

WHILE Chaucer was making for us pictures of English life, in the sister kingdom across the rugged Cheviots another poet was singing to a ruder people. This poet was John Barbour, Archdeacon of Aberdeen. An older man than Chaucer, born perhaps twenty years before the English poet, he died only five years earlier. So that for many years these two lived and wrote at the same time.

But the book by which Barbour is remembered best is very different from that by which we remember Chaucer. Barbour's best-known book is called *The Bruce,* and in it, instead of the quiet tales of middle-class people, we hear throughout the clash and clang of battle. Here once again we have the hero of romance. Here once again history and story are mingled, and Robert the Bruce swings his battle-ax and wings his faultless arrow, saving his people from the English yoke.

The music of *The Bruce* cannot compare with the music of the *Tales,* but the spirit throughout is one of manliness, of delight in noble deeds and noble thoughts. Barbour's way of telling his stories is simple and straightforward. It is full of stern battle, yet there are lines of tender beauty, but nowhere do we find anything like the quiet laughter and humor of Chaucer. And that is not wonderful, for those were stern times in Scotland, and *The Bruce* is as much an outcome of those times as were the

Tales or *Piers Ploughman* an outcome of the times in England.

But if to Chaucer belongs the title of "Father of English Poetry," to Barbour belongs that of "Father of Scottish Poetry and Scottish History." He, indeed, calls the language he wrote in "Inglis," but it is a different English from that of Chaucer. They were both founded on Anglo-Saxon, but instead of growing into modern English, Barbour's tongue grew into what was known later as "braid Scots." All the quotations that I am going to give you from the poem I have turned into modern English, for, although they lose a great deal in beauty, it makes them easier for every one to understand. For even to the Scots boys and girls who read this book there are many words in the original that would need translating, although they are words still used by every one who speaks Scots to this day. In one page of twenty-seven lines taken at random we find sixteen such words. They are, micht, nicht, licht, weel, gane, ane, nane, stane, rowit, mirk, nocht, brocht, mair, sperit at, sair, hert. For those who are Scots it is interesting to know how little the language of the people has changed in five hundred years.

As of many another of our early poets, we know little of Barbour's life. He was Archdeacon of Aberdeen, as already said, and in 1357 he received a safe-conduct from Edward III. to allow him to travel to Oxford with three companions. In those days there was not as yet any university in Scotland. The monasteries still held their place as centers of learning. But already the fame of Oxford had reached the northern kingdom, and Barbour was anxious to share in the treasures of learning to be found there. At the moment there was peace between the two countries, but hate was not dead, it only slumbered. So a safe-conduct or passport was necessary for any Scotsman who would travel through England in safety.

"Edward the King unto his lieges greeting," it ran. "Know ye that we have taken under our protection (at the request of David de Bruce) John Barbour, Archdeacon of Aberdeen, with the scholars in his company, in coming into our kingdom of England, in order to study in the university of Oxford, and perform his scholastic exercises, and in remaining there and in returning to his own country of Scotland. And we hereby grant him our safe-conduct, which is to continue in force for one year."

Barbour was given two other safe-conducts, one to allow him again to visit Oxford, and another to allow him to pass through England on his way to France. Besides this, we know that Barbour received a pension from the King of Scotland, and that he held his archdeaconry until his death; and that is almost all that we know certainly of his life.

The Bruce is the great national poem, Robert the Bruce the great national hero of Scotland. But although *The Bruce* concerns Scotland in the first place, it is of interest to every one, for it is full of thrilling stories of knightly deeds, many of which are true. "The fine poem deserves to be better known," says one of its editors.[1] "It is a proud thing for a country to have given a subject for such an Odyssey, and to have had so early in its literature a poet worthy to celebrate it." And it is little wonder that Barbour wrote so stirringly of his hero, for he lived not many years after the events took place, and when he was a schoolboy Robert the Bruce was still reigning over Scotland.

In the beginning of his book Barbour says:—

> "Stories to read are delightful,
> Supposing even they be naught but fable;
> Then should stories that true were,
> And that were said in good manner,

---

[1] Cosmo Innes

Have double pleasantness in hearing.
The first pleasantness is the telling
And the other is the truthfulness
That shows the thing right as it was
And such things that are likand
To man's hearing are pleasant,
Therefore I would fain set my will,
If my wit may suffice thereto,
To put in writ a truthful story,
That it last aye forth in memory,
So that no time of length it let,
Nor gar it wholly be forgot."

So he will, he says, tell the tale of "stalwart folk that lived erst while," of "King Robert of Scotland that hardy was of heart and hand," and of "Sir James of Douglas that in his time so worthy was" that his fame reached into far lands. Then he ends this preface with a prayer that God will give him grace, "so that I say naught but soothfast thing."

The story begins with describing the state of Scotland after the death of Alexander III., when Edward I. ruled in England. Alexander had been a good king, but at his death the heir to the throne was a little girl, the Maid of Norway. She was not even in Scotland, but was far across the sea. And as this child-queen came sailing to her kingdom she died on board ship, and so never saw the land over which she ruled.

Then came a sad time for Scotland. "The land six year and more i-faith lay desolate," for there was no other near heir to the throne, and thirteen nobles claimed it. At last, as they could not agree which had the best right, they asked King Edward of England to decide for them.

As you know, it had been the dream of every King of England to be King of Scotland too. And now Edward I saw his chance to make that dream come true. He chose as King the man who had, perhaps, the greatest right to the throne, John Balliol. But he made him promise to hold the crown as a vassal to the King of England.

This, however, the Scots would not suffer. Freedom they had ever loved, and freedom they would have. No man, they said, whether he were chosen King or no, had power to make them thralls of England.

> "Oh! Freedom is a noble thing!
> Freedom makes a man to have liking,
> Freedom all solace to man gives,
> He lives at ease that freely lives
> A noble heart may have no ease,
> Nor nothing else that may him please,
> If freedom faileth; for free delight
> Is desired before all other thing
> Nor he that aye has lived free
> May not know well the quality,
> The anger, nor the wretched doom
> That joinéd is to foul thraldom."

So sang Barbour, and so the passionate hearts of the Scots cried through all the wretched years that followed the crowning of John Balliol. And when at last they had greatest need, a leader arose to show them the way to freedom. Robert the Bruce, throwing off his sloth and forgetfulness of his country, became their King and hero. He was crowned and received the homage of his barons, but well he knew that was but the beginning.

> "To maintain what he had begun
> He wist, ere all the land was won,
> He should find full hard bargaining
> With him that was of England King,
> For there was none in life so fell,
> So stubborn, nor so cruel"

Then began a long struggle between two gallant men, Robert of Scotland and Edward of England. At first things went ill with the Bruce. He lost many men in

battle, others forsook him, and for a time he lived a hunted
outlaw among the hills.

> "He durst not to the plains y-go
> For all the commons went him fro,
> That for their lives were full fain
> To pass to the English peace again."

But in all his struggles Bruce kept a good heart and
comforted his men.

> " 'For discomfort,' as then said he,
> 'Is the worst thing that may be;
> For through mickle discomforting
> Men fall oft into despairing.
> And if a man despairing be,
> Then truly vanquished is he ' "

Yet even while Bruce comforted his men he bade them
be brave, and said: —

> "And if that them were set a choice,
> To die, or to live cowardly,
> They should ever die chivalrously."

He told them stories, too, of the heroes of olden times
who, after much suffering, had in the end won the victory
over their enemies.   Thus the days passed, and winter
settled down on the bleak mountains.   Then the case of
Robert and his men grew worse and worse, and they almost
lost hope.   But at length, with many adventures, the
winter came to an end.   Spring returned again, and with
spring hope.

CHAPTER XXVII

BARBOUR—"THE BRUCE," THE END OF THE STRUGGLE

> " 'Twas in spring, when winter tide
> With his blasts, terrible to bide
> Was overcome; and birdies small,
> As throstle and the nightingale,
> Began right merrily to sing,
> And to make in their singing
> Sundrie notes, and varied sounds,
> And melody pleasant to hear,
> And the trees began to blow
> With buds, and bright blossom also,
> To win the covering of their heads
> Which wicked winter had them riven,
> And every grove began to spring "

It was in spring that Bruce and his men gathered to the island of Arran, off the west coast of Scotland, and there Bruce made up his mind to make another fight for the crown. A messenger was therefore sent over to the mainland, and it was arranged that if he found friends there, if he thought it was safe for the King to come, he should, at a certain place, light a great fire as a signal. Anxiously Bruce watched for the light, and at last he saw it. Then joyfully the men launched their boat, and the King and his few faithful followers set out.

> "They rowéd fast with all their might,
> Till that upon them fell the night,
> That it wox mirk[1] in great manner
> So that they wist not where they were,
> For they no needle had, nor stone,

---

[1] Dark.

> But rowéd always in one way,
> Steering always upon the fire
> That they saw burning bright and clear.
> It was but adventure that them led,
> And they in short time so them sped
> That at the fire arrived they,
> And went to land but [1] mair delay "

On shore the messenger was eagerly and anxiously awaiting them, and with a "sare hert" he told the King that the fire was none of his. Far from there being friends around, the English, he said, swarmed in all the land.

> "Were in the castle there beside,
> Full filléd of despite and pride."

There was no hope of success.

> "Then said the King in full great ire,
> 'Traitor, why made thou on the fire?'
> 'Ah sire,' he said, 'so God me see
> That fire was never made on for me.
> No ere this night I wist it not
> But when I wist it weel [2] I thocht
> That you and all your company
> In haste would put you to the sea.
> For this I come to meet you here,
> To tell the perils that may appear ' "

The King, vexed and disappointed, turned to his followers for advice. What was best to do, he asked. Edward Bruce, the King's brave brother, was the first to answer.

> "And said, 'I say you sickerly,
> There shall no perils that may be
> Drive me eftsoons into the sea;
> Mine adventure here take will I
> Whether it be easeful or angry.'
> 'Brother,' he said, 'since you will so
> It is good that we together take
> Disease and ease, or pain or play
> After as God will us purvey ' "

---

[1] Without.   [2] Well

And so, taking courage, they set out in the darkness, and attacked the town, and took it with great slaughter.

> "In such afray they bode that night
> Till in the morn, that day was bright,
> And then ceaséd partly
> The noise, the slaughter, and the cry."

Thus once again the fierce struggle was begun. But this time the Bruce was successful. From town after town, from castle after castle the enemy was driven out, till only Stirling was left to the English. It was near this town, on the field of Bannockburn, that the last great struggle took place. Brave King Edward I. was dead by this time, but his son, Edward II., led the army. It was the greatest army that had ever entered Scotland, but the Scots won the day and won freedom at the same time. I cannot tell you of this great battle, nor of all the adventures which led up to it. These you must read in other books, one day, I hope, in Barbour's *Bruce* itself.

From the day of Bannockburn, Barbour tells us, Robert the Bruce grew great.

> "His men were rich, and his country
> Abounded well with corn and cattle,
> And of all kind other richness;
> Mirth, solace, and eke blithness
> Was in the land all commonly,
> For ilk man blith was and jolly."

And here Barbour ends the first part of his poem. In the second part he goes on to tell us of how the Bruces carried war into Ireland, of how they overran Northumberland, and of how at length true peace was made. Then King Robert's little son David, who was but five, was married to Joan, the seven-year-old sister of King Edward III. Thus, after war, came rest and ease to both countries.

But King Robert did not live long to enjoy his well-earned rest. He died, and all the land was filled with mourning and sorrow.

> "'All our defense,' they said, 'alas!
> And he that all our comfort was,
> Our wit and all our governing,
> Is brought, alas, here to ending;
>
> .   .   .   .   .
>
> Alas! what shall we do or say?
> For in life while he lasted, aye
> By all our foes dred were we,
> And in many a far country
> Of our worship ran the renown,
> And that was all for his person'"

Barbour ends his book by telling of how the Douglas set out to carry the heart of the Bruce to Palestine, and of how he fell fighting in Spain, and of how his dead body and the King's heart were brought back to Scotland.

Barbour was born about six years after the battle of Bannockburn. As a boy he must have heard many stories of these stirring times from those who had taken part in them. He must have known many a woman who had lost husband or father in the great struggle. He may even have met King Robert himself. And as a boy he must have shared in the sorrow that fell upon the land when its hero died. He must have remembered, when he grew up, how the people mourned when the dead body of the Douglas and the heart of the gallant Bruce were brought home from Spain. But in spite of Barbour's prayer to be kept from saying "ought but soothfast thing," we must not take *The Bruce* too seriously. If King Robert was a true King he was also a true hero of romance. We must not take all *The Bruce* as serious history, but while allowing for the truth of much, we must also allow something for the poet's worship of his hero, a hero, too, who lived so near the time in which he wrote. We must allow something for the feelings of a poet who so passionately loved the freedom for which that hero fought.

BOOKS TO READ

There is, so far as I know, no modernized version of *The Bruce,* but there are many books illustrative of the text In this connection may be read *Robert the Bruce* (Children's Heroes Series), by Jeannie Lang, Chapters XXIV to XLIV. *Scotland's Story,* by H E Marshall; *The Lord of the Isles,* by Sir Walter Scott, *Castle Dangerous,* by Sir Walter Scott; chapters relating to this period in *Tales of a Grandfather,* by Sir Walter Scott, "The Heart of the Bruce" in *Lays of the Scottish Cavaliers,* by Aytoun The most available version of *The Brus* in old "Inglis," edited by W M. Mackenzie.

CHAPTER XXVIII

A POET KING

The Bruce is a book which is the outcome of the history of the times. It is the outcome of the quarrels between England and Scotland, and of Scotland's struggle for freedom. Now we come to another poet, and another poem which was the outcome of the quarrels between England and Scotland. For although Scotland's freedom was never again in danger, the quarrels between the two countries were, unhappily, not over.

In 1399, as we know, Henry IV. wrested the crown of England from Richard II. The new King proved no friend to Scotland, for he desired, as those before him had desired, to rule both countries. Henry lost no chance, therefore, by which he might gain his end So when in 1405 the King of Scotland sent his little son James to be educated in France, the English attacked the ship in which he sailed and took him prisoner. Instead, then, of going as a guest to the court of France, the Prince was carried as a prisoner to the court of England. When the old King heard the sad news he died, and James, captive though he was, became King of Scotland.

Those were again troublous times in Scotland. The captive King's uncle was chosen as Regent to rule in his absence. But he, wishing to rule himself, had no desire that his nephew should be set free. So through the reigns of Henry IV and of Henry V. James remained a prisoner. But although a prisoner he was not harshly treated, and the Kings of England took care that he should receive an

164

education worthy of a prince. James was taught to read and write English, French, and Latin. He was taught to fence and wrestle, and indeed to do everything as a knight should. Prince James was a willing pupil; he loved his books, and looked forward to the coming of his teachers, who lightened the loneliness of his prison.

"But," says a Frenchman who has written a beautiful little book about this captive King, "'stone walls do not a prison make, nor iron bars a cage'; the soul of the child, who grew to be a youth, was never a prisoner. Behind the thick walls of the Tower, built long ago by the Conqueror, he studied. Guards watched over him, but his spirit was far away voyaging in the realms of poetry. And in these thought journeys, sitting at his little window, with a big book upon his knee, he visited the famous places which the *Gesta Romanorum* unrolled before him. . . . The 'noble senator' Boece taught him resignation. William de Lorris took him by the hand and led him to the garden of the Rose. The illustrious Chaucer invited him to follow the gay troop of pilgrims along the highroad to Canterbury. The grave Gower, announcing in advance a sermon of several hours, begged him to be seated, and to the murmur of his wise talk, his head leaning on the window frame, the child slept peacefully.

"Thus passed the years, and the chief change that they brought was a change of prison. After the Tower it was the Castle of Nottingham, another citadel of the Norman time, then Evesham, then again the Tower when Henry V. came to the throne, and at last, and this was by contrast almost liberty, the Castle of Windsor." [1]

And thus for eighteen years the Prince lived a life half-real, half-dream. The gray days followed each other without change, without adventure. But the brilliant throng of kings and queens, of knights and ladies, of

[1] J J Jusserand, *Le Roman d un Roi d'Écosse*

pilgrims and lovers, and all the make-believe people of storyland stood out all the brighter for the grayness of the background. And perhaps to the Prince in his quiet tower the storied people were more real than the living, who only now and again came to visit him. For the storied people were with him always, while the living came and went again and were lost to him in the great world without, of which he knew scarce anything. But at last across this twilight life, which was more than half a dream, there struck one day a flash of sunshine. Then to the patient, studious prisoner all was changed. Life was no longer a twilight dream, but real. He knew how deep joy might be, how sharp sorrow. Life was worth living, he learned, freedom worth having, and at length freedom came, and the Prince returned to his country a free King and a happy lover.

How all this happened King James has told us himself in a book called *The King's Quair*, which means the King's little book, which he wrote while he was still a prisoner in England.

King James tells us how one night he could not sleep, try as he might. He lay tossing and tumbling, "but sleep for craft on earth might I no more." So at last, "knowing no better wile," he took a book hoping "to borrow a sleep" by reading. But instead of bringing sleep, the book only made him more and more wide awake. At length he says:—

> "Mine eyen gan to smart for studying,
> My book I shut, and at my head it laid,
> And down I lay but [1] any tarrying."

Again he lay thinking and tossing upon his bed until he was weary.

> "Then I listened suddenly,
> And soon I heard the bell to matins ring,

---

[1] Without

And up I rose, no longer would I lie
But now, how trow ye? such a fantasy
Fell me to mind, that aye methought the bell
Said to me, 'Tell on man what thee befell'

Thought I tho' to myself, 'What may this be?
This is mine own imagining,
It is no life [1] that speaketh unto me;
It is a bell, or that impression
Of my thought causeth this illusion,
That maketh me think so nicely in this wise';
And so befell as I shall you devise"

Prince James says he had already wasted much ink and paper on writing, yet at the bidding of the bell he decided to write some new thing. So up he rose,

"And forth-with-all my pen in hand I took,
And made a + and thus began my book"

Prince James then tells of his past life, of how, when he was a lad, his father sent him across the sea in a ship, and of how he was taken prisoner and found himself in "Straight ward and strong prison" "without comfort in sorrow." And there full often he bemoaned his fate, asking what crime was his that he should be shut up within four walls when other men were free.

"Bewailing in my chamber thus alone,
Despairing of all joy and remedy,
Out wearied with my thought and woe begone,
Unto the window gan I walk in haste,
To see the world and folk that went forbye,
As for the time though I of mirths food
Might have no more, to look it did me good."

Beneath the tower in which the Prince was imprisoned lay a beautiful garden. It was set about with hawthorn hedges and juniper bushes, and on the small, green branches sat a little nightingale, which sang so loud and

[1] Living person

clear "that all the garden and the walls rang right with the song." Prince James leaned from his window listening to the song of the birds, and watching them as they hopped from branch to branch, preening themselves in the early sunshine and twittering to their mates. And as he watched he envied the birds, and wondered why he should be a thrall while they were free.

> "And therewith cast I down mine eyes again,
> Whereas I saw, walking under the tower
> Full secretly, new coming her to play,
> The fairest and the freshest young flower
> That ever I saw methought, before that hour,
> For which sudden abate, anon astart,
> The blood of all my body to my heart"

A lovely lady was walking in the garden, a lady more lovely than he had dreamed any one might be. Her hair was golden, and wreathed with flowers. Her dress was rich, and jewels sparkled on her white throat. Spellbound, he stood a while watching the lovely lady. He could do nothing but gaze.

> "No wonder was; for why my wits all
> Were so overcome with pleasance and delight,
> Only through letting of mine eyes down fall,
> That suddenly my heart became her thrall,
> For ever of free will."

Thus, from the first moment in which he saw her, James loved the beautiful lady After a few minutes he drew in his head lest she might see him and be angry with him for watching her. But soon he leaned out again, for while she was in the garden he felt he must watch and see her walk "so womanly."

So he stood still at the window, and although the lady was far off in the garden, and could not hear him, he whispered to her, telling of his love. "O sweet," he said, "are you an earthly creature, or are you a goddess? How shall I do reverence to you enough, for I love you? And you, if you will not love me too, why, then, have you come? Have you but come to add to the misery of a poor prisoner?"

Prince James looked, and longed, and sighed, and envied the little dog with which the lovely lady played. Then he scolded the little birds because they sang no more. "Where are the songs you chanted this morning?" he asked. "Why do you not sing now? Do you not see that the most beautiful lady in all the world is come into your garden?" Then to the nightingale he cried, "Lift up thine heart and sing with good intent. If thou would sing well ever in thy life, here is i-faith the time—here is the time, or else never."

Then it seemed to the Prince as if, in answer to his words, all the birds sang more sweetly than ever before. And what they sang was a love-song to his lady. And she, walking under the tender green of the May trees, looked upward, and listened to their sweet songs, while James watched her and loved her more and more.

> "And when she walkéd had a little while
> Under the sweet green boughs bent,
> Her fair fresh face as white as any snow,
> She turnéd has, and forth her ways went;
> But then began my sickness and torment
> To see her go, and follow I not might,
> Methought the day was turnéd into night."

Then, indeed, the day was dark for the Prince. The beautiful lady in going had left him more lonely than before. Now he truly knew what it was to be a prisoner. All day long he knelt at the window, watching, and longing, and not knowing by what means he might see his lady again. At last night came, and worn out in heart and mind he leaned his head against the cold rough stone and slept.

CHAPTER XXIX

THE DEATH OF THE POET KING

As Prince James slept he dreamed that a sudden great light shone into his prison, making bright all the room. A voice cried, "I bring thee comfort and healing, be not afraid." Then the light passed as suddenly as it had come, and the Prince went forth from his prison, no man saying him nay.

> "And hastily by both the arms twain
> I was araiséd up into the air,
> Caught in a cloud of crystal clear and fair."

And so through "air and water and hot fire" he was carried, seeing and hearing many wonders, till he awoke to find himself still kneeling by his window.

Was it all a dream, Prince James asked himself, even the vision of the lovely lady in the garden? At that thought his heart grew heavy. Then, as if to comfort him, a dove flew in at his window carrying in her mouth a sprig of gilliflowers. Upon the stalks in golden letters were written the words, "Awake! Awake! lover, I bring thee glad news."

And so the story had a happy ending, for Prince James knew that the lovely lady of the garden loved him. "And if you think," he says, "that I have written a great deal about a very little thing, I say this to you:—

> "Who that from hell hath creepéd once to heaven
> Would after one thank for joy not make six or seven,
> And every wight his own sweet or sore
> Has most in mind: I can say you no more."

170

Then, in an outburst of joy, he thanks and blesses everything that has led up to this happy day, which has brought him under "Love's yoke which easy is and sure." Even his exile and his prison he thanks.

> "And thankéd be the fair castle wall
> Whereas I whileome lookéd forth and leant"

7

The King's Quair reminds us very much of Chaucer's work. All through it there are lines which might have been written by Chaucer, and in the last verse James speaks of Gower and Chaucer as his "masters dear." Of Gower I have said nothing in this book, because there is not room to tell of every one, and he is not so important as some or so interesting as others. So I leave you to learn about him later. It is to Chaucer, too, much more than to Gower that James owes his music. And if he is grave like Gower rather than merry like Chaucer, we must remember that for nineteen years he had lived a captive, so that it was natural his verse should be somber as his life had been. And though there is no laughter in this poem, it shows a power of feeling joy as well as sorrow, which makes us sad when we remember how long the poet was shut away from common human life.

The King's Quair is written in verses of seven lines. Chaucer used this kind of verse, but because King James used it too, and used it so well, it came to be called the Rhyme Royal.

King James's story had a happy ending. A story with a happy ending must end of course with a wedding, and so did this one. The King of England, now Henry vi., was only a child. But those who ruled for him were quite pleased when they heard that Prince James had fallen in love with the beautiful lady of the garden, for she was the King's cousin, Lady Jane Beaufort. They set James free and willingly consented that he should marry his lady, for in this way they hoped to bind England and Scotland together, and put an end to wars between the two countries. So there was a very grand wedding in London when the lovely lady of the garden became Queen of Scotland. And then these two, a King and Queen, yet happy as any simple lovers, journeyed northward to their kingdom.

They were received with great rejoicing and crowned at Scone. But the new King soon found, that during the long years he had been kept a prisoner in England his kingdom had fallen into wild disorder. Sternly he set himself to bring order out of disorder, and the wilfull, lawless nobles soon found to their surprise that the gentle poet had a will of iron and a hand of steel, and that he could wield his sword and scepter as skillfully as his pen.

James I. righted much that was wrong. In doing it he made for himself many enemies. But of all that he did or tried to do in the twelve years that he ruled you will read in history books. Here I will only tell you of his sad death.

In 1436 James decided to spend Christmas at Perth, a town he loved. As he neared the river Forth, which he had to cross on his way, an aged woman came to him crying in a loud voice, "My Lord King, if ye cross this water ye shall never return again in life"

Now the King had read a prophecy in which it was said that a King of Scotland should be slain that same year. So wondering what this might mean, he sent a knight to speak with the woman. But the knight could make nothing of her, and returning to the King he said, "Sir, take no heed of yon woman's words, for she is old and foolish, and wots not what she sayeth." So the King rode on.

Christmas went by quietly and peacefully, and the New Year came, and still the King lingered in Perth. The winter days passed pleasantly in reading, walking, and tennis-playing; the evenings in chess-playing, music, and story-telling.

But one night, as James was chatting and laughing with the Queen and her ladies before going to bed, a great noise was heard. The sound of many feet, the clatter of armor mingled with wild cries was borne to the quiet room, and through the high windows flashed the light of many torches

At once the King guessed that he was betrayed. The Queen and her ladies ran hastily to the door to shut it. But the locks had been broken and the bolts carried away, so that it could not be fastened.

In vain James looked round. Way of escape there was none. Alone, unarmed, he could neither guard the ladies nor save himself. Crying to them to keep fast the door as best they might, he sprang to the window, hoping by his great strength to wrench the iron bars from their places and escape that way. But, alas, they were so strongly set in the stone that he could not move them, "for which cause the King was ugly astonied."[1]

Then turning to the fire James seized the tongs, "and under his feet he mightily brast up a plank of the chamber,"[2] and leaping down into the vault beneath he let the plank fall again into its place. By this vault the King might have escaped, for until three days before there had been a hole leading from it to the open air. But as he played tennis his balls often rolled into this hole and were lost. So he had ordered it to be built up.

There was nothing, then, for the King to do but wait. Meanwhile the noise grew louder and louder, the traitors came nearer and nearer. One brave lady named Catherine Douglas, hoping to keep them out, and so save the King, thrust her arm through the iron loops on the door where the great bolt should have been. But against the savage force without, her frail, white arm was useless. The door was burst open. Wounded and bleeding, Catherine Douglas was thrown aside and the wild horde stormed into the room.

[1] *The Dethe of the Kynge of Scottis*   .   [2] The same.

It was not long ere the King's hiding-place was found, and one of the traitors leaped down beside him with a great knife in his hand. "And the King, doubting him for his life, caught him mightily by the shoulders, and with full great violence cast him under his feet. For the King was of his person and stature a man right manly strong."[1]

Seeing this, another traitor leaped down to help his fellow. "And the King caught him manly by the neck, and cast him above that other. And so he defouled them both under him that all a long month after men might see how strongly the King had holden them by the throats."[2]

Fiercely the King struggled with his enemies, trying to wrench their knives from them so that he might defend himself. But it was in vain. Seeing him grow weary a third traitor, the King's greatest enemy, Robert Grahame, leaped down too into the vault, "with a horrible and mortal weapon in his hand, and therewithal he smote him through the body, and therewithal the good King fell down."[3]

And thus the poet King died with sixteen wounds in his brave heart and many more in his body. So at the long last our story has a sad ending. But we have to remember that for twelve years King James had a happy life, and that as he had loved his lady at the first so he loved her to the end, and was true to her.

Besides *The King's Quair,* there are a few other short poems which some people think King James wrote. They are very different from the *Quair,* being more like the ballads of the people, and most people think now that James did not write them. But because they are different is no real reason for thinking that they are not his. For James was quite clever enough, we may believe, to write in more than one way.

Besides these doubtful poems, there is one other poem

---

[1] *The Dethe of the Kynge of Scottis.*   The same.   [3] The same.

of three verses about which no one has any doubt. I will
give you one verse here, for it seems in tune with the
King's own life and sudden death.

> "Be not our proud in thy prosperite,
> Be not o'er proud in thy prosperity,
> For as it cumis, sa will it pass away;
> For as it comes, so will it pass away;
> Thy tym to compt is short, thou may weille se
> Thy time to count is short, thou mayst well see
> For of green gres soyn cumis walowit hay,
> For of green grass soon cometh withered hay,
> Labour in trewth, quhill licht is of the day.
> Labour in truth, while light is of the day
> Trust maist in God, for he best gyd thee can,
> Trust most in God, for he best guide thee can,
> And for ilk inch he wil thee quyt a span "
> And for each inch he will thee requite a span.

BOOKS TO READ

An illustration of this chapter may be read *The Fair Maid of Perth,* by Sir
Walter Scott, *The King's Tragedy* (poetry), by D G. Rossetti in his *Poetical
Works.* The best version of *The King's Quair* in the ancient text is by W. W. Skeat.

CHAPTER XXX

DUNBAR—THE WEDDING OF THE THISTLE AND THE ROSE

THE fifteenth century, the century in which King James I. reigned and died, has been called the "Golden Age of Scottish Poetry," because of the number of poets who lived and wrote then. And so, although I am only going to speak of one other Scottish poet at present, you must remember that there were at this time many more. But of them all William Dunbar is counted the greatest. And although I do not think you will care to read his poems for a very long time to come, I write about him here both because he was a great poet and because with one of his poems, *The Thistle and the Rose,* he takes us back, as it were, over the Border into England once more.

William Dunbar was perhaps born in 1460 and began his life when James III. began his reign. He was of noble family, but there is little to know about his life, and as with Chaucer, what we learn about the man himself we learn chiefly from his writings. We know, however, that he went to the University of St. Andrews, and that it was intended that he should go into the Church. In those days in Scotland there were only two things a gentleman might be—either he must be a soldier or a priest. Dunbar's friends, perhaps seeing that he was fond of books, thought it best to make him a priest. But indeed he had made a better soldier. For a time, however, although he was quite unsuited for such a life, he became a friar. As a preaching friar he wandered far.

176

"For in every town and place
 Of all England from Berwick to Calais,
 I have in my habit made good cheer
 In friar's weed full fairly have I fleichet,[1]
 In it have I in pulpit gone and preached,
 In Dernton kirk and eke in Canterbury,
 In it I passed at Dover o'er the ferry
 Through Picardy, and there the people teachéd"

Dunbar himself knew that he had no calling to be a
friar or preacher. He confesses that

"As long as I did bear the friar's style
 In me, God wot, was many wrink and wile,
 In me was falseness every wight to flatter,
 Which might be banished by no holy water;
 I was aye ready all men to beguile"

So after a time we find him no longer a friar, but a
courtier. Soon we find him, like Chaucer, being sent on
business to the Continent for his King, James IV. Like
Chaucer he receives pensions; like Chaucer, too, he knows
sometimes what it is to be poor, and he has left more than
one poem in which he prays the King to remember his old
and faithful servant and not leave him in want. We
find him also begging the King for a Church living, for
although he had no mind to be a friar, he wanted a living,
perhaps merely that he might be sure of a home in his old
age. But for some reason the King never gave him what
he asked.

We have nearly ninety poems of Dunbar, none of them
very long. But although he is a far better poet than
Barbour, or even perhaps than James I., he is not for you
so interesting in the meantime. First, his language is
very hard to understand. One reason for this is that he
knows so many words and uses them all. "He language
had at large," says one of his fellow poets and countrymen.[2]

---

[1] Flattered.   [2] Sir David Lyndsay

And so, although his thought is always clear, it is not always easy to follow it through his strange words. Second, his charm as a poet lies not so much in what he tells, not so much in his story, as in the way that he tells it. And so, even if you are already beginning to care for words and the way in which they are used, you may not yet care so much that you can enjoy poetry written in a tongue which, to us is almost a foreign tongue. But if some day you care enough about it to master this old-world poet, you will find that there is a wonderful variety in his poems. He can be glad and sad, tender and fierce. Sometimes he seems to smile gently upon the sins and sorrows of his day, at other times he pours forth upon them words of savage scorn, grim and terrible. But when we take all his work together, we find that we have such a picture of the times in which he lived as perhaps only Chaucer besides has given us.

For us the most interesting poem is *The Thistle and the Rose.* This was written when Margaret, the daughter of King Henry VII. of England, came to be the wife of King James IV. of Scotland. Dunbar was the "Rhymer of Scotland," that is the poet-laureate of his day, and so, as was natural, he made a poem upon this great event. For a poet-laureate is the King's poet, and it is his duty to make poems on all the great things that may happen to the King. For this he receives a certain amount of money and a cask of wine every year. But it is the honor and not the reward which is now prized.

Dunbar begins by telling us that he lay dreaming one May morning. You will find when you come to read much of the poetry of those days, that poets were very fond of making use of a dream by which to tell a story. It was then a May morning when Dunbar lay asleep.

"When March was with varying winds past,
And April had, with her silver showers,

> Tane leave of nature with an orient blast,
> And pleasant May, that mother is of flowers,
> Had made the birds to begin their hours [1]
> Among the tender arbours red and white,
> Whose harmony to hear it was delight"

Then it seemed that May, in the form of a beautiful lady, stood beside his bed. She called to him, "Sluggard, awake anon for shame, and in mine honor go write something."

> " 'What,' quoth I, 'shall I uprise at morrow?'
> For in this May few birdies heard I sing
> 'They have more cause to weep and plain their sorrow,
> Thy air it is not wholesome or benign!' "

"Nevertheless rise," said May. And so the lazy poet rose and followed the lady into a lovely garden. Here he saw many wonderful and beautiful sights. He saw all the birds, and beasts, and flowers in the world pass before Dame Nature.

> "Then calléd she all flowers that grew in field,
> Discerning all their fashions and properties;
> Upon the awful Thistle she beheld,
> And saw him keepéd [2] by a bush of spears;
> Considering him so able for the wars,
> A radiant crown of rubies she him gave,
> And said, 'In field go forth, and fend the lave [3]
>
> And, since thou art a king, be thou discreet,
> Herb without virtue hold thou not of such price
> As herb of virtue and of odour sweet;
> And let no nettle vile, and full of vice,
> Mate him to the goodly fleur-de-lis,
> Nor let no wild weed full of churlishness
> Compare her to the lily's nobleness
>
> Nor hold thou no other flower in such dainty
> As the fresh Rose, of colour red and white,
> For if thou dost, hurt is thine honesty

---

[1] Orisons—morning prayers   [2] Guarded.   [3] Rest = others.

> Considering that no flower is so perfect,
> So full of virtue, pleasance and delight,
> So full of blissful angelic beauty,
> Imperial birth, honour and dignity.' "

By the Thistle, of course, Dunbar means James IV., and by the Rose the Princess Margaret.

Then to the Rose Dame Nature spoke, and crowned her with "a costly crown with shining rubies bright." When that was done all the flowers rejoiced, crying out, "Hail be thou, richest Rose." Then all the birds—the thrush, the lark, the nightingale—cried "Hail," and "the common voice uprose of birdies small" till all the garden rang with joy.

> "Then all the birdies sang with such a shout,
> That I anon awoke where that I lay,
> And with a start I turnéd me about
> To see this court but all were went away:
> Then up I leanéd, half yet in fear,
> And thus I wrote, as ye have heard to forrow,[1]
> Of lusty May upon the nineth morrow "

Thus did Dunbar sing of the wedding of the Thistle and the Rose. It was a marriage by which the two peoples hoped once more to bring a lasting peace between the two countries. And although the hope was not at once fulfilled, it was a hundred years later. For upon the death of Elizabeth, James VI. of Scotland, the great-grandson of Margaret Tudor and James Stuart, received the crown of England also, thus joining the two rival countries. Then came the true marriage of the Thistle and the Rose.

Meanwhile, as long as Henry VII. remained upon the throne, there was peace between the two peoples. But when Henry VIII. began to rule, his brother-in-law of Scotland soon found cause to quarrel with him Then once again the Thistle and the Rose met, not in peace, but in war. On the red field of Flodden once again the blood of

---

[1] Before=already.

a Scottish King stained the grass. Once again Scotland was plunged in tears.

After "that most dolent day" [1] we hear no more of Dunbar. It is thought by some that he, as many another knight, courtier and priest, laid down his life fighting for his King, and that he fell on Flodden field. By others it is thought that he lived to return to Scotland, and that the Queen gave to him one of the now many vacant Church livings, and that there he spent his last days in quietness and peace.

This may have been so. For although Dunbar makes no mention of Flodden in his poems, it is possible that he may have done so in some that are lost. But where this great poet lies taking his last rest we do not know. It may be he was laid in some quiet country churchyard. It may be he met death suddenly amid the din and horror of battle.

BOOKS TO READ

In illustration of this chapter may be read "Edinburgh after Flodden" in *Lays of the Scottish Cavaliers*, by W. E. Aytoun   The best edition of the *Poems of Dunbar* in the original is edited by J. Small

[1] Sir David Lyndsay.

CHAPTER XXXI

AT THE SIGN OF THE RED PALE

If the fifteenth century has been called the Golden Age of Scottish poetry, it was also the dullest age in English literature. During the fifteenth century few books were written in England. One reason for this was that in England it was a time of foreign and of civil war. The century opened in war with Wales, it continued in war with France. Then for thirty years the wars of the Roses laid desolate the land. They ended at length in 1485 with Bosworth field, by which Henry VII. became King.

But in spite of all the wars and strife, the making of books did not quite cease. And if only a few books were written, it was because it was a time of rebirth and new life as well as a time of war and death. For it was in the fifteenth century that printing was discovered. Then it was that the listening time was really done. Men began to use their eyes rather than their ears. They saw as they had never before seen.

Books began to grow many and cheap. More and more people learned to read, and this helped to settle our language into a form that was to last. French still, although it was no longer the language of the court or of the people, had an influence on our speech. People traveled little, and in different parts of the country different dialects, which were almost like different languages, were spoken. We have seen that the "Inglis" of Scotland differed from Chaucer's English, and the language of the north of

182

England differed from it just as much   But when printed books increased in number quickly, when every man could see for himself what the printed words looked like, these differences began to die out.   Then our English, as a literary language, was born.

It was Caxton, you remember, who was the first English printer.   We have already heard of him when following the Arthur story as the printer of Malory's *Morte d'Arthur*. But Caxton was not only a printer, he was author, editor, printer, publisher and bookseller all in one.

William Caxton, as he himself tells us, was born in Kent in the Weald.   But exactly where or when we do not know, although it may have been about the year 1420. Neither do we know who or what his father was.   Some people think that he may have been a mercer or cloth merchant, because later Caxton was apprenticed to one of the richest cloth merchants of London.   In those days no man was allowed to begin business for himself until he had served for a number of years as an apprentice.   When he had served his time, and then only, was he admitted into the company and allowed to trade for himself.   As the Mercers' Company was one of the wealthiest and most powerful of the merchant companies, they were very careful of whom they admitted as apprentices.   Therefore it would seem that really Caxton's family was "of great repute of old, and genteel-like," as an old manuscript says.[1]

Caxton's master died before he had finished his apprenticeship, so he had to find a new master, and very soon he left England and went to Bruges.   There he remained for thirty-five years.

In those days there was much trade between England and Flanders (Belgium we now call the country) in wool and cloth, and there was a little colony of English merchants in Bruges.   There Caxton steadily rose in

[1] Harleian MS, 5910.

importance until he became "Governor of the English Nation beyond the seas." As Governor he had great power, and ruled over his merchant adventurers as if he had been a king.

But even with all his other work, with his trading and ruling to attend to, Caxton found time to read and write, and he began to translate from the French a book of stories called the *Recuyell* [1] *of the Histories of Troy.* This is a book full of the stories of Greek heroes and of the ancient town of Troy.

Caxton was not very well pleased with his work, however—he "fell into despair of it," he says—and for two years he put it aside and wrote no more.

In 1468 Princess Margaret, the sister of King Edward IV., married the Duke of Burgundy and came to live in Flanders, for in those days Flanders was under the rule of the Dukes of Burgundy. Princess Margaret soon heard of the Englishman William Caxton who had made his home in Bruges. She liked him and encouraged him to go on with his writing, and after a time he gave up his post of Governor of the English and entered the service of the Princess. We do not know what post Caxton held in the household of the Princess, but it was one of honor we may feel sure.

It was at the bidding of the Princess, whose "dreadful command I durst in no wise disobey," that Caxton finished the translation of his book of stories. And as at this time there were no stories written in English prose (poetry only being still used for stories), the book was a great success. The Duchess was delighted and rewarded Caxton well, and besides that so many other people wished to read it that he soon grew tired of making copies. It was then that he decided to learn the new and wonderful art of printing, which was already known in Flanders. So it

---

[1] Collection, from the French word *recueillir*, to gather.

came about that the first book ever printed in English was not printed in England, but somewhere on the Continent. It was printed some time before 1477, perhaps in 1474.

If in manuscript the book had been a success, it was now much more of one. And we may believe that it was this success that made Caxton leave Bruges and go home to England in order to begin life anew as a printer there.

Many a time, as Governor of the English Nation over the seas, he had sent forth richly laden vessels. But had he known it, none was so richly laden as that which now sailed homeward bearing a printing-press.

At Westminster, within the precincts of the Abbey, Caxton found a house and set up his printing-press. And there, not far from the great west door of the Abbey he, already an elderly man, began his new busy life. His house came to be known as the house of the Red Pale from the sign that he set up. It was probably a shield with a red line down the middle of it, called in heraldry a pale. And from here Caxton sent out the first printed advertisement known in England. "If it please any man spiritual or temporal," he says, to buy a certain book. "let him come to Westminster in to the Almonry at the Red Pale and he shall have them good cheap." The advertisement ended with some Latin words which we might translate, "Please do not pull down the advertisement."

The first book that Caxton is known to have printed in England was called *The Dictes*[1] *and Sayings of the Philosophers.* This was also a translation from French, not, however, of Caxton's own writing. It was translated by Earl Rivers, who asked Caxton to revise it, which he did, adding a chapter and writing a prologue.

To the people of Caxton's day printing seemed a marvelous thing So marvelous did it seem that some of them thought it could only be done by the help of evil

---

[1] Another word for sayings, from the French *dire,* to say

spirits. It is strange to think that in those days, when anything new and wonderful was discovered, people at once thought that it must be the work of evil spirits. That it might be the work of good spirits never seemed to occur to them.

Printing, indeed, was a wonderful thing. For now, instead of taking weeks and months to make one copy of a book, a man could make dozens or even hundreds at once. And this made books so cheap that many more people could buy them, and so people were encouraged both to read and write. Instead of gathering together to hear one man read out of a book, each man could buy a copy for himself. At the end of one of his books Caxton begs folk to notice "that it is not written with pen and ink as other books be, to the end that every man may have them at once. For all the books of this story called the *Recuyell of the Histories of Troy* thus imprinted as ye see here were begun on one day and also finished in one day." We who live in a world of books can hardly grasp what that meant to the people of Caxton's time.

For fourteen years Caxton lived a busy life, translating, editing, and printing. Besides that he must have led a busy social life, for he was a favorite with Edward IV., and with his successors Richard III. and Henry VII. too. Great nobles visited his workshop. sent him gifts, and eagerly bought and read his books. The wealthy merchants, his old companions in trade, were glad still to claim him as a friend. Great ladies courted, flattered, and encouraged him. He married, too, and had children, though we know nothing of his home life. Altogether his days were full and busy, and we may believe that he was happy.

But at length Caxton's useful, busy life came to an end. On the last day of it he was still translating a book from French. He finished it only a few hours before he died

We know this, although we do not know the exact date of his death. For his pupil and follower, who carried on his work afterwards, says on the title-page of this book that it was "finished at the last day of his life."

Caxton was buried in the church near which he had worked—St. Margaret's, Westminster. He was laid to rest with some ceremony as a man of importance, for in the account-books of the parish we find these entries:—

> "At burying of William Caxton for four torches 6s 8d
> For the bell at same burying 6d."

This was much more than was usually spent at the burial of ordinary people in those days.

Among the many books which Caxton printed we must not forget Sir Thomas Malory's *Morte d'Arthur,* which we spoke of out of its place in following the story of Arthur in chapter viii. Perhaps you would like to turn back and read it over again now.

As we have said, Caxton was not merely a printer. He was an author too. But although he translated books both from French and Dutch, it is perhaps to his delightful prefaces more than to anything else that he owes his title of author. Yet it must be owned that sometimes they are not all quite his own, but parts are taken wholesale from other men's works or are translated from the French. We are apt to look upon a preface as something dull which may be left unread. But when you come to read Caxton's books, you may perhaps like his prefaces as much as anything else about them. In one he tells of his difficulties about the language, because different people spoke it so differently. He tells how once he began to translate a book, but "when I saw the fair and strange terms therein, I doubted that it should not please some gentlemen which late blamed me, saying that in my translations I had over curious terms, which could not be understood by common people, and desired me to use old and homely terms in my translations. And fain would I satisfy every man. And so to do I took an old book and read therein, and certainly the English was so rude and broad that I could not well understand it. . . . And certainly our language now used varieth far from that which was used and spoken when I was born. .... And that common English that is spoken in one shire varyeth from another. In-so-much that in my days it happened that certain merchants were in a ship in Thames, for to have sailed over the sea into Zealand. For lack of wind they tarried at Foreland, and went to land for to refresh them.

"And one of them, named Sheffield, a mercer, came into an house and asked for meat. And especially he asked for eggs. And the good wife answered that she could speak no French. And the merchant was angry, for he also could speak no French, but would have had eggs, and she understood him not.

"And then at last another said that he would have eyren. Then the good wife said that she understood him well. So what should a man in these days now write, eggs or eyren? Certainly it is hard to please every man by cause of diversity and change of language. . . .

"And some honest and great clerks have been with me, and desired me to write the most curious terms that I could find. And thus between plain, rude, and curious I stand abashed. But in my judgement the common terms that be daily used, be lighter to be understood than the old and ancient English."

In another book Caxton tells us that he knows his own "simpleness and unperfectness" in both French and English. "For in France was I never, and was born and learned my English in Kent, in the Weald, where I doubt not is spoken as broad and rude English as in any place in England."

So you see our English was by no means yet settled. But printing, perhaps, did more than anything else to settle it.

We know that Caxton printed at least one hundred and two editions of books. And you will be surprised to hear that of all these only two or three were books of poetry. Here we have a sure sign that the singing time was nearly over. I do not mean that we are to have no more singers, for most of our greatest are still to come. But from this time prose had shaken off its fetters. It was no longer to be used only for sermons, for prayers, for teaching. It was to take its place beside poetry as a means of enjoyment—as literature. Literature, then, was no longer the affair of the market-place and the banqueting-hall, but of a man's own fireside and quiet study. It was no longer the affair of the crowd, but of each man to himself alone.

The chief poems which Caxton printed were Chaucer's. In one place he calls Chaucer "The worshipful father and first founder and embellisher of ornate eloquence in our English." Here, I think, he shows that he was trying to follow the advice of "those honest and great clerks" who told him he should write "the most curious terms" that he could find. But certainly he admired Chaucer very greatly. In the preface to his second edition of the *Canterbury Tales* he says, "Great thank, laud and honour ought to be given unto the clerks, poets" and others who have written "noble books." "Among whom especially before all others, we ought to give a singular laud unto that noble and great philosopher, Geoffrey Chaucer." Then Caxton goes on to tell us how hard he had found it to get a correct copy of Chaucer's poems, "For I find many of the said books which writers have abridged it, and many things left out: and in some places have set verses that he never made nor set in his book."

This shows us how quickly stories became changed in

the days when everything was copied by hand. When Caxton wrote these words Chaucer had not been dead more than about eighty years, yet already it was not easy to find a good copy of his works.

And if stories changed, the language changed just as quickly. Caxton tells us that the language was changing so fast that he found it hard to read books written at the time he was born. His own language is very Frenchy, perhaps because he translated so many of his books from French. He not only uses words which are almost French, but arranges his sentences in a French manner. He often, too, drops the *e* in *the,* just as in French the *e* or *a* in *le* and *la* is dropped before a vowel. This you will often find in old English books. "The abbey" becomes *thabbay,* "the English" *thenglish.* Caxton writes, too, *thensygnementys* for "the teaching." Here we have the dropped *e* and also the French word *enseignement* used instead of "teaching." But these were only last struggles of a foreign tongue. The triumphant English we now possess was already taking form.

But it was not by printing alone that in the fifteenth century men's eyes were opened to new wonder. They were also opened to the wonder of new worlds far over the sea. For the fifteenth century was the age of discovery, and of all the world's first great sailors. It was the time when America and the western isles were discovered, when the Cape of Good Hope was first rounded, and the new way to India found. So with the whole world urged to action by the knowledge of these new lands, with imagination wakened by the tales of marvels to be seen there, with a new desire to see and do stirring in men's minds, it was not wonderful that there should be little new writing. The fifteenth century was the age of new action and new worlds. The new thought was to follow.

CHAPTER XXXII

ABOUT THE BEGINNING OF THE THEATER

MANY of you have, no doubt, been to the theater. You have seen pantomimes and *Peter Pan,* perhaps; perhaps, too, a play of Shakespeare,—a comedy, it may be, which made you laugh, or even a tragedy which made you want to cry, or at least left you sad. Some of you, too, have been to "Pageants," and some may even have been to an oratorio, which last may have been sung in a church.

But did you ever wonder how plays and theaters came to be? Did you ever think that there was a time when in all the length and breadth of the land there was no theater, when there were no plays either merry or sad? Yet it was so. But at a very early time the people of England began to act. And, strange as it may seem to us now, the earliest plays were acted by monks and took place in church. And it is from these very early monkish plays that the theater with its different kinds of plays, that pageants and even oratorios have sprung.

In this chapter I am going to talk about these beginnings of the English theater and of its literature. All plays taken together are called the drama, and the writers of them are called dramatists, from a Greek word *dran,* to act or do. For dramas are written not to be read merely, but also to be acted.

To trace the English drama from its beginnings we must go a long way back from the reigns of Henry VII. and of Henry VIII., down to which the life of Dunbar has brought us. We must go back to the days when the

191

priests were the only learned people in the land, when the monasteries were the only schools.

If we would picture to ourselves what these first English plays were like, we must not think of a brilliantly lighted theater planked out and fine with red and gold and white such as we know. We must think rather of some dim old church. Stately pillars rise around us, and the outline of the arches is lost in the high twilight of the roof. Behind the quaintly dressed players gleams the great crucifix with its strange, sad figure and outstretched arms which, under the flickering light of the high altar candles, seems to stir to life. And beyond the circle of light, in the soft darkness of the nave, the silent people kneel or stand to watch.

It was in such solemn surroundings that our first plays were played. And the stories that were acted were Bible stories. There was no thought of irreverence in such acting. On the contrary, these plays were performed "to exort the mindes of common people to good devotion and holesome doctrine."

You remember when Caedmon sang, he made his songs of the stories of Genesis and Exodus. And in this way, in those bookless days, the people were taught the Bible stories. But you know that what we learn by our ears is much harder to remember than what we learn by our eyes. If we are only told a thing we may easily forget it. But if we have seen it, or seen a picture of it, we remember it much more easily. In those far-off days, however, there were as few pictures as there were books in England. And so the priests and monks fell upon the plan of acting the Bible stories and the stories of the saints, so that the people might see and better understand.

These plays which the monks made were called Mystery or Miracle plays. I cannot tell you the exact date of our first Miracle plays, but the earliest that we know of certainly was acted at the end of the eleventh or beginning of the twelfth century. It is not unreasonable to suppose, however, that there had been still earlier plays of which we know nothing. For the Miracle plays did not spring all at once to life, they began gradually, and the beginnings can be traced as far back as the ninth century. In an old book of rules for Winchester Cathedral, written about 959, there are directions given for showing the death and resurrection of Christ in dumb show chiefly, with just a few Latin sentences to explain it. By degrees these plays grew longer and fuller, until in them the whole story of man from the Creation to the Day of Judgment was acted in what was called a cycle or circle of short acts or plays.

But although these plays were looked upon as an act of religion, they were not all solemn. At times, above the grave tones of the monks or the solemn chanting of the choir, laughter rang out. For some of the characters were meant to be funny, and the watching crowd knew and greeted them as such even before they spoke, just as we know and greet the jester or the clown.

The demons were generally funny, and Noah's wife, who argued about going into the ark. The shepherds, also, watching their flocks by night, were almost sure to make the people laugh.

But there were solemn moments, too, when the people reverently listened to the grave words of God the Father, or to those, tender and loving, of Mary, the Virgin Mother. And when the shepherds neared the manger where lay the wondrous Babe, all jesting ceased. Here there was nothing but tender, if simple and unlearned, adoration.

In those early days Latin was the tongue of the Church, and the Miracle plays were at first said in Latin. But as the common folk could not understand what was said, the plays were chiefly shown in dumb show. Soon, however, Latin was given up, and the plays were acted in English. Then by degrees the churches grew too small to hold the great crowds of people who wished to see the plays, and so they were acted outside the church door in the churchyard, on a stage built level with the steps. The church, then, could be made to represent heaven, where God and the angels dwelt. The stage itself was the world, and below it was hell, from out of which came smoke and sometimes flames, and whence might be heard groans and cries and the clanking of chains.

But the playing of Mysteries and Miracles at the church doors had soon to be given up. For the people, in their excitement, forgot the respect due to the dead. They trampled upon the graves and destroyed the tombs in their eagerness to see. And when the play was over the grave-yard was a sorry sight with trodden grass and broken headstones. So by degrees it came about that these plays lost their connection with the churches, and were no more played in or near them. They were, instead, played in some open space about the town, such as the market-place. Then, too, the players ceased to be monks and priests, and the acting was taken up by the people themselves. It was then that the playing came into the hands of the trade guilds.

Nowadays we hear a great deal about "trades unions." But in those far-off days such things were unknown. Each trade, however, had its own guild by which the members of it were bound together. Each guild had its patron saint, and after a time the members of a guild began to act a play on their saint's day in his honor. Later still the guilds all worked together, and all acted their plays on one day. This was Corpus Christi Day, a feast founded by Pope Urban IV. in 1264. As this feast was in summer, it was a very good time to act the plays, for the weather was warm and the days were long. The plays often began very early in the morning as soon as it was light, and lasted all day.

The Miracles were now acted on a movable stage.

This stage was called a pageant, and the play which was acted on it was also in time called a pageant. The stage was made in two stories. The upper part was open all round, and upon this the acting took place. The under part was curtained all round, and here the actors dressed. From here, too, they came out, and when they had finished their parts they went back again within the curtains.

The movable stages were, of course, not very large, so sometimes more than one was needed for a play. At other times the players overflowed, as it were, into the audience. "Here Herod rages on the pageant and in the street also" is one stage direction. The devils, too, often ran among the people, partly to amuse them and partly to frighten and show them what might happen if they remained wicked. At the Creation, animals of all kinds which had been kept chained up were let loose suddenly, and ran among the people, while pigeons set free from cages flew over their heads. Indeed, everything seems to have been done to make the people feel the plays as real as possible.

The pageants were on wheels, and as soon as a play was over at the first appointed place, the stage was dragged by men to the next place and the play again began. In an old MS. we are told, "The places where they played them was in every streete. They begane first at the abay gates, and when the first pagiante was played, it was wheeled to the highe crosse befor the mayor, and soe to every streete. And soe every streete had a pagiant playinge before them at one time, till all the pagiantes for the daye appoynted weare played. And when one pagiante was neare ended worde was broughte from streete to streete, that soe they mighte come in place thereof, exceedinge orderly. And all the streetes have theire pagiantes afore them all at one time playinge togeather."[1]

[1] Harleian MS., 1918

Thus, if a man kept his place all a long summer's day, he might see pass before him pageant after pageant until he had seen the whole story of the world, from the Creation to the Day of Judgment.

In time nearly every town of any size in England had its own cycle of plays, but only four of these have come down to us. These are the York, the Chester, the Wakefield, and the Coventry cycles. Perhaps the most interesting of them all are the Wakefield plays. They are also called the Townley plays, from the name of the family who possessed the manuscript for a long time.

Year after year the same guild acted the same play. And it really seemed as if the pageant was in many cases chosen to suit the trade of the players. The water-drawers of Chester, for instance, acted the Flood. In York the shipwrights acted the building of the ark, the fishmongers the Flood, and the gold-beaters and money-workers the three Kings out of the East.

The members of each guild tried to make their pageant as fine as they could. Indeed, they were expected to do so, for in 1394 we find the Mayor of York ordering the craftsmen "to bring forth their pageants in order and course by good players, well arrayed and openly speaking, upon pain of losing of 100 shillings, to be paid to the chamber without any pardon." [1]

So, in order to supply everything that was needful, each member of a guild paid what was called "pageant silver." Accounts of how this money was spent were carefully kept. A few of these have come down to us, and some of the items and prices paid sound very funny now.

> "Paid for setting the world of fire 5d
> For making and mending of the black souls hose 6d.

---

[1] Thomas Sharp, *Dissertation on the Pageants*

THE DEMONS WERE GENERALLY FUNNY!

> For a pair of new hose and mending of the old for the white
> souls 18d.
> Paid for mending Pilate's hat 4d "

The actors, too, were paid. Here are some of the prices:—

> "To Fawson for hanging Judas 4d.
> Paid to Fawson for cock crowing 4d."

Some got much more than others. Pilate, for instance, who was an important character, got 4s., while two angels, only got 8d. between them. But while the rehearsing and acting were going on the players received their food, and when it was all over they wound up with a great supper.

CHAPTER XXXIII

HOW THE SHEPHERDS WATCHED THEIR FLOCKS

In this chapter I am going to give you a part of one of the Townley plays to show you what the beginnings of our drama were like.

Although our forefathers tried to make the pageants as real as possible, they had, of course, no scenery, but acted on a little bare platform. They never thought either that the stories they acted had taken place long ago and in lands far away, where dress and manners and even climate were all very different from what they were in England.

For instance, in the Shepherd's play, of which I am going to tell, the first shepherd comes in shivering with cold. For though he is acting in summer he must make believe that it is Christmas-time, for on Christmas Day Christ was born. And Christmas-time in England, he knows, is cold. What it may be in far-off Palestine he neither knows nor cares.

> "Lord, what these weathers are cold! and I am ill happed;
> I am near hand dulled so long have I napped;
> My legs they fold, my fingers are chapped,
> It is not as I would, for I am all lapped
>   In sorrow
> In storm and tempest,
> Now in the east, now in the west,
> Woe is him has never rest
>   Mid-day or morrow "

In this strain the shepherd grumbles until the second comes. He, too, complains of the cold.

198

"The frost so hideous, they water mine een,
　　No he!
Now is dry, now is wet,
Now is snow, now is sleet.
When my shoon freeze to my feet,
　　It is not all easy"

So they talk until the third shepherd comes. He, too, grumbles.

"Was never syne Noah's floods such floods seen;
　Winds and rains so rude, and storms so keen"

The first two ask the third shepherd where the sheep are. "Sir," he replies,

"This same day at morn
I left them i the corn
　When they rang lauds
They had pasture good they cannot go wrong"

That is all right, say the others, and so they settle to sing a song, when a neighbor named Mak comes along. They greet the newcomer with jests. But the second shepherd is suspicious of him.

"Thus late as thou goes,
What will men suppose?
And thou hast no ill nose
For stealing of sheep."

"I am true as steel," says Mak. "All men wot it. But a sickness I feel that holds me full hot," and so, he says, he is obliged to walk about at night for coolness.

The shepherds are all very weary and want to sleep. But just to make things quite safe, they bid Mak lie down between them so that he cannot move without awaking them. Mak lies down as he is bid, but he does not sleep, and as soon as the others are all snoring he softly rises and "borrows" a sheep.

Quickly he goes home with it and knocks at his cottage door. "How, Gill, art thou in? Get us a light."

"Who makes such din this time of night?" answers his wife from within.

When she hears that it is Mak she unbars the door, but when she sees what her husband brings she is afraid.

"By the naked neck thou art like to hang," she says.

"I have often escaped before," replies Mak.

"But so long goes the pot to the water, men say, at last comes it home broken," cries Gill.

But the question is, now that they have the sheep, how is it to be hid from the shepherds. For Mak feels sure that they will suspect him when they find out that a sheep is missing.

Gill has a plan. She will swaddle the sheep like a new-born baby and lay it in the cradle. This being done, Mak returns to the shepherds, whom he finds still sleeping, and lies down again beside them. Presently they all awake and rouse Mak, who still pretends to sleep. He, after some talk, goes home, and the shepherds go off to seek and count their sheep, agreeing to meet again at the "crooked thorn."

Soon the shepherds find that one sheep is missing, and suspecting Mak of having stolen it they follow him home. They find him sitting by the cradle singing a lullaby to the new-born baby, while Gill lies in bed groaning and pretending to be very ill. Mak greets the shepherds in a friendly way, but bids them speak softly and not walk about, as his wife is ill and the baby asleep.

But the shepherds will not be put off with words. They search the house, but can find nothing.

"All work we in vain as well may we go.
  Bother it!
I can find no flesh
Hard or nesh,[1]
Salt or fresh,
  But two toom [2] platters "

---

[1] Soft.   [2] Empty.

Meanwhile, Gill from her bed cries out at them, calling them thieves. "Ye come to rob us. I swear if ever I you beguiled, that I eat this child that lies in this cradle."

The shepherds at length begin to be sorry that they have been so unjust as to suspect Mak. They wish to make friends again. But Mak will not be friends "Farewell, all three, and glad I am to see you go," he cries.

So the shepherds go a little sadly. "Fair winds may there be, but love there is none this year," says one.

"Gave ye the child anything?" says another.

"I trow not a farthing."

"Then back will I go," says the third shepherd, "abide ye there."

And back he goes full of his kindly thought. "Mak," he says, "with your leave let me give your bairn but sixpence."

But Mak still pretends to be sulky, and will not let him come near the child. By this time all the shepherds have come back. One wants to kiss the baby, and bends over the cradle. Suddenly he starts back. What a nose! The deceit is found out and the shepherds are very angry. Yet even in their anger they can hardly help laughing. Mak and Gill, however, are ready of wit. They will not own to the theft. It is a changeling child, they say.

> "He was taken with an elf,
> 5   I saw it myself,
> When the clock struck twelve was he foreshapen,"

says Gill.

But the shepherds will not be deceived a second time. They resolve to punish Mak, but let him off after having tossed him in a blanket until they are tired and he is sore and sorry for himself.

This sheepstealing scene shows how those who wrote the play tried to catch the interest of the people. For every one who saw this scene could understand it. Sheep-stealing was a very common crime in England in those days, and was often punished by death. Probably every one who saw the play knew of such cases, and the writers used this scene as a link between the everyday life, which was near at hand and easy to understand, and the story of the birth of Christ, which was so far off and hard to understand.

And it is now, when the shepherds are resting from their hard work of beating Mak, that they hear the angels sing "Glory to God in the highest." From this point on all the jesting ceases, and in its rough way the play is reverent and loving.

The angel speaks.

"Rise, herdmen, quickly, for now is he born
That shall take from the fiend what Adam was lorn;
That demon to spoil this night is he born,
God is made your friend now at this morn.
  He behests
At Bethlehem go see,
There lies that fre [1]
In a crib full poorly
  Betwixt two beasties"

The shepherds hear the words of the angel, and looking upward see the guiding star. Wondering at the music, talking of the prophecies of David and Isaiah, they hasten to Bethlehem and find the lowly stable. Here, with a mixture of awe and tenderness, the shepherds greet the Holy Child. It is half as if they spoke to the God they feared. half as if they played with some little helpless baby who was their very own. They mingle simple things of everyday life with their awe. They give him gifts, but their simple minds can imagine no other than those they might give to their own children.

[1] Noble

The first shepherd greets the child with the words:—

> "Hail, comely and clean! Hail, young child!
> Hail, maker as methinks of a maiden so mild.
> Thou hast warred, I ween, the demon so wild."

Then he gives as his gift a bob of cherries.
The second shepherd speaks:—

> "Hail! sovereign saviour! for thee have we sought
> Hail, noble child and flower that all thing hast wrought.
> Hail, full of favour, that made all of nought
> Hail! I kneel and I cower! A bird have I brought
>   To my bairn
> Hail, little tiny mop,
> Of our creed thou art crop,[1]
> I would drink to thy health,
>   Little Day Star!"

The third shepherd speaks:—

> "Hail! darling dear full of Godhead!
> I pray thee be near when that I have need!
> Hail! sweet is thy cheer! My heart would bleed
> To see thee sit here in so poor weed
>   With no pennies.
> Hail! put forth thy dall.[2]
> I bring thee but a ball:
> Have and play thee with all
>   And go to the tennis."

And so the pageant of the shepherds comes to an end, and they return home rejoicing.

This play gives us a good idea of how the Miracles wound themselves about the lives of the people. It gives us a good idea of the rudeness of the times when such jesting with what we hold as sacred seemed not amiss. It gives, too, the first gleam of what we might call true comedy in English.

[1] Head   [2] Hand.

CHAPTER XXXIV

THE STORY OF EVERYMAN

A LITTLE later than the Miracle and Mystery plays came another sort of play called the Moralities. In these, instead of representing real people, the actors represented thoughts, feelings and deeds, good and bad. Truth, for instance, would be shown as a beautiful lady; Lying as an ugly old man, and so on. These plays were meant to teach just as the Miracles were meant to teach. But instead of teaching the Bible stories, they were made to show men the ugliness of sin and the beauty of goodness. When we go to the theater now we only think of being amused, and it is strange to remember that all acting was at first meant to teach.

The very first of our Moralities seems to have been a play of the Lord's Prayer. It was acted in the reign of Edward III. or some time after 1327. But that has long been lost, and we know nothing of it but its name. There are several other Moralities, however, which have come down to us of a later date, the earliest being of the fifteenth century, and of them perhaps the most interesting is *Everyman.*

But we cannot claim *Everyman* altogether as English literature, for it is translated from, or at least founded upon, a Dutch play. Yet it is the best of all the Moralities which have come down to us, and may have been translated into English about 1480. In its own time it must have been thought well of, or no one would have troubled to

204

translate it. But, however popular it was long ago, for hundreds of years it had lain almost forgotten, unread except by a very few, and never acted at all, until some one drew it from its dark hiding-place and once more put it upon the stage. Since then, during the last few years, it has been acted often. And as, happily, the actors have tried to perform it in the simple fashion in which it must have been done long ago, we can get from it a very good idea of the plays which pleased our forefathers. On the title-page of *Everyman* we read: "Here beginneth a treatise how the high Father of heaven sendeth Death to summon every creature to come to give a count of their lives in this world, and is in the manner of a moral play." So in the play we learn how Death comes to Everyman and bids him follow him.

But Everyman is gay and young. He loves life, he has many friends, the world to him is beautiful, he cannot leave it. So he prays Death to let him stay, offers him gold and riches if he will but put off the matter until another day.

But Death is stern. "Thee availeth not to cry, weep and pray," he says, "but haste thee lightly that thou wert gone the journey."

Then seeing that go he must, Everyman thinks that at least he will have company on the journey. So he turns to his friends. But, alas, none will go with him. One by one they leave him. Then Everyman cries in despair:—

> "O to whom shall I make my moan
> For to go with me in that heavy journey?
> First Fellowship said he would with me gone,
> His words were very pleasant and gay,
> But afterward he left me alone
> Then spake I to my kinsmen all in despair,
> And also they gave me words fair,
> They lacked no fair speaking,
> But all forsake me in the ending"

So at last Everyman turns him to his Good Deeds—his Good Deeds, whom he had almost forgotten and who lies bound and in prison by reason of his sins. And Good Deeds consents to go with him on the dread journey. With him come others, too, among them Knowledge and Strength. But at the last these, too, turn back. Only Good Deeds is true, only Good Deeds stands by him to the end with comforting words. And so the play ends; the body of Everyman is laid in the grave, but we know that his soul goes home to God.

This play is meant to picture the life of every man or woman, and to show how unhappy we may be in the end if we have not tried to be good in this world.

> "This moral men may have in mind,
> The hearers take it of worth old and young,
> And forsake Pride, for he deceiveth you in the end,
> And remember Beauty, Five Wits, Strength, and Discretion,
> They all at the last do Everyman forsake,
> Save his Good Deeds; these doth he take
> And beware,—an they be small,
> Before God he hath no help at all.
> None excuse may be there for Everyman."

BOOK TO READ

Everyman A Morality (Everyman's Library).

CHAPTER XXXV

HOW A POET COMFORTED A GIRL

PERHAPS the best Morality of which we know the author's name is *Magnificence,* by John Skelton. But, especially after *Everyman,* it is dull reading for little people, and it is not in order to speak of this play that I write about Skelton.

John Skelton lived in the stormy times of Henry VIII., and he is called sometimes our first poet-laureate. But he was not poet-laureate as we now understand it, he was not the King's poet. The title only meant that he had taken a degree in grammar and Latin verse, and had been given a laurel wreath by the university which gave the degree. It was in this way that Skelton was made laureate, first by Oxford, then by Louvain in Belgium, and thirdly by Cambridge, so that in his day he was considered a learned man and a great poet. He was a friend of Caxton and helped him with one of his books. "I pray, maister Skelton, late created poet-laureate in the university of Oxenford," says Caxton, "to oversee and correct this said book."

John Skelton, like so many other literary men of those days, was a priest. He studied, perhaps, both at Oxford and at Cambridge, and became tutor to Prince, afterwards King, Henry VIII. We do not know if he had an easy time with his royal pupil or not, but in one of his poems he tells us that "The honour of England I learned to spell" and "acquainted him with the Muses nine."

207

The days of Henry VIII. were troublous times for thinking people. The King was a tyrant, and the people of England were finding it harder than ever to bow to a tyrant while the world was awakening to new thought, and new desires for freedom, both in religion and in life.

The Reformation had begun. The teaching of Piers Ploughman, the preaching of Wyclif, had long since almost been forgotten, but it had never altogether died out. The evils in the Church and in high places were as bad as ever, and Skelton, himself a priest, preached against them. He attacked others, even though he himself sinned against the laws of priesthood. For he was married, and in those days marriage was forbidden to clergymen, and his life was not so fair as it might have been.

At first Wolsey, the great Cardinal and friend of Henry VIII., was Skelton's friend too. But Skelton's tongue was mocking and bitter. "He was a sharp satirist, but with more railing and scoffery than became a poet-laureate," [1] said one. The Cardinal became an enemy, and the railing tongue was turned against him. In a poem called *Colin Cloute* Skelton pointed out the evils of his day and at the same time pointed the finger of scorn at Wolsey. Colin Cloute, like Piers Ploughman, was meant to mean the simple good Englishman.

> "Thus I Colin Cloute,
> As I go about,
> And wandering as I walk,
> There the people talk
> Men say, for silver and gold
> Mitres are bought and sold"

And again:--

> "Laymen say indeed.
> How they (the priests) take no heed
> Their silly sheep to feed,

---

[1] George Puttenham

> But pluck away and pull
> The fleeces of their wool."

But he adds:—

> "Of no good bishop speak I,
> Nor good priest I decry,
> Good friar, nor good chanon,[1]
> Good nun, nor good canon,
> Good monk, nor good clerk,
> Nor yet no good work
> But my recounting is
> Of them that do amiss"

Yet, although Skelton said he would not decry any good man or any good work, his spirit was a mocking one. He was fond of harsh jests and rude laughter, and no person or thing was too high or too holy to escape his sharp wit. "He was doubtless a pleasant conceited fellow, and of a very sharp wit," says a writer about sixty years later, "exceeding bold, and would nip to the very quick when he once set hold." [2]

And being bold as bitter, and having set hold with hatred upon Wolsey, he in another poem called *Why come ye not to Court?* and in still another called *Speake, Parrot,* wrote directly against the Cardinal. Yet although Skelton railed against the Cardinal and against the evils in the Church, he was no Protestant. He believed in the Church of Rome, and would have been sorry to think that he had helped the "heretics."

Wolsey was still powerful, and he made up his mind to silence his enemy, so Skelton found himself more than once in prison, and at last to escape the Cardinal's anger he was forced to take sanctuary in Westminster. There he remained until he died a few months before his great enemy fell from power.

As many of Skelton's poems were thus about quarrels

[1] Same as canon   [2] William Webbe.

over religion and politics, much of the interest in them has died. Yet, as he himself says,

> "For although my rhyme is ragged,
> Tattered and jagged,
> Rudely rain-beaten,
> Rusty and moth eaten,
> If ye take well therewith,
> It hath in it some pith."

And it is well to remember the name of Colin Cloute at least, because a later and much greater poet borrowed that name for one of his own poems, as you shall hear.

But the poem which keeps most interest for us is one which perhaps at the time it was written was thought least important. It is called *The Book of Philip Sparrow.* And this poem shows us that Skelton was not always bitter and biting. For it is neither bitter nor coarse, but is a dainty and tender lament written for a schoolgirl whose sparrow had been killed by a cat. It is written in the same short lines as *Colin Cloute* and others of Skelton's poems —"breathless rhymes," [1] they have been called. These short lines remind us somewhat of the old Anglo-Saxon short half-lines, except that they rime. They are called after their author "Skeltonical."

What chiefly makes *The Book of Philip Sparrow* interesting is that it is the original of our nursery rime *Who Killed Cock Robin?* It is written in the form of a dirge, and many people were shocked at that, for they said that it was but another form of mockery that this jesting priest had chosen with which to divert himself. But I think that little Jane Scoupe at school in the nunnery at Carowe would dry her eyes and smile when she read it. She must have been pleased that the famous poet, who had been the King's tutor and friend and who had been both

[1] Bishop Hall

the friend and enemy of the great Cardinal, should trouble
to write such a long poem all about her sparrow.

Here are a few quotations from it:—

"Pla ce bo,[1]
Who is there who?
Di le sci,
Dame Margery;
Fa re my my,
Wherefore and why why?
For the soul of Philip Sparrow
That was late slain at Carowe,
Among the nuns black,
For that sweet soul's sake,
And for all sparrows' souls,
Set in our bead rolls,
Pater Noster qui,
With an Ave Mari,
And with the corner of a creed,
The more shall be your need.

.   .   .   .

I wept and I wailed,
The tears down hailed,
But nothing it availed
To call Philip again,
That Gib our cat hath slain.
   Gib, I say, our cat
Worried her on that
Which I loved best
It cannot be expressed
My sorrowful heaviness
And all without redress.

.   .   .   .

It had a velvet cap,
And would sit upon my lap,
And seek after small worms,
And sometimes white bread-crumbs.

.   .   .   .

---

[1] Placebo is the first word of the first chant in the service for the dead
Skelton has here made it into three words   The chant is called the Placebo from
the first word, see also page 214

Sometimes he would gasp
When he saw a wasp,
A fly or a gnat
He would fly at that,
And prettily he would pant
When he saw an ant;
Lord, how he would fly
After the butterfly.
And when I said Phip, Phip
Then he would leap and skip,
And take me by the lip.
Alas, it will me slo,[1]
That Philip is gone me fro.

.   .   .   .

For it would come and go,
And fly so to and fro;
And on me it would leap
When I was asleep,
And his feathers shake,
Wherewith he would make
Me often for to wake

.   .   .   .

That vengeance I ask and cry,
By way of exclamation,
On all the whole nation
Of cats wild and tame.
God send them sorrow and shame!
That cat especially
That slew so cruelly
My little pretty sparrow
That I brought up at Carowe.
　O cat of churlish kind,
The fiend was in thy mind,
When thou my bird untwined [2]
I would thou hadst been blind
The leopards savage,
The lions in their rage,
Might catch thee in their paws
And gnaw thee in their jaws

.   .   .   .   .

---

[1] Slay   [2] Tore to pieces

These villainous false cats,
Were made for mice and rats,
And not for birdies small

.   .   .

Alas, mine heart it slayeth
My Philip's doleful death,
When I remember it,
How prettily it would sit,
Many times and oft,
Upon my finger aloft.

.   .   .

To weep with me, look that ye come,
All manner of birds of your kind;
So none be left behind,
To mourning look that ye fall
With dolorous songs funeral,
Some to sing, and some to say,
Some to weep, and some to pray,
Every bird in his lay.
The goldfinch and the wagtail,
The gangling jay to rail,
The flecked pie to chatter
Of the dolorous matter;
The robin redbreast,
He shall be the priest,
The requiem mass to sing,
Softly warbling,
With help of the red sparrow,
And the chattering swallow,
This hearse for to hallow;
The lark with his lung too,
The chaffinch and the martinet also;

.   .   .

The lusty chanting nightingale,
The popinjay to tell her tale,
That peepeth oft in the glass,
Shall read the Gospel at mass;
The mavis with her whistle
Shall read there the Epistle,
But with a large and a long
To keep just plain song.

The peacock so proud,
Because his voice is loud,
And hath a glorious tail
He shall sing the grayle; [1]
The owl that is so foul
Must help us to howl.

. . .

At the Placebo
We may not forego
The chanting of the daw
The stork also,
That maketh her nest
In chimnies to rest.

. . .

The ostrich that will eat
A horseshoe so great,
In the stead of meat,
Such fervent heat
His stomach doth gnaw.
He cannot well fly
Nor sing tuneably

. . .

The best that we can
To make him our bellman,
And let him ring the bells,
He can do nothing else.
Chanticlere our cock
Must tell what is of the clock
By the astrology
That he hath naturally
Conceived and caught,
And was never taught

. . .

To Jupiter I call
Of heaven imperial
That Philip may fly
Above the starry sky
To greet the pretty wren
That is our Lady's hen,
Amen, amen, amen.

---

[1] Gradual=the part of the mass between Epistle and Gospel

CHAPTER XXXVI

THE RENAISSANCE

RENAISSANCE means rebirth, and to make you understand
something of what the word means in our literature I must
take you a long way. You have been told that the
fifteenth century was a dull time in English literature,
but that it was also a time of new action and new life,
for the discovery of new worlds and the discovery of printing had opened men's eyes and minds to new wonders.
There was a third event which added to this new life by
bringing new thought and new learning to England. That
was the taking of Constantinople by the Turks.

It seems difficult to understand how the taking of
Constantinople could have any effect on our literature.
I will try to explain, but in order to do so clearly I must go
back to the time of the Romans.

All of you have read English history, and there you read
of the Romans. You know what a clever and conquering
people they were, and how they subdued all the wild tribes
who lived in the countries around them. Besides conquering all the barbarians around them, the Romans conquered
another people who were not barbarians, but who were
in some ways more civilized than themselves. These
were the Greeks. They had a great literature, they were
more learned and quite as skilled in the arts of peace as the
Romans. Yet in 146 B.C., long before the Romans came
to our little island, Greece became a Roman province.

Nearly five hundred years later there sat upon the

throne an Emperor named Constantine. And he, although Rome was still pagan, became a Christian. He was, besides, a great and powerful ruler. His court was brilliant, glittering with all the golden splendor of those far-off times. But although Rome was still pagan, Greece, a Roman province, had become Christian. And in this Christian province Constantine made up his mind to build a New Rome.

In those days the boundaries of Greece stretched far further than they do now, and it was upon the shores of the Bosphorus that Constantine built his new capital. There was already an ancient town there named Byzantium, but he transformed it into a new and splendid city. The Emperor willed it to be called New Rome, but instead the people called it the city of Constantine, and we know it now as Constantinople.

When Constantinople was founded it was a Roman city. All the rulers were Roman, all the high posts were filled by Romans, and Latin was the speech of the people. But in Constantinople it happened as it had happened in England after the Conquest. In England, for a time after the Conquest, the rulers were French and the language was French, but gradually all that passed away, and the language and the rulers became English once more. So it was in Constantinople. By degrees it became a Greek city, the rulers became Greek, and Greek was the language spoken.

In building a second capital Constantine had weakened his Empire. Soon it was split in two, and there arose a western and an eastern Empire. As time went on the Western Empire with Rome at its head declined and fell, while the Eastern Empire with Constantinople as its capital grew great. But it grew into a Greek Empire. Even very clever people cannot tell the exact date at which the Roman Empire came to an end and the Greek or

Byzantine Empire, as it is called, began. So we need not trouble about that. All that is needful for us to understand now is that Constantinople was a Christian city, a Greek city, and a treasure-house of Greek learning and literature.

Thus Constantinople was the Christian outpost of Europe. For hundreds of years the Byzantine Empire stood as a barrier against the Saracen hosts of Asia. It might have stood still longer, but sad to say, this barrier was first broken down by the Christians themselves. For in 1204 the armies of the fourth Crusade, which had gathered to fight the heathen, turned their swords, to their shame be it said, against the Christian people of the Greek Empire. Constantinople was taken, plundered, and destroyed by these "pious brigands," [1] and the last of the Byzantine Emperors was first blinded and then flung from a high tower, so that his body fell shattered to pieces on the paving-stones of his own capital.

Baldwin, Count of Flanders, one of the great leaders of the Crusade, was then crowned by his followers and acknowledged Emperor of the East. But the once great Empire was now broken up, and out of it three lesser Empires, as well as many smaller states, were formed.

Baldwin did not long rule as Emperor of the East, and the Greeks after a time succeeded in regaining Constantinople from the western Christians. But although for nearly two hundred years longer they kept it, the Empire was dying and lifeless. And by degrees, as the power of Greece grew less, the power of Turkey grew greater. At length in 1453 the Sultan Mohammed II. attacked Constantinople. Then the Cross, which for a thousand years and more had stood upon the ramparts of Christendom, went down before the Crescent.

Constantine XI., the last of the Greek Emperors, knelt

[1] George Finlay, *History of Greece.*

in the great church of St. Sophia to receive for the last time the Holy Sacrament. Then mounting his horse he rode forth to battle. Fighting for his kingdom and his faith he fell, and over his dead body the young Sultan and his soldiers rode into the ruined city. Then in the church, where but a few hours before the fallen Emperor had knelt and prayed to Christ, the Sultan bowed himself in thanks and praise to Allah and Mohammed.

And now we come to the point where the taking of Constantinople and the fall of the Greek Empire touches our literature.

In Constantinople the ancient learning and literature of the Greeks had lived on year after year. The city was full of scholars who knew, and loved, and studied the Greek authors. But now, before the terror of the Turk, driven forth by the fear of slavery and disgrace, these Greek scholars fled. They fled to Italy. And although in their flight they had to leave goods and wealth behind, they came laden with precious manuscripts from the libraries of Constantinople.

These fugitive Greeks brought to the Italians a learning which was to them new and strange. Soon all over Europe the news of the New Learning spread. Then across the Alps scholars thronged from every country in Europe to listen and to learn.

I do not think I can quite make you understand what this New Learning was. It was indeed but the old learning of Greece. Yet there was in it something that can never grow old, for it was human. It made men turn away from idle dreaming and begin to learn that the world we live in is real. They began to realize that there was something more than a past and a future. There was the present. So, instead of giving all their time to vague wonderings of what might be, of what never had been, and what never could be, they began to take an interest in life

as it was and in man as he was. They began to see that
human life with all its joys and sorrows was, after all, the
most interesting thing to man.

It was a New Birth, and men called it so. For that is
the meaning of Renaissance. Many things besides the fall
of Constantinople helped towards this New Birth. The
discovery of new worlds by daring sailors like Columbus
and Cabot, and the discovery of printing were among them.
But the touchstone of the New Learning was the knowledge of Greek, which had been to the greater part of
Europe a lost tongue. On this side of the Alps there was
not a school or college in which it could be learned. So to
Italy, where the Greek scholars had found a refuge, those
who wished to learn flocked.

Among them were some Oxford scholars. Chief of
these were three, whose names you will learn to know well
when you come to read more about this time. They were
William Grocyn, "the most upright and best of all Britons," [1] Thomas Linacre, and John Colet. These men, returning from Italy full of the New Learning, began to teach
Greek at Oxford. And it is strange now to think that there
were many then who were bitterly against such teaching.
The students even formed themselves into two parties, for
and against. They were called Greeks and Trojans, and
between these two parties many a fierce fight took place,
for the quarrel did not end in words, but often in blows.

The New Learning, however, conquered. And so
keenly did men feel the human interests of such things as
were now taught, that we have come to call grammar,
rhetoric, poetry, Greek and Latin the Humanities, and
the professor who teaches these things the professor of
Humanity.

[1] Erasmus.

CHAPTER XXXVII

THE LAND OF NOWHERE

WHILE the New Learning was stirring England, and Greek was being for the first time taught in Oxford, a young student of fourteen came to the University there. This student was named Thomas More. He was the son of a lawyer who became a judge, and as a little boy he had been a page in the household of Morton, the Archbishop of Canterbury.

The Archbishop was quick to see that the boy was clever. "This child here waiting at the table, whoever will live to see it, will prove a marvellous man," [1] he would say. And so he persuaded More's father to send the boy to Oxford to study law.

Thomas remained only two years at Oxford, for old Sir John, fearing he was learning too much Greek and literature and not enough law, called his son home and sent him to study law in London. It must have been a disappointment to the boy to be taken from the clever friends he had made in Oxford, and from the books and studies that he loved, to be set instead to read dry law-books. But Thomas More was most sunny-tempered. Nothing made him sulky or cross. So now he settled down quietly to his new life, and in a very short time became a famous and learned lawyer.

It was after More left Oxford that he met the man who became his dearest friend. This was Desiderius

[1] William Roper, *The Mirrour of Virtue.*

Erasmus, a learned Dutchman. He was eleven years
older than More and he could speak no English, but that
did not prevent them becoming friends, as they both
could speak Latin easily and well. They had much in
common. Erasmus was of the same lively, merry wit as
More, they both loved literature and the Greek learning,
and so the two became fast friends. And it helps us
to understand the power which Latin still held over our
literature, and indeed over all the literature of Europe,
when we remember that these two friends spoke to each
other and wrote and jested in Latin as easily as they
might have done in English. Erasmus was one of the most
famous men of his time. He was one who did much in
his day to free men's minds, one who helped men to think
for themselves. So although he had directly perhaps
little to do with English literature, it is well to remember
him as the friend of More. "My affection for the man is
so great," wrote Erasmus once, "that if he bade me dance
a hornpipe, I should do at once what he bid me."

Although More was so merry and witty, religion got a
strong hold upon him, and at one time he thought of
becoming a monk. But his friends persuaded him to
give up that idea, and after a time he decided to marry.
He chose his wife in a somewhat quaint manner. Among
his friends there was a gentleman who had three daughters.
More liked the second one best, "for that he thought her
the fairest and best favoured." [1] But he married the eldest
because it seemed to him "that it would be both great
grief and some shame also to the oldest to see her younger
sister preferred before her in marriage. He then, of a
certain pity, framed his fancy toward her, and soon after
married her." [2]

Although he chose his wife so quaintly More's home
was a very happy one. He loved nothing better than to

[1] W. Roper   [2] The same

live a simple family life with his wife and children round him. After six years his wife died, but he quickly married again. And although his second wife was "a simple ignorant woman and somewhat worldly too," with a sharp tongue and short temper, she was kind to her step-children and the home was still a happy one.

More was a great public man, but he was first a father and head of his own house. He says: "While I spend almost all the day abroad amongst others, and the residue at home among mine own, I leave to myself, I mean to my book, no time. For when I come home, I must commen with my wife, chatter with my children, and talk with my servants. All the which things I reckon and account among business, forasmuch as they must of necessity be done, and done must they needs be unless a man will be stranger in his own house. And in any wise a man must so fashion and order his conditions and so appoint and dispose himself, that he be merry, jocund and pleasant among them, whom either Nature hath provided or chance hath made, or he himself hath chosen to be the fellows and companions of his life, so that with too much gentle behaviour and familiarity he do not mar them, and by too much sufferance of his servants make them his masters."

At a time, too, when education was thought little necessary for girls, More taught his daughters as carefully as his sons. His eldest daughter Margaret (Mog, as he loved to call her) was so clever that learned men praised and rewarded her. When his children married they did not leave home, but came with their husbands and wives to live at Chelsea in the beautiful home More had built there. So the family was never divided, and More gathered a "school" of children and grandchildren round him.

More soon became a great man. Henry vii., indeed, did

not love him, so More did not rise to power while he lived.
But Henry vii. died and his son Henry viii. ruled. The
great Chancellor, Cardinal Wolsey, became More's friend,
and presently he was sent on business for the King to
Bruges.

It was while More was about the King's business in
Belgium that he wrote the greater part of the book by
which he is best remembered. This book is called *Utopia*.
The name means "nowhere," from two Greek words, *"ou,"*
no, and *"topos,"* a place.

The *Utopia*, like so many other books of which we have
read, was the outcome of the times in which the writer lived.
When More looked round upon the England that he knew
he saw many things that were wrong. He was a man
loyal to his King, yet he could not pretend to think that
the King ruled only for the good of his people and not for
his own pleasure. There was evil, misery, and suffering
in all the land. More longed to make people see that
things were wrong; he longed to set the wrong right. So
to teach men how to do this he invented a land of Nowhere
in which there was no evil or injustice, in which every one
was happy and good. He wrote so well about that make-
believe land that from then till now every one who reads
Utopia sees the beauty of More's idea. But every one, too,
thinks that this land where everything is right is an
impossible land. Thus More gave a new word to our language, and when we think some idea beautiful but impossible we call it "Utopian."

As it was the times that made More write his book,
so it was the times that gave him the form of it.

In those days, as you know, men's minds were stirred
by the discovery of new lands and chiefly by the discovery
of America. And although it was Columbus who first
discovered America, he did not give his name to the new
country. It was, instead, named after the Italian explorer

Amerigo Vespucci. Amerigo wrote a book about his voyages, and it was from this book that More got some of his ideas for the *Utopia*.

More makes believe that one day in Antwerp he saw a man "well stricken in age, with a black sun-burned face, a long beard, and a cloak cast homely about his shoulders, whom by his favour and apparel forthwith I judged to be a mariner."

This man was called Raphael Hythlodaye and had been with Amerigo Vespucci in the three last of his voyages, "saving that in the last voyage he came not home again with him." For on that voyage Hythlodaye asked to be left behind. And after Amerigo had gone home he, with five friends, set forth upon a further voyage of discovery. In their travels they saw many marvelous and fearful things, and at length came to the wonderful land of Nowhere. "But what he told us that he saw, in every country where he came, it were very long to declare."

More asked many questions of this great traveler. "But as for monsters, because they be no news, of them we were nothing inquisitive. . . . But to find citizens ruled by good and wholesome laws, that is an exceeding rare and hard thing!"

The whole story of the *Utopia* is told in the form of talks between Hythlodaye, More, and his friend Peter Giles. And More mixes what is real and what is imaginary so quaintly that it is not wonderful that many of the people of his own day thought that Utopia was a real place. Peter Giles, for instance, was a real man and a friend of More, while Hythlodaye was imaginary, his name being made of Greek words meaning Cunning Babbler. Nearly all the names of the towns, rivers, and people of whom Hythlodaye tells were also made from Greek words and have some meaning. For instance, Achoriens means people-who-have-no-place-on-earth, Amaurote a-phantom-city, and so on.

More takes a great deal of trouble to keep up the mystery of this strange land. It was not wonderful that he should, for under the pretense of a story he said hard things about the laws and ill-government of England, things which it was treason to whisper. In those days treason was a terrible word covering a great deal, and death and torture were like to be the fate of any one who spoke his mind too freely.

But More knew that it would be a hard matter to make things better in England. As he makes Hythlodaye say, it is no use trying to improve things in a blundering fashion. It is of no use trying by fear to drive into people's heads things they have no mind to learn. Neither must you "forsake the ship in a tempest, because you cannot rule and keep down the winds." But "you must with a crafty wile and subtile train, study and endeavour yourself, as much as in you lieth, to handle the matter wittily and handsomely for the purpose. And that which you cannot turn to good, so to order it that it be not very bad. For it is not possible for all things to be well, unless all men were good: which I think will not be yet in these good many years."

The *Utopia* is divided into two books. The first and shorter gives us what we might call the machinery of the tale. It tells of the meeting with Hythlodaye and More's first talk with him. It is not until the beginning of the second book that we really hear about Utopia. And I think if you read the book soon, I would advise you to begin with the second part, which More wrote first. In the second book we have most of the story, but the first book helps us to understand More's own times and explains what he was trying to do in writing his tale.

At the beginning of this book I told you that we should

have to talk of many books which for the present, at least, you could not hope to like, but which you must be content to be told are good and worth reading. I may be wrong, but I think *Utopia* is one of these. Yet as Cresacre More, More's great-grandson, speaking of his great-grandfather's writing, says, he "seasoned always the troublesomeness of the matter with some merry jests or pleasant tales, as it were sugar, whereby we drink up the more willingly these wholesome drugs . . . which kind of writing he hath used in all his works, so that none can ever be weary to read them, though they be never so long."

And even if you like the book now, you will both like and understand it much better when you know a little about politics. You will then see, too, how difficult it is to know when More is in earnest and when he is merely poking fun, for More loved to jest. Yet as his grandson, who wrote a life of him, tells us, "Whatsoever jest he brought forth, he never laughed at any himself, but spoke always so sadly, that few could see by his look whether he spoke in earnest or in jest."

It would take too long to tell all about the wonderful island of Utopia and its people, but I must tell you a little of it and how they regarded money. All men in this land were equal. No man was idle, neither was any man over-burdened with labor, for every one had to work six hours a day. No man was rich, no man was poor, for "though no man have anything, yet every man is rich," for the State gave him everything that he needed. So money was hardly of any use, and gold and silver and precious jewels were despised.

"In the meantime gold and silver, whereof money is made, they do so use, as none of them doth more esteem it, than the very nature of the thing deserveth. And then who doth not plainly see how far it is under iron? as without the which men can no better live than without fire and water: whereas to gold and silver nature hath given no use that we may not well lack, if that the folly of men had not set it in higher estimation for the rareness sake. But, of the contrary part, Nature, as a most tender and loving mother, hath placed the best and most necessary things open abroad, as the air, the water, and the earth itself; and hath removed and hid farthest from us vain and unprofitable things."

Yet as other countries still prized money, gold and silver was sometimes needed by the Utopians. But, thought the wise King and his counselors, if we lock it up in towers and take great care of it, the people may begin to think that gold is of value for itself, they will begin to think that we are keeping something precious from them. So to set this right they fell upon a plan. It was this. "For whereas they eat and drink in earthen and glass vessels, which indeed be curiously and properly made, and yet be of very small value; of gold and silver they make other vessels that serve for most vile uses, not only in their common halls, but in every man's private house. Furthermore of the same metals they make great chains with fetters and gyves, wherein they tie their bondmen. Finally, whosoever for any offense be infamed, by their ears hang rings of gold, upon their fingers they wear rings of gold, and about their necks chains of gold; and in conclusion their heads be tied about with gold.

"Thus, by all means that may be, they procure to have gold and silver among them in reproach and infamy. And therefore these metals, which other nations do as grievously and sorrowfully forego, as in a manner from their own lives, if they should altogether at once be taken from the Utopians, no man there would think that he had lost the worth of a farthing.

"They gather also pearls by the seaside, and diamonds and carbuncles upon certain rocks. Yet they seek not for

them, but by chance finding them they cut and polish
them. And therewith they deck their young infants.
Which, like as in the first years of their childhood they
make much and be fond and proud of such ornaments, so
when they be a little more grown in years and discretion,
perceiving that none but children do wear such toys and
trifles, they lay them away even of their own shamefast-
ness, without any bidding of their parents, even as our
children when they wax big, do caste away nuts, brooches
and dolls. Therefore these laws and customs, which be
so far different from all other nations, how divers fancies
also and minds they do cause, did I never so plainly
perceive, as in the Ambassadors of the Anemolians.

"These Ambassadors came to Amaurote whiles I was
there. And because they came to entreat of great and
weighty matters, three citizens a piece out of every city
(of Utopia) were come thither before them. But all the
Ambassadors of the next countries, which had been there
before, and knew the fashions and manners of the Utopians,
among whom they perceived no honour given to sumptuous and costly apparel, silks to be contemned, gold also
to be infamed and reproachful, were wont to come thither
in very homely and simple apparel. But the Anemolians,
because they dwell far thence, and had very little acquaintance with them, hearing that they were all apparelled alike, and that very rudely and homely, thinking
them not to have the things which they did not wear,
being therefore more proud than wise, determined in the
gorgeousness of their apparel to represent very gods, and
with the bright shining and glistering of their gay clothing
to dazzle the eyes of the silly poor Utopians.

"So there came in three Ambassadors with a hundred
servants all apparelled in changeable colours; the most
of them in silks; the Ambassadors themselves (for at
home in their own country they were noble men) in cloth

of gold, with great chains of gold, with gold hanging at their ears, with gold rings upon their fingers, with brooches and aglettes [1] of gold upon their caps, which glistered full of pearls and precious stones; to be short, trimmed and adorned with all those things, which among the Utopians were either the punishment of bondmen, or the reproach of infamed persons, or else trifles for young children to play withall.

"Therefore it would have done a man good at his heart to have seen how proudly they displayed their peacocks' feathers; how much they made of their painted sheathes; and how loftily they set forth and advanced themselves, when they compared their gallant apparel with the poor raiment of the Utopians. For all the people were swarmed forth into the streets.

"And on the other side it was no less pleasure to consider how much they were deceived, and how far they missed of their purpose; being contrary ways taken than they thought they should have been. For to the eyes of all the Utopians, except very few, which had been in other countries for some reasonable cause, all that gorgeousness of apparel seemed shameful and reproachful; in so much that they most reverently saluted the vilest and most abject of them for lords; passing over the Ambassadors themselves without any honour; judging them by their wearing of golden chains to be bondmen.

"Yea, you should have seen children also that had cast away their pearls and precious stones, when they saw the like sticking upon the Ambassadors' caps, dig and push their mothers under the sides, saying thus to them: 'Look, mother, how great a lubber doth yet wear pearls and precious stones, as though he were a little child still.'

"But the mother, yea, and that also in good earnest:

---

[1] Hanging ornaments.

'Peace, son,' saith she, 'I think he be some of the Ambassadors' fools.'

"Some found fault with their golden chains, as to no use nor purpose; being so small and weak, that a bondman might easily break them; and again so wide and large, that, when it pleased him, he might cast them off, and run away at liberty whither he would.

"But when the Ambassadors had been there a day or two, and saw so great abundance of gold so lightly esteemed, yea, in no less reproach that it was with them in honour; and, besides that, more gold in the chains and gyves of one fugitive bondman, than all the costly ornaments of their three was worth; they began a-bate their courage, and for very shame laid away all that gorgeous array whereof they were so proud; and especially when they had talked familiarly with the Utopians, and had learned all their fashions and opinions. For they marvel that any man be so foolish as to have delight and pleasure in the glistering of a little trifling stone, which may behold any of the stars, or else the sun itself; or that any man is so mad as to count himself the nobler for the smaller or finer thread of wool, which self-same wool (be it now in never so fine a spun thread) did once a sheep wear, and yet was she all that time no other thing than a sheep."

CHAPTER XXXVIII

THE DEATH OF SIR THOMAS MORE

THERE is much that is quaint, much that is deeply wise, in More's *Utopia,* still no one is likely to agree with all he says, or to think that we could all be happy in a world such as he describes. For one thing, to those of us who love color it would seem a dull world indeed were we all forced to dress in coarse-spun, undyed sheep's wool, and if jewels and gold with all their lovely lights and gleamings were but the signs of degradation. Each one who reads it may find something in the *Utopia* that he would rather have otherwise. But each one, too, will find something to make him think.

More was not the first to write about a happy land where every one lived in peace and where only justice reigned. And if he got some of his ideas of the island from the discoveries of the New World, he got many more from the New Learning. For long before, Plato, a Greek writer, had told of a land very like Utopia in his book called the *Republic.* And the New Learning had made that book known to the people of England.

We think of the *Utopia* as English literature, yet we must remember that More wrote it in Latin, and it was not translated into English until several years after his death. The first English translation was made by Ralph Robinson, and although since then there have been other translations which in some ways are more correct, there has never been one with more charm. For Robinson's

231

quaint English keeps for us something of the spirit of More's time and of More's self in a way no modern and more perfect translation can.

The *Utopia* was not written for one time or for one people. Even before it was translated into English it had been translated into Dutch, Italian, German, and French and was largely read all over the Continent. It is still read to-day by all who are interested in the life of the people, by all who think that in "this best of all possible worlds" things might still be made better.

More wrote many other books both in English and in Latin and besides being a busy author he led a busy life. For blustering, burly, selfish King Henry loved the gentle, witty lawyer, and again and again made use of his wits. "And so from time to time was he by the King advanced, continuing in his singular favour and trusty service twenty years and above." [1]

It was not only for his business cleverness that King Henry loved Sir Thomas. It was for his merry, witty talk. When business was done and supper-time came, the King and Queen would call for him "to be merry with them." Thus it came about that Sir Thomas could hardly ever get home to his wife and children, where he most longed to be. Then he began to pretend to be less clever than he was, so that the King might not want so much of his company. But Henry would sometimes follow More to his home at Chelsea, where he had built a beautiful house. Sometimes he came quite unexpectedly to dinner. Once he came, "and after dinner, in a fair garden of his, walked with him by the space of an hour, holding his arm about his neck." As soon as the King was gone, More's son-in-law said to him that he should be happy seeing the King was so friendly with him, for with no other man was he so familiar, not even with Wolsey.

[1] W. Roper

"I thank our Lord," answered More, "I find in his Grace a very good lord indeed, and I believe he doth as singularly favour me as any subject within the realm. Howbeit, son Roper, I may tell thee, I have no cause to be proud thereof, for if my head would win him a castle in France it should not fail to go."

And Sir Thomas was not wrong. Meanwhile, however, the King heaped favor upon him. He became Treasurer of the Exchequer, Speaker of the House of Commons, Chancellor of the Duchy of Lancaster, and last of all Lord Chancellor of England. This was a very great honor. And as More was a layman the honor was for him greater than usual. For he was the first layman to be made Chancellor. Until then the Chancellor had always been some powerful Churchman.

More was not eager for these honors. He would much rather have lived a simple family life, but bluff King Hal was no easy master to serve. If he chose to honor a man and set him high, that man could but submit. So, as Erasmus says, More was dragged into public life and honor, and being thus dragged in troubles were not slow to follow.

Henry grew tired of his wife, Queen Catherine, but the Pope would not allow him to divorce her so that he might marry another. Then Henry quarreled with the Pope. The Pope, he said, should no longer have power in England. He should no longer be head of the Church, but the people must henceforth look to the King as such. This More could not do. He tried to keep out of the quarrel. He was true to his King as king, but he felt that he must be true to his religion too. To him the Pope was the representative of Christ on earth, and he could look to no other as head of the Church. When first More had come into the King's service, Henry bade him "first look unto God, and after God unto him." Of this his Chancellor now reminded him, and laying down his seal of office he went home, hoping to live the rest of his days in peace.

But that was not to be. "It is perilous striving with princes," said a friend. "I would wish you somewhat to incline to the King's pleasure. The anger of princes is death."

"Is that all?" replied More calmly; "then in good faith the difference between you and me is but this, that I shall die to-day and you to-morrow."

So it fell out. There came a day when messengers came to More's happy home, and the beloved father was led away to imprisonment and death.

For fifteen months he was kept in the Tower. During all that time his cheerful steadfastness did not waver. He wrote long letters to his children, and chiefly to Meg, his best-loved daughter. When pen and ink were taken away from him, he still wrote with coal. In these months he became an old man, bent and crippled with disease. But though his body was feeble his mind was clear, his spirit bright as ever. No threats or promises could shake his purpose. He could not and would not own Henry as head of the Church.

At last the end came. In Westminster Hall More was tried for treason and found guilty. From Westminster through the thronging streets he was led back again to the Tower. In front of the prisoner an ax was carried, the edge being turned towards him. That was the sign to all who saw that he was to die.

As the sad procession reached the Tower Wharf there was a pause. A young and beautiful woman darted from the crowd, and caring not for the soldiers who surrounded him, unafraid of their swords and halberds, she reached the old man's side, and threw herself sobbing on his breast. It was Margaret, More's beloved daughter, who, fearing that never again she might see her father, thus came in the open street to say farewell. She clung to him and kissed him in sight of all again and again, but no word could she say save "Oh, my father! oh, my father!"

Then Sir Thomas, holding her tenderly, comforted and blessed her, and at last she took her arms from about his neck and he passed on. But Margaret could not yet leave him. Scarcely had she gone ten steps than suddenly she turned back. Once more breaking through the guard she threw her arms about him. Not a word did Sir Thomas say, but as he held her there the tears fell fast from his eyes, while from the crowd around broke the sound of weeping. Even the guards wept for pity. But at last, with full and heavy hearts, father and daughter parted.

"Dear Meg," Sir Thomas wrote for the last time, "I never liked your manner better towards me than when you kissed me last. For I like when daughterly love and dear charity hath no leisure to look to worldly courtesy."

Next day he died cheerfully as he had lived. To the last he jested in his quaint fashion. The scaffold was so badly built that it was ready to fall, so Sir Thomas, jesting, turned to the lieutenant. "I pray you, Master Lieutenant," he said, "see me safe up, and for my coming down let me shift for myself." He desired the people to pray for him, and having kissed the executioner in token of forgiveness, he laid his head upon the block. "So passed Sir Thomas More out of the world to God." His death was mourned by many far and near. "Had we been master of such a servant," said the Emperor Charles when he heard of it, "we would rather have lost the best city of our dominions than have lost such a worthy counselor."

More died for his faith, that of the Catholic Church. He, as others, saw with grief that there was much within the Church that needed to be made better, but he trusted it would be made better. To break away from the Church, to doubt the headship of the Pope, seemed to him such wickedness that he hated the Reformers and wrote against them. And although in Utopia he allowed his happy people to have full freedom in matters of religion, in real life he treated sternly and even cruelly those Protestants with whom he had to deal.

Yet the Reformation was stirring all the world, and while Sir Thomas More cheerfully and steadfastly died for the Catholic faith, there were others in England who as cheerfully lived, worked, and died for the Protestant faith. We have little to do with these Reformers in this book, except in so far as they touch our literature, and it is to them that we owe our present Bible.

First William Tyndale, amid difficulties and trials, translated afresh the New and part of the Old Testament, and died the death of a martyr in 1536.

Miles Coverdale followed him with a complete translation in happier times. For Henry viii., for his own purposes, wished to spread a knowledge of the Bible, and commanded that a copy of Coverdale's Bible should be placed in every parish church. And although Coverdale was not so great a scholar as Tyndale, his language was fine and stately, with a musical ring about the words, and to this day we still keep his version of the Psalms in the Prayer Book.

Other versions of the Bible followed these, until in 1611, in the reign of James i. and vi., the translation which we use to-day was at length published. That has stood and still stands the test of time. And, had we no other reason to treasure it, we would still for its simple musical language look upon it as one of the fine things in our literature.

BOOKS TO READ

Life of Sir Thomas More (King's Classics, modern English), by W Roper (his son-in-law) *Utopia* (King's Classics, modern English), translated by R Robinson *Utopia* (old English), edited by Churton Collins

CHAPTER XXXIX

HOW THE SONNET CAME TO ENGLAND

Upon a January day in 1527 two gaily decked barges met upon the Thames. In the one sat a man of forty. His fair hair and beard were already touched with gray. His face was grave and thoughtful, and his eyes gave to it a curious expression, for the right was dull and sightless, while with the left he looked about him sharply. This was Sir John Russell, gentleman of the Privy Chamber, soldier, ambassador, and favorite of King Henry VIII. Fighting in the King's French wars he had lost the sight of his right eye. Since then he had led a busy life in court and camp, passing through many perilous adventures in the service of his master, and now once again by the King's commands he was about to set forth for Italy.

As the other barge drew near Russell saw that in it there sat Thomas Wyatt, a young poet and courtier of twenty-three. He was tall and handsome, and his thick dark hair framed a pale, clever face which now looked listless. But as his dreamy poet's eyes met those of Sir John they lighted up. The two men greeted each other familiarly. "Whither away," cried Wyatt, for he saw that Russell was prepared for a journey.

"To Italy, sent by the King."

To Italy, the land of Poetry! The idea fired the poet's soul.

"And I," at once he answered, "will, if you please, ask leave, get money, and go with you."

237

"No man more welcome," answered the ambassador, and so it was settled between them. The money and the leave were both forthcoming, and Thomas Wyatt passed to Italy. This chance meeting and this visit to Italy are of importance to our literature, because they led to a new kind of poem being written in English. This was the Sonnet.

The Sonnet is a poem of fourteen lines, and is perhaps the most difficult kind of poem to write. It is divided into two parts. The first part has eight lines and ought only to have two rimes. That is, supposing we take words riming with love and king for our rimes, four lines must rime with love and four with king. The rimes, too, must come in a certain order. The first, fourth, fifth and eighth lines must rime, and the second, third, sixth, and seventh. This first part is called the octave, from the Latin word *octo*, eight. The second part contains six lines, and is therefore called the sextet, from the Latin word *sex*, meaning six. The sextet may have either two or three rimes, and these may be arranged in almost any order. But a correct sonnet ought not to end with a couplet, that is two riming lines. However, very many good writers in English do so end their sonnets.

As the sonnet is so bound about with rules, it often makes the thought which it expresses sound a little unreal. And for that very reason it suited the times in which Wyatt lived. In those far-off days every knight had a lady whom he vowed to serve and love. He took her side in every quarrel, and if he were a poet, or even if he were not, he wrote verses in her honor, and sighed and died for her. The lady was not supposed to do anything in return: she might at most smile upon her knight or drop her glove, that he might be made happy by picking it up. In fact, the more disdainful the lady might be the better it was, for then the poet could write the more passionate verses. For all this love and service was make-believe. It was merely a fashion and not meant to be taken seriously. A man might have a wife whom he loved dearly, and yet write poems in honor of another lady without thought of wrong. The sonnet, having something very artificial in it, just suited this make-believe love.

Petrarch, the great Italian poet, from whom you remember Chaucer had learned much, and whom perhaps he had once met, made use of this kind of poem. In his sonnets he told his love of a fair lady, Laura, and made her famous for all time.

Of course, when Wyatt came to Italy Petrarch had long been dead. But his poems were as living as in the days of Chaucer, and it was from Petrarch's works that Wyatt learned this new kind of poem, and it was he who first made use of it in English. He, too, like Petrarch, addressed his sonnets to a lady, and the lady he took for his love was Queen Anne Boleyn. As he is the first, he is perhaps one of the roughest of our sonnet writers, but into his sonnets he wrought something of manly strength. He does not sigh so much as other poets of the age. He says, in fact, "If I serve my lady faithfully I deserve reward." Here is one of his sonnets, which he calls "The lover compareth his state to a ship in perilous storm tossed by the sea."

> "My galley chargéd with forgetfulness,
> Through sharpe seas in winter's night doth pass,
> 'Tween rock and rock, and eke my foe (alas)
> That is my lord, steereth with cruelness·
> And every oar a thought in readiness,
> As though that death were light in such a case.
> An endless wind doth tear the sail apace,
> Of forcéd sighs and trusty fearfulness;
> A rain of tears, a cloud of dark disdain,
> Have done the wearied cords great hinderance:
> Wreathéd with error and with ignorance,
> The stars be hid, that lead me to this pain,
> Drownéd is reason that should me comfort,
> And I remain, despairing of the port."

It is not perfect, it is not even Wyatt's best sonnet, but it is one of the most simple. To make it run smoothly we must sound the *ed* in these words ending in *ed* as a separate syllable, and we must put a final *e* to sharp in the second line and sound that. Then you see the rimes are not very good. To begin with, the first eight all have sounds of *s*. Then "alas" and "pass" do not rime with "case" and "apace," nor do "comfort" and "port." I point these things out, so that later on you may see for yourselves how much more polished and elegant a thing the sonnet becomes.

Although Wyatt was our first sonnet writer, some of his poems which are not sonnets are much more musical, especially some he wrote for music. Perhaps best of all you will like his satire *Of the mean and sure estate.* A satire is a poem which holds up to scorn and ridicule wickedness, folly, or stupidity. It is the sword of literature, and often its edge was keen, its point sharp.

> "My mother's maids when they do sew and spin,
> They sing a song made of the fieldish mouse;
> That for because her livelod [1] was but thin
> Would needs go see her townish sister's house
>
> .   .   .   .   .
>
> 'My sister,' quoth she, 'hath a living good,
> And hence from me she dwelleth not a mile,
> In cold and storm she lieth warm and dry
> In bed of down. The dirt doth not defile
> Her tender foot, she labours not as I.
> Richly she feeds, and at the rich man's cost;
> And for her meat she need not crave nor cry
> By sea, by land, of delicates [2] the most,
> Her caterer seeks, and spareth for no peril.
> She feeds on boil meat, bake meat and roast,
> And hath, therefore, no whit of charge or travail.'
>
> .   .   .   .   .   .

---

[1] Livelihood   [2] Delicacies

So forth she goes, trusting of all this wealth
With her sister her part so for to shape,
That if she might there keep herself in health,
To live a Lady, while her life do last.
And to the door now is she come by stealth,
And with her foot anon she scrapes full fast.
Th' other for fear durst not well scarce appear,
Of every noise so was the wretch aghast.
At last she askéd softly who was there;
And in her language as well as she could,
'Peep,' quoth the other, 'sister, I am here'
'Peace,' quoth the town mouse, 'why speaketh thou so
    loud?'
But by the hand she took her fair and well
'Welcome,' quoth she, 'my sister by the Rood.'
She feasted her that joy it was to tell
The fare they had, they drank the wine so clear;
And as to purpose now and then it fell,
So cheered her with, 'How, sister, what cheer.'
Amid this joy befell a sorry chance,
That welladay, the stranger bought full dear
The fare she had. For as she looked ascance,
Under a stool she spied two flaming eyes,
In a round head, with sharp ears. In France
Was never mouse so feared, for the unwise
Had not ere seen such beast before
Yet had nature taught her after her guise
To know her foe, and dread him evermore.
The town mouse fled, she knew whither to go;
The other had no shift, but wonders sore,
Fear'd of her life! At home she wished her tho';
And to the door, alas! as she did skip
(The heaven it would, lo, and eke her chance was so)
At the threshold her silly foot did trip;
And ere she might recover it again,
The traitor Cat had caught her by the hip
And made her there against her will remain,
That had forgot her poor surety and rest,
For seeming wealth, wherein she thought to reign "

That is not the end of the poem. Wyatt points the
moral. "Alas," he says, "how men do seek the best and find

the worst." "Although thy head were hooped with gold," thou canst not rid thyself of care. Content thyself, then, with what is allotted thee and use it well.

This satire Wyatt wrote while living quietly in the country, having barely escaped with his life from the King's wrath. But although he escaped the scaffold, he died soon after in his King's service. Riding on the King's business in the autumn of 1542 he became overheated, fell into a fever, and died. He was buried at Sherborne. No stone marks his resting-place, but his friend and fellow-poet, Henry Howard, Earl of Surrey, wrote a noble elegy:—

> "A head, where Wisdom mysteries did frame;
> Whose hammers beat still, in that lively brain,
> As on a stithy[1] where that some work of fame
> Was daily wrought, to turn to Britain's gain
>
> .   .   .
>
> A hand, that taught what might be said in rhyme,
> That Chaucer reft the glory of his wit.
> A mark, the which (unperfected for time)
> Some may approach; but never none shall hit!'"

BOOK TO READ

Early Sixteenth-Century Lyrics (Belle Lettres Series), edited by F. M. Padelford (original spelling)

[1] Anvil.

CHAPTER XL

THE BEGINNING OF BLANK VERSE

THE poet with whose verses the last chapter ended was named Henry Howard, Earl of Surrey. The son of a noble and ancient house, Surrey lived a gay life in court and camp. Proud, hot-headed, quick-tempered, he was often in trouble, more than once in prison. In youth he was called "the most foolish proud boy in England," and at the age of thirty, still young and gay and full of life, he died upon the scaffold. Accused of treason, yet innocent, he fell a victim to "the wrath of princes," the wrath of that hot-headed King Henry VIII. Surrey lived at the same time as Wyatt and, although he was fourteen years younger, was his friend. Together they are the forerunners of our modern poetry. They are nearly always spoken of together—Wyatt and Surrey—Surrey and Wyatt. Like Wyatt, Surrey followed the Italian poets. Like Wyatt he wrote sonnets; but whereas Wyatt's are rough, Surrey's are smooth and musical, although he does not keep the rules about rime endings. One who wrote not long after the time of Wyatt and Surrey says of them, "Sir Thomas Wyatt, the elder, and Henry, Earl of Surrey, were the two chieftains, who, having travelled in Italy, and there tasted the sweet and stately measures and style of the Italian poesie . . . greatly polished our rude and homely manner of vulgar poesie from that it had been before, and for that cause may justly be said the first reformers of our English metre and style. . . . I repute

243

them for the two chief lanterns of light to all others that have since employed their pens on English poesie." [1]

A later writer [2] has called Surrey the "first refiner" of our language. And just as there comes a time in our own lives when we begin to care not only for the story, but for the words in which a story is told and for the way in which those words are used, so, too, there comes such a time in the life of a nation, and this time for England we may perhaps date from Wyatt and Surrey. Before then there were men who tried to use the best words in the best way, but they did it unknowingly, as birds might sing. The language, too, in which they wrote was still a growing thing. When Surrey wrote it had nearly reached its finished state, and he helped to finish and polish it.

As the fashion was, Surrey chose a lady to whom to address his verses. She was the little Lady Elizabeth Fitz-Gerald, whose father had died a broken-hearted prisoner in the Tower. She was only ten when Surrey made her famous in song, under the name of Geraldine. Here is a sonnet in which he, seeing the joy of all nature at the coming of Spring, mourns that his lady is still unkind:

> "The sweet season, that bud and bloom forth brings,
> With green hath clad the hill, and eke the vale,
> The nightingale with feathers new she sings·
> The turtle to her mate hath told her tale
> Summer is come, for every spray now springs,
> The hart hath hung his old head on the pale,
> The buck in haste his winter coat he flings;
> The fishes float with new repairéd scale,
> The adder all her slough away she slings;
> The swift swallow pursueth the flies small;
> The busy-bee her honey now she mings. [3]
> Winter is worn that was the flowers' bale
> And thus I see among these pleasant things
> Each care decays, and yet my sorrow springs"

---

[1] G Puttenham, *Art of English Poesie*　　　　　　[2] W. J. Courthope,
[3] Mingles.

Besides following Wyatt in making the sonnet known to English readers, Surrey was the first to write in blank verse, that is in long ten-syllabled lines which do not rime. This is a kind of poetry in which some of the grandest poems in our language are written, and we should remember Surrey as the first maker of it. For with very little change the rules which Surrey laid down have been followed by our best poets ever since, so from the sixteenth century till now there has been far less change in our poetry than in the five centuries before. You can see this for yourself if you compare Surrey's poetry with Laya-mon's or Langland's, and then with some of the blank verse near the end of this book.

It was in translating part of Virgil's *Æneid* that Surrey used blank verse. Virgil was an ancient Roman poet, born 70 B.C., who in his book called the *Æneid* told of the wanderings and adventures of Æneas, and part of this poem Surrey translated into English.

This is how he tells of the way in which Æneas saved his old father by carrying him on his shoulders out of the burning town of Troy when "The crackling flame was heard throughout the walls, and more and more the burning heat drew near."

> "My shoulders broad,
> And layéd neck with garments 'gan I spread,
> And thereon cast a yellow lion's skin;
> And thereupon my burden I receive.
> Young Iulus clasped in my right hand,
> Followeth me fast, with unequal pace,
> And at my back my wife. Thus did we pass
> By places shadowed most with the night,
> And me, whom late the dart which enemies threw,
> Nor press of Argive routs could make amaz'd,
> Each whisp'ring wind hath power now to fray,
> And every sound to move my doubtful mind.
> So much I dread my burden and my fere.[1]

---

[1] Companion.

And now we 'gan draw near unto the gate,
Right well escap'd the danger, as me thought,
When that at hand a sound of feet we heard.
My father then, gazing throughout the dark,
Cried on me, 'Flee, son! they are at hand.'
With that, bright shields, and shene [1] armours I saw
But then, I know not what unfriendly god
My troubled wit from me bereft for fear.
For while I ran by the most secret streets,
Eschewing still the common haunted track,
From me, catif, alas! bereavéd was
Creusa then, my spouse; I wot not how,
Whether by fate, or missing of the way,
Or that she was by weariness retain'd;
But never sith these eyes might her behold.
Nor did I yet perceive that she was lost,
Nor never backward turnéd I my mind,
Till we came to the hill whereon there stood
The old temple dedicate to Ceres

And when that we were there assembled all,
She was only away deceiving us,
Her spouse, her son, and all her company
What god or man did I not then accuse,
Near wode [2] for ire? or what more cruel chance
Did hap to me in all Troy's overthrow?"

---

[1] Bright.   [2] Mad

CHAPTER XLI

SPENSER—THE "SHEPHERD'S CALENDAR"

WHEN Henry signed Surrey's death-warrant he himself was near death, and not many weeks later the proud and violent king met his end. Then followed for England changeful times. After Protestant Edward came for a tragic few days Lady Jane. Then followed the short, sad reign of Catholic Mary, who, dying, left the throne free for her brilliant sister Elizabeth. Those years, from the death of King Henry VIII. to the end of the first twenty years of Elizabeth's reign, were years of action rather than of production. They were years of struggle, during which England was swayed to and fro in the fight of religions. They were years during which the fury of the storm of the Reformation worked itself out. But although they were such unquiet years they were also years of growth, and at the end of that time there blossomed forth one of the fairest seasons of our literature.

We call the whole group of authors who sprang up at this time the Elizabethans, after the name of the Queen in whose reign they lived and wrote. And to those of us who know even a very little of the time, the word calls up a brilliant vision. Great names come crowding to our minds, names of poets, dramatists, historians, philosophers, divines. It would be impossible to tell of all in this book, so we must choose the greatest from the noble array. And foremost among them comes Edmund Spenser, for "the glory of the new literature broke in England with Edmund Spenser." [1]

If we could stand aside, as it were, and take a wide view of all our early literature, it would seem as if the names of Chaucer and Spenser stood out above all others like great mountains. The others are valleys between. They are pleasant fields in which to wander, in which to gather flowers, not landmarks for all the world like Chaucer and Spenser. And although it is easier and safer for children to wander in the meadows and gather meadow flowers, they still may look up to the mountains and hope to climb them some day.

Edmund Spenser was born in London in 1552, and was the son of a poor clothworker or tailor. He went to school at the Merchant Taylors' School, which had then been newly founded. That his father was very poor we know, for Edmund Spenser's name appears among "certain poor scholars of the schools about London" who received money and clothes from a fund left by a rich man to help poor children at school.

When he was about seventeen Edmund went to Cambridge, receiving for his journey a sum of ten shillings from the fund from which he had already received help at school. He entered college as a sizar, that is, in return for doing the work of a servant he received free board and lodging in his college. A sizar's life was not always a happy one, for many of the other scholars or gentlemen commoners looked down upon them because of their poverty. And this poverty they could not hide, for the sizars were obliged to wear a different cap and gown from that of the gentlemen commoners.

But of how Spenser fared at college we know nothing, except that he was often ill and that he made two lifelong friends. That he loved his university, however, we learn

[1] J. R. Green, *History of English People*

from his poems, when he tenderly speaks of "my mother Cambridge." [1] When he left college Spenser was twenty-three. He was poor and, it would seem, ill, so he did not return to London, but went to live with relatives in the country in Lancashire. And there about "the wasteful woods and forest wide" [2] he wandered, gathering new life and strength, taking all a poet's joy in the beauty and the freedom of a country life, "for ylike to me was liberty and life," [3] he says. And here among the pleasant woods he met a fair lady named Rosalind, "the widow's daughter of the glen." [4]

Who Rosalind really was no one knows. She would never have been heard of had not Spenser taken her for his lady and made songs to her. Spenser's love for Rosalind was, however, more real than the fashionable poet's passion. He truly loved Rosalind, but she did not love him, and she soon married some one else. Then all his joy in the summer and the sunshine was made dark.

> "Thus is my summer worn away and wasted,
> Thus is my harvest hastened all to rathe; [5]
> The ear that budded fair is burnt and blasted,
> And all my hopéd gain is turned to scathe·
> Of all the seed, that in my youth was sown,
> Was naught but brakes and brambles to be mown " [6]

At twenty-four life seemed ended, for "Love is a cureless sorrow." [7]

> "Winter is come, that blows the baleful breath,
> And after Winter cometh timely death." [8]

And now, when he was feeling miserable, lonely, desolate an old college friend wrote to him begging him to come to London. Spenser went, and through his friend he came to

---

[1] *Faery Queen*, book IV. canto xi
[3] The same, December.
[5] Early
[7] The same, August
[2] *Shepherd's Calendar*, December
[4] The same, April
[6] *Shepherd's Calendar*, December.
[8] The same, December.

know Sir Philip Sidney, a true gentleman and a poet like himself, who in turn made him known to the great Earl of Leicester, Elizabeth's favorite.

Spenser thought his heart had been broken and that his life was done. But hearts do not break easily. Life is not done at twenty-four. After a time Spenser found that there was still much to live for. The great Earl became the poet's friend and patron, and gave him a post as secretary in his house. For in those days no man could live by writing alone. Poetry was still a graceful toy for the rich. If a poor man wished to toy with it, he must either starve or find a rich friend to be his patron, to give him work to do that would leave him time to write also. Such a friend Spenser found in Leicester. In the Earl's house the poor tailor's son met many of the greatest men of the court of Queen Elizabeth. On the Earl's business he went to Ireland and to the Continent, seeing new sights, meeting the men and women of the great world, so that a new and brilliant life seemed opening for him.

Yet when, a few years later, Spenser published his first great poem, it did not tell of courts or courtiers, but of simple country sights and sounds. This book is called the *Shepherd's Calendar,* as it contains twelve poems, one for every month of the year.

In it Spenser sings of his fair lost lady Rosalind, and he himself appears under the name of Colin Clout. The name is taken, as you will remember, from John Skelton's poem.

Spenser called his poems Æclogues, from a Greek word meaning Goatherds' Tales, "Though indeed few goatherds have to do herein." He dedicated them to Sir Philip Sidney as "the president of noblesse and of chivalrie."

> "Go, little book. Thy self present,
> As child whose parent is unkent,
> To him that is the president
> Of Noblesse and of Chivalrie;

And if that Envy bark at thee,
As sure it will, for succour flee
Under the shadow of his wing;
And, askéd who thee forth did bring;
A shepherd's swain, say, did thee sing,
All as his straying flock he fed;
And when his honour hath thee read
Crave pardon for my hardyhood
But, if that any ask thy name,
Say, 'thou wert basebegot with blame'
For thy thereof thou takest shame,
And, when thou art past jeopardy,
Come tell me what was said of mee,
And I will send more after thee"

The *Shepherd's Calendar* made the new poet famous. Spenser was advanced at court, and soon after went to Ireland in the train of the Lord-Deputy as Secretary of State. At that time Ireland was filled with storm and anger, with revolt against English rule, with strife among the Irish nobles themselves. Spain also was eagerly looking to Ireland as a point from which to strike at England. War, misery, poverty were abroad in all the land. Yet amid the horrid sights and sounds of battle Spenser found time to write.

After eight years spent in the north of Ireland, Spenser was given a post which took him south. His new home was the old castle of Kilcolman in Cork. It was surrounded by fair wooded country, but to Spenser it seemed a desert. He had gone to Ireland as to exile, hoping that it was merely a stepping-stone to some great appointment in England, whither he longed to return. Now after eight years he found himself still in exile. He had no love for Ireland, and felt himself lonely and forsaken there. But soon there came another great Elizabethan to share his loneliness. This was Sir Walter Raleigh, who, being out of favor with his Queen, took refuge in his Irish estates until her anger should pass.

The two great men, thus alone among the wild Irish, made friends, and they had many a talk together. There within the gray stone walls of the old ivy-covered castle Spenser read the first part of his book, the *Faery Queen,* to Raleigh. Spenser had long been at work upon this great poem. It was divided into parts, and each part was called a book. Three books were now finished, and Raleigh, loud in his praises of them, persuaded the poet to bring them over to England to have them published.

In a poem called *Colin Clout's come home again,* which Spenser wrote a few years later, he tells in his own poetic way of these meetings and talks, and of how Raleigh persuaded him to go to England, there to publish his poem. In *Colin Clout* Spenser calls both himself and Raleigh shepherds. For just as at one time it was the fashion to write poems in the form of a dream, so in Spenser's day it was the fashion to write poems called pastorals, in which the authors made believe that all their characters were shepherds and shepherdesses.

> "One day, quothe he, I sat (as was my trade)
> Under the foot of Mole, that mountain hoare,
> Keeping my sheep amongst the cooly shade,
> Of the green alders by the Mulla's [1] shore:
> There a strange shepherd chanst to find me out,
> Whether alluréd by my pipe's delight,
> Whose pleasing sound y-shrilléd far about,
> Or thither led by chance, I know not right:
> Whom when I askéd from what place he came,
> And how he hight, himself he did y-clep,
> The Shepherd of the Ocean by name,
> And said he came far from the main sea deep.
> He sitting me beside in that same shade,
> Provokéd me to play some pleasant fit; [2]
> And, when he heard the music that I made,
> He found himself full greatly pleased at it."

[1] River Awbeg   [2] Strain

Spenser tells then how the "other shepherd" sang:—

> "His song was all a lamentable lay,
> Of great unkindness, and of usage hard,
> Of Cynthia, the Lady of the Sea,
> That from her presence faultless him debarred.
>
> .   .   .   .   .   .
>
> When thus our pipes we both had wearied well,
> And each an end of singing made,
> He gan to cast great liking to my lore,
> And great disliking to my luckless lot,
> That banished had myself, like wight forlore,
> Into that waste, where I was quite forgot:
> The which to leave henceforth he counselled me,
> Unmeet for man in whom was ought regardful,
> And wend with him his Cynthia to see,
> Whose grace was great, and bounty most rewardful.
>
> .   .   .   .   .   .
>
> So what with hope of good, and hate of ill
> He me persuaded forth with him to fare."

Queen Elizabeth received Spenser kindly, and was so delighted with the *Faery Queen* that she ordered Lord Burleigh to pay the poet £100 a year.

"What!" grumbled the Lord Treasurer, "it is not in reason. So much for a mere song!"

"Then give him," said the Queen, "what is reason," to which he consented.

But, says an old writer, "he was so busied, belike about matters of higher concernment, that Spenser received no reward." [1] In the long-run, however, he did receive £50 a year, as much as £400 would be now. But it did not seem to Spenser to be enough to allow him to give up his post in Ireland and live in England. So back to Ireland he went once more, with a grudge in his heart against Lord Burleigh.

[1] Thomas Fuller.

CHAPTER XLII

SPENSER—THE "FAERY QUEEN"

Spenser's plan for the *Faery Queen* was a very great one. He meant to write a poem in twelve books, each book containing the adventures of a knight who was to show forth one virtue. And if these were well received he purposed to write twelve more. Only the first three books were as yet published, but they made him far more famous than the *Shepherd's Calendar* had done. For never since Chaucer had such poetry been written. In the *Faery Queen* Spenser has, as he says, changed his "oaten reed" for "trumpets stern," and sings no longer now of shepherds and their loves, but of "knights and ladies gentle deeds" of "fierce wars and faithful loves."

The first three books tell the adventures of the Red Cross Knight St. George, or Holiness; of Sir Guyon, or Temperance; and of the Lady Britomartis, or Chastity. The whole poem is an allegory. Everywhere we are meant to see a hidden meaning. But sometimes the allegory is very confused and hard to follow. So at first, in any case, it is best to enjoy the story and the beautiful poetry, and not trouble about the second meaning. Spenser plunges us at once into the very middle of the story. He begins:

> "A gentle Knight was pricking on the plain,
> Yclad in mighty arms and silver shield,
> Wherein old dints of deep wounds did remain,
> The cruel marks of many a bloody field,
> Yet arms till that time did he never wield
> His angry steed did chide his foaming bit,
> As much disdaining to the curb to yield·

Full jolly knight he seem'd, and fair did sit,
As one for knightly jousts and fierce encounters fit.

But on his breast a bloody cross he bore,
The dear remembrance of his dying Lord,
For whose sweet sake that glorious badge he wore,
And dead as living ever him ador'd;
Upon his shield the like was also scor'd."

And by the side of this Knight rode a lovely Lady upon a snow-white ass. Her dress, too, was snow-white, but over it she wore a black cloak, "as one that inly mourned," and it "seemed in her heart some hidden care she had."

So the story begins; but why these two, the grave and gallant Knight and the sad and lovely Lady, are riding forth together we should not know until the middle of the seventh canto, were it not for a letter which Spenser wrote to Raleigh and printed in the beginning of his book. In it he tells us not only who these two are, but also his whole great design. He writes this letter, he says, "knowing how doubtfully all allegories may be construed," and this book of his "being a continued allegory, or dark conceit," he thought it good to explain. Having told how he means to write of twenty-four knights who shall represent twenty-four virtues, he goes on to tell us that the Faery Queen kept her yearly feast twelve days, upon which twelve days the occasions of the first twelve adventures happened, which, being undertaken by twelve knights, are told of in these twelve books.

The first was this. At the beginning of the feast a tall, clownish young man knelt before the Queen of the Fairies asking as a boon that to him might be given the first adventure that might befall. "That being granted he rested him on the floor, unfit through his rusticity for a better place.

"Soon after entered a fair Lady in mourning weeds, riding on a white ass with a Dwarf behind her leading a warlike steed, that bore the arms of a knight, and his spear in the Dwarf's hand.

"She, falling before the Queen of Fairies, complained that her Father and Mother, an ancient King and Queen, had been by a huge Dragon many years shut up in a brasen Castle, who thence suffered them not to issue." And therefore she prayed the Fairy Queen to give her a knight who would slay the Dragon.

Then the "clownish person" started up and demanded the adventure The Queen was astonished, the maid unwilling, yet he begged so hard that the Queen consented. The Lady, however, told him that unless the armor she had brought would serve him he could not succeed. But when he put the armor on "he seemed the goodliest man in all that company, and was well liked of that Lady. And eftsoons taking on him knighthood, and mounting on that strange courser, he went forth with her on that adventure, where beginneth the first book, viz.:

> " 'A gentle Knight was pricking on the plain,' etc "

The story goes on to tell how the Knight, who is the Red Cross Knight St. George, and the Lady, who is called Una, rode on followed by the Dwarf. At length in the wide forest they lost their way and came upon the lair of a terrible She-Dragon. "Fly, fly," quoth then the fearful Dwarf, "this is no place for living men."

> "But full of fire and greedy hardiment,
> The youthful Knight could not for ought be stayed;
> But forth unto the darksome hole he went,
> And lookéd in: his glistering armour made
> A little glooming light, much like a shade,
> By which he saw the ugly monster plain,
> Half like a serpent horribly displayed,
> But th'other half did woman's shape retain,
> Most loathsome, filthy, foul, and full of vile disdain."

There was a fearful fight between the Knight and the

Dragon, whose name is Error, but at length the Knight conquered. The terrible beast lay dead "reft of her baleful head," and the Knight, mounting upon his charger, once more rode onwards with his Lady.

> "At length they chanced to meet upon the way
> An aged sire, in long black weeds yclad,
> His feet all bare, his beard all hoary grey,
> And by his belt his book he hanging had,
> Sober he seemed, and very sagely sad,
> And to the ground his eyes were lowly bent,
> Simple in show, and void of malice bad,
> And all the way he prayéd, as he went,
> And often knocked his breast, as one that did repent."

The Knight and this aged man greeted each other fair and courteously, and as evening was now fallen the godly father bade the travelers come to his Hermitage for the night. This the Knight and Lady gladly did, and soon were peacefully sleeping beneath the humble roof.

But the seeming godly father was a wicked magician. While his guests slept he wove evil spells about them, and calling a wicked dream he bade it sit at the Knight's head and whisper lies to him. This the wicked dream did till that it made the Knight believe his Lady to be bad and false. Then early in the morning the Red Cross Knight rose and, believing his Lady to be unworthy, he rode sadly away, leaving her alone.

Soon, as he rode along, he met a Saracen whose name was Sansfoy, or without faith, "full large of limb and every joint he was, and caréd not for God or man a point."

> "He had a fair companion of his way,
> A goodly Lady clad in scarlet red,
> Purfled with gold and pearl of rich assay,
> And like a Persian mitre on her head
> She wore, with crowns and riches garnishéd,

> The which her lavish lovers to her gave;
> Her wanton palfrey all was overspread
> With tinsell trappings, woven like a wave,
> Whose bridle rang with golden bells and bosses brave."

The Red Cross Knight fought and conquered Sansfoy Then he rode onward with the dead giant's companion, the lady Duessa, whom he believed to be good because he was "too simple and too true" to know her wicked.

Meanwhile Una, forsaken and woeful, wandered far and wide seeking her lost Knight. But nowhere could she hear tidings of him. At length one day, weary of her quest, she got off her ass and lay down to rest in the thick wood, where "her angel's face made a sunshine in the shady place."

Then out of the thickest of the wood a ramping lion rushed suddenly.

> "It fortuned out of the thickest wood
> A ramping Lion rushed suddenly,
> Hunting full greedy after savage blood
> Soon as the royal virgin he did spy,
> With gaping mouth at her ran greedily
> To have at once devoured her tender corse "

But as he came near the sleeping Lady the Lion's rage suddenly melted. Instead of killing Una, he licked her weary feet and white hands with fawning tongue. From being her enemy he became her guardian. And so for many a day the Lion stayed with Una, guarding her from all harm. But in her wanderings she at length met with Sansloy, the brother of Sansfoy, who killed the Lion and carried Una off into the darksome wood.

But here in her direst need Una found new friends in a troupe of fauns and satyrs who were playing in the forest.

> "Whom when the raging Saracen espied,
> A rude, misshapen, monstrous rabblement,
> Whose like he never saw, he durst not bide,
> But got his ready steed, and fast away gan ride."

Then the fauns and satyrs gathered round the Lady, wondering at her beauty, pitying her "fair blubbered face."

But Una shook with fear. These terrible shapes, half goat, half human, struck her dumb with horror: "Ne word to speak, ne joint to move she had."

> "The savage nation feel her secret smart
> And read her sorrow in her count'nance sad;
> Their frowning foreheads with rough horns yclad,
> And rustic horror all aside do lay,
> And gently grinning shew a semblance glad
> To comfort her, and fear to put away."

They kneel upon the ground, they kiss her feet, and at last, sure that they mean her no harm, Una rises and goes with them.

Rejoicing, singing songs, honoring her as their Queen, waving branches, scattering flowers beneath her feet, they lead her to their chief Sylvanus. He, too, receives her kindly, and in the wood she lives with these wild creatures until there she finds a new knight named Satyrane, with whom she once more sets forth to seek the Red Cross Knight.

Meanwhile Duessa had led the Red Cross Knight to the house of Pride.

> "A stately Palace built of squaréd brick,
> Which cunningly was without mortar laid,
> Whose walls were high, but nothing strong, nor thick,
> And golden foil all over them displayed,
> That purest sky with brightness they dismayed.
> High lifted up were many lofty towers
> And goodly galleries far overlaid,
> Full of fair windows, and delightful bowers,
> And on the top a dial told the timely hours
>
> It was a goodly heap for to behold,
> And spake the praises of the workman's wit,
> But full great pity, that so fair a mould
> Did on so weak foundation ever sit,

> For on a sandy hill, that still did flit,
> And fall away, it mounted was full high,
> And every breath of heaven shakéd it,
> And all the hinder parts, that few could spy,
> Were ruinous and old, but painted cunningly "

Here the Knight met Sansjoy, the third of the Saracen brothers, and another fearful fight took place.

> "The Saracen was stout, and wondrous strong,
> And heapéd blows like iron hammers great
> For after blood and vengeance he did long
> The Knight was fierce, and full of youthly heat,
> And doubled strokes like dreaded thunder's threat,
> For all for praise and honour he did fight.
> Both striken strike, and beaten both do beat
> That from their shields forth flyeth fiery light,
> And helmets hewen deep, show marks of either's might "

At last a charmed cloud hid the Saracen from the Knight's sight. So the fight ended, and the Knight, sorely wounded, was "laid in sumptuous bed, where many skilful leeches him abide."

But as he lay there weak and ill the Dwarf came to warn him, for he had spied

> "Where, in a dungeon deep, huge numbers lay
> Of caitiff wretched thralls, that wailéd night and day,
>
> .   .   .   .   .   .
>
> Whose case when as the careful Dwarf had told,
> And made ensample of their mournful sight
> Unto his master, he no longer would
> There dwell in peril of like painful plight,
> But early rose, and ere that dawning light
> Discovered had the world to heaven wide,
> He by a privy postern took his flight,
> That of no envious eyes he might be spied,
> For doubtless death ensued, if any him descried."

When the false Duessa discovered that the Red Cross Knight had fled, she followed him and found him resting beside a fountain. Not knowing that the water was en-

chanted, he drank of it, and at once all his manly strength
ebbed away, and he became faint and feeble. Then, when
he was too weak to hold a sword or spear, he saw a fearful
sight:—

> "With sturdy steps came stalking in his sight,
> An hideous Giant horrible and high,
> That with his tallness seemed to threat the sky,
> The ground eke groanéd under him for dread,
> His living like saw never living eye,
> Nor durst behold; his stature did exceed
> The height of three the tallest sons of mortal seed."

Towards the Knight, so weak that he could scarcely
hold his sword, this Giant came stalking. Weak as he was,
the Knight made ready to fight. But

> "The Giant strake so mainly merciless,
> That could have overthrown a stony tower;
> And were not heavenly grace that did him bless,
> He had been powdered all as thin as flour."

As the Giant struck at him, the Knight leapt aside and
the blow fell harmless. But so mighty was it that the wind
of it threw him to the ground, where he lay senseless. And
ere he woke out of his swoon the Giant took him up, and

> "Him to his castle brought with hasty force
> And in a dungeon deep him threw without remorse."

Duessa then became the Giant's lady. "He gave her
gold and purple pall to wear," and set a triple crown upon
her head. For steed he gave her a fearsome dragon with
fiery eyes and seven heads, so that all who saw her went
in dread and awe.

The Dwarf, seeing his master thus overthrown and made
prisoner, gathered his armor and set forth to tell his evil
tidings and find help. He had not gone far before he met
the Lady Una. To her he told his sad news, and she with
grief in her heart turned with him to find the dark dungeon

in which her Knight lay. On her way she met another knight. This was Prince Arthur. And he, learning of her sorrow, went with her promising aid. Guided by the Dwarf they reached the castle of the Giant, and here a fearful fight took place in which Prince Arthur conquered Duessa's Dragon and killed the Giant. Then he entered the castle,

> "Where living creature none he did espy.
> Then gan he loudly through the house to call;
> But no man cared to answer to his cry;
> There reigned a solemn silence over all,
> Nor voice was heard, nor wight was seen in bower or hall.
>
> At last, with creeping crooked pace forth came
> An old, old man with beard as white as snow;
> That on a staff his feeble steps did frame,
> And guide his weary gate both to and fro,
> For his eyesight him failéd long ago;
> And on his arm a bunch of keys he bore,
> The which unuséd rust did overgrow;
> Those were the keys of every inner door,
> But he could not them use, but kept them still in store."

And what was strange and terrible about this old man was that his head was twisted upon his shoulders, so that although he walked towards the knight his face looked backward.

Seeing his gray hairs and venerable look Prince Arthur asked him gently where all the folk of the castle were.

"I cannot tell," answered the old man. And to every question he replied, "I cannot tell," until the knight, impatient of delay, seized the keys from his arm. Door after door the Prince Arthur opened, seeing many strange, sad sights. But nowhere could he find the captive Knight.

> "At last he came unto an iron door,
> That fast was locked, but key found not at all,
> Amongst that bunch to open it withal."

But there was a little grating in the door through which

Prince Arthur called. A hollow, dreary, murmuring voice replied. It was the voice of the Red Cross Knight, which, when the champion heard, "with furious force and indignation fell" he rent that iron door and entered in.

Once more the Red Cross Knight was free and reunited to his Lady, while the false Duessa was unmasked and shown to be a bad old witch, who fled away "to the wasteful wilderness apace."

But the Red Cross Knight was still so weak and feeble that Despair almost persuaded him to kill himself. Seeing this, Una led him to the house of Holiness, where he stayed until once more he was strong and well. Here he learned that he was St. George. "Thou," he is told,

> "Shalt be a saint, and thine own nation's friend
> And patron. Thou St George shalt callèd be,
> St. George of merry England, the sign of victory"

Once more strong of arm, full of new courage, the Knight set forth with Una, and soon they reached her home, where the dreadful Dragon raged.

Here the most fierce fight of all takes place. Three days it is renewed, and on the third day the Dragon is conquered

> "So down he fell, and forth his life did breathe
> That vanished into smoke and clouds swift;
> So down he fell, that th' earth him underneath
> Did groan, as feeble so great load to lift;
> So down he fell, as an huge rocky clift
> Whose false foundation waves have washed away,
> With dreadful poise is from the mainland rift
> And rolling down, great Neptune doth dismay;
> So down he fell, and like an heapèd mountain lay"

Thus all ends happily. The aged King and Queen are rescued from the brazen tower in which the Dragon had imprisoned them, and Una and the Knight are married.

That is the story of the first book of the *Faery Queen*.

In it Spenser has made great use of the legend of St. George and the Dragon. The Red Cross of his Knight, "the dear remembrance of his dying Lord," was in those days the flag of England, and is still the Red Cross of our Union Jack. And besides the allegory the poem has something of history in it. The great people of Spenser's day play their parts there. Thus Duessa, sad to say, is meant to be the fair, unhappy Queen of Scots, the wicked magician is the Pope, and so on. But we need scarcely trouble about all that. I repeat that meantime it is enough for you to enjoy the story and the poetry.

CHAPTER XLIII

SPENSER—HIS LAST DAYS

THERE are so many books now published which tell the stories of the *Faery Queen,* and tell them well, that you may think I hardly need have told one here. But few of these books give the poet's own words, and I have told the story here giving quotations from the poem in the hope that you will read them and learn from them to love Spenser's own words. I hope that long after you have forgotten my words you will remember Spenser's, that they will remain in your mind as glowing word-pictures, and make you anxious to read more of the poem from which they are taken.

Spenser has been called the poet's poet,[1] he might also be called the painter's poet, for on every page almost we find a word-picture, rich in color, rich in detail. Each person as he comes upon the scene is described for us so that we may see him with our mind's eye. The whole poem blazes with color, it glows and gleams with the glamor of fairyland. Spenser more than any other poet has the old Celtic love of beauty, yet so far as we know there was in him no drop of Celtic blood. He loved neither the Irishman nor Ireland. To him his life there was an exile, yet perhaps even in spite of himself he breathed in the land of fairies and of "little people" something of their magic: his fingers, unwittingly perhaps, touched the golden and ivory gate so that he entered in and saw.

[1] Charles Lamb.

265

That it is a fairyland and no real world which Spenser opens to us is the great difference between Chaucer and him. Chaucer gives us real men and women who love and hate, who sin and sorrow. He is humorous, he is coarse, and he is real. Spenser has humor too, but we seldom see him smile. There are, we may be glad, few coarse lines in Spenser, but he is artificial. He took the tone of his time—the tone of pretense. It was the fashion to make-believe, yet, underneath all the make-believe, men were still men, not wholly good nor wholly bad. But underneath the brilliant trappings of Spenser's knights and ladies, shepherds and shepherdesses, there seldom beats a human heart. He takes us to dreamland, and when we lay down the book we wake up to real life. Beauty first and last is what holds us in Spenser's poems—beauty of description, beauty of thought, beauty of sound. As it has been said, " 'A thing of beauty is a joy forever,' and that is the secret of the enduring life of the *Faery Queen.*" [1]

Spenser invented for himself a new stanza of nine lines and made it famous, so that we call it after him, the Spenserian Stanza. It was like Chaucer's stanza of seven lines, called the Rhyme Royal, with two lines more added.

Spenser admired Chaucer above all poets. He called him "The Well of English undefiled," [2] and after many hundred years we still feel the truth of the description. He uses many of Chaucer's words, which even then had grown old-fashioned and were little used. So much is this so that a glossary written by a friend of Spenser, in which old words were explained, was published with the *Shepherd's Calendar.* But whether old or new, Spenser's power of using words and of weaving them together was wonderful.

He weaves his wonderful words in such wonderful

[1] Courthorpe, *History of English Poetry*
[2] *Faery Queen,* book iv. canto ii.

fashion that they sound like what he describes. Is there anything more drowsy than his description of the abode of sleep:

> "And more, to lull him in his slumber soft,
> A trickling stream from high rock tumbling down,
> And ever drizzling rain upon the loft
> Mix'd with a murmuring wind, much like the sound
> Of swarming bees, did cast him in a swound,[1]
> No other noise nor peoples' troublous cries,
> As still are wont t' annoy the walléd town,
> Might there be heard; but careless quiet lies
> Wrapt in eternal silence, far from enemies"

So all through the poem we are enchanted or lulled by the glamor of words.

The *Faery Queen* made Spenser as a poet famous, but, as we know, it did not bring him enough to live on in England. It did not bring him the fame he sought nor make him great among the statesmen of the land. Among the courtiers of Queen Elizabeth he counted for little. So he returned to Ireland a disappointed man. It was now he wrote *Colin Clout's come home again,* from which I have already given you some quotations. He published also another book of poems and then he fell in love. He forgot his beautiful Rosalind, who had been so hard-hearted, and gave his love to another lady who in her turn loved him, and to whom he was happily married. This lady, too, he made famous in his verse. As the fashion was, he wrote to her a series of sonnets, in one of which we learn that her name was Elizabeth. He writes to the three Elizabeths, his mother, his Queen, and

> "The third, my love, my life's last ornament,
> By whom my spirit out of dust was raised"

But more famous still than the sonnets is the *Epithalamion* or wedding hymn which he wrote in his lady's

---

[1] Swoon

honor, and which ever since has been looked on as the most glorious love-song in the English language, so full is it of exultant, worshipful happiness.

It was now, too, that Spenser wrote *Astrophel,* a sadly beautiful dirge for the death of his friend and fellow-poet, Sir Philip Sidney. He gave his verses as "fittest flowers to deck his mournful hearse."

Just before his marriage Spenser finished three more books of the *Faery Queen,* and the following year he took them to London to publish them. The three books were on Friendship, on Justice, and on Courtesy. They were received as joyfully as the first three. The poet remained for nearly a year in London still writing busily. Then he returned to Ireland. There he passed a few more years, and then came the end.

Ireland, which had always been unquiet, always restless, under the oppressive hand of England, now broke out into wild rebellion. The maddened Irish had no love or respect for the English poet. Kilcolman Castle was sacked and burned, and Spenser fled with his wife and children to Cork, homeless and wellnigh ruined. A little later Spenser himself went on to London, hoping perhaps to better his fortunes, and there in a Westminster inn, disappointed, ill, shattered in hopes and health, he lay down to die.

As men count years, he was still young, for he was only forty-seven. He had dreamed that he had still time before him to make life a success. For as men counted success in those days, Spenser was a failure. He had failed to make a name among the statesmen of the age. He failed to make a fortune, he lived poor and he died poor. As a poet he was a sublime success. He dedicated the *Faery Queen* to Elizabeth "to live with the eternity of her fame," and it is not too much to believe that even should the deeds of Elizabeth be forgotten the fame of Spenser will endure.

And the poets of Spenser's own day knew that in him they had lost a master, and they mourned for him as such. They buried him in Westminster not far from Chaucer. His bier was carried by poets, who, as they stood beside his grave, threw into it poems in which they told of his glory and their own grief. And so they left "The Prince of Poets in his tyme, whose divine spirit needs no other witnesse than the workes which he left behind him." [1]

BOOKS TO READ

Tales from Spenser (Told to Children Series)   *Una and the Red Cross Knight,* by N. G. Royde Smith (has many quotations)   *Tales from the Faerie Queene,* by C L. Thomson (prose)   *The Faerie Queene* (verse, sixteenth century spelling). *Faerie Queene,* book I., by Professor W. H Hudson   *Complete Works* (Globe Edition), edited by R Morris   *Britomart,* edited by May E Litchfield, is the story of Britomart taken from scattered portions in books III, IV., and V. in original poetry, spelling modernized

[1] The first epitaph engraved on Spenser's tomb

CHAPTER XLIV

ABOUT THE FIRST THEATERS

In the beginnings of our literature there were two men who, we might say, were the fountain-heads. These were the gay minstrel abroad in the world singing in hall and market-place, and the patient monk at work in cell or cloister. And as year by year our literature grew, strengthened and broadened, we might say it flowed on in two streams. It flowed in two streams which were ever joining, mingling, separating again, for the monk and the minstrel spoke to man each in his own way. The monk made his appeal to the eye as with patient care he copied, painted and made his manuscript beautiful with gold and colors. The minstrel made his appeal to the ear with music and with song. Then after a time the streams seemed to join, and the monk when he played the miracle-plays seemed to be taking the minstrel's part. Here was an appeal both to eye and ear. Instead of illuminating the silent parchment he made living pictures illustrate spoken words. Then followed a time when the streams once more divided and church and stage parted. The strolling players and the trade guilds took the place both of the minstrel and of the monkish actors. the monk went back once more to his quiet cell, and the minstrel gradually disappeared.

So year after year went on. By slow degrees times changed, and our literature changed with the times. But looking backward we can see that the poet is the development of the minstrel, the prose writer the development of

the monkish chronicler and copyist. Prose at first was
only used for grave matters, for history, for religious works,
for dry treatises which were hardly literature, which were
not meant for enjoyment but only for use and for teaching.
But by degrees people began to use prose for story-telling,
for enjoyment. More and more prose began to be written
for amusement until at last it has quite taken the place
of poetry. Nowadays many people are not at all fond
of poetry. They are rather apt to think that a poetry
book is but dull reading, and they much prefer plain prose.
It may amuse those who feel like that to remember that
hundreds of years ago it was just the other way round.
Then it was prose that was considered dull—hence we
have the word prosy.

All poetry was at first written to be sung, sung too
perhaps with some gesture, so that the hearers might the
better understand the story. Then by degrees poets got
further and further away from that, until poets like Spenser
wrote with no such idea. But while poets like Spenser
wrote their stories to be read, another class of poets was
growing up who intended their poems to be spoken and
acted. These were the dramatists.

So you see that the minstrel stream divided into two.
There was now the poet who wrote his poems to be
read in quiet and the poet who wrote his, if not to be
sung, at least to be spoken aloud. But there had been,
as we have seen, a time when the minstrel and
the monkish stream had touched, a time when the monk,
using the minstrel's art, had taught the people through
ear and eye together. For the idea of the Miracle and
Morality plays was, you remember, to teach. So, long
after the monks had ceased to act, those who wrote poems
to be acted felt that they must teach something. Thus
after the Miracle plays came the Moralities, which sometimes were very long and dull. They were followed by

Interludes which were much the same as Moralities but were shorter, and as their name shows were meant to come in the middle of something else, for the word comes from two Latin words, "inter" between and "ludus" a play. An Interlude may have been first used, perhaps, as a kind of break in a long feast.

The Miracle plays had only been acted once a year, first by the monks and later by the trade guilds. But the taste for plays grew, and soon bands of players strolled about the country acting in towns and villages. These strolling players often made a good deal of money. But though the people crowded willingly to see and hear, the magistrates did not love these players, and they were looked upon as little better than rogues and vagabonds. Then it became the fashion for great lords to have their own company of players, and they, when their masters did not need them, also traveled about to the surrounding villages acting wherever they went. This taste for acting grew strong in the people of England. And if in the life of the Middle Ages there was always room for story-telling, in the life of Tudor England there was always room for acting and shows.

These shows were called by various names, Pageants, Masques, Interludes, Mummings or Disguisings, and on every great or little occasion there was sure to be something of the sort. If the King or Queen went on a journey he or she was entertained by pageants on the way. If a royal visitor came to the court of England there were pageants in his honor. A birthday, a christening, a wedding or a victory would all be celebrated by pageants, and in these plays people of all classes took part. School-children acted, University students acted, the learned lawyers of Inns of Court acted, great lords and ladies acted, and even at times the King and Queen themselves took part. And although many of these shows, especially the pageants, were merely shows, without any

words, many, on the other hand, had words. Thus with
so much acting and love of acting it was not wonderful
that a crowd of dramatists sprang up.

Then, too, plays began to be divided into tragedies and
comedies. A tragedy is a play which shows the sad side of
life and which has a mournful ending. The word really
means a goat-song, and comes from two Greek words,
"*tragos*" a goat and "*ode*" a song. It was so called either
because the oldest tragedies were acted while a goat was
sacrificed, or because the actors themselves wore clothes
made of goat-skins. A comedy is a play which shows the
merry side of life and has a happy ending. This word too
comes from two Greek words, "*komos*," a revel, and "*ode*,"
a song. The Greek word for village is also "*komo*," so a
comedy may at first have meant a village revel or merry-
making. "Tragedy," it has been said, "is poetry in its
deepest earnest; comedy is poetry in unlimited jest." [1]
But the old Moralities were neither the one nor the other,
neither tragedy nor comedy. They did not touch life
keenly enough to awaken horror or pain. They were often
sad, but not with that sadness which we have come to call
tragic, they were often indeed merely dull, and although
there was always a funny character to make laughter, it was
by no means unlimited jest. The Interludes came next,
after the Moralities, with a little more human interest and
a little more fun, and from them it was easy to pass to real
comedies.

A play named *Ralph Roister Doister* is generally looked
upon as the first real English comedy. It was written by
Nicholas Udall, headmaster first of Eton and then of Westminster, for the boys of one or other school. It was probably for those of Westminster that it was written, and
may have been acted about 1552.

The hero, if one may call him so, who gives his name to

[1] Coleridge.

the play, is a vain, silly swaggerer. He thinks every woman who sees him is in love with him. So he makes up his mind to marry a rich and beautiful widow named Christian Custance.

Not being a very good scholar, Ralph gets some one else to write a love-letter for him, but when he copies it he puts all the stops in the wrong places, which makes the sense quite different from what he had intended, and instead of being full of pretty things the letter is full of insults.

Dame Custance will have nothing to say to such a stupid lover, "I will not be served with a fool in no wise. When I choose a husband I hope to take a man," she says. In revenge for her scorn Ralph Roister Doister threatens to burn the dame's house down, and sets off to attack it with his servants. The widow, however, meets him with her handmaidens. There is a free fight (which, no doubt, the schoolboy actors enjoyed), but the widow gets the best of it, and Ralph is driven off.

Our first real tragedy was not written until ten years after our first comedy. This first tragedy was written by Thomas Norton and Thomas Sackville, Earl of Dorset. It was acted by the gentlemen of the Inner Temple "before the Queen's most excellent Majestie in her highness' Court of Whitehall the 18th day of January, 1561."

Chaucer tells us that a tragedy is a story

> "Of him that stood in great prosperitie,
> And is yfallen out of high degree
> Into miserie, and endeth wretchedly." [1]

So our early tragedies were all taken from sad stories in the old Chronicle histories. And this first tragedy, written by Norton and Sackville, is called *Gorboduc,* and is founded upon the legend of Gorboduc, King of Britain. The story is told, though not quite in the same way, by Geoffrey of

[1] Prologue to the "Monk's Tale," *Canterbury Tales.*

Monmouth, our old friend, by Matthew of Westminster, and by others of the old chroniclers. For in writing a poem or play it is not necessary to keep strictly to history. As Sir Philip Sidney, Spenser's friend, says: "Do they not know that a tragedy is tied to the laws of Poesie and not of History, not bound to follow the story, but, having liberty, either to fain a quite new matter, or to frame the history to the most tragical convenience?" [1]

The story goes that Gorboduc, King of Britain, divided his realm during his lifetime between his sons Ferrex and Porrex. But the brothers quarreled, and the younger killed the elder. The mother, who loved her eldest son most, then killed the younger in revenge. Next the people, angry at such cruelty, rose in rebellion and killed both father and mother. The nobles then gathered and defeated the rebels. And lastly, for want of an heir to the throne, "they fell to civil war," and the land for a long time was desolate and miserable.

In the play none of these fearful murders happen on the stage. They are only reported by messengers. There is also a chorus of old sage men of Britain who, at the end of each act, chant of what has happened. When you come to read Greek plays you will see that this is more like Greek than English tragedy, and it thus shows the influence of the New Learning upon our literature. But, on the other hand, in a Greek drama there was never more than one scene, and all the action was supposed to take place on one day. This was called preserving the unities of time and place, and no Greek drama which did not observe them would have been thought good. In *Gorboduc* there are several scenes, and the action, although we are not told how long, must last over several months at least. So that although *Gorboduc* owed something to the New Learning, which had made men study Greek, it owed as much to the

[1] Sidney, *Apologie for Poetrie*.

old English Miracle plays. Later on when you come to read more about the history of our drama you will learn a great deal about what we owe to the Greeks, but here I will not trouble you with it.

You remember that in the Morality plays there was no scenery. And still, although in the new plays which were now being written the scene was supposed to change from place to place, there was no attempt to make the stage look like these places. The stage was merely a plain platform, and when the scene changed a board was hung up with "This is a Palace" or "This is a Street" and the imagination of the audience had to do the rest.

That some people felt the absurdity of this we learn from a book by Sir Philip Sidney. In it he says, "You shall have Asia of the one side, and Affrick of the other, and so many other under kingdoms, that the Player, when he cometh in, must ever begin with telling where he is, or else the tale will not be conceived. Now you shall have three ladies walk to gather flowers, and then we must believe the stage to be a garden. By and by, we hear news of shipwreck in the same place, and then we are to blame if we accept it not for a Rock. Upon the back of that, comes out a hideous Monster, with fire and smoke, and then the miserable beholders are bound to take it for a cave. While in the meantime two Armies fly in, represented with four swords and bucklers, and then what hard heart will not receive it for a pitched field?" [1]

If the actors of the Elizabethan time had no scenery they made up for the lack of it by splendid and gorgeous dressing. But it was the dressing of the day. The play might be supposed to take place in Greece or Rome or Ancient Britain, it mattered not. The actors dressed after the fashion of their own day. And neither actors nor audience saw anything funny in it. To them it was not

[1] *An Apologie for Poetrie,* published 1595.

funny that an ancient British king should wear doublet and
hose, nor that his soldiers should discharge firearms in a
scene supposed to take place hundreds of years before
gunpowder had been invented. But we must remember
that in those days dress meant much more than it does now.
Dress helped to tell the story. Men then might not dress
according to their likes and dislikes, they were obliged to
dress according to their rank. Therefore it helped the
Elizabethan onlooker to understand the play when he saw
a king, a courtier, or a butcher come on to the stage dressed
as he knew a king, a courtier, or a butcher dressed. Had
he seen a man of the sixth century dressed as a man of the
sixth century he would not have known to what class he
belonged and would not have understood the play nearly
so well.

But besides having no scenery, the people of England
had at first no theaters. Plays were acted in halls, in the
dining-halls of the great or in the guild halls belonging to
the various trades. It was not until 1575 that the first
theater was built in London. This first theater was so
successful that soon another was built and still another,
until in or near London there were no fewer than twelve.
But these theaters were very unlike the theaters we know
now. They were really more like the places where people
went to see cock-fights and bear-baiting. They were round,
and except over the stage there was no roof. The rich
onlookers who could afford to pay well sat in "boxes" on
the stage itself, and the other onlookers sat or stood in the
uncovered parts. Part of a theater is still called the pit,
which helps to remind us that the first theaters may have
served as "cock-pits" or "bear-pits" too as well as theaters.
For a long time, too, the theater was a man's amusement
just as bear-baiting or cock-fighting had been. There
were no actresses, the women's parts were taken by boys,
and at first ladies when they came to look on wore masks

so that they might not be known, as they were rather ashamed of being seen at a theater.

And now that the love of plays and shows had grown so great that it had been found worth while to build special places in which to act, you may be sure that there was no lack of play-writers. There were indeed many of whom I should like to tell you, but in this book there is no room to tell of all. To show you how many dramatists arose in this great acting age 1 will give you a list of the greatest, all of whom were born between 1552 and 1585. After Nicholas Udall and Thomas Norton and Thomas Sackville, the writers of our first comedy and first tragedy, there came:—

George Peel.	Francis Beaumont.
John Lyly.	John Fletcher.
Thomas Kyd.	John Webster.
Robert Greene.	Philip Massinger.
Christopher Marlowe.	John Ford.
William Shakespeare.	Thomas Heywood.
Ben Jonson.	

It would be impossible to tell you of all these, so I shall choose only two, and first I shall tell you of the greatest of them—Shakespeare. He shines out from among the others like a bright star in a clear sky. He is, however, not a lonely star, for all around him cluster others. They are bright, too, and if he were not there we might think some of them even very bright, yet he outshines them all. He forces our eyes to turn to him, and not only our eyes but the eyes of the whole world. For all over the world, wherever poetry is read and plays are played, the name of William Shakespeare is known and reverenced.

CHAPTER XLV

SHAKESPEARE—THE BOY

ONE April morning nearly three hundred and fifty years ago there was stir and bustle in a goodly house in the little country town of Stratford-on-Avon. The neighbors went in and out with nods and smiles and mysterious whisperings. Then there was a sound of clinking of glasses and of laughter, for it became known that to John and Mary Shakespeare a son had been born, and presently there was brought to be shown to the company "The infant mewling and puking in the nurse's arms." It was a great event for the father and mother, something of an event for Stratford-on-Avon, for John Shakespeare was a man of importance. He was a well-to-do merchant, an alderman of the little town. He seems to have done business in several ways, for we are told that he was a glover, a butcher, and a corn and wool dealer. No doubt he grew his own corn, and reared and killed his own sheep, making gloves from the skins, and selling the wool and flesh. His wife, too, came of a good yeoman family who farmed their own land, and no doubt John Shakespeare did business with his kinsfolk in both corn and sheep. And although he could perhaps not read, and could not write even his own name, he was a lucky business man and prosperous. So he was well considered by his neighbors and had a comfortable house in Henley Street, built of rough plastered stone and dark strong wood work.

And now this April morning John Shakespeare's heart

was glad. Already he had had two children, two little girls, but they had both died. Now he had a son who would surely live to grow strong and great, to be a comfort in his old age and carry on his business when he could no longer work. It was a great day for John Shakespeare. How little he knew that it was a great day for all the world and for all time.

Three days after he was born the tiny baby was christened. And the name his father and mother gave him was William. After this three months passed happily. Then one of the fearful plagues which used to sweep over the land, when people lived in dark and dirty houses in dark and dirty streets, attacked Stratford-on-Avon. Jolly John Shakespeare and Mary, his wife, must have been anxious of heart, fearful lest the plague should visit their home. John did what he could to stay it. He helped the stricken people with money and goods, and presently the plague passed away, and the life of the dearly loved little son was safe.

Years passed on, and the house in Henley Street grew ever more noisy with chattering tongues and pattering feet, until little Will had two sisters and two brothers to keep him company.

Then, although his father and mother could neither of them write themselves, they decided that their children should be taught, so William was sent to the Grammar School. He was, I think, fonder of the blue sky and the slow-flowing river and the deep dark woods that grew about his home than of the low-roofed schoolroom. He went perhaps

> "A whining schoolboy, with his satchel
> And shining morning face, creeping like snail
> Unwillingly to school"

But we do not know. And whether he liked school or not, at least we know that later, when he came to write plays, he made fun of schoolmasters. He knew "little Latin and less Greek," [1] said a friend in after life, but then that friend was very learned and might think "little" that which we might take for "a good deal." Indeed, another old writer says "he understood Latin pretty well." [2]

We know little either of Shakespeare's school hours or play hours, but once or twice at least he may have seen a play or pageant. His father went on prospering and was made chief bailiff of the town, and while in that office he entertained twice at least troups of strolling players, the Queen's Company and the Earl of Worcester's Company. It is very likely that little Will was taken to see the plays they acted. Then when he was eleven years old there was great excitement in the country town, for Queen Elizabeth came to visit the great Earl of Leicester at his castle of Kenilworth, not sixteen miles away. There were great doings then, and the Queen was received with all the magnificence and pomp that money could procure and imagination invent. Some of these grand shows Shakespeare must have seen.

Long afterwards he remembered perhaps how one evening he had stood among the crowd tiptoeing and eager to catch a glimpse of the great Queen as she sat enthroned on a golden chair. Her red-gold hair gleamed and glittered with jewels under the flickering torchlight. Around her stood a crowd of nobles and ladies only less brilliant than she. Then, as William gazed and gazed, his eyes aching with the dazzling lights, there was a movement in the surging crowd, a murmur of "ohs" and "ahs." And, turning, the boy saw another lady, another Queen, appear from out the dark shadow of the trees. Stately and slowly she moved across the grass. Then following her came a winged boy with golden bow and arrows. This was the God of Love, who roamed the world shooting his

[1] Ben Jonson   [2] John Aubrey.

love arrows at the hearts of men and women, making them love each other. He aimed, he shot, the arrow flew, but the god missed his aim and the lady passed on, beautiful, cold, free, as before. Love could not touch her, he followed her but in vain.

It was with such pageants, such allegories, that her people flattered Queen Elizabeth, for many men laid their hearts at her feet, but she in return never gave her own. She was the woman above all others to be loved, to be worshiped, but herself remained in "maiden meditation fancy-free." The memory of those brilliant days stayed with the poet-child. They were sun-gilt, as childish memories are, and in after years he wrote:

> "That very time I saw (but thou couldst not)
> Flying between the cold moon and the earth,
> Cupid all arm'd. A certain aim he took
> At a fair vestal, throned by the West,
> And loos'd his love-shaft smartly from his bow,
> As it should pierce a hundred thousand hearts,
> But I might see young Cupid's fiery shaft
> Quench'd in the chaste beams of the watery moon,
> And the imperial votaress passed on,
> In maiden meditation, fancy-free
> Yet mark'd I where the bolt of Cupid fell
> It fell upon a little western flower;
> Before, milk-white; now, purple with love's wound,
> And maidens call it love-in-idleness." [1]

Some time after John Shakespeare became chief bailiff his fortunes turned. From being rich he became poor. Bit by bit he was obliged to sell his own and his wife's property. So little Will was taken away from school at the age of thirteen, and set to earn his own living as a butcher—his father's trade, we are told. But if he ever was a butcher he was, nevertheless, an actor and a poet, "and when he killed a calf he would do it in a high

[1] *Midsummer Night's Dream*, Act II Scene i

style and make a speech." [1] How Shakespeare fared in this new work we do not know, but we may fancy him when work was done wandering along the pretty country lanes, or losing himself in the forest of Arden, which lay not far from his home, "the poet's eye in a fine frenzy rolling," and singing to himself:

> "Jog on, jog on, the footpath way,
> And merrily hent the stile-a;
> A merry heart goes all the day,
> Your sad tires in a mile-a " [2]

He knew the lore of fields and woods, of trees and flowers, and birds and beasts. He sang of

> "The ousel-cock so black of hue,
> With orange-tawny bill,
> The throstle with his note so true,
> The wren with little quill.
> The finch, the sparrow, and the lark,
> The plain-song cuckoo gray,
> Whose note full many a man doth mark,
> And dares not answer nay." [3]

He remembered, perhaps, in after years his rambles by the slow-flowing Avon, when he wrote:

> "He makes sweet music with th' enamell'd stones,
> Giving a gentle kiss to every sedge
> He overtaketh in his pilgrimage;
> And so by many winding nooks he strays,
> With willing sport, to the wide ocean " [4]

He knew the times of the flowers. In spring he marked

> "the daffodils,
> That come before the swallow dares, and take
> The winds of March with beauty." [5]

---

[1] John Aubrey.
[2] *Winter's Tale*, Act IV Scene II
[3] *Midsummer Night's Dream*, Act III Scene i
[4] *Two Gentlemen of Verona*, Act II Scene VII
[5] *Winter's Tale.*

Of summer flowers he tells us

> "Hot lavender, mints, savory, marjoram;
> The marigold, that goes to bed wi' the sun,
> And with him rises weeping; these are flowers
> Of middle summer " [1]

He knew that "a lapwing runs close by the ground," that choughs are "russet-pated." He knew all the beauty that is to be found throughout the country year.

Sometimes in his country wanderings Shakespeare got into mischief too. He had a daring spirit, and on quiet dark nights he would creep silently about the woods snaring rabbits or hunting deer. But we are told "he was given to all unluckiness in stealing venison and rabbits." [2] He was often caught, sometimes got a good beating, and sometimes was sent to prison.

So the years passed on, and we know little of what happened in them. Some people like to think that Shakespeare was a schoolmaster for a time, others that he was a clerk in a lawyer's office. He may have been one or other, but we do not know. What we do know is that when he was eighteen he took a great step. He married. We can imagine him making love-songs then. Perhaps he sang:

> "O mistress mine, where are you roaming?
> O, stay and hear; your true-love's coming,
>   That can sing both high and low
> Trip no further, pretty sweeting;
> Journeys end in lovers' meeting,
>   Every wise man's son doth know
>
> What is love? 'tis not hereafter;
> Present mirth hath present laughter,
>   What's to come is still unsure
> In delay there lies no plenty,
> Then come kiss me, sweet-and-twenty;
>   Youth's a stuff will not endure." [3]

---

[1] *Winter's Tale*   [2] Archdeacon Davies   [3] *Twelfth Night*

The lady whom Shakespeare married was named Anne Hathaway. She came of farmer folk like Shakespeare's own mother. She was eight years older than her boyish lover, but beyond that we know little of Anne Hathaway, for Shakespeare never anywhere mentions his wife.

A little while after their marriage a daughter was born to Anne and William Shakespeare. Nearly two years later a little boy and girl came to them. The boy died when he was about eleven, and only the two little girls, Judith and Susanna, lived to grow up.

In spite of the fact that Shakespeare had now a wife and children to look after, he had not settled down. He was still wild, and being caught once more in stealing game he left Stratford and went to London.

CHAPTER XLVI

SHAKESPEARE—THE MAN

When Shakespeare first went to London he had a hard life. He found no better work to do than that of holding horses outside the theater doors. In those days the plays took place in the afternoon, and as many of the fine folk who came to watch them rode on horseback, some one was needed to look after the horses until the play was over. But poor though this work was, Shakespeare seems to have done it well, and he became such a favorite that he had several boys under him who were long known as "Shakespeare's boys." Their master, however, soon left work outside the theater for work inside. And now began the busiest years of his life, for he both acted and wrote. At first it may be he only altered and improved the plays of others. But soon he began to write plays that were all his own. Yet Shakespeare, like Chaucer, never invented any of his own stories. There is only one play of his, called *Love's Labor's Lost,* the story of which is not to be found in some earlier book. That, too, may have been founded on another story which is now lost.

When you come to know Shakespeare's plays well you will find it very interesting to follow his stories to their sources. That of *King Lear,* which is one of Shakespeare's great romantic historical plays, is, for instance, to be found in Geoffrey of Monmouth, in Wace's *Brut,* and in Layamon's *Brut.* But it was from none of these that Shakespeare took the story, but from the chronicle of a man named

266

Holinshed who lived and wrote in the time of Queen Elizabeth, he in his turn having taken it from some one of the earlier sources.

For, after all, in spite of the thousands of books that have been written since the world began, there are only a certain number of stories which great writers have told again and again in varying ways. One instance of this we saw when in the beginning of this book we followed the story of Arthur.

But although Shakespeare borrowed his plots from others, when he had borrowed them he made them all his own. He made his people so vivid and so true that he makes us forget that they are not real people. We can hardly realize that they never lived, that they never walked and talked, and cried and laughed, loved and hated, in this world just as we do. And this is so because the stage to him is life and life a stage. "All the world's a stage," he says,

> "And all the men and women merely players:
> They have their exits and their entrances
> And one man in his time plays many parts,
> His acts being seven ages." [1]

And again he tells us:

> "Life's but a walking shadow; a poor player,
> That struts and frets his hour upon the stage
> And then is heard no more." [2]

It is from Shakespeare's works that we get the clearest picture of Elizabethan times. And yet, although we learn from him so much of what people did in those days, of how they talked and even of how they thought, the chief thing that we feel about Shakespeare's characters is, not that they are Elizabethan, but that they are human, that they are like ourselves, that they think, and say, and do, things which we ourselves might think, and say, and do.

[1] *As You Like It.*   [2] *Macbeth.*

There are many books we read which we think of as very pretty, very quaint, very interesting—but old-fashioned. But Shakespeare can never be old-fashioned, because, although he is the outcome of his own times, and gives us all the flavor of his own times, he gives us much more. He understood human nature, he saw beneath the outward dress, and painted for us real men and women. And although fashion in dress and modes of living may change, human nature does not change. "He was not of an age but for all time," it was said of him about seven years after his death, and now that nearly three hundred years have come and gone we still acknowledge the truth of those words.

Shakespeare's men and women speak and act and feel in the main as we might now. Many of his people we feel are our brothers and sisters. And to this human interest he adds something more, for he leads us too through "unpathed waters" to "the undreamed shores" of fairyland.

Shakespeare's writing time was short. Before he left Stratford he wrote nothing unless it may have been a few scoffing verses against the Justice of the Peace who punished him for poaching. But these, if they were ever written, are lost. In the last few years of his life he wrote little or nothing. Thus the number of his writing years was not more than twenty to twenty-five, but in that time he wrote thirty-seven plays, two long poems, and a hundred and fifty-six sonnets. At one time he must have written two plays every year. And when you come to know these plays well you will wonder at the greatness of the task.

Shakespeare writes his plays sometimes in rime, sometimes in blank verse, sometimes in prose, at times using all these in one play. In this he showed how free he was from rules. For, until he wrote, plays had been written in rime or blank verse only.

For the sake of convenience Shakespeare's plays have been divided into histories, tragedies and comedies. But it is not always easy to draw the line and decide to which class a play belongs. They are like life. Life is not all laughter, nor is it all tears. Neither are Shakespeare's comedies all laughter, and some of his tragedies would seem at times to be too deep for tears, full only of fierce, dark sorrow—and yet there is laughter in them too.

Besides being divided into histories, tragedies and comedies they have been divided in another way, into three periods of time. The first was when Shakespeare was trying his hand, when he was brimming over with the joy of the new full life of London. The second was when some dark sorrow lay over his life, we know not what, when the pain and mystery and the irony of living seems to strike him hard. Then he wrote his great tragedies. The third was when he had gained peace again, when life seemed to flow calmly and smoothly, and this period lasted until the end.

We know very little of Shakespeare's life in London. As an actor he never made a great name, never acted the chief character in a play. But he acted sometimes in his own plays and took the part, we are told, of a ghost in one, and of a servant in another, neither of them great parts. He acted, too, in plays written by other people. But it was as a writer that he made a name, and that so quickly that others grew jealous of him. One called him "an upstart Crow, beautified in our feathers . . . in his own conceit the only Shake-scene in the country." [1]   But for the most part Shakespeare made friends even of rival authors, and many of them loved him well. He was good-tempered, merry, witty, and kindly, a most lovable man. "He was a handsome, well-shaped man, very good company, and a

[1] Robert Greene, *A groatsworth of Wit bought with a million of repentance.*

very ready and pleasant smooth wit," [1] said one. "I loved the man and do honor his memory, on this side idolatry as much as any. He was indeed honest and of an open and free nature," [2] said another. Others still called him a good fellow, gentle Shakespeare, sweet Master Shakespeare. I should like to think, too, that Spenser called him "our pleasant Willy." But wise folk tell us that these words were not spoken of Shakespeare but of some one else whose name was not William at all.

And so although outside his work we get only glimpses of the man, these glimpses taken together with his writings show us Will Shakespeare as a big-hearted man, a man who understood all and forgave all. He understood the little joys and sorrows that make up life. He understood the struggle to be good, and would not scorn people too greatly when they were bad. "Children, we feel sure," says one of the latest writers about him, "did not stop their talk when he came near them, but continued in the happy assurance that it was only Master Shakespeare." [3] And so if children find his plays hard to read yet a while they may at least learn to know his stories and learn to love his name—it is only Master Shakespeare. But they must remember that learning to know Shakespeare's stories through the words of other people is only half a joy. The full joy of Shakespeare can only come when we are able to read his plays in his very own words. But that will come all the more easily and quickly to us if we first know his stories well.

There are parts in some of Shakespeare's plays that many people find coarse. But Shakespeare is not really coarse. We remember the vision sent to St. Peter which taught him that there was nothing common or unclean. Shakespeare had seen that vision. In life there is nothing common or unclean, if we only look at it in the right way.

[1] John Aubrey.   [2] Ben Jonson.   [3] Prof Raleigh

And Shakespeare speaks of everything that touches life most nearly. He uses words that we do not use now; he speaks of things we do not speak of now; but it was the fashion of his day to be more open and plain spoken than we are. And if we remember that, there is very little in Shakespeare that need hurt us even if there is a great deal which we cannot understand. And when you come to read some of the writers of Shakespeare's age and see that in them the laughter is often brutal, the horror of tragedy often coarse and crude, you will wonder more than ever how Shakespeare made his laughter so sweet and sunny, and how, instead of revolting us, he touches our hearts with his horror and pain.

About eleven years passed after Shakespeare left Stratford before he returned there again. But once having returned, he often paid visits to his old home. And he came now no more as a poor wild lad given to poaching. He came as a man of wealth and fame. He bought the best house in Stratford, called New Place, as well as a good deal of land. So before John Shakespeare died he saw his family once more important in the town.

Then as the years went on Shakespeare gave up all connection with London and the theater and settled down to a quiet country life. He planted trees, managed his estate, and showed that though he was the world's master-poet he was a good business man too. Everything prospered with him, his two daughters married well, and comfortably, and when not more than forty-three he held his first grandchild in his arms. It may be he looked forward to many happy peaceful years when death took him. He died of fever, brought on, no doubt, by the evil smells and bad air by which people lived surrounded in those days before they had learned to be clean in house and street.

Shakespeare was only fifty-two when he died. It was

in the springtime of 1616 that he died, breathing his last upon

> "The uncertain glory of an April day
> Which now shows all the beauty of the sun
> And by and by a cloud takes all away." [1]

He was buried in Stratford Parish Church, and on his grave was placed a bust of the poet. That bust and an engraving in the beginning of the first great edition of his works are the only two real portraits of Shakespeare. Both were done after his death, and yet perhaps there is no face more well known to us than that of the greatest of all poets.

Beneath the bust are written these lines:

> "Stay, passenger, why goest thou by so fast?
> Read, if thou-canst, whom envious Death hath plast·
> Within this monument, Shakespeare with whome
> Quick nature dide whose name doth deck ys tombe,
> Far more than cost, sith all yt he hath writt,
> Leaves living art but page to serve his witt."

Upon a slab over the grave is carved:

> "Good frend, for Jesus' sake forbeare
> To digg the dust encloased heare;
> Bleste be ye man yt spares thes stones,
> And curst be he yt moves my bones."

And so our greatest poet lies not beneath the great arch of Westminster but in the quiet church of the little country town in which he was born.

[1] *Two Gentlemen of Verona.*

CHAPTER XLVII

SHAKESPEARE—"THE MERCHANT OF VENICE"

In this chapter I am going to tell you in a few words the story of one of Shakespeare's plays called *The Merchant of Venice*. It is founded on an Italian story, one of a collection made by Ser Giovanni Fiorentino.

The merchant of Venice was a rich young man called Antonio. When the story opens he had ventured all his money in trading expeditions to the East and other lands. In two months' time he expects the return of his ships and hopes then to make a great deal of money. But meantime he has none to spare, and when his great friend Bassanio comes to borrow of him he cannot give him any.

Bassanio's need is urgent, for he loves the beautiful lady Portia and desires to marry her. This lady was so lovely and so rich that her fame had spread over all the world till "the four winds blow in from every coast renowned suitors." Bassanio would be among these suitors, but alas he has no money, not even enough to pay for the journey to Belmont where the lovely lady lived. Yet if he wait two months until Antonio's ships return it may be too late, and Portia may be married to another. So to supply his friend's need Antonio decides to borrow the money, and soon a Jew named Shylock is found who is willing to lend it. For Shylock was a money-lender. He lent money to people who had need of it and charged them interest. That is, besides having to pay back the full sum they had borrowed they had also to pay some extra money in return for the loan.

293

In those days Jews were ill-treated and despised, and there was great hatred between them and Christians. And Shylock especially hated Antonio, because not only did he rail against Jews and insult them, but he also lent money without demanding interest, thereby spoiling Shylock's trade. So now the Jew lays a trap for Antonio, hoping to catch him and be revenged upon his enemy. He will lend the money, he says, and he will charge no interest, but if the loan be not repaid in three months Antonio must pay as forfeit a pound of his own flesh, which Shylock may cut from any part of his body that he chooses.

To this strange bargain Antonio consents. It is but a jest, he thinks.

> "Content in faith, I'll seal to such a bond,
> And say, there is much kindness in the Jew."

But Bassanio is uneasy. "I like not fair terms," he says, "and a villain mind. You shall not seal to such a bond for me." But Antonio insists and the bond is sealed.

All being settled, Bassanio receives the money, and before he sets off to woo his lady he gives a supper to all his friends, to which he also invites Shylock. Shylock goes to this supper although to his daughter Jessica he says,

> "But wherefore should I go?
> I am not bid for love; they flatter me.
> But yet I'll go in hate, to feed upon
> The prodigal Christian."

But Jessica does not join her father in his hatred of all Christians. She indeed has given her heart to one of the hated race, and well knowing that her father will never allow her to marry him, she, that night while he is at supper with Bassanio, dresses herself in boy's clothes and steals away, taking with her a great quantity of jewels and money.

When Shylock discovers his loss he is mad with grief and rage. He runs about the streets crying for justice.

> "Justice! the law! my ducats, and my daughter!
> A sealed bag, two sealed bags of ducats,
> Of double ducats stol'n from me by my daughter!"

And all the wild boys in Venice follow after him mocking him and crying, "His stones, his daughter and his ducats!"

So finding nowhere love or sympathy but everywhere only mockery and cruel laughter, Shylock vows vengeance. The world has treated him ill, and he will repay the world with ill, and chiefly against Antonio does his anger grow bitter.

Then Antonio's friends shake their heads and say, "Let him beware the hatred of the Jew." They look gravely at each other, for it is whispered abroad that "Antonio hath a ship of rich lading wreck'd on the narrow seas."

Then let Antonio beware.

"Thou wilt not take his flesh," says one of the young merchant's friends to Shylock. "What's that good for?"

"To bait fish withal," snarls the Jew. "If it will feed nothing else it will feed my revenge. He hath disgraced me, and hindered me half a million; laughed at my losses, mocked at my gains, scorned my nation, thwarted my bargains, cooled my friends, heated mine enemies; and what's his reason? I am a Jew. Hath not a Jew eyes? Hath not a Jew hands, organs, dimensions, senses, affections, passions? Fed with the same food, hurt with the same weapons, subject to the same diseases, healed by the same means, warmed and cooled by the same winter and summer, as a Christian is? If you prick us, do we not bleed? If you tickle us, do we not laugh? If you poison us, do we not die? If you wrong us, shall we not revenge? If we are like you in the rest, we will resemble you in that. If a Jew wrong a Christian, what is his humility? Revenge. If a Christian wrong a Jew, what should his sufferance be by Christian example? Why, revenge. The villainy you teach me, I will execute, and it shall go hard but I will better the instruction."

Then let Antonio beware.

Meantime in Belmont many lovers come to woo fair Portia. With high hope they come, with anger and disappointment they go away. None can win the lady's hand. For there is a riddle here of which none knows the meaning.

When a suitor presents himself and asks for the lady's hand in marriage, he is shown three caskets, one of gold, one of silver, and one of lead. Upon the golden one is written the words, "Who chooseth me, shall gain what many men desire"; upon the silver casket are the words, "Who chooseth me, shall get as much as he deserves"; and upon the leaden one, "Who chooseth me, must give and hazard all he hath." And only whoso chooseth aright, each suitor is told, can win the lady.

This trial of all suitors had been ordered by Portia's father ere he died, so that only a worthy and true man might win his daughter. Some suitors choose the gold, some the silver casket, but all, princes, barons, counts, and dukes, alike choose wrong.

At length Bassanio comes. Already he loves Portia, and she loves him. There is no need of any trial of the caskets. Yet it must be. Her father's will must be obeyed. But what if he choose wrong. That is Portia's fear.

> "I pray you, tarry; pause a day or two
> Before you hazard; for, in choosing wrong,
> I lose your company,"

she says.

But Bassanio cannot wait:—

> "Let me choose;
> For, as I am, I live upon the rack."

And so he stands before the caskets, longing to make
a choice, yet fearful. The gold he rejects, the silver too,
and lays his hand upon the leaden casket. He opens it.
Oh, joy! within is a portrait of his lady. He has chosen
aright. Yet he can scarce believe his happiness.

"I am," he says,

> "Like one of two contending in a prize,
> That thinks he hath done well in people's eyes,
> Hearing applause, and universal shout,
> Giddy in spirit, still gazing in a doubt
> Whether those peals of praise be his or no;
> So, thrice fair lady, stand I, even so;
> As doubtful whether what I see be true,
> Until confirm'd, sign'd, ratifi'd by you"

And Portia, happy, triumphant, humble, no longer
the great lady with untold wealth, with lands and palaces
and radiant beauty, but merely a woman who has given
her love, answers:—

> "You see me, Lord Bassanio, where I stand,
> Such as I am· though, for myself alone,
> I would not be ambitious in my wish,
> To wish myself much better; yet, for you,
> I would be trebled twenty times myself;
> A thousand times more fair, ten thousand times
> More rich;
> That only to stand high on your account,
> I might in virtues, beauties, livings, friends,
> Exceed account· but the full sum of me
> Is sum of something. which, to term in gross,
> Is an unlesson'd girl, unschool'd, unpractis'd,

> Happy in this, she is not yet so old
> But she may learn, happier than this,
> She is not bred so dull but she can learn;
> Happiest of all, is, that her gentle spirit
> Commits itself to yours to be directed,
> As from her lord, her governor, her king.
> Myself, and what is mine, to you, and yours
> Is now converted; but now I was the lord
> Of this fair mansion, master of my servants,
> Queen o'er myself; and even now, but now,
> This house, these servants, and this same myself,
> Are yours, my lord"

Then as a pledge of all her love Portia gives to Bassanio a ring, and bids him never part from it so long as he shall live. And Bassanio taking it, gladly swears to keep it forever.

> "But when this ring
> Parts from this finger, then parts life from hence;
> O, then be bold to say, Bassanio's dead"

And then as if to make the joy complete, it is discovered that Portia's lady in waiting, Nerissa, and Bassanio's friend, Gratiano, also love each other, and they all agree to be married on the same day.

In the midst of this happiness the runaway couple, Lorenzo and Jessica, arrive from Venice with another of Antonio's friends who brings a letter to Bassanio. As Bassanio reads the letter all the gladness fades from his face. He grows pale and trembles. Anxiously Portia asks what troubles him.

> "I am half yourself,
> And I must freely have the half of anything
> That this same paper brings you"

And Bassanio answers:—

> "O sweet Portia,
> Here are a few of the unpleasant'st words
> That ever blotted paper! Gentle lady,

When I did first impart my love to you,
I freely told you, all the wealth I had
Ran in my veins, I was a gentleman,
And then I told you true: and yet, dear lady,
Rating myself at nothing, you shall see
How much I was a braggart. when I told you
My state was nothing, I should then have told you
That I was worse than nothing."

He is worse than nothing, for he is in debt to his friend, and that friend for him is now in danger of his life. For the three months allowed by Shylock for the payment of the debt are over, and as not one of Antonio's ships has returned, he cannot pay the money. Many friends have offered to pay for him, but Shylock will have none of their gold. He does not want it. What he wants is revenge. He wants Antonio's life, and well he knows if a pound of flesh be cut from this poor merchant's breast he must die.

And all for three thousand ducats! "Oh," cries Portia when she hears, "what a paltry sum! Pay the Jew ten times the money and tear up the bond, rather than that Antonio shall lose a single hair through Bassanio's fault."

"It is no use," she is told, "Shylock will have his bond, and nothing but his bond."

If that be so, then must Bassanio hasten to his friend to comfort him at least. So the wedding is hurried on, and immediately after it Bassanio and Gratiano haste away, leaving their new made wives behind them.

But Portia has no mind to sit at home and do nothing while her husband's friend is in danger of his life. As soon as Bassanio has gone, she gives her house into the keeping of Lorenzo and sets out for Venice. From her cousin, the great lawyer Bellario, she borrows lawyer's robes for herself, and those of a lawyer's clerk for Nerissa. And thus disguised, they reach Venice safely.

This part of the story has brought us to the fourth act

of the play, and when the curtain rises on this act we see
the Court of Justice in Venice. The Duke and all his
courtiers are present, the prisoner Antonio, with Bassanio,
and many others of his friends. Shylock is called in. The
Duke tries to soften the Jew's heart and make him turn
to mercy, in vain. Bassanio also tries in vain, and still
Bellario, to whom the Duke has sent for aid, comes not.

At this moment Nerissa, dressed as a lawyer's clerk,
enters, bearing a letter. The letter is from Bellario recommending a young lawyer named Balthazar to plead
Antonio's cause. This is, of course, none other than Portia. She is admitted, and at once begins the case. "You
stand within his danger, do you not?" she says to Antonio.

"ANTONIO I do
PORTIA Then must the Jew be merciful.
SHYLOCK. On what compulsion must I? tell me that.
PORTIA The quality of mercy is not strained;
    It droppeth, as the gentle rain from heaven
    Upon the place beneath, it is twice blessed,
    It blesseth him that gives, and him that takes·
    'Tis mightiest in the mightiest; it becomes
    The thronéd monarch better than his crown;
    His scepter shows the force of temporal power,
    The attribute to awe and majesty,
    Wherein doth sit the dread and fear of kings;
    But mercy is above this sceptr'd sway,
    It is enthronéd in the hearts of kings,
    It is an attribute to God himself;
    And earthly power doth then show likest God's
    When mercy seasons justice. Therefore, Jew,
    Though justice be thy plea, consider this—
    That in the course of justice, none of us
    Shall see salvation: we do pray for mercy,
    And that same prayer doth teach us all to render
    The deeds of mercy I have spoke thus much,
    To mitigate the justice of thy plea,
    Which if thou follow, this strict court of Venice
    Must needs give sentence 'gainst the merchant there.

SHYLOCK My deeds upon my head! I crave the law,
    The penalty and forfeit of my bond
PORTIA Is he not able to discharge the money?
BASSANIO. Yes, here I tender it for him in the court,
    Yea, twice the sum. if that will not suffice,
    I will be bound to pay it ten times o'er,
    On forfeit of my hands, my head, my heart:
    If this will not suffice, it must appear
    That malice bears down truth And I beseech you
    Wrest once the law to your authority.
    To do a great right, do a little wrong;
    And curb this cruel devil of his will
PORTIA. It must not be, there is no power in Venice
    Can alter a decree established:
    'Twill be recorded for a precedent,
    And many an error, by the same example,
    Will rush into the state; it cannot be.
SHYLOCK A Daniel come to judgement! yea, a Daniel!
    O wise young judge, how I do honour thee!
PORTIA. I pray you, let me look upon the bond
SHYLOCK. Here 'tis, most reverend doctor, here it is
PORTIA Shylock, there's thrice thy money offered thee.
SHYLOCK An oath, an oath, I have an oath in heaven:
    Shall I lay perjury upon my soul?
    No, not for Venice.
PORTIA.   Why, this bond is forfeit·
    And lawfully by this the Jew may claim
    A pound of flesh, to be by him cut off
    Nearest the merchant's heart. Be merciful,
    Take thrice thy money; bid me tear the bond
SHYLOCK. When it is paid according to the tenour.
    It doth appear you are a worthy judge;
    You know the law, your exposition
    Hath been most sound; I charge you by the law,
    Whereof you are a well-deserving pillar,
    Proceed to judgment· by my soul I swear,
    There is no power in the tongue of man
    To alter me. I stay here on my bond
ANTONIO. Most heartily I do beseech the court
    To give the judgement
PORTIA.   Why then, thus it is.
    You must prepare your bosom for his knife.

SHYLOCK. O noble judge! O excellent young man!
PORTIA For the intent and purpose of the law
    Hath full relation to the penalty,
    Which here appeareth due upon the bond.
SHYLOCK. 'Tis very true: O wise and upright judge!
    How much more elder art thou than thy looks!
PORTIA. Therefore, lay bare your bosom
SHYLOCK.   Ay, his breast·
    So says the bond;—Doth it not, noble judge?
    Nearest his heart, those are the very words.
PORTIA It is so   Are there balance here, to weigh
    The flesh?
SHYLOCK I have them ready
PORTIA. Have by some surgeon, Shylock, on your charge,
    To stop his wounds, lest he do bleed to death
SHYLOCK. Is it so nominated in the bond?
PORTIA It is not so express'd But what of that?
    'Twere good you do so much for charity.
SHYLOCK I cannot find it; 'tis not in the bond
PORTIA. Come, merchant, have you anything to say?"

Antonio answers, "But little." He is prepared for
death, and takes leave of Bassanio. But Shylock is impatient. "We trifle time," he cries; "I pray thee, pursue
sentence."

"PORTIA.   A pound of that same merchant's flesh is thine;
    The court awards it, and the law doth give it.
SHYLOCK.   Most rightful judge!
PORTIA   And you must cut this flesh from off his breast,
    The law allows it, and the court awards it
SHYLOCK.   Most learned judge!—A sentence; come, prepare.
PORTIA.   Tarry a little,—there is something else.
    This bond doth give thee here no jot of blood;
    The words expressly are, a pound of flesh,
    Take then thy bond, take thou thy pound of flesh:
    But, in the cutting it, if thou dost shed
    One drop of Christian blood, thy lands and goods
    Are, by the laws of Venice, confiscate
    Unto the state of Venice.
GRATIANO.   O upright judge!—Mark, Jew;—O learned judge!
SHYLOCK.   Is that the law?

PORTIA.   Thyself shall see the act;
  For, as thou urgest justice, be assur'd,
  Thou shalt have justice, more than thou desir'st
GRATIANO.   O learned judge,—Mark, Jew;—a learned judge!
SHYLOCK.   I take this offer then,—pay the bond thrice,
  And let the Christian go
BASSANIO   Here is the money.
PORTIA   Soft;
  The Jew shall have all justice;—soft;—no haste;—
  He shall have nothing but the penalty.
GRATIANO.   O Jew! An upright judge, a learned judge!
PORTIA.   Therefore, prepare thee to cut off the flesh.
  Shed thou no blood; nor cut thou less, nor more,
  But just a pound of flesh: if thou tak'st more,
  Or less, than a just pound,—be it but so much
  As makes it light, or heavy, in the substance,
  Or the division of the twentieth part
  Of one poor scruple,—nay, if the scale do turn
  But in the estimation of a hair,—
  Thou diest, and all thy goods are confiscate.
GRATIANO.   A second Daniel, a Daniel, Jew!
  Now, infidel, I have thee on the hip
PORTIA.   Why doth the Jew pause? Take thy forfeiture.
SHYLOCK.   Give me my principal, and let me go.
BASSANIO.   I have it ready for thee; here it is
PORTIA.   He hath refus'd it in the open court,
  He shall have merely justice, and his bond
GRATIANO.   A Daniel, still say I; a second Daniel!
  I thank thee, Jew, for teaching me that word
SHYLOCK.   Shall I not have barely my principal?
PORTIA   Thou shalt have nothing but the forfeiture,
  To be so taken at thy peril, Jew."

So, seeing himself beaten on all points, the Jew would leave the court. But not yet is he allowed to go. Not until he has been fined for attempting to take the life of a Venetian citizen, not until he is humiliated, and so heaped with disgrace and insult that we are sorry for him, is he allowed to creep away.

The learned lawyer is loaded with thanks, and Bassanio wishes to pay him nobly for his pains. But he will take nothing; nothing, that is, but the ring which glitters on Bassanio's finger. That Bassanio cannot give—it is his wife's present and he has promised never to part with it. At that the lawyer pretends anger. "I see, sir," he says:—

> "You are liberal in offers:
> You taught me first to beg, and now, methinks,
> You teach me how a beggar should be answered"

Hardly have they parted than Bassanio repents his seemingly churlish action. Has not this young man saved his friend from death, and himself from disgrace? Portia will surely understand that his request could not be refused, and so he sends Gratiano after him with the ring. Gratiano gives the ring to the lawyer, and the seeming clerk begs Gratiano for his ring, which he, following his friend's example, gives.

In the last act of the play all the friends are gathered again at Belmont. After some merry teasing upon the subject of the rings the truth is told, and Bassanio and Gratiano learn that the skillful lawyer and his clerk were none other than their young and clever wives.

BOOKS TO READ

Among the best books of Shakespeare's stories are· *Stories from Shakespeare*, by Jeanie Lang *The Shakespeare Story-Book*, by Mary M'Leod. *Tales from Shakespeare* (Everyman's Library), by C and M. Lamb.

LIST OF SHAKESPEARE'S PLAYS

Histories.—Henry VI (three parts), Richard III , Richard II , King John; Henry IV (two parts), Henry v., Henry VIII. (doubtful if Shakespeare's).

Tragedies—Titus Andronicus; Romeo and Juliet; Julius Cæsar; Hamlet; Othello, King Lear, Macbeth; Timon of Athens; Antony and Cleopatra, Coriolanus.

Comedies—Love's Labour's Lost; Two Gentlemen of Verona; Comedy of Errors, Merchant of Venice; Taming of the Shrew, A Midsummer Night's Dream, All's Well that Ends Well; Merry Wives of Windsor; Much Ado About Nothing; As You Like It; Twelfth Night; Troilus and Cressida; Measure for Measure, Pericles; Cymbeline; The Tempest; A Winter's Tale

CHAPTER XLVIII

JONSON—"EVERY MAN IN HIS HUMOUR"

OF all the dramatists who were Shakespeare's friends, of those who wrote before him, with him, and just after him, we have little room to tell. But there is one who stands almost as far above them all as Shakespeare stands above him. This is Ben Jonson, and of him we must speak.

Ben Jonson's life began in poverty, his father dying before he was born, and leaving his widow poorly provided for. When Ben was about two years old his mother married again, and this second husband was a bricklayer. Ben, however, tells us that his own father was a gentleman, belonging to a good old Scottish Border family, and that he had lost all his estates in the reign of Queen Mary. But about the truth of this we do not know, for Ben was a bragger and a swaggerer. He may not have belonged to this Scottish family, and he may have had no estates to lose. Ben first went to a little school at St. Martin's-in-the-fields in London. There, somehow, the second master of Westminster School came to know of him, became his friend, and took him to Westminster, where he paid for his schooling. But when Ben left school he had to earn a living in some way, so he became a bricklayer like his step-father, when "having a trowell in his hand he had a book in his pocket." [1]

He did not long remain a bricklayer. however, for he

[1] Fuller

could not endure the life, and next we find him a soldier
in the Netherlands. We know very little of what he did
as a soldier, and soon he was home again in England.
Here he married. His wife was a good woman, but with a
sharp tongue, and the marriage does not seem to have
been very happy. And although they had several children,
all of them died young.

And now, like Shakespeare, Jonson became an actor.
Like Shakespeare too, he wrote plays. His first play is
that by which he is best known, called *Every Man in His
Humour*. By a man's humor, Jonson means his chief
characteristic, one man, for instance, showing himself
jealous, another boastful, and so on.

It will be a long time before you will care to read *Every
Man in His Humour,* for there is a great deal in it that you
would neither understand nor like. It is a play of the
manners and customs of Elizabethan times which are so
unlike ours that we have little sympathy with them. And
that is the difference between Ben Jonson and Shakespeare.
Shakespeare, although he wrote of his own time, wrote for
all time; Jonson wrote of his own time for his own time.
Yet, in *Every Man in His Humour* there is at least one
character worthy to live beside Shakespeare's, and that
is the blustering, boastful Captain Bobadill. He talks
very grandly, but when it comes to fighting, he thinks it
best to run away and live to fight another day. If only
to know Captain Bobadill it will repay you to read *Every
Man in His Humour* when you grow up.

Here is a scene in which he shows his "humor"
delightfully:—

"Bobadill. I am a gentleman, and live here obscure, and to myself.
But were I known to Her Majesty and the Lords—observe me—
I would undertake, upon this poor head and life, for the public
benefit of the State, not only to spare the entire lives of her
subjects in general, but to save the one half, nay, three parts,

of her yearly charge in holding war, and against what enemy soever   And how would I do it, think you?

EDWARD KNOWELL.   Nay, I know not, nor can I conceive.

BOBADILL.   Why thus, sir   I would select nineteen more, to myself, throughout the land   Gentlemen, they should be of good spirit, strong and able constitution   I would choose them by an instinct, a character that I have.   And I would teach these nineteen the special rules, as your punto,[1] your reverso, your stoccata, your imbroccata, your passada, your montanto; till they could all play very near, or altogether, as well as myself.   This done, say the enemy were forty thousand strong, we twenty would come into the field the tenth of March, or thereabouts, and we would challenge twenty of the enemy.   They could not in their honour refuse us.   Well, we would kill them   Challenge twenty more, kill them, twenty more, kill them, twenty more, kill them too   And thus would we kill every man his twenty a day.   That's twenty score.   Twenty score, that's two hundred   Two hundred a day, five days a thousand   Forty thousand; forty times five, five times forty, two hundred days kills them all up by computation.   And this will I venture my poor gentleman-like carcase to perform, provided there be no treason practised upon us, by fair and discreet manhood; that is, civilly by the sword

EDWARD KNOWELL.   Why! are you so sure of your hand, Captain, at all times?

BOBADILL.   Tut! never miss thrust, upon my reputation with you

EDWARD KNOWELL.   I would not stand in Downright's state then, an you meet him, for the wealth of any one street in London"

(Knowell says this because Bobadill and Downright have had a quarrel, and Downright wishes to fight the Captain.)

"BOBADILL.   Why, sir, you mistake me.   If he were here now, by this welkin, I would not draw my weapon on him.   Let this gentleman do his mind; but I will bastinado him, by the bright sun, wherever I meet him

MATTHEW.   Faith, and I'll have a fling at him, at my distance.

EDWARD KNOWELL.   Ods so, look where he is! yonder he goes.

[DOWNRIGHT *crosses the stage.*

DOWNRIGHT.   What peevish luck have I, I cannot meet with these bragging rascals?

---

[1] This and the following are names of various passes and thrusts used in fencing. Punto is a direct hit, reverso a backward blow, and so on.

BOBADILL. It is not he, is it?

EDWARD KNOWELL. Yes, faith, it is he

MATTHEW. I'll be hanged then if that were he.

EDWARD KNOWELL. Sir, keep your hanging good for some greater
matter, for I assure you that was he.

STEPHEN Upon my reputation, it was he.

BOBADILL Had I thought it had been he, he must not have gone so.
But I can hardly be induced to believe it was he yet.

EDWARD KNOWELL. That I think, sir—   [Re-enter DOWNRIGHT.
But see, he is come again.

DOWNRIGHT. O, Pharaoh's foot, have I found you? Come, draw, to
your tools Draw, gipsy, or I'll thrash you.

BOBADILL Gentlemen of valour, I do believe in thee. Hear me—

DOWNRIGHT. Draw your weapon then

BOBADILL. Tall man, I never thought on it till now——Body of me, I
had a warrant of the peace served on me, even now as I came
along, by a water-bearer. This gentleman saw it, Master Matthew.

DOWNRIGHT. 'Sdeath! you will not draw then!

[DOWNRIGHT disarms BOBADILL and beats him.
MATTHEW runs away.

BOBADILL. Hold! hold! under thy favour forbear!

DOWNRIGHT. Prate again, as you like this, you foist[1] you. Your
consort is gone Had he staid he had shared with you, sir.

[Exit DOWNRIGHT.

BOBADILL Well, gentlemen, bear witness, I was bound to the peace,
by this good day.

EDWARD KNOWELL. No, faith, it's an ill day, Captain, never reckon
it other. But, say you were bound to the peace, the law allows
you to defend yourself That will prove but a poor excuse.

BOBADILL. I cannot tell, sir. I desire good construction in fair sort.
I never sustained the like disgrace, by heaven! Sure I was
struck with a planet thence, for I had no power to touch my
weapon.

EDWARD KNOWELL. Ay, like enough, I have heard of many that
have been beaten under a planet. Go, get you to a surgeon!
'Slid! and these be your tricks, your passadoes, and your mon-
tantos, I'll none of them."

When *Every Man in His Humour* was acted, Shakespeare took a part in it. He and Jonson must have met
each other often, must have known each other well. At

_____
[1] Fraud.

the Mermaid Tavern all the wits used to gather. For there was a kind of club founded by Sir Walter Raleigh, and here the clever men of the day met to smoke and talk, and drink not a little. And among all the clever men Jonson soon came to be acknowledged as the king and leader. We have a pleasant picture of these friendly meetings by a man who lived then. "Many were the wit-combats," he says, "betwixt Shakespeare and Ben Jonson, which two I behold like a Spanish great gallion and an English Man of War: Master Jonson (like the former) was built far higher in learning; solid, but slow in his performances. Shakespeare, with the English Man of War, lesser in bulk but lighter in sailing, could turn with all tides, tack about, and take advantage of all winds, by the quickness of his wit and invention." [1]

Another writer says in a letter to Ben,

"What things have we seen,
Done at the Mermaid! heard words that have been
So nimble, and so full of subtile flame
As if that every one from whence they came
Had meant to put his whole wit in a jest" [2]

And so we get a picture of Ben lording it in taverns. A great good fellow, a stout fellow, he rolls his huge bulk about laying down the law.

So the years went on. Big Ben wrote and fought, quarreled and made friends, drank and talked, living always on the verge of poverty. At length, in 1603, the great Queen Elizabeth died, and James of Scotland came to the English throne. All the way as he journeyed he was greeted with rejoicing. There were everywhere plays and feasts given in his honor, and soon after he arrived in London a Masque written by Jonson was played before him. The new king was fond of such enter-

[1] Thomas Fuller, *Worthies.*
[2] F. Beaumont, *Letter to Ben Jonson.*

tainments. He smiled upon Master Ben Jonson, and life became for him easier and brighter.

But shortly after this, Jonson, with two others, wrote a play in which some things were said against the Scots. With a Scottish king surrounded by Scottish lords, that was dangerous. All three soon found themselves in prison and came near losing their noses and ears. This was not the first time that Ben had been in prison, for soon after *Every Man in His Humour* was acted, he quarreled for some unknown reason with another actor. In the foolish fashion of the day they fought a duel over it, and Ben killed the other man. For this he was seized and put in prison, and just escaped being hanged. He was left off only with the loss of all his goods and a brand on the left thumb.

Now once more Jonson escaped. When he was set free, his friends gave a great feast to show their joy. But Ben had not learned his lesson, and at least once again he found himself in prison because of something he had written.

But in spite of these things the King continued to smile upon Ben Jonson. He gave him a pension and made him poet laureate, and it was now that he began to write the Masques for which he became famous. These Masques were dainty poetic little plays written for the court and often acted by the Queen and her ladies. There was much singing and dancing in them, and the dresses of the actors were gorgeous beyond description. And besides this, while the ordinary stage was still without any scenery, Inigo Jones, the greatest architect in the land, joined Ben Jonson in making his plays splendid by inventing scenery for them. This scenery was beautiful and elaborate, and was sometimes changed two or three times during the play. One of these plays called *The Masque of Blackness* was acted by the Queen and her ladies in 1605, and when we read the description of the scenery it makes us wonder and smile too at the remembrance of Wall and the Man in the Moon of which Shakespeare made such fun a few years earlier, and of which you will read in *A Midsummer Night's Dream*.

Besides his Masques, Jonson wrote two tragedies, and a number of comedies, as well as other poems. But for a great part of his life, the part that must have been the easiest and brightest, he wrote Masques for the King and court and not for the ordinary stage. He knew his own power in this kind of writing well, and he was not modest. "Next himself," he said, "only Fletcher and Chapman could make a mask."[1] He found, too, good friends among the nobles. With one he lived for five years, another gave him money to buy books, and his library became his great joy and pride.

Ben Jonson traveled too. For a time he traveled in France with Sir Walter Raleigh's son, while Sir Walter himself was shut up in the Tower. But Jonson's most famous journey is his walk to Scotland. He liked to believe that he belonged to a famous Border family, and wished to visit the land of his forefathers. So in the midsummer of 1618 he set out. We do not know how long he took to his lengthy walk, but in September he was comfortably settled in Leith, being "worthily entertained" by all the greatest and most learned men of the day. He had money enough for all his wants, for he was able to give a gold piece and two and twenty shillings to another poet less well off than himself. He was given the freedom of the city of Edinburgh and more than £200 was spent on a great feast in his honor. About Christmas he went to pay a visit to a well-known Scottish poet, William Drummond, who lived in a beautiful house called Hawthornden, a few miles from Edinburgh. There he stayed

---

[1] Conversation of Ben Jonson with Drummond of Hawthornden.

two or three weeks, during which time he and his host had
many a long talk together, discussing men and books.
Drummond wrote down all that he could remember of these
talks, and it is from them that we learn a good deal of what
we know about our poet, a good deal, perhaps, not to his
credit. We learn from them that he was vain and boastful,
a loud talker and a deep drinker. Yet there is something
about this big blustering Ben that we cannot help but like.

In January sometime, Jonson set his face homeward,
and reached London in April or May, having taken nearly
a year to pay his visit. He must have been pleased with
his journey, for on his return he wrote a poem about
Scotland. Nothing of it has come down to us, however,
except one line in which he calls Edinburgh "The heart of
Scotland, Britain's other eye."

The years passed for Jonson, if not in wealth, at least
in such comfort as his way of life allowed. For we cannot
ever think of him as happy in his own home by his own
fireside. He is rather a king in Clubland spending his
all freely, and taking no thought for the morrow. But
in 1625 King James died, and although the new King
Charles still continued the poet's pension, his tastes were
different from those of his father, and Jonson found himself and his Masques neglected. His health began to fail
too, and his library, which he dearly loved, was burned,
together with many of his unpublished manuscripts, and
so he fell on evil days.

Forgotten at court, Jonson began once more to write
for the stage. But now that he had to write for bread, it
almost seemed as if his pen had lost its charm. The plays
he wrote added nothing to his fame. They were badly
received. And so at last, in trouble for to-morrow's bread,
without wife or child to comfort him, he died on 8th
August, 1637.

He was buried in Westminster, and it was intended

to raise a fine tomb over his grave. But times were growing troublous, and the monument was still lacking, when
a lover of the poet, Sir John Young of Great Milton, in
Oxfordshire, came to do honor to his tomb. Finding it
unmarked, he paid a workman 1s. 6d. to carve above the
poet's resting-place the words, "O rare Ben Jonson."
And perhaps these simple words have done more to keep
alive the memory of the poet than any splendid monument
could have done.

CHAPTER XLIX

JONSON—"THE SAD SHEPHERD"

ALTHOUGH Ben Jonson's days ended sadly, although his later plays showed failing powers, he left behind him unfinished a Masque called *The Sad Shepherd* which is perhaps more beautiful and more full of music than anything he ever wrote. For Ben's charm did not lie in the music of his words but in the strength of his drawing of character. As another poet has said of him, "Ben as a rule—a rule which is proved by the exception—was one of the singers who could not sing; though, like Dryden, he could intone most admirably." [1]

The Sad Shepherd is a tale of Robin Hood. Here once more we find an old story being used again, for we have already heard of Robin Hood in the ballads. Robin Hood makes a great feast to all the shepherds and shepherdesses round about. All are glad to come, save one Æglamon, the Sad Shepherd, whose love, Earine, has, he believes, been drowned. But later in the play we learn that Earine is not dead, but that a wicked witch, Mother Maudlin, has enchanted her, and shut her up in a tree. She had done this in order to force Earine to give up Æglamon, her true lover, and marry her own wretched son Lorel.

When the play begins, Æglamon passes over the stage mourning for his lost love.

[1] Swinburne

314

"Here she was wont to go¹ and here¹ and here¹
Just where those daisies, pinks, and violets grow,
The world may find the spring by following her,
For other print her airy steps ne'er left
Her treading would not bend a blade of grass,
Or shake the downy blow-ball from his stalk¹
But like the soft west wind she shot along,
And where she went the flowers took thickest root—
As she had sowed them with her odorous foot"

Robin Hood has left Maid Marian, Friar Tuck, Little
John, and all his merry men to hunt the deer and make
ready the feast. And Tuck says:

"And I, the chaplain, here am left to be
Steward to-day, and charge you all in fee,
To don your liveries, see the bower dressed,
And fit the fine devices for the feast"

So some make ready the bower, the tables and the
seats, while Maid Marian, Little John and others set out
to hunt. Presently they return successful, having killed
a fine stag. Robin, too, comes home, and after loving
greetings, listens to the tale of the hunt. Then Marian
tells how, when the huntsmen cut up the stag, they threw
the bone called the raven's bone to one that sat and
croaked for it.

"Now o'er head sat a raven,
On a sere bough, a grown great bird, and hoarse¹
Who, all the while the deer was breaking up
So croaked and cried for it, as all the huntsmen,
Especially old Scathlock, thought it ominous;
Swore it was Mother Maudlin, whom he met
At the day-dawn, just as he roused the deer
Out of his lair."

Mother Maudlin was a wretched old witch, and Scathlock says he is yet more sure that the raven was she,
because in her own form he has just seen her broiling the
raven's bone by the fire, sitting "In the chimley nuik

within." While the talk went on Maid Marian had gone away. Now she returns and begins to quarrel with Robin Hood. Venison is much too good for such folk as he and his men, she says; "A starved mutton carcase would better fit their palates," and she orders Scathlock to take the venison to Mother Maudlin. Those around can scarce believe their ears, for

> "Robin and his Marian are the sum and talk
> Of all that breathe here in the green-wood walk."

Such is their love for each other. They are "The turtles of the wood," "The billing pair." No one is more astonished than Robin Hood, as he cries:

> "I dare not trust the faith of mine own senses,
> I fear mine eyes and ears: this is not Marian!
> Nor am I Robin Hood! I pray you ask her,
> Ask her, good shepherds, ask her all for me:
> Or rather ask yourselves, if she be she,
> Or I be I."

But Maid Marian only scolds the more, and at last goes away leaving the others in sad bewilderment. Of course this was not Maid Marian at all, but Mother Maudlin, the old witch, who had taken her form in order to make mischief.

Meanwhile the real Maid Marian discovers that the venison has been sent away to Mother Maudlin's. With tears in her eyes she declares that she gave no such orders, and Scathlock is sent to bring it back.

When Mother Maudlin comes to thank Maid Marian for her present, she is told that no such present was ever intended, and so she in anger curses the cook, casting spells upon him:

> "The spit stand still, no broches turn
> Before the fire, but let it burn
> Both sides and haunches, till the whole
> Converted be into one coal.

The pain we call St. Anton's fire,
The gout, or what we can desire,
To cramp a cook in every limb,
Before they dine yet, seize on him"

Soon Friar Tuck comes in. "Hear you how," he says,

"Poor Tom the cook is taken! all his joints
Do crack, as if his limbs were tied with points.
His whole frame slackens; and a kind of rack,
Runs down along the spindils of his back;
A gout, or cramp, now seizeth on his head,
Then falls into his feet; his knees are lead;
And he can stir his either hand no more
Than a dead stump, to his office, as before."

He is bewitched, that is certain. And certain too it is
that Mother Maudlin has done it. So Robin and his men
set out to hunt for her, while Friar Tuck and Much the
Miller's son stay to look after the dinner in the poor cook's
stead. Robin soon meets Mother Maudlin who has again
taken the form of Maid Marian. But this time Robin sus-
pects her. He seizes the witch by her enchanted belt.
It breaks, and she comes back to her own shape, and
Robin goes off, leaving her cursing.

Mother Maudlin then calls for Puck-hairy, her goblin.
He appears, crying:

"At your beck, madam."
"O Puck my goblin! I have lost my belt,
The strong thief, Robin Outlaw, forced it from me,"

wails Mother Maudlin. But Puck-hairy pays little attention to her complaints.

"They are other clouds and blacker threat you, dame,
You must be wary, and pull in your sails,
And yield unto the weather of the tempest
You think your power's infinite as your malice,
And would do all your anger prompts you to,
But you must wait occasions, and obey them:
Sail in an egg-shell, make a straw your mast,

A cobweb all your cloth, and pass unseen,
Till you have 'scaped the rocks that are about you.
MAUDLIN. What rocks about me?
PUCK. I do love, madam,
To show you all your dangers—when you're past them!
Come, follow me, I'll once more be your pilot,
And you shall thank me.
MAUDLIN. Lucky, my loved Goblin!'"

And here the play breaks off suddenly, for Jonson died and left it so. It was finished by another writer [1] later on, but with none of Jonson's skill, and reading the continuation we feel that all the interest is gone. However, you will be glad to know that everything comes right. The good people get happily married and all the bad people become good, even the wicked old witch, Mother Maudlin.

[1] F. G Waldron.

CHAPTER L

RALEIGH—"THE REVENGE"

SOME of you may have seen a picture of a brown-faced sailor sitting by the seashore, telling stories of travel and adventure to two boys. The one boy lies upon the sand with his chin in his hands listening but carelessly, the other with his hands clasped about his knees listens eagerly. His face is rapt, his eyes the eyes of a poet and a dreamer. This picture is called *The Boyhood of Raleigh,* and was painted by one of our great painters, Sir John Millais. In it he pictures a scene that we should like to believe was common in Sir Walter Raleigh's boyhood, but we cannot tell if it were really so or not. Beyond the fact that he was born in a white-walled thatched-roofed farmhouse, near Budleigh Salterton in Devonshire, about the year 1552, we know nothing of Raleigh's childhood. But from the rising ground near Hayes Barton, the house in which he was born, we catch sight of the sea. It seems not too much to believe that many a time Walter and his brother Carew, wandered through the woods and over the common the two and a half miles to the bay. So that from his earliest days Walter Raleigh breathed in a love and knowledge of the sea. We like to think these things, but we can only make believe to ourselves as Millais did when he went to Budleigh Salterton and painted that picture.

When still quite a boy, Walter Raleigh went to Oriel College, Oxford, but we know nothing of what he did there,

and the next we hear of him is that he is fighting for the
Huguenots in France.   How long he remained in France,
and what he did there beyond this fighting, we do not know.
But this we know, that when he went to France he was
a mere boy, with no knowledge of fighting, no knowledge
of the world.   When he left he was a man and a tried
soldier, a captain and leader of men.

When next we hear of Raleigh he is in Ireland fighting
the rebels.   There he did some brave deeds, some cruel
deeds, there he lived to the full the life of a soldier as it was
in those rough times, making all Ireland ring with his
name.   But although Raleigh had won for himself a name
among soldiers, he was as yet unknown to the Queen; his
fortune was still unmade.

You have all heard the story of how Raleigh first met
the Queen.   The first notice we have of this story is in a
book from which I have already quoted more than once—
The Worthies of England.

"This Captain Raleigh," says Fuller, "coming out of
Ireland to the English Court in good habit (his clothes
being then a considerable part of his estate), found the
Queen walking, till, meeting with a plashy place, she
seemed to scruple going thereon.   Presently Raleigh cast
and spread his new plush cloak on the ground, whereon
the Queen trod gently, rewarding him afterwards with
many suits for his so free and seasonable tender of so fair
a foot cloth."

Thomas Fuller, who wrote the book in which this story
is found, was only a boy of ten when Raleigh died, so he
could not have known the great man himself, but he must
have heard many stories about him from those who had,
and we need not disbelieve this one.   It is one of those things
which might very well have happened even if it did not.

And whether Raleigh first came into Queen Elizabeth's
notice in this manner or not, after he did become known to

her, he soon rose in her favor. He rose so quickly that he almost feared the giddy height to which he rose. According to another story of Fuller's, "This made him write in a glasse window, obvious to the Queen's eye,

'Fain would I climb, yet fear I to fall'

"Her Majesty, either espying or being shown it, did underwrite:

'If thy heart fails thee, climb not at all.'

"However he at last climbed up by the stairs of his own desert."

Honors and favors were heaped upon Raleigh, and from being a poor soldier and country gentleman he became rich and powerful, the lord of lands in five counties, and Captain of the Queen's Own Body-Guard. Haughty of manner, splendid in dress, loving jewels more than even a woman does, Raleigh became as fine a courtier as he was a brave soldier. But soldier though Raleigh was, courtier though he was, loving ease and wealth and fine clothes, he was at heart a sailor and adventurer, and the sea he had loved as a boy called to him.

Like many another of his age Raleigh, hearing the call of the waves ever in his ears, felt the desire to explore tug at his heart-strings. For in those days America had been discovered, and the quest for the famous North-West passage had begun. And Raleigh longed to set forth with other men to conquer new worlds, to find new paths across the waves. But above all he longed to fight the Spaniards, who were the great sea kings of those days. Raleigh however could not be a courtier and a sailor at one and the same time. He was meanwhile high in the Queen's favor, and she would not let him go from her. So all that Raleigh could do, was to venture his money, and fit out a ship to which he gave his own name. This he sent to sail along with others under the command of his step-brother Sir Humphrey Gilbert, who was setting out upon a voyage of discovery. It was on this voyage that Sir Humphrey found and claimed Newfoundland as an English possession, setting up there "the Arms of England in-graven in lead and infixed upon a pillar of wood." [1] But the expedition was unfortunate, most of the men and ships were lost, Sir Humphrey himself being drowned on his way home. He was brave and fearless to the last. "We are as near to Heaven by sea as by land," he said, a short time before his ship went down. One vessel only "in great torment of weather and peril of drowning" [2] reached home safely, "all the men tired with the tediousness of so unprofitable a voyage to their seeming." Yet though they knew it not they had helped to lay the foundation of Greater Britain.

Nothing daunted by this loss, six months later Raleigh sent out another expedition. This time it was to the land south of Newfoundland that the ships took their way. There they set up the arms of England, and named the new possession Virginia in honor of the virgin Queen. This expedition was little more successful than Sir Humphrey Gilbert's, but nothing seemed to discourage Raleigh. He was bent on founding a colony, and again and yet again he sent out ships and men, spending all the wealth which the Queen heaped upon him in trying to extend her dominions beyond the seas. Hope was strong within him. "I shall yet live to see it an English nation," he said.

And while Raleigh's captains tried to found a new England in the New World, Raleigh himself worked at home to bring order into the vast estates the Queen had given to him in Ireland. This land had belonged to the

[1] Hakluyt's *Voyages.*   [2] The same

rebel Earl of Desmond. At one time no doubt it had been fertile, but rebellion and war had laid it waste. "The land was so barren both of man and beast that whosoever did travel from one end of all Munster . . . . he should not meet man, woman, or child, saving in cities or towns, nor yet see any beast, save foxes, wolves, or the ravening beasts." And barren and desolate as it was when Raleigh received it, it soon became known as the best tilled land in all the country-side. For he brought workers and tenants from his old Devon home to take the place of the beggared or slain Irish. He introduced new and better ways of tilling, and also he brought to Ireland a strange new root. For it is interesting to remember that it was in Raleigh's Irish estates that potatoes were first grown in our Islands.

Raleigh took a great interest in these estates, so perhaps it was not altogether a hardship to him, finding himself out of favor with his Queen, to go to Ireland for a time. And although they had known each other before, it was then that his friendship with Spenser began. Spenser read his *Faery Queen* to Raleigh, and perhaps Raleigh read to Spenser his poem *Cynthia* written in honor of Queen Elizabeth. But of that poem nearly all has been lost. Elizabeth was not as yet very angry with Raleigh, still he felt the loss of her favor, for Spenser tells us:—

> "His song was all a lamentable lay,
> Of great unkindness and of usage hard,
> Of Cynthia, the Lady of the Sea,
> Which from her presence faultless him debarred.
> And ever and anon with singults[1] rife,
> He cried out, to make his undersong,
> 'Ah! my love's Queen, and goddess of my life,
> Who shal me pity when thou doest me wrong?'"[2]

---

[1] Sobs   [2] *"Colin Clout's come home again"*

But Raleigh soon decided to return to court, and persuaded Spenser

> "To wend with him his Cynthia to see,
>   Whose grace was great and bounty most rewardful" [1]

You know how Spenser was received and how he fared. But Raleigh himself after he had introduced his friend did not stay long at court. Quarrels with his rivals soon drove him forth again.

It was soon after this that he published the first writing which gives him a claim to the name of author. This was an account of the fight between a little ship called the *Revenge* and a Spanish fleet.

Although with the destruction of the Invincible Armada the sea power of Spain had been crippled, it had not been utterly broken, and still whenever Spanish and English ships met on the seas, there was sure to be battle. It being known that a fleet of Spanish treasure-ships would pass the Azores, islands in mid-Atlantic, a fleet of English ships under Lord Thomas Howard was sent to attack them. But the English ships had to wait so long at the Azores for the coming of the Spanish fleet that the news of the intended attack reached Spain, and the Spaniards sent a strong fleet to help and protect their treasure-ships. The English in turn hearing of this sent a swift little boat to warn Lord Thomas. The warning arrived almost too late. Many of the Englishmen were sick and ashore, and before all could be gathered the fleet of fifty-three great Spanish ships was upon them. Still Lord Thomas managed to slip away. Only the last ship, the *Revenge,* commanded by the Rear-Admiral Sir Richard Grenville, lost the wind and was caught between two great squadrons of the Spanish. Whereupon Sir Richard "was persuaded," Sir Walter says, "by the Master and

[1] *Colin Clout*

others to cut his main-sail, and cast about, and to trust to the sailing of the ship. . . . But Sir Richard utterly refused to turn from the enemy, alleging that he would rather choose to die, than to dishonour himself, his country, and her Majesty's ship, persuading his company that he would pass through the two squadrons, in despite of them."

For a little time it seemed as if Sir Richard's daring might succeed. But a great ship, the *San Philip,* came between him and the wind "and coming towards him, becalmed his sails in such sort, as the ship could neither make way, nor feel the helm: so huge and high-carged[1] was the Spanish ship. . . . The fight thus beginning at three of the clock of the afternoon continued very terrible all that evening. But the great *San Philip* having received the lower tier of the *Revenge,* discharged with cross-bar shot, shifted herself with all diligence from her sides, utterly misliking her first entertainment. . . . The Spanish ships were filled with companies of soldiers, in some two hundred, besides the mariners; in some five, in others eight hundred. In ours there were none at all beside the mariners, but the servants of the commanders and some few voluntary gentlemen only." And yet the Spaniards "were still repulsed, again and again, and at all times beaten back into their own ships, or into the seas."

In the beginning of the fight one little store ship of the English fleet hovered near. It was small and of no use in fighting. Now it came close to the *Revenge* and the Captain asked Sir Richard what he should do, and "Sir Richard bid him save himself, and leave him to his fortune." So the gallant *Revenge* was left to fight alone. For fifteen hours the battle lasted, Sir Richard himself was sorely wounded, and when far into the night the fighting ceased, two of the Spanish vessels were sunk "and in many other of the Spanish ships great slaughter was made." "But

---

[1] The meaning of the word is uncertain It may be high-charged

the Spanish ships which attempted to board the *Revenge,* as they were wounded and beaten off, so always others came in their places, she having never less than two mighty galleons by her sides and aboard her. So that ere the morning, from three of the clock the day before, there had fifteen several Armadas [1] assailed her. And all so ill approved their entertainment, as they were, by the break of day, far more willing to hearken to a composition [2] than hastily to make any more assaults or entries.

"But as the day increased so our men decreased. And as the light grew more and more, by so much more grew our discomforts. For none appeared in sight but enemies, saving one small ship called the *Pilgrim,* commanded by Jacob Whiddon, who hovered all night to see the success. But in the morning bearing with the *Revenge,* she was hunted like a hare amongst many ravenous hounds, but escaped.

"All the powder of the *Revenge* to the last barrel was now spent, all her pikes broken, forty of her best men slain, and the most part of the rest hurt. In the beginning of the fight she had but one hundred free from sickness and four score and ten sick, laid in hold upon the ballast. A small troop to man such a ship, and a weak garrison to resist so mighty an army. By those hundred all was sustained, the volleys, boarding and enterings of fifteen ships of war, besides those which beat her at large.

"On the contrary, the Spanish were always supplied with soldiers brought from every squadron; all manner of arms and powder at will. Unto ours there remained no comfort at all, no hope, no supply either of ships, men, or weapons; the masts all beaten overboard, all her tackle cut asunder, her upper work altogether razed, and in effect evened she was with the water, but the very foundation of a ship, nothing being left overhead for flight or defence.

[1] Armada here means merely a Spanish ship of war.
[2] An arrangement to cease fighting on both sides.

"Sir Richard finding himself in this distress and unable any longer to make resistance, having endured in this fifteen hours' fight the assault of fifteen several Armadas, all by turns aboard him, and by estimation eight hundred shot of great artillery besides many assaults and entries; and (seeing) that himself and the ship must needs be possessed of the enemy who were now all cast in a ring round about him, the *Revenge* not able to move one way or another, but as she was moved by the waves and billow of the sea, commanded the Master Gunner, whom he knew to be a most resolute man, to split and sink the ship, that thereby nothing might remain of glory or victory to the Spaniards: seeing in so many hours' fight, and with so great a navy, they were not able to take her, having had fifteen hours' time, above ten thousand men, and fifty and three sail of men of war to perform it withal. And (he) persuaded the company, or as many as he could induce, to yield themselves unto God, and to the mercy of none else, but as they had, like valiant resolute men, repulsed so many enemies, they should not now shorten the honour of their nation, by prolonging their own lives by a few hours, or a few days. The Master Gunner readily condescended and divers others. But the Captain and the Master were of another opinion, and besought Sir Richard to have care of them, alleging that the Spaniard would be as ready to entertain a composition as they were willing to offer the same. And (they said) that there being divers sufficient and valiant men yet living, and whose wounds were not mortal, they might do their country and their Prince acceptable service hereafter. And whereas Sir Richard alleged that the Spaniards should never glory to have taken one ship of her Majesty, seeing they had so long and so notably defended themselves; they answered that the ship had six foot water in hold, three shot under water, which were so weakly stopped as with the first working of the sea, she must needs sink, and was besides so crushed and bruised, as she could never be removed out of the place.

"And as the matter was thus in dispute, and Sir Richard refusing to hearken to any of those reasons, the Master of the *Revenge* (while the Captain won unto him the greater party) was convoyed aboard the *General Don Alfonso Baçan*. Who (finding none overhasty to enter the *Revenge* again, doubting lest Sir Richard would have blown them up and himself, and perceiving by the report of the Master of the *Revenge* his dangerous disposition) yielded that all their lives should be saved, the company sent for England, and the better sort to pay such reasonable ransom as their estate would bear, and in the mean season to be free from galley or imprisonment To this he so much the better condescended as well, as I have said, for fear of further loss and mischief to themselves, as also for the desire he had to recover Sir Richard Grenville, whom for his notable valour he seemed greatly to honour and admire.

"When this answer was returned, and that safety of life was promised, the common sort being now at the end of their peril the most drew back from Sir Richard and the Master Gunner, (it) being no hard matter to dissuade men from death to life. The Master Gunner finding himself and Sir Richard thus prevented and matsered by the greater number, would have slain himself with a sword, had he not been by force with-held and locked into his cabin. Then the General sent many boats aboard the *Revenge,* and divers of our men fearing Sir Richard's disposition, stole away aboard the *General* and other ships. Sir Richard thus over-matched was sent unto by Alfonso Baçan to remove out of the *Revenge,* the ship being marvellous unsavoury, filled with blood and bodies of dead, and wounded men, like a slaughterhouse.

"Sir Richard answered he might do with his body what he list, for he esteemed it not. And as he was carried out of the ship he swooned, and reviving again desired the company to pray for him.

"The General used Sir Richard with all humanity, and left nothing unattempted that tended to his recovery, highly commending his valour and worthiness, and greatly bewailing the danger in which he was, being unto them a rare spectacle, and a resolution seldom approved, to see one ship turn toward so many enemies, to endure the charge and boarding of so many huge Armadas, and to resist and repel the assaults and entries of so many soldiers.

"There were slain and drowned in this fight well near one thousand of the enemies, and two special commanders . . . . besides divers others of special account.

"Sir Richard died as it is said, the second or third day aboard the *General* and was by them greatly bewailed. What became of his body, whether it were buried in the sea or on the land, we know not. The comfort that remaineth to his friends is, that he hath ended his life honourably in respect of the reputation won to his nation and country and of the same to his posterity, and that being dead, he hath not outlived his own honour."

This gallant fight of the little *Revenge* against the huge navy of Spain is one of the great things in the story of the sea; that is why I have chosen it out of all that Sir Walter wrote to give you as a specimen of English prose in Queen Elizabeth's time. As long as brave deeds are remembered, it will be told how Sir Richard Grenville "walled round with wooden castles on the wave" bid defiance to the might and pride of Spain, "hoping the splendour of some lucky star." [1] The fight was a hopeless one from the very beginning, but it was as gallant a one as ever took place. Even his foes were forced to admire

[1] Gervase Markham

Sir Richard's dauntless courage, for when he was carried aboard Don Alfonso's ship "the captains and gentlemen went to visit him, and to comfort him in his hard fortune, wondering at his courageous stout heart for that he showed not any sign of faintness nor changing of colour. But feeling the hour of death to approach, he spake these words in Spanish and said, 'Here die I, Richard Grenville, with a joyful and quiet mind, for that I have ended my life as a true soldier ought to do, and hath fought for his country, Queen, religion, and honour, whereby my soul most joyful departeth out of this body, and shall always leave behind it an everlasting fame of a valiant and true soldier that hath done his duty as he was bound to do.' When he had finished these or other like words he gave up the Ghost, with great and stout courage, and no man could perceive any true signs of heaviness in him." [1]

Poets of the time made ballads of this fight. Raleigh wrote of it as you have just read, and in our own day the great laureate Lord Tennyson made the story live again in his poem *The Revenge.* Tennyson tells how after the fight a great storm arose:

"And or ever that evening ended a great gale blew
And a wave like the wave that is raised by an earthquake grew,
Till it smote on their hulls and their sails and their masts and their flags,
And the whole sea plunged and fell on the shot-shatter'd navy of Spain.
And the little *Revenge* herself went down by the island crags
To be lost evermore in the main."

So neither the gallant captain nor his little ship were led home to the triumph of Spain.

It is interesting to remember that had it not been for the caprice of the Queen, Raleigh himself would have been in Sir Richard Grenville's place. For he had orders to go on this voyage, but at the last moment he was recalled, and Sir Richard was sent instead.

[1] Linschoten's Large Testimony in *Hakluyt's Voyages*

CHAPTER LI

RALEIGH—"THE HISTORY OF THE WORLD"

Soon after the fight with the *Revenge,* the King of Spain made ready more ships to attack England. Raleigh then persuaded Queen Elizabeth that it would be well to be beforehand with the Spaniards and attack their ships at Panama. So to this end a fleet was gathered together. But the Queen sent only two ships, various gentlemen provided others, and Raleigh spent every penny of his own that he could gather in fitting out the remainder. He was himself chosen Admiral of the Fleet. So at length he started on an expedition after his own heart.

But he had not gone far, when a swift messenger was sent to him ordering him to return. Unwillingly he obeyed, and when he reached home he was at once sent to the Tower a prisoner. This time the Queen was really angry with him; in her eyes Raleigh's crime was a deep one, for he had fallen in love with one of her own maids of honor, Mistress Elizabeth Throgmorton, and the Queen had discovered it. Elizabeth allowed none of her favorites to love any one but herself, so she punished Raleigh by sending him to the Tower.

Mistress Throgmorton was also made a prisoner. After a time, however, both prisoners were set free, though they were banished from court. They married and went to live at Sherborne where Raleigh busied himself improving his beautiful house and laying out the garden. For though set free Raleigh was still in disgrace. But we may believe that he found some recompense for his Queen's anger in his wife's love.

In his wife Raleigh found a life-long comrade. Through all good and evil fortune she stood by him, she shared his hopes and desires, she sold her lands to give him money for his voyages, she shared imprisonment with him when it came again, and after his death she never ceased to mourn his loss. How Raleigh loved her in return we learn from the few letters written to her which have come down to us. She is "Sweetheart" "Dearest Bess," and he tells to her his troubles and his hopes as to a staunch and true friend.

We cannot follow Raleigh through all his restless life, it was so full and varied that the story of it would fill a long book. He loved fighting and adventure, he loved books too, and soon we find him back in London meeting Ben Jonson and Shakespeare, and all the great writers of the age at the Mermaid Club. For Raleigh knew all the great men of his day, among them Sir Robert Bruce Cotton of whom you heard in connection with the adventures of the Beowulf Manuscript.

But soon, in spite of his love for his wife, in spite of his interest in his beautiful home, in spite of his many friends, Raleigh's restless spirit again drove him to the sea, and he set out on a voyage of discovery and adventure. This time he sailed to Guiana in South America, in search of Eldorado, the fabled city of gold. And this time he was not called back by the Queen, but although he reached South America and sailed up the Orinoco and the Caroni he "returned a beggar and withered"[1] without having found the fabled city. Yet his belief in it was as strong as ever. He had not found the fabled city but he believed it was to be found, and when he came home he wrote an account of his journey because some of his enemies said

[1] Raleigh's *Discovery of Guiana.*

that he had never been to Guiana at all but had been hiding in Cornwall all the time. In this book he said that he was ready again to "lie hard, to fare worse, to be subjected to perils, to diseases, to ill savours, to be parched and withered"[1] if in the end he might succeed.

Raleigh was ready to set off again at once to discover more of Guiana. But instead he joined the Fleet and went to fight the Spanish, who were once more threatening England, and of all enemies Raleigh considered the Spaniards the greatest.

Once again the English won a splendid victory over Spain. Before the town of Cadiz eight English ships captured or destroyed thirty Spanish great and little. They took the town of Cadiz and razed its fortifications to the ground. Raleigh bore himself well in this fight, so well, indeed, that even his rival, Essex, was bound to confess "that which he did in the sea-service could not be bettered."

And now after five years' banishment from the Queen's favor, Raleigh was once more received at court. But we cannot follow all the ups and downs of his court life, for we are told "Sir Walter Raleigh was in and out at court, so often that he was commonly called the tennis ball of fortune." And so the years went on. Raleigh became a Member of Parliament, and was made Governor of Jersey. He fought and traveled, attended to his estates in Ireland, to his business in Cornwall, to his governorship in Jersey. He led a stirring, busy life, fulfilling his many duties, fighting his enemies, until in 1603 the great Queen, whose smile or frown had meant so much to him, died.

Then soon after the new king came to the throne, it was seen that Raleigh's day at court was indeed at an end. For James had been told that Sir Walter was among those

[1] Raleigh's *Discovery of Guiana.*

who were unwilling to receive him as king. Therefore he was little disposed to look graciously on the handsome daring soldier-sailor.

One by one Raleigh's posts of honor were taken from him. He was accused of treason and once more found himself a prisoner in the Tower. He was tried, and in spite of the fact that nothing was proved against him, he was condemned to die. The sentence was changed, however, to imprisonment for life.

Raleigh was not left quite lonely in the Tower. His wife and children, whom he dearly loved, were allowed to come to live beside him. The governor was kind to him and allowed his renowned prisoner to use his garden. And there in a little hen-house Raleigh amused himself by making experiments in chemistry, and discovering among other things how to distill fresh water from salt water. He found new friends too in the Queen and in her young son Henry, Prince of Wales. It was a strange friendship and a warm one that grew between the gallant boy-prince of ten and the tried man of fifty. Prince Henry loved to visit Raleigh in the Tower and listen to the tales of his brave doings by sea and land in the days when he was free. Raleigh helped Prince Henry to build a model ship, and the Prince asked Raleigh's advice and talked over with him all his troubles. His generous young heart grieved at the thought of his friend's misfortunes. "Who but my father would keep such a bird in such a cage," he said with boyish indignation.

And it was for this boy friend that Raleigh began the book by which we know him best, his *History of the World.* Never has such a great work been attempted by a captive. To write the history of even one country must mean much labor, much reading, much thought. To write a history of the world still more. And I have told you about Raleigh because with him begins an interest in history beyond the bounds of our own island. Before him our historians had only written of England.

It gives us some idea of the large courage of Raleigh's mind when we remember that he was over fifty when he began this tremendous piece of work for the sake of a boy he loved. Raleigh labored at this book for seven years or more. He was allowed to have his own books in prison. Sir Robert Cotton lent him others, and learned friends came to talk over his book with him and help him. And so the pile of written sheets grew. But the book was never finished, for long before the first volume was ready the brave young prince for whom it was written died.

To Raleigh, this was the cruellest blow fate ever dealt him, for with the death of Prince Henry died his hope of freedom. In spite of his long imprisonment, Raleigh had never lost hope of one day regaining his freedom. Prince Henry just before his death had wrung an unwilling promise from the King his father that Raleigh should be set free. But when the Prince died the King forgot his promise.

"O eloquent, just and mighty death!" Raleigh says in the last lines of his book, "whom none could advise, thou hast persuaded, what none hath dared, thou hast done; and whom all the world hath flattered, thou only hast cast out of the world and despised; thou hast drawn together all the far stretching greatness, all the pride, cruelty, and ambition of man, and covered it all over with these two narrow words Hic Jacet.

"Lastly, whereas this book by the title it hath, calls itself, the first part of *The General History of the World*, implying a second and third volume, which I also intended and have hewn out, besides many other discouragements, persuading my silence, it hath pleased God to take that glorious prince out of the world, to whom they were directed; whose unspeakable and never enough lamented loss hath taught me to say with Job, my heart is turned to mourning and my organ into the voice of them that weep."

Raleigh begins his great book with the Creation and brings it down to the third Macedonian war, which ended in 168 B.C. So you see he did not get far. But although when he began he had intended to write much more, he never meant to bring his history down to his own time. "I know that it will be said by many," he writes in his preface, "that 1 might have been more pleasing to the reader if I had written the story of mine own times, having been permitted to draw water as near the well-head as another. To this I answer that whosoever in writing a modern history, shall follow truth too near the heels, it may haply strike out his teeth."

Raleigh feels it much safer to write "of the elder times." But even so, he says there may be people who will think "that in speaking of the past I point at the present," and that under the names of those long dead he is showing the vices of people who are alive. "But this I cannot help though innocent," he says.

Raleigh's fears were not without ground and at one time his history was forbidden by King James "for being too saucy in censuring princes. He took it much to heart, for he thought he had won his spurs and pleased the King extraordinarily." He had hoped to please the King and win freedom again, but his hopes were shattered.

At last, however, the door of his prison was opened. It was a golden key that opened it. For Raleigh promised, if he were set free, to seek once more the fabled Golden City, and this time he swore to find it and bring home treasure untold to his master the King.

So once more the imprisoned sea-bird was free, and gathering men and ships he set forth on his last voyage. He set forth bearing with him all his hopes, all his fortune.

For both Raleigh and his wife almost beggared themselves to get money to fit out the fleet, and with him as captain sailed his young son Walter.

A year later Raleigh returned. But he returned without his son, with hopes broken, fortune lost. Many fights and storms had he endured, many hardships suffered, but he had not found the Golden City. His money was spent, his ships shattered, his men in mutiny, and hardest of all to bear, his young son Walter lay dead in far Guiana, slain in a fight with Spaniards. How Raleigh grieved we learn from his letter to his wife, "I was loath to write," he says, "because I knew not how to comfort you; and, God knows, I never knew what sorrow meant till now. . . . Comfort your heart, dearest Bess, I shall sorrow for us both, I shall sorrow less because I have not long to sorrow, because not long to live. . . . I have written but that letter, for my brains are broken, and it is a torment for me to write, and especially of misery. . . . The Lord bless and comfort you that you may bear patiently the death of your most valiant son."

Raleigh came home a sad and ruined man, and had the pity of the King been as easily aroused as his fear of the Spaniards he had surely been allowed to live out the rest of his life in peaceful quiet. But James, who shuddered at the sight of a drawn sword, feared the Spaniards and had patched up an imaginary peace with them. And now when the Spanish Ambassador rushed into the King's Chamber crying "Pirates! Pirates!" Raleigh's fate was sealed.

Raleigh had broken the peace in land belonging to "our dear brother the King of Spain" said James, therefore he must die.

Thus once again, Raleigh found himself lodged in the Tower. But so clearly did he show that he had broken no peace where no peace was, that it was found impossible to put him to death because of what he had done in Guiana. He was condemned to death, therefore, on the old charge of treason passed upon him nearly fifteen years before. He met death bravely and smiling. Clad in splendid clothes such as he loved, he mounted the scaffold and made his farewell speech to those around.

" 'Tis a sharp medicine, but it is a sound cure for all diseases," he said smiling to the Sheriff as he felt the edge of the ax. Then he laid his head upon the block.

"Thus," says the first writer of Raleigh's life, "have we seen how Sir Walter Raleigh who had been one of the greatest scourges of Spain, was made a sacrifice to it."

"So may we say to the memory of this worthy knight," says Fuller, " 'Repose yourself in this our Catalogue under what topic you please, statesman, seaman, soldier, learned writer or what not.' His worth unlocks our cabinets and provides both room and welcome to entertain him . . . so dexterous was he in all his undertakings in Court, in camp, by sea, by land, with sword, with pen." [1]

BOOK TO READ

Westward Ho! by Charles Kingsley may be read in illustration of this chapter.

---

[1] Fuller's *Worthies.*

CHAPTER LII

BACON—NEW WAYS OF WISDOM

WHEN we are little, there are many things we cannot understand; we puzzle about them a good deal perhaps, and then we ask questions. And sometimes the grown-ups answer our questions and make the puzzling things clear to us, sometimes they answer yet do not make the puzzling things any clearer to us, and sometimes they tell us not to trouble, that we will understand when we grow older. Then we wish we could grow older quick, for it seems such a long time to wait for an answer. But worst of all, sometimes the grown-ups tell us not to talk so much and not to ask so many questions.

The fact is, though perhaps I ought not to tell you, grown-ups don't know everything. That is not any disgrace either, for of course no one can know everything, not even father or mother. And just as there are things which puzzle little folks, there are things which puzzle big folks. And just as among little folks there are some who ask more questions and who "want to know" more than others, so among grown-ups there are some who more than others seek for the answer to those puzzling questions. These people we call philosophers. The word comes from two Greek words, *philos* loving, *sophos* wise, and means loving wisdom. In this chapter I am going to tell you about Francis Bacon, the great philosopher who lived in the times of Elizabeth and James. I do not think that I can quite make you understand what philosophy really means, or what his learned books were about, nor do I think you will care to read them for a long time to come. But you will find the life of Francis Bacon very interesting. It is well, too, to know about Bacon, for with him began a new kind of search for wisdom. The old searchers after truth had tried to settle the questions which puzzled them by turning to imaginary things, and by mere thinking. Bacon said that we must answer these questions by studying not what was imaginary, but what was real—by studying nature. So Bacon was not only a lover of truth but was also the first of our scientists of to-day. Scientist comes from the Latin word *scio* to know, and Science means that which we know by watching things and trying things, —by making experiments. And although Bacon did not himself find out anything new and useful to man, he pointed out the road upon which others were to travel.

It was upon a cold day in January in 1560 that Francis Bacon "came crying into the world."[1] He was born in a fine house and was the child of great people, his father being Sir Nicholas Bacon, Lord Keeper of the Great Seal. But although his father was one of the most important men in the kingdom, we know little about Francis as a boy. We know that he met the Queen and that he must have been a clever little boy, for she would playfully call him her "young Lord Keeper." Once too when she asked him how old he was, he answered, "Two years younger than your Majesty's happy reign." So if you know when Elizabeth began to reign you will easily remember when Bacon was born.

Francis was the youngest of a big family, and when he was little more than twelve years old he went to Trinity College, Cambridge. Even in those days, when people went to college early, this was young.

[1] James Spedding.

For three years Bacon remained at college and then
he went to France with the English ambassador. While
he was in France his father died and Bacon returned
home. At eighteen he thus found himself a poor lad with
his future to make and only his father's great name and
his own wits to help him. He made up his mind to
take Law as his profession. So he set himself quietly
to study.

He worked hard, for from the very beginning he meant
to get on, he meant to be rich and powerful. So he bowed
low before the great, he wrote letters to them full of
flattery, he begged and promised.

Bacon is like a man with two faces. We look at one
and we see a kindly face full of pity and sorrow for all
wrong and pain that men must suffer, we see there a longing to help man, to be his friend. We look at the other
face and there we see the greed of gain, the desire for
power and place. Yet it may be that Bacon only strove
to be great so that he might have more power and free-
down to be pitiful. In spite of Bacon's hard work, in spite
of his flattery and begging, he did not rise fast. After five
years we find him indeed a barrister and a Member of
Parliament, but among the many great men of his age he
was still of little account. He had not made his mark,
in spite of the fact that the great Lord Burleigh was his
uncle, in spite of the fact that Elizabeth had liked him as
a boy. Post after post for which he begged was given to
other men. He was, he said himself, "like a child following a bird, which when he is nearest flieth away and lighteth
a little before, and then the child after it again, and so in
infinitum. I am weary of it."

But one friend at court he found in the Earl of Essex,
the favorite of Elizabeth, the rival of Raleigh. Essex,
however, who could win so much favor for himself, could
win none for Francis Bacon. Being able to win nothing

from the Queen, on his own account Essex gave his friend an estate worth about £1800. But although that may have been some comfort to Bacon, it did not win for him greatness in the eyes of the world, the only greatness for which he longed. As to the Queen, she made use of him when it pleased her, but she had no love for him. "Though she cheered him much with the bounty of her countenance," says an early writer of Bacon's life, his friend and chaplain,[1] "yet she never cheered him with the bounty of her hand." It was, alas, that bounty of the hand that Bacon begged for and stooped for all through his life. Yet he cared nothing for money for its own sake, for what he had, he spent carelessly. He loved to keep high state, he loved grandeur, and was always in debt.

Essex through all his brilliant years when the Queen smiled upon him stuck by his friend, for him he spent his "power, might, authority and amity" in vain. When the dark hours came and Essex fell into disgrace, it was Bacon who forgot his friendship.

You will read in history-books of how Essex, against the Queen's orders, left Ireland, and coming to London, burst into her presence one morning before she was dressed. You will read of how he was disgraced and imprisoned. At first Bacon did what he could for his friend, and it was through his help that Essex was set free. But even then, Bacon wrote to the Earl, "I confess I love some things much better than I love your lordship, as the Queen's service, her quiet and contentment, her honour, her favour, the good of my country, and the like. Yet I love few persons better than yourself, both for gratitude's sake, and for your own virtues."

Set free, Essex rushed into passionate, futile rebellion. Again he was made prisoner and tried for high treason. It was then that Bacon had to choose between friend and

---

[1] William Rawley

Queen. He chose his Queen and appeared in court against his friend. To do anything else, Bacon told himself, had been utterly useless. Essex was now of no more use to him, he was too surely fallen. To cling to him could do no good, but would only bring the Queen's anger upon himself also. And yet he had written: "It is friendship when a man can say to himself, I love this man without respect of utility. . . . I make him a portion of my own wishes."

He wrote that as a young man, later he saw nothing in friendship beyond use.

The trial of Essex must have been a brilliant scene. The Earl himself, young, fair of face, splendidly clad, stood at the bar. He showed no fear, his bearing was as proud and bold as ever, "but whether his courage were borrowed and put on for the time or natural, it were hard to judge."[1] The Lord Treasurer, the Lord High Steward, too, were there and twenty-five peers, nine earls, and sixteen barons to try the case. Among the learned counsel sat Bacon, a disappointed man of forty. There was nothing to single him out from his fellows save that he was the Earl's friend, and as such might be looked upon to do his best to save him.

As the trial went on, however, Bacon spoke, not to save, but to condemn. Did no memory of past kindliness cross his mind as he likened his friend to "Cain, that first murderer," as he complained to the court that too much favor was shown to the prisoner, that he had never before heard "so silly a defense of such great and notorious treasons." The Earl answered in his own defense again and yet again. But at length he was silent. His case was hopeless, and he was condemned to death. He was executed on 25th February, 1601.

Perhaps Bacon could not have saved his friend from

[1] John Chamberlain.

death, but had he used his wit to try at least to save instead of helping to condemn, he would have kept his own name from a dark blot. But a greater betrayal of friendship was yet to follow. Though Essex had been wild and foolish the people loved him, and now they murmured against the Queen for causing his death. Then it was thought well, that they should know all the blackness of his misdeeds, and it was Bacon who was called upon to write the story of them.

Even from this he did not shrink, for he hoped for great rewards. But, as before, the Queen used him, and withheld "the bounty of her hand"; from her he received no State appointment. He did indeed receive £1200 in money. It was scarcely as much as Essex had once given him out of friendship. To Bacon it seemed too small a reward for his betrayal of his friend, even although it had seemed to mean loyalty to his Queen. "The Queen hath done somewhat for me," he wrote, "though not in the proportion I hoped." And so in debt and with a blotted name, Bacon lived on until Queen Elizabeth died. But with the new King his fortunes began to rise. First he was made Sir Francis Bacon, then from one honor to another he rose until he became at last Lord High Chancellor of England, the highest judge in the land. A few months later, he was made a peer with the title of Baron Verulam. A few years later at the age of sixty he went still one step higher and became Viscount St. Albans.

Bacon chose the name of Baron Verulam from the name of the old Roman city Verulamium which was afterwards called St. Albans. It was near St. Albans that Bacon had built himself a splendid house, laid out a beautiful garden, and planted fine trees, and there he kept as great state as the King himself.

He had now reached his highest power. He had published his great work called the *Novum Organum* or *New*

Instrument in which he taught men a new way of wisdom. He was the greatest judge in the land and a peer of the realm. He had married too, but he never had any children, and we know little of his home life.

It seemed as if at last he had all he could wish for, as if his life would end in a blaze of glory. But instead of that in a few short weeks after he became Viscount St. Albans, he was a disgraced and fallen man.

He had always loved splendor and pomp, he had always spent more than he could afford. Now he was accused of taking bribes, that is, he was accused of taking money from people and, instead of judging fairly, of judging in favor of those who had given him most money. He was accused, in fact, of selling justice. That he should sell justice is the blackest charge that can be brought against a judge. At first Bacon could not believe that any one would dare to attack him. But when he heard that it was true, he sank beneath the disgrace, he made no resistance. His health gave way. On his sick-bed he owned that he had taken presents, yet to the end he protested that he had judged justly. He had taken the bribes indeed, but they had made no difference to his judgments. He had not sold justice.

He made his confession and stood to it. "My lords," he said, "it is my act, my hand, my heart. I beseech your lordships be merciful to a broken reed."

Bacon was condemned to pay a fine of £40,000, to be imprisoned during the King's pleasure, never more to have office of any kind, never to sit in Parliament, "nor come within the verge of the Court."

"I was the justest judge that was in England these fifty years," said Bacon afterwards. "But it was the justest censure in Parliament that was these two hundred years."

Bacon's punishment was not as heavy as at first sight

it seems, for the fine was forgiven him, and "the king's pleasure," made his imprisonment in the Tower only a matter of a few days.

And now that his life was shipwrecked, though he never ceased to long to return to his old greatness, he gave all his time to writing and to science. He spent many peaceful hours in the garden that he loved. "His lordship," we are told, "was a very contemplative person, and was wont to contemplate in his delicious walks." He was generally accompanied by one of the gentlemen of his household "that attended him with ink and paper ready to set down presently his thoughts." [1]

He was not soured or bitter. "Though his fortunes may have changed," says one of his household,[2] "yet I never saw any change in his mien, his words, or his deeds, towards any man. But he was always the same both in sorrow and joy, as a philosopher ought to be."

Bacon was now shut out from honorable work in the world, but he had no desire to be idle. "I have read in books," he wrote, "that it is accounted a great bliss to have Leisure with Honour. That was never my fortune. For time was I had Honour without Leisure; and now I have Leisure without Honour. But my desire is now to have Leisure without Loitering." So now he lived as he himself said "a long cleansing week of five years." Then the end came.

It was Bacon's thirst for knowledge that caused his death. One winter day when the snow lay on the ground he drove out in his coach. Suddenly as he drove along looking at the white-covered fields and roads around, the thought came to him that food might be kept good by means of snow as easily as by salt. He resolved to try, so, stopping his coach, he went into a poor woman's cottage and bought a hen. The woman killed and made

'BACON WAS GENERALLY ACCOMPANIED BY A GENTLEMAN OF HIS HOUSEHOLD,
WHO WAS READY TO SET DOWN HIS THOUGHTS'

ready the hen, but Bacon was so eager about his experiment that he stuffed it himself with snow. In doing this he was so chilled by the cold that he became suddenly ill, too ill to return home. He was taken to a house near "where they put him into a good bed warmed with a pan"[1] and there after a few days he died.

This little story of how Bacon came by his death gives a good idea of how he tried to make use of his philosophy. He was not content with thinking and speculating, that is, looking at ideas. Speculate comes from the Latin *speculari,* to spy out. He wanted to experiment too. And although in those days no one had thought about it, we now know that Bacon was quite right and that meat can be kept by freezing it. And it is pleasant to know that before Bacon died he was able to write that the experiment had succeeded "excellently well."

In his will Bacon left his name and memory "to men's charitable speeches, to foreign nations and to the next ages," and he was right to do so, for in spite of all the dark shadows that hang about his name men still call him great. We remember him as a great man among great men; we remember him as the fore-runner of modern science; we remember him for the splendid English in which he wrote.

And yet, although Bacon's English is clear, strong, and fine, although Elizabethan English perhaps reached in him its highest point, he himself despised English. He did not believe that it was a language that would live. And as he wanted his books to be read by people all over the world and in all time to come, he wrote his greatest books in Latin. He grieved that he had wasted time in writing English, and he had much that he wrote in English translated into Latin during his lifetime.

It seems strange to us now that in an age when Spenser and Shakespeare had shown the world what the English

[1] J. Aubrey

tongue had power to do that any man should have been able to disbelieve in its greatness. But so it was, and Bacon translated his books into Latin so that they might live when English books "were not."

I will not weary you with a list of all the books Bacon wrote. Although it is not considered his greatest work, that by which most people know him is his *Book of Essays*. By an essay, Bacon meant a testing or proving. In the short chapters of his essays he tries and proves many things such as Friendship, Study, Honor; and when you come to read these essays you will be surprised to find how many of the sentences are known to you already. They have become "household words," and without knowing it we repeat Bacon's wisdom. But we miss in them something of human kindliness. Bacon's wisdom is cool, calm, and calculating, and we long sometimes for a little warmth, a little passion, and not so much "use."

The essays are best known, but the *New Atlantis* is the book that you will best like to read, for it is something of a story, and of it I will tell you a little in the next chapter.

CHAPTER LIII

BACON—THE HAPPY ISLAND

ATLANTIS was a fabled island of the Greeks which lay somewhere in the Western Sea. That island, it was pretended, sank beneath the waves and was lost, and Bacon makes believe that he finds another island something like it in the Pacific Ocean and calls it the New Atlantis. Here, as in More's Utopia, the people living under just and wise laws, are happy and good. Perhaps some day you will be interested enough to read these two books together and compare them. Then one great difference will strike you at once. In the Utopia all is dull and gray, only children are pleased with jewels, only prisoners are loaded with golden chains. In the New Atlantis jewels and gold gleam and flash, the love of splendor and color shows itself almost in every page.

Bacon wastes no time in explanations but launches right into the middle of his story. "We sailed from Peru," he says, "(where we had continued by the space of one whole year) for China and Japan, by the South Sea, taking with us victuals for twelve months." And through all the story we are not told who the "we" were or what their names or business. There were, we learn, fifty-one persons in all on board the ship. After some months' good sailing they met with storms of wind. They were driven about now here, now there. Their food began to fail, and finding themselves in the midst of the greatest wilderness of

349

waters in the world, they gave themselves up as lost. But presently one evening they saw upon one hand what seemed like darker clouds, but which in the end proved to be land.

"And after an hour and a half's sailing, we entered into a good haven, being the port of a fair city, not great indeed, but well built, and that gave a pleasant view from the sea.

"And we, thinking every minute long till we were on land, came close to the shore, and offered to land. But straightways we saw divers of the people, with bastons in their hands, as it were forbidding us to land; yet without any cries or fierceness, but only as warning us off by signs that they made. Whereupon being not a little discomforted, we were advising with ourselves what we should do. During which time there made forth to us a small boat, with about eight persons in it; whereof one of them had in his hand a tipstaff [1] of a yellow cane, tipped at both ends with blue, who came aboard our ship, without any show of distrust at all. And when he saw one of our number present himself somewhat before the rest, he drew forth a little scroll of parchment (somewhat yellower than our parchment, and shining like the leaves of writing-tables, but otherwise soft and flexible), and delivered it to our foremost man. In which scroll were written in ancient Hebrew, and in ancient Greek, and in good Latin of the School, and in Spanish, these words: 'Land ye not, none of you. And provide to be gone from this coast within sixteen days, except ye have further time given you. Meanwhile, if ye want fresh water, or victual, or help for your sick, or that your ship needeth repair, write down your wants, and ye shall have that which belongeth to mercy.'

"This scroll was signed with a stamp of Cherubim's

[1] Staff of office.

wings, not spread but hanging downwards, and by them a cross

"This being delivered, the officer returned, and left only a servant with us to receive our answer. Consulting thereupon among ourselves, we were much perplexed. The denial of landing and hasty warning us away troubled us much. On the other side, to find that the people had languages and were so full of humanity, did comfort us not a little. And above all, the sign of the cross to that instrument was to us a great rejoicing, and as it were a certain presage of good.

"Our answer was in the Spanish tongue: 'That for our ship, it was well; for we had rather met with calms and contrary winds than any tempests. For our sick, they were many, and in very ill case, so that if they were not permitted to land, they ran danger of their lives.'

"Our other wants we set down in particular; adding, 'that we had some little store of merchandise, which if it pleased them to deal for, it might supply our wants without being chargeable unto them.'

"We offered some reward in pistolets unto the servant, and a piece of crimson velvet to be presented to the officer. But the servant took them not, nor would scarce look upon them; and so left us, and went back in another little boat which was sent for him."

About three hours after the answer had been sent, the ship was visited by another great man from the island. "He had on him a gown with wide sleeves, of a kind of water chamelot of an excellent azure colour, far more glossy than ours. His under apparel was green, and so was his hat, being in the form of a turban, daintily made, and not so huge as the Turkish turbans. And the locks of his hair came down below the brims of it. A reverend man was he to behold.

"He came in a boat, gilt in some part of it, with four persons more only in that boat, and was followed by another boat, wherein were some twenty. When he was come within a flight shot of our ship, signs were made to us that we should send forth some to meet him upon the water; which we presently did in our shipboat, sending the principal man amongst us save one, and four of our number with him.

"When we were come within six yards of their boat they called to us to stay, and not to approach further; which we did. And thereupon the man whom I before described stood up, and with a loud voice in Spanish, asked 'Are ye Christians?'

"We answered, 'We were'; fearing the less, because of the cross we had seen in the subscription.

"At which answer the said person lifted up his right hand towards heaven, and drew it softly to his mouth (which is the gesture they use when they thank God) and then said: 'If ye will swear (all of you) by the merits of the Saviour that ye are no pirates, nor have shed blood lawfully nor unlawfully within forty days past, you may have licence to come on land.'

"We said, 'We were all ready to take that oath.'

"Whereupon one of those that were with him, being (as it seemed) a notary, made an entry of this act. Which done, another of the attendants of the great person, which was with him in the same boat, after his lord had spoken a little to him, said aloud: 'My lord would have you know, that it is not of pride or greatness that he cometh out aboard your ship; but for that in your answer you declare that you have many sick amongst you, he was warned by the Conservator of Health of the city that he should keep a distance.'

"We bowed ourselves towards him, and answered, 'We were his humble servants; and accounted for great honour and singular humanity towards us that which was already done; but hoped well that the nature of the sickness of our men was not infectious.'

"So he returned; and a while after came the notary to us aboard our ship, holding in his hand a fruit of that country, like an orange, but of colour between orange-tawny and scarlet, which cast a most excellent odour. He used it (as it seemeth) for a preservative against infection.

"He gave us our oath; 'By the name of Jesus and of his merits,' and after told us that the next day by six of the clock in the morning we should be sent to, and brought to the Strangers' House (so he called it), where we should be accommodated of things both for our whole and for our sick.

"So he left us. And when we offered him some pistolets he smiling said, 'He must not be twice paid for one labour,' meaning, as I take it, that he had salary sufficient of the State for his service. For (as I after learned) they call an officer that taketh rewards, *twice paid*."

So next morning the people landed from the ship, and Bacon goes on to tell us of the wonderful things they saw and learned in the island. The most wonderful thing was a place called Solomon's House. In describing it Bacon was describing such a house as he hoped one day to see in England. It was a great establishment in which everything that might be of use to mankind was studied and taught. And Bacon speaks of many things which were only guessed at in his time. He speaks of high towers wherein people watched "winds, rain, snow, hail and some of the fiery meteors also." To-day we have observatories. He speaks of "help for the sight far above spectacles and glasses," also "glasses and means to see small and minute bodies perfectly and distinctly, as the shapes and colours of small flies and worms, grains and flaws in gems, which cannot otherwise be seen." To-day we have the microscope. He says "we have also means to convey sounds in trunks and pipes, in strange lines and distances," yet in those days no one had dreamed of a telephone. "We imitate also flights of birds; we have some degrees of flying in the air. We have ships and boats for going under water," yet in those days stories of flying-ships or torpedoes would have been treated as fairy tales.

Bacon did not finish *The New Atlantis*. "The rest was not perfected" are the last words in the book and it was not published until after his death. These words might almost have been written of Bacon himself. A great writer, a great man,—but "The rest was not perfected." He put his trust in princes and he fell. Yet into the land of knowledge—

> "Bacon, like Moses, led us forth at last;
> The barren wilderness he passed,
> Did on the very border stand
> Of the blest promised land,
> And from the mountain's top of his exalted wit
> Saw it himself and shew'd us it
> But life did never to one man allow
> Time to discover worlds and conquer too;
> Nor can so short a line sufficient be,
> To fathom the vast depths of nature's sea.
> The work he did we ought t'admire,
> And were unjust if we should more require
> From his few years, divided twixt th' excess
> Of low affliction and high happiness
> For who on things remote can fix his sight
> That's always in a triumph or a fight " [1]

You will like to know, that less than forty years after Bacon's death a society called The Royal Society was founded. This is a Society which interests itself in scientific study and research, and is the oldest of its kind

[1] Abraham Cowley, *To the Royal Society*.

in Great Britain.   It was Bacon's fancy of Solomon's House which led men to found this Society.   Bacon was the great man whose "true imagination"[1] set it on foot, and although many years have passed since then, the Royal Society still keeps its place in the forefront of Science.

BOOKS TO READ

The New Atlantis, edited by G D W. Bevan, modern spelling (for schools).
The New Atlantis, edited by G C. Moore Smith, in old spelling (for schools).

[1] Thomas Sprat, *History of Royal Society*, 1667.

CHAPTER LIV

ABOUT SOME LYRIC POETS

BEFORE either Ben Jonson or Bacon died, a second Stuart king sat on the throne of England. This was Charles I. the son of James VI. and I. The spacious days of Queen Elizabeth were over and gone, and the temper of the people was changing. Elizabeth had been a tyrant but the people of England had yielded to her tyranny. James, too, was a tyrant, but the people struggled with him, and in the struggle they grew stronger. In the days of Elizabeth the religion of England was still unsettled. James decided that the religion of England must be Episcopal, but as the reign of James went on, England became more and more Puritan and the breach between King and people grew wide, for James was no Puritan nor was Charles after him.

As the temper of the people changed, the literature changed too. As England grew Puritan, the people began to look askance at the theater, for the Puritans had always been its enemies. Puritan ideas drew the great mass of thinking people.

For one reason or another the plays that were written became by degrees poorer and poorer. They were coarse too, many of them so much so that we do not care to read them now. But people wrote such stories as the playgoers of those days liked, and from them we can judge how low the taste of England had fallen. However, there were people in England in those days who revolted against this taste, and in 1642, when the great struggle between King and Parliament had begun, all theaters were closed by order of Parliament. So for a time the life of English drama paused.

But while dramatic poetry declined, lyric poetry flourished. Lyric comes from the Greek word *lura,* a lyre, and all lyric poetry was at one time meant to be sung. Now we use the word for any short poem whether meant to be sung or not. In the times of James and Charles there were many lyric poets. Especially in the time of Charles it was natural that poets should write lyrics rather than longer poems. For a time of strong action, of fierce struggle was beginning, and amid the clash of arms men had no leisure to sit in the study and ponder long and quietly. But life brought with it many sharp and quick moments, and these could be best expressed in lyric poetry. And as was natural when religion was more and more being mixed with politics, when life was forcing people to think about religion whether they would or not, many of these lyric poets were religious poets. Indeed this is the great time of English religious poetry. So these lyric poets were divided into two classes, the religious poets and the court poets, gay cavaliers these last who sang love-songs, love-songs, too, in which we often seem to hear the clash of swords. For if these brave and careless cavaliers loved gayly, they fought and died as gayly as they loved.

Later on when you come to read more in English literature, you will learn to know many of these poets. In this book we have not room to tell about them or even to mention their names. Their stories are bound up with the stories of the times, and many of them fought and suffered for their king. But I will give you one or two poems which may make you want to know more about the writers of them.

Here are two written by Richard Lovelace, the very model of a gay cavalier. While he was at Oxford, King

Charles saw him and made him M.A. or Master of Arts, not for his learning, but because of his beautiful face. He went to court and made love and sang songs gayly. He went to battle and fought and sang as gayly, he went to prison and still sang. To the cause of his King he clung through all, and when Charles was dead and Cromwell ruled with his stern hand, and song was hushed in England, he died miserably in a poor London alley.

The first of these songs was written by Lovelace while he was in prison for having presented a petition to the House of Commons asking that King Charles might be restored to the throne.

TO ALTHEA FROM PRISON

"When love with unconfinéd wings
　　Hovers within my gates,
And my divine Althea brings
　　To whisper at the grates;
When I lye tangled in her haire,
　　And fettered to her eye,
The gods, that wanton in the aire,
　　Know no such liberty

"When (like committed linnets) I
　　With shriller throat shall sing
The sweetness, mercy, majesty,
　　And glories of my King.
When I shall voyce aloud, how good
　　He is, how great should be,
Enlargéd winds, that curle the flood,
　　Know no such liberty

"Stone walls do not a prison make,
　　Nor iron bars a cage,
Mindes innocent and quiet take
　　That for an hermitage;
If I have freedome in my love,
　　And in my soule am free,
Angels alone that soar above
　　Enjoy such liberty."

TO LUCASTA GOING TO THE WARRES

"Tell me not (sweet) I am unkinde,
   That from the nunnerie
Of thy chaste heart and quiet minde
   To warre and armes I flie

"True a new Mistresse now I chase,
   The first foe in the field,
And with a stronger faith embrace
   A sword, a horse, a shield.

"Yet this inconstancy is such
   As you, too, shall adore,
I could not love thee, dear, so much,
   Lov'd I not Honour more."

James Graham, Marquis of Montrose, was another
cavalier poet whose fine, sad story you will read in history.
He loved his King and fought and suffered for him, and
when he heard that he was dead he drew his sword and
wrote a poem with its point:

"Great, Good, and Just, could I but rate
My grief, and thy too rigid fate,
I'd weep the world in such a strain
As it should deluge once again
But since thy loud-tongued blood demands supplies
More from Briareus' hands than Argus' eyes,
I'll sing thy obsequies with trumpet sounds
And write thine epitaph in blood and wounds"

He wrote, too, a famous song known as Montrose's
Love-song.   Here it is:—

"My dear and only love, I pray
   This noble world of thee,
Be governed by no other sway
   But purest monarchie.

"For if confusion have a part
   Which vertuous souls abhore,
And hold a synod in thy heart,
   I'll never love thee more

"Like Alexander I will reign,
　　And I will reign alone,
My thoughts shall evermore disdain
　　A rival on my throne

"He either fears his fate too much
　　Or his deserts are small,
That puts it not unto the touch,
　　To win or lose it all

"But I must rule and govern still,
　　And always give the law,
And have each subject at my will,
　　And all to stand in awe.

"But 'gainst my battery if I find
　　Thou shun'st the prize so sore,
As that thou set'st me up a blind
　　I'll never love thee more

"If in the Empire of thy heart,
　　Where I should solely be,
Another do pretend a part,
　　And dares to vie with me·

"Or if committees thou erect,
　　And goes on such a score,
I'll sing and laugh at thy neglect,
　　And never love thee more

"But if thou wilt be constant then,
　　And faithful to thy word,
I'll make thee glorious with my pen
　　And famous by my sword

"I'll serve thee in such noble ways
　　Was never heard before,
I'll crown and deck thee all with bays
　　And love thee more and more."

In these few cavalier songs we can see the spirit of the times. There is gay carelessness of death, strong courage in misfortune, passionate loyalty. There is, too, the proud spirit of the tyrant, which is gentle and loving when obeyed, harsh and cruel if disobeyed.

There is another song by a cavalier poet which I should like to give you. It is a love-song, too, but it does not tell of these stormy times, or ring with the noise of battle. Rather it takes us away to a peaceful summer morning before the sun is up, when everything is still, when the dew trembles on every blade of grass, and the air is fresh and cool, and sweet with summer scents. And in this cool freshness we hear the song of the lark:

"The lark now leaves his wat'ry nest,
And, climbing, shakes his dewy wings;
He takes this window for the east,
And to implore your light, he sings,
'Awake, awake! the Moon will never rise,
Till she can dress her beauty at your eyes'

"The merchant bows unto the seaman's star,
The ploughman from the Sun his season takes;
But still the lover wonders what they are,
Who look for day before his mistress wakes.
'Awake, awake! break thro' your veils of lawn!
Then draw your curtains, and begin the dawn.'"

That was written by William Davenant, poet-laureate. It is one of our most beautiful songs, and he is remembered by it far more than by his long epic poem called *Gondibert* which few people now read. But I think you will agree with me that his name is worthy of being remembered for that one song alone.

CHAPTER LV

HERBERT—THE PARSON POET

HAVING told you a little about the songs of the cavaliers
I must now tell you something about the religious poets
who were a feature of the age. Of all our religious poets,
of this time at least, George Herbert is the greatest. He
was born in 1593 near the town of Montgomery, and was
the son of a noble family, but his father died when he was
little more than three, leaving his mother to bring up
George with his nine brothers and sisters.

George Herbert's mother was a good and beautiful
woman, and she loved her children so well that the poet
said afterwards she had been twice a mother to him.

At twelve he was sent to Westminster school where we
are told "the beauties of his pretty behaviour shined" so
that he seemed "to become the care of Heaven and of a
particular good angel to guard and guide him." [1]

At fifteen he went to Trinity College, Cambridge. And
now, although separated from his "dear and careful
Mother" [1] he did not forget her or all that she had taught
him. Already he was a poet. We find him sending verses
as a New Year gift to his mother and writing to her that
"my poor abilities in poetry shall be all and ever consecrated to God's glory."

As the years went on Herbert worked hard and became
a gently good, as well as a learned man, and in time he was
given the post of Public Orator at the University. This

[1] Izaak Walton.

362

post brought him into touch with the court and with the King. Of this George Herbert was glad, for although he was a good and saintly man, he longed to be a courtier. Often now he went to court hoping for some great post. But James i. died in 1625 and with him died George Herbert's hope of rising to be great in the world.

For a time, then, he left court and went into the country, and there he passed through a great struggle with himself. The question he had to settle was "whether he should return to the painted pleasure of a court life" or become a priest.

In the end he decided to become a priest, and when a friend tried to dissuade him from the calling as one too much below his birth, he answered: "It hath been judged formerly, that the domestic servants of the King of Heaven should be of the noblest families on earth. And though the iniquity of late times have made clergymen meanly valued, and the sacred name of priest contemptible, yet I will labor to make it honorable. . . . And I will labor to be like my Saviour, by making humility lovely in the eyes of all men, and by following the merciful and meek example of my dear Jesus."

But before Herbert was fully ordained a great change came into his life. The Church of England was now Protestant and priests were allowed to marry, and George Herbert married. The story of how he met his wife is pretty.

Herbert was such a cheerful and good man that he had many friends. It was said, indeed, that he had no enemy. Among his many friends was one named Danvers, who loved him so much that he said nothing would make him so happy as that George should marry one of his nine daughters. But specially he wished him to marry his daughter Jane, for he loved her best, and would think of no more happy fate for her than to be the wife of such a

man as George Herbert. He talked of George so much
to Jane that she loved him without having seen him.
George too heard of Jane and wished to meet her. And
at last after a long time they met. Each had heard so
much about the other that they seemed to know one
another already, and like the prince and princess in a fairy
tale, they loved at once, and three days later they were
married.

Soon after this, George Herbert was offered the living
of Bemerton near Salisbury. But although he had already made up his mind to become a priest he was as yet
only a deacon. This sudden offer made him fearful. He
began again to question himself and wonder if he was good
enough for such a high calling. For a month he fasted
and prayed over it. But in the end Laud, Bishop of
London, assured him "that the refusal of it was a sin." So
Herbert put off his sword and gay silken clothes, and putting on the long dark robe of a priest turned his back for
ever to thoughts of a court life. "I now look back upon my
aspiring thoughts," he said, "and think myself more happy
than if I had attained what I so ambitiously thirsted for.
I can now behold the court with an impartial eye, and see
plainly that it is made up of fraud and titles and flattery,
and many other such empty, imaginary, painted pleasures."
And having turned his back on all gayety, he began the life
which earned for him the name of "saintly George Herbert."
He taught his people, preached to them, and prayed with
them so lovingly that they loved him in return. "Some
of the meaner sort of his parish did so love and reverence
Mr. Herbert that they would let their plough rest when
Mr. Herbert's saint's bell rang to prayers, that they might
also offer their devotions to God with him; and would
then return back to their plough. And his most holy
life was such, that it begot such reverence to God and
to him, that they thought themselves the happier when

they carried Mr. Herbert's blessing back with them to their labour." [1]

But he did not only preach, he practised too. I must tell you just one story to show you how he practiced. Herbert was very fond of music; he sang, and played too, upon the lute and viol. One day as he was walking into Salisbury to play with some friends "he saw a poor man with a poorer horse, which was fallen under his load. They were both in distress and needed present help. This Mr. Herbert perceiving put off his canonical coat, and helped the poor man to unload, and after to load his horse. The poor man blest him for it, and he blest the poor man, and was so like the Good Samaritan that he gave him money to refresh both himself and his horse, and told him, that if he loved himself, he should be merciful to his beast. Thus he left the poor man.

"And at his coming to his musical friends at Salisbury, they began to wonder that Mr. George Herbert, which used to be so trim and clean, came into that company so soiled and discomposed. But he told them the occasion. And when one of the company told him, he had disparaged himself by so dirty an employment, his answer was: that the thought of what he had done would prove music to him at midnight, and the omission of it would have upbraided and made discord in his conscience whensoever he should pass by that place. 'For if I be bound to pray for all that be in distress, I am sure that I am bound, so far as it is in my power, to practice what I pray for. And though I do not wish for the like occasion every day, yet let me tell you, I would not willingly pass one day of my life without comforting a sad soul or shewing mercy. And I praise God for this occasion.

" 'And now let's tune our instruments ' " [2]

This story reminds us that besides being a parson Her-

[1] Walton   The same.

bert was a courtier and a fine gentleman. His courtly friends were surprised that he should lower himself by helping a poor man with his own hands. But that is just one thing that we have to remember about Herbert, he had nothing of the Puritan in him, he was a cavalier, a courtier, yet he showed the world that it was possible to be these and still be a good man. He did not believe that any honest work was a "dirty employment." In one of his poems he says:

> "Teach me my God and King,
> In all things Thee to see,
> And what I do in anything
> To do it as for Thee.
>
> . . . . .
>
> "All may of Thee Partake:
> Nothing can be so mean
> Which with his tincture (for Thy sake)
> Will not grow bright and clean.
>
> "A Servant with this clause
> Makes drudgery divine;
> Who sweeps a room as for Thy laws
> Makes that and th' action fine
>
> "This is the famous stone
> That turneth all to gold;
> For that which God doth touch and own
> Cannot for less be told." [1]

I have told you the story about Herbert and the poor man in the words of Izaak Walton, the first writer of a life of George Herbert. I hope some day you will read that life and also the other books Walton wrote, for although we have not room for him in this book, his books are one of the delights of our literature which await you.

In all Herbert's work among his people, his wife was his companion and help, and the people loved her as much as they loved their parson. "Love followed her," says Walton, "in all places as inseparably as shadows follow substances in sunshine."

[1] Counted

Besides living thus for his people Herbert almost rebuilt the church and rectory both of which he found very
ruined. And when he had made an end of rebuilding
he carved these words upon the chimney in the hall of
the Rectory:

> "If thou chance for to find
> A new house to thy mind,
> And built without thy cost;
> Be good to the poor,
> As God gives thee Store
> And then my labor's not lost."

His life, one would think, was busy enough, and full
enough, yet amid it all he found time to write. Besides
many poems he wrote for his own guidance a book called
The Country Parson. It is a book, says Walton, "so full of
plain, prudent, and useful rules that that country parson
that can spare 12d. and yet wants it is scarce excusable."

But Herbert's happy, useful days at Bemerton were
all too short. In 1632, before he had held his living three
years, he died, and was buried by his sorrowing people
beneath the altar of his own little church.

It was not until after his death that his poems were
published. On his death-bed he left the book in which
he had written them to a friend. "Desire him to read it,"
he said, "and if he can think it may turn to the advantage
of any dejected poor soul, let it be made public. If not let
him burn it."

The book was published under the name of *The Temple.*
All the poems are short except the first, called *The Church
Porch.* From that I will quote a few lines. It begins:

> "Thou whose sweet youth and early hopes enchance
> Thy rate and price, and mark thee for a treasure,
> Hearken unto a Verser, who may chance
> Ryme thee to good, and make a bait of pleasure.
> A verse may find him who a sermon flies,
> And turn delight into a sacrifice.

"Lie not, but let thy heart be true to God,
Thy mouth to it, thy actions to them both:
Cowards tell lies, and those that fear the rod;
The stormy-working soul spits lies and froth
    Dare to be true: nothing can need a lie,
    A fault which needs it most, grows two thereby.

    .   .   .   .   .   .

"Art thou a magistrate? then be severe:
If studious, copy fair what Time hath blurr'd,
Redeem truth from his jaws: if soldier,
Chase brave employment with a naked sword
    Throughout the world. Fool not; for all may have,
    If they dare try, a glorious life, or grave.

    .   .   .   .   .   .

"Do all things like a man, not sneakingly;
Think the King sees thee still; for his King does.
Simpring is but a lay-hypocrisy;
Give it a corner and the clue undoes
    Who fears to do ill sets himself to task,
    Who fears to do well sure should wear a mask."

There is all the strong courage in these lines of the
courtier-parson. They make us remember that before
he put on his priest's robe he wore a sword. They are full
of the fearless goodness that was the mark of his gentle
soul. And now, to end the chapter, I will give you another
little poem full of beauty and tenderness. It is called
The Pulley. Herbert often gave quaint names to his
poems, names which at first sight seem to have little meaning. Perhaps you may be able to find out why this is
called *The Pulley.*

    "When God at first made man,
Having a glass of blessings standing by,
'Let us,' said He, 'pour on him all we can;
Let the world's riches which disperséd lie,
    Contract into a span.'

    "So strength first made way,
Then beauty flowed, then wisdom, honour, pleasure;
When almost all was out, God made a stay,
Perceiving that, alone of all His treasure,
    Rest in the bottom lay.

" 'For if I should,' said He,
'Bestow this jewel on My creature,
He would adore My gifts instead of Me,
And rest in Nature, not the God of Nature:
    So both should losers be.

" 'Yet let him keep the rest,
But keep them with repining restlessness,
Let him be rich and weary, that at least,
If goodness lead him not, yet weariness
    May toss him to my breast.' "

CHAPTER LVI

HERRICK AND MARVELL—OF BLOSSOMS AND BOWERS

ANOTHER poet of this age, Robert Herrick, in himself joined the two styles of poetry of which we have been speaking, for he was both a love poet and a religious poet.

He was born in 1591 and was the son of an old, well-to-do family, his father being a London goldsmith. But, like Herbert, he lost his father when he was but a tiny child. Like Herbert again he went to Westminster School and later to Cambridge. But before he went to Cambridge he was apprenticed to his uncle, who was a goldsmith, as his brother, Herrick's father, had been. Robert, however, never finished his apprenticeship. He found out, we may suppose, that he had no liking for the jeweler's craft, that his hand was meant to create jewels of another kind. So he left his uncle's workshop and went to Cambridge, although he was already much beyond the usual age at which boys then went to college. Like Herbert he went to college meaning to study for the Church. But according to our present-day ideas he seems little fitted to have been a priest. For although we know little more than a few bare facts about Herrick's life, when we have read his poems and looked at his portrait we can draw for ourselves a clear picture of the man, and the picture will not fit in with our ideas of priesthood.

In some ways therefore, as we have seen, though there was an outward likeness between the lives of Herbert and of Herrick, it was only an outward likeness. Herbert was tender and kindly, the very model of a Christian gentleman. Herrick was a jolly old Pagan, full of a rollicking joy in life. Even in appearance these two poets were different. Herbert was tall and thin with a quiet face and eyes which were truly "homes of silent prayer." In Herrick's face is something gross, his great Roman nose and thick curly hair seem to suit his pleasure-loving nature. There is nothing spiritual about him.

After Herrick left college we know little of his life for eight or nine years. He lived in London, met Ben Jonson and all the other poets and writers who flocked about great Ben. He went to court no doubt, and all the time he wrote poems. It was a gay and cheerful life which, when at length he was given the living of Dean Prior in Devonshire, he found it hard to leave.

It was then that he wrote his farewell to poetry. He says:—

> "I, my desires screw from thee, and direct
> Them and my thoughts to that sublim'd respect
> And conscience unto priesthood "

It was hard to go. But yet he pretends at least to be resigned, and he ends by saying:—

> "The crown of duty is our duty: Well—
> Doing's the fruit of doing well   Farewell "

For eighteen years Herrick lived in his Devonshire home, and we know little of these years. But he thought sadly at times of the gay days that were gone. "Ah, Ben!" he writes to Jonson,

> "Say how, or when
> Shall we thy guests
> Meet at those lyric feasts
> Made at the Sun,
> The Dog, the Triple Tun?

Where we such clusters had,
As made us nobly wild, not mad,
And yet each verse of thine
Out-did the meat, out-did the frolic wine."

Yet he was not without comforts and companions in his country parsonage. His good and faithful servant Prue kept house for him, and he surrounded himself with pets. He had a pet lamb, a dog, a cat, and even a pet pig which he taught to drink out of a mug.

"Though Clock,
To tell how night draws hence, I've none,
A Cock
I have, to sing how day draws on
I have
A maid (my Prue) by good luck sent,
To save
That little, Fates me gave or lent.
A Hen
I keep, which, creeking[1] day by day,
Tells when
She goes her long white egg to lay
A Goose
I have, which, with a jealous ear,
Lets loose
Her tongue, to tell what danger's near.
A Lamb
I keep, tame, with my morsels fed,
Whose Dam
An orphan left him, lately dead
A Cat
I keep, that plays about my house,
Grown fat
With eating many a miching[2] mouse.
To these
A Tracy[3] I do keep, whereby
I please
The more my rural privacy,

---

[1] Clucking   [2] Thieving   [3] His spaniel.

> Which are
> But toys to give my heart some ease;
> Where care
> None is, slight things do lightly please."

But Herrick did not love his country home and parish or his people. We are told that the gentry round about loved him "for his florid and witty discourses." But his people do not seem to have loved these same discourses, for we are also told that one day in anger he threw his sermon from the pulpit at them because they did not listen attentively. He says:—

> "More discontents I never had,
>   Since I was born, than here,
> Where I have been, and still am sad,
>   In this dull Devonshire"

Yet though Herrick hated Devonshire, or at least said so, it was this same wild country that called forth some of his finest poems. He himself knew that, for in the next lines he goes on to say:—

> "Yet, justly too, I must confess
>   I ne'er invented such
> Ennobled numbers for the press,
>   Than where I loathed so much."

Yet it is not the ruggedness of the Devon land we feel in Herrick's poems. We feel rather the beauty of flowers, the warmth of sun, the softness of spring winds, and see the greening trees, the morning dews, the soft rains. It is as if he had not let his eyes wander over the wild Devonshire moorlands, but had confined them to his own lovely garden and orchard meadow, for he speaks of the "dewbespangled herb and tree," the "damasked meadows," the "silver shedding brooks." Hardly any English poet has written so tenderly of flowers as Herrick. One of the best known of these flower poems is *To Daffodils*.

"Fair Daffodils, we weep to see
 You haste away so soon,
As yet the early-rising sun
 Has not attain'd his noon.
     Stay, stay,
 Until the hasting day
     Has run
 But to the Even-song;
And, having pray'd together, we
 Will go with you along

We have short time to stay, as you,
 We have as short a spring,
As quick a growth to meet decay,
 As you, or anything
     We die
 As your hours do, and dry
     Away,
 Like to the summer's rain,
Or as the pearls of morning's dew,
 Ne'er to be found again."

And here is part of a song for May morning:—

"Get up, get up for shame, the blooming morn
Upon her wings presents the god unshorn
 See how Aurora throws her fair
 Fresh-quilted colours through the air:
 Get up, sweet slug-a-bed, and see
 The dew bespangling herb and tree,
Each flower has wept and bow'd toward the east
Above an hour since; yet you not dress'd;
 Nay! not so much as out of bed?
 When all the birds have matins said
 And sung their thankful hymns, 'tis sin,
 Nay, profanation to keep in,
Whenas a thousand virgins on this day
Spring, sooner than the lark, to fetch in May.

Rise and put on your foliage, and be seen
To come forth, like the Spring-time, fresh and green

And sweet as Flora   Take no care
For jewels for your gown or hair;
Fear not; the leaves will strew
Gems in abundance upon you.
Besides, the childhood of the day has kept,
Against you come, some orient pearls unwept;
Come and receive them while the light
Hangs on the dew-locks of the night:
And Titan on the eastern hill
Retires himself, or else stands still
Till you come forth   Wash, dress, be brief in praying;
Few beads are best when once we go a-Maying."

Another well-known poem of Herrick's is:—

"Gather ye rosebuds while ye may,
   Old Time is still a-flying·
And this same flower that smiles to-day,
   To-morrow will be dying.

The glorious lamp of Heaven, the Sun,
   The higher he's a-getting,
The sooner will his race be run,
   And nearer he's to setting.

That age is best, which is the first,
   When Youth and Blood are warmer:
But being spent, the worse, and worst
   Times still succeed the former

Then be not coy, but use your time,
   And while ye may, go marry;
For having lost but once your prime,
   You may for ever tarry"

Herrick only published one book. He called it *The Hesperides, or the works both Human and Divine.* The "divine" part although published in the same book, has a separate name, being called his *Noble Numbers.* The Hesperides, from whom he took the name of his book, were lovely maidens who dwelt in a beautiful garden far away on the verge of the ocean. The maidens sang beautifully, so Herrick took their name for his book, for it might well be that the songs they sang were such as his. This garden of the Hesperides was sometimes thought to be the same as the fabled island of Atlantis of which we have already heard. And it was here that, guarded by a dreadful dragon, grew the golden apples which Earth gave to Hera on her marriage with Zeus.

The *Hesperides* is a collection of more than a thousand short poems, a few of which you have already read in this chapter. They are not connected with each other, but tell of all manner of things.

Herrick was a religious poet too, and here is something that he wrote for children in his *Noble Numbers*. It is called *To his Saviour, a Child: A Present by a Child*.

> "Go, pretty child, and bear this flower
> Unto thy little Saviour;
> And tell him, by that bud now blown,
> He is the Rose of Sharon known
> When thou hast said so, stick it there
> Upon his bib or stomacher;
> And tell Him, for good handsel too,
> That thou hast brought a whistle new,
> Made of a clear, straight oaten reed,
> To charm his cries at time of need
> Tell Him, for coral, thou hast none,
> But if thou hadst, He should have one;
> But poor thou art, and known to be
> Even as moneyless as He
> Lastly, if thou canst win a kiss
> From those mellifluous lips of His;
> Then never take a second on,
> To spoil the first impression"

Herrick wrote also several graces for children. Here is one:—

> "What God gives, and what we take
> 'Tis a gift for Christ His sake

Be the meal of beans and peas,
God be thanked for those and these:
Have we flesh, or have we fish,
All are fragments from His dish.
He His Church save, and the king;
And our peace here, like a Spring,
Make it ever flourishing"

While Herrick lived his quiet, dull life and wrote poetry in the depths of Devonshire, the country was being torn asunder and tossed from horror to horror by the great Civil War. Men took sides and fought for Parliament or for King. Year by year the quarrel grew. What was begun at Edgehill ended at Naseby where the King's cause was utterly lost. Then, although Herrick took no part in the fighting, he suffered with the vanquished, for he was a Royalist at heart. He was turned out of his living to make room for a Parliament man. He left his parish without regret.

"Deanbourne, farewell, I never look to see
Deane, or thy warty incivility.
Thy rocky bottom, that doth tear thy streams,
And makes them frantic, ev'n to all extremes;
To my content, I never should behold,
Were thy streams silver, or thy rocks all gold
Rocky thou art, and rocky we discover
Thy men: and rocky are thy ways all over.
O men, O manners, now and ever known
To be a rocky generation
A people currish, churlish as the seas;
And rude, almost, as rudest savages:
With whom I did, and may re-sojourn when
Rocks turn to rivers, rivers turn to men"

Hastening to London, he threw off his sober priest's robe, and once more putting on the gay dress worn by the gentlemen of his day he forgot the troubles and the duties of a country parson.

Rejoicing in his freedom, he cried:—

> "London my home is: though by hard fate sent
> Into a long and irksome banishment,
> Yet since called back; henceforward let me be,
> O native country, repossess'd by thee"

He had no money, but he had many wealthy friends, so he lived, we may believe, merrily enough for the next fifteen years. It was during these years that the *Hesperides* was first published, although for a long time before many people had known his poems, for they had been handed about among his friends in manuscript.

So the years passed for Herrick we hardly know how. In the great world Cromwell died and Charles II. returned to England to claim the throne of his fathers. Then it would seem that Herrick had not found all the joy he had hoped for in London, for two years later, although rocks had not turned to rivers, nor rivers to men, he went back to his "loathed Devonshire."

After that, all that we know of him is that at Dean Prior "Robert Herrick vicker was buried ye 15th day of October 1674." Thus in twilight ends the life of the greatest lyric poet of the seventeenth century.

All the lyric poets of whom I have told you were Royalists, but the Puritans too had their poets, and before ending this chapter I would like to tell you a little of Andrew Marvell, a Parliamentary poet.

If Herrick was a lover of flowers, Marvell was a lover of gardens, woods and meadows. The garden poet he has been called. He felt himself in touch with Nature:—

> "Thus I, easy philosopher,
> Among the birds and trees confer,
> And little now to make me wants,
> Or of the fowls or of the plants:
> Give me but wings as they, and I
> Straight floating in the air shall fly;

Or turn me but, and you shall see
I was but an inverted tree." [1]

Yet although Marvell loved Nature, he did not live, like Herrick, far from the stir of war, but took his part in the strife of the times. He was an important man in his day. He was known to Cromwell and was a friend of Milton, a poet much greater than himself. He was a member of Parliament, and wrote much prose, but the quarrels in the cause of which it was written are matters of bygone days, and although some of it is still interesting, it is for his poetry rather that we remember and love him. Although Marvell was a Parliamentarian, he did not love Cromwell blindly, and he could admire what was fine in King Charles. He could say of Cromwell:—

"Though his Government did a tyrant resemble,
He made England great, and his enemies tremble" [2]

And no one perhaps wrote with more grave sorrow of the death of Charles than did Marvell, and that too in a poem which, strangely enough, was written in honor of Cromwell.

"He nothing common did, or mean,
Upon that memorable scene,
    But with his keener eye
    The axe's edge did try:
Nor called the gods with vulgar spite
To vindicate his helpless right,
    But bowed his comely head,
    Down, as upon a bed." [3]

At Cromwell's death he wrote:—

"Thee, many ages hence, in martial verse
Shall the English soldier, ere he charge, rehearse;

---

[1] *Appleton House, to the Lord Fairfax*
[2] *A Dialogue between two Horses*
[3] *An Horatian ode upon Cromwell's return from Ireland*

Singing of thee, inflame himself to fight
And, with the name of Cromwell, armies fright." [1]

But all Marvell's writings were not political, and one of
his prettiest poems was written about a girl mourning for
a lost pet.

"The wanton troopers riding by
Have shot my fawn, and it will die.
Ungentle men! they cannot thrive
Who killed thee. Thou ne'er didst alive
Them any harm: alas! nor could
Thy death yet do them any good.

.   .   .   .

With sweetest milk and sugar, first
I it at my own fingers nurs'd,
And as it grew, so every day
It wax'd more sweet and white than they.
It had so sweet a breath! And oft
I blushed to see its foot so soft,
And white (shall I say than my hand?)
Nay, any lady's of the land.
  It is a wondrous thing how fleet
'Twas on those little silver feet;
With what a pretty skipping grace
It oft would challenge me to race;
And when 't had left me far away.
'Twould stay, and run again, and stay;
For it was nimbler much than hinds,
And trod as if on the four winds.
  I have a garden of my own,
But so with roses overgrown
And lilies, that you would it guess
To be a little wilderness;
And all the spring-time of the year
It only loved to be there.
Among the lilies, I
Have sought it oft, where it should lie

---

[1] *Upon the Death of the Lord Protector.*

Yet could not, till itself would rise,
Find it, although before mine eyes;
For in the flaxen lilies' shade,
It like a bank of lilies laid
Upon the roses it would feed,
Until its lips even seemed to bleed;
And then to me 'twould boldly trip
And plant those roses on my lip.

.   .   .   .   .

Now my sweet fawn is vanish'd to
Whither the swans and turtles go;
In fair Elysium to endure,
With milk-white lambs and ermines pure,
O do not run too fast for I
Will but bespeak thy grave, and die "

After the Restoration Marvell wrote satires, a kind of
poem of which you had an early and mild example in the
fable of the two mice by Surrey, a kind of poem of which
we will soon hear much more.   In these satires Marvell
poured out all the wrath of a Puritan upon the evils of his
day.   Marvell's satires were so witty and so outspoken
that once or twice he was in danger of punishment because
of them.   But once at least the King himself saved a book
of his from being destroyed, for by every one "from the
King down to the tradesman his books were read with
great pleasure." [1]   Yet he had many enemies, and when he
died suddenly in August, 1678, many people thought that
he had been poisoned.   He was the last, we may say, of the
seventeenth-century lyric poets.

Besides the lyric writers there were many prose writers
in the seventeenth century who are among the men to be
remembered.   But their books, although some day you
will love them, would not interest you yet.   They tell no
story, they are long, they have not, like poetry, a lilt or
rhythm to carry one on.   It would be an effort to read

[1] Burnet.

them. If I tried to explain to you wherein the charm of them lies I fear the charm would fly, for it is impossible to imprison the sunbeam or find the foundations of the rainbow. It is better therefore to leave these books until the years come in which it will be no effort to read them, but a joy.

CHAPTER LVII

MILTON—SIGHT AND GROWTH

"There is but one Milton,"[1] there is, too, but one Shakespeare, yet John Milton, far more than William Shakespeare, stands a lonely figure in our literature. Shakespeare was a dramatist among dramatists. We can see how there were those who led up to him, and others again who led away from him. From each he differs in being greater, he outshines them all. Shakespeare was a man among men. He loved and sinned with men, he was homely and kindly, and we can take him to our hearts. Milton both in his life and work was cold and lonely. He was a master without scholars, a leader without followers. Him we can admire, but cannot love with an understanding love. Yet although we love Shakespeare we can find throughout all his works hardly a line upon which we can place a finger and say here Shakespeare speaks of himself, here he shows what he himself thought and felt. Shakespeare understood human nature so well that he could see through another's eyes and so forget himself. But over and over again in Milton's work we see himself. Over and over again we can say here Milton speaks of himself, here he shows us his own heart, his own pain. He is one of the most self-ful of all poets. He has none of the dramatic power of Shakespeare, he cannot look through another's eyes, so he sees things only from one standpoint and that his own. He stands far apart from us, and is

[1] Professor Raleigh.

322

almost inhumanly cold. That is the reason why so many of us find him hard to love.

When, on a bleak December day in 1606, more than three hundred years ago, Milton was born, Elizabeth was dead, and James of Scotland sat upon the throne, but many of the great Elizabethans still lived. Shakespeare was still writing, still acting, although he had become a man of wealth and importance and the owner of New Place. Ben Jonson was at the very height of his fame, the favorite alike of Court and Commons. Bacon was just rising to power and greatness, his *Novum Organum* still to come. Raleigh, in prison, was eating his heart out in the desire for freedom, trying to while away the dreary hours with chemical experiments, his great history not yet begun. Of the crowd of lyric writers some were boys at college, some but children in the nursery, and some still unborn. Yet in spite of the many writers who lived at or about the same time, Milton stands alone in our literature.

John Milton was the son of a London scrivener, that is, a kind of lawyer. He was well-to-do and a Puritan. Milton's home, however, must have been brighter than many a Puritan home, for his father loved music, and not only played well, but also composed. He taught his son to play too, and all through his life Milton loved music.

John was a pretty little boy with long golden brown hair, a fair face and dark gray eyes. But to many a strict Puritan, beauty was an abomination, and we are told that one of Milton's schoolmasters "was a Puritan in Essex who cut his hair short." No doubt to him a boy with long hair was unseemly. John was the eldest and much beloved son of his father, who perhaps petted and spoiled him. He was clever as well as pretty, and already at the age of ten he was looked upon by his family as a poet. He was very studious, for besides going to St. Paul's School he had a private tutor. Even with that he was not satisfied, but studied alone far into the night. "When he went to schoole, when he was very young," we are told, "he studied hard and sate up very late: commonly till twelve or one at night. And his father ordered the mayde to sitt up for him. And in those years he composed many copies of verses, which might well become a riper age."[1] We can imagine to ourselves the silence of the house, when all the Puritan household had been long abed. We can picture the warm quiet room where sits the little fair-haired boy poring over his books by the light of flickering candles, while in the shadow a stern-faced white-capped Puritan woman waits. She sits very straight in her chair, her worn hands are folded, her eyes heavy with sleep. Sometimes she nods. Then with a start she shakes herself wide awake again, murmuring softly that it is no hour for any Christian body to be out o' bed, wondering that her master should allow so young a child to keep so long over his books. Still she has her orders, so with a patient sigh she folds her hands again and waits. Thus early did Milton begin to shape his own course and to live a life apart from others.

At sixteen Milton went to Christ's College, Cambridge. And here he earned for himself the name of the Lady of Christ's, both because of his beautiful face and slender figure, and because he stood haughtily aloof from amusements which seemed to him coarse or bad. In going to Cambridge, Milton had meant to study for the Church. But all through life he stood for liberty. "He thought that man was made only for rebellion," said a later writer.[2] As a child he had gone his own way, and as he grew older he found it harder and harder to agree with all that the Church taught—"till coming to some maturity of years, and perceiving what tyranny had invaded in the Church, that he who would take orders must subscribe slave, and

[1] Aubrey   [2] Johnson.

take an oath withal. . . . I thought it better to prefer a blameless silence before the sacred office of speaking, bought and begun with servitude and forswearing." Thus was he, he says, "church-outed by the Prelates." [1] Milton could not, with a free conscience, become a clergyman, so having taken his degree he went home to his father, who now lived in the country at Horton. He left Cambridge without regrets. No thrill of pleasure seemed to have warmed his heart in after days when he looked back upon the young years spent beside the Cam.

Milton went home to his father's house without any settled plan of life. He had not made up his mind what he was to be, he was only sure that he could not be a clergyman. His father was well off, but not wealthy. He had no great estates to manage, and he must have wished his eldest son to do and be something in the world, yet he did not urge it upon him. Milton himself, however, was not quite at rest, as his sonnet *On his being arrived to the age of twenty-three* shows:—

> "How soon hath Time, the subtle thief of youth,
> Stolen on his wing my three-and-twentieth year:
> My hasting days fly on with full career,
> But my late Spring no bud or blossom show'th
> Perhaps my semblance might deceive the truth,
> That I to manhood am arriv'd so near,
> And inward ripeness doth much less appear,
> That some more timely happy spirits endu'th.
> Yet be it less or more, or soon or slow,
> It shall be still in strictest measure even
> To that same lot, however mean, or high,
> Toward which Time leads me, and the Will of Heaven;
> All is, if I have grace to use it so,
> As ever in my great Task-Master's eye"

Yet dissatisfied as he sometimes was, he was very sure of himself, and for five years he let his wings grow, as he

[1] *The Reason of Church Government,* book II

himself said. But these years were not altogether lost,
for if both day and night Milton roamed the meadows
about his home in seeming idleness, he was drinking in all
the beauty of earth and sky, flower and field, storing his
memory with sights and sounds that were to be a treasure to him in after days. He studied hard, too, rang-
ing at will through Greek and Latin literature. "No
delay, no rest, no care or thought almost of anything
holds me aside until I reach the end I am making for,
and round off, as it were, some great period of my studies,"
he says to a friend. And as the outcome of these
five fallow years Milton has left us some of his most
beautiful poems. They have not the stately grandeur of
his later works, but they are natural and easy, and at
times full of a joyousness which we never find in him again.
And before we can admire his great poem which he wrote
later, we may love the beauty of *L'Allegro, Il Penseroso*
and *Lycidas*, which he wrote now.

L'Allegro and *Il Penseroso* are two poems which picture two moods in which the poet looks at life. They
are two moods which come to every one, the mirthful and
the sad. *L'Allegro* pictures the happy mood. Here the
man "who has, in his heart, cause for contentment" sings.
And the poem fairly dances with delight of being as it
follows the day from dawn till evening shadows fall. It
begins by bidding "loathéd Melancholy" begone "'Mongst
horrid shapes, and shrieks, and sights unholy," and by
bidding come "heart-easing Mirth."

> "Haste thee, nymph, and bring with thee
> Jest and youthful Jollity,
> Quips and cranks, and wanton wiles,
> Nods and becks, and wretchéd smiles,
> Such as hang on Hebe's cheek,
> And love to live in dimple sleek;
> Sport that wrinkled Care derides,
> And Laughter holding both his sides

Come, and trip it as ye go
On the light fantastic toe.

To hear the lark begin his flight,
And singing startle the dull night,
From his watch-tower in the skies,
Till the dappled dawn doth rise."

These are a few lines from the opening of the poem which you must read for yourselves, for if I quoted all that is beautiful in it I should quote the whole.

Il Penseroso pictures the thoughtful mood, or mood of gentle Melancholy. Here Mirth is banished, "Hence fair deluding joys, the brood of Folly, and hail divinest Melancholy." The poem moves with more stately measure, "with even step, and musing gait," from evening through the moonlit night till morn. It ends with the poet's desire to live a peaceful studious life.

"But let my due feet never fail
To walk the studious cloisters pale;
And love the high embowéd roof,
With antique pillars massy proof,
And storied windows richly dight,
Casting a dim religious light
There let the pealing organ blow
To the full-voic'd choir below,
In service high, and anthems clear,
As may with sweetness through mine ear,
Dissolve me into ecstasies,
And bring all Heaven before mine eyes."

In *Lycidas* Milton mourns the death of a friend who was drowned while crossing the Irish Channel. He took the name from an Italian poem, which told of the sad death of another Lycidas. The verse moves with even more stately measure than *Il Penseroso*.

"Bitter constraint, and sad occasion dear,
Compels me to disturb your season due.

For Lycidas is dead, dead ere his prime,
Young Lycidas, and hath not left his peer:
Who would not sing for Lycidas? he knew
Himself to sing, and build the lofty rhyme.

. . . . . .

Fame is the spur that the clear spirit doth raise,
(That last infirmity of noble minds)
To scorn delights, and live laborious days,
But the fair guerdon when we hope to find,
And think to burst out into sudden blaze,
Comes the blind Fury with th' abhorréd shears,
And slits the thin-spun life."

It was during these early years spent at Horton, too, that Milton wrote his masque of *Comus*. It is strange to find a Puritan poet writing a masque, for Puritans looked darkly on all acting. It is strange to find that, in spite of the Puritan dislike to acting, the last and, perhaps, the best masque in our language should be written by a Puritan, and that not ten years before all the theaters in the land were closed by Puritan orders. But although, in many ways, Milton was sternly Puritan, these were only the better ways. He had no hatred of beauty, "God has instilled into me a vehement love of the beautiful," he says.

The masque of *Comus* was written for a great entertainment given by the Earl of Bridgewater, at Ludlow Castle, and three of his children took part in it. In a darksome wood, so the story runs, the enchanter, Comus, lived with his rabble rout, half brute, half man. For to all who passed through the wood Comus offered a glass from which, if any drank,—

"Their human countenance,
Th' express resemblance of the gods, is changed
Into some brutish form of wolf, or bear,
Or ounce, or tiger, hog. or bearded goat.
All other parts remaining as they were"

And they, forgetting their home and friends, henceforth live riotously with Comus.

Through this wood a Lady and her two brothers pass, and on the way the Lady is separated from her brothers and loses her way. As she wanders about she is discovered by Comus who, disguising himself as a shepherd, offers her shelter in his "low but loyal cottage." The Lady, innocent and trusting, follows him. But instead of leading her to a cottage he leads her to his palace. There the Lady is placed in an enchanted chair from which she cannot rise, and Comus tempts her to drink from his magic glass. The Lady refuses, and with his magic wand Comus turns her to seeming stone.

Meanwhile the brothers have met a Guardian Spirit, also disguised as a shepherd, and he warns them of their sister's danger. Guided by him they set out to find her. Reaching the palace, they rush in, sword in hand. They dash the magic glass to the ground and break it in pieces and put Comus and his rabble to flight. But though the Lady is thus saved she remains motionless and stony in her chair.

"What, have ye let the false enchanter scape?" the Guardian Spirit cries. "Oh, ye mistook, ye should have snatched his wand and bound him fast." Without his rod reversed and backward-muttered incantations they cannot free the Lady. Yet there is another means. Sabrina, the nymph of the Severn, may save her. So the Spirit calls upon her for aid.

> "Sabrina fair,
> Listen where thou art sitting
> Under the glassy, cool, translucent wave,
> In twisted braids of lilies knitting
> The loose train of thy amber-dropping hair,
> Listen for dear honour's sake,
> Goddess of the silver lake,
> 　　　　Listen and save."

Sabrina comes, and sprinkling water on the Lady, breaks the charm.

"Brightest Lady, look on me,
Thus I sprinkle on thy breast
Drops that from my fountain pure
I have kept of precious cure,
Thrice upon thy fingers' tip,
Thrice upon thy rubied lip,
Next this marble venomed seat,
Smeared with gums of glutinous heat,
I touch with chaste palms moist and cold.
Now the spell hath lost its hold "

The Lady is free and, greatly rejoicing, the Guardian Spirit leads her, with her brothers, safe to their father's home.

All these poems of which I have told you, Milton wrote during the quiet years spent at Horton. But at length these days came to an end. He began to feel his life in the country cramped and narrow. He longed to go out into the great wide world and see something of all the beauties and wonder of it. Italy, which had called so many of our poets, called him. Once more his kindly father let him do as he would. He gave him money, provided him with a servant, and sent him forth on his travels. For more than a year Milton wandered, chiefly among the sunny cities of Italy. He meant to stray still further to Sicily and Greece, but news from home called him back, "The sad news of Civil War." "I thought it base," he said, "that while my fellow-countrymen were fighting at home for liberty, I should be traveling abroad at ease."

When Milton returned home he did not go back to Horton, but set up house in London. Here he began to teach his two nephews, his sister's children, who were boys of nine and ten. Their father had died, their mother married again, and Milton not only taught the boys, but took them to live with him. He found pleasure, it would seem, in teaching, for soon his little class grew, and he began to teach other boys, the sons of friends.

Milton was a good master, but a severe one. The boys were kept long hours at their lessons, and we are told that in a year's time they could read a Latin author at sight, and within three years they went through the best Latin and Greek poets. But "as he was severe on one hand, so he was most familiar and free in his conversation to those to whom most sour in his way of education."[1] He himself showed the example of "hard study and spare diet,"[2] for besides teaching the boys he worked and wrote steadily, study being ever the "grand affair of his life."[3] Only now and again he went to see "young sparks" of his acquaintance, "and now and then to keep a gawdy-day."[4] It is scarce to be imagined that a gawdy-day in which John Milton took part could have been very riotous.

Then after Milton had been leading this severe quiet life for about four years, a strange thing happened. One day he set off on a journey. He told no one why he went. Every one thought it was but a pleasure jaunt. He was away about a month, then "home he returns a married man that went out a bachelor."[5] We can imagine how surprised the little boys would be to find that their grave teacher of thirty-four had brought home a wife, a wife, too, who was little more than a girl a few years older than themselves. And as it was a surprise to them it is still a surprise to all who read and write about Milton's life to this day. With the new wife came several of her friends, and so the quiet house was made gay with feasting and merriment for a few days; for strange to say, Milton, the stern Puritan, had married a Royalist lady, the daughter of a cavalier. After these few merry days the gay friends left, and the young bride remained behind with her grave and learned husband, in her new quiet home. But to poor little Mary Milton, used to a great house and much merry coming and going, the life she now led seemed dull beyond

<hr>

[1] Aubrey.   [2] Philips   [3] The same   [4] The same   [5] The same.

bearing. She was not clever; indeed, she was rather stupid, so after having led a "philosophical life" for about a month, she begged to be allowed to go back to her mother.

Milton let her go on the understanding that she should return to him in a month or two. But the time appointed came and went without any sign of a returning wife. Milton wrote to her and got no answer. Several times he wrote, and still no answer. Then he sent a messenger. But the messenger returned without an answer, or at least without a pleasing one. He had indeed been "dismissed with some sort of contempt."

It would seem the cavalier family regretted having given a daughter in marriage to the Puritan poet. The poet, on his side, now resolved to cast out forever from his heart and home his truant wife. He set himself harder than before to the task of writing and teaching. He hid his aching heart and hurt pride as best he might beneath a calm and stern bearing. But life had changed for him. Up to this time all had gone as he wished. Ever since, when a boy of twelve, he had sat till midnight over his books with a patient waiting-maid beside him, those around had smoothed his path in life for him. His will had been law until a girl of seventeen defied him.

Time went on, the King's cause was all but hopeless. Many a cavalier had lost all in his defense, among them those of Mary Milton's family. Driven from their home, knowing hardly where to turn for shelter, they bethought them of Mary's slighted husband. He was on the winning side, and a man of growing importance. Beneath his roof Mary at least would be safe.

The poor little runaway wife, we may believe, was afraid to face her angry husband. But helped both by his friends and her own a meeting was arranged. Milton had a friend to whose house he often went, and in this

house his wife was hid one day when the poet came to pay
a visit. While Milton waited for his friend he was surprised, for when the door opened there came from the
adjoining room, not his friend, but "one whom he thought
to have never seen more." Mary his wife came to him,
and sinking upon her knees before him begged to be forgiven. Long after, in his great poem, Milton seems to
describe the scene when he makes Adam cry out to Eve
after the Fall, "Out of my sight, thou serpent! That
name best befits thee."

> "But Eve,
> Not so repulsed, with tears that ceased not flowing,
> And tresses all disordered, at his feet
> Fell humble, and, embracing them, besought
> His peace; and thus proceeded in her plaint·
>   'Forsake me not thus, Adam! Witness, Heaven,
> What love sincere, and reverence in my heart
> I bear thee, and unweeting have offended,
> Unhappily deceived! Thy suppliant
> I beg, and clasp thy knees. Bereave me not,
> Whereon I live, thy gentle looks, thy aid,
> Thy counsel in this uttermost distress,
> My only strength and stay. Forlorn of thee,
> Whither shall I betake me? where subsist?
> While yet we live, scarce one short hour perhaps,
> Between us two let there be peace'
>   .   .   .   .   .
> She ended weeping; and her lowly plight,
> Immovable till peace obtained from fault
> Acknowledged and deplored, in Adam wrought
> Commiseration. Soon his heart relented
> Towards her, his life so late and sole delight,
> Now at his feet submissive in distress,
> Creature so fair his reconcilement seeking,
> His counsel, whom she had displeased, his aid;
> As one disarmed, his anger all he lost,
> And thus with peaceful words upraised her soon."

Milton thus took back to his home his wandering wife

and not her only, but also her father, mother, and homeless brothers and sisters. So although he had moved to a larger house, it was now full to overflowing, for besides all this Royalist family he had living with him his pupils and his own old father.

CHAPTER LVIII

MILTON—DARKNESS AND DEATH

AND now for twenty years the pen of Milton was used, not for poetry, but for prose. The poet became a politician. Victory was still uncertain, and Milton poured out book after book in support of the Puritan cause. These books are full of wrath and scorn and all the bitter passion of the time. They have hardly a place in true literature, so we may pass them over glad that Milton found it possible to spend his bitterness in prose and leave his poetry what it is.

One only of his prose works is still remembered and still read for its splendid English. That is *Areopagitica,* a passionate appeal for a free press. Milton desired that a man should have not only freedom of thought, but freedom to write down and print and publish these thoughts. But the rulers of England, ever since printing had been introduced, had thought otherwise, and by law no book could be printed until it had been licensed, and no man might set up a printing press without permission from Government. To Milton this was tyranny. "As good almost kill a man as kill a good book," he said, and again "Give me the liberty to know, to utter, and to argue freely according to my conscience above all liberties." He held the licensing law in contempt, and to show his contempt he published *Areopagitica* without a license and without giving the printer's or bookseller's name. It was not the first time Milton had done this, and his enemies tried to use it against him to bring him into trouble. But he had become by this time too important a man, and nothing came of it.

Time went on, the bitter struggle between King and people came to an end. The people triumphed, and the King laid his head upon the block. Britain was without ruler other than Parliament. It was then, one March day in 1649, that a few grave-faced, somber-clad men knocked at the door of Milton's house We can imagine them tramping into the poet's low-roofed study, their heavy shoes resounding on the bare floor, their sad faces shaded with their tall black hats. And there, in sing-song voices, they tell the astonished man that they come from Parliament to ask him to be Secretary for Foreign Tongues.

Milton was astonished, but he accepted the post. And now his life became a very busy one. It had been decided that all letters to foreign powers should be written in Latin, but many Governments wrote to England in their own languages. Milton had to translate these letters, answer them in Latin, and also write little books or pamphlets in answer to those which were written against the Government.

It was while he was busy with this, while he was pouring out bitter abuse upon his enemies or upon the enemies of his party, that his great misfortune fell upon him. He became blind. He had had many warnings. He had been told to be careful of his eyes, for the sight of one had long been gone. But in spite of all warnings he still worked on, and at length became quite blind.

His enemies jeered at him, and said it was a judgment upon him for his wicked writing. But never for a moment did Milton's spirit quail. He had always been sure of himself, sure of his mission in life, sufficient for himself. And now that the horror of darkness shut him off from others, shut him still more into himself, his heart did not fail him. Blind at forty-three, he wrote:—

"When I consider how my light is spent,
Ere half my days, in this dark world and wide,
And that one talent which is death to hide,
Lodg'd with me useless, though my soul more bent
To serve therewith my Maker, and present
My true account, lest He, returning, chide,
'Doth God exact day labour, light denied?'
I fondly ask but Patience, to prevent
That murmur, soon replies, 'God doth not need
Either man's work, or His own gifts, who best
Bear His mild yoke, they serve Him best. His state
Is kingly; thousands at His bidding speed,
And post o'er land and ocean without rest;
They also serve who only stand and wait'"

Milton meant to take up this new burden patiently, but at forty-three, with all the vigor of life still stirring in him, he could not meekly fold his hands to stand and wait. Indeed, his greatest work was still to come. Blind though he was, he did not give up his post of Latin Secretary. He still remained Chief Secretary, and others worked under him, among them Andrew Marvell, the poet. He still gave all his brain and learning to the service of his country, while others supplied his lacking eyesight. But now in the same year Fate dealt him another blow. His wife died. Perhaps there had never been any great love or understanding between these two, for Milton's understanding of all women was unhappy. But now, when he had most need of a woman's kindly help and sympathy, she went from him leaving to his blind care three motherless girls, the eldest of whom was only six years old.

We know little of Milton's home life during the next years. But it cannot have been a happy one. His children ran wild. He tried to teach them in some sort. He was dependent now on others to read to him, and he made his daughters take their share of this. He succeeded in teaching them to read in several languages, but

they understood not a word of what they read, so it was
no wonder that they looked upon it as a wearisome task.
They grew up with neither love for nor understanding of
their stern blind father. To them he was not the great
poet whose name should be one of the triumphs of English
Literature. He was merely a severe father and hard
taskmaster.

Four years after his first wife died Milton married
again. This lady he never saw, but she was gentle and
kind, and he loved her. For fifteen months she wrought
peace and order in his home, then she too died, leaving
her husband more lonely than before. He mourned her
loss in poetic words. He dreamed she came to him one
night:—

> "Came vested all in white, pure as her mind,
> Her face was veil'd; yet to my fancied sight
> Love, sweetness, goodness, in her person shin'd
> So clear, as in no face with more delight
> But O, as to embrace me she inclin'd,
> I wak'd, she fled; and day brought back my night."

With this sonnet (for those lines are part of the last
sonnet Milton ever wrote) it would seem as if a new period
began with Milton, his second period of poetry writing.
Who knows but that it was the sharp sorrow of his loss
which sent him back to poetry. For throughout Milton's
life we can see that it was always something outside himself
which made him write poetry. He did not sing like the
birds because he must, but because he was asked to sing
by some person, or made to sing by some circumstance.

However that may be, it was now that Milton began his
greatest work, *Paradise Lost*. Twenty years before the
thought had come to him that he would write a grand epic.
We have scarcely spoken of an epic since that first of all
our epics, the Story of Beowulf. And although others
had written epics, Milton is to be remembered as the

writer of the great English epic. At first he thought of
taking Arthur for his hero, but as more and more he saw
what a mass of fable had gathered round Arthur, as more
and more he saw how plain a hero Arthur seemed, stripped
of that fable, his mind turned from the subject. And
when, at last, after twenty years of almost unbroken
silence as a poet, he once more let his organ voice be heard,
it was not a man he spoke of, but Man. He told the story
which Caedmon a thousand years before had told of the
war in heaven, of the temptation and fall of man, and of
how Adam and Eve were driven out of the happy garden.

> "Of man's first disobedience, and the fruit
> Of that forbidden tree, whose mortal taste
> Brought death into the world, and all our woe,
> With loss of Eden, till one greater Man
> Restore us, and regain the blissful seat,
> Sing, Heavenly Muse."

You will remember, or if you look back to Chapter XIII.
you can read again about the old poet Caedmon and what
he wrote It was in 1655 that Junius published the so-
called Caedmon Manuscript, and Milton, who was so great
a student, no doubt heard of it and found some one to
read it to him And perhaps these poems helped to
decide him in his choice, although many years before he
had thought of writing on the subject.

Perhaps when you are older it may interest you to read
the poems of Milton and the poems of Caedmon together.
Then you will see how far ahead of the old poet Milton is
in smooth beauty of verse, how far behind him sometimes
in tender knowledge of man and woman. But I do not
think you can hope to read *Paradise Lost* with true pleasure yet a while. It is a long poem in blank verse,
much of it will seem dull to you, and you will find it hard
to be interested in Adam and Eve. For Milton set himself
a task of enormous difficulty when he tried to interest

common men and women in people who were without sin,
who knew not good nor evil. Yet if conceit, if self-assur-
ance, if the want of the larger charity which helps us to
understand another's faults, are sins, then Adam sinned
long before he left Milton's Paradise. In fact, Adam is
often a bore, and at times he proves himself no gentleman
in the highest and best meaning of the word.

But in spite of Adam, in spite of everything that can be
said against it, *Paradise Lost* remains a splendid poem.
Never, perhaps, has the English language been used more
nobly, never has blank verse taken on such stately measure.
Milton does not make pictures for us, like some poets, like
Spenser, for instance; he sings to us. He sings to us, not
like the gay minstrel with his lute, but in stately measured
tones, which remind us most of solemn organ chords.
His voice comes to us, too, out of a poet's country through
which, if we would find our way, we must put our hand in
his and let him guide us while he sings. And only when
we come to love "the best words in the best order" can we
truly enjoy Milton's *Paradise Lost.*

Milton fails at times to interest us in Adam, but he does
interest us in the Bad Angel Satan, and it has been said
over and over again that Satan is his true hero. And
with such a man as Milton this was hardly to be wondered
at. All his life had been a cry for liberty—liberty even
when it bordered on rebellion. And so he could not fail
to make his arch rebel grand, and even in his last degradation we somehow pity him, while feeling that he is almost
too high for pity. Listen to Satan's cry of sorrow and
defiance when he finds himself cast out from Heaven:—

> " 'Is this the region, this the soil, the clime,'
> Said then the lost Archangel, 'this the seat
> That we must change for heaven?'—this mournful gloom
> For that celestial light? Be it so, since he
> Who now is sovran can dispose and bid

What shall be right, farthest from him is best,
Whom reason hath equalled, force hath made supreme
Above his equals. Farewell, happy fields,
Where joy for ever dwells! Hail, horrors! hail,
Infernal world! and thou, profoundest Hell
Receive thy new possessor—one who brings
A mind not to be changed by place or time,
The mind is its own place, and in itself
Can make a Heaven of Hell, a Hell of Heaven.
What matter where, if I be still the same,
And what I should be, all but less than he
Whom thunder hath made greater? Here at least
We shall be free, the Almighty hath not built
Here for his envy, will not drive us hence,
Here we may reign secure, and, in my choice,
To reign is worth ambition, though in Hell
Better to reign in Hell than serve in Heaven'"

Then in contrast to this outburst of regal defiance, read
the last beautiful lines of the poem and see in what softened
mood of submission Milton pictures our first parents as
they leave the Happy Garden:—

"In either hand the hastening Angel caught
Our lingering parents, and to the eastern gate
Led them direct, and down the cliff as fast
To the subjected plain—then disappeared.
They, looking back, all the eastern side beheld
Of Paradise, so late their happy seat,
Waved over by that flaming brand; the gate
With dreadful faces thronged and fiery arms
Some natural tears they dropped, but wiped them soon;
The world was all before them, where to choose
Their place of rest, and Providence their guide
They, hand in hand, with wandering steps and slow,
Through Eden took their solitary way."

Milton worked slowly at this grand poem. Being blind
he had now to depend on others to write out what poetry
he made in his own mind, so it was written "in a parcel of
ten, twenty, or thirty verses at a time by whatever hand

came next." We are told that when he was dictating sometimes he sat leaning back sideways in an easy-chair, with his leg flung over the arm. Sometimes he dictated from his bed, and if in the middle of the night lines came to him, whatever time it was he would ring for one of his daughters to write them down for him, lest the thought should be lost ere morning.

We are told, too, that he wrote very little in summer. For he said himself that it was in winter and spring that his poetic fancy seemed to come best to him, and that what he wrote at other times did not please him. "So that in all the years he was about this poem, he may be said to have spent but half his time therein."[1]

But now, while Milton's mind was full of splendid images, while in spite of the discomfort and loneliness of his misruled home, he was adding line to line of splendid sounding English, great changes came over the land.

Oliver Cromwell died. To him succeeded his son Richard. But his weak hands could not hold the scepter. He could not bind together a rebel people as great Oliver had done. In a few months he gave up the task, and little more than a year later the people who had wept at the death of the great Protector, were madly rejoicing at the return of a despot.

With a Stuart king upon the throne, there was no safety for the rebel poet who had used all the power of his wit and learning against the Royal cause. Pity for his blindness might not save him. So listening to the warnings of his friends, he fled into hiding somewhere in the city of London, "a place of retirement and abscondence."

But after a time the danger passed, and Milton crept forth from his hiding-place. It was perhaps pity for his blind helplessness, perhaps contempt for his powerlessness, that saved him, who can tell? His books were burned by

[1] Philips.

the common hangman, and he found himself in prison for a short time, but he was soon released. While others were dying for their cause, the blind poet whose trumpet call had been Liberty! Liberty! was contemptuously allowed to live.

Now indeed had Milton fallen on dark and evil days. He had escaped with his life and was free. But all that he had worked for during the past twenty years he saw shattered as at one blow. He saw his friends suffering imprisonment and death, himself forsaken and beggared. He found no sympathy at home. His daughters, who had not loved their father in his days of wealth and ease, loved him still less in poverty. They sold his books, cheated him with the housekeeping money, and in every way added to his unhappiness. At length, as a way out of the misery and confusion of his home, Milton married for the third time.

The new wife was a placid, kindly woman. She managed the house, managed too the wild, unruly girls as no one had managed them before. She saw the folly of keeping them, wholly untamed and half-educated as they were, at home, and persuaded her husband to let them learn something by which they might earn a living. So they went out into the world "to learn some curious and ingenious sorts of manufacture, that are proper for women to learn, particularly embroideries in gold and silver."

Thus for the last few years of his life Milton was surrounded by peace and content such as he had never before known. All through life he had never had any one to love him deeply except his father and his mother, whose love for him was perhaps not all wise. Those who had loved him in part had feared him too, and the fear outdid the love. But now in the evening of his days, if no perfect love came to him, he found at least kindly understanding. His wife admired him and cared for him. She had a fair face and pretty voice, and it is pleasant to picture the gray-haired poet sitting at his organ playing while his wife sings. He cannot see the sun gleam and play in her golden hair, or the quick color come and go in her fair face, but at least he can take joy in the sound of her sweet fresh voice.

It was soon after this third marriage that *Paradise Lost* was finished and published. And even in those wild Restoration days, when laughter and pleasure alone were sought, men acknowledged the beauty and grandeur of this grave poem. "This man cuts us all out, and the ancients too," said Dryden, another and younger poet.

People now came to visit the author of *Paradise Lost,* as before they had come to visit great Cromwell's secretary. We have a pleasant picture of him sitting in his garden at the door of his house on sunny days to enjoy the fresh air, for of the many houses in which Milton lived not one was without a garden. There, even when the sun did not shine, wrapt in a great coat of coarse gray cloth, he received his visitors. Or when the weather was colder he sat in an upstairs room hung with rusty green. He wore no sword, as it was the fashion in those days to do, and his clothes were black. His long, light gray hair fell in waves round his pale but not colorless face, and the sad gray eyes with which he seemed to look upon his visitors were still clear and beautiful.

Life had now come for Milton to a peaceful evening time, but his work was not yet finished. He had two great poems still to write.

One was *Paradise Regained*. In this he shows how man's lost happiness was found again in Christ. Here is a second temptation, the temptation in the wilderness, but this time Satan is defeated, Christ victorious.

The second poem was *Samson Agonistes,* which tells the tragic story of Samson in his blindness. And no one reading it can fail to see that it is the story too of Milton in his blindness. It is Milton himself who speaks when he makes Samson exclaim:—

> "O loss of sight, of thee I most complain!
> Blind among enemies O worse than chains,
> Dungeon, or beggary, or decrepit age!
> Light, the prime work of God, to me is extinct,
> And all her various objects of delight
> Annulled, which might in part my grief have eased.
> Inferior to the vilest now become
> Of man or worm· the vilest here excel me,
> They creep, yet see; I, dark in light, exposed
> To daily fraud, contempt, abuse, and wrong,
> Within doors, or without, still as a fool,
> In power of others, never in my own;—
> Scarce half I seem to live, dead more than half.
> O dark, dark, dark, amid the blaze of noon,
> Irrecoverably dark, total eclipse
> Without all hope of day!"

This was Milton's last poem. He lived still four years longer and still wrote. But his singing days were over, and what he now wrote was in prose. His life's work was done, and one dark November evening in 1674 he peacefully died.

> "Thy soul was like a Star, and dwelt apart·
> Thou hadst a voice whose sound was like the sea:
> Pure as the naked heavens, majestic, free,
> So didst thou travel on life's common way." [1]

---

[1] Wordsworth.

CHAPTER LIX

BUNYAN—"THE PILGRIM'S PROGRESS"

THE second great Puritan writer of England was John Bunyan. He was born in 1628, more than twenty years after Milton. His father was a tinker. A tinker! The word makes us think of ragged, weather-worn men and women who wander about the countryside. They carry bundles of old umbrellas, and sometimes a battered kettle or two. They live, who knows how? they sleep, who knows where? Sometimes in our walks we come across a charred round patch upon the grass in some quiet nook by the roadside, and we know the tinkers have been there, and can imagine all sorts of stories about them Or sometimes, better still, we find them really there by the roadside boiling a mysterious three-legged black kettle over a fire of sticks.

But John Bunyan's father was not this kind of tinker. He did not wander about the countryside, but lived at the little village of Elstow, about a mile from the town of Bedford, as his father had before him. He was a poor and honest workman who mended his neighbors' kettles and pans, and did his best to keep his family in decent comfort.

One thing which shows this is that little John was sent to school. In those days learning, even learning to read and write, was not the just due of every one. It was only for the well-to-do. "But yet," says Bunyan himself, "notwithstanding the meanness and inconsiderableness of my parents, it pleased God to put it into their hearts to put me to school, to learn me both to read and write."

Bunyan was born when the struggle between King and people was beginning to be felt, and was a great boy of fourteen when at last the armies of King and Parliament met on the battlefield of Edgehill. To many this struggle was a struggle for freedom in religion. From end to end of our island the question of religion was the burning question of the day. Religion had wrought itself into the lives of people. In those days of few books the Bible was the one book which might be found in almost every house. The people carried it in their hands, and its words were ever on their lips. But the religion which came to be the religion of more than half the people of England was a stern one. They forgot the Testament of Love, they remembered only the Testament of Wrath. They made the narrow way narrower, and they believed that any who strayed from it would be punished terribly and eternally. It was into this stern world that little John Bunyan was born, and just as a stern religious struggle was going on in England so a stern religious struggle went on within his little heart. He heard people round him talk of sins and death, of a dreadful day of judgment, of wrath to come. These things laid hold of his childish mind and he began to believe that in the sight of God he must be a desperate sinner. Dreadful dreams came to him at night. He dreamed that the Evil One was trying to carry him off to a darksome place there to be "bound down with the chains and bonds of darkness, unto the judgment of the great day." Such dreams made night terrible to him.

Bunyan tells us that he swore and told lies and that he was the ringleader in all the wickedness of the village. But perhaps he was not so bad as he would have us believe, for he was always very severe in his judgments of himself. Perhaps he was not worse than many other boys who did not feel that they had sinned beyond all forgiveness. And in spite of his awful thoughts and terrifying dreams

Bunyan still went on being a naughty boy; he still told lies and swore.

At length he left school and became a tinker like his father. But all England was being drawn into war, and so Bunyan, when about seventeen, became a soldier.

Strange to say we do not know upon which side he fought. Some people think that because his father belonged to the Church of England that he must have fought on the King's side. But that is nothing to go by, for many people belonged to that Church for old custom's sake who had no opinions one way or another, and who took no side until forced by the war to do so. It seems much more likely that Bunyan, so Puritan in all his ways of thought, should fight for the Puritan side. But we do not know. He was not long a soldier, we do not know quite how long, it was perhaps only a few months. But during these few months his life was saved by, what seemed to him afterwards to have been a miracle.

"When I was a soldier," he says, "I, with others, were drawn out to go to such a place to besiege it. But when I was just ready to go one of the company desired to go in my room. To which, when I had consented, he took my place. And coming to the siege, as he stood sentinel, he was shot in the head with a musket bullet, and died.

"Here, as I said, were judgments and mercy, but neither of them did awaken my soul to righteousness. Wherefore I sinned still, and grew more and more rebellious against God."

So whether Bunyan served in the Royal army, where he might have heard oaths, or in the Parliamentarian, where he might have heard godly songs and prayers, he still went on his way as before.

Some time after Bunyan left the army, and while he was still very young, he married. Both he and his wife were, he says, "as poor as poor might be, not having so much household stuff as a dish or a spoon betwixt us both. Yet this she had for her part, *The Plain Man's Pathway to Heaven* and *The Practice of Piety,* which her father had left her when he died."

These two books Bunyan read with his wife, picking up again the art of reading, which he had been taught at school, and which he had since almost forgotten. He began now to go a great deal to church, and one of his chief pleasures was helping to ring the bells. To him the services were a joy. He loved the singing, the altar with its candles, the rich robes, the white surplices, and everything that made the service beautiful. Yet the terrible struggle between good and evil in his soul went on. He seemed to hear voices in the air, good voices and bad voices, voices that accused him, voices that tempted. He was a most miserable man, and seemed to himself to be one of the most wicked, and yet perhaps the worst thing he could accuse himself of doing was playing games on Sunday, and pleasing himself by bell-ringing. He gave up his bell-ringing because it was a temptation to vanity. "Yet my mind hankered, therefore I would go to the steeple house and look on, though I durst not ring." One by one he gave up all the things he loved, things that even if we think them wrong do not seem to us to merit everlasting punishment. But at last the long struggle ended and his tortured mind found rest in the love of Christ.

Bunyan himself tells us the story of this long fight in a book called *Grace Abounding to the Chief of Sinners.* As we read we cannot help but see that Bunyan was never a very wicked man, but merely a man with a very tender conscience. Things which seemed to other men trifles were to him deadly sins; and although he was so stern to himself, to others he showed a fatherly tenderness which makes us feel that this rough tinker was no narrow Puritan, but a broad-minded, large-hearted Christian. And now that

Bunyan had found peace he became a Baptist, and joined the church of a man whom he calls "the holy Mr. Gifford." Gifford had been an officer in the Royal army. He had been wild and drunken, but repenting of his evil ways had become a preacher. Now, until he died some years later, he was Bunyan's fast friend.

In the same year as Bunyan lost his friend his wife too died, and he was left alone with four children, two of them little girls, one of whom was blind. She was, because of that, all the more dear to him. "She lay nearer to my heart than all beside," he says.

And now Bunyan's friends found out his great gift of speech. They begged him to preach, but he was so humble and modest that at first he refused. At length, however, he was over-persuaded. He began his career as a minister and soon became famous. People came from long distances to hear him, and he preached not only in Elstow and Bedford but in all the country round   He preached, not only in churches, but in barns and in fields, by the roadside or in the market-place, anywhere, in fact, where he could gather an audience.

It was while Cromwell ruled that Bunyan began this ministry. But in spite of all the battles that had been fought for religious freedom, there was as yet no real religious freedom in England. Each party, as it became powerful, tried to tyrannize over every other party, and no one was allowed to preach without a license. The Presbyterians were now in power; Bunyan was a Baptist, and some of the Presbyterians would gladly have silenced him. Yet during Cromwell's lifetime he went his way in peace. Then the Restoration came. A few months later Bunyan was arrested for preaching without a license. Those who now ruled "were angry with the tinker because he strove to mend souls as well as kettles and pans." [1] Before he was

[1] Henry Deane.

taken prisoner Bunyan was warned of his danger, and if he had "been minded to have played the coward" he might have escaped. But he would not try to save himself. "If I should now run to make an escape," he said, "it will be a very ill savour in the country. For what will my weak and newly-converted brethren think of it but that I was not so strong in deed as I was in word."

So Bunyan was taken prisoner. Even then he might have been at once set free would he have promised not to preach. But to all persuasions he replied, "I durst not leave off that work which God has called me to."

Thus Bunyan's long imprisonment of twelve years began. He had married again by this time, and the parting with his wife and children was hard for him, and harder still for the young wife left behind "all smayed at the news." But although she was dismayed she was brave of heart, and she at once set about eagerly doing all she could to free her husband. She went to London, she ventured into the House of Lords, and there pleaded for him. Touched by her earnestness and her helplessness the Lords treated her kindly. But they told her they could do nothing for her and that she must plead her case before the ordinary judges.

So back to Bedford she went, and with beating heart and trembling limbs sought out the judges. Again she was kindly received, but again her petition was of no avail. The law was the law. Bunyan had broken the law and must suffer. He would not promise to cease from preaching, she would as little promise for him. "My lord," she said, "he dares not leave off preaching as long as he can speak."

So it was all useless labor, neither side could or would give way one inch. Bursting into tears the poor young wife turned away. But she wept "not so much because they were so hard-hearted against me and my husband, but to think what a sad account such poor creatures will have to give at the coming of the Lord, when they shall then answer for all things whatsoever they have done in the body, whether it be good, or whether it be bad."

Seeing there was no help for it, Bunyan set himself bravely to endure his imprisonment. And, in truth, this was not very severe. Strangely enough he was allowed to preach to his fellow-prisoners, he was even at one time allowed to go to church. But the great thing for us is that he wrote books. Already, before his imprisonment, he had written several books, and now he wrote that for which he is most famous, the *Pilgrim's Progress*.

It is a book so well known and so well loved that I think I need say little about it. In the form of a dream Bunyan tells, as you know, the story of Christian who sets out on his long and difficult pilgrimage from the City of Destruction to the City of the Blest. He tells of all Christian's trials and adventures on the way, of how he encounters giants and lions, of how he fights with a great demon, and of how at length he arrives at his journey's end in safety. A great writer has said, "There is no book in our literature on which we would so readily stake the fame of the old unpolluted English language, no book which shows so well how rich that language is in its own proper wealth, and how little it has been improved by all that it has borrowed." [1]

For the power of imagination this writer places Bunyan by the side of Milton. Although there were many clever men in England towards the end of the seventeenth century, there were only two minds which had great powers of imagination. "One of those minds produced the *Paradise Lost*, the other the *Pilgrim's Progress*." That is very great praise, and yet although Milton and Bunyan are

[1] Macaulay

thus placed side by side no two writers are more widely apart Milton's writing is full of the proofs of his learning, his English is fine and stately, but it is full of words made from Latin words. As an early writer on him said, "Milton's language is English, but it is Milton's English." [1]

On the other hand, Bunyan's writing is most simple. He uses strong, plain, purely English words. There is hardly one word in all his writings which a man who knows his Bible cannot easily understand. And it was from the Bible that Bunyan gathered nearly all his learning. He knew it from end to end, and the poetry and grandeur of its language filled his soul. But he read other books, too, among them, we feel sure, the *Faery Queen*. Some day you may like to compare the adventures of the Red Cross Knight with the adventures of Christian. And perhaps in all the *Faery Queen* you will find nothing so real and exciting as Christian's fight with Apollyon. Apollyon comes from a Greek word meaning the destroyer. This is how Bunyan tells of the fight:—

"But now in this Valley of Humiliation poor Christian was hard put to it. For he had gone but a little way before he espied a Foul Fiend coming over the field to meet him. His name is Apollyon. Then did Christian begin to be afraid and to cast in his mind whether to go back or to stand his ground. But he considered again, that he had no armour for his back, and therefore thought that to turn the back to him might give him greater advantage, with ease, to pierce him with his darts. Therefore he resolved to venture and stand his ground. For, he thought, had I no more in mine eye than the saving of my life, 'twould be the best way to stand.

"So he went on, and Apollyon met him. Now the Monster was hideous to behold. He was clothed with

[1] Richardson.

scales like a fish, and they are his pride. He had wings like a dragon, feet like a bear, and out of his belly came fire and smoke. And his mouth was as the mouth of a lion. When he came up to Christian he beheld him with a disdainful countenance, and thus began to question him.

"APOLLYON. Whence came you? and whither are you bound?

"CHRISTIAN. I am come from the City of Destruction, which is the place of all evil, and am going to the City of Zion."

After this Apollyon argued with Christian, trying to persuade him to give up his pilgrimage and return to his evil ways. But Christian would listen to nothing that Apollyon could say.

"Then Apollyon straddled quite over the whole breadth of the Way and said, 'I am void of fear in this matter. Prepare thyself to die, for I swear by my Infernal Den that thou shalt go no further. Here will I spill thy soul!'

"And with that he threw a flaming dart at his heart. But Christian had a shield in his hand, with which he caught it, and so prevented the danger of that.

"Then did Christian draw, for he saw it was time to bestir him, and Apollyon as fast made at him, throwing darts as thick as hail, by the which, notwithstanding all that Christian could do to avoid it, Apollyon wounded him in his head, his hand, and foot. This made Christian give a little back. Apollyon therefore followed his work amain, and Christian again took courage and resisted as manfully as he could. This sore combat lasted for above half a day, even till Christian was almost quite spent. For you must know that Christian, by reason of his wounds, must needs grow weaker and weaker.

"Then Apollyon espying his opportunity began to gather up close to Christian, and wrestling with him gave him a dreadful fall. And with that Christian's sword flew out of his hand. Then said Apollyon, 'I am sure of thee now.' And with that he had almost pressed him to death so that Christian began to despair of life. But, as God would have it, while Apollyon was fetching his last blow, thereby to make a full end of this good man, Christian nimbly reached out his hand for his sword and caught it, saying, 'Rejoice not against me, O mine Enemy! when I fall I shall arise!' and with that gave him a deadly thrust which made him give back, as one that had received his mortal wound.

"Christian perceiving that made at him again, saying, 'Nay in all these things we are more than conquerors through Him that loved us.' And with that Apollyon spread forth his dragon's wings and sped him away, and Christian saw him no more."

Bunyan wrote a second part or sequel to the *Pilgrim's Progress,* in which he tells of the adventures of Christian's wife and children on their way to Zion. But the story does not interest us as the story of Christian does. Because we love Christian we are glad to know that his wife and children escaped destruction, but except that they belong to him we do not really care about them.

Bunyan wrote several other books. The best known are *The Holy War* and *Grace Abounding. The Holy War* might be called a *Paradise Lost* and *Regained* in homely prose. It tells much the same story, the story of the struggle between Good and Evil for the possession of man's soul.

In *Grace Abounding* Bunyan tells of his own struggle with evil, and it is from that book that we learn much of what we know of his life.

He also wrote the *Life and Death of Mr. Badman.* Instead of telling how a good man struggles with evil and at last wins rest, it tells of how a bad man yields always to evil and comes at last to a sad end. It is not a pretty story, and is one, I think, which you will not care to read.

Bunyan, too, wrote a good deal of rime, but for the most part it can hardly be called poetry. It is for his prose that we remember him. Yet who would willingly part with the song of the shepherd-boy in the second part of the *Pilgrim's Progress:*—

> "He that is down needs fear no fall;
>   He that is low, no pride
> He that is humble, ever shall
>   Have God to be his guide
>
> I am content with what I have,
>   Little be it or much
> And, Lord, contentment still I crave,
>   Because thou savest such.
>
> Fullness to such a burden is
>   That go on pilgrimage
> Here little, and hereafter bliss,
>   Is best from age to age"

When Bunyan had been in prison for six years he was set free, but as he at once began to preach he was immediately seized and reimprisoned. He remained shut up for six years longer. Then King Charles II. passed an Act called the Declaration of Indulgence. By this Act all the severe laws against those who did not conform to the Church of England were done away with, and, in consequence, Bunyan was set free. Charles passed this Act, not because he was sorry for the Nonconformists—as all who would not conform to the Church of England were called—but because he wished to free the Roman Catholics, and he could not do that without freeing the Nonconformists too. Two years later Bunyan was again imprisoned because "in contempt of his Majesty's good laws he preached or teached in other manner than according to the Liturgy or practice of the Church of England." But this time his imprisonment lasted only six months. And I must tell you that many people now think that it was during this later short imprisonment that Bunyan wrote the *Pilgrim's Progress,* and not during the earlier and longer.

The rest of Bunyan's life passed peacefully and happily. But we know few details of it, for "he seems to have been too busy to keep any records of his busy life." [1] We know at least that it was busy. He was now a licensed preacher, and if the people had flocked to hear him before his imprisonment they flocked in far greater numbers now. Even learned men came to hear him. "I marvel," said King Charles to one, "that a learned man such as you can sit and listen to an unlearned tinker."

"May it please your Majesty," replied he, "I would gladly give up all my learning if I could preach like that tinker."

Bunyan became the head of the Baptist Church. Near and far he traveled, preaching and teaching, honored and beloved wherever he went. And his word had such power, his commands such weight, that people playfully called him Bishop Bunyan. Yet he was "not puffed up in prosperity, nor shaken in adversity, always holding the golden mean." [2]

Death found Bunyan still busy, still kindly. A young man who lived at Reading had offended his father so greatly that the father cast him off. In his trouble the young man came to Bunyan. He at once mounted his horse and rode off to Reading. There he saw the angry father, and persuaded him to make peace with his repentant son.

Glad at his success, Bunyan rode on to London where he meant to preach. But the weather was bad, the roads were heavy with mud, he was overtaken by a storm of rain, and ere he could find shelter he was soaked to the

[1] Brown   [2] Charles Doe

DURING HIS IMPRISONMENT BUNYAN WROTE THE "PILGRIM'S PROGRESS"

skin. He arrived at length at a friend's house wet and weary and shaking with fever. He went to bed never to rise again. The time had come when, like Christian, he must cross the river which all must cross "where there is no bridge to go over and the river very deep." But Bunyan, like Christian, was held up by Hope. He well knew the words, "When thou passest through the waters I will be with thee, and through the rivers they shall not overflow thee." And so he crossed over.

And may we not believe that Bunyan, when he reached the other side, heard again, as he had once before heard in his immortal dream, "all the bells in the city ring again with joy," and that it was said unto him, "Enter ye into the joy of our Lord"?

CHAPTER LX

DRYDEN—THE NEW POETRY

"The life of Dryden may be said to comprehend a history of the literature of England, and its changes, during nearly half a century." With these words Sir Walter Scott, himself a great writer, began his life of John Dryden. Yet although John Dryden stands for so much in the story of our literature, as a man we know little of him. As a writer his influence on the age in which he lived was tremendous. As a man he is more shadowy than almost any other greater writer. We seem to know Chaucer, and Spenser, and Milton, and even Shakespeare a little, but to know Dryden in himself seems impossible. We can only know him through his works, and through his age. And in him we find the expression of his age.

With Milton ended the great romantic school of poetry. He was indeed as one born out of time, a lonely giant. He died and left no follower. With Dryden began a new school of poetry, which was to be the type of English poetry for a hundred and fifty years to come. This is called the classical school, and the rime which the classical poets used is called the heroic couplet. It is a long ten-syllabled line, and rimes in couplets, as, for instance:—

> "He sought the storms; but, for a calm unfit,
> Would stem too nigh the sands, to boast his wit,
> Great wits are sure to madness near allied,
> And thin partitions do their bounds divide " [1]

---

[1] *Absalom and Achitophel*

Dryden did not invent the heroic couplet, but it was he who first made it famous. "It was he," says Scott, "who first showed that the English language was capable of uniting smoothness and strength." But when you come to read Dryden's poems you may perhaps feel that in gaining the smoothness of Art they have lost something of the beauty of Nature. The perfect lines with their regular sounding rimes almost weary us at length, and we are glad to turn to the rougher beauty of some earlier poet.

But before speaking more of what Dryden did let me tell you a little of what we know of his life.

John Dryden was the son of a Northamptonshire gentleman who had a small estate and a large family, for John was the eldest of fourteen children. The family was a Puritan one, although in 1631, when John was born, the Civil War had not yet begun.

When John Dryden left school he went, like nearly all the poets, to Cambridge. Of what he did at college we know very little. He may have been wild, for more than once he got into trouble, and once he was "rebuked on the head" for speaking scornfully of some nobleman. He was seven years at Cambridge, but he looked back on these years with no joy. He had no love for his University, and even wrote:—

> "Oxford to him a dearer name shall be,
> Than his own Mother University"

Already at college Dryden had begun to write poetry, but his poem on the death of Cromwell is perhaps the first that is worth remembering:—

> "Swift and relentless through the land he past,
> Like that bold Greek, who did the East subdue;
> And made to battles such heroic haste
> As if on wings of victory he flew

He fought secure of fortune as of fame,
Till by new maps the island might be shown
Of conquests, which he strewed where'er he came,
Thick as the galaxy with stars is sown

Nor was he like those stars which only shine,
When to pale mariners they storms portend,
He had a calmer influence, and his mien
Did love and majesty together blend.

Nor died he when his ebbing fame went less,
But when fresh laurels courted him to live
He seemed but to prevent some new success,
As if above what triumphs earth could give.

His ashes in a peaceful urn shall rest;
His name a great example stands to show,
How strangely high endeavours may be blessed,
Where piety and valour jointly go "

So wrote Dryden. But after the death of Cromwell
came the Restoration. Dryden had been able to admire
Cromwell, but although he came of a Puritan family he
could never have been a Puritan at heart. What we learn
of him in his writings shows us that. He was not of the
stern stuff which makes martyrs and heroes. There was
no reason why he should suffer for a cause in which he did
not whole-heartedly believe. So Dryden turned Royalist,
and the very next poem he wrote was *On the Happy
Restoration and Return of His Majesty Charles the Second.*

"How easy 'tis when destiny proves kind,
With full-spread sails to run before the wind!" [1]

So Dryden ran before the wind.

About three years after the Restoration Dryden
married an earl's daughter, Lady Elizabeth Howard.
We know very little about their life together, but they had
three children of whom they were very fond.

[1] *Astræa Redux*

With the Restoration came the re-opening of the theaters, and for fourteen years Dryden was known as a dramatic poet. There is little need to tell you anything about his plays, for you would not like to read them. During the reign of Puritanism in England the people had been forbidden even innocent pleasures. The Maypole dances had been banished, games and laughter were frowned upon. Now that these too stern laws had been taken away, people plunged madly into pleasure: laughter became coarse, merriment became riotous. Puritan England had lost the sense of where innocent pleasure ends and wickedness begins. In another way Restoration England did the same. The people of the Restoration saw fun and laughter in plays which seem to us now simply vulgar and coarse as well as dull. The coarseness, too, is not the coarseness of an ignorant people who know no better, but rather of a people who do know better and who yet prefer to be coarse. I do not mean to say that there are no well-drawn characters, no beautiful lines, in Dryden's plays, for that would not be true. Many of them are clever, the songs in them are often beautiful, but nearly all are unpleasant to read. The taste of the Restoration times condemned Dryden to write in a way unworthy of himself for money. "Neither money nor honour—that in two words was the position of writers after the Restoration." [1]

> "And Dryden, in immortal strain,
> Had raised the table-round again
> But that a ribald King and Court
> Bade him toil on to make them sport,
> Demanding for their niggard pay,
> Fit for their souls, a loser lay" [2]

Had Dryden written nothing but plays we should not remember him as one of our great poets. Yet it was

[1] Beljame, *Le Public et les Hommes de Lettres en Angleterre.*
[2] Walter Scott, *Marmion.*

during this time of play-writing that Dryden was made Poet Laureate and Historiographer Royal with the salary of £200 a year and a butt of sack. It was after he became Poet Laureate that Dryden began to write his satires, the poems for which he is most famous. Although a satire is a poem which holds wickedness up to scorn, sometimes it was used, not against the wicked and the foolish, but against those who merely differed from the writer in politics or religion or any other way of life or thought. Such was Dryden's best satire—thought by some people the best in the English language. It is called *Absalom and Achitophel.* To understand it we must know and understand the history of the times. Here in the guise of the old Bible story Dryden seeks to hold Lord Shaftesbury up to scorn because he tried to have a law passed which would prevent the King's brother James from succeeding to the throne, and which would instead place the Duke of Monmouth there. When the poem was published Shaftesbury was in the Tower awaiting his trial for high treason. The poem had a great effect, but Shaftesbury was nevertheless set free.

In spite of the fine sounding lines you will perhaps never care to read *Absalom and Achitophel* save as a footnote to history. But Dryden's was the age of satire. Those he wrote called forth others. He was surrounded and followed by many imitators, and it is well to remember Dryden as the greatest of them all. His satires were so powerful, too, that the people against whom they were directed felt them keenly, and no wonder. "There are passages in Dryden's satires in which every couplet has not only the force but the sound of a slap in the face," says a recent writer.[1]

Among the younger writers Dryden took the place Ben Jonson used to hold. He kinged it in the coffee-house,

[1] Saintsbury

then the fashionable place at which the wits gathered, as Jonson had in the tavern. He was given the most honored seat, in summer by the window, in winter by the fire. And although he was not a great talker like Jonson, the young wits crowded around him, eager for the honor of a word or a pinch from the great man's snuff-box.

Besides his plays and satires Dryden wrote a poem in support of the English Church called *Religio Laici*. Then a few years later, when Charles ii. died and James ii. came to the throne, Dryden turned Roman Catholic and wrote a poem called *The Hind and the Panther* in praise of the Church of Rome.

But the reign of James ii. was short. The "Glorious Revolution" came, and with a Protestant King and Queen upon the throne, the Catholic Poet Laureate lost his post and pension and all his other appointments. Dryden was now nearly sixty; and although he had made what was then a good deal of money by his plays and other poems he had spent it freely, and always seemed in need. Now he had to face want and poverty. But he faced them bravely. Dryden all his life had been a flatterer; he had always sailed with the wind. Now, whether he could not or would not, he changed no more, he flattered no more. A kind friend, it is said, still continued to pay him the two hundred pounds he had received as Poet Laureate, and he now wrote more plays which brought him money. Then, thus late in life, he began the work which for you at present will have the greatest interest. Dryden was a great poet, but he could create nothing, he had to have given him ideas upon which to work. Now he began translations from Latin poets, and for those who cannot read them in the original they are still a great pleasure and delight.

True, Dryden did not translate literally, that is word for word. He paraphrased rather, and in doing so he Drydenized the originals, often adding whole lines of his

own. Among his translations was Virgil's *Æneid,* which
long before, you remember, Surrey had begun in blank
verse. But blank verse was not what the age in which
Dryden lived desired, and he knew it. So he wrote
in rimed couplets. Long before this he had turned
Milton's *Paradise Lost* into rimed couplets, making it
into an opera, which he called *The State of Innocence.*
An opera is a play set to music, but this opera was never
set to music, and never sung or acted. Dryden, we
know, admired Milton's poetry greatly. "This man cuts
us all out," he had said. Yet he thought he could make
the poem still better, and asked Milton's leave to turn
it into rime. "Ay, you may tag my verses if you will,"
replied the great blind man.

It is interesting to compare the two poems, and when
you come to read *The State of Innocence* you will find that
not all the verses are "tagged." So that in places you
can compare Milton's blank verse with Dryden's. And
although Dryden must have thought he was improving
Milton's poem, he says himself: "Truly I should be sorry,
for my own sake, that any one should take the pains to
compare them (the poems) together, the original being,
undoubtedly, one of the greatest, most noble, and most
sublime poems which either this age or nation has produced."

Dryden begins his poem with the speech of Satan, Lucifer
he calls him, on finding himself cast out from heaven:—

> "Is this the seat our conqueror has given?
> And this the climate we must change for heaven?
> These regions and this realm my wars have got;
> This mournful empire is the loser's lot;
> In liquid burnings, or on dry, to dwell,
> Is all the sad variety of hell"

If you turn back to page 401 you can compare this with
Milton's own version.

Besides translating some Latin and a few Greek poems Dryden translated stories from Boccaccio, Chaucer's old friend, and last of all he translated Chaucer himself into Drydenese. For in Dryden's day Chaucer's language had already become so old-fashioned that few people troubled to read him. "It is so obsolete," says Dryden, "that his sense is scarce to be understood." "I find some people are offended that I have turned these tales into modern English, because they think them unworthy of my pains, and look on Chaucer as a dry, old-fashioned wit not worthy reviving."

Again he says: "But there are other judges, who think I ought not to have translated Chaucer into English, out of a quite contrary notion. They suppose there is a certain veneration due to his old language, and that it is little less than profanation and sacrilege to alter it. They are further of opinion that somewhat of his good sense will suffer in this transfusion, and much of the beauty of his thoughts will infallibly be lost, which appear with more grace in their old habit." I think all of us who can read Chaucer in his own language must agree with these judges. But Dryden goes on to say he does not write for such, but for those who cannot read Chaucer's English. Are they who can understand Chaucer to deprive the greater part of their countrymen of the same advantage, and hoard him up, as misers do their gold, only to look on it themselves and hinder others from making use of it? he asks.

This is very good reasoning, and all that can be said against it is that when Dryden has done with Chaucer, although he tells the same tales, they are no longer Chaucer's but Dryden's. The spirit is changed. But that you will be able to feel only when you grow older and are able to read the two and balance them one against the other. Dryden translated only a few of the *Canterbury Tales,* and the one he liked best was the knight's tale of

Palamon and Arcite. He published it in a book which he called *Fables,* and it is, I think, as a narrative or story-telling poet in these fables, and in his translations, that he keeps most interest for the young people of to-day.

You have by this time, I hope, read the story of Palamon and Arcite at least in *Tales* from Chaucer, and here I will give you a few lines first from Dryden and then from Chaucer, so that you can judge for yourselves of the difference. In them the poets describe Emelia as she appeared on that May morning when Palamon first looked forth from his prison and saw her walk in the garden:—

> "Thus year by year they pass, and day by day,
> Till once,—'twas on the morn of cheerful May,—
> The young Emila, fairer to be seen
> Than the fair lily on the flowery green,
> More flesh than May herself in blossoms new,
> For with the rosy colour strove her hue,
> Waked, as her custom was, before the day,
> To do the observance due to sprightly May;
> For sprightly May commands our youth to keep
> The vigils of her night, and breaks their sluggard sleep;
> Each gentle breast with kindly warmth she moves;
> Inspires new flames, revives extinguished loves
> In this remembrance, Emily, ere day,
> Arose, and dressed herself in rich array,
> Fresh as the month, and as the morning fair,
> Adown her shoulders fell her length of hair;
> A ribbon did the braided tresses bind,
> The rest was loose, and wantoned in the wind:
> Aurora had but newly chased the night,
> And purpled o'er the sky with blushing light,
> When to the garden walk she took her way,
> To sport and trip along in cool of day,
> And offer maiden vows in honour of the May.
> At every turn she made a little stand,
> And thrust among the thorns her lily hand
> To draw the rose, and every rose she drew,
> She shook the stalk, and brushed away the dew,

Then party-coloured flowers of white and red
She wove, to make a garland for her head
This done, she sung and carolled out so clear,
That men and angels might rejoice to hear,
Even wondering Philomel forgot to sing,
And learned from her to welcome in the Spring."

That is Dryden's, and this is how Chaucer tells of the
same May morning:—

"This passeth yeer by yeer, and day by day,
Till it fel oones in a morwe of May
That Emelie, that fairer was to scene
Than is the lilie on his stalke grene,
And fressher than the May with floures newe—
For with the rose colour strof hire hewe,
I not which was the fairer of hem two—
Er it were day, as was hir wone to do,
She was arisen and al redy dight.
For May wol have no sloggardye anight.
The seson priketh every gentil herte,
And maketh him out of his sleep to sterte,
And seith, 'Arise and do thin observance'.
This maked Emelye have remembrance
To don honour to May, and for to rise
I-clothed was she fressh for to devise,
Hir yelowe heer was broyded in a tresse,
Behinde hir bak, a yerde long I gesse;
And in the gardyn at the sunne upriste
She walketh up and doun, and as hir liste
She gadereth floures, party white and rede,
To make a subtil garland for hir hede,
And as an angel hevenly she song."

In this quotation from Chaucer I have not changed the
old spelling into modern as I did in the chapter on Chaucer,
so that you may see the difference between the two styles
more clearly.

If you can see the difference between these two quotations you can see the difference between the poetry of
Dryden's age and all that went before him. It is the

difference between art and nature. Chaucer sings like a bird, Dryden like a trained conceit singer who knows that people are listening to him. There is room for both in life. We want and need both.

If you can feel the difference between Chaucer and Dryden you will understand in part what I meant by saying that Dryden was the expression of his time. For in Restoration times the taste was for art rather than for natural beauty. The taste was for what was clever, witty, and polished rather than for the simple, stately grandeur of what was real and true. Poetry was utterly changed. It no longer went to the heart but to the brain. Dryden's poetry does not make the tears start to our eye or the blood come to our cheek, but it flatters our ear with its smoothness and elegance; it tickles our fancy with its wit.

You will understand still better what the feeling of the times was when I tell you that Dryden, with the help of another poet, re-wrote Shakespeare's *Tempest* and made it to suit the fashion of the day. In doing so they utterly spoiled it. As literature it is worthless; as helping us to understand the history of those times it is useful. But although *The Tempest,* as re-written by Dryden, is bad, one of the best of his plays is founded upon another of Shakespeare's. This play is called *All for Love or the World Well Lost,* and is founded upon Shakespeare's *Antony and Cleopatra.* It is not written in Dryden's favorite heroic couplet but in blank verse. "In my style," he says, "I have professed to imitate the divine Shakespeare, which, that I might perform more freely, I have disencumbered myself from rhyme. Not that I condemn my former way, but that this is more proper to my present purpose." And when you come to read this play you will find that, master as Dryden was of the heroic couplet, he could write, too, when he chose, fine blank verse.

Perhaps the best-known of all Dryden's shorter poems

is the ode called *Alexander's Feast*. It was written for a
London musical society, which gave a concert each year
on St. Cecilia's day, when an original ode was sung in her
honor. Dryden in this ode, which was sung in 1697,
pictures Timotheus, the famous Greek musician and poet,
singing before Alexander, at a great feast which was held
after the conquest of Persia. Alexander listens while

> "The lovely Thais, by his side,
> Sate like a blooming Eastern bride,
> In flower of youth and beauty's pride.
> Happy, happy, happy pair!
> None but the brave,
> None but the brave,
> None but the brave deserves the fair!"

As Timotheus sings he stirs at will his hearers' hearts to
love, to pity, or to revenge.

> "Timotheus, to his breathing flute
> And sounding lyre,
> Could swell the soul to rage, or kindle soft desire."

But those were heathen times. In Christian times came
St. Cecilia and she

> "Enlarged the former narrow bounds,
> And added length to solemn sounds,
> With nature's Mother-wit, and arts unknown before.
> Let old Timotheus yield the prize.
> Or both divide the crown:
> He raised a mortal to the skies
> She drew an angel down"

Dryden was a great poet, and he dominated his own age
and the age to come. But besides being a poet he was a
great prose-writer. His prose is clear and fine and almost
modern. We do not have to follow him through sentences
so long that we lose the sense before we come to the end.
"He found English of brick and left it marble," says a late

writer, and when we read his prose we almost believe that
saying to be true. He was the first of modern critics, that
is he was able to judge the works of others surely and well.
And many of his criticisms of men were so true that
we accept them now even as they were accepted then.
Here is what he says of Chaucer in his preface to *The
Fables*:—

"He [Chaucer] must have been a man of a most
wonderful comprehensive nature, because as it has been
truly observed of him, he has taken into the compass of
his *Canterbury Tales* the various manners and humours (as
we now call them) of the whole English nation, in his age.
Not a single character has escaped him. All his pilgrims
are severally distinguished from each other; and not only
in their inclinations, but in their very physiognomies and
persons. . . . The matter and manner of their tales, and
of their telling, are so suited to their different educations,
humours, and callings, that each of them would be im-
proper in any other mouth. Even the grave and serious
characters are distinguished by their several sorts of
gravity. Their discourses are such as belong to their age,
their calling, and their breeding; such as are becoming to
them and to them only. Some of his persons are vicious,
and some virtuous; some are unlearned, or (as Chaucer
calls them) lewd, and some are learned. Even the ribaldry
of the low characters is different: the Reeve, the Miller, and
the Cook, are several men, and distinguished from each other
as much as the mincing Lady-Prioress and the broad-
speaking, gap-toothed Wife of Bath. . . . It is sufficient
to say, according to the proverb, that here is God's plenty.
We have our forefathers and great-grand-dames all before
us, as they were in Chaucer's days. Their general characters are still remaining in mankind, and even in England,
though they are called by other names than those of monks,
and friars, and canons, and lady abbesses, and nuns;

for mankind is ever the same, and nothing lost out of nature though everything is altered."

The Fables was the last book Dryden wrote. He was growing to be an old man, and a few months after it was published he became very ill. "John Dryden, Esq., the famous poet, lies a-dying," said the newspapers on the 30th April, 1700. On May Morning he closed his eyes for ever, just as

"Aurora had but newly chased the night,
And purpled o'er the sky with blushing light."

CHAPTER LXI

DEFOE—THE FIRST NEWSPAPERS

To almost every house in the land, as regular as the milk-man, more regular than the postman, there comes each morning the newspaper boy. To most of us breakfast means, as well as things to eat, mother pouring out the tea and father reading the newspaper. As mother passes father's tea she says, "Anything in the paper, John?" And how often he answers, "Nothing, nothing whatever."

Although father says there is nothing in the paper there is a great deal of reading in it, that we can see. And now comes the question, Who writes it all? Who writes this thin, flat book of six or eight great pages which every morning we buy for a penny or a halfpenny? But perhaps you think it does not matter who writes the newspaper, for the newspaper is not literature. Literature means real books with covers—dear possessions to be loved and taken care of, to be read and read again. But a newspaper is hardly read at all when it is crumpled up and used to light the fire. And no one minds, for who could love a newspaper, who care to treasure it, and read it again and yet again?

We do not want even to read yesterday's newspapers, for newspapers seem to hold for us only the interest of the day. The very name by which they used to be called, journal, seems to tell us that, for it comes from the French word *"jour,"* meaning "a day." Newspapers give us the news *of* the day *for* the day. Yet in them we find the history of our own times, and we are constantly kept in mind of how important they are in our everyday life by such

434

phrases as "the freedom of the Press," "the opinion of the Press," the Press meaning all the newspapers, journals and magazines and the people who write for them.

So we come back again to our question, Who writes for the newspapers? The answer is, the journalists. A newspaper is not all the work of one man, but of many whose names we seldom know, but who work together so that each morning we may have our paper. And in this chapter I want to tell you about one of our first real journalists, Daniel Defoe. Of course you know of him already, for he wrote *Robinson Crusoe,* and he is perhaps your favorite author. But before he was an author he was a journalist, and as I say one of our first.

For there was a time when there were no newspapers, nothing for father to read at breakfast-time, and no old newspapers to crumple up and light fires with. The first real printed English newspaper was called the *Weekly News.* It was published in 1622, while King Charles I. was still upon the throne.

But this first paper and others that came after it were very small. The whole paper was not so large as a page of one of our present halfpenny papers. The news was told baldly without any remarks upon it, and when there was not enough news it was the fashion to fill up the space with chapters from the Bible. Sometimes, too, a space was left blank on purpose, so that those who bought the paper in town might write in their own little bit of news before sending it off to country friends.

Defoe was one of the first to change this, to write articles and comments upon the news. Gradually newspapers became plentiful. And when Government by party became the settled form of our Government, each party had its own newspaper and used it to help on its own side and abuse the other.

Milton and Dryden were really journalists; Milton

when he wrote his political pamphlets, and Dryden when he wrote *Absalom and Achitophel* and other poems of that kind. But they were poets first, journalists by accident. Defoe was a journalist first, though by nature ever a story-teller.

Daniel Defoe, born in 1661, was the son of a London butcher named James Foe. Why Daniel, who prided himself on being a true-born Englishman, Frenchified his name by adding a "De" to it we do not know, and he was over forty before he changed plain Foe into Defoe.

Daniel's father and mother were Puritans, and he was sent to school with the idea that he should become a Nonconformist minister. But Defoe did not become a minister; perhaps he felt he was unsuited for such solemn duty. "The pulpit," he says later, "is none of my office. It was my disaster first to be set apart for, and then to be set apart from the honor of that sacred employ."

Defoe never went to college, and because of this many a time in later days his enemies taunted him with being ignorant and unlearned. He felt these taunts bitterly, and again and again answered them in his writings "I have been in my time pretty well master of five languages," he says in one place. "I have also, illiterate though I am, made a little progress in science. I have read Euclid's Elements. . . . I have read logic. . . . I went some length in physics. . . . I thought myself master of geography and to possess sufficient skill in astronomy." Yet he says I am "no scholar."

When Defoe left school he went into the office of a merchant hosier. It was while he was in this office that King Charles II. died and King James II. came to the throne. Almost at once there followed the Duke of Monmouth's rebellion. The Duke was a Protestant and James was a Catholic. There were many in the land who feared a Catholic King, and who believed too that the Duke had more right to the throne than James, so they joined the rebellion. Among them was Daniel. But the Rebellion came to nothing. In a few weeks the Duke's army was scattered in flight, and he himself a wretched prisoner in the Tower.

Happier than many of his comrades, Defoe succeeded in escaping death or even punishment. Secretly and safely he returned to London and there quietly again took up his trade of merchant hosier. But he did not lose his interest in the affairs of his country. And when the glorious Revolution came he was one of those who rode out to meet and welcome William the Deliverer.

But perhaps he allowed politics to take up too much of his time and thought, for although he was a good business man he failed and had to hide from those to whom he owed money. But soon we find him setting to work again to mend his fortunes. He became first secretary to and then part owner of a tile and brick factory, and in a few years made enough money to pay off all his old debts.

By this time Defoe had begun to write, and was already known as a clever author. Now some one wrote a book accusing William among many other "crimes" of being a foreigner. Defoe says, "this filled me with a kind of rage"; and he replied with a poem called *The True-born Englishman.* It became popular at once, thousands of copies being sold in the first few months. Every one read it from the King in his palace to the workman in his hut, and long afterwards Defoe was content to sign his books "By the author of 'The True-born Englishman.'" It made Defoe known to the King. "This poem," he said, "was the occasion of my being known to his Majesty." He was received and employed by him and "above the capacity of my deserving, rewarded." He was given a small appointment in the Civil Service. All his life after Defoe loved King William and was his staunch friend, using all the power of his clever pen to make the unloved Dutch King better understood of his people. But when King William died and Queen Anne ruled in his stead Defoe fell on evil times.

In those days the quarrels about religion were not yet over. There was a party in the Church which would very willingly have seen the Nonconformists or Dissenters persecuted. This party was now in power, and the Dissenters were like to have an evil time. To show how wrong persecution was, Defoe wrote a little pamphlet which he called *The Shortest Way with the Dissenters*. He wrote as if he were very angry indeed with the Dissenters. He said they had been far too kindly treated, and that if he had his way he would make a law that "whoever was found at a conventicle should be banished the nation, and the preacher be hanged. We should soon see an end of the tale—they would all come to Church, and one age would make us all one again."

Defoe meant this for satire. A satire is, you remember, a work which holds up folly or wickedness to ridicule. He meant to show the High Churchmen how absurd and wicked was their desire to punish the Dissenters for worshiping God in their own way. He meant to make the world laugh at them. But at first the High Churchmen did not see that it was meant to ridicule them. They greeted the author of this pamphlet as a friend and ally. The Dissenters did not see the satire either, and found in the writer a new and most bitter enemy.

But when at last Defoe's meaning became plain the High Church party was very angry, and resolved to punish him. Defoe fled into hiding. But a reward of fifty pounds was offered for his discovery, and, "rather than others should be ruined by his mistake," Defoe gave himself up.

For having written "a scandalous and seditious pamphlet" Defoe was condemned to pay a large fine, to stand three times in the pillory, and to be imprisoned during the Queen's pleasure. Thus quickly did Fortune's wheel turn round. "I have seen the rough side of the world as well as the smooth," he said long after. "I have, in less than half a year, tasted the difference between the closet of a King, and the dungeon of Newgate."

The pillory was a terrible punishment. In a public place, raised on a platform, in full view of the passing crowd, the victim stood. Round his neck was a heavy collar of wood, and in this collar his hands were also confined. Thus he stood helpless, unable to protect himself either from the sun or rain or from the insults of the crowd. For a man in the pillory was a fitting object for laughter and rude jests. To be jeered at, to have mud thrown at him, was part of his punishment.

But for Defoe it was a triumph rather than a punishment. To the common people he was already a hero. So they formed a guard round him to protect him from the mud and rotten eggs his enemies would have thrown. They themselves threw flowers, they wreathed the pillory with roses and with laurel till it seemed a place of honor rather than of disgrace. They sang songs in his praise and drank to his health and wished those who had sent him there stood in his place. Thus through all the long, hot July hours Defoe was upheld and comforted in his disgrace. And to show that his spirit was untouched by his sentence he wrote *A Hymn to the Pillory*. This was bought and read and shouted in the ears of his enemies by thousands of the people. It was a more daring satire than even *The Shortest Way*. In the end of it Defoe calls upon the Pillory, "Thou Bugbear of the Law," to speak and say why he stands there:—

> "Tell them, it was, because he was too bold,
> And told those truths which should not have been told!
> Extol the justice of the land,
> Who punish what they will not understand!
>
> Tell them, he stands exalted there
> For speaking what we would not hear
> And yet he might have been secure,
> Had he said less, or would he have said more!

Tell them the men that placed him here
Are scandals to the Times!
Are at a loss to find his guilt,
And can't commit his crimes!'"

But although Defoe's friends could take the sting out of the terrible hours during which he stood as an object for mockery they could do little else for him. So he went back to prison to remain there during the Queen's pleasure.

This, of course, meant ruin to him. For himself he could bear it, but he had a wife and children, and to know that they were in poverty and bitter want was his hardest punishment.

From prison Defoe could not manage his factory. He had to let that go, losing with it thousands of pounds. For the second time he saw himself ruined. But he had still left to him his pen and his undaunted courage. So, besides writing many pamphlets in prison, Defoe started a paper called the *Review*. It appeared at first once, then twice, and at last three times a week. Unlike our papers of to-day, which are written by many hands, Defoe wrote the whole of the *Review* himself, and continued to do so for years. It contained very little news and many articles, and when we turn these worn and yellowing pages we find much that, interesting in those days, has lost interest for us. But we also find articles which, worded in clear, strong, truly English English, seem to us as fresh and full of life as when they were written more than two hundred years ago. We find as well much that is of keen historical interest, and we gain some idea of the undaunted courage of the author when we remember that the first numbers of the *Review* at least were penned in a loathsome prison where highwaymen, pirates, cut-throats, and common thieves were his chief companions.

CHAPTER LXII

DEFOE—"ROBINSON CRUSOE"

For more than a year and a half Defoe remained in prison; then he was set free.

A new Government had come into power. It was pointed out to the Queen that it was a mistake to make an enemy of so clever an author as Defoe. Then he was set at liberty, but on condition that he should use his pen to support the Government. So although Defoe was now free to all seeming, this was really the beginning of bondage. He was no longer free in mind, and by degrees he became a mere hanger-on of Government, selling the support of his pen to whichever party was in power.

We cannot follow him through all the twists and turns of his politics, nor through all his ups and downs in life, nor mention all the two hundred and fifty books and pamphlets that he wrote. It was an adventurous life he led, full of dark and shadowy passages which we cannot understand and so perhaps cannot pardon. But whether he sold his pen or no we are bound to confess that Defoe's desire was towards the good, towards peace, union, and justice.

One thing he fought for with all his buoyant strength was the Union between England and Scotland. It had been the desire of William III. ere he died, it had now become the still stronger desire of Queen Anne and her ministers. So Defoe took "a long winter, a chargeable, and, as it proved, hazardous journey" to Scotland. There he threw himself into the struggle, doing all he could for the Union. He has left for us a history of that struggle,[1] which perhaps better than any other makes us realize the unrest of the Scottish people, the anger, the fear, the indecision, with which they were filled. "People went up and down wondering and amazed, expecting every day strange events, afraid of peace, afraid of war. Many knew not which way to fix their resolutions. They could not be clear for the Union, yet they saw death at the door in its breaking off—Death to their liberty, to their religion, and to their country." Better than any other he gives a picture of the "infinite struggles, clamor, railing, and tumult of party." Let me give, in his own words, a description of a riot in the streets of Edinburgh:—

"The rabble by shouting and noise having increased their numbers to several thousands, they began with Sir Patrick Johnston, who was one of the treaters, and the year before had been Lord Provost. First they assaulted his lodgings with stones and sticks, and curses not a few. But his windows being too high they came up the stairs to his door, and fell to work at it with sledges or great hammers. And had they broke it open in their first fury, he had, without doubt, been torn to pieces without mercy; and this only because he was a treater in the Commission to England, for, before that, no man was so well beloved as he, over the whole city.

"His lady, in the utmost despair with this fright, came to the window, with two candles in her hand, that she might be known; and cried out, for God's sake to call the guards. An honest Apothecary in the town, who knew her voice, and saw the distress she was in, and to whom the family, under God, is obliged for their deliverance, ran immediately down to the town guard. But they would not stir without the Lord Provost's order. But that

[1] *History of the Union of Great Britain*

being soon obtained, one Captain Richardson, who commanded, taking about thirty men with him, marched bravely up to them; and making his way with great resolution through the crowd, they flying, but throwing stones, and hallooing at him, and his men. He seized the foot of the staircase; and then boldly went up, cleared the stair, and took six of the rabble in the very act, and so delivered the gentleman and his family.

"But this did not put a stop to the general tumult, though it delivered this particular family. For the rabble, by this time, were prodigiously increased, and went roving up and down the town, breaking the windows of the Members of Parliament and insulting them in their coaches in the streets. They put out all the lights that they might not be discovered. And the author of this had one great stone thrown at him for but looking out of a window. For they suffered nobody to look out, especially with any lights, lest they should know faces, and inform against them afterwards.

"By this time it was about eight or nine o'clock at night, and now they were absolute masters of the city. And it was reported they were going to shut up all the ports.[1] The Lord Commissioner being informed of that, sent a party of the foot guards, and took possession of the Netherbow, which is a gate in the middle of the High Street, as Temple Bar between the City of London and the Court.

"The city was now in a terrible fright, and everybody was under concern for their friends. The rabble went raving about the streets till midnight, frequently beating drums, raising more people. When my Lord Commissioner being informed, there were a thousand of the seamen and rabble come up from Leith; and apprehending if it were suffered to go on, it might come to a dangerous head, and

[1] Gates in the City Wall

be out of his power to suppress, he sent for the Lord Provost, and demanded that the guards should march into the city.

"The Lord Provost, after some difficulty, yielded; though it was alleged, that it was what never was known in Edinburgh before. About one o'clock in the morning a battalion of the guards entered the town, marched up to the Parliament Close, and took post in all the avenues of the city, which prevented the resolutions taken to insult the houses of the rest of the treaters. The rabble were entirely reduced by this, and gradually dispersed, and so the tumult ended."

Although Defoe did all he could to bring the Union about he felt for and with the poor distracted people. He saw that amid the strife of parties, proud, ignorant, mistaken, it may be, the people were still swayed by love of country, love of freedom.

Even after the Union was accomplished Defoe remained in Scotland. He still wrote his *Review* every week, and filled it so full of Union matters that his readers began to think he could speak of nothing else and that he was growing dull. In his *Review* he writes:—

"Nothing but Union, Union, says one now that wants diversion; I am quite tired of it, and we hope, 'tis as good as over now. Prithee, good Mr. Review, let's have now and then a touch of something else to make us merry." But Defoe assures his readers he means to go on writing about the Union until he can see some prospect of calm among the men who are trying to make dispeace. "Then I shall be the first that shall cease calling upon them to Peace."

The years went on, Defoe always living a stormy life amid the clash of party politics, always writing, writing. More than once his noisy, journalistic pen brought him to prison. But he was never a prisoner long, never long

silenced. Yet although Defoe wrote so much and lived at a
time when England was full of witty writers he was outside
the charmed circle of wits who pretended not to know of
his existence. "One of these authors," says another writer,
"(the fellow that was pilloried, I have forgotten his name),
is indeed so grave, sententious, dogmatical a rogue that
there is no enduring him."[1]

At length when Defoe was nearly sixty years old he
wrote the book which has brought him world-wide and enduring fame. Need I tell you of that book? Surely not.
For who does not know *Robinson Crusoe,* or, as the first
title ran, "The Life and Strange Surprising Adventures of
Robinson Crusoe, of York, Mariner, who lived eight-and-
twenty years all alone in an uninhabited Island on the
Coast of America near the Mouth of the great River
Oroonoque, having been cast on shore by shipwreck,
wherein all the men perished but himself. With an account
how he was at last strangely delivered by Pirates. Written
by himself." In those days, you see, they were not afraid
of long titles The book, too, is long. "Yet," as another
great writer says,[2] "was there ever anything written by mere
man that was wished longer by its readers, except *Don
Quixote, Robinson Crusoe,* and the *Pilgrim's Progress?*"

The book was a tremendous success. It pleased the
men and women and children of two hundred years ago
as much as it pleases them to-day. Within a few months
four editions had been sold. Since then, till now, there
has never been a time when *Robinson Crusoe* has not been
read. The editions of it have been countless. It has been
edited and re-edited, it has been translated and abridged,
turned into shorthand and into poetry, and published in
every form imaginable, and at every price, from one penny
to many pounds.

Defoe got the idea of his story from the adventures

[1] Jonathan Swift.   [2] Samuel Johnson.

of a Scots sailor named Alexander Selkirk. This sailor quarreled with his captain, and was set ashore upon an uninhabited island where he remained alone for more than four years. At the end of that time he was rescued by a passing ship and brought home to England. Out of this slender tale Defoe made his fascinating story so full of adventure.

What holds us in the story is its seeming truth. As we read it we forget altogether that it is only a story, we feel sure that Crusoe really lived, that all his adventures really happened. And if you ever read any more of Defoe's books you will find that this feeling runs through them all. Defoe was, in fact, a born story-teller—like Sir John Mandeville. With an amazing show of truth he was continually deceiving people. "He was a great, a truly great liar, perhaps the greatest liar that ever lived." [1]

Finding that *Robinson Crusoe* was such a success, Defoe began to write other stories. He wrote of thieves, pirates and rogues. These stories have the same show of truth as *Robinson Crusoe*. Defoe, no doubt, got the ideas for them from the stories of the rogues with whom he mixed in prison. But they have nearly all been forgotten, for although they are clever the heroes and heroines are coarse and the story of their adventures is unpleasant reading. Yet as history, showing us the state of the people in the days of Queen Anne and of George I., they are useful.

Defoe was now well off. He had built himself a handsome house surrounded by a pleasant garden. He had carriages and horses and lived in good style with his wife and beautiful daughters. There seemed to be no reason why he should not live happily and at ease for the rest of his life. But suddenly one day, for some unknown reason, he fled from his comfortable home into hiding. Why he did this no one can tell. For two years he lived a home-

[1] William Minto.

less, skulking fugitive. Then in 1731 he died, if not in poverty at least in loneliness and distress of mind.

BOOKS TO READ

Robinson Crusoe, abridged by John Lang. *Robinson Crusoe*, retold by Edith Robarts, illustrated by J. Hassall, R I. *Robinson Crusoe* (Everyman's Library)

CHAPTER LXIII

SWIFT—THE "JOURNAL TO STELLA"

WE all know what it is to feel hurt and angry, to feel that
we are misunderstood, that no one loves us. At such times
it may be we want to hurt ourselves so that in some
mysterious way we may hurt those who do not love us.
We long to die so that they may be sorry. But these
feelings do not come often and they soon pass. We cry
ourselves to sleep perhaps and wake up to find the evil
thoughts are gone. We forget all about them, or if we
remember them we remember to smile at our own foolish-
ness, for we know that after all we are understood, we are
loved. And when we grow old enough to look back upon
those times, although we may remember the pain of them,
we can see that sometimes they came from our own fault,
it was not that we were misunderstood so much as that we
were misunderstanding. Yet whether it be our own
fault or not, when such times do come, the world seems
very dark and life seems full of pain. Then think of what
a whole life filled with these evil thoughts must be. Think
of a whole life made terrible with bitter feelings. That
would be misery indeed.

Yet when we read the sad story of the life of Jonathan
Swift who has in *Gulliver's Travels* given to countless
children, and grown-up people too, countless hours of
pleasure, we are forced to believe that so he passed a
great part of his life. Swift was misunderstood and
misunderstanding. It was not that he had no love given

448

to him, for all his life through he found women to love him.
But it was his unhappiness that he took that love only to
turn it to bitterness in his heart, that he took that love so
as to leave a stain on him and it ever after. He had friendship too. But in the hands stretched out to help him in
his need he saw only insult. In the kindness that was
given to him he saw only a grudging charity, and yet he
was angry with the world and with man that he did not
receive more.

In the life of Jonathan Swift there are things which
puzzle even the wisest. Children would find those things
still harder to understand, so I will not try to explain them,
but will tell you a little that you will readily follow about
the life of this lonely man with the biting pen and aching
heart.

Jonathan Swift's father and mother were very poor, so
poor indeed that their friends said it was folly for them to
marry. And when after about two years of married life
the husband died, he left his young wife burdened with
debts and with a little baby girl to keep. It was not until
a few months after his father's death that Jonathan was
born.

His mother was a brave-hearted, cheerful woman, and
although her little son came to her in the midst of such
sorrow she no doubt loved him, and his nurse loved him
too. Little Jonathan's father and mother were English,
but because he was born in Dublin, and because he spent
a great deal of his life there, he has sometimes been looked
upon as an Irishman.

Jonathan's nurse was also an Englishwoman, and when
he was about a year old she was called home to England
to a dying friend. She saw that she must go to her friend,
but she loved her baby-charge so much that she could not
bear to part from him. He had been a sickly child, often
ill, but that seemed only to make him dearer to her. She

held him in her arms thinking how empty they would feel without their dear burden. She kissed him, jealous at the thought that he might learn to know and love another nurse, and she felt that she could not part with him. Making up her mind that she would not, she wrapped him up warmly and slipped quietly from the house carrying the baby in her arms. She then ran quickly to the boat, crept on board, and was well out on the Irish Sea before it was discovered that she had stolen little Jonathan from his mother. Mrs. Swift was poor, Jonathan was not strong, so the fond and daring nurse was allowed by the mother to keep her little charge until he was nearly four. Thus for three years little Jonathan lived with his nurse at Whitehaven, growing strong and brown in the sea air. She looked after him lovingly, and besides feeding and clothing him, taught him so well that Swift tells us himself, though it seems a little hard to believe, that he could spell and could read any chapter in the Bible before he was three.

After Jonathan's return to Ireland his uncle, Godwin Swift, seems to have taken charge of him, and when he was six to have sent him to a good school. His mother, meanwhile, went home to her own people in England, and although mother and son loved each other they were little together all through life. At fourteen Godwin Swift sent his nephew from school to Trinity College, Dublin. But Swift was by this time old enough to know that he was living on the charity of his uncle and the knowledge was bitter to his proud spirit. Instead of spurring him on the knowledge weighed him down. He became gloomy, idle, and wild. He afterwards said he was a dunce at college and "was stopped of his degree for dulness and insufficiency." But although at first the examiners refused to pass him, he was later, for some reason, given a special degree, granted by favor rather than gained by desert "in a manner little to his credit," says bitter Swift. Jona-

than gave his uncle neither love nor thanks for his schooling. "He gave me the education of a dog," was how he
spoke of it years after. Yet he had been sent to the best
school in Ireland and to college later. But perhaps it was
not so much the gift as the manner of giving which Swift
scorned. We cannot tell.

Soon after Jonathan left college he went to live in the
house of Sir William Temple. Temple was a great man in
his day. He had been an Ambassador, the friend of kings
and princes, and he considered himself something of a
scholar. To him Swift acted as a kind of secretary. To
a proud man the post of secretary or chaplain in a great
house was, in those days, no happy one. It was a position
something between that of a servant and a friend, and in it
Swift's haughty soul suffered torments. Sir William, no
doubt, meant to be kind, but he was cold and condescend-
ing, and not a little pompous and conceited. Swift's fierce
pride was ready to fancy insults where none were meant,
he resented being "treated like a schoolboy," and during
the years he passed in Sir William's house he gathered a
store of bitterness against the world in his heart.

But in spite of all his miseries real or imaginary, Swift
had at least one pleasure. Among the many people
making up the great household there was a little girl of
seven named Esther Johnson. She was a delicate little
girl with large eyes and black hair. She and Swift soon
grew to be friends, and he spent his happiest hours teaching
her to read and write. It is pleasant to think of the gloomy,
untrained genius throwing off his gloom and bending all
his talents to the task of teaching and amusing this little
delicate child of seven.

With intervals between, Swift remained in Sir William's
household for about five years. Here he began to write
poetry, but when he showed his poems to Dryden, who was
a distant kinsman, he got little encouragement. "Cousin

Swift," said the great man, "you will never be a poet." Here was another blow from a hostile world which Swift could never either forget or forgive.

As the years went on Swift found his position grow more and more irksome. At last he began to think of entering the Church as a means of earning an independent livelihood and becoming his own master. And one day, having a quarrel with Sir William, he left his house in a passion and went back to Ireland. Here after some trouble he was made a priest and received a little seaside parish worth about a hundred pounds a year.

Swift was now his own master, but he found it dull. He had so few parishioners that it is said he used to go down to the seashore and skiff stones in order to gather a congregation. For he thought if the people would not come to hear sermons they would come at least to stare at the mad clergyman, and for years he was remembered as the "mad clergyman." And now because he found his freedom dull, and for various other reasons, when Sir William asked him to come back he gladly came. This time he was much happier as a member of Sir William's household than he had been before.

It was now that Swift wrote the two little books which first made him famous. These were *The Battle of the Books* and *A Tale of a Tub. The Battle of the Books* rose out of a silly quarrel in which Sir William Temple had taken part as to whether the ancient or the modern writers were the best. Swift took Temple's side and wrote to prove that the ancient writers were best. But, as it has been said, he wrote so cleverly that he proved the opposite against his will, for nowhere in the writings of the ancients is there anything so full of humor and satire as *The Battle of the Books.*

Swift imagines a real battle to have taken place among the books in the King's library at St. James's Palace. The books leave the shelves, some on horseback, some on foot, and armed with sword and spear throw themselves into the fray, but we are left quite uncertain as to who gained the victory. This little book is a satire, and, like all Swift's famous satires, is in prose not in poetry. In the preface he says, "Satire is a sort of glass, wherein beholders do generally discover everybody's face but their own; which is the chief reason for that kind reception it meets with in the world, and that so very few are offended with it." It is not a book that you will care to read for a long time, for to find it interesting you must know both a good deal about Swift's own times and about the books that fight the battle.

You will not care either for *A Tale of a Tub*. And yet it is the book above all others which one must read, and read with understanding, if one would get even a little knowledge of Swift's special genius. It was the book, nevertheless, which more than any other stood in his way in after life.

A Tale of a Tub like *The Battle of the Books* is a satire, and Swift wrote it to show up the abuses of the Church. He tells the story of three brothers, Peter, Martin and Jack. Peter represents the Roman Catholic, Martin the Anglican, and Jack the Presbyterian Church. He meant, he says, to turn the laugh only against Peter and Jack. That may be so, but his treatment of Martin cannot be called reverent. Indeed, reverence was impossible to Swift. There is much good to be said of him. There was a fierce righteousness about his spirit which made him a better parish priest than many a more pious man. He hated shams, he hated cant, he hated bondage. "Dr. Swift," it was said, "hated all fanatics: all fanatics hated Dr. Swift." [1] But with all his uprightness and breadth he was neither devout nor reverent.

When Sir William Temple died Swift went back to

[1] Lord Orrery

Ireland, and after a little time he once more received a Church living there. But here, as before, his parish was very small, so that sometimes he had only his clerk as congregation. Then he would begin the service with "Dearly beloved Roger, the Scripture moveth you and me." instead of "Dearly beloved brethren," as the Prayer Book has it.

Sir William had left Swift some money; he had also left some to Esther Johnson, the little girl Swift used to teach. She had grown into a beautiful and witty woman, and now she too, with a friend, went to Ireland, and for the rest of her life lived there near Swift.

The strange friendship between these two, between Esther Johnson and Swift, is one of the puzzles in Swift's life. That they loved each other, that they were life-long friends, every one knows. But were they ever married? Were they man and wife? That question remains unanswered.

Esther is the Persian word for star; Stella the Latin. Swift called his girl-friend Stella, and as Stella she has become famous in our literature. For when Swift was away from home he wrote letters to her which we now have under the name of the *Journal to Stella*. Here we see the great man in another light. Here he is no longer armed with lightning, his pen is no longer dipped in poison, but in friendly, simple fashion he tells all that happens to him day by day. He tells what he thinks and what he feels, where and when he dines, when he gets up, and when he goes to bed, all the gossiping details interesting to one who loves us and whom we love. And with it all we get a picture of the times in which he lived, of the politics of the day, of the great men he moved among. Swift always addresses both Stella and her companion Mistress Dingley, and the letters are everywhere full of tender, childish nonsense. He invented what he called a "little language," using all sorts of quaint and babyish words and strange strings of capital letters, M. D., for instance, meaning my dears, M. E., Madam Elderly, or D. D., Dear Dingley, and so on. Throughout, too, we come on little bits of doggerel rimes, bad puns, simple jokes, mixed up with scraps of politics, with threatenings of war, with party quarrels, with all kinds of stray fragments of news which bring the life of the times vividly before us. The letters were never meant for any one but Stella and Mistress Dingley to see, and sometimes when we are reading the affectionate nonsense we feel as if no one ought to have seen it but these two. And yet it gives us one whole side of Swift that we should never have known but for it. It is not easy to give an idea of this book, it must be read to be understood, but I will give you a few extracts from it:—

"Pshaw, I must be writing to those dear saucy brats every night, whether I will or no, let me have what business I will, or come home ever so late, or be ever so sleepy; but an old saying and a true one,

> 'Be you lords, or be you earls,
> You must write to saucy girls'

"I was to-day at Court and saw Raymond among the beefeaters, staying to see the Queen; so I put him in a better station, made two or three dozen of bows, and went to Church, and then to Court again to pick up a dinner, as I did with Sir John Stanley, and then we went to visit Lord Mountjoy, and just now left him, and 'tis near eleven at night, young women."

Or again:—

"The Queen was abroad to-day in order to hunt, but finding it disposed to rain she kept in her coach; she hunts in a chaise with one horse, which she drives herself, and drives furiously, like Jehu, and is a mighty hunter, like

Nimrod. Dingley has heard of Nimrod, but not Stella, for it is in the Bible. . . . The Queen and I were going to take the air this afternoon, but not together: and were both hindered by a sudden rain. Her coaches and chaises all went back, and the guards too; and I scoured into the marketplace for shelter."

Another day he writes:—

"Pish, sirrahs, put a date always at the bottom of your letter, as well as the top, that I may know when you send it; your last is of November 3, yet I had others at the same time, written a fortnight after. . . . Pray let us have no more bussiness, but busyness. Take me if I know how to spell it! Your wrong spelling, Madam Stella, has put me out: it does not look right; let me see, bussiness, busyness, business, bisyness, bisness, bysness; faith, I know not which is right, I think the second; I believe I never writ the word in my life before; yes, sure I must, though; business, busyness, bisyness.—I have perplexed myself, and can't do it. Prithee ask Walls. Business, I fancy that's right Yes it is, I looked in my own pamphlet, and found it twice in ten lines, to convince you that I never writ it before. O, now I see it as plain as can be; so yours is only an s too much."

CHAPTER LXIV

SWIFT—"GULLIVER'S TRAVELS"

DURING the years in which Swift found time to write these playful letters to Stella he was growing into a man of power. Like Defoe he was a journalist, but one of far more authority. The power of his pen was such that he was courted by his friends, feared by his enemies. He threw himself into the struggle of party, first as a Whig, then as a Tory; but as a friend said of him later, "He was neither Whig nor Tory, neither Jacobite nor Republican. He was Dr. Swift."[1] He was now, he says:—

> "Grown old in politicks and wit,
> Caress'd by ministers of State,
> Of half mankind the dread and hate"[2]

And he felt that he deserved reward for what he had done for his party. He thought that he should have been made a bishop. But even in those days, when little thought was given to the fitness of a man for such a position, the Queen steadily refused to make the author of *A Tale of a Tub* a bishop.

Again Swift felt that he was unjustly treated, and even when he was at length made Dean of St. Patrick's that consoled him little. He longed for power, and owned that he was never so happy as when treated like a lord. He longed for wealth, for "wealth," he said, "is liberty, and liberty is a blessing fittest for a philosopher." And if Swift was displeased at being made only a Dean, the Irish people

---

[1] Lord Orrery. [2] *Cadenus and Vanessa.*

457

were equally displeased with him as their Dean. As he rode through the streets of Dublin to take possession of his Deanery, the people threw stones and mud at him and hooted him as he passed. The clergy, too, made his work as Dean as hard as possible. But Swift set himself to conquer them, and soon he had his own way even in trifles.

We cannot follow Swift through all his political adventures and writings. In those days the misgovernment of Ireland was terrible, and Swift, although he loved neither Ireland nor the Irish, fought for their rights until, from being hated by them, he became the idol of the people, and those who had thrown mud and stones now cheered him as he passed. Wherever he went he was received with honor, his birthday was kept as a day of rejoicing, and to this day Swift is held in remembrance by Irishmen with gratitude. But even in his hour of triumph Swift was a lonely and discontented man as we may learn from his letters.

It was now that he published the book upon which his fame most surely rests—*Gulliver's Travels.* It is a book which has given pleasure to numberless people ever since. Yet Swift said himself: "The chief end I propose to myself in all my labours is to vex the world rather than divert it, and if I could compass that design without hurting my own person or fortune, I would be the most indefatigable writer you have ever seen. . . . I hate and detest that animal called man, although I heartily love John, Peter, Thomas, and so forth. . . . Upon this great foundation of misanthropy, the whole building of my *Travels* is erected."

But whether Swift at the time vexed the world with *Gulliver* or not, ever since he has succeeded in diverting it. *Gulliver's Travels* is an allegory and a satire, but there is no need now to do more than enjoy it as a story.

The story is divided into four parts. In the first

Captain Lemuel Gulliver being wrecked finds himself upon an island where all the people are so small that he can pick them up in his thumb and finger, and it requires six hundred of their beds to make one for him.

In the second part Gulliver comes to a country where the people are giants. They are so large that they in their turn can lift Gulliver up between thumb and finger.

In the third voyage Gulliver is taken by pirates and at last lands upon a flying island, and from there he passes on to other wonderful places.

In the fourth his men mutiny and put him ashore on an unknown land. There he finds that horses are the rulers, and a terrible kind of degraded human being their slaves and servants.

In the last part the satire is too bitter, the degradation of man too terribly insisted upon to make it pleasant reading, and altogether the first two stories are the most interesting.

Here is how Swift tells us of Gulliver's arrival in Lilliput, the country of the tiny folk. After the shipwreck and a long battle with the waves he has at length reached land:—

"I lay down on the grass, which was very short and soft, where I slept sounder than ever I remember to have done in my life, and, as I reckoned, about nine hours; for when I awaked, it was just daylight. I attempted to rise, but was not able to stir: for as I happened to lie on my back, I found my arms and legs were strongly fastened on each side to the ground; and my hair, which was long and thick, tied down in the same manner.

"I could only look upwards, the sun began to grow hot, and the light offended my eyes. I heard a confused noise about me, but in the posture I lay, could see nothing except the sky. In a little time I felt something alive moving on my left leg, which advancing gently forward over my breast, came almost up to my chin; when bending my eyes downwards as much as I could, I perceived it to be a human creature not six inches high, with a bow and arrow in his hands, and a quiver at his back.

"In the meantime, I felt at least fifty more of the same kind (as I conjectured) following the first. I was in the utmost astonishment, and roared so loud, that they all ran back in a fright; and some of them, as I was afterwards told, were hurt with the falls they got by leaping from my sides upon the ground. However, they soon returned, and one of them, who ventured so far as to get a full sight of my face, lifting up his hands and eyes by way of admiration, cried out in a shrill, but distinct voice, *Hekinah degul*: the others repeated the same words several times, but then I knew not what they meant.

"I lay all this while, as the reader may believe, in great uneasiness: at length, struggling to get loose, I had the fortune to break the strings, and wrench out the pegs that fastened my left arm to the ground; for, by lifting it up to my face, I discovered the methods they had taken to bind me, and at the same time with a violent pull, which gave me excessive pain, I a little loosened the strings that tied down my hair on the left side, so that I was just able to turn my head about two inches.

"But the creatures ran off a second time, before I could seize them; whereupon there was a great shout in a very shrill accent, and after it ceased, I heard one of them cry aloud *Tolgo phonac*; when in an instant I felt above an hundred arrows discharged on my left hand, which pricked me like so many needles; and besides, they shot another flight into the air, as we do bombs in Europe, whereof many, I suppose, fell on my body (though I felt them not) and some on my face, which I immediately covered with my left hand.

"When this shower of arrows was over, I fell a-groaning with grief and pain, and then striving again to get loose, they discharged another volley larger than the first, and some of them attempted with spears to stick me in the sides, but, by good luck, I had on a buff jerkin, which they could not pierce."

Gulliver decided that the best thing he could do was to lie still until night came and then, having his left hand already loose, he would soon be able to free himself. However, he did not need to wait so long, for very soon, by orders of a mannikin, who seemed to have great authority over the others, his head was set free. The little man then made a long speech, not a word of which Gulliver understood, but he replied meekly, showing by signs that he had no wicked intentions against the tiny folk and that he was also very hungry.

"The *Hurgo* (for so they call a great lord, as I afterwards learnt) understood me very well. He commanded that several ladders should be applied to my sides, on which above an hundred of the inhabitants mounted and walked towards my mouth, laden with baskets full of meat, which had been provided and sent thither by the King's orders, upon the first intelligence he received of me. I observed there was the flesh of several animals, but could not distinguish them by the taste. There were shoulders, legs, and loins, shaped like those of mutton, and very well dressed, but smaller than the wings of a lark. I ate them by two or three at a mouthful, and took three loaves at a time, about the bigness of musket bullets. They supplied me as fast as they could, showing a thousand marks of wonder and astonishment at my bulk and appetite. I then made another sign that I wanted drink. They found by my eating, that a small quantity would not suffice me; and being a most ingenious people, they slung up with great dexterity one of their largest hogsheads, then rolled it towards my hand, and beat out the top; I drank it off at a draught, which I might well do, for it did not hold half a pint, and tasted like a small wine of Burgundy, but much more delicious. They brought me a second hogshead, which I drank in the same manner, and made signs for more, but they had none to give me. When I had performed these wonders, they shouted for joy, and danced upon my breast, repeating several times as they did at first *Hekinah degul.*"

And now having introduced you and Gulliver to the Lilliputians, I must leave you to hear about his further adventures among them from the book itself. There you will learn how Gulliver received his freedom, and how he lived happily among the little people until at length Swift falls upon the quaint idea of having him impeached for treason. Gulliver then, hearing of this danger, escapes, and after a few more adventures arrives at home.

As a contrast to what you have just read you may like to hear of Gulliver's first adventures in Brobdingnag, the land of giants. Gulliver had been found by a farmer and carried home. When the farmer's wife first saw him "she screamed and ran back, as women in England do at the sight of a toad or a spider." However, when she saw that he was only a tiny man, she soon grew fond of him.

"It was about twelve at noon, and a servant brought in dinner. It was only one substantial dish of meat (fit for the plain condition of an husbandman) in a dish of about four-and-twenty foot diameter. The company were the farmer and his wife, three children, and an old grandmother. When they were sat down, the farmer placed me at some distance from him on the table, which was thirty foot high from the floor. I was in a terrible fright, and kept as far as I could from the edge for fear of falling. The wife minced a bit of meat, then crumbled some bread on a trencher, and placed it before me. I made her a low bow, took out my knife and fork, and fell to eat, which gave them exceeding delight. The mistress sent her maid for a small dram cup, which held about two gallons, and filled it with drink. I took up the vessel with much difficulty in both hands, and in a most respectful manner drank to her ladyship's health, expressing the words as loud as I could in English, which made the company laugh so heartily, that I was almost deafened with the noise. . . .

"In the midst of dinner, my mistress's favourite cat leapt into her lap. I heard a noise behind me like that of a dozen stocking-weavers at work; and turning my head, I found it proceeded from the purring of this animal, who seemed to be three times larger than an ox, as I computed by the view of her head, and one of her paws, while her mistress was feeding and stroking her. The fierceness of this creature's countenance altogether discomposed me; though I stood at the further end of the table, above fifty foot off; and although my mistress held her fast for fear she might give a spring, and seize me in her talons. But it happened there was no danger; for the cat took not the least notice of me when my master placed me within three yards of her. And as I have been always told, and found true by experience in my travels, that flying, or discovering fear before a fierce animal, is a certain way to make it pursue or attack you, so I resolved in this dangerous juncture to show no manner of concern. I walked with intrepidity five or six times before the very head of the cat, and came within half a yard of her; whereupon she drew herself back, as if she were more afraid of me."

When it was published *Gulliver's Travels* was at once a great success. Ten days after it appeared, two poets wrote to Swift that "the whole town, men, women, and children are quite full of it."

For nearly twenty years longer Swift lived, then sad to say the life of the man who wrote for us these fascinating tales closed in gloom without relief. Stella, his life-long friend, died. That left him forlorn and desolate. Then, as the years passed, darker and darker gloom settled upon his spirit. Disease crept over both mind and body, he was tortured by pain, and when at length the pain left him he sank into torpor. It was not madness that had come upon him, but a dumb stupor. For more than two years he lived, but it was a living death. Without memory, without hope, the great genius had become the voiceless ruin of a man. But at length a merciful end came. On an October day in 1745 Swift died. He who had torn his own heart with restless bitterness, who had suffered and caused others to suffer, had at last found rest.

He was buried at dead of night in his own cathedral and laid by Stella's side, and over his grave were carved words chosen by himself which tol the wayfarer that Jonathan Swift had gone "Where savage indignation can no longer tear at his heart. Go, wayfarer, and imitate, if thou canst, a man who did all a man may do as a valiant champion of liberty."

BOOKS TO READ

Stories of Gulliver, by J Lang *Gulliver's Travels* *Gulliver's Travels* (Everyman's Library).

Note·—These two last are both the same text and are illustrated by A Rackham It is the edition in Temple Classics for Young People that is recommended, not that in the Temple Classics.

CHAPTER LXV

ADDISON—THE "SPECTATOR"

SWIFT's wit makes us laugh, but it leaves us on the whole, perhaps, a little sad. Now we come to a satirist of quite another spirit whose wit, it has been said, "makes us laugh and leaves us good and happy." [1]

Joseph Addison was the son of a Dean. He was born in 1672 in the quaint little thatched parsonage of Milston, a Wiltshire village, not far from that strange monument of ancient days, Stonehenge. When he was old enough Joseph was sent first to schools near his home, and then a little later to the famous Charterhouse in London. Of his schooldays we know little, but we can guess, for one story that has come down to us, that he was a shy, nervous boy. It is said that once, having done something a little wrong, he was so afraid of what punishment might follow that he ran away. He hid in a wood, sleeping in a hollow tree and feeding on wild berries until he was found and taken home to his parents.

At Charterhouse Joseph met another boy named Dick Steele, and these two became fast friends although they were very different from each other. For Dick was merry, noisy, and fun-loving, and although Joseph loved fun too it was in a quiet, shy way. Dick, who was a few weeks older than Joseph, was the son of a well-to-do lawyer. He was born in Ireland, but did not

[1] Thackeray.

465

remain there long. For, as both his father and mother died when he was still a little boy, he was brought to England to be taken care of by an uncle.

From Charterhouse Joseph and Dick both went to Oxford, but to different Colleges. Dick left the University without taking his degree and became a soldier, while Joseph stayed many years and became a man of learning.

Joseph Addison had gone to College with the idea of becoming a clergyman like his father, but after a time he gave up that idea, and turned his thoughts to politics. The politicians of the day were always on the lookout for clever men, who, by their writings, would help to sway the people to their way of thinking. Already at college Addison had become known by his Latin poetry, and three Whig statesmen thought so highly of it that they offered him a pension of £300 a year to allow him to travel on the Continent and learn French, and so add to his learning as to be able to help their side by his writing. Addison accepted the pension and set out on his travels. For four years he wandered about the Continent, adding to his store of knowledge of men and books, meeting many of the foremost men of letters of his day. But long before he returned home his friends had fallen from power and his pension was stopped. So back in London we find him cheerfully betaking himself to a poor lodging up three flights of stairs, hoping for something to turn up.

These were the days of the War of the Spanish Succession and of the brilliant victories of Marlborough of which you have read in the history of the time of Anne. Blenheim had been fought. All England was ringing with the praises of the great General in prose and verse. But the verse was poor, and it seemed to those in power that this great victory ought to be celebrated more worthily, so the Lord Treasurer looked about him for some one who could sing of it in fitting fashion. The right person, however, seemed hard to find, and the laureate of the day, an honest gentleman named Nahum Tate, who could hardly be called a poet, was quite unable for the task. To help the Lord Treasurer out of his difficulty one of the great men who had already befriended Addison suggested him as a suitable writer. And so one morning Addison was surprised in his little garret by a visit from no less a person than the Chancellor of the Exchequer.

A shy boy at school, Addison had grown into a shy, retiring man, and no doubt he was not a little taken aback at a visit from so great a personage. The Chancellor, however, soon put him at his ease, told him what he had come about, and begged him to undertake the work. "In short, the Chancellor said so many obliging things, and in so graceful a manner, as gave Mr. Addison the utmost spirit and encouragement to begin that poem, which he afterwards published and entitled *The Campaign*." [1]

The poem was a great success, and besides being paid for the work, Addison received a Government post, so once more life ran smoothly for him. He had now both money and leisure. His Government duties left him time to write, and in the next few years he published a delightful book of his travels, and an opera.

Shy, humorous, courteous, Addison steadily grew popular. Everything went well with him. "If he had a mind to be chosen king he would hardly be refused," said Swift. He, however, only became a member of Parliament. But he was too shy ever to make a speech, and presently he went to Ireland as Secretary of State. Swift and Addison already knew each other, and Addison had sent a copy of his travels to Swift as "to the most agreeable companion, the truest friend, and the greatest genius of his age." Now in Ireland they saw much of

[1] Budgell, *Memories of the Boyles*

each other, and although they were, as Swift himself says, as different as black and white, they became fast friends. And even later, in those days of bitter party feeling, when Swift left his own side and became a Tory, though their friendship cooled, they never became enemies. Swift's bitter pen was never turned against his old friend. Addison with all his humor and his satire never attacked any man personally, so their relations continued friendly and courteous to the end.

In the *Journal to Stella* we find many entries about this difficulty between the friends, "Mr. Addison and I are as different as black and white, and I believe our friendship will go off by this business of party. But I love him still as much as ever, though we seldom meet." "All our friendship and dearness are off. We are civil acquaintance, talk words of course, of when we shall meet, and that's all. Is it not odd?" Then later the first bitterness of difference seems to pass, and Swift tells how he went to Addison's for supper. "We were very good company, and I yet know no man half so agreeable to me as he is."

It was while Addison was in Ireland that Richard Steele started a paper called the *Tatler*. When Addison found out that it was his old friend Dick who had started the *Tatler* he offered to help. And he helped to such good purpose that Steele says, "I fared like a distressed prince who calls in a powerful neighbour to his aid. I was undone by my own auxiliary; when I had once called him in, I could not subsist without dependence on him."

This was the beginning of a long literary partnership that has become famous. Never perhaps were two friends more different in character. Yet, says Steele, long after, speaking of himself and Addison, "There never was a more strict friendship than between those gentlemen, nor had they ever any difference but what proceeded from their different way of pursuing the same thing. The one with patience, foresight, and temperate address, always waited and stemmed the torrent; while the other often plunged himself into it, and was as often taken out by the temper of him who stood weeping on the brink for his safety, whom he could not dissuade from leaping into it. . . . When they met they were as unreserved as boys, and talked of the greatest affairs, upon which they saw where they differed, without pressing (what they knew impossible) to convert each other." [1]

The *Tatler,* like Defoe's *Review,* was a leaflet of two or three pages, published three times a week. The *Review* and other papers of the same kind no doubt prepared the way for the *Tatler.* But the latter was written with far greater genius, and while the *Review* is almost forgotten the *Tatler* is still remembered and still read.

In the first number Steele announced that:—"All accounts of gallantry, pleasure and entertainment, shall be under the article of White's Chocolate-House; Poetry under that of Wills' Coffee-House; learning under the title of Grecian; foreign and domestic news you will have from Saint James's Coffee-House; and what else I have to offer on any other subject shall be dated from my own apartment."

The coffee-houses and chocolate-houses were the clubs of the day. It was there the wits gathered together to talk, just as in the days of Ben Jonson they gathered at the Mermaid Tavern. And in these still nearly newspaperless days it was in the coffee-houses that the latest news, whether of politics or literature or sheer gossip, was heard and discussed. At one coffee-house chiefly statesmen and politicians would gather, at another poets and wits, and so on. So Steele dated each

[1] Steele in the *Theatre,* 12

article from the coffee-house at which the subject of it would most naturally be discussed.

Steele meant the *Tatler* to be a newspaper in which one might find all the news of the day, but he also meant it to be something more.

You have heard that, after the Restoration, many of the books that were written, and plays that were acted, were coarse and wicked, and the people who read these books and watched these plays led coarse and wicked lives. And now a rollicking soldier, noisy, good-hearted Dick Steele, "a rake among scholars, and a scholar among rakes"[1] made up his mind to try to make things better and give people something sweet and clean to read daily. The *Tatler*, especially after Addison joined with Steele in producing it, was a great success. But, as time went on, although it continued to be a newspaper, gradually more room was given to fiction than to fact, and to essays on all manner of subjects than to the news of the day. For Addison is among the greatest of our essayists. But although these essays were often meant to teach something, neither Steele nor Addison are always trying to be moral or enforce a lesson. At times the papers fairly bubble with fun. One of the best humorous articles in the *Tatler* is one in which Addison gives a pretended newly found story by our old friend Sir John Mandeville. It is perhaps as delightful a lying tale as any that "learned and worthy knight" ever invented. Here is a part of it:—

"We were separated by a storm in the latitude of 73, insomuch that only the ship which I was in, with a Dutch and French vessel, got safe into a creek of Nova Zembla. We landed, in order to refit our vessels, and store ourselves with provisions. The crew of each vessel made themselves a cabin of turf and wood, at some distance from

[1] Macaulay.

each other, to fence themselves againts the inclemencies of the weather, which was severe beyond imagination.

"We soon observed, that in talking to one another we lost several of our words, and could not hear one another at above two yards' distance, and that too when we sat very near the fire. After much perplexity, I found that our words froze in the air before they could reach the ears of the persons to whom they were spoken I was soon confirmed in this conjecture, when, upon the increase of the cold, the whole company grew dumb, or rather deaf. For every man was sensible, as we afterwards found, that he spoke as well as ever, but the sounds no sooner took air than they were condensed and lost.

"It was now a miserable spectacle to see us nodding and gaping at one another, every man talking, and no man heard. One might observe a seaman that could hail a ship at a league distance, beckoning with his hands, straining his lungs, and tearing his throat, but all in vain.

"We continued here three weeks in this dismal plight. At length, upon a turn of wind, the air about us began to thaw. Our cabin was immediately filled with a dry clattering sound, which I afterwards found to be the crackling of consonants that broke above our heads, and were often mixed with a gentle hissing, which I imputed to the letter S, that occurs so frequently in the English tongue.

"I soon after felt a breeze of whispers rushing by my ear; for those, being of a soft and gentle substance, immediately liquified in the warm wind that blew across our cabin. These were soon followed by syllables and short words, and at length by entire sentences, that melted sooner or later, as they were more or less congealed; so that we now heard everything that had been spoken during the whole three weeks that we had been silent; if I may use that expression.

"It was now very early in the morning, and yet, to my surprise, I heard somebody say, 'Sir John, it is midnight, and time for the ship's crew to go to bed.' This I knew to be the pilot's voice, and upon recollecting myself I concluded that he had spoken these words to me some days before, though I could not hear them before the present thaw. My reader will easily imagine how the whole crew was amazed to hear every man talking, and seeing no man opening his mouth."

When the confusion of voices was pretty well over Sir John proposed a visit to the Dutch cabin, and so they set out. "At about half a mile's distance from our cabin, we heard the groanings of a bear, which at first startled us. But upon inquiry we were informed by some of our company, that he was dead, and now lay in salt, having been killed upon that very spot about a fortnight before, in the time of the frost."

Having reached the Dutch cabin the company was almost stunned by the confusion of sounds, and could not make out a word for about half an hour. This, Sir John thinks, was because the Dutch language being so much harsher than ours it "wanted more time than ours to melt and become audible."

Next they visited the French cabin and here Sir John says, "I was convinced of an error into which I had before fallen. For I had fancied, that for the freezing of the sound, it was necessary for it to be wrapped up, and, as it were, preserved in breath. But I found my mistake, when I heard the sound of a kit playing a minuet over our heads."

The kit was a small violin to the sound of which the Frenchmen had danced to amuse themselves while they were deaf or dumb. How it was that the kit could be heard during the frost and yet still be heard in the thaw we are not told. Sir John gave very good reasons, says

Addison, but as they are somewhat long "I pass over them in silence." [1]

Addison and Steele carried on the *Tatler* for two years, then it was stopped to make way for a far more famous paper called the *Spectator*. But meanwhile the Whigs fell from power and Addison lost his Government post. In twelve months, he said to a friend, he lost a place worth two thousand pounds a year, an estate in the Indies, and, worst of all, his lady-love. Who the lady-love was is not known, but doubtless she was some great lady ready enough to marry a Secretary of State, but not a poor scribbler.

As Addison had now no Government post, it left him all the more time for writing, and his essays in the *Spectator* are what we chiefly remember him by.

The *Spectator* was still further from the ordinary newspaper than the *Tatler*. It was more perhaps what our modern magazines are meant to be, but, instead of being published once a week or once a month, it was published every morning.

In order to give interest to the paper, instead of dating the articles from various coffee-houses, as had been done in the *Tatler,* Addison and Steele between them imagined a club. And it is the doings of these members, their characters, and their lives, which supply subjects for many of the articles. In the first numbers of the *Spectator* these members are described to us.

First of all there is the Spectator himself. He is the editor of the paper. It is he who with kindly humorous smile and grave twinkle in his eye is to be seen everywhere. He is seen, and he sees and listens, but seldom opens his lips. "In short," he says, "I have acted in all the parts of my life as a looker-on." And that is the meaning of Spectator—the looker-on. This on-looker, there can be

[1] *Tatler*, 254.

little doubt, was meant to be a picture of Addison himself. In a later paper he tells us that "he was a man of a very short face, extremely addicted to silence . . . and was a great humorist in all parts of his life." [1] And when you come to know Mr. Spectator well, I think you will love this grave humorist.

After Mr. Spectator, the chief member of the Club was Sir Roger de Coverley. "His great-grandfather was inventor of that famous country dance which is called after him. All who know that shire (in which he lives), are very well acquainted with the parts and merits of Sir Roger. He is a gentleman that is very singular in his behaviour, but his singularities proceed from his good sense, and are contradictions to the manners of the world, only as he thinks the world is in the wrong." He was careless of fashion in dress, and wore a coat and doublet which, he used laughingly to say, had been in and out twelve times since he first wore it. "He is now in his fifty-sixth year, cheerful, gay, and hearty; keeps a good house both in town and country; a great lover of mankind; but there is such a mirthful cast in his behaviour, that he is rather beloved than esteemed. His tenants grow rich, his servants look satisfied. All the young women profess love to him and the young men are glad of his company. When he comes into a house he calls the servants by their names, and talks all the way upstairs to a visit."

Next came a lawyer of the Inner Temple, who had become a lawyer not because he wanted to be one, but because he wanted to please his old father. He had been sent to London to study the laws of the land, but he liked much better to study those of the stage. "He is an excellent critic, and the time of the play is his hour of business. Exactly at five he passes through New Inn,

[1] *Spectator*, 101.

crosses through Russell Court, and takes a turn at Wills' till the play begins. He has his shoes rubbed and his periwig powdered at the barber's as you go into the Rose."

Next comes Sir Andrew Freeport, "a merchant of great eminence in the City of London." "He abounds in several frugal maxims, amongst which the greatest favorite is, 'A penny saved is a penny got.'"

"Next to Sir Andrew in the Club room sits Captain Sentry, a gentleman of great courage, good understanding, but invincible modesty. He was some years a captain, and behaved himself with great gallantry in several engagements and at several sieges. But having a small estate of his own, and being next heir to Sir Roger, he has quitted a way of life in which no man can rise suitably to his merit, who is not something of a courtier as well as a soldier. The military part of his life has furnished him with many adventures, in the relation of which he is very agreeable to the company, for he is never over-bearing, though accustomed to command men in the utmost degree below him, nor ever too obsequious, from an habit of obeying men highly above him.

"But that our society may not appear a set of humorists, unacquainted with the gallantries and pleasures of the age, we have among us the gallant Will Honeycomb, a gentleman who, according to his years, should be in the decline of his life. But having ever been very careful of his person, and always had a very easy fortune, time has made but very little impression, either by wrinkles on his forehead, or traces in his brain. His person is well turned, of a good height. He is very ready at that sort of discourse with which men usually entertain women. He has all his life dressed very well, and remembers habits as others do men. He can smile when one speaks to him, and laugh easily." He is in fact an old beau, a regular man about town, "a well-bred, fine gentleman," yet no great scholar, "he spelt like a gentleman and not like a scholar." [1] he says.

Last of all there is a clergyman, a man of "general learning, great sanctity of life, and the most exact breeding." He seldom comes to the Club, "but when he does it adds to every man else a new enjoyment of himself."

This setting forth of the characters in the story will remind you a little perhaps of Chaucer in his Prologue to the *Canterbury Tales*. As he there gives us a clear picture of England in the time of Edward III., so Addison gives us a clear picture of England in the time of Anne. And although the essays are in the main unconnected, the slight story of these characters runs through them, weaving them into a whole. You may pick up a volume of the *Spectator* and read an essay here or there at will with enjoyment, or you may read the whole six hundred one after the other and find in them a slight but interesting story.

You know that the books many of your grown-up friends read most are called novels. But in the days when Joseph Addison and Richard Steele wrote the *Spectator,* there were no novels. Even Defoe's stories had not yet appeared, and it was therefore a new delight for our forefathers to have the adventures of the Spectator Club each day with their morning cup of tea or chocolate. "Mr. Spectator," writes one lady, "your paper is part of my tea equipage, and my servant knows my humour so well, that calling for my breakfast this morning (it being past my usual hour) she answered, the *Spectator* was not yet come in, but that the tea-kettle boiled, and she expected it every moment."

Thus the *Spectator* had then become part of everyday. life just as our morning newspapers have now, and there must have been many regrets among the readers when

[1] *Spectator,* 105

one member of the supposed Club died, another married and settled down, and so on until at length the Club was entirely dispersed and the *Spectator* ceased to appear. It may interest you to know that the paper we now call the *Spectator* was not begun until more than a hundred years after its great namesake ceased to appear, the first number being published in 1828.

It was after the *Spectator* ceased that Addison published his tragedy called *Cato*. Cato was a great Roman who rebelled against the authority of Cæsar and in the end killed himself. His is a story out of which a good tragedy might be made. But Addison's genius is not dramatic, and the play does not touch our hearts as Shakespeare's tragedies do. Yet, although we cannot look upon Addison's *Cato* as a really great tragedy, there are lines in it which every one remembers and quotes, although they may not know where they come from. Such are, for instance, "Who deliberates is lost," and

> " 'Tis not in mortals to command success,
> But we'll do more, Sempronius, we'll deserve it."

But although *Cato* is not really great, the writer was perhaps the most popular man of his day, and so his tragedy was a tremendous success. With *Cato* Addison reached the highest point of his fame as an author in his own day, but now we remember him much more as a writer of delightful essays, and as the creator or at least the perfecter of Sir Roger, for to Steel is due the first invention of the worthy knight.

Fortune still smiled on Addison. When George I. came to the throne, the Whigs once more returned to power, and Addison again became Secretary for Ireland. He still wrote, both on behalf of his Government and to please himself.

And now, in 1716, when he was already a man of forty-four, Addison married. His wife was the Dowager Countess of Warwick, and perhaps she was that great lady whom he had lost a few years before when he lost his post of Secretary of State. Of all Addison's pleasant prosperous life these last years ought to have been the most pleasant and most prosperous. But it has been said that his marriage was not happy, and that plain Mr. Addison was glad at times to escape from the stately grandeur of his own home and from the great lady, his wife, to drink and smoke with his friends and "subjects" at his favorite coffee-house. For Addison held sway and was surrounded by his little court of literary admirers, as Dryden and Ben Jonson before him.

But whether Addison was happy in his married life or not, one sorrow he did have. Between his old friend, Dick Steele, and himself a coldness grew up. They disagreed over politics. Steele thought himself ill-used by his party. His impatient, impetuous temper was hurt at the cool balance of his friend's, and so they quarreled. "I ask no favour of Mr. Secretary Addison," writes Steele angrily. During life the quarrel was never made up, but after Addison died Steele spoke of his friend in his old generous manner. Under his new honors and labors Addison's health soon gave way. He suffered much from asthma, and in 1718 gave up his Government post. A little more than a year later he died.

He met his end cheerfully and peacefully. "See how a Christian can die," he said to his wild stepson, the Earl of Warwick, who came to say farewell to his stepfather.

The funeral took place at dead of night in Westminster Abbey. Whig and Tory alike joined in mourning, and as the torchlight procession wound slowly through the dim isles, the organ played and the choir sang a funeral hymn.

> "How silent did his old companions tread,
> By midnight lamps, the mansions of the dead,

Thro' breathing statues, then unheeded things,
Thro' rows of warriors, and thro' walks of Kings!
What awe did the slow solemn knell inspire,
The pealing organ, and the pausing choir,
The duties by the lawn-robed prelate paid,
And the last words, that dust to dust conveyed!
While speechless o'er thy closing grave we bend,
Accept these tears, thou dear departed Friend!" [1]

So our great essayist was laid to rest, but it was not until many years had come and gone that a statue in his honor was placed in the Poets' Corner. This, says Lord Macaulay, himself a great writer, was "a mark of national respect due to the unsullied statesman, to the accomplished scholar, to the master of pure English eloquence, to the consummate painter of life and manners. It was due, above all, to the great satirist, who alone knew how to use ridicule without abusing it, who, without inflicting a wound, effected a great social reform, and who reconciled wit with virtue, after a long and disastrous separation, during which wit had been led astray by profligacy, and virtue by fanaticism."

BOOKS TO READ

Sir Roger de Coverley *The Coverley Papers*, edited by O. M. Myers.

[1] T. Tickell.

CHAPTER LXVI

STEELE—THE SOLDIER AUTHOR

You have heard a little about Dick Steele in connection with Joseph Addison. Steele is always overshadowed by his great friend, for whom he had such a generous admiration that he was glad to be so overshadowed. But in this chapter I mean to tell you a little more about him.

He was born, you know, in Dublin in 1671, and early lost his father. About this he tells us himself in one of the *Tatlers*:

"The first sense of sorrow I ever knew was upon the death of my father, at which time I was not quite five years of age, but was rather amazed at what all the house meant, than possessed with a real understanding, why nobody was willing to play with me. I remember I went into the room where his body lay, and my mother sat weeping alone by it. I had my battledore in my hand, and fell abeating the coffin, and calling 'Papa,' for, I know not how, I had some slight idea that he was locked up there. My mother catched me in her arms, and, transported beyond all patience of the silent grief she was before in, she almost smothered me in her embrace, and told me, in a flood of tears, Papa could not hear me, and would play with me no more, for they were going to put him under ground, whence he could never come to us again." [1]

[1] *Tatler*, 181

Steele's sad, beautiful mother died soon after her husband, and little Dick was left more lonely than ever. His uncle took charge of him, and sent him to Charterhouse, where he met Addison. From there he went to Oxford, but left without taking a degree. "A drum passing by," he says, "being a lover of music, I listed myself for a soldier."[1] "He mounted a war horse, with a great sword in his hand, and planted himself behind King William the Third against Lewis the Fourteenth." But he says when he cocked his hat, and put on a broad sword, jack boots, and shoulder belt, he did not know his own powers as a writer, he did not know then that he should ever be able to "demolish a fortified town with a goosequill."[2] So Steele became a "wretched common trooper," or, to put it more politely, a gentleman volunteer. But he was not long in becoming an ensign, and about five years later he got his commission as captain.

In those days the life of a soldier was wild and rough. Drinking and swearing were perhaps the least among the follies and wickedness they were given to, and Dick Steele was as ready as any other to join in all the wildness going. But in spite of his faults and failings his heart was kind and tender. He had no love of wickedness though he could not resist temptation. So the dashing soldier astonished his companions by publishing a little book called the *Christian Hero*. It was a little book written to show that no man could be truly great who was not religious. He wrote it at odd minutes when his day's work was over, when his mind had time "in the silent watch of the night to run over the busy dream of the day." He wrote it at first for his own use, "to make him ashamed of understanding and seeming to feel what was virtuous and yet living so quite contrary a life." Afterwards he resolved to publish it for the good of others.

[1] *Tatler*, 89.   [2] *Theatre*, 11.

But among Steele's gay companions the book had little effect except to make them laugh at him and draw comparisons between the lightness of his words and actions, and the seriousness of the ideas set forth in his *Christian Hero*. He found himself slighted instead of encouraged, and "from being thought no undelightful companion, was soon reckoned a disagreeable fellow." [1] So he took to writing plays, for "nothing can make the town so fond of a man as a successful play."

The plays of the Restoration had been very coarse. Those of Steele show the beginning of a taste for better things, "Tho' full of incidents that move laughter, virtue and vice appear just as they ought to do," he says of his first comedy. But although we may still find Steele's plays rather amusing, it is not as a dramatist that we remember him, but as an essayist.

Steele led a happy-go-lucky life, nearly always cheerful and in debt. His plays brought him in some money, he received a Government appointment which brought him more, and when he was about thirty-three he married a rich widow. Still he was always in debt, always in want of money.

In about a year Steele's wife died, and he was shortly married to another well-off lady. About this time he left the army, it is thought, although we do not know quite surely, and for long afterwards he was called Captain Steele.

Steele wrote a great many letters to his second wife, both before and after his marriage. She kept them all, and from them we can learn a good deal of this warmhearted, weak-willed, harum-scarum husband. She is "Dearest Creature," "Dear Wife," "Dear Prue" (her name, by the way, was Mary), and sometimes "Ruler," "Absolute Governess," and he "Your devoted obedient Husband,"

[1] *Apology for himself and his Writings.*

"Your faithful, tender Husband." Many of the letters are about money troubles. We gather from them that Dick Steele loved his wife, but as he was a gay and careless spendthrift and she was a proud beauty, a "scornful lady," for neither of them was life always easy.

It was about two years after this second marriage that Steele suddenly began the *Tatler*. He did not write under his own name, but under that of Isaac Bickerstaff, a name which Swift had made use of in writing one of his satires. As has been said, the genius of Steele has been overshadowed by that of Addison, for Steele had such a whole-hearted admiration for his friend that he was ready to give him all the praise. And yet it is nearly always to Steele that we owe the ideas which were later worked out and perfected by Addison.

It is to Steele, too, that we owe the first pictures of English family life. It has been said that he "was the first of our writers who really seemed to admire and respect women," [1] and if we add "after the Restoration" we come very near the truth. Steele had a tender heart towards children too, and in more than one paper his love of them shows itself. Indeed, as we read we cannot help believing that in real life Captain Dick had many child-friends. Here is how he tells of a visit to a friend's house:—

"I am, as it were, at home at that house, and every member of it knows me for their well-wisher. I cannot indeed express the pleasure it is, to be met by the children with so much joy as I am when I go thither. The boys and girls strive who shall come first, when they think it is I that am knocking at the door. And that child which loses the race to me, runs back again to tell the father it is Mr. Bickerstaff.

"This day I was led in by a pretty girl, that we all thought must have forgot me, for the family has been out of town these two years. Her knowing me again was a

[1] Thackeray

mighty subject with us, and took up our discourse at the
first entrance. After which they began to rally me upon
a thousand little stories they heard in the country about my
marriage to one of my neighbor's daughters. Upon
which the gentleman, my friend, said, 'Nay, if Mr.
Bickerstaff marries a child of any of his old companions,
I hope mine shall have the preference. There's Mistress
Mary is now sixteen, and would make him as fine a widow
as the best of them.' "

After dinner the mother and children leave the two
friends together. The father speaks of his love for his
wife, and his fears for her health.

" 'Ah, you little understand, you that have lived a
bachelor, how great a pleasure there is in being really
beloved. Her face is to me more beautiful than when I first
saw it. In her examination of her household affairs, she
shows a certain fearfulness to find a fault, which makes
her servants obey her like children, and the meanest we
have has an ingenuous shame for an offence, not always
to be seen in children in other families. I speak freely to
you, my old friend. Ever since her sickness, things that
gave me the quickest joy before, turn now to a certain
anxiety. As the children play in the next room, I know
the poor things by their steps, and am considering what
they must do, should they lose their mother in their
tender years. The pleasure I used to take in telling my
boy stories of the battles, and asking my girl questions
about the disposal of her baby, and the gossiping of it, is
turned into inward reflection and melancholy.' The poor
gentleman would have gone on much longer with his sad
forebodings, but his wife returning, and seeing by his grave
face what he had been talking about, said, with a smile,
'Mr. Bickerstaff, don't believe a word of what he tells you.
I shall still live to have you for my second, as I have often
promised you, unless he takes more care of himself than he

has done since his coming to town. You must know, he tells me, that he finds London is a much more healthy place than the country, for he sees several of his old acquaintance and school-fellows are here, young fellows with fair, full-bottomed periwigs. I could scarce keep him this morning from going out open-breasted.'" And so they sat and chatted pleasantly until, "on a sudden, we were alarmed with the noise of a drum, and immediately entered my little godson to give me a point of war.[1] His mother, between laughing and chiding, would have put him out of the room, but I would not part with him so. I found, upon conversation with him, though he was a little noisy in his mirth, that the child had excellent parts, and was a great master of all the learning on the other side of eight years old. I perceived him to be a very great historian in *Æsop's Fables;* but he frankly declared to me his mind, that he did not delight in that learning, because he did not believe they were true. For which reason I found he had very much turned his studies, for about a twelve-month past, into the lives and adventures of *Don Bellianis of Greece, Guy of Warwick,* the *Seven Champions,* and other historians of that age.

"I could not but observe the satisfaction the father took in the forwardness of his son, and that these diversions might turn to some profit, I found the boy had made remarks which might be of service to him during the course of his whole life. He would tell you the mismanagements of John Hickathrift, find fault with the passionate temper in Bevis of Southampton, and loved St. George for being the champion of England; and by this means had his thoughts insensibly moulded into the notions of discretion, virtue, and honour.

"I was extolling his accomplishments, when the mother told me that the little girl who led me in this morning

[1] A strain of war-like music.

was, in her way, a better scholar than he. 'Betty,' says she, 'deals chiefly in fairies and sprites, and sometimes, in a winter night, will terrify the maids with her accounts, till they are afraid to go up to bed.'

"I sat with them till it was very late, sometimes in merry, sometimes in serious discourse, with this particular pleasure which gives the only true relish to all conversation, a sense that every one of us liked each other. I went home considering the different conditions of a married life and that of a bachelor. And I must confess it struck me with a secret concern to reflect that, whenever I go off, I shall leave no traces behind me. In this pensive mood I returned to my family, that is to say, to my maid, my dog, and my cat, who only can be the better or worse for what happens to me." [1]

You will be sorry to know that, a few *Tatlers* further on, the kind mother of this happy family dies. But Steele was himself so much touched by the thought of all the misery he was bringing upon the others by giving such a sad ending to his story, that he could not go on with the paper, and Addison had to finish it for him.

The *Spectator,* you know, succeeded the *Tatler,* and it was while writing for the *Spectator* that Steele took seriously to politics. He became a member of Parliament and wrote hot political articles. He and Swift crossed swords more than once, and from being friends became enemies. But Steele's temper was too hot, his pen too hasty. The Tories were in power, and he was a Whig, and he presently found himself expelled from the House of Commons for "uttering seditious libels." Shut out from politics, Steele turned once more to essay-writing, and published, one after the other, several papers of the same style as the *Spectator,* but none of them lived long.

Better days, however, were coming. Queen Anne died,

[1] *Tatler, 96*

and King George became king in 1714, the Whigs returned to power, Steele again received a Government post, again he sat in Parliament, and a few months later he was knighted, and became Sir Richard Steele. We cannot follow him through all his projects, adventures, and writings. He was made one of the commissioners for the forfeited estates of the Scottish lords who had taken part in the '15, and upon this business he went several times to Scotland. The first time he went was in the autumn of 1717. But before that Lady Steele had gone to Wales to look after her estates there. While she was there Dick wrote many letters to her, some of which are full of tenderness for his children. They show us something too of the happy-go-lucky household in the absence of the careful mistress. In one he says:—

"Your son at the present writing is mighty well employed in tumbling on the floor of the room, and sweeping the sand with a feather. He grows a most delightful child, and very full of play and spirit. He is also a very great scholar. He can read his primer, and I have brought down my *Virgil*. He makes most shrewd remarks about the pictures. We are very intimate friends and play-fellows. He begins to be very ragged, and I hope I shall be pardoned if I equip him with new clothes and frocks." Or again:—"The brats, my girls, stand on each side of the table, and Molly says what I am writing now is about her new coat. Bess is with me till she has new clothes. Miss Moll has taken upon her to hold the sand-box,[1] and is so impertinent in her office that I cannot write more. But you are to take this letter as from your three best friends, Besse, Moll, and their Father.

'Moll bids me let you know that she fell down just now and did not hurt herself.''

Soon after this Steele set out for Scotland, and although

[1] In those days there was no blotting-paper, and sand was used to dry the ink.

the business which brought him could not have been welcome to many a Scottish gentleman, he himself was well received. They forgot the Whig official in the famous writer. In Edinburgh he was feasted and fêted. "You cannot imagine," wrote Steele, "the civilities and honours I had done me there. I never lay better, ate or drank better, or conversed with men of better sense than there." Poets and authors greeted him in verse, he was "Kind Richy Spec, the friend to a' distressed," "Dear Spec," and many stories are told of his doings among these new-found friends. He paid several later visits to Scotland, but about a year after his return from this first short visit Steele had a great sorrow. His wife died. "This is to let you know," he writes to a cousin, "that my dear and honoured wife departed this life last night."

And now that his children were motherless, Steele, when he was away from them, wrote to them, always tender, often funny, letters. It is Betty, the eldest, he addresses, she is "Dear Child," "My dear Daughter," "My good Girlie." He bids them be good and grow like their mother. "I have observed that your sister," he says in one letter, "has for the first time written the initial or first letters of her name. Tell her I am highly delighted to see her subscription in such fair letters. And how many fine things those two letters stand for when she writes them. M. S. is Milk and Sugar, Mirth and Safety, Music and Songs, Meat and Sauce, as well as Molly and Spot, and Mary and Steele." I think the children must have loved their kind father who wrote such pretty nonsense to them.

So with ups and downs the years passed. However much money Steele got he never seemed to have any, and in spite of all his carelessness and jovialness, there is something sad in these last years of his life. He quarreled with, and then for ever lost his life-long friend, Joseph Addison. His two sons died, and at length, broken in health, troubled about money, he went to spend his last days in Carmarthen in Wales. Here we have a last pleasant picture of him being carried out on a summer's evening to watch the country lads and lasses dance. And with his own hand, paralyzed though it was, he would write an order for a new gown to be given to the best dancer. And here in Carmarthen, in 1729, he died and was buried in the Church of St. Peter.

BOOKS TO READ

Essays of Richard Steele, selected and edited by L E Steele   *Steele Selections from the Tatler, Spectator, and Guardian,* edited by Austin Dobson

CHAPTER LXVII

POPE—THE "RAPE OF THE LOCK"

As you have already guessed by the number of prose
writers you have been reading about, this age, the age of
the last Stuarts and the first Georges, was not a poetic
one. It was an age of art and posturing. It was an age
of fierce and passionate party strife—strife between
Whig and Tory which almost amounted to civil war,
but instead of using swords and guns the men who took
part in the strife used pen and ink. They played the game
without any rules of fair play. No weapon was too vile
or mean to be used if by it the enemy might be injured.

You have often been told that it is rude to make
personal remarks, but the age of Anne was the age of
personal remarks, and they were not considered rude.
The more cruel and pointed they were, the more clever
they were thought to be. To be stupid or ugly are not
sins. They ought not to be causes of scorn and laughter,
but in the age of Anne they were accepted as such. And
if the enemy was worsted in the fight he took his revenge
by holding up to ridicule the person of his victor. To
raise the unkind laughter of the world against an enemy
was the great thing to be aimed at. Added to this, too,
the age was one of common sense. All this does not make
for poetry, yet in this age there was one poet, who,
although he does not rank among our greatest poets,
was still great, and perhaps had he lived in a less artificial
age he might have been greater still.

490

This poet was Alexander Pope, the son of a well-to-do Catholic linen-draper. He was born in London in 1688, but soon afterwards his father retired from business, and went to live in a little village not far from Windsor.

Alexander was an only son. He had one step-sister, but she was a good many years older than he, and he seems never to have had any child companions or real childhood. He must always have been delicate, yet as a child his face was "round, plump, pretty, and of a fresh complexion." [1] He is said, too, to have been very sweet tempered, but his father and mother spoilt him not a little, and when he grew up he lost that sweetness of temper. Yet, unlike many spoilt children, Pope never forgot the reverence due to father and mother. He repaid their love with love as warm, and in their old age he tended and cared for them fondly.

As Pope was a delicate boy he got little regular schooling. He learned to write by copying the printed letters in books, and was first taught to read by an aunt, and later by a priest, but still at home. After a time he was at school for a few years, but he went from one school to another, never staying long at any, and so never learning much. He says indeed that he unlearned at two of his schools all that he had learned at another. By the time he was twelve he was once more at home reading what he liked and learning what he liked, and he read and studied so greedily that he made himself ill.

Pope loved the stories of the Greek and Roman heroes, but he did not care for the hard work needed to learn to read them in the original with ease, and contented himself with translations. He was so fond of these stories that while still a little boy he made a play from the *Iliad* which was acted by the boys of one of his schools.

[1] Spence, *Anecdotes*.

Very early Pope began to write poetry. He read a great deal, and two of his favorite poets were Spenser and Dryden. His great idea was to become a poet also, and in this his father encouraged him. Although no poet himself he would set his little son to make verses upon different subjects. "He was pretty difficult in being pleased," says Pope's mother, "and used often to send him back to new turn them; 'These are not good rhymes,' he would say."

There is a story told that Pope admired Dryden's poetry so much that he persuaded a friend to take him one day to London, to the coffee-house where Dryden used to hold his little court. There he saw the great man, who spoke to him and gave him a shilling for some verses he wrote. But the story is a very doubtful one, as Dryden died when Pope was twelve years old, and for some time before that he had been too ill to go to coffee-houses. But that Pope's admiration for Dryden was very sincere and very great we know, for he chose him as his model. Like Dryden, Pope wrote in the heroic couplet, and in his hands it became much more neat and polished than ever it did in the hands of the older poet.

Pope saw Dryden only once, even if the story is true; but with another old poet, a dramatist, he struck up a great friendship. This poet was named Wycherley, but by the time that Pope came to know him Wycherley had grown old and feeble, all his best work was done, and people were perhaps beginning to forget him. So he was pleased with the admiration of the boy poet fifty years younger than himself, and glad to accept his help. At first this flattered Pope's vanity, but after a little he quarreled with his old friend and left him. This was the first of Pope's literary quarrels, of which he had many.

Already, as a boy, Pope was becoming known. He had published a few short poems, and others were handed

about in manuscript among his friends.   "That young
fellow will either be a madman or make a very great poet," [1]
said one man after meeting him when he was about fourteen.   All the praise and attention which Pope received
pleased him much.   But he took it only as his due, and his
great ambition was to make people believe that he had
been a wonderfully clever child, and that he had begun
to write when he was very young.   He says of himself
with something of pompousness, "I lisp'd in numbers,
for the numbers came."

Pope's keenest desire was to be a poet, and few poets
have rushed so quickly into fame.   He received few of the
buffets which young authors have as a rule to bear.
Instead, many a kindly helping hand was stretched out
to him by the great men of the day, for there was much
in this young genius to draw out the pity of others.   He
was fragile and sickly.   As a full grown man he stood
only four feet six inches high.   His body was bent and
deformed, and so frail that he had to be strapped in canvas
to give him some support.   His fine face was lined by pain,
for he suffered from racking headaches, and indeed his
life was one long disease.   Yet in spite of constant pain
this little crooked boy, with his "little, tender, crazy
carcass," as Wycherley called it, wrote the most astonishing
poetry in a style which in his own day was considered the
finest that could be written.

It is not surprising then that his poems were greeted
with kindly wonder, mixed it may be with a little envy.
Unhappily Pope saw only the envy and overlooked the
kindliness.   Perhaps it was that his crooked little body
had warped the great mind it held, but certain it is, as
Pope grew to manhood his thirst for praise and glory
increased, and with it his distrust and envy of others.
And many of the ways he took to add to his own fame,

[1] Edmund Smith

and take away from that of others, were mean and tortuous to the last degree. Deceit and crooked ways seemed necessary to him. It has been said that he hardly drank tea without a stratagem, and that he played the politician about cabbages and turnips.[1]

He begged his own letters back from the friends to whom they were written. He altered them, changed the dates, and published them. Then he raised a great outcry pretending that they had been stolen from him and published without his knowledge. Such ways led to quarrels and strife while he was alive, and since his death they have puzzled every one who has tried to write about him. All his life through he was hardly ever without a literary quarrel of some sort, some of his poems indeed being called forth merely by these quarrels.

But though many of Pope's poems led to quarrels, and some were written with the desire to provoke them, one of his most famous poems was, on the other hand, written to bring peace between two angry families. This poem is called the *Rape of the Lock*—rape meaning theft, and the lock not the lock of a door, but a lock of hair.

A gay young lord had stolen a lock of a beautiful young lady's hair, and she was so angry about it that there was a coolness between the two families. A friend then came to Pope to ask him if he could not do something to appease the angry lady. So Pope took up his pen and wrote a mock-heroic poem making friendly fun of the whole matter. But although Pope's intention was kindly his success was not complete. The families did not entirely see the joke, and Pope writes to a friend, "The celebrated lady herself is offended, and, what is stranger, not at herself, but me."

But the poem remains one of the most delightful of

[1] Lady Bolingbroke.

airy trifles in our language. And that it should be so airy is a triumph of Pope's genius, for it is written in the heroic couplet, one of the most mechanical forms of English verse.

Addison called it "a delicious little thing" and the very salt of wit.

Another and later writer says of it—"It is the most exquisite specimen of filigree work ever invented. It is made of gauze and silver spangles. . . . Airs, languid airs, breathe around, the atmosphere is perfumed with affectation. A toilet is described with the solemnity of an altar raised to the goddess of vanity, and the history of a silver bodkin is given with all the pomp of heraldry. No pains are spared, no profusion of ornament, no splendour of poetic diction to set off the meanest things. . . . It is the perfection of the mock-heroic." [1]

Pope begins the poem by describing Belinda, the heroine, awaking from sleep. He tells how her guardian sylph brings a morning dream to warn her of coming danger. In the dream she is told that all around her unnumbered fairy spirits fly guarding her from evil—

"Of these am I, who thy protection claim,
A watchful sprite, and Ariel is my name
Late, as I ranged the crystal wilds of air,
In the clear mirror of thy ruling star
I saw, alas! some dread event impend,
Ere to the main this morning sun descend.
But heaven reveals not what, or how, or where:
Warned by the sylph, oh pious maid, beware!
This to disclose is all thy guardian can
Beware of all, but most beware of Man!"

Then Shock, Belinda's dog,

"Who thought she slept too long,
Leaped up, and waked his mistress with his tongue"

---

[1] Hazlitt.

So Belinda rises and is dressed. While her maid seems to do the work,

> "The busy sylphs surround their darling care,
> These set the head, and those divide the hair,
> Some fold the sleeve, whilst others plait the gown;
> And Betty's praised for labours not her own."

Next Belinda set out upon the Thames to go by boat to Hampton Court, and as she sat in her gayly decorated boat she looked so beautiful that every eye was turned to gaze upon her—

> "On her white breast a sparkling cross she wore,
> Which Jews might kiss, and infidels adore"

She was so beautiful and graceful that it seemed as if she could have no faults, or—

> "If to her share some female errors fall,
> Look in her face, and you'll forget them all.
> This nymph, to the destruction of mankind,
> Nourished two locks, which graceful hung behind
> In equal curls, and well conspired to deck,
> With shining ringlets, the smoothe iv'ry neck
> Love in these labyrinths his slaves detains,
> And mighty hearts are held in slender chains.
> With hairy springes we the birds betray,
> Slight lines of hair surprise the finny prey,
> Fair tresses man's imperial race insnare,
> And beauty draws us with a single hair."

The "Adventurous Baron" next appears upon the scene. He, greatly admiring Belinda's shining locks, longs to possess one, and makes up his mind that he will. And, as the painted vessel glided down the Thames, Belinda smiled, and all the world was gay, only Ariel alone was sad and disturbed, for he felt some evil, he knew not what, was hanging over his mistress. So he gathered all his company and bade them watch more warily than before over their charge. Some must guard the watch, some the fan, "And thou Crispissa, tend her fav'rite lock," he says. And woe betide that sprite who shall be careless or neglectful!

"Whatever spirit, careless of his charge,
His post neglects, or leaves the fair at large,
Shall feel sharp vengeance soon o'ertake his sins,
Be stopped in vials, or transfixed with pins,
Or plunged in lakes of bitter washes lie,
Or wedged, whole ages in a bodkin's eye."

So the watchful sprites flew off to their places—

"Some, orb in orb, around the nymph extend;
Some thrid [1] the mazy ringlets of her hair,
Some hang upon the pendants of her ear."

The day went on, Belinda sat down to play cards. After the game coffee was brought, and "while frequent cups prolong the rich repast," Belinda unthinkingly gave the Baron a pair of scissors. Then indeed the hour of fate struck. The Baron standing behind Belinda found the temptation too great. He opened the scissors and drew near—

"Swift to the lock a thousand sprites repair,
A thousand wings by turns blow back the hair;
And thrice they twitched the diamond in her ear;
Thrice she looked back, and thrice the foe drew near."

But at last "the fatal engine" closed upon the lock. Even to the last, one wretched sylph struggling to save the lock clung to it. It was in vain, "Fate urged the shears, and cut the sylph in twain." Then, while Belinda cried aloud in anger, the Baron shouted in triumph and rejoiced over his spoil.

The poem goes on to tell how Umbriel, a dusky melancholy sprite, in order to make the quarrel worse, flew off

[1] Slipped through

to the witch Spleen, and returned with a bag full of "sighs,
sobs, and passions, and the war of tongues," "soft sorrows,
melting griefs, and flowing tears," and emptied it over
Belinda's head. She—

> "Then raging to Sir Plume repairs,
> And bids her beau demand the precious hairs
> Sir Plume, of amber snuff-box justly vain,
> And the nice conduct of a clouded cane,
> With earnest eyes, and round unthinking face,
> He first the snuff-box opened, then the case."

Sir Plume, not famous for brains, put on a very bold,
determined air, and fiercely attacked the Baron—"My
Lord," he cried, "why, what! you must return the lock!
You must be civil. Plague on 't! 'tis past a jest—nay
prithee, give her the hair." And as he spoke he tapped
his snuff-box daintily.

But in spite of this valiant champion of fair ladies in
distress, the Baron would not return the lock. So a
deadly battle followed in which the ladies fought against
the gentlemen, and in which the sprites also took part.
The weapons were only frowns and angry glances—

> "A beau and witling perished in the throng,
> One died in metaphor, and one in song.
>
> .   .   .   .   .
>
> A mournful glance Sir Fopling upwards cast,
> 'Those eyes were made so killing,' was his last"

Belinda, however, at length disarmed the Baron with
a pinch of snuff, and threatened his life with a hair pin.
And so the battle ends. But alas!—

> "The lock, obtained with guilt and kept with pain,
> In ev'ry place is sought, but sought in vain"

During the fight it has been caught up to the skies—

> "A sudden star, it shot through liquid air,
> And drew behind a radiant trail of hair"

Thus, says the poet, Belinda has no longer need to mourn her lost lock, for it will be famous to the end of time as a bright star among the stars—

> "Then cease, bright nymph! to mourn thy ravished hair,
> Which adds new glory to the starry sphere!
> Not all the tresses that fair head can boast,
> Shall draw such envy as the lock you lost.
> For after all the murders of your eye,
> When, after millions slain, yourself shall die;
> When those fair suns shall set, as set they must,
> And all those tresses shall be laid in dust,
> This lock the Muse shall consecrate to fame,
> And midst the stars inscribe Belinda's name"

When Pope first published this poem there was nothing about fairies in it. Afterwards he thought of the fairies, but Addison advised him not to alter the poem, as it was so delightful as it was. Pope, however, did not take the advice, but added the fairy part, thereby greatly improving the poem. This caused a quarrel with Addison, for Pope thought he had given him bad advice through jealousy. A little later this quarrel was made much worse. Pope translated and published a version of the *Iliad,* and at the same time a friend of Addison did so too. This made Pope bitterly angry, for he believed that the translation was Addison's own and that he had published it to injure the sale of his. From this you see how easily Pope's anger and jealousy were aroused, and will not wonder that his life was a long record of quarrels.

Pope need not have been jealous of Addison's friend, for his own translation of Homer was a great success, and people soon forgot the other. He translated not only the *Iliad,* but with the help of two lesser poets the *Odyssey* also. Both poems were done in the fashionable heroic couplet, and Pope made so much money by them that he was able to live in comfort ever after. And it is interesting to remember that Pope was the first poet who was able to live in comfort entirely on what he made by his writing.

Pope now took a house at Twickenham, and there he spent many happy hours planning and laying out his garden, and building a grotto with shells and stones and bits of looking-glass. The house has long ago been pulled down and the garden altered, but the grotto still remains, a sight for the curious.

It has been said that to write in the heroic couplet "is an art as mechanical as that of mending a kettle or shoeing a horse, and may be learned by any human being who has sense enough to learn anything." [1] And although this is not all true, it is so far true that it is almost impossible to tell which books of the *Odyssey* were written by Pope, and which by the men who helped him. But, taken as a whole, the *Odyssey* is not so good as the *Iliad*. Scholars tell us that in neither the one nor the other is the feeling of the original poetry kept. Pope did not know enough Greek to enter into the spirit of it, and he worked mostly from translations. Even had he been able to enter into the true spirit he would have found it hard to keep that spirit in his translation, using as he did the artificial heroic couplet. For Homer's poetry is not artificial, but simple and natural like our own early poetry. "A pretty poem, Mr. Pope, but you must not call it Homer," said a friend [2] when he read it, and his judgment is still for the most part the judgment of to-day.

It was after he had finished the *Odyssey* that Pope wrote his most famous satire, called the *Dunciad*. In this he insulted and held up to ridicule all stupid or dull authors, all dunces, and all those whom he considered his enemies. It is very clever, but a poem full of malice and hatred does not make very pleasant reading. For most of us, too, the interest it had has vanished, as many

[1] Macaulay.   [2] Bentley

of the people at whom Pope levied his malice are forgotten, or only remembered because he made them famous by adding their names to his roll of dunces. But in Pope's own day the *Dunciad* called forth cries of anger and revenge from the victims, and involved the author in still more quarrels.

Pope wrote many more poems, the chief being the *Essay on Criticism* and the *Essay on Man*. But his translations of Homer and the *Rape of the Lock* are those you will like best in the meantime. As a whole Pope is perhaps not much read now, yet many of his lines have become household words, and when you come to read him you will be surprised to find how many familiar quotations are taken from his poems. Perhaps no one of our poets except Shakespeare is more quoted. And yet he seldom says anything which touches the heart. When we enjoy his poetry we enjoy it with the brain. It gives us pleasure rather as the glitter of a diamond than as the perfume of a rose.

In spite of his crooked, sickly little body Pope lived to be fifty-six, and one evening in May 1744 he died peacefully in his home at Twickenham, and was buried in the church there, near the monument which he had put up to the memory of his father and mother.

There is so much that is disagreeable and mean in Pope that we are apt to lose sight of what was good in him altogether. We have to remind ourselves that he was a good and affectionate son, and that he was loving to the friends with whom he did not quarrel. Yet these can hardly be counted as great merits. Perhaps his greatest merit is that he kept his independence in an age when writers fawned upon patrons or accepted bribes from Whig or Tory. Pope held on his own way, looking for favors neither from one side nor from the other. And when we think of his frail little body, this sturdy independence of mind is all the more wonderful. From Pope we date the beginning of the time when a writer could live honorably by his pen, and had no need to flatter a patron, or sell his genius to politics or party. But Pope stood alone in this independence, and he never had to fight for it. A happy chance, we might say, made him free. For while his brother writers all around him were still held in the chains of patronage, Pope having more money than some did not need to bow to it, and having less greed than others did not choose to bow to it, in order to add to his wealth. And in the following chapter we come to another man who in the next generation fought for freedom, won it, and thereby helped to free others. This man was the famous Dr. Samuel Johnson. —

BOOKS TO READ

Pope's Iliad, edited by A. J. Church   *Pope's Odyssey*, edited by A. J Church.

NOTE —As an introduction to Pōpe's *Homer* the following books may be read.—

Stories from the Iliad, by Jeannie Lang   *Stories from the Odyssey*, by Jeannie Lang   *The Children's Iliad*, by A. J. Church.   *The Children's Odyssey*, by A. J Church.

/

CHAPTER LXVIII

JOHNSON—DAYS OF STRUGGLE

Samuel Johnson was the son of a country bookseller, and he was born at Lichfield in 1709. He was a big, strong boy, but he suffered from a dreadful disease known then as the King's Evil. It left scars upon his good-looking face, and nearly robbed him of his eyesight. In those days people still believed that this dreadful disease would be cured if the person suffering from it was touched by a royal hand. So when he was two, little Samuel was taken to London by his father and mother, and there he was "touched" by Queen Anne. Samuel had a wonderful memory, and although he had been so young at the time, all his life after he kept a kind of awed remembrance of a stately lady who wore a long black hood and sparkling diamonds. The touch of the Queen's soft white hand did the poor little sick child no good, and it is quaint to remember that the great learned doctor thought it might be because he had been touched by the wrong royal hand. He might have been cured perhaps had he been taken to Rome and touched by the hand of a Stuart. For Johnson was a Tory, and all his life he remained at heart a Jacobite.

At school Samuel learned easily and read greedily all kinds of books. He loved poetry most, and read Shakespeare when he was so young that he was frightened at finding himself alone while reading about the ghost in *Hamlet*. Yet he was idle at his tasks and had not

503

altogether an easy time, for when asked long years after how he became such a splendid Latin scholar, he replied, "My master whipt me very well, without that, sir, I should have done nothing."

Samuel learned so easily that, though he was idle, he knew more than any of the other boys. He ruled them too. Three of them used to come every morning to carry their stout comrade to school. Johnson mounted on the back of one, and the other two supported him, one on each side. In winter when he was too lazy to skate or slide himself they pulled him about on the ice by a garter tied round his waist. Thus early did Johnson show his power over his fellows.

At sixteen Samuel left school, and for two years idled about his father's shop, reading everything that came in his way. He devoured books. He did not read them carefully, but quickly, tearing the heart out of them. He cared for nothing else but reading, and once when his father was ill and unable to attend to his bookstall, he asked his son to do it for him. Samuel refused. But the memory of his disobedience and unkindliness stayed with him, and more than fifty years after, as an old and worn man, he stood bare-headed in the wind and rain for an hour in the market-place, upon the spot where his father's stall had stood. This he did as a penance for that one act of disobedience.

Johnson's father was a bookworm, like his son, rather than a tradesman. He knew and loved his books, but he made little money by them. A student himself, he was proud of his studious boy, and wanted to send him to college. But he was miserably poor and could not afford it. A well-off friend, however, offered to help, and so at eighteen Samuel went to Oxford.

Here he remained three years. Those years were not altogether happy ones, for Johnson's huge ungainly figure, and shabby, patched clothes were matters for laughter among his fellow-students. He became a sloven in his dress. His gown was tattered and his linen dirty, and his toes showed through his boots. Yet when some one, meaning no doubt to be kind, placed a new pair at his door, he kicked them away in anger. He would not stoop to accept charity. But in spite of his poverty and shabby clothes, he was a leader at college as he had been at school, and might often be seen at his college gates with a crowd of young men round him, "entertaining them with wit and keeping them from their studies." [1]

After remaining about three years at college, Johnson left without taking a degree. Perhaps poverty had something to do with that. At any rate, with a great deal of strange, unordered learning and no degree, and with his fortune still to make, Samuel returned to his poverty-stricken home. There in a few months the father died, leaving to his son an inheritance of forty pounds.

With forty pounds not much is to be done, and Samuel became an usher, or under-master in a school. He was little fitted to teach, and the months which followed were to him a torture, and all his life after he looked back on them with something of horror.

After a few months, he left the school where he had been so unhappy, and went to Birmingham to be near an old schoolfellow. Here he managed to live somehow, doing odd bits of writing, and here he met the lady who became his wife.

Johnson was now twenty-five and a strange-looking figure. He was tall and lank, and his huge bones seemed to start out of his lean body. His face was deeply marked with scars, and although he was very near-sighted, his gray eyes were bright and wild, so wild at times that they frightened those upon whom they were turned. He wore

[1] Boswell.

his own hair, which was coarse and straight, and in an age when every man wore a wig this made him look absurd. He had a trick of making queer gestures with hands and feet. He would shake his head and roll himself about, and would mutter to himself until strangers thought that he was an idiot.

And this queer genius fell in love with a widow lady more than twenty years older than himself. She, we are told, was coarse, fat, and unlovely, but she was not without brains, for she saw beneath the strange outside of her young lover. "This is the most sensible man that I ever saw in my life," she said, after talking with him. So this strange couple married. "Sir," said Johnson afterwards, "it was a love-marriage on both sides." And there can be no doubt that Samuel loved his wife devotedly while she lived, and treasured her memory tenderly after her death

Mrs. Johnson had a little money, and so Samuel returned to his native town and there opened a school. An advertisement appeared in the papers, "At Edial, near Lichfield, in Staffordshire, young gentlemen are boarded and taught the Latin and Greek languages, by Samuel Johnson." But Johnson was quite unfitted to be a teacher, and the school did not prosper. "His schoolroom," says another writer, "must have resembled an ogre's den," and only two or three boys came to it. Among them was David Garrick, who afterwards became a famous actor and amused the world by imitating his friend and old schoolmaster, the great Sam, as well as his elderly wife.

After struggling with his school for more than a year, Johnson resolved to give it up and go to London, there to seek his fortune. Leaving his wife at Lichfield, he set off with his friend and pupil, David Garrick, as he afterwards said, "With twopence halfpenny in my pocket, and thou, Davy, with three halfpence in thine."

The days of the later Stuarts and the first of the

Georges were the great days of patronage. When a writer of genius appeared, noblemen and others, who were powerful and wealthy, were eager to become his patron, and have his books dedicated to them. So although the dunces among writers remained terribly poor, almost every man of genius was sure of a comfortable life. But although he gained this by his writing, it was not because the people liked his books, but because one man liked them or was eager to have his name upon them, and therefore became his patron. The patron, then, either himself helped his pet writer, or got for him some government employment. After a time this fashion ceased, and instead of taking his book to a patron, a writer took it to a bookseller, and sold it to him for as much money as he could. And so began the modern way of publishing books.

But when Johnson came to London to try his fortune as a writer, it was just the time between. The patron had not quite vanished, the bookseller had not yet taken his place. Never had writinng been more badly paid, never had it been more difficult to make a living by it. "The trade of author was at about one of its lowest ebbs when Johnson embarked on it." [1]

Johnson had brought with him to London a tragedy more than half written, but when he took it to the booksellers they showed no eagerness to publish it, or indeed anything else that he might write. Looking at him they saw no genius, but only a huge and uncouth country youth One bookseller, seeing his great body, advised him rather to try his luck as a porter than as a writer. But, in spite of rebuffs and disappointments, Johnson would not give in. When he had money enough he lived in mean lodgings, when he had none, hungry, ragged, and cold, he roamed about the streets, making friends with other strange, forlorn men of genius, and sharing their miseries.

[1] Carlyle.

But if Johnson starved he never cringed, and once when a bookseller spoke rudely to him he knocked him down with one of his own books. A beggar or not, Johnson demanded the respect due to a man. At school and college he had dominated his fellows, he dominated now. But the need of fighting for respect made him rough. And ever after his manner with friend and foe alike was rude and brusque.

The misery of this time was such that long years after Johnson burst into tears at the memory of it. But it did not conquer him, he conquered it. He got work to do at last, and became one of the first newspaper reporters.

Nowadays, during the debates in Parliament there are numbers of newspapers reporters who take down all that is said in shorthand, and who afterwards write out the debates for their various newspapers. In Johnson's day no such thing had been thought of. He did not hear the debates, but wrote his accounts of them from a few notes given to him by some one who had heard them. The speeches which appeared in the paper were thus really Johnson's, and had very little resemblance to what had been said in the House. And being a Tory, Johnson took good care, as he afterwards confessed, "that the Whig dogs should not have the best of it." After a time, however, Johnson began to think this so-called reporting was not quite honest, and gave it up. He found other literary work to do, and soon, although he was still poor, he had enough money to make it possible for his wife to join him in London.

Among other things he wrote one or two poems and the life of Richard Savage, a strange, wild genius with whom he had wandered the streets in the days of his worst poverty. The tragedy called *Irene* which Johnson had brought with him to London was at length after twelve years produced by Garrick, who had by that time become a famous actor. Johnson had, however, no dramatic genius. "When Johnson writes tragedy," said Garrick, " 'declamation roars and passion sleeps':[1] when Shakespeare wrote, he dipped the pen in his own heart." Garrick did what he could with the play, but it was a failure, and although Johnson continued to believe that it was good, he wrote no more tragedies.

The story of *Irene* is one of the fall of Constantinople in 1453. After Mahomet had taken Constantinople he fell in love with a fair Greek maiden whose name was Irene. The Sultan begged her to become a Mohammedan so that he might marry her. To this Irene consented, but when his soldiers heard of it they were so angry that they formed a conspiracy to dethrone their ruler.

Hearing of this Mahomet resolved to make an end of the conspiracy and rescue his throne from danger. Calling all his nobles together he bade Irene appear before him. Then catching her by the hair with one hand and drawing his sword with the other he at one blow struck off her head. This deed filled all who saw it with terror and wonder. But turning to his nobles Mahomet cried, "Now by this, judge if your Emperor is able to bridle his affections or not."

It seems as if there were here a story which might be made to stir our hearts, but Johnson makes it merely dull. In his long words and fine-sounding sentences we catch no thrill of real life. The play is artificial and cold, and moves us neither to wonder nor sorrow.

Johnson's play was a failure, but by that time he had begun the great work which was to name him and single him out from the rest of the world as Dictionary Johnson. To make a complete dictionary of a language is a tre-

---

[1] Garrick is here quoting from one of Johnson's own poems in which he describes the decline of the drama at the Restoration.

mendous work. Johnson thought that it would take three years. It took, instead, seven.

But during these seven years he also wrote other things and steadily added to his fame. He started a paper after the model of the *Spectator,* called the *Rambler.* This paper was continued for about two years, Johnson writing all but five of the essays. After that he wrote many essays in a paper called the *Adventurer,* and, later still, for two years he wrote for another paper a series of articles called the *Idler.*

But none of these can we compare with the *Spectator.* Johnson never for a moment loses sight of "a grand moral end." There is in his essays much sound common sense, but they are lumbering and heavy. We get from them no such picture of the times as we get from the *Spectator,* and, although they are not altogether without humor, it is a humor that not seldom reminds us of the dancing of an elephant. This is partly because, as Johnson said himself, he is inclined to "use too big words and too many of them."

In the days when Johnson wrote, this style was greatly admired, but now we have come back to thinking that the simplest words are best, or, at least, that we must suit our words to our subject. And if we tell a fairy tale (as Johnson once did) we must not use words of five syllables when words of two will better give the feeling of the tale. Yet there are many pleasant half-hours to be spent in dipping here and there into the volumes of the *Rambler* or the *Idler.* I will give you in the next chapter, as a specimen of Johnson's prose, part of one of the essays from the *Idler.* It is the story of a man who sets forth upon a very ordinary journey and who makes as great a tale of it as he had been upon a voyage of discovery in some untraveled land.

CHAPTER LXIX

JOHNSON—THE END OF THE JOURNEY

"I supped three nights ago with my friend Will Marvel. His affairs obliged him lately to take a journey into Devonshire, from which he has just returned. He knows me to be a very patient hearer, and was glad of my company, as it gave him an opportunity of disburdening himself, by a minute relation of the casualties of his expedition.

"Will is not one of those who go out and return with nothing to tell. He has a story of his travels, which will strike a home-bred citizen with horror, and has in ten days suffered so often the extremes of terror and joy, that he is in doubt whether he shall ever again expose either his body or his mind to such danger and fatigue.

"When he left London the morning was bright, and a fair day was promised. But Will is born to struggle with difficulties. That happened to him, which has sometimes, perhaps, happened to others. Before he had gone more than ten miles, it began to rain. What course was to be taken? His soul disdained to turn back. He did what the King of Prussia might have done; he flapped his hat, buttoned up his cape, and went forwards, fortifying his mind by the stoical consolation, that whatever is violent will be short."

So, with such adventures, the first day passes, and reaching his inn, after a good supper, Will Marvel goes to bed and sleeps soundly. But during the night he is

511

wakened "by a shower beating against his windows with such violence as to threaten the dissolution of nature." Thus he knows that the next day will have its troubles. "He joined himself, however, to a company that was travelling the same way, and came safely to the place of dinner, though every step of his horse dashed the mud in the air."

In the afternoon he went on alone, passing "collections of water," puddles doubtless, the depth of which it was impossible to guess, and looking back upon the ride he marvels at his rash daring. "But what a man undertakes he must perform, and Marvel hates a coward at his heart.

"Few that lie warm in their beds think what others undergo, who have, perhaps, been as tenderly educated, and have as acute sensations as themselves. My friend was now to lodge the second night almost fifty miles from home, in a house which he never had seen before, among people to whom he was totally a stranger, not knowing whether the next man he should meet would prove good or bad; but seeing an inn of a good appearance, he rode resolutely into the yard; and knowing that respect is often paid in proportion as it is claimed, delivered his injunctions to the ostler with spirit, and, entering the house, called vigorously about him.

"On the third day up rose the sun and Mr. Marvel. His troubles and dangers were now such as he wishes no other man ever to encounter." The way was lonely, often for two miles together he met not a single soul with whom he could speak, and, looking at the bleak fields and naked trees, he wished himself safe home again. His only consolation was that he suffered these terrors of the way alone. Had, for instance, his friend the "Idler" been there he could have done nothing but lie down and die.

"At last the sun set and all the horrors of darkness

came upon him. . . . Yet he went forward along a path which he could no longer see, sometimes rushing suddenly into water, and sometimes encumbered with stiff clay, ignorant whither he was going, and uncertain whether his next step might not be the last.

"In this dismal gloom of nocturnal peregrination his horse unexpectedly stood still. Marvel had heard many relations of the instinct of horses, and was in doubt what danger might be at hand. Sometimes he fancied that he was on the bank of a river still and deep, and sometimes that a dead body lay across the track. He sat still awhile to recollect his thoughts; and as he was about to alight and explore the darkness, out stepped a man with a lantern, and opened the turnpike. He hired a guide to the town, arrived in safety, and slept in quiet.

"The rest of his journey was nothing but danger. He climbed and descended precipices on which vulgar mortals tremble to look; he passed marshes like the *Serbonian bog,*[1] *where armies whole* have sunk; he forded rivers where the current roared like the Egre or the Severn; or ventured himself on bridges that trembled under him, from which he looked down on foaming whirlpools, or dreadful abysses; he wandered over houseless heaths, amidst all the rage of the elements, with the snow driving in his face, and the tempest howling in his ears.

"Such are the colours in which Marvel paints his adventures. He has accustomed himself to sounding words and hyperbolical images, till he has lost the power of true description. In a road, through which the heaviest carriages pass without difficulty, and the post-boy every day and night goes and returns, he meets with hardships

---

[1] Lake Serbonis in Egypt Sand being blown over it by the winds gave it the appearance of solid ground, whereas it was a bog
    "A gulf profound as that Serbonian bog . .
    Where armies whole have sunk."—MILTON.

like those which are endured in Siberian deserts, and missed nothing of romantic danger but a giant and a dragon. When his dreadful story is told in proper terms, it is only that the way was dirty in winter, and that he experienced the common vicissitudes of rain and sunshine."

I am afraid you will find a good many "too big" words in that. But if I changed them to others more simple you would get no idea of the way in which Johnson wrote, and I hope those you do not understand you will look up in the dictionary. It will not be Johnson's own dictionary, however, for that has grown old-fashioned. and its place has been taken by later ones. For some of Johnson's meanings were not correct, and when these mistakes were pointed out to him he was not in the least ashamed. Once a lady asked him how he came to say that the pastern was the knee of a horse, and he calmly replied, "Ignorance, madam, pure ignorance." "Dictionaries are like watches," he said, "the worst is better than none, and the best cannot be expected to go quite true."

With some words, instead of giving the original meaning, he gave a personal meaning, that is he allowed his own sense of humor, feelings or politics, to color the meaning. For instance, he disliked the Scots, so for the meaning of Oats he gave, "A grain which in England is generally given to horses, but in Scotland supports the people." He disliked the Excise duty, so he called it "A hateful tax levied by wretches hired by those to whom excise is paid." For this last meaning he came very near being punished for libel.

When Johnson thought of beginning the dictionary he wrote about it to Lord Chesterfield, a great man and fine gentleman of the day. As the fashion was, Johnson had chosen this great man for his patron. But Lord Chesterfield, although his vanity was flattered at the idea of having a book dedicated to him, was too delicate a fine gentleman to wish to have anything to do with a man he considered poor. "He throws anywhere but down his throat," he said, "whatever he means to drink, and mangles what he means to carve. . .   The utmost I can do for him is to consider him a respectable Hottentot." So, when Johnson had called several times and been told that his lordship was not at home. or had been kept waiting for hours before he was received, he grew angry, and marched away never to return, vowing that he had done with patrons for ever.

The years went on, and Johnson saw nothing of his patron. When, however, the dictionary was nearly done, Lord Chesterfield let it be known that he would be pleased to have it dedicated to him. But Johnson would have none of it. He wrote a letter which was the "Blast of Doom, proclaiming into the ear of Lord Chesterfield, and, through him, of the listening world, that patronage would be no more!" [1]

"Seven years, my Lord, have now passed," wrote Johnson, "since I waited in your outward rooms and was repulsed from your door; during which time I have been pushing on my work through difficulties of which it is useless to complain, and have brought it at last to the verge of publication without one act of assistance, one word of encouragement, and one smile of favour. Such treatment I did not expect, for I never had a patron before. . . .

"Is not a patron, my Lord, one who looks with unconcern on a man struggling for life in the water, and when he has reached the ground cumbers him with help? The notice which you have been pleased to take of my labours, had it been early, had been kind; but it has been delayed till I am indifferent, and cannot enjoy it; till I

[1] Carlyle.

am solitary, and cannot impart it; till I am known, and do not want it."

There was an end of patronage so far as Johnson was concerned, and it was the beginning of the end of it with others. Great Sam had roared, he had asserted himself, and with the publication of his dictionary he became "The Great Cham [1] of literature." [2]

He had by this time founded a club of literary men which met at "a famous beef-steak house," and here he lorded it over his fellows as his bulky namesake had done more than a hundred years before. In many ways there was a great likeness between these two. They were both big and stout (for Sam was now stout). They were loud-voiced and dictatorial. They both drank a great deal, but Ben, alas, drank wine overmuch, as was common in his day, while Sam drank endless cups of tea, seventeen or eighteen it might be at a sitting, indeed he called himself a hardened and shameless tea-drinker. But, above all, their likeness lies in the fact that they both dominated the literary men of their period; they were kings and rulers. They laid down the law and settled who was great and who little among the writers of the day. And it was not merely the friends around Johnson who heard him talk, who listened to his judgments about books and writers. The world outside listened, too, to what he had to say, and you will remember that it was he who utterly condemned Macpherson's pretended poems of Ossian, "that pious three-quarters fraud" [3] of which you have already read in chapter iv.

Johnson had always spent much of his time in taverns, and was now more than ever free to do so. For while he was still working at his dictionary he suffered a great grief in the death of his wife. He had loved her truly

---

[1] A Tartar word for prince or chief.   [2] Smollett.
[3] A. Lang.

and never ceased to mourn her loss. But though he had lost his wife, he did not remain solitary in his home, for he opened his doors to a queer collection of waifs and strays —three women and a man, upon whom he took pity because no one else would. They were ungrateful and undeserving, and quarreled constantly among themselves, so that his home could have been no peaceful spot. "Williams hates everybody," he writes; "Levett hates Desmoulins and does not love Williams; Desmoulins hates them both; Poll loves none of them." It does not sound peaceful or happy.

Some years after the death of Johnson's wife his mother died at the age of ninety, and although he had not been with her for many years, that too was a grief. The poor lady had had very little to live on, and she left some debts. Johnson himself was still struggling with poverty. He had no money, so to pay his mother's few debts, and also the expenses of her funeral, he sat down to write a story. In a week he had finished *Rasselas, Prince of Abyssinia.*

The story of Rasselas is that of a prince who is shut up in the Happy Valley until the time shall come for him to ascend the throne of his fathers. Everything was done to make life in the Happy Valley peaceful and joyful, but Rasselas grew weary of it; to him it became but a prison of pleasure, and at last, with his favorite sister, he escaped out into the world. The story tells then of their search for happiness. But perfect happiness they cannot find, and discovering this, they decide to return to the Happy Valley.

There is a vein of sadness throughout the book. It ends as it were with a big question mark, with a "conclusion in which nothing is concluded." For the position of the prince and his sister was unchanged, and they had not found what they sought. Is it to be found at all? The

story is a revelation of Johnson himself. He never saw
life joyously, and at times he had fits of deep melancholy
which he fought against as against a madness. "I
inherited," he said, "a vile melancholy from my father,
which has made me mad all my life, at least not sober,"
and his long struggle with poverty helped to deepen this
melancholy.

But a year or two after *Rasselas* was written, a great
change came in Johnson's life, which gave him comfort
and security for the rest of his days. George III. had
come to the throne. He thought that he would like to
do something for literature, and offered Johnson a pension
of three hundred pounds a year.

Johnson was now a man of fifty-four. He was acknowledged as the greatest man of letters of his day, yet he was
still poor. Three hundred pounds seemed to him wealth,
but he hesitated to accept it. He was an ardent Tory and
hated the House of Hanover. In his dictionary he had
called a pension "an allowance made to any one without an
equivalent. In England it is generally understood to mean
pay given to a state hireling for treason to his country."
A pensioner he had said was "A slave of state hired by a
stipend to obey his master." Was he then to become a
traitor to his country and a slave of state?

But after a little persuasion Johnson yielded, as the
pension would be given to him, he was told, not for
anything that he would do, but for what he had done.
"It is true," he said afterwards, with a smile, "that I
cannot now curse the House of Hanover; nor would it
be decent for me to drink King James's health in the wine
that King George gives me money to pay for. But, sir, I
think that the pleasure of cursing the House of Hanover,
and drinking King James's health, are amply overbalanced
by three hundred pounds a year."

Johnson had always been indolent. It was perhaps

only poverty that had forced him to write, and now that he was comfortably provided for he became more indolent still.   He reproached himself, made good resolutions, and prayed over this fault, but still he remained slothful and idle.   He would lie abed till two o'clock, and sit up half the night talking, and an addition of Shakespeare which he had promised years before got no further on. An edition of another man's works often means a great deal of labor in making notes and comments.   This is especially so if hundreds of years have passed since the book was first written and the language has had time to change, and Johnson felt little inclined for this labor.   But at length he was goaded into working upon his Shakespeare by some spiteful verses on his idleness, written by a political enemy, and after long delay it appeared.

Just a little before this a young Scotsman named James Boswell got to know the great man.   He worshiped Johnson and spent as much time with him as he could. It was a strange friendship which grew up between these two.   The great man bullied and insulted yet loved the little man, and the little man accepted all the insults gladly, happy to be allowed to be near his hero on any conditions whatever.   He treasured every word that Johnson spoke and noted his every action.   Nothing was was too small or trivial for his loving observation.   He asked Johnson questions and made remarks, foolish or otherwise, in order to draw him out and make him talk, and afterwards he set down everything in a notebook.

And when Johnson was dead Boswell wrote his life. It is one of the most wonderful lives ever written—perhaps the most wonderful.   And when we have read it we seem to know Johnson as well as if we had lived with him. We see and know him in all his greatness and all his little-ness, in all his weakness and all his might.

It was with Boswell that Johnson made his most

famous journey, his tour to Scotland. For, like his name-sake, Ben, he too visited Scotland. But he traveled in a more comfortable manner, and his journey was a much longer one, for he went as far as the Hebrides. It was a wonderful expedition for a man of sixty-four, especially in those days when there were no trains and little ease in the way of traveling, and when much of it had to be done on rough ponies or in open boats.

On his return Johnson wrote an account of this journey which did not altogether please some of the Scots. But indeed, although Johnson did not love the Scots, there is little in his book at which to take offense.

Johnson's last work was a series of short lives of some of the English poets from the seventeenth century onwards. It is generally looked upon as his best. And although some of the poets of whom he wrote are almost forgotten, and although we may think that he was wrong in his criticisms of many of the others, this is the book of Johnson's which is still most read. For it must be owned that the great Sam is not much read now, although he is such an important figure in the history of our literature. It is as a person that we remember him, not as a writer. He stamped his personality, as it is called, upon his age. Boswell caught that personality and preserved it for us, so that, for generation after generation, Johnson lives as no other character in English literature lives. Boswell gave a new meaning to the word biographer, that is the writer of a life, and now when a great man has had no one to write his life well, we say "He lacks a Boswell."

Boswell after a time joined the famous club at which Johnson and his friends met together and talked. Johnson loved to argue, and he made a point of always getting the best of an argument. If he could not do so by reason, he simply roared his opponent down and silenced him by sheer rudeness. "There is no arguing with Johnson,"

"THERE IS NO ARGUING WITH JOHNSON," SAID GOLDSMITH, "FOR WHEN HIS

said one of his friends, Oliver Goldsmith, "for when his pistol misses fire he knocks you down with the butt end of it." And perhaps Goldy, as Johnson called him, had to suffer more rudeness from him than any of his friends save Bozzy. Yet the three were often to be found together, and it was Goldsmith who said of Johnson, "No man alive has a more tender heart. He has nothing of the bear but his skin."

And indeed in Johnson's outward appearance there was much of the bear. He was a sloven in dress. His clothes were shabby and thrown on anyhow. "I have no passion for clean linen," he said himself. At table he made strange noises and ate greedily, yet in spite of all that, added to his noted temper and rude manners, men loved him and sought his company more than that of any other writer of his day, for "within that shaggy exterior of his there beat a heart warm as a mother's, soft as a little child's." [1]

After Johnson received his pension we may look upon him as a lumbering vessel which has weathered many a strong sea and has now safely come to port. His life was henceforth easy. He received honorary degrees, first from Dublin and then from Oxford, so that he became Dr. Johnson. For two-and-twenty years he enjoyed his pension, his freedom and his honors; then, in 1784, surrounded by his friends, he died in London, and was buried in Westminster Abbey.

BOOKS TO READ

Rasselas, Prince of Abyssinia   A Journey to the Western Islands of Scotland.

[1] Carlyle.

CHAPTER LXX

GOLDSMITH—THE VAGABOND

THE kind of book which is most written and read nowadays is called a novel. But we have not yet spoken much about this kind of book, for until now there were no novels in our meaning of the word. There were romances such as *Havelok the Dane* and *Morte d'Arthur,* later still tales such as those of Defoe, and the modern novel is the outcome of such tales and romances, but it is usually supposed to be more like real life than a romance. In a romance we may have giants and fairies, things beyond nature and above nature. A novel is supposed to tell only of what could happen, without the help of anything outside everyday life. This is a kind of writing in which the English have become very clever, and now, as I said, more novels than any other kinds of book are written. But only a few of these are good enough to take a place in our literature, and very many are not worth reading or remembering at all.

The first real novel in the modern sense was written by Samuel Richardson, and published in 1740. Quickly after that there arose several other novel writers whose books became famous. These still stand high in the literature of our land, but as nothing in them would be interesting to you for many years to come we need not trouble about them now. There is, however, one novel of this early time which I feel sure you would like, and of

522

it and its author I shall tell you something. The book I mean is called *The Vicar of Wakefield,* and it was written by Oliver Goldsmith.

Oliver Goldsmith was born in 1728 in Pallas, a little out-of-the-way Irish village. His father was a clergyman and farmer, with a large family and very little money. He was a dear, simple, kindly man.

> "A man he was to all the country dear,
> And passing rich with forty pounds a year."

Two years after Oliver was born his father moved to Lissoy, another and better parish. Little Oliver began to learn very early, but his first teacher thought him stupid: "Never was there such a dull boy," she said. She managed, however, to teach him the alphabet, and at six he went to the village school of Lissoy. Paddy Byrne, the master here, was an old soldier. He had fought under Marlborough, he had wandered the world seeking and finding adventures. His head was full of tales of wild exploits, of battles, of ghosts and fairies too, for he was an Irishman and knew and loved the Celtic lore. Besides all this he wrote poetry.

To his schoolmaster's stories little Oliver listened eagerly. He listened, too, to the ballads sung by Peggy, the dairymaid, and to the wild music of the blind harper, Turlogh O'Carolan, the last Irish minstrel. All these things sank into the heart of the shy, little, ugly boy who seemed so stupid to his schoolfellows. He learned to read, and devoured all the romances and tales of adventure upon which he could lay hands, and in imitation of his schoolmaster he began to write poetry.

For three years Oliver remained under the care of his vagabond teacher. He looked up to him with a kind of awed wonder, and many years afterwards he drew a picture of him in his poem *The Deserted Village.*

"There, in his noisy mansion, skilled to rule,
The village master taught his little school.
A man severe he was, and stern to view,
I knew him well, and every truant knew·
Well had the boding tremblers learn'd to trace
The day's disasters in his morning face,
Full well they laugh'd, with counterfeited glee
At all his jokes, for many a joke had he,
Full well the busy whisper circing round
Convey'd the dismal tidings when he frown'd
Yet he was kind, or, if severe in aught,
The love he bore to learning was in fault;
The village all declared how much he knew:
'Twas certain he could write, and cypher too;
Lands he could measure, terms and tides presage,
And ev'n the story ran—that he could gauge
In arguing, too, the parson own'd his skill;
For ev'n though vanquish'd, he could argue still,
While words of learned length and thund'ring sound,
Amazed the gazing rustics ranged around,
And still they gazed, and still the wonder grew,
That one small head should carry all he knew."

But after three years of school under wonderful Paddy Byrne, Goldsmith became very ill with smallpox. He nearly died of it, and when he grew better he was plainer than ever, for his face was scarred and pitted by the disease. Goldsmith had been shy before his illness, and now when people laughed at his pock-marked face he grew more shy and sensitive still. For the next seven years he was moved about from school to school, always looked upon by his fellows as dull of wit, but good at games, and always in the forefront in mischief.

At length, when Goldsmith was nearly seventeen, he went to Trinity College, Dublin, as a sizar. As you know, in those days sizars had to wear a different dress from the commoners. Oliver's elder brother had gone as a commoner and Oliver had hoped to do the same. But as his father could not afford the money he was obliged, much

against his will, to go as a sizar. Indeed had it not been
for the kindness of an uncle he could not have gone to
college at all.

Awkward and shy, keen to feel insults whether intended
or not, Goldsmith hated his position as sizar. He did not
like his tutor either, who was a coarse, rough man, so his
life at college was not altogether happy. He was constantly in want of money, for when he had any his purse
was always open to others. At times when he was much
in need he wrote street ballads for five shillings each, and
would steal out at night to have the joy of hearing them
sung in the street.

Goldsmith was idle and wild, and at the end of two
years he quarreled with his tutor, sold his books, and
ran away to Cork. He meant to go on board a ship,
and sail away for ever from a land where he had been so
unhappy. But he had little money, and what he had was
soon spent, and at last, almost starving. having lived for
three days on a shilling, he turned homewards again.
Peace was made with his tutor, and Goldsmith went back
to college, and stayed there until two years later when
he took his degree.

His father was now dead and it was necessary for
Oliver to earn his own living. All his family wished him
to be a clergyman, but he "did not deem himself good
enough for it." However, he yielded to their persuasions,
and presented himself to his bishop. But the bishop
would not ordain him—why is not known, but it was said
that he was offended with Goldsmith for coming to be
ordained dressed in scarlet breeches.

After this failure Oliver tried teaching and became a
tutor, but in a very short time he gave that up. Next
his uncle, thinking that he would make a lawyer of him,
gave him £50 and sent him off to London to study law
there. Goldsmith lost the money in Dublin, and came home

penniless. Some time after this a gentleman remarked that he would make an excellent medical man, and again his uncle gave him money and sent him off to Edinburgh, this time as a medical student. So he said his last good-by to home and Ireland and set out.

In Scotland Goldsmith lived for a year and a half traveling about, enjoying life, and, it may be, studying. Then, in his happy-go-lucky way, he decided it would be well to go to Holland to finish his medical studies there. Off he started with little money in his pocket, and many debts behind him. After not a few adventures he arrived at length in Leyden. Here passing a florist's shop he saw some bulbs which he knew his uncle wanted. So in he ran to the shop, bought them, and sent them off to Ireland. The money with which he bought the bulbs was borrowed, and now he left Leyden to make the tour of Europe, burdened already with debt, with one guinea in his pocket, and one clean shirt and a flute as his luggage.

Thus on foot he wandered through Belgium, Germany, Switzerland, Italy, and France. In the villages he played upon his flute to pay for his food and his night's lodging.

> "Yet would the village praise my wondrous power,
> And dance, forgetful of the noon-tide hour.
> Alike all ages. Dames of ancient days
> Have led their children through the mirthful maze,
> And the gay grandsire, skill'd in gestic lore,
> Has frisk'd beneath the burthen of threescore " [1]

In the towns where no one listened to his flute, and in Italy where almost every peasant played better than he, he entered the colleges and disputed. For in those days many of the colleges and monasteries on the Continent kept certain days for arguments upon subjects of philosophy "for which, if the champion opposes with any dexterity, he can gain a gratuity in money, a dinner, and a bed for one night."

[1] *The Traveller.*

Thus from town to town, from village to village, Goldsmith wandered, until at the end of a year he found himself back among his countrymen, penniless and alone in London streets.

Here we have glimpses of him, a sorry figure in rusty black and tarnished gold, his pockets stuffed with papers, now assisting in a chemist's shop, now practicing as a doctor among those as poor as himself, now struggling to get a footing in the realm of literature, now passing his days miserably as an usher in a school. At length he gained more or less constant work in writing magazine articles, reviews, and children's books. By slow degrees his name became known. He met Johnson and became a member of his famous club. It is said that the first time those two great men met Johnson took special care in dressing himself. He put on a new suit of clothes and a newly powdered wig. When asked by a friend why he was so particular he replied, "Why, sir, I hear that Goldsmith is a very great sloven, and justifies his disregard for cleanliness and decency by quoting my example. I wish this night to show him a better example." But although Goldsmith was now beginning to be well known, he still lived in poor lodgings. He had only one chair, and when a visitor came he was given the chair while Oliver sat on the window ledge. When he had money he led an idle, easy life until it was spent. He was always generous. His hand was always open to help others, but he often forgot to pay his just debts. At length one day his landlady, finding he could not pay his rent, arrested him for debt.

In great distress Goldsmith wrote to Johnson begging him to come to his aid. Johnson sent him a guinea, promising to come to him as soon as possible. When Johnson arrived at Goldsmith's lodging, "I perceived," he says, "that he had already changed my guinea, and had got a bottle of Madeira and a glass before him. I put the cork into the bottle, desired him to be calm, and began to talk to him of the means by which he might be extricated. He then told me that he had a novel ready for the press, which he produced to me. I looked into it, and saw its merits, told the landlady I should soon return, and having gone to a bookseller sold it for sixty pounds. I brought Goldsmith the money, and he discharged his rent, not without rating his landlady in high tone for having used him so ill."

The novel which thus set Goldsmith free for the moment was the famous *Vicar of Wakefield* "There are an hundred faults in this thing," says Goldsmith himself, and if we agree with him there we also agree with him when he goes on to say, "and an hundred things might be said to prove them beauties. But it is needless. A book may be amusing with numerous errors, or it may be very dull without a single absurdity. The hero of this piece unites in himself the three greatest characters upon earth: he is a priest, an husbandman, and the father of a family. He is drawn as ready to teach, and ready to obey: as simple in affluence, and majestic in adversity." When we have made the acquaintance of the Vicar we find ourselves the richer for a lifelong friend. His gentle dignity, his simple faith, his sly and tender humor, all make us love him.

In the *Vicar of Wakefield* Goldsmith drew for us a picture of quiet, fireside family life such as no one before, or perhaps since, has drawn. Yet he himself was a homeless man. Since a boy of sixteen he had been a wanderer, a lonely vagabond, dwelling beneath stranger roofs. But it was the memory of his childish days that made it possible for him to write such a book, and in learning to know and love gentle Dr. Primrose we learn to know Oliver's father, Charles Goldsmith.

CHAPTER LXXI

GOLDSMITH—"THE VICAR OF WAKEFIELD"

"I CHOSE my wife," says Dr. Primrose in the beginning of the book, "as she did her wedding gown, not for a fine, glossy surface, but such qualities as would wear well. To do her justice, she was a good-natured, notable woman; and as for breeding, there were few county ladies who could show more. She could read any English book without much spelling; but for pickling, preserving, and cooking, none could excel her. She prided herself also upon being an excellent contriver in housekeeping; though I could never find that we grew richer with her contrivances."

Of his children he says, "Our eldest son was named George, after his uncle, who left us ten thousand pounds. Our second child, a girl, I intended to call, after her aunt, Grissel; but my wife, who had been reading romances, insisted upon her being called Olivia. In less than another year we had another daughter, and now I was determined that Grissel should be her name; but a rich relation taking a fancy to stand god-mother, the girl was by her directions called Sophia; so that we had two romantic names in the family; but I solemnly protest I had no hand in it. Moses was our next; and, after an interval of twelve years, we had two sons more." These two youngest boys were called Dick and Bill.

This is the family we learn to know in the "Vicar." When the story opens Olivia is just eighteen, Sophia

seventeen, and they are both very beautiful girls. At
first Dr. Primrose is well off and lives comfortably in a
fine house, but before the story goes far he loses all his
money, and is obliged to go with his family to a poor
living in another part of the country. Here, instead of
their handsome house, they have a tiny four-roomed
cottage, with whitewashed walls and thatched roof, for
a home. It is a very quiet country life which they have
now to live, and yet when you come to read the book you
will find that quite a number of exciting things happen
to them.

The dear doctor soon settles down to his changed
life, but his wife and her beautiful daughters try hard to
be as fine as they were before, and as grand, if not grander,
than their neighbors. This desire leads to not a few
of their adventures. Among other things they decide
to have their portraits painted. This is how Dr. Primrose
tells of it: "My wife and daughters happening to return
a visit to neighbour Flamborough's, found that family
had lately got their pictures drawn by a limner, who
travelled the country, and took likenesses for fifteen
shillings a-head. As this family and ours had long a sort
of rivalry in point of taste, our spirit took the alarm at
this stolen march upon us; and, notwithstanding all I
could say, and I said much, it was resolved that we should
have our pictures done too.

"Having therefore engaged the limner (for what
could I do?) our next deliberation was, to show the
superiority of our taste in the attitudes. As for our
neighbour's family, there were seven of them; and they
were drawn with seven oranges, a thing quite out of taste,
no variety in life, no composition in the world. We
desired to have something in a higher style, and after
many debates, at length came to a unanimous resolution,
of being drawn together, in one large historical family-

piece. This would be cheaper, since one frame would serve for all, and it would be infinitely more genteel; for all families of any taste were now drawn in the same manner.

"As we did not immediately recollect an historical subject to hit us, we were contented each with being drawn as independent historical figures. My wife desired to be represented as Venus, and the painter was instructed not to be too frugal of his diamonds in her stomacher and hair. Her two little ones were to be as cupids by her side; while I in my gown and band, was to present her with my books on the Whistonian controversy. Olivia would be drawn as an amazon, sitting upon a bank of flowers, dressed in a green Joseph,[1] richly laced with gold, and a whip in her hand. Sophia was to be a shepherdess, with as many sheep as the painter could put in for nothing; and Moses was to be dressed out with a hat and white feather.

"Our taste so much pleased the Squire that he insisted on being put in as one of the family, in the character of Alexander the Great, at Olivia's feet. This was considered by us all as an indication of his desire to be introduced into the family; not could we refuse his request. The painter was therefore set to work; and as he wrought with assiduity and expedition, in less than four days the whole was completed. The piece was large; and it must be owned he did not spare his colours; for which my wife gave him great encomiums.

"We were all perfectly satisfied with his performance; but an unfortunate circumstance had not occurred until the picture was finished, which now struck us with dismay. It was so very large, that we had no place in the house to fix it. How we all came to disregard so material a point is inconceivable; but certain it is, we had been all greatly remiss. The picture, therefore, instead of gratifying our

[1] A coat with capes worn by ladies in the eighteenth century for riding

vanity, as we hoped, leaned, in a most mortifying manner, against the kitchen wall, where the canvas was stretched and painted, much too large to be got through any of the doors, and the jest of all our neighbours. One compared it to Robinson Crusoe's long-boat, too large to be removed; another thought it more resembled a reel in a bottle; some wondered how it could be got out, but still more were amazed how it ever got in."

For the rest of the troubles and adventures of the good Vicar and his family you must go to the book itself. In the end all comes right, and we leave the Vicar surrounded by his family with Dick and Bill sitting on his knee. "I had nothing now this side the grave to wait for," he says; "all my cares were over; my pleasure was unspeakable." Even if you do not at first understand all of this book I think it will repay you to read it, for on almost every page you will find touches of gentle humor. We feel that no one but a man of simple childlike heart could have written such a book, and when we have closed it we feel better and happier for having read it.

But delightful though we find the *Vicar of Wakefield,* the bookseller who bought it did not think highly enough of it to publish it at once. Meanwhile Goldsmith published a poem called *The Traveller.* His own wanderings on the Continent gave him the subject for this poem, for Goldsmith, like Milton, put something of himself into all his best works. *The Traveller* was such a success that the bookseller thought it worth while to publish the *Vicar of Wakefield.*

Goldsmith was now famous, but he was still poor. He lived in a miserable garret doing all manner of literary work for bread. Among the things he wrote was a play called *The Good Natured Man.* It was a success, and brought him in £500.

Goldsmith now left his garret, took a fine set of rooms,

furnished them grandly, and gave dinner-parties and card-
parties to his friends.   These were the days of Goldy's
splendor.   He no longer footed it in the great world in
rusty black and tarnished gold, but in blue silk breeches,
and coat with silken linings and golden buttons.   He
dined with great people; he strutted in innocent vanity,
delighted to shine in the world, to see and be seen, although
in Johnson's company he could never really shine.   Sam
was a great talker, and it was said Goldsmith "wrote like an
angel and spoke like poor Poll."   His friends called him
Doctor, although where he took his medical degree no one
knows, and he certainly had no other degree given to him
as an honor as Johnson had.   So Johnson was Dr. major,
Goldsmith only Dr. minor.

But soon these days of wealth were over; soon Goldsmith's money was all spent, and once again he had to
sit down to grinding work.   He wrote many things, but
the next great work he published was another poem, *The
Deserted Village.*

The Deserted Village, like *The Traveller,* is written in
the heroic couplet which, since the days of Dryden, had
held its ground as the best form of English poetry.   In
these poems the couplet has reached its very highest level,
for although his rimes are smooth and polished Goldsmith has wrought into them something of tender grace
and pathos which sets them above the diamond-like glitter
of Pope's lines.   His couplets are transformed by the
Celtic touch.

The poem tells the story of a village which had once
been happy and flourishing, but which is now quite deserted
and fallen to ruins.   The village is thought by some people
to have been Lissoy, where Oliver had lived as a boy, but
others think this cannot be, for they say no Irish village
was ever so peaceful and industrious as Goldsmith pictures
his village to have been.   But we must remember that

the poet had not seen his home since childhood, and that he looked back upon it through the golden haze of memory. It is in this poem that we have the picture of Oliver's old schoolmaster which I have already given you. Here, too, we have a picture of the kindly village parson who may be taken both from Oliver's father and from his brother Henry. Probably he had his brother most in mind, for Henry Goldsmith had but lately died, "and I loved him better than most other men," said the poet sadly in the dedication of this poem—

"Near yonder copse, where once the garden smiled,
And still where many a garden flower grows wild,
There, where a few torn shrubs the place disclose,
The village preacher's modest mansion rose.
A man he was to all the country dear,
And passing rich with forty pounds a year;
Remote from towns he ran his godly race,
Nor e'er had changed, nor wish'd to change, his place:
Unpractis'd he to fawn, or seek for power,
By doctrines fashion'd to the varying hour;
Far other aims his heart had learn'd to prize,
More skill'd to raise the wretched than to rise.
His house was known to all the vagrant train;
He chid their wand'rings, but relieved their pain
The long-remember'd beggar was his guest,
Whose beard descending swept his aged breast,
The ruin'd spendthrift, now no longer proud,
Claim'd kindred there, and had his claims allow'd;
The broken soldier, kindly bade to stay,
Sat by his fire, and talk'd the night away,
Wept o'er his wounds, or, tales of sorrow done,
Shoulder'd his crutch, and showed how fields were won.
Pleased with his guests, the good man learn'd to glow,
And quite forgot their vices in their woe;
Careless their merits or their faults to scan,
His pity gave ere charity began.
Thus to relieve the wretched was his pride,
And ev'n his failings lean'd to virtue's side,
But in his duty prompt, at every call,
He watch'd and wept, he pray'd and felt for all;

At church, with meek and unaffected grace,
His looks adorn'd the venerable place,
Truth from his lips prevail'd with double sway,
And fools, who came to scoff, remain'd to pray.
The service past, around the pious man,
With steady zeal, each honest rustic ran,
Ev'n children followed with endearing wile,
And pluck'd his gown, to share the good man's smile
His ready smile a parent's warmth exprest;
Their welfare pleased him, and their eaies distrest:
To them his heart, his love, his griefs were given,
But all his serious thoughts had rest in heaven.
As some tall cliff that lifts its awful form,
Swells from the vale, and midway leaves the storm,
Though round its breast the rolling clouds are spread,
Eternal sunshine settles on its head "

Goldsmith's last great work was a comedy named *She Stoops to Conquer*. It is said that the idea for this play was given to him by something which happened to himself when a boy.

The last time that Goldsmith returned home from school he made his journey on horseback. The horse was borrowed or hired, but he had a guinea in his pocket, and he felt very grown up and grand. He had to spend one night on the way, and as evening came on he asked a passing stranger to direct him to the best house, meaning the best in the neighborhood. The stranger happened to be the village wag, and seeing the schoolboy swagger, and the manly airs of sixteen, he, in fun, directed him to the squire's house. There the boy arrived, handed over his horse with a lordly air to a groom, marched into the house and ordered supper and a bottle of wine. In the manner of the times, in drinking his wine he invited his landlord to join him as a real grown-up man might have done. The squire saw the joke and fell in with it, and not until next morning did the boy discover his mistake.

The comedy founded on this adventure was a great success, and no wonder, for it bubbles over with fun and laughter. Some day you will read the play, perhaps too, you may see it acted, for it is still sometimes acted. In any case it makes very good reading.

But Goldsmith did not long enjoy the new fame this comedy brought him. In the spring of 1774, less than a year after it appeared, the kindly spendthrift author lay dead. He was only forty-five.

The beginning of Goldsmith's life had been a struggle with poverty; the end was a struggle with debt. By his writing he made what was in those days a good deal of money, but he could not keep it. To give him money was like pouring water into a sieve "Is your mind at ease," asked his doctor as he lay dying. "No, it is not," answered Goldsmith. Those were his last words.

"Of poor dear Dr. Goldsmith," wrote Johnson, "there is little to be told more than the papers have made public. He died of a fever, made, I am afraid, more violent by uneasiness of mind. His debts began to be heavy, and all his resources were exhausted. Sir Joshua [1] is of opinion that he owed not less than two thousand pounds. Was ever poet so trusted before?"

Goldsmith was buried in the graveyard of the Temple Church, but his tomb is unmarked, and where he lies no one knows. His sorrowing friends, however, placed a tablet to his memory in Westminster, so that his name at least is recorded upon the roll of the great dead who lie gathered there.

BOOK TO READ

The Vicar of Wakefield (Everyman's Library)

[1] Sir Joshua Reynolds, the famous painter

CHAPTER LXXII

BURNS—THE PLOWMAN POET

Should auld acquaintance be forgot,
    And never brought to min'?
Should auld acquaintance be forgot,
    And days o' lang syne?

      For auld lang syne, my dear,
      For auld lang syne,
      We'll tak a cup o' kindness yet,
      For auld lang syne.

We twa hae run about the braes,
    And pu'd the gowans fine,
But we've wander'd mony a weary foot,
    Sin auld lang syne.

      For auld lang syne, etc.

We twa hae paidl't i' the burn,
    Frae mornin' sun till dine [1]
But seas between us braid hae roar'd,
    Sin auld lang syne

      For auld lang syne, etc.

And here's a hand, my trusty fiere, [2]
    And gie's a hand o' thine;
And we'll tak a right guid-willie waught, [3]
    For auld lang syne

      For auld lang syne, etc

---

[1] Dinner.   [2] Companion   [3] Drink

And surely ye'll be your pint-stowp,[1]
And surely I'll be mine,
And we'll tak a cup o' kindness yet,
For auld lang syne.

For auld lang syne, my dear,
For auld lang syne,
We'll tak a cup o' kindness yet,
For auld lang syne

No song, perhaps, is so familiar to English-speaking people as that with which this chapter begins. In the back woods of Canada, in far Australia, on the wide South African veldt, wherever English-speaking people meet and gather, they join hands to sing that song. To the merriest gathering it comes as a fitting close. It is the hymn of home, of treasured friendships, and of old memories, just as "God save the King" is the hymn of loyalty, and yet it is written in Scots, which English tongues can hardly pronounce, and many words of which to English ears hardly carry a meaning. But the plaintive melody and the pathetic force of the rhythm grip the heart. There is no need to understand every word of this "glad kind greeting" [2] any more than there is need to understand what some great musician means by every note which his violin sings forth.

The writer of that song was, like Caedmon long ago, a son of the soil, he, too, was a "heaven-taught ploughman." [3]

While Goldsmith lay a-dying in London, in the breezy Scottish Lowlands a big rough lad of fifteen called Robert Burns was following his father's plow by day, poring over Shakespeare, the *Spectator,* and Pope's *Homer,* of nights, not knowing that in years to come he was to be remembered as our greatest song writer. Robert was the

---

[1] Measure.   [2] Carlyle.   [3] Henry Mackenzie

Burns had been farmer folk
m Burns had fallen on evil
1ome he drifted to Ayrshire,
ge of Alloway as a gardener.
built himself a mud cottage.
1" and a kitchen, whitewashed
kitchen there was a fireplace,
d, and little else beyond the

in the wild January weather
1. Scarcely a week later, one
frail home was blown in. So
1ed as if the whole wall might
, and the storm, the baby and
neighbor's house. There they
their own cottage was again
rough entry into the world for

Burns went on working as a
was about seven he took a
1hant, and removed there with

o make his farm pay, to feed
his brothers and sisters, who
him. But, poor though he
p his mind that his children
: Robert went daily to school,
sent away somewhere else,
vas left without any teacher,
hbors joined together to pay
1ot pay enough to give him a
d to stay with each family in
.

a grave-faced, serious, small
r Gilbert were the cleverest

scholars in the little school. Chief among their school books was the Bible and a collection of English prose and verse. It was from the last that Burns first came to know Addison's works, for in this book he found the "Vision of Mirza" and other *Spectator* tales, and loved them.

Robert had a splendid memory. In school hours he stored his mind with the grand grave tales of the Bible, and with the stately English of Addison; out of school hours he listened to the tales and songs of an old woman who sang to him, or told him stories of fairies and brownies, of witches and warlocks, of giants, enchanted towns, dragons, and what not. The first books he read out of school were a *Life of Hannibal,* the great Carthagenian general, and a *Life of Wallace,* the great Scottish hero; this last being lent him by the blacksmith. These books excited little Robert so much that if ever a recruiting sergeant came to his village, he would strut up and down in raptures after the drum and bagpipe, and long to be tall enough to be a soldier. The story of Wallace, too, awoke in his heart a love of Scotland and all things Scottish, which remained with him his whole life through. At times he would steal away by himself to read the brave, sad story, and weep over the hard fate of his hero. And as he was in the Wallace country he wandered near and far exploring every spot where his hero might have been

After a year or two the second schoolmaster went away as the other had done. Then all the schooling the Burns children had was from their father in the long winter evenings after the farm work for the day was over.

And so the years went on, the family at Mount Oliphant living a hard and sparing life. For years they never knew what it was to have meat for dinner, yet when Robert was thirteen his father managed to send him and Gilbert week about to a school two or three miles away.

He could not send them both together, for he could neither afford to pay two fees, nor could he spare both boys at once, as already the children helped with the farm work.

At fifteen Robert was his father's chief laborer. He was a very good plowman, and no one in all the country-side could wield the scythe or the threshing-flail with so much skill and vigor. He worked hard, yet he found time to read, borrowing books from whoever would lend them. Thus, before he was fifteen, he had read Shakespeare, and Pope, and the *Spectator,* besides a good many other books which would seem to most boys of to-day very dull indeed. But the book he liked best was a collection of songs. He carried it about with him. "I pored over them," he says, "driving my cart, or walking to labour, song by song, verse by verse."

Thus the years passed, as Burns himself says, in the "cheerless gloom of a hermit, with the unceasing toil of a galley-slave." Then when Robert was about nineteen his father made another move to the farm of Lochlea, about ten miles off. It was a larger and better farm, and for three or four years the family lived in comfort. In one of Burns's own poems, *The Cotter's Saturday Night,* we get some idea of the simple home life these kindly God-fearing peasants led—

"November chill blaws loud wi' angry sugh;[1]
  The short'ning winter-day is near a close;
The miry beasts retreating frae the pleugh;
  The black'ning trains o' craws to their repose;
  The toil-worn Cotter frae his labour goes,
This night his weekly moil is at an end,
  Collects his spades, his mattocks, and his hoes,
Hoping the morn in ease and rest to spend,
And weary, o'er the moor, his course does hameward bend.

---

[1] Whistling sound.

"At length his lonely cot appears in view,
  Beneath the shelter of an aged tree;
Th' expectant wee-things, toddlin, stacher [1] through
  To meet their dad, wi' flichterin [2] noise and glee
  His wee bit ingle, blinkin bonnily,
His clean hearth-stane, his thriftie wifie's smile,
  The lisping infant prattling on his knee,
Does a' his weary carking cares beguile,
An' makes him quite forget his labour and his toil.

"Belyve,[3] the elder bairns come drapping in,
  At service out, amang the farmers roun',
Some ca' the pleugh, some herd, some tentie [4] rin
  A cannie [5] errand to a neebor town
  Their eldest hope, their Jenny, woman grown,
In youthfu' bloom, love sparkling in her e'e,
  Comes hame, perhaps, to show a braw new gown,
Or deposite her sair-won penny-fee,[6]
To help her parents dear, if they in hardship be.

"With joy unfeign'd, brothers and sisters meet,
  An' each for other's weelfare kindly spiers [7]
The social hours, swift-wing'd, unnotic'd, fleet;
  Each tells the uncos [8] that he sees or hears;
  The parents, partial, eye their hopeful years;
Anticipation forward points the view.
  The mother, wi' her needle and her sheers,
Gars auld claes look amaist as weel's the new [9]
The father mixes a' wi' admonition due.

·   ·   ·   ·   ·   ·   ·

"The cheerfu' supper done, wi' serious face,
  They, round the ingle, form a circle wide;
The sire turns o'er, wi' patriarchal grace,
  The big ha'-Bible, ance his father's pride:
  His bonnet rev'rently is laid aside,

---

[1] Stagger.   [2] To run with outspread arms.
[3] In a little   [4] Carefully.
[6] Not difficult.   [5] Wages paid in money.
[7] Asks after.   [8] Strange things
[9] Makes old clothes look almost as good as new.

His lyart haffets [1] wearing thin an' bare,
  Those strains that once did sweet in Zion glide,
He wales [2] a portion with judicious care,
And "Let us worship God!" he says, with solemn air.

.   .   .   .

Then homeward all take off their sev'ral way;
  The youngling cottagers retire to rest·
The parent-pair their secret homage pay,
  And proffer up to Heaven the warm request,
  That He who stills the raven's clam'rous nest,
And decks the lily fair in flow'ry pride,
  Would, in the way His wisdom sees the best,
For them and for their little ones provide,
But, chiefly, in their hearts with grace divine preside."

As Robert grew to be a man the changes in his somber life were few. But once he spent a summer on the coast learning how to measure and survey land. In this he made good progress. "But," he says, "I made a greater progress in the knowledge of mankind." For it was a smuggling district. Robert came to know the men who carried on the unlawful trade, and so was present at many a wild and riotous scene, and saw men in new lights. He had already begun to write poetry, now he began to write letters too. He did not write with the idea alone of giving his friends news of him. He wrote to improve his power of language. He came across a book of letters of the wits of Queen Anne's reign, and these he pored over, eager to make his own style as good.

When Robert was twenty-two he again left home. This time he went to the little seaport town of Irvine to learn flax dressing. For on the farm the father and brothers had begun to grow flax, and it was thought well that one of them should know how to prepare it for spinning.

[1] The gray hair on his temples   [2] Chooses

Here Robert got into evil company and trouble. He sinned and repented and sinned again. We find him writing to his father, "As for this world, I despair of ever making a figure in it. I am not formed for the bustle of the busy, nor the flutter of the gay. I shall never again be capable of entering into such scenes." Burns knew himself to be a man of faults. The knowledge of his own weakness, perhaps, made him kindly to others. In one of his poems he wrote—

> "Then gently scan your brother man,
>   Still gentler sister woman,
> Tho' they may gang a kennin wrang,[1]
>   To step aside is human:
> One point must still be greatly dark,
>   The moving *why* they do it;
> And just as lamely can ye mark
>   How far perhaps they rue it.

> "Who made the heart, 'tis He alone
>   Decidedly can try us.
> He knows each chord, its various tone,
>   Each spring its various bias:
> Then at the balance let's be mute,
>   We never can adjust it;
> What's done we partly may compute,
>   But know not what's resisted."

Bad fortune, too, followed Burns. The shop in which he was engaged was set on fire, and he was left "like a true poet, not worth a sixpence."

So leaving the troubles and temptations of Irvine behind, he carried home a smirched name to his father's house.

Here, too, troubles were gathering. Bad harvests were followed by money difficulties, and, weighed down with all his cares, William Burns died. The brothers had already taken another farm named Mossgiel. Soon

[1] A very little wrong.

after the father's death the whole family went to live there.

Robert meant to settle down and be a regular farmer. "Come, go to, I will be wise," he said. He read farming books and bought a little diary in which he meant to write down farming notes. But the farming notes often turned out to be scraps of poetry.

The next four years of Burns's life were eventful years, for though he worked hard as he guided the plow or swung the scythe, he wove songs in his head. And as he followed his trade year in year out, from summer to winter, from winter to summer, he learned all the secrets of the earth and sky, of the hedgerow and the field.

How everything that was beautiful and tender and helpless in nature appealed to him we know from his poems. There is the field mouse—the "wee sleekit,[1] cow'rin', tim'rous beastie," whose nest he turned up and destroyed in his November plowing. "Poor little mouse, I would not hurt you," he says—

> "Thy wee bit housie, too, in ruin;
> Its silly wa's the win's are strewin'!"

And thou poor mousie art turned out into the cold, bleak, winter weather!—

> "But, Mousie, thou art no thy lane,
> In proving foresight may be vain;
> The best laid schemes o' mice an' men,
> Gang aft agley,[2]
> An' lea'e us nought but grief and pain
> For promis'd joy"

It goes to his heart to destroy the early daisies with the plow—

> "Wee, modest, crimson-tipped flow'r,
> Thou's met me in an evil hour;

---

[1] Smooth   [2] Go often wrong

> For I maun crush amang the stoure
>> Thy slender stem.
> To spare thee now is past my pow'r,
>> Thou bonnie gem.
>
> "Alas! it's no thy neebor sweet,
> The bonnie lark, companion meet,
> Bending thee 'mang the dewy weet,
>> Wi' spreckl'd breast,
> When upward springing, blythe, to greet
>> The purpling east.
>
> "Cauld blew the bitter-biting North
> Upon thy early, humble birth,
> Yet cheerfully thou glinted forth
>> Amid the storm,
> Scarce rear'd above the parent earth
>> Thy tender form.
>
> "The flaunting flow'rs our gardens yield,
> High shelt'ring woods and wa's maun shield;
> But thou, beneath the random bield [1]
>> O' clod or stane,
> Adorns the histie stibble-field,[2]
>> Unseen, alane
>
> "There, in thy scanty mantle clad,
> Thy snawie bosom sunward spread,
> Thou lifts thy unassuming head
>> In humble guise;
> But now the share uptears thy bed,
>> And low thou lies!"

Burns wrote love songs too, for he was constantly in love—often to his discredit, and at length he married Jean Armour, Scots fashion, by writing a paper saying that they were man and wife and giving it to her. This was enough in those days to make a marriage. But Burns had no money; the brothers' farm had not pros-

---

[1] Shelter. [2] Bare stubble field

pered, and Jean's father, a stern old Scotsman, would have nothing to say to Robert, who was in his opinion a bad man, and a wild, unstable, penniless rimester. He made his daughter burn her "lines," thus in his idea putting an end to the marriage.

Robert at this was both hurt and angry, and made up his mind to leave Scotland for ever and never see his wife and children more. He got a post as overseer on an estate in Jamaica, but money to pay for his passage he had none. In order to get money some friends proposed that he should publish his poems. This he did, and the book was such a success that instead of going to Jamaica as an unknown exile Burns went to Edinburgh to be entertained, fêted, and flattered by the greatest men of the day.

All the fine ladies and gentlemen were eager to see the plowman poet. The fuss they made over him was enough to turn the head of a lesser man. But in spite of all the flattery, Burns, though pleased and glad, remained as simple as before. He moved among the grand people in their silks and velvets clad in homespun clothes "like a farmer dressed in his best to dine with the laird" [1] as easily as he had moved among his humble friends. He held himself with that proud independence which later made him write—

> "Is there for honest poverty
>   That hangs his head, and a' that?
> The coward slave, we pass him by,
>   We dare be poor for a' that!
> For a' that, and a' that,
>   Our toils obscure, and a' that,
> The rank is but the guinea stamp,
>   The man's the gowd for a' that.

---

[1] Scott.

> "What though on hamely fare we dine,
>   Wear hodden grey, and a' that,
> Gie fools their silks. and knaves their wine,
>   A man's a man for a' that
> For a' that and a' that,
>   Their tinsel show, and a' that;
> The honest man, though e'er sae poor,
>   Is king o' men for a' that."

After spending a brilliant winter in Edinburgh, Burns set off on several tours through his native land, visiting many of the places famous in Scottish history. But, as the months went on, he began to be restless in his seeming idleness. The smiles of the great world would not keep hunger from the door; he feared that his fame might be only a nine days' wonder, so he decided to return to his farming. He took a farm a few miles from Dumfries, and although since he had been parted from his Jean he had forgotten her time and again and made love to many another, he and she were now married, this time in good truth. From now onward it was that Burns wrote some of his most beautiful songs, and it is for his songs that we remember him. Some of them are his own entirely, and some are founded upon old songs that had been handed on for generations by the people from father to son, but had never been written down until Burns heard them and saved them from being forgotten. But in every case he left the song a far more beautiful thing than he found it. None of them perhaps is more beautiful than that he now wrote to his Jean—

> "Of a' the airts [1] the wind can blaw,
>   I dearly like the west,
> For there the bonnie lassie lives,
>   The lassie I lo'e best.

---

[1] Directions

The wild-woods grow and rivers row,[1]
  And mony a hill between;
But day and night my fancy's flight
  Is ever wi' my Jean

"I see her in the dewy flowers,
  I see her sweet and fair:
I hear her in the tunefu' birds,
  I hear her charm the air;
There's not a bonnie flower that springs
  By fountain, shaw,[2] or green,
There's not a bonnie bird that sings
  But minds me o' my Jean "

But farming and song-making did not seem to go together, and on his new farm Burns succeeded little better than on any that he had tried before. He thought to add to his livelihood by turning an excise man, that is, an officer whose work is to put down smuggling, to collect the duty on whisky, and to see that none upon which duty has not been paid is sold. One of his fine Edinburgh friends got an appointment for him, and he began his duties, and it would seem fulfilled them well. But this mode of life was for Burns a failure. In discharge of his duties he had to ride hundreds of miles in all kinds of weathers. He became worn out by the fatigue of it, and it brought him into the temptation of drinking too much. Things went with him from bad to worse, and at length he died at the age of thirty-six, worn out by toil and sin and suffering.

In many ways his was a misspent life "at once unfinished and a ruin "[3] His was the poet's soul bound in the body of clay. He was an unhappy man, and we cannot but pity him, and yet remember him with gratitude for the beautiful songs he gave us. In his own words we may say—

[1] Roll   [2] Wood   [3] Carlyle.

"Is there a man, whose judgment clear,
Can others teach the course to steer,
Yet runs, himself, life's mad career,
  Wild as the wave?
Here pause—and, through the starting tear,
  Survey this grave "

Burns was a true son of the soil. There is no art in his songs but only nature. Apart from his melody what strikes us most is his truth; he sang of what he saw, of what he felt and knew. He knew the Scottish peasant through and through. Grave and humorous, simple and cunning, honest and hypocritical, proud and independent—every phase of him is to be found in Burns's poems. He knew love too; and in every phase—happy and unhappy, worthy and unworthy—he sings of it. But it is of love in truth that he sings. Here we have no more the make-believe of the Elizabethan age, no longer the stilted measure of the Georgian. The day of the heroic couplet is done; with Burns we come back to nature.

BOOK TO READ

Selected Works of Robert Burns, edited by R Sutherland

Note.—This is probably the best selection for juvenile readers.

CHAPTER LXXIII

COWPER—"THE TASK"

WHILE Burns was weaving his wonderful songs among the Lowland hills of Scotland, another lover of nature was telling of placid English life, of simple everyday doings, in a quiet little country town in England. This man was William Cowper.

Cowper was the son of a clergyman. He was born in 1731 and became a barrister, but it seemed a profession for which he was little fitted. He was shy and morbidly religious, and he also liked literature much better than law. Still he continued his way of life until, when he was thirty-two, he was offered a post as Clerk of the Journals of the House of Lords. He wished to accept the post, but was told he must stand an examination at the bar of the House of Lords.

This was more than his nervous, sensitive nature could bear. Rather than face the trial he decided to die. Three times he tried to kill himself. Three times he failed. Then the darkness of madness closed in upon him. Religious terrors seized him, and for many months he suffered agonies of mind. But at length his tortured brain found rest, and he became once more a sane man.

Then he made up his mind to leave London, and all the excitements of a life for which he was not fit, and after a few changes here and there he settled down to a peaceful life with a clergyman and his wife, named Unwin. And when after two years Mr. Unwin died, Cowper still lived with his widow. With her he moved to Olney in

Buckinghamshire. It was here that, together with the curate, John Newton, Cowper wrote the Olney hymns, many of which are still well loved to-day. Perhaps one of the best is that beginning—

"God moves in a mysterious way,
His wonders to perform,
He plants His footsteps in the sea,
And rides upon the storm"

It was written when Cowper felt again the darkness of insanity closing in upon him. Once again he tried to end his life, but again the storm passed.

Cowper was already a man of nearly fifty when these hymns first appeared. Shortly afterwards he published another volume of poems in the style of Pope.

It was after this that Cowper found another friend who brought some brightness into his life. Lady Austen, a widow, took a house near Cowper and Mrs. Unwin, and became a third in their friendship. It was she who told Cowper the story of John Gilpin. The story tickled his fancy so that he woke in the night with laughter over it. He decided to make a ballad of the story, and next day the ballad was finished. I think I need hardly give you any quotation here. You all know that—

"John Gilpin was a citizen
Of credit and renown,
A train-band captain eke was he
Of famous London town."

And you have heard his adventures on the anniversary of his wedding day.

John Gilpin was first published in a magazine, and there it was seen by an actor famous in his day, who took it for a recitation. It at once became a success, and thousands of copies were sold.

It was Lady Austen, too, who urged Cowper to his

greatest work, *The Task*. She wanted him to try blank
verse, but he objected that he had nothing to write about.
"You can write upon any subject," replied Lady Austen,
"write upon the sofa."

So Cowper accepted the task thus set for him, and
began to write. The first book of *The Task* is called *The
Sofa*, and through all the six books we follow the course of
his simple country life. It is the epic of simplicity, at once
pathetic and playful. Its tuneful, easy blank verse never
rises to the grandeur of Milton's, yet there are fine passages
in it. Though Cowper lived a retired and uneventful
life, the great questions of his day found an echo in his
heart. Canada had been won and the American States lost
when he wrote—

"England, with all thy faults, I love thee still—
My Country! and, while yet a nook is left
Where English minds and manners may be found,
Shall be constrained to love thee.

   .   .   .   .

Time was when it was praise and boast enough
In every clime, and travel where we might,
That we were born her children; praise enough
To fill the ambition of a private man,
That Chatham's language was his mother tongue,
And Wolfe's great name compatriot with his own.
Farewell those honours, and farewell with them
The hope of such hereafter! they have fallen
Each in his field of glory: one in arms,
And one in council—Wolfe upon the lap
Of smiling Victory that moment won,
And Chatham heart-sick of his country's shame
They made us many soldiers. Chatham, still
Consulting England's happiness at home,
Secured it by an unforgiving frown,
If any wronged her. Wolfe, where'er he fought,
Put so much of his heart into his act,
That his example had a magnet's force,
And all were swift to follow where all loved."

These lines are from the second book of *The Task* called *The Timepiece*. The third is called *The Garden*, the fourth *The Winter Evening*. There we have the well-known picture of a quiet evening by the cozy fireside. The post boy has come "with spattered boots, strapped waist, and frozen locks." He has brought letters and the newspaper—

"Now stir the fire, and close the shutters fast,
Let fall the curtains, wheel the sofa round,
And, while the bubbling and loud-hissing urn
Throws up a steamy column, and the cups,
That cheer but not inebriate, wait on each,
So let us welcome peaceful evening in."

The poem ends with two books called *The Winter Morning Walk* and *The Winter Walk at Noon*. Though not grand, *The Task* is worth reading. It is, too, an easily read, and easily understood poem, and through it all we feel the love of nature, the return to romance and simplicity. In the last book we see Cowper's love of animals. There he sings, "If not the virtues, yet the worth, of brutes."

Cowper loved animals tenderly and understood them in a wonderful manner. He tamed some hares and made them famous in his verse. And when he felt madness coming upon him he often found relief in his interest in these pets. One of his poems tells how Cowper scolded his spaniel Beau for killing a little baby bird "not because you were hungry," says the poet, "but out of naughtiness." Here is Beau's reply—

"Sir, when I flew to seize the bird
In spite of your command,
A louder voice than yours I heard,
And harder to withstand

"You cried 'Forbear!'—but in my breast
A mightier cried 'Proceed!'—
'Twas nature, sir, whose strong behest
Impelled me to the deed.

"Yet much as nature I respect,
 I ventured once to break
(As you perhaps may recollect)
 Her precept for your sake;

"And when your linnet on a day,
 Passing his prison door,
Had fluttered all his strength away
 And panting pressed the floor,

"Well knowing him a sacred thing
 Not destined to my tooth,
I only kissed his ruffled wing
 And licked the feathers smooth.

"Let my obedience then excuse
 My disobedience now,
Nor some reproof yourself refuse
 From your aggrieved Bow-wow;

"If killing birds be such a crime
 (Which I can hardly see),
What think you, sir, of killing Time
 With verse addressed to me?"

As Cowper's life went on, the terrible lapses into insanity became more frequent, but his sweet and kindly temper won him many friends, and he still wrote a great deal. And among the many things he wrote, his letters to his friends were not the least interesting. They are among the best letters in our language.

Perhaps Cowper's greatest accomplishment, though not his greatest work, was a translation of *Homer*. He had never considered Pope's *Homer* good, and he wished to leave to the world a better. Cowper's version was published in 1791, and he fondly believed that it would take the place of Pope's. But although Cowper's may be more correct, it is plain and dry, and while Pope's is still read and remembered, Cowper's is forgotten.

Indeed, that Cowper is remembered at all is due more to his shorter poems such as *Boadicea* and *The Wreck of the Royal George,* and chiefly, perhaps, to *John Gilpin,* which in its own way is a treasure that we would not be without. Other of his shorter poems are full of a simple pathos and gentle humor. The last he wrote was called *The Castaway,* and the verse with which it ends describes not unfittingly the close of his own life. For his mind sank ever deeper into the shadow of madness until he died in April 1800—

> "No voice divine the storm allayed,
>   No light propitious shone;
> When, snatched from all effectual aid,
>   We perished, each alone:
> But I beneath a rougher sea,
> And whelmed in deeper gulfs than he "

Cowper was never a power in our literature, but he was a forerunner, "the forerunner of the great Restoration of our liteature."[1] and unlike most forerunners he was popular in his own day. And although it is faint, like the scent of forgotten rose leaves, his poetry still keeps a charm and sweetness for those who will look for it.

[1] Macaulay.

CHAPTER LXXIV

WORDSWORTH—THE POET OF NATURE

COWPER was as a straw blown along the path; he had no force in himself, he showed the direction of the wind. Now we come to one who was not only a far greater poet, but who was a force in our literature. This man was William Wordsworth. He was the apostle of simplicity, the prophet of nature. He sang of the simplest things, of the common happenings of everyday life, and that too a simple life.

His desire was to choose words only which were really used by men in everyday talk, "and, at the same time, to throw over them a certain colouring of the imagination."

He chose to sing of humble life because there men's thoughts and feelings were more free from art and restraint, there they spoke a plainer, more forceful language, there they were in touch with all that was lasting and true in Nature. Here then, you will say, is the poet for us, the poet who tells of simple things in simple words, such as we can understand. And yet, perhaps, strange as it may seem, there is no poet who makes less appeal to young minds than does Wordsworth.

In reading poetry, though we may not always understand every word of it, we want to feel the thrill and glamour of it. And when Wordsworth remembers his own rules and keeps to them there is no

557

glamour, and his simplicity is apt to seem to us mere silliness.

When we are very young we cannot walk alone, and are glad of a kindly helping hand to guide our footsteps. In learning to read, as in learning to walk, it is at first well to trust to a guiding hand. And in learning to read poetry it is at first well to use selections chosen for us by those wiser than ourselves. Later, when we can go alone, we take a man's whole work, and choose for ourselves what we will most love in it. And it is only by making use of this power of choice that we can really enjoy what is best. But of all our great writers Wordsworth is perhaps the last in the reading of whose works we willingly go alone. He is perhaps the writer who gains most by being read in selections. Indeed, for some of us there never comes a time when we care to read his whole works.

For if we take his whole works, at times we plow through pages of dry-as-dust argument where there is never a glimmer of that beauty which makes poetry a joy, till we grow weary of it. Then suddenly there springs to our eye a line of truest beauty which sets our senses atingle with delight, and all our labor is more than paid. And if our great poets were to be judged by single lines or single stanzas we may safely say that Wordsworth would be placed high among them. He is so placed, but it is rather by the love of the few than by the voice of the many.

I am not trying to make you afraid of reading Wordsworth, I am only warning you that you must not go to him expecting to gather flowers. You must go expecting to and willing to dig for gold. Yet although Wordsworth gives us broad deserts of prose in his poetry, he himself knew the joy of words in lovely sequence.

He tells us that when he was ten years old, or less, already his mind—

"With conscious pleasure opened to the charm
Of words in tuneful order, found them sweet
For their own *sakes,* a passion, and a power;
And phrases pleased me chosen for delight,
For pomp, or love " [1]

When Wordsworth first published his poems they were received with scorn, and he was treated with neglect greater even than most great poets have had to endure. But in time the tide turned and people came at last to acknowledge that Wordsworth was not only a poet, but a great one. He showed men a new way of poetry; he proved to them that nightingale was as poetical a word as Philomel, that it was possible to speak of the sun and the moon as the sun and the moon, and not as Phœbus and Diana. Phœbus, Diana, and Philomel are, with the thoughts they convey, beautiful in their right places, but so are sun, moon, and nightingale.

Wordsworth tried to make men see with new eyes the little everyday things that they had looked upon week by week and year by year until they had grown common. He tried to make them see these things again with "the glory and the freshness of a dream." [2]

Wordsworth fought the battle of the simple word, and phrase, and thought, and won it. And the poets who came after him, and not the poets only, but the prose writers too, whether they acknowledged it or not, whether they knew it or not, entered as by right into the possession of the kingdom which he had won for them.

And now let me tell you a little of the life of this nature poet.

William Wordsworth was born at Cockermouth in Cumberland in 1770. He was the second son of John Wordsworth, a lawyer, and law agent for the Earl of Lonsdale. William's mother died when he was still a

---

[1] *Prelude,* book v.   [2] Ode, *Intimations of Immortality.*

very small boy, and he remembered little about her. He remembered dimly that one day as he was going to church, she pinned some flowers into his coat. He remembered seeing her once lying in an easy chair when she was ill, and that was nearly all.

Before Wordsworth lost his mother he had a happy out-door childhood. He spent long days playing about in garden and orchard, or on the banks of the Derwent, with his friends and brothers and his sister Dorothy. In one of his long poems called *The Prelude,* which is a history of his own young life, he tells of these happy childish hours. In other of his poems he tells of the love and comradeship that there was between himself and his sister, though she was two years younger—

> "Oh! pleasant, pleasant were the days,
> The time, when, in our childish plays,
> My sister Emmeline and I
> Together chased the butterfly!
> A very hunter did I rush
> Upon the prey —with leaps and springs
> I followed on from brake to bush;
> But she, God love her! feared to brush
> The dust from off its wings "[1]

Together they spied out the sparrows' nests and watched the tiny nestlings as they grew, the big rough boy learning much from his tender-hearted, gentle sister. In after years he said—

> "She gave me eyes, she gave me ears;
> And humble cares, and delicate fears,
> A heart, the fountain of sweet tears;
> And love, and thought, and joy."[2]

When the mother died these happy days for brother and sister together were done, for Willie went to school

[1] *To a Butterfly.*   [2] *The Sparrow's Nest.*

at Hawkshead with his brothers, and Dorothy was sent
to live with her grandfather at Penrith.

But Wordsworth's school-time was happy too. Hawkshead was among the beautiful lake and mountain scenery
that he loved. He had a great deal of freedom, and out
of school hours could take long rambles, day and night too.
When moon and stars were shining he would wander
among the hills until the spirit of the place laid hold of
him, and he says—

> "I heard among the solitary hills
> Low breathings coming after me, and sounds
> Of undistinguishable motion, steps
> Almost as silent as the turf they trod." [1]

Wordsworth fished and bird-nested, climbing perilous
crags and slippery rocks to find rare eggs. In summer
he and his companions rowed upon the lake, in winter
they skated.

> "And in the frosty season, when the sun
> Was set, and visible for many a mile
> The cottage windows blazed through twilight gloom,
> I heeded not their summons· happy time
> It was indeed for all of us—for me
> A time of rapture! Clear and loud
> The village clock tolled six,—I wheeled about,
> Proud and exulting like an untired horse
> That cares not for his home   All shod with steel,
> We hissed along the polished ice in games
>
> .   .   .   .   .
>
> We were a noisy crew; the sun in heaven
> Beheld not vales more beautiful than ours;
> Nor saw a band in happiness and joy
> Richer, or worthier of the ground they trod." [2]

Yet among all this noisy boyish fun and laughter, Wordsworth's strange, keen love of nature took root and grew.
At times he says—

[1] *Prelude,* book i   [2] *Prelude,* book 1

"Even *then* I felt
Gleams like the flashing of a shield·—the earth
And common face of nature spake to me
Rememberable things"[1]

He read, too, what he liked, spending many happy hours over *Gulliver's Travels,* and the *Tale of a Tub, Don Quixote,* and the *Arabian Nights.*

While Wordsworth was still at school his father died. His uncles then took charge of him, and after he left school sent him to Cambridge. Wordsworth did nothing great at college. He took his degree without honors, and left Cambridge still undecided what his career in life was to be. He did not feel himself good enough for the Church. He did not care for law, but rather liked the idea of being a soldier. That idea, however, he also gave up, and for a time he drifted.

In those days one of the world's great dramas was being enacted. The French Revolution had begun. With the great struggle the poet's heart was stirred, his imagination fired. It seemed to him that a new dawn of freedom and joy and peace was breaking on the world, and "France lured him forth." He crossed the Channel, and for two years he lived through all the storm and stress of the Revolution. He might have ended his life in the fearful Reign of Terror which was coming on, had not his friends in England called him home. He left France full of pity, and sorrow, and disappointment, for no reign of peace had come, and the desire for Liberty had been swallowed up in the desire for Empire.

In spite of his years of travel, in spite of the fact that it was necessary for him to earn his living, Wordsworth was still unsettled as to what his work in life was to be, when a friend dying left him nine hundred pounds. With Wordsworth's simple tastes this sum was enough to live

[1] *Prelude,* book i

upon for several years, so he asked his dearly loved sister Dorothy to make her home with him, and together they settled down to a simple cottage life in Dorsetshire. It was a happy thing for Wordsworth that he found such a comrade in his sister. From first to last she was his friend and helper, cheering and soothing him when need be—

> "Her voice was like a hidden bird that sang,
> The thought of her was like a flash of light,
> Or an unseen companionship, a breath
> Of fragrance independent of the wind "

Another poet, Samuel Taylor Coleridge, whom William and Dorothy Wordsworth now met, calls her "Wordsworth's exquisite sister." "She is a woman indeed, in mind I mean, and in heart. . . . In every motion her innocent soul out-beams so brightly that who saw her would say 'Guilt was a thing impossible with her.' "

CHAPTER LXXV

WORDSWORTH AND COLERIDGE—THE LAKE POETS

AFTER Coleridge and Wordsworth once met they soon became fast friends, and in order to be near Coleridge the Wordsworths moved to another house near Nether Stowey in Somersetshire.

Coleridge was two years or more younger than Wordsworth, having been born in 1772. He was the thirteenth child of his father, who was a clergyman. As a boy he was sensitive and lonely, liking better to day-dream by himself than to play with his fellows. While still a mere child he loved books. Before he was five he had read the *Arabian Nights,* and he peopled his day dreams with giants and genii, slaves and fair princesses. When he was ten he went to school at Christ's Hospital, the Blue-coat School. Here he met Charles Lamb, who also became a writer, and whose *Essays* and *Tales from Shakespeare* I hope you will soon read.

At school even his fellows saw how clever Coleridge was. He read greedily and talked with any one who would listen and answer. In his lonely wanderings about London on "leave days" he was delighted if he could induce any stray passer-by to talk, especially, he says, if he was dressed in black. No subject came amiss to him, religion, philosophy, science, or poetry. From school Coleridge went to Cambridge, but after a time, getting into trouble and debt, he ran away and enlisted in a cavalry regiment under the name of Silas Tomkyn Comberback.

In a few months, however, he was discovered, and his brothers bought him out. He then went back to Cambridge, but left again at the end of the same year without taking a degree.

Meantime, while on a visit to Oxford, he had met Southey, another poet who was at this time a student there.

Robert Southey was born in 1774, and was the son of a Bristol linen draper, but he was brought up chiefly by an aunt in Bath. At fourteen he went to school at Westminster, and later to Balliol College, Oxford. When Coleridge met him he was just twenty, and Coleridge twenty-two. Like Wordsworth, they were both fired with enthusiasm for the French Revolution, and they soon became friends.

With some others of like mind they formed a little society, which they called the Pantisocracy, from Greek words meaning all-equal-rule. They decided that they should all marry and then emigrate to the banks of the Susquehanna (chosen, it has been said, because of its beautiful name), and there form a little Utopia. Property was to be in common, each man laboring on the land two hours a day in order to provide food for the company. But the fine scheme came to nothing, for meanwhile none of the company had enough money to pay for his passage to the banks of the beautiful-sounding river. Coleridge and Southey, however, carried out part of the program. They both married, their wives being sisters.

Coleridge, about the same time as he married, published a volume of poems. But as this did not bring him wealth he then tried various other ways of making a living. He began a weekly paper which ceased after a few numbers, he lectured on history, and preached in various Unitarian chapels. Then after a time he settled at Nether Stowey, where he was living when he met Wordsworth.

The two poets, as has been said, at once became friends, Coleridge having a deep and whole-hearted admiration for Wordsworth's genius. "I speak with heartfelt sincerity," he says, "and I think unblinded judgment, when I tell you that I feel a little man by his side."

The two friends had many walks and talks together, shaping their ideas of what poetry should be. They at length decided to publish a book together to be called *Lyrical Ballads*.

In this book there was published the poem which of all that Coleridge wrote is the best known, *The Ancient Mariner*. It tells how this old old sailor stops a guest who is going to a wedding, and bids him hear a tale. The wedding guest does not wish to stay, but the old man holds him with his skinny hand—

> "He holds him with his glittering eye—
> The Wedding Guest stood still,
> And listens like a three years' child:
> The Mariner hath his will "

He hath his will, and tells how the ship sailed forth gayly, and how it met after a time with storms, and cold, and fog, until at last it was all beset with ice. Then when to the sailors all hope seemed lost, an albatross came sailing through the fog. With joy they hailed it, the only living thing in that wilderness of ice. They fed it with delight—

> "It ate the food it ne'er had eat,
> And round and round it flew:
> The ice did split with a thunder-fit;
> The helmsman steered us through !"

Then on they gladly sailed, the albatross following, until one day the Ancient Mariner, in a mad moment, shot the beautiful bird. In punishment for this deed terrible disasters fell upon that ship and its crew. Under a

blazing sun, in a hot and slimy sea filled with creeping,
crawling things, they were becalmed—

> "Day after day, day after day,
>   We stuck, nor breath nor motion;
> As idle as a painted ship
>   Upon a painted ocean"

Then plague and death came, and every man died except
the guilty Mariner—

> "Alone, alone, all, all alone,
>   Alone on a wide, wide sea;
> And never a saint took pity on
>   My soul in agony.
>
> .   .   .   .   .
>
> "I looked to heaven, and tried to pray;
>   But or ever a prayer had gush'd,
> A wicked whisper came, and made
>   My heart as dry as dust."

But one day as the Mariner watched the water snakes, the
only living things in all that dreadful waste, he blessed
them unaware, merely because they were alive. That self-
same moment, he found that he could pray, and the
albatross, which his fellows in their anger had hung about
his neck, dropped from it, and fell like lead into the sea.
Then, relieved from his terrible agony of soul, the Mariner
slept, and when he woke he found that the dreadful
drought was over, and that it was raining. Oh, blessed
relief! But more terrors still he had to endure until at
last the ship drifted homeward—

> "Oh, dream of joy! is this indeed
>   The lighthouse top I see?
> Is this the hill? is this the kirk?
>   Is this mine own countree?
>
> "We drifted o'er the Harbour-bar,
>   And I with sobs did pray—
> 'O let me be awake, my God!
>   Or let me sleep alway.' "

The ship had indeed reached home, but in the harbor it suddenly sank like lead. Only the Mariner was saved.

When once more he came to land, he told his tale to a holy hermit and was shriven, but ever and anon afterward an agony comes upon him and forces him to tell the tale again, even as he has just done to the wedding guest. And thus he ends his story—

> "He prayeth best, who loveth best
> All things both great and small;
> For the dear God, who loveth us,
> He made and loveth all "

Then he goes, leaving the wondering wedding guest alone.

> "The Mariner, whose eye is bright,
> Whose beard with age is hoar,
> Is gone, and now the Wedding Guest
> Turned from the Bridegroom's door.
>
> "He went, like one that hath been stunned,
> And is of sense forlorn
> A sadder and a wiser man
> He rose the morrow morn."

Among the poems which Wordsworth wrote for the book of *Lyrical Ballads,* was one which every one knows, *We are Seven.* In another, called *Lines written in Early Spring,* he gives as it were the text of all his nature poems, and his creed, for here he tells us that he believes that all things in Nature, bird and flower alike, feel.

> "I heard a thousand blended notes,
> While in a grove I sate reclined,
> In that sweet mood when pleasant thoughts
> Bring sad thoughts to the mind.
>
> "In her fair works did Nature link
> The human soul that through me ran;
> And much it griev'd my heart to think
> What man has made of man

"Through primrose tufts, in that sweet bower,
　The periwinkle trailed its wreaths;
And 'tis my faith that every flower
　Enjoys the air it breathes.

"The birds around me hopp'd and play'd,
　Their thoughts I cannot measure.—
But the least motion that they made,
　It seemed a thrill of pleasure

"The budding twigs spread out their fan,
　To catch the breezy air;
And I must think, do all I can,
　That there was pleasure there.

"If this belief from heaven be sent,
　If such be Nature's holy plan,
Have I not reason to lament
　What man has made of man?"

The book was not a success. People did not understand *The Ancient Mariner,* and they laughed at Wordsworth's simple lyrics, although the last poem in the book, *Tintern Abbey,* has since become famous, and is acknowledged as one of the treasures of our literature.

And now, as this new book was not a success, and as he did not seem able to make enough money as a poet, Coleridge seriously began to think of becoming a Unitarian preacher altogether. But the Wedgwoods, the famous potters, wealthy men with cultured minds and kindly hearts, offered him one hundred and fifty pounds a year if he would give himself up to poetry and philosophy. After some hesitation, Coleridge consented, and that winter he set off for a visit to Germany with the Wordsworths.

It was on their return from this visit that Wordsworth again changed his home and went to live at Dove Cottage, near Grasmere, in the Lake District, which as a boy he had known and loved. And here, among the hills, he made his home for the rest of his life.

The days at Grasmere flowed along peacefully and almost without an event. Wordsworth published a second volume of lyrical ballads, and then went on writing and working steadily at his long poem *The Prelude,* in which he told the story of his early life.

Coleridge soon followed his friend, and settled at Greta Hall, Keswick, and there was much coming and going between Dove Cottage and Greta Hall. At Greta Hall there were two houses under one roof, and soon Southey took the second house and came to live beside his brother-in-law, Coleridge. And so these three poets, having thus drifted together, came to be called the Lake Poets, although Southey's poetry had little in common with that of either Wordsworth or Coleridge.

It seemed hardly to break the peaceful flow of life at Dove Cottage, when, in 1802, Wordsworth married his old playmate and schoolfellow, Mary Hutchinson. They had known each other all their lives, and marriage was a natural and lovely ending to their friendship. Of her Wordsworth wrote—

> "She was a Phantom of delight
> When first she gleamed upon my sight;
> A lovely Apparition, sent
> To be a moment's ornament;
> Her eyes as stars of Twilight fair;
> Like Twilight's, too, her dusky hair;
> But all things else about her drawn
> From May-time and the cheerful Dawn;
> A dancing Shape, an Image gay,
> To haunt, to startle, and waylay.
>
> "I saw her upon nearer view,
> A Spirit, yet a woman too!
> Her household motions light and free,
> And steps of virgin-liberty;
> A countenance in which did meet
> Sweet records, promises as sweet,

A Creature not too bright and good
For human nature's daily food;
For transient sorrows, simple wiles,
Praise, blame, love, kisses, tears, and smiles.

"And now I see with eye serene
The very pulse of the machine;
A Being breathing thoughtful breath,
A Traveller between life and death;
The reason firm, the temperate will,
Endurance, foresight, strength, and skill;
A perfect Woman, nobly planned,
To warn, to comfort, and command;
And yet a Spirit still, and bright
With something of angelic light."

The years passed in quiet fashion, with friendly comings and goings, with journeys here and there, now to Scotland, now to the Continent.

Children were born, friends died, and once or twice the Wordsworths changed their house until they finally settled at Rydal Mount, and there the poet remained for the rest of his long life. And all the time, for more than fifty years, Wordsworth steadily wrote, but it is not too much to say that all his best work was done in the twenty years between 1798 and 1818.

Besides *The Prelude,* of which we have already spoken, Wordsworth's other long poems are *The Excursion* and *The White Doe of Rylstone. The White Doe* is a story of the days of Queen Elizabeth, of the days when England was still in the midst of religious struggle. There was a rebellion in Yorkshire, in which the old lord of Rylstone fought vainly if gallantly for the Old Religion, and he and his sons died the death of rebels. Of all the family only the gentle Emily remained "doomed to be the last leaf on a blasted tree" About the country-side she wandered alone accompanied only by a white doe. In time she, too, died, then for many years the doe was seen alone. It was often to be seen in the churchyard during service, and after service it would go away with the rest of the congregation.

The Excursion, though a long poem, is only part of what Wordsworth meant to write. He meant in three books to give his opinions on Man, Nature, and Society, and the whole was to be called *The Recluse.* To this great work *The Prelude* was to be the introduction, hence its name. But Wordsworth never finished his great design and *The Excursion* remains a fragment. Much of *The Excursion* cannot be called poetry at all. Yet, as one of Wordsworth's great admirers has said:[1] "In deserts of preaching we find delightful oases of poetry." There is little action in *The Excursion,* and much of it is merely dull descriptions and conversations. So I would not advise you to read it for a long time to come, but to try rather to understand some of Wordsworth's shorter poems, although at times their names may seem less inviting.

One of the most beautiful of all his poems Wordsworth calls by the cumbrous name of *Intimations of Immortality from recollections of Early Childhood.* This is his way of saying that when we are small we are nearer the wonder-world than when we grow up, and that when we first open our eyes on this world they have not quite forgotten the wonderful sights they saw in that eternity whence we came, for the soul has no beginning, therefore no ending. I will give you here one verse of this poem:—

> "Our birth is but a sleep and a forgetting:
> The Soul that rises with us, our life's Star,
>   Hath had elsewhere its setting,
>   And cometh from afar;
>   Not in entire forgetfulness,
>   And not in utter nakedness,

---

[1] Morley.

But trailing clouds of glory do we come
    From God, who is our home
Heaven lies about us in our infancy!
Shades of the prison-house begin to close
    Upon the growing Boy,
But He beholds the light, and whence it flows,
    He sees it in his joy;
The Youth, who daily further from the east
    Must travel, still is Nature's Priest,
    And by the vision splendid
    Is on his way attended;
At length the Man perceives it die away,
And fade into the light of common day."

Wordsworth, for the times in which he lived, traveled a good deal, and in his comings and goings he made many new friends and met all the great literary men of his day. And by slow degrees his poetry won its way, and the younger men looked up to him as to a master. The great, too, came to see in him a power. Since 1813 Southey had been Laureate, and when in 1843 he died, the honor was given to Wordsworth. He was now an old man of seventy-three, and although he still wrote a few poems, he wrote nothing as Laureate, except an ode in honor of the Prince Consort when he became Chancellor of Cambridge University. Now, as he grew old, one by one death bade his friends to leave him—

"Like clouds that rake the mountain summits,
Or waves that own no curbing hand,
How fast has brother followed brother,
From sunshine to the sunless land!

"Yet I whose lids from infant slumber
Were earlier raised, remain to hear
A timid voice, that asks in whispers
'Who next will drop and disappear?' " [1]

---

[1] *Upon the Death of James Hogg*

At length in 1850, at the age of eighty, he too closed his eyes, and went "From sunshine to the sunless land."

> "But where will Europe's latter hour
> Again find Wordsworth's healing power?
> Others will teach us how to dare,
> And against fear our breast to steel;
> Others will strengthen us to bear—
> But who, ah! who, will make us feel?"[1]

BOOKS TO READ

Poems of Wordsworth, selected by C L Thomson. *Selections,* by Matthew Arnold.

[1] Arnold.

CHAPTER LXXVI

COLERIDGE AND SOUTHEY—SUNSHINE AND SHADOW

LONG before Wordsworth closed his eyes on this world, Coleridge, in some ways a greater poet than his friend, had gone to his last rest. Wordsworth had a happy, loving understanding of the little things of real life. He had an "exquisite regard for common things," but his words have seldom the glamour, the something which we cannot put into words which makes us see beyond things seen. This Coleridge had. It is not only his magic of words, it is this trembling touch upon the unknown, the unearthly beauty and sadness of which he makes us conscious in his poems that marks him as great.

And yet all that Coleridge has left us which reaches the very highest is very little. But as has been said, "No English poet can be put above Coleridge when only quality and not quantity is demanded."[1] Of *The Ancient Mariner* I have already told you, although perhaps it is too full of fearsomeness for you to read yet. Next to it stands *Christabel,* which is unfinished. It is too full of mysterious glamour to translate into mere prose, so I will not try to tell the story, but here are a few lines which are very often quoted—

> "Alas! they had been friends in youth;
> But whispering tongues can poison truth;
> And Constancy lives in realms above;
> And Life is thorny, and Youth is vain;
> And to be wroth with one we love,
> Doth work like madness in the brain.

---

[1] Stainsbury.

And thus it chanced, as I divine,
With Roland and Sir Leoline.
Each spake words of high disdain
And insult to his heart's best brother:
They parted—ne'er to meet again!
But never either found another
To free the hollow heart from paining;
They stood aloof, the scars remaining,
Like cliffs which had been rent asunder;
A dreary sea now flows between;—
But neither heat, nor frost, nor thunder,
Shall wholly do away, I ween,
The marks of that which once had been "

Coleridge's singing time was short. All his best poetry had been written before he went to live at Keswick. There his health, which had never been good, gave way. Unhappy in his home, and racked with bodily pain, he at length began to use opium in order to find relief. The habit to which he soon became a slave made shipwreck of his life. He had always been unstable of purpose and weak of will, never keeping to one course long. He had tried journalism, he tried lecturing, he planned books which were never written. His life was a record of beginnings. As each new plan failed he yielded easily to the temptation of living on his friends. He had always been restless in mind, now he became as restless in body as in mind. He left his home, and after wanderings now here now there, he at length found a home in London with kind, understanding friends. Of him here we have a pathetic picture drawn by another great man.[1] "The good man—he was now getting old, towards sixty perhaps, and gave you the idea of a life that had been full of sufferings; a life heavy-laden, half-vanquished, still swimming painfully in seas of manifold physical and other bewilderment. Brow and head were round and of massive weight, but the face was flabby and irresolute. The deep

---

[1] Carlyle.

eyes, of a light hazel, were as full of sorrow as of inspiration, confused pain looked mildly from them, as in a kind of mild astonishment. The whole figure and air, good and amiable otherwise, might be called flabby and irresolute, expressive of weakness under possibility of strength, . . . a heavy-laden, high-aspiring, and surely much suffering man."

And yet to this broken-down giant men crowded eagerly to hear him talk. Never, perhaps, since the great Sam had held his court had such a talker been heard. And although there was no Boswell near to make these conversations live again, the poet's nephew, Henry Nelson Coleridge, gathered some of his sayings together into a book which he called *Table Talk*. With his good friends Coleridge spent all his remaining life from 1816 till 1834, when he died.

Meanwhile his children and his home were left to the care of others. And when Coleridge threw off his home ties and duties it was upon Southey that the burden chiefly fell. And Southey, kindly and generous, loving his own children fondly, loved and cared for his nephews and nieces too. We cannot regard Southey as one of our great poets, but when we read his letters, we must love him as a man. He wrote several long poems, the two best known perhaps are *The Curse of Kehama* and *Thalaba,* the one a Hindoo, the other a Mahometan story, but he is better remembered by his short poems, such as *The Battle of Blenheim* and *The Inchcape Rock.*

For forty years Southey lived at Greta Hall, and from his letters we get the pleasantest picture of the home-loving, nonsense-loving "comical papa" who had kept the heart of a boy, even when his hair grew gray—

"A man he is by nature merry,
Somewhat Tom-foolish, and comical very;
Who has gone through the world, not mindful of pelf,
Upon easy terms, thank Heaven, with himself."

He loved his books and he loved the little curly-headed children that gathered about him with pattering feet and chattering tongues, and never wished to be absent from them. "Oh dear, oh dear," he says, "there is such a comfort in one's old coat and old shoes, one's armchair and own fireside, one's own writing-desk and own library— with a little girl climbing up my neck, and saying, 'Don't go to London, papa—you must stay with Edith'; and a little boy, whom I have taught to speak the language of cats, dogs, cuckoos, and jackasses, etc., before he can articulate a word of his own; there is such a comfort in all these things, that transportation to London for four or five weeks seems a heavier punishment than any sins of mine deserve."

And so we see him spending long hours, long years, among his books, hoping for lasting fame from his poems, and meantime earning with his prose food for hungry little mouths, shoes for nimble little feet, with just a trifle over for books, and still more books. For Southey loved books, and his big library was lined with them. There were thousands there, many in beautiful bindings, glowing in soft coloring, gleaming with pale gold, for he loved to clothe his treasures in fitting garments. When a new box of books comes he rejoices. "I shall be happier," he says, "than if his Majesty King George IV. were to give orders that I should be clothed in purple, and sleep upon gold, and have a chain about my neck, and sit next him because of my wisdom and be called his cousin."

We think of Southey first as a poet, but it is perhaps as a prose writer that his fame will last longest, and above all as a biographer, that is as a writer of people's lives. During the busy years at Greta Hall he wrote about a hundred books, several of them biographies—among them a life of Nelson, which is one of the best short lives ever written. Some day I hope you will read it, both for the sake of Southey's clear, simple style, and for the sake of the brave man of whom he writes. You might also, I think, like his lives of Bunyan and Cowper, both of whom you have heard of in this book.

Another book which Southey wrote is called *The Doctor*. This is a whimsical, rambling jumble, which can hardly be called a story; a mixture of quotations and original work, of nonsense and earnest. And in the middle of it what do you think you come upon? Why our old nursery friend, *The Three Bears*. Southey trusts that this book will suit every one, "that the lamb may wade in it, though the elephant may swim, and also that it will be found 'very entertaining to the ladies.'" Indeed he flatters himself that it will be found profitable for "old and young, for men and for women, the married and the single, the idle and the studious, the merry and the sad; and that it may sometimes inspire the thoughtless with thought, and sometimes beguile the careful of their cares." But if it is to be quite perfect it must have a chapter for children—

"Prick up your ears then,
My good little women and men;

and ye who are neither so little nor so good, *favete linguis*,[1] for here follows the story of the Three Bears." So there it is. "One of them was a Little, Small, Wee Bear; and one was a Middle-sized Bear, and the other was a Great, Huge Bear"—and from the way it is told, I think we may be sure that Uncle Robert or comical papa often told stories with a circle of eager, bright faces round him. For he says—

"And 'twas in my vocation
For their recreation
That so I should sing;
Because I was Laureate
To them and the King"

---

[1] Be silent

As the years went on Southey received other honors besides the Laureateship. He was offered a baronetcy which he refused. He was "ell-ell-deed" by Oxford, as he quaintly puts it in his letters to his children. And when he tells them about it he says, "Little girls, you know it might be proper for me now to wear a large wig, and to be called Doctor Southey and to become very severe, and leave off being a comical papa. . . . However, I shall not come home in my wig, neither shall I wear my robes at home."

It is sad to think that this kindly heart had to bear the buffetings of ill fortune. Two of his dearly loved children died, then he was parted from his wife by worse than death, for she became insane and remained so until she died. Eight years later Robert Southey was laid beside her in the churchyard under the shadow of Skiddaw. "I hope his life will not be forgotten," says Macaulay, "for it is sublime in its simplicity, its energy, its honour, its affection. . . . His letters are worth piles of epics, and are sure to last among us, as long as kind hearts like to sympathise with goodness and purity and love and upright life."

BOOKS TO READ

Southey: *Poems*, chosen by E Dowden *Life of Nelson* (Everyman's Library).
Coleridge: *Lyrical Poems*, chosen by A T. Quiller-Couch.

CHAPTER LXXVII

SCOTT—THE AWAKENING OF ROMANCE

THE 15th of August 1771 was a lucky day for all the boys and girls and grown-up people too of the English-speaking race, for on that day Walter Scott was born in Edinburgh. Literature had already begun to shake off its fetters of art. Romance had begun to stir in her long sleep, for six years before sturdy baby Walter was born, Bishop Percy had published a book called *Reliques of Ancient English Poetry*. In this book he had gathered together many old ballads and songs, such as those of *Robin Hood* and *Patrick Spens*. They had almost been forgotten, and yet they are poems which stir the heart with their plaintive notes, telling as they do—

> "Of old, unhappy, far-off things,
> And battles long ago;
> Or is it some more humble lay,
> Familiar matter of to-day?
> Some natural sorrow, loss, or pain,
> That has been, and may be again!" [1]

Bishop Percy, like a knight of old, laid his lance in rest and tilted against the prickly briar hedge that had grown up around the Sleeping Beauty, Romance. But he could not win through and wake the princess. And although Burns and Wordsworth, Coleridge and Southey, all knowing it or not, fought on his side, it was left for another knight to break through the hedge and make us free

[1] Wordsworth

581

of the Enchanted Land. And that knight's name was Walter—Sir Walter, too—for, like a true knight, he won his title in the service of his lady.

Little Walter's father was a kindly Scots lawyer, but he came of a good old Border family, "A hardy race who never shrunk from war."[1] Among his forbears had been wild moss-troopers and cattle-reivers, lairds of their own lands, as powerful as kings in their own countryside. There were stories enough of their bold and daring deeds to fill many books, so that we feel that Walter had been born into a heritage of Romance.

Walter was a strong, healthy child, but when he was about eighteen months old he had an illness which left him lame in his right leg. Everything was done that could be done to restore the lost power, and although it was partly regained, Scott walked with a limp to the end of his days. Meanwhile he had a by no means unhappy childhood. He spent a great deal of time at the farm belonging to his grandfather. Little Wat was a winsome laddie, and the whole household loved him. On fine days he was carried out and laid down among the crags and rocks, beside an old shepherd who tended his sheep and little Walter too, telling him strange tales the while—

> "Of forayers, who, with headlong force,
> Down from that strength had spurr'd their horse,
> Their southern rapine to renew,
> Far in the distant Cheviots blue,
> And, home returning, fill'd the hall
> With revel, wassel-rout, and brawl."[2]

At other times Walter listened to the stories of his grandmother, hearing all about the wild doings of his forbears, or the brave deeds of Bruce and Wallace. He was taken to the seaside, to Bath, and to London, and at length, grown into a sturdy little boy, though still lame,

[1] Leyden [2] Marmion

he went back to his father's house in Edinburgh. Here he says he soon felt the change from being a single indulged brat, to becoming the member of a large family.

He now went to school, but did not show himself to be very clever. He was not a dunce, but an "incorrigibly idle imp," and in spite of his lameness he was better at games than at lessons. In some ways, owing to his idleness, he was behind his fellows, on the other hand he had read far more than they. And now he read everything he could, in season and out of season. Pope's *Homer*, Shakespeare, Ossian, and especially Spenser were among his favorites. Then one happy day he came upon a volume of Percy's *Reliques*. All one summer day he read and read, forgetting the world, forgetting even to be hungry. After that he was for ever entertaining his schoolfellows with scraps of tragic ballads, and as soon as he could scrape enough money together, he bought a copy of the book for himself.

So the years passed, Walter left school, went to Edinburgh University, and began to study law. It was at this time, as a boy of sixteen, that for the first and only time he met Robert Burns, who had just come to Edinburgh, and was delighted at receiving a kind word and look from the poet. He still found time to read a great deal, to ride, and to take long, rambling walks, for, in spite of his limp, he was a great walker and could go twenty or thirty miles. Indeed he used to tramp the countryside so far and so long that his father would say he feared his son was born to be nothing better than a wandering peddler.

After a time it was decided that Walter should be a barrister, or, as it is called in Scotland, an advocate, and in 1792 he was called to the Bar. His work as an advocate was at first not very constant, and it left him plenty of time for long, rambling excursions or raids, as he used to call them, in different parts of Scotland and in the north of England. He traveled about, listening to the ballads of the country folk, gathering tales, storing his mind with memories of people and places. "He was making himself a' the time," said a friend who went with him, "but he didna ken maybe what he was about till years had passed. At first he thought o' little, I daresay, but the queerness and the fun."

It was in an expedition to the English Lakes with his brother and a friend that Scott met his wife. One day while out riding he saw a lady also riding. She had raven black hair and deep brown eyes, which found a way at once to the poet's heart. In true poet fashion he loved her. That night there was a ball, and though Walter Scott could not dance, he went to the ball and met his lady love. She was Charlotte Margaret Carpenter, the daughter of a Frenchman who had taken refuge in England from the fury of the Revolution. Walter was able to win his lady's heart, and before the end of the year had married her and carried her off to Scotland.

Two or three years after his marriage, Scott published a book of Border Ballads. It was the outcome of his wanderings in the Border country. In it Scott had gathered together many ballads which he had heard from the country folk, but he altered and bettered them as he thought fit, and among them were new ballads by himself and some of his friends.

The book was only a moderate success, but in it we may find the germ of all Scott's later triumphs. For it was the spirit of these ballads with which his mind was so full which made it possible for him to write the Metrical Romances that made him famous.

It is now many chapters since we spoke of Metrical Romances. They were, you remember, the chief literature from the twelfth to the fifteenth century, which time was also the time of the early ballads. And now that people had begun again to see the beauty of ballads, they were ready also to turn again to the simplicity of Metrical Romances. These rime stories which Scott now began to write, burst on our Island with the splendor of something new, and yet it was simply the old-time spirit in which Scott had steeped himself, which found a new birth—a Renascence. Scott was a stalwart Border chieftain born out of time. But as another writer says, instead of harrying cattle and cracking crowns, this Border chief was appointed to be the song-singer and pleasant tale-teller to Britain and to Europe. "It was the time for such a new literature; and this Walter Scott was the man for it." [1]

> "The mightiest chiefs of British song
> Scorn'd not such legends to prolong:
> They gleam through Spenser's elfin dream,
> And mix in Milton's heavenly theme " [2]

The first of Scott's song stories was called *The Lay of the Last Minstrel*. In it he pictures an old minstrel, the last of all his race, wandering neglected and despised about the countryside. But at Newark Castle, the seat of the Duchess of Buccleuch, he receives kindly entertainment.

> "When kindness had his wants supplied,
> And the old man was gratified,
> Began to rise his minstrel pride:
> And he began to talk anon,
> Of good Earl Francis, dead and gone,
> And of Earl Walter, rest him, God!
> A braver ne'er to battle rode,
> And how full many a tale he knew,
> Of the old warriors of Buccleuch;
> And, would the noble Duchess deign
> To listen to an old man's strain,

---

[1] Carlyle.   [2] *Marmion.*

Though stiff his hand, his voice though weak,
He thought even yet, the sooth to speak,
That, if she loved the harp to hear,
He could make music to her ear "

This humble boon was granted. The minstrel was led
to the room of state where sat the noble-hearted Duchess
with her ladies, and there began his lay. You must read
The Lay itself to learn about William of Deloraine, the
Goblin Page, the Lady Margaret, and Lord Cranstoun,
and all the rest. The meter in which Scott wrote was
taken from Coleridge's *Christabel.* For, though it was
not yet published, it had long been in manuscript, and
Scott had heard part of it repeated by a friend.

The Lay of the Last Minstrel was a success. From
henceforth Scott was an author. But he had no need to
write for money, as money came to him in other ways.
So none of the struggles of a rising author fell to his lot.
His career was simply a triumphant march. And good-
natured, courteous, happy-hearted Scott took his triumphs
joyously.

Other poems followed *The Lay,* the best being *Marmion*
and *The Lady of the Lake.* Scott's son-in-law says, "*The
Lay* is, I should say, generally considered as the most
natural and original, *Marmion* as the most powerful and
splendid, *The Lady of the Lake* as the most interesting,
romantic, picturesque, and graceful of his great poems."
Fame and money poured in upon Scott, and not upon him
only, but upon Scotland. For the new poet had sung the
beauties of the rugged country so well that hundreds of
English flocked to see it for themselves. Scotland became
the fashion, and has remained so ever since.

In 1799 Scott had been appointed Sheriff-deputy
of Selkirkshire, and as this obliged him to live part of the
year at least in the district, he rented a house not far from
Selkirk. But now that he saw himself becoming wealthy,

he bought an estate in his beloved Border country and began to build the house of Abbotsford. To this house he and his family removed in May 1812. Here, amid the noise of carpenters and masons, with only one room fit to sit in, and that shared by chattering children, he went on with his work. To a friend he writes, "As for the house and the poem, there are twelve masons hammering at the one, and one poor noddle at the other—so they are both in progress."

It was at Abbotsford that Scott made his home for the rest of his life. Here he put off the gown and wig of a barrister, and played the part of a country gentleman. He rode about accompanied by his children and his friends, and followed by his dogs. He fished, and walked, and learned to know every one around, high and low. He was beloved by all the countryside, for he was kindly and courteous to all, and was "aye the gentleman." He would sit and talk with a poor man in his cottage, listening to his tales of long ago, with the same ease and friendliness as he would entertain the great in his own beautiful house. And that house was always thronged with visitors, invited and uninvited, with friends who came out of love of the genial host, with strangers who came out of curiosity to see the great novelist. For great as was Scott's fame as a poet, it was nothing to the fame he earned as a story-teller.

The first story he published was called *Waverley, or 'Tis Sixty Years Since.* He had begun to write this tale years before, but had put it aside as some of his friends did not think well of it. One day he came upon the manuscript by accident, thought himself that the story was worth something, and resolved to publish it. Finishing the writing in three weeks he published the novel without putting his name upon the title-page. He did this, he said, because he thought it was not quite dignified for a grave advocate and Sheriff of the county to write novels. The book was a wild success, everybody read it, everybody was eager to know who the author was. Many people guessed that it was Scott, but, for more than ten years, he would not own to it. At public dinners when the health of the author of *Waverley* was drunk, people would look meaningly at Scott, but he would appear quite unconcerned, and drink the health and cheer with the rest. To keep the mystery up he even reviewed his own books. And so curiosity grew. Who was this Great Unknown, this Wizard of the North?

Waverley is a story of Jacobite times, of the rebellion of '45. The hero, Edward Waverley, who is no such great hero either, his author calling him indeed "a sneaking piece of imbecility," gives his name to the book. He meets Bonnie Prince Charlie, is present at the famous ball at Holyrood, fights at the battle of Prestonpans, and marches with the rebel army into England.

Thus we have the beginning of the historical novel. Scott takes real people, and real incidents, and with them he interweaves the story of the fortunes of make-believe people and make-believe incidents. Scott does not always keep quite strictly to facts. He is of the same mind as the old poet Davenant who thought it folly to take away the liberty of a poet and fetter his feet in the shackles of an historian. Why, he asked, should a poet not make and mend a story and frame it more delightfully, merely because austere historians have entered into a bond to truth. So Scott takes liberties with history, but he always gives us the spirit of the times of which he writes. Thus in one sense he is true to history. And perhaps from *Waverley* we get a better idea of the state of Scotland, at the time of the last Jacobite rebellion, than from any number of histories. In the next chapter Scott himself shall give you an account of the battle of Prestonpans.

SCOTT WOULD SIT AND TALK WITH A POOR MAN IN HIS COTTAGE.

CHAPTER LXXVIII

SCOTT—"THE WIZARD OF THE NORTH"

"The army, moving by its right from off the ground on
which they had rested, soon entered the path through the
morass, conducting their march with astonishing silence
and great rapidity. The mist had not risen to the higher
grounds, so that for some time they had the advantage
of starlight. But this was lost as the stars faded before
approaching day, and the head of the marching column,
continuing its descent, plunged as it were into the heavy
ocean of fog, which rolled its white waves over the whole
plain, and over the sea by which it was bounded. Some
difficulties were now to be encountered, inseparable from
darkness, a narrow, broken, and marshy path, and the
necessity of preserving union in the march. These,
however, were less inconvenient to Highlanders, from
their habits of life, than they would have been to any
other troops, and they continued a steady and swift
movement.

.　　　.　　　.　　　.　　　.

"The clan of Fergus had now gained the firm plain,
which had lately borne a large crop of corn. But the
harvest was gathered in, and the expanse was unbroken
by trees, bush, or interruption of any kind. The rest of
the army were following fast, when they heard the drums
of the enemy beat the general. Surprise, however, had
made no part of their plan, so they were not disconcerted
by this intimation that the foe was upon his guard and

prepared to receive them. It only hastened their dispositions for the combat, which were very simple.

. . . . .

"'Down with your plaid, Waverley,' cried Fergus, throwing off his own; 'we'll win silks for our tartans before the sun is above the sea.'

"The clansmen on every side stripped their plaids, prepared their arms, and there was an awful pause of about three minutes, during which the men, pulling off their bonnets, raised their faces to heaven, and uttered a short prayer; then pulled their bonnets over their brows, and began to move forward at first slowly. Waverley felt his heart at that moment throb as it would have burst his bosom. It was not fear, it was not ardour—it was a compound of both, a new and deeply energetic impulse, that with its first emotion chilled and astounded, then fevered and maddened his mind. The sounds around him combined to exalt his enthusiasm; the pipes played, and the clans rushed forward, each in its own dark column. As they advanced they mended their pace, and the muttering sounds of the men to each other began to swell into a wild cry. At this moment, the sun, which was now risen above the horizon, dispelled the mist. The vapours rose like a curtain, and showed the two armies in the act of closing. The line of the regulars was formed directly fronting the attack of the Highlanders; it glittered with the appointments of a complete army, and was flanked by cavalry and artillery. But the sight impressed no terror on the assailants.

"'Forward, sons of Ivor,' cried their chief, 'or the Camerons will draw the first blood!' They rushed on with a tremendous yell.

"The rest is well known. The horse, who were commanded to charge the advancing Highlanders in the flank, received an irregular fire from their fusees as they ran on, and, seized with a disgraceful panic, wavered, halted, disbanded, and galloped from the field. The artillerymen, deserted by the cavalry, fled after discharging their pieces, and the Highlanders, who dropped their guns when fired, and drew their broadswords, rushed with headlong fury against the infantry.

"The English infantry, trained in the wars in Flanders, stood their ground with great courage. But their extended files were pierced and broken in many places by the close masses of the clans; and in the personal struggle which ensued, the nature of the Highlanders' weapons, and their extraordinary fierceness and activity, gave them a decided superiority over those who had been accustomed to trust much to their array and discipline, and felt that the one was broken and the other useless.

"Loud shouts now echoed over the whole field. The battle was fought and won, and the whole baggage, artillery, and military stores of the regular army remained in possession of the victors. Never was a victory more complete."

Such is Scott's picture of the battle of Prestonpans. And throughout the whole book we have wonderful pictures of Scottish life as it then was—pictures of robbers' caves, and chieftains' halls, of the chiefs themselves, and their followers, of mountain, loch, and glen, all drawn with such a true and living touch that we cannot forget them.

After *Waverley* other novels followed fast, each one adding to the reputation of the unknown author, and now, from the name of the first, we call them all the Waverley Novels.

Scott's was one of the most wonderful successes—perhaps the most wonderful—that has ever been known in our literature. "As long as Sir Walter Scott wrote poetry," said a friend, "there was neither man nor woman ever thought of either reading or writing anything but poetry. But the instant that he gave over writing poetry, there was neither man nor woman ever read it more! All turned to tales and novels." [1]

Everybody read The Novels, from the King to the shepherd. Friends, money, and fame came tumbling in upon the author. He had refused to be made Poet Laureate, and passed the honor on to Southey, but he accepted a baronetcy. He added wing after wing to his beautiful house, and acre after acre to his land, and rejoiced in being laird of Abbotsford.

The speed with which Scott wrote was marvelous. His house was always full of visitors, yet he always had time to entertain them. He was never known to refuse to see a friend, gentle or simple, and was courteous even to the bores who daily invaded his home. He had unbounded energy. He rose early in the morning, and before the rest of the family was astir had finished more than half of his daily task of writing. Thus by twelve o'clock he was free to entertain his guests.

If ever man was happy and succesful, Scott seemed to be that man. But suddenly all his fair prospects were darkened over. Sir Walter was in some degree a partner in the business both of his publisher and his printer. Now both publisher and printer failed, and Scott found himself ruined with them. At fifty-five he was not only a ruined man, but loaded with a terrible debt of £117,000.

It was a staggering blow, and most men would have been utterly crushed by it. Not so Scott. He was proud, proud of his old name and of his new-founded baronial hall. He was stout of heart too. At fifty-five he began life again, determined with his pen to wipe out

[1] James Hogg

the debt. Many were the hands stretched out to help him; rich men offered their thousands, poor men their scanty savings, but Scott refused help from both rich and poor. His own hand must wipe out the debt, he said. Time was all he asked. So with splendid courage and determination, the like of which has perhaps never been known, he set to work.

But evil days had begun for Sir Walter. Scarcely four months after the crash, his wife died, and so he lost a companion of nearly thirty years. "I think my heart will break," he cries in the first bitterness of sorrow. "Lonely, aged, deprived of my family, an impoverished, an embarrassed man." But dogged courage comes to him again. "Well, that is over, and if it cannot be forgotten must be remembered with patience." So day after day he bent to his work. Every morning saw his appointed task done. Besides novels and articles he wrote a *History of Napoleon,* a marvelous book, considering it was written in eighteen months.

Then Scott began the book which will be the first of all his books to interest you, *The Tales of a Grandfather.* This is a history of Scotland, and it was written for his grandson John Hugh Lockhart, or Hugh Littlejohn as he is called in *The Tales.* "I will make," said Scott, "if possible, a book that a child shall understand, yet a man shall feel some temptation to peruse should he chance to take it up."

Hugh Littlejohn was a delicate boy, indeed he had not long to live, but many a happy day he spent, this summer (1827), riding about the woods of Abbotsford with his kind grandfather, listening to the tales he told. For Scott, too, the rides were a joy, and helped to make him forget his troubles. When he had told his tale in such a simple way that Littlejohn understood, he returned home and wrote it down.

In the December of the same year the first part of *The*

Tales was published, and at once was a tremendous success, a success as great almost as any of the novels. Hugh Littlejohn liked *The Tales* too. "Dear Grandpapa," he writes, "I thank you for the books. I like my own picture and the Scottish chief: I am going to read them as fast as I can."

Two more volumes of *Tales* followed. Then there was no need to write more for the dearly loved grandson, as a year or two later, when he was only eleven, poor Littlejohn died. But already the kind grandfather was near his end also, the tremendous effort which he made to force himself to work beyond his strength could not be kept up. His health broke down under it. Still he struggled on, but at last, yielding to his friends' entreaties, he went to Italy in search of health and strength. It gives us some idea of the high place Sir Walter had won for himself in the hearts of the people, when we learn that his health seemed a national concern, and that a warship was sent to take him on his journey. But the journey was of no avail. Among the great hills and blue lakes of Italy Scott longed for the lesser hills and grayer lochs of Scotland. So he turned homewards. And at home, in his beloved Abbotsford, in the still splendor of an autumn day, with the meadow-scented air he loved fanning his face, and the sound of rippling Tweed in his ears, he closed his eyes for ever. In the grass-grown ruin of Dryburgh Abbey, not far from his home, he was laid to rest, while the whole countryside mourned Sir Walter.

Before he died Scott had paid £70,000 of his debt, an enormous sum for one man to make by his pen in six years. He died in the happy belief that all was paid, as indeed it all was. For after the author's death, his books still brought in a great deal of money, so that in fifteen years the debt was wiped out.

I have not told you any of Scott's stories here, because,

unlike many of the books we have spoken of, they are easily to be had. And the time will soon come, if it has not come already, when you can read Sir Walter's books, just as he wrote them. It is best, I think, that you should read them so, for Sir Walter Scott is perhaps the first of all our great writers nearly the whole of whose books a child can read without help. You will find many long descriptions in them, but do not let them frighten you. You need not read them all the first time, and very likely you will want to read them the second time.

But perhaps before you read his novels you will like to read his Metrical Romances. For when we are children— big children perhaps, but still children—is the time to read them. Long ago in the twelfth century, when the people of England were simple and unlearned, they loved Metrical Romances, and we when we are simple and unlearned may love them too. Many of these old romances, however, are hard to get, and they are written in a language hard for many of us to understand. But Sir Walter Scott, in the nineteenth century, has recreated for us all the charm of those old tales. For this then, let us thank and remember him.

> "His legendary song could tell
> Of ancient deeds, so long forgot;
> Of feuds, whose memory was not;
> Of forests, now laid waste and bare;
> Of towers, which harbour now the hare;
> Of manners, long since chang'd and gone;
> Of chiefs, who under their grey stone
> So long had slept, that fickle Fame
> Had blotted from her rolls their name,
> And twin'd round some new minion's head
> The fading wreath for which they bled." [1]

---

[1] *Lay of the Last Minstrel.*

CHAPTER LXXIX

BYRON—"CHILDE HAROLD'S PILGRIMAGE"

When Sir Walter Scott ceased to write Metrical Romances, he said it was because Byron had beaten him. But the metrical romances of these two poets are widely different. With Sir Walter we are up among the hills, out on the wide moorland. With him we tramp the heather, and ford the rushing streams; his poems are full of healthy, generous life. With Byron we seem rather to be in the close air of a theater. His poems do not tell of a rough and vigorous life, but of luxury and softness; of tyrants and slaves, of beautiful houris and dreadful villains. And in the villains we always seem to see Byron himself, who tries to impress us with the fact that he is indeed a very "bold, bad man." In his poetry there is something artificial, which takes us backward to the time of Pope, rather than forward with the nature poets.

The boyhood of George Gordon Byron was a sad one. He came of an ancient and noble family, but one which in its later generations had become feeble almost to madness. His father, who was called Mad Jack, was wild and worthless, his mother was a wealthy woman, but weak and passionate, and in a short time after her marriage her husband spent nearly all her money. Mrs. Byron then took her little baby and went to live quietly in Aberdeen on what was left of her fortune.

She was a weak and passionate woman, and sometimes she petted and spoiled her little boy, sometimes she treated

596

him cruelly, calling him "a lame brat," than which nothing could hurt him more, for poor little George was born lame, and all his life long he felt sore and angry about it. To him too had been given the passionate temper of both father and mother, and when he was angry he would fall into "silent rages," bite pieces out of saucers, or tear his pinafores to bits.

Meanwhile, while in Aberdeen Mrs. Byron struggled to live on £130 a year, in Newstead Abbey, near Notting-ham, there lived a queer, half-mad, old grand-uncle, who had earned for himself the name of "the wicked lord." He knew well enough that when he died the little boy in Aberdeen, with the pretty face and lame foot, would become Lord Byron. He might have taken some interest in his nephew, and seen at least that he was sent to school, and given an education to fit him for his future place in the world. But that was not "the wicked lord's" way. He paid no attention to the little boy in Aberdeen. Indeed, it is said that he hated him, and that he cut down his trees and despoiled Newstead as much as he could, in order to leave his heir as poor a heritage as possible.

But when George was ten this old uncle died. Then mother and son said good-by to Aberdeen, and traveled southwards to take possession of their great house and broad lands. But the heritage was not so great as at first sight would appear, for the house was so ruinous that it was scarcely fit to live in, and the wicked lord had sold some of the land. However, as the sale was unlawful, after much trouble the land was recovered.

Byron had now to take his place among boys of his own class, and when he was thirteen he was sent to school at Harrow. But he hated school. He was shy as "a wild mountain colt" and somewhat snobbish, and at first was most unpopular.

As he says himself, however, he "fought his way very

fairly" and he formed some friendships, passionately, as he did everything. In spite of his lameness, he was good at sports, especially at swimming. He was brave, and even if his snobbishness earned for him the nickname of the "Old English Baron," his comrades admired his spirit, and in the end, instead of being unpopular, he led—often to mischief. "1 was," he says, "always cricketing—rebelling—fighting, rowing (from *row,* not *boat*-rowing, a different practice), and in all manner of mischiefs." Yet, wild though he was, of his headmaster he ever kept a kindly remembrance. "Dr. Drury," he says, "whom I plagued sufficiently too, was the best, the kindest friend I ever had."

Byron hated Harrow until his last year and a half there; then he liked it. And when he knew he must leave and go to Cambridge, he was so unhappy that he counted the days that remained, not with joy at the thought of leaving, but with sorrow.

At Cambridge he felt himself lonely and miserable at first, as he had at school. But there too he soon made friends. He found plenty of time for games, he rode and shot, rejoiced in feats of swimming and diving. He wrote poetry also, which he afterwards published under the name of *Hours of Idleness.* It was a good name for the book, for indeed he was so idle in his proper studies, that the wonder is that he was able to take his degree.

It was in 1807, at the age of nineteen, that Lord Byron published his *Hours of Idleness,* with a rather pompous preface. The poems were not great, some of them indeed were nothing less than mawkish, but perhaps they did not deserve the slashing review which appeared in the *Edinburgh Review.* The *Edinburgh Review* was a magazine given at this time to criticising authors very severely, and Byron had to suffer no more than other and greater poets. But he trembled with indignation, and his anger called forth his first really good poem, called *English Bards and Scotch Reviewers.* It is a satire after the style of Pope, and in it Byron lashes not only his reviewers, but also other writers of his day. His criticisms are, many of them, quite wrong, and in after years when he came to know the men he now decried, he regretted this poem, and declared it should never be printed again. But it is still included in his works. Perhaps having just read about Sir Walter Scott, it may amuse you to read what Byron has to say of him.

> "Thus Lays of Minstrels—may they be the last!—
> On half-strung harps whine mournful to the blast.
> While mountain spirits prate to river sprites,
> That dames may listen to the sound at nights;
>
> .   .   .   .
>
> Next view in state, proud prancing on his roan,
> The golden-crested haughty Marmion,
> Now forging scrolls, now foremost in the fight,
> Not quite a felon, yet but half a knight,
> The gibbet or the field prepared to grace;
> A mighty mixture of the great and base.
> And think'st thou, Scott! by vain conceit perchance,
> On public taste to foist thy stale romance."

Then after a sneer at Scott for making money by his poems, Byron concludes with this passage:—

> "These are the themes that claim our plaudits now;
> These are the bards to whom the muse must bow;
> While Milton, Dryden, Pope, alike forgot,
> Resign their hallowed bays to Walter Scott."

When people read this satire, they realized that a new poet had appeared. But it was not until Byron published his first long poem, called *Childe Harold's Pilgrimage,* that he became famous. Then his success was sudden and amazing. "I woke up one morning and found myself famous," he says. "His fame," says another poet and friend who wrote his life,[1] "seemed to spring up like the palace of a fairy tale, in a night." He was praised and lauded by high and low. Every one was eager to know him, and for a time he became the spoiled darling of society.

Childe Harold is a long poem of four cantos, but now only two cantos were published. The third was added in 1816, the fourth in 1818. It is written in the Spenserian stanza, with here and there songs and ballads in other meters, and in the first few verses there is even an affectation of Spenserian wording. But the poet soon grew tired of that, and returned to his own English. Childe is used in the ancient sense of knight, and the poem tells of the wanderings of a gloomy, vicious, world-worn man.

There is very little story in *Childe Harold*. The poem is more a series of descriptions and a record of the thoughts that are called forth by the places through which the traveler passes. It is indeed a poetic diary. The pilgrim visits many famous spots, among them the field of Waterloo, where but a few months before the fate of Europe had been decided. To us the battle of Waterloo is a long way off. To Byron it was still a deed of yesterday. As he approaches the field he feels that he is on sacred ground.

> "Stop!—for thy tread is on an Empire's dust!
> An Earthquake's spoil is sepulchred below!
> Is the spot marked with no colossal bust?
> Nor column trophied for triumphal show?
> None; but the moral's truth tells simpler so,
> As the ground was before, thus let it be,—
> How that red rain hath made the harvest grow!
> And is this all the world has gain'd by thee,
> Thou first and last of fields! kingmaking victory?"

---

[1] Moore

Then in thought Byron goes over all that took place that fateful day.

"There was a sound of revelry by night,
And Belgium's capital had gather'd then
Her beauty and her chivalry, and bright
The lamps shone o'er fair women and brave men;
A thousand hearts beat happily; and when
Music arose with its voluptuous swell,
Soft eyes look'd love to eyes which spake again,
And all went merry as a marriage bell;
But hush! hark! a deep sound strikes a rising knell!

"Did ye not hear it?—No; 'twas but the wind,
Or the car rattling o'er the stony street;
On with the dance! let joy be unconfined,
No sleep till morn, when Youth and Pleasure meet
To chase the glowing hours with flying feet
But hark!—that heavy sound breaks in once more,
As if the clouds its echo would repeat;
And nearer, clearer, deadlier than before!
Arm! arm! it is—it is—the cannon's opening roar!

.   .   .   .

"Ah! then and there was hurrying to and fro,
And gathering tears, and tremblings of distress,
And checks all pale, which but an hour ago
Blush'd at the praise of their own loveliness,
And there were sudden partings, such as press
The life from out young hearts, and choking sighs
Which ne'er might be repeated; who could guess
If ever more should meet those mutual eyes,
Since upon night so sweet such awful morn could rise!

"And there was mounting in hot haste, the steed,
The mustering squadron, and the clattering car,
Went pouring forward with impetuous speed,
And swiftly forming in the ranks of war,
And the deep thunder peal on peal afar;
And near, the beat of the alarming drum
Roused up the soldier ere the morning star;
While throng'd the citizens with terror dumb,
Or whispering, with white lips—'The foe! they come! they come!'"

And then thinking of the battle lost by the great conqueror
of Europe, the poet mourns for him—

> "Conqueror and captive of the earth art thou!
> She trembles at thee still, and thy wild name
> Was ne'er more bruited in men's minds than now
> That thou are nothing, save the jest of Fame,
> Who woo'd thee once, thy vassal, and became
> The flatterer of thy fierceness, till thou wert
> A god unto thyself; nor less the same
> To thee astounded kingdoms all inert,
> Who deem'd thee for a time whate'er thou didst assert

> "Oh, more or less than man—in high or low,
> Battling with nations, flying from the field;
> Now making monarchs' necks thy footstool, now
> More than thy meanest soldier taught to yield;
> An empire thou couldst crush, command, rebuild,
> But govern not thy pettiest passion, nor,
> However deeply in men's spirits skill'd,
> Look through thine own, nor curb the lust of war,
> Nor learn that tempted Fate will leave the loftiest Star."

These are a few verses from one of the best known parts
of *Childe Harold*. There are many other verses equally
well known. They have become the possession of almost
every schoolboy. Some of them you will read in school
books, and when you are grown up and able to distinguish
between what is vulgar and what is good and beautiful
in it, I hope you will read the whole poem.

For two years Byron was as popular as man might be.
Then came a change. From the time that he was a child
he had always been in love, first with one and then with
another. His heart was tinder, ever ready to take fire.
Now he married. At first all went well. One little baby
girl was born. Then troubles came, troubles which have
never been explained, and for which we need not seek an
explanation now, and one day Lady Byron left her husband never to return.

The world which had petted and spoiled the poet now turned from the man. He was abused and decried; instead of being courted he was shunned. So in anger and disgust, Byron left the country where he found no sympathy. He never returned to it, the rest of his life being spent as a wanderer upon the Continent.

It was to a great extent a misspent life, and yet, while Byron wasted himself in unworthy ways, he wrote constantly and rapidly, pouring out volumes of poetry at a speed equaled only by Scott. He wrote tragedies, metrical romances, lyrics, and everything that he wrote was read—not only at home, but on the Continent. And one thing that we must remember Byron for is that he made English literature Continental. "Before he came," says an Italian patriot and writer,[1] "all that was known of English literature was the French translation of Shakespeare. It is since Byron that we Continentalists have learned to study Shakespeare and other English writers. From him dates the sympathy of all the true-hearted amongst us for this land of liberty. He led the genius of Britain on a pilgrimage throughout all Europe."

Much that Byron wrote was almost worthless. He has none of the haunting sense of the beauty of words in perfect order that marks the greatest poets. He has no passion for the correct use of words, and often his song seems tuneless and sometimes vulgar. For in Byron's undisciplined, turgid soul there is a strain of coarseness and vulgarity which not seldom shows itself in his poetry, spoiling some of his most beautiful lines. His poetry is egotistical too, that is, it is full of himself. And again and again it has been said that Byron was always his own hero. "He never had more than a single subject—himself. No man has ever pushed egotism further than he."[2] In all his dark and gloomy heroes we

---

[1] Mazzini   [2] Scherer

see Lord Byron, and it is not only himself which he gives to the world's gaze, but his wrongs and his sorrows. Yet in spite of all its faults, there is enough that is purely beautiful in his work to give Byron rank as a poet. He has been placed on a level with Wordsworth. One cultured writer whose judgment on literature we listen to with respect has said: "Wordsworth and Byron stand out by themselves. When the year 1900 is turned, and our nation comes to recount her poetic glories of the century which has then just ended, the first names with her will be these."[1] But there are many who will deny him this high rank. "He can only claim to be acknowledged as a poet of the third class," says another great poet,[2] "who now and then rises into the second, but speedily relapses into the lower element where he was born." And yet another has said that his poetry fills the great space through which our literature has moved from the time of Johnson to the time of Wordsworth. "It touches the *Essay of Man*[3] at the one extremity, and *The Excursion* at the other."[4] So you see Byron's place in our literature is hardly settled yet.

When Byron left England he fled from the contempt of his fellows. His life on the Continent did little to lessen that contempt. But before he died he redeemed his name from the scorner.

Long ago, you remember, at the time of the Renaissance, Greece had been conquered by the Turks. Hundreds of years passed, and Greece remained in a state of slavery. But by degrees new life began to stir among the people, and in 1821 a war of independence broke out. At first the other countries in Europe stood aloof, but gradually their sympathies were drawn to the little nation making so gallant a fight for freedom.

And this struggle woke all that was generous in the

[1] Arnold   [2] Swinburne   [3] By Pope   [4] Macaulay.

heart of Byron, the worn man of the world. Like his own *Childe Harold,* "With pleasure drugg'd he almost long'd for woe." So to Greece he went, and the last nine months of his life were spent to such good purpose that when he died the whole Greek nation mourned. He had hoped to die sword in hand, but that was not to be. His body was worn with reckless living, and could ill bear any strain. One day, when out for a long ride, he became heated, and then soaked by a shower of rain. Rheumatic fever followed, and ten days later he lay dead. He was only thirty-six.

All Greece mourned for the loss of such a generous friend. Cities vied with each other for the honor of his tomb. And when his friends decided that his body should be carried home to England, homage as to a prince was paid to it as it passed through the streets on its last journey.

"The sword, the banner, and the field,
Glory and Greece, around me see!
The Spartan, borne upon his shield,
Was not more free.

"Awake! (not Greece—she *is* awake!)
Awake! my spirit! Think through *whom*
Thy life-blood tracks its parent lake,
And then strike home!

"Tread those reviving passions down,
Unworthy manhood! unto thee
Indifferent should the smile or frown
Of Beauty be.

"If thou regrett'st thy youth, *why live?*
The land of honourable death
Is here:—up to the field, and give
Away thy breath!

"Seek out—less often sought than found—
A soldier's grave, for thee the best;
Then look around, and choose thy ground
And take thy rest "

These lines are from Byron's last poem, written on his thirty-sixth birthday.

CHAPTER LXXX

SHELLEY—THE POET OF LOVE

WHEN Byron wandered upon the Continent he met and made friends with another poet, a greater than himself. This poet was called Percy Bysshe Shelley, and of him I am going to tell you something in this chapter.

On the 4th of August, 1792, Percy Bysshe Shelley was born at Field Place, near the village of Warnham, in Sussex. His father, "a well-meaning, ill-doing, wrong-headed man," was of a good family, and heir to a baronetcy. His mother was a beautiful woman.

Of the early childhood of Bysshe we know nothing, except that at the age of six he was daily taught Latin by a clergyman.

When we next hear of him he is a big boy, the hero of the nursery with four little sisters, and a wee, toddling, baby brother, to all of whom he loved to play big brother. His sisters would often sit on his knee and listen to the wonderful tales he told. There were stories of the Great Tortoise which lived in a pond near. True, the Great Tortoise was never seen, but that made it all the more mysterious and wonderful, and any unusual noise was put down to the Great Tortoise. There were other stories about the Great Old Snake which lived in the garden. This really was seen, and perhaps it was the same serpent which two hundred years before had been known to lurk about the countryside. "He could jut out his neck an ell," it was said, "and cast his venom about four rods; a serpent of countenance very proud, at the sight or hearing of men or cattle, raising his head seeming to listen and look about with great arrogancy." But if it was this same serpent it had lost its venom, and in the days when Bysshe and his sisters played about the garden, they looked upon it as a friend. One day, however, a gardener killed it by mistake, when he was cutting the grass with a scythe. So there was an end of the Great Old Snake. But the Tortoise and the Snake were not the only wonderful things about Field Place. There was a big garret which was never used, with beneath it a secret room, the only entrance to which was through a plank in the garret floor. This, according to the big brother, was the dwelling-place of an alchemist "old and grey with a long beard." Here with his lamp and magic books he wrought his wonders, and "Some day" the eager children were promised a visit to him. Meanwhile Bysshe himself played the alchemist, and with his sisters dressed up in strange costumes to represent fiends or spirits he ran about with liquid fire until this dangerous play was stopped. Then he made an electric battery and amused himself by giving his sisters "shocks" to the secret terror of at least one of them whose heart would sink with fear when she saw her brother appear with a roll of brown paper, a bit of wire, and a bottle. But one day she could not hide her terror any longer, and after that the kind big brother never worried her any more to have shocks.

Sometimes, too, their games took them further afield, and led by Bysshe the children went on long rambles through woods and meadows, climbing walls and scrambling through hedges, and coming home tired and muddy. Bysshe was so happy with his sisters and little brother that he decided to buy a little girl and bring her up as his own. One day a little gypsy girl came to the back door, and he thought she would do very well. His father and mother, however, thought otherwise, so the little girl was not bought.

But the boy who was so lively with his sisters, at times was quiet and thoughtful. Sometimes he would slip out of the house on moonlight nights. His anxious parents would then send an old servant after him, who would return to say that "Master Bysshe only took a walk, and came back again." A very strange form of amusement it must have seemed to his plain matter-of-fact father.

But now these careless happy days came to an end, or only returned during holiday times, for when Bysshe was ten years old he was sent to school.

Shelley went first to a private school, and after a year or two to Eton, but at neither was he happy. And although he had been so merry at home, at school he was looked upon as a strange unsociable creature. He refused to fag for the bigger boys. He never joined in the ordinary school games, and would wander about by himself reading, or watching the clouds and the birds. He read all kinds of books, liking best those which told of haunted castles, robbers, giants, murderers, and other eerie subjects. He liked chemistry too, and was more than once brought into trouble by the daring experiments he made. Shelley was very brave and never afraid of anything except what was base and low. To the few who loved him he was gentle, but most of his schoolfellows took delight in tormenting him. And when goaded into wrath he showed that he could be fierce.

Shelley soon began to write, and while still at school, at the age of sixteen, he published a novel for which he received £40. A little later he and one of his sisters published a book of poems together.

From Eton Shelley went to Oxford. Here he remained for a few months reading hard. "He was to be found, book in hand, at all hours; reading in season and out of season; at table, in bed, and especially during a walk." But he read more what pleased himself than what pleased the college authorities. He wrote too, and among the things he wrote was a little leaflet of a few pages which seemed to the fellows of his college a dangerous attack upon religion. They summoned Shelley to appear before them, and as he refused to answer their questions he was expelled. Shelley had given himself the name of Atheist. It is a very ugly name, meaning one who denies the existence of God. Looking back now we can see that it was too harsh and ugly a name for Shelley. The paper for which he was expelled, even if it was wicked, was the work of a rash, impetuous boy, not the reasoned wickedness of a grown man. But the deed was done, and Shelley was thrown out into the world, for his father, sorely vexed and troubled, not knowing how to control his wild colt of a son, refused to allow him to return home. So Shelley remained in London. Here he went often to visit his sisters at school, and came to know one of their school friends, Harriet Westbrook. She was a pretty, good-tempered girl of sixteen with "hair like a poet's dream." [1] Shelley thought that she too was oppressed and ill-used as he had been. She loved him, he liked her, so they decided to get married, and ran away to Scotland and were married in Edinburgh. Shelley was nineteen and his little bride sixteen.

This boy and girl marriage was a terrible mistake, and three years later husband and wife separated.

I can tell you very little more of Shelley's life, some of it was wrong, much of it was sad, as it could hardly fail to be following on this wrong beginning. When you grow older you will be able to read it with charity and understanding. Meantime keep the picture of the kindly big brother, and imagine him growing into a lovable

[1] Hogg

and brave man, into a poet who wins our hearts almost unawares by the beauty of his poetry, his poetry which has been called "a beautiful dream of the future." Of some of it I shall now tell you a little.

Very early Shelley began to publish poetry, but most of it was not worthy of a truly great poet. His first really fine poem is *Alastor.* It is written in blank verse, and represents a poet seeking in vain for his ideal of what is truly lovely and beautiful. Being unable to find that which he seeks, he dies. The poem is full of beautiful description, but it is sad, and in the picture of the poet we seem to see Shelley himself. Other long poems followed, poems which are both terrible and beautiful, but many years must pass before you try to read them. For Shelley's poetry is more vague, his meaning more elusive, than that of almost any other poet of whom we have spoken. It is rather for Shelley's shorter poems, his lyrics, that I would try to gain your love at present, for although he wrote *The Cenci,* the best tragedy of his time, a tragedy which by its terror and pain links him with Shakespeare, it is as a lyric poet that we love Shelley. "Here," says another poet,[1] "Shelley forgets that he is anything but a poet, forgets sometimes that he is anything but a child. . . He plays truant from earth, slips through the wicket of fancy into heaven's meadow, and goes gathering stars." And of all our poets, Shelley is the least earthly, the most spiritual. But he loved the beautiful world, the sea and sky, and when we have heard him sing of the clouds and the skylark, of the wind and the waves, of—

"The fresh Earth in new leaves drest,
 And the starry night;
Autumn evening, and the morn
When the golden mists are born,"[2]

---

[1] Francis Thompson   [2] *Song.*

when we have heard him sing of these, and have understood with our heart, they have an added meaning for us. We love and understand the song of the skylark better for having heard Shelley sing of it.

"Hail to thee, blithe spirit!
  Bird thou never wert,
That from heaven, or near it,
  Pourest thy full heart
In profuse strains of unpremeditated art.

"Higher still and higher,
  From the earth thou springest
Like a cloud of fire;
  The deep blue thou wingest,
And singing still dost soar, and soaring ever singest.

"In the golden lightening
  Of the sunken sun,
O'er which clouds are brightening,
  Thou dost float and run;
Like an unbodied joy whose race is just begun.

"The pale purple even
  Melts around thy flight;
Like a star of heaven,
  In the broad daylight,
Thou art unseen, but yet I hear thy shrill delight

.   .   .   .

"All the earth and air
  With thy voice is loud,
As, when night is bare,
  From one lonely cloud
The moon rains out her beams, and heaven is overflowed

"What thou art we know not;
  What is most like thee?
From rainbow clouds there flow not
  Drops so bright to see,
As from thy presence showers a rain of melody.

"Like a poet hidden
    In the light of thought,
Singing hymns unbidden,
    Till the world is wrought
In sympathy with hopes and fears it heeded not:

"Like a high-born maiden
    In a palace tower,
Soothing her love-laden
    Soul a secret hour
With music sweet as love, which overflows her bower.

   .   .   .   .

"Teach us, sprite or bird,
    What sweet thoughts are thine;
I have never heard
    Praise of love or wine
That panted forth a flood of rapture so divine.

   .   .   .   .

"We look before and after,
    And pine for what is not:
Our sincerest laughter
    With some pain is fraught;
The sweetest songs are those that tell of saddest thought.

"Yet if we could scorn
    Hate, and pride, and fear;
If we were things born
    Not to shed a tear,
I know not how thy joy we ever should come near.

"Better than all measures
    Of delightful sound,
Better than all treasures
    That in books are found,
Thy skill to poet were, thou scorner of the ground!

"Teach me half the gladness
    That thy brain must know;
Such harmonious madness
    From my lips would flow,
The world would listen then, as I am listening now!"

As we listen to the lark singing we look upward and
see the light summer clouds driving over the blue sky.
They, too, have a song which once the listening poet
heard.

"I bring fresh showers for the thirsty flowers,
From the seas and the streams,
I bear light shades for the leaves when laid
In their noonday dreams
From my wings are shaken the dews that waken
The sweet buds every one,
When rocked to rest on their mother's breast,
As she dances about the sun
I wield the flail of the lashing hail,
And whiten the green plains under,
And then again I dissolve it in rain,
And laugh as I pass in thunder

"I sift the snow on the mountains below,
And their great pines groan aghast,
And all the night 'tis my pillow white,
While asleep in the arms of the blast.
Sublime on the towers of my skiey bowers,
Lightning my pilot sits,
In a cavern under is fettered the thunder,
It struggles and howls at fits,
Over earth and ocean with gentle motion
This pilot is guiding me,
Lured by the love of the genii that move
In the depths of the purple sea;
Over the rills, and the crags, and the hills,
Over the lakes and the plains,
Wherever he dream, under mountain or stream,
The spirit he loves remains;
And I all the while bask in heaven's blue smile,
Whilst he is dissolving in rains.

.   .   .   .

"I bind the sun's throne with the burning zone,
And the moon's with a girdle of pearl
The volcanoes are dim, and the stars reel and swim
When the whirlwinds my banner unfurl

From cape to cape, with a bridge-like shape,
    Over a torrent sea,
Sunbeam-proof, I hang like a roof,
    The mountains its columns be
The triumphal arch through which I march,
    With hurricane, fire, and snow,
When the powers of the air are chained to my chair,
    In the million-coloured bow;
The sphere-fire above its soft colours wove,
    While the moist earth was laughing below.

"I am the daughter of earth and water,
    And the nursling of the sky
I pass through the pores of the ocean and shores;
    I change, but I cannot die.
For after the rain, when with never a stain,
    The pavilion of heaven is bare,
And the winds and sunbeams with their convex gleams,
    Build up the blue dome of air,
I silently laugh at my own cenotaph,
    And out of the caverns of rain,
Like a child from the womb, like a ghost from the tomb,
    I arise and unbuild it again"

That is one of Shelley's happiest poems. For most of his poems have at least a tone of sadness, even the joyous song of the skylark leaves us with a sigh on our lips, "our sincerest laughter with some pain is fraught." But *The Cloud* is full only of joy and movement, and of the laughter of innocent mischief. It is as if we saw the boy Shelley again.

We find his sadness, too, in his *Ode to the West Wind*, but it ends on a note of hope. Here are the last verses—

"Make me thy lyre, even as the forest is
What if my leaves are falling like its own!
The tumult of thy mighty harmonies

"Will take from both a deep autumnal tone,
Sweet though in sadness. Be thou, spirit fierce,
My spirit! Be thou me, impetuous one!

"Drive my dead thoughts over the universe
Like withered leaves to quicken a new birth;
And by the incantation of this verse,

"Scatter, as from an unextinguished hearth
Ashes and sparks, my words among mankind!
Be through my lips to unawakened earth

"The trumpet of a prophecy! O wind,
If Winter comes, can Spring be far behind?"

Shelley sang of Love as well as of the beauty of all things. Here is a little poem, some lines of which are often quoted—

"One word is too often profaned
For me to profane it,
One feeling too falsely disdained
For thee to disdain it,
One hope is too like despair
For prudence to smother,
And Pity from thee more dear
Than that from another.

"I can give not what men call love,
But wilt thou accept not
The worship the heart lifts above
And the Heavens reject not.
The desire of the moth for the star,
Of the night for the morrow,
The devotion of something afar
From the sphere of our sorrow?"

And when his heart was crushed with the knowledge of the wrong and cruelty in the world, it was through love alone that he saw the way to better and lovelier things. "To purify life of its misery and evil was the ruling passion of his soul,"[1] said one who loved him and knew him perhaps better than any living being. And it was through love and the beauty of love that he hoped for the triumph of human weal.

[1] Mary Shelley.

The ideas of the Revolution touched him as they had touched Byron and Wordsworth, and although Wordsworth turned away from them disappointed, Shelley held on hopefully.

> "To suffer woes which Hope thinks infinite;
> To forgive wrongs darker than death or night;
> To defy Power, which seems omnipotent;
> To love, and bear; to hope till Hope creates
> From its own wreck the thing it contemplates:
> Neither to change, nor falter, nor repent;
> This, like thy glory, Titan! is to be
> Good, great and joyous, beautiful and free;
> This is alone Life, Joy, Empire, and Victory!" [1]

One of Shelley's last poems was an elegy called *Adonais*. Under the name of Adonais, he mourns for the death of another poet, John Keats, who died at twenty-six. Shelley believed when he wrote the poem that Keats had been done to death by the cruel criticisms of his poems, that he had died of a broken heart, because the world neither understood nor sympathized with his poetry. Shelley himself knew what it was to suffer from unkind criticisms, and so he understood the feelings of another poet. But although Keats did suffer something from neglect and cruelty, he died of consumption, not of a broken heart.

Adonais ranks with *Lycidas* as one of the most beautiful elegies in our language. In it, Shelley calls upon everything, upon every thought and feeling, upon all poets, to weep for the loss of Adonais.

> "All he had loved, and moulded into thought
> From shape, and hue, and odour, and sweet sound,
> Lamented Adonais Morning sought
> Her eastern watch-tower, and her hair unbound,
> Wet with the tears which should adorn the ground,

---

[1] *Prometheus Unbound.*

Dimmed the aerial eyes that kindle day;
Afar the melancholy thunder moaned,
Pale ocean in unquiet slumber lay,
And the wild winds flew around, sobbing in their dismay

.   .   .   .

"The mountain shepherds came,
Their garlands sere, their magic mantles rent;
The Pilgrim of Eternity,[1] whose fame
Over his living head like Heaven is bent,
An early but enduring monument,
Came, veiling all the lightnings of his song
In sorrow; from her wilds Ierne[2] sent
The sweetest lyrist of her saddest wrong,
And love taught grief to fall like music from his tongue."

He pictures himself, too, among the mourners—

"'Midst others of less note, came one frail Form,
A phantom among men, companionless
As the last cloud of an expiring storm,
Whose thunder is its knell"

Shelley mourned for Keats, little knowing that soon others would mourn for himself. Little more than a year after writing this poem he too lay dead.

Shelley had passed much of his time on the Continent, and in 1822 he was living in a lonely spot on the shores of the Bay of Spezia. He always loved the sea, and he here spent many happy hours sailing about the bay in his boat the *Don Juan*. Hearing that a friend had arrived from England he sailed to Leghorn to welcome him.

Shelley met his friend, and after a week spent with him and with Lord Byron, he set out for home. The little boat never reached its port, for on the journey it was wrecked, we shall never know how. A few days later Shelley's dead body was thrown by the waves upon the sandy shore. In his pocket was found a copy of Keats's poems doubled back, as if he had been reading to the last

---

[1] Lord Byron   [2] Ierne=Ireland sends Thomas Moore to mourn

moment and hastily thrust the book into his pocket. The body was cremated upon the shore, and the ashes were buried in the Protestant cemetery at Rome, not far from the grave of Keats. "It is an open space among the ruins, covered in winter with violets and daisies. It might make one in love with death, to think that one should be buried in so sweet a place." So Shelley himself had written in the preface to *Adonais*.

Over his grave was placed a simple stone with the date of his birth and death and the words "Cor Cordium"— heart of hearts. Beneath these words are some lines from the *Tempest* which Shelley had loved—

> "Nothing of him doth fade
> But doth suffer a sea-change
> Into something rich and strange."

BOOK TO READ

Poems of Shelley, selected and arranged for use in schools, by E E Speight

CHAPTER LXXXI

KEATS—THE POET OF BEAUTY

JOHN KEATS, the poet whose death Shelley mourned in *Adonais,* was by a few years the younger, having been born in 1795. He was born, too, in very different circumstances, for whereas Shelley was the eldest son of a country gentleman, John Keats, was the eldest son of a stableman.

As a boy Thomas Keats had come to London and found a situation as ostler in some livery stables. He was clever and steady, and before he was twenty had risen to be head ostler and married his master's daughter. Keats then became manager of the stables, and his father-in-law, who was comfortably off, went away to live in the country. John's parents were not poor, nor were they common people. In all they had four children, two boys besides John, and a little girl, and they determined to give their children a good education. They would have liked to send their boys to Harrow, but finding that would cost too much they sent them to a smaller school at Enfield. It was a good school, with a large playground, and John seems to have had a happy time there. He was a little chap for his years, but a manly little fellow, broad shouldered and strong. He was full of spirits and fond of fun, and in spite of his passionate temper, every one liked him. He was not particularly fond of lessons, but he did them easily and then turned to other things. What he liked best was fighting. "He

620

would fight any one," says one of his old schoolfellows,[1] "morning, noon, and night, his brothers among the rest It was meat and drink to him." "Yet," says another, "no one ever had an angry word to say of him, and they loved him not only for his terrier-like courage, but for his generosity, his high-mindedness, and his utter ignorance of what was mean or base." But although John was so much loved, and although he was generally so bright and merry, he had miserable times too He had fits of melancholy, but when these came he would go to his brothers and pour out all his grief to them. This made him feel better, and he troubled no one else with his moods.

Very soon after John went to school his father was killed by a fall from his horse, his grandfather died too, and his mother married again. But the marriage was not happy, and she soon left her new husband and went to live with her own mother at Edmonton. So for five years John's life was spent between school and his grand-mother's house. They were a happy family. The brothers loved each other though they jangled and fought, and they loved their mother and little sister too.

So the years went on, and John showed not the slightest sign of being a poet. Some doggerel rimes he wrote to his sister show the boy he was, not very unlike other boys.

> "There was a naughty boy,
> And a naughty boy was he:
> He kept little fishes
> In washing-tubs three,
>   In spite
>   Of the might
>   Of the maid,
>   Nor afraid
> Of his granny good
> He often would

---

[1] E. Holmes.

Hurly-burly
Get up early
　　And go
By hook or crook
To the brook,
And bring home
Miller's Thumb,
Tittlebat
Not over fat,
Minnows small
As the stall
Of a glove,
Not above
　　The size
　　Of a nice
Little baby's
Little fingers."

After John had been at school some time he suddenly began to care for books. He began to read and read greedily, he won all the literature prizes, and even on half-holidays he could hardly be driven out to join in the games of his comrades, preferring rather to sit in the quiet schoolroom translating from Latin or French, and even when he was driven forth he went book in hand.

It was while John was still at school that his mother died and all her children were placed under the care of a guardian. As John was now fifteen, their guardian took him from school, and it was decided to make him a doctor. He was apprenticed, in the fashion of the day, to a surgeon at Edmonton, for five years. Keats seems to have been quite pleased with this arrangement. His new studies still left him time to read. He was within walking distance of his old school, and many a summer afternoon he spent reading in the garden with Cowden Clarke, the son of his old schoolmaster, in whom Keats had found a friend. From this friend he borrowed Spenser's *Faery Queen,* and having read it a new wonder-world seemed opened to him. "He ramped through the scenes of the romance like a young horse turned into a spring meadow,"[1] and all through Keats's poetry we find the love of beautiful coloring and of gorgeous detail that we also find in Spenser. It was Spenser that awakened in Keats his sleeping gift of song, and the first verses which he wrote were in imitation of the Elizabethan poet.

From Spenser Keats learned how poetry might be gemmed, how it might glow with color. But there was another source from which he was to learn what pure and severe beauty might mean. This source was the poetry of Homer. Keats knew nothing of Greek, yet all his poetry shows the influence of Greece. At school he had loved the Greek myths and had read them in English. Now among the books he read with his friend Cowden Clarke was a translation of Homer. It was not Pope's translation but an earlier one by Chapman. The two friends began to read it one evening, and so keen was Keats's delight that at times he shouted aloud in joy; so intense was his interest that they read on and on until the morning light put out their candles. In the dawning of the day the young poet went home quivering with delight. It was for him truly the dawning of a new day. For him still another new world had opened, and his spirit exulted. The voice of this great master poet awoke in him an answering voice, and before many hours had passed Cowden Clarke had in his hands Keats's sonnet *On first looking into Chapman's Homer*. The lines that Spenser had called forth were a mere imitation; Homer called forth Keats's first really great poem.

> "Much have I travell'd in the realms of gold,
> And many goodly states and kingdoms seen;
> Round many Western islands have I been
> Which bards in fealty to Apollo hold

---

[1] Cowden Clarke.

Oft of one wide expanse had I been told,
That deep-brow'd Homer ruled as his demesne·
Yet did I never breathe its pure serene
Till I heard Chapman speak out loud and bold:
Then felt I like some watcher of the skies
When a new planet swims into his ken,
Or like stout Cortez when with eagle eyes
He star'd at the Pacific—and all his men
Look'd at each other with a wild surmise—
Silent, upon a peak in Darien."

For some unexplained reason Keats broke his apprenticeship to the surgeon at Edmonton after four years. He did not however give up the idea of becoming a doctor, and he went on with his studies at the London hospitals. Keats was by this time about nineteen. He was small— only about five feet—so that his fellow-students called him "little Keats." But his face was fine, and out of it looked eyes "like those of a wild gipsy-maid set in the face of a young god." He was a steady student, although he did "scribble doggerel rhymes" among his notes, and he passed his examinations well. Yet the work was all against the grain. More and more he began to feel that nothing but poetry mattered, that for him it was the real business of life. It was hard to study when even a sunbeam had power to set his thoughts astray. "There came a sunbeam into the room," once he said to a friend, "and with it a whole troop of creatures floating in the ray, and I was off with them to Oberon and Fairyland."

Keats gradually made several friends among the young writers of the day. One of these printed a few of the young poet's sonnets in his paper the *Examiner,* and in 1817 Keats published a volume of poems. This was his good-by to medicine, for although very little notice was taken of the book and very few copies were sold, Keats henceforth took poetry for his life work.

The life of Keats was short, and it had no great adventures in it. He lived much now with his two brothers until the elder, George, married and emigrated to America, and the younger, Tom, who had always been an invalid, died. He went excursions too, with his friends or by himself to country or seaside places, or sometimes he would spend days and nights in the hospitable homes of his friends. And all the time he wrote letters which reveal to us his steadfast, true self, and poems which show how he climbed the steps of fame.

Undismayed at the ill success of his first book, the next year he published his long poem *Endymion.*

Endymion was a fabled Grecian youth whose beauty was so great that Selene, the cold moon, loved him. He fell asleep upon the hill of Latmus, and while he slept Selene came to him and kissed him. Out of this simple story Keats made a long poem of four books or parts. Into it he wove many other stories, his imagination leading him through strange and wondrous scenery. The poem is not perfect—it is rambling and disconnected— the story of Endymion being but the finest thread to hold a string of beads and priceless pearls together.

The first book is merely a long introduction, but it opens with unforgettable lines—

> "A thing of beauty is a joy for ever;
> Its loveliness increases; it will never
> Pass into nothingness, but still will keep
> A bower quiet for us, and a sleep
> Full of sweet dreams, and health, and quiet breathing."

Then the poet tells us what are the things of beauty of which he thinks.

> "Such the sun, the moon,
> Trees old, and young, sprouting a shady boon
> For simple sheep; and such are daffodils
> With the green world they live in, and clear rills

That for themselves a cooling covert make
'Gainst the hot season; the mid forest brake,
Rich with a sprinkling of fair musk-rose blooms,
And such too is the grandeur of the dooms
We have imagined for the mighty dead;
All lovely tales that we have heard or read,
An endless fountain of immortal drink
Pouring unto us from the heaven's brink."

But although throughout the long poem there are lovely passages, and one or two most beautiful lyrics, the critics of the day saw only the faults of which *Endymion* is full, and the poem was received with a storm of abuse.

Soon after Keats published this poem, he, with a friend, set out on a walking tour to the Lake Country and to Scotland. This was Keats's first sight of real mountains, and he gloried in the grand scenery, but said ' human nature is finer." When Keats set out there was not a sign of the invalid about him. He walked twenty or thirty miles a day and cheerfully bore the discomforts of travel. But the tour proved too much for his strength. He caught a bad cold and sore throat, and was ordered home by the doctor. He went by boat, arriving brown, shabby, and almost shoeless, among his London friends.

Keats never quite recovered his good health, and other griefs and troubles crowded in upon him. It was after his return from this tour that his dearly loved brother, Tom, died. Cruel criticisms of his poetry hurt him at the same time, and he was in trouble about money, for the family guardian had not proved a good manager. And now to this already overcharged heart something else was added. Keats fell in love. The lady he loved was young and beautiful, but commonplace. Keats himself describes her when he first met her as "beautiful and elegant, graceful, silly, fashionable, and strange." Her beauty and her strangeness won for her a way to the poet's heart. Love, however, brought to him no joyful rest, but rather passionate, jealous restlessness. Yet in spite of all his troubles, Keats continued to write poems which will ever be remembered as among the most beautiful in our language.

Like Scott and Byron, Keats wrote metrical romances. One of these, *Isabella, or the Pot of Basil,* is founded upon a tale of Boccaccio, that old master to whom so many poets have gone for inspiration. In Keats's romances there is no war-cry, no clash of swords as in Scott's, and the luxury is altogether different from Byron's. There is in them that trembling sense of beauty which opens to us wide windows into fairyland. They are simple stories veiled in the glamour of lovely words, and full of the rich color and the magic of the middle ages. But here as elsewhere in Keats's poetry what we lack is the touch of human sorrow. Keats wrote of nature with all Wordsworth's insight and truth, and with far greater magic of words. He understood the mystery of nature, but of the mystery of the heart of man it was not his to sing. He lived in a world apart. The terror and beauty of real life hardly touched him. Alone of all the poets of his day he was unmoved by the French Revolution, and all that it stood for.

Some day you will read Keats's metrical romances, and now I will give you a few verses from some of his odes, for in his odes we have Keats's poetry at its very best. Here are some verses from his ode *On a Grecian Urn.* You have seen such a vase, perhaps, with beautiful sculptured figures on it, dancing maidens and piping shepherds.

"Heard melodies are sweet, but those unheard
Are sweeter; therefore, ye soft pipes, play on,
Not to the sensual ear, but, more endear'd,
Pipe to the spirit ditties of no tone;

Fair youth, beneath the trees, thou canst not leave
Thy song, nor ever can those trees be bare;
Bold Lover, never, never canst thou kiss,
Though winning near the goal—yet, do not grieve;
She cannot fade, though thou hast not thy bliss,
For ever wilt thou love, and she be fair!

"Ah, happy, happy boughs! that cannot shed
Your leaves, nor ever bid the Spring adieu;
And, happy melodist, unwearied,
For ever piping songs for ever new;
More happy love! more happy, happy love!
For ever warm and still to be enjoy'd,
For ever panting, and for ever young;
All breathing human passion far above,
That leaves a heart high-sorrowful and cloy'd,
A burning forehead, and a parching tongue.

"O Attic shape! Fair attitude! with brede[1]
Of marble men and maidens over-wrought,
With forest branches and the trodden weed,
Thou, silent form, dost tease us out of thought
As doth eternity: Cold Pastoral!
When old age shall this generation waste,
Thou shalt remain, in midst of other woe
Than ours, a friend to man, to whom thou say'st,
'Beauty is truth, truth beauty,'—that is all
Ye know on earth, and all ye need to know."

In these last lines we have the dominant note in
Keats's song. beauty and the love of beauty. What is true
must be beautiful, and just in so far as we move away from
truth we lose what is beautiful. Nothing is so ugly as a lie.

And now remembering how Shelley sang of the skylark you will like to read how his brother poet sang of the
nightingale.

"My heart aches, and a drowsy numbness pains
My sense, as though of hemlock I had drunk,
Or emptied some dull opiate to the drains
One minute past, and Lethe-wards had sunk·

---

[1] Embroidery.

'Tis not through envy of thy happy lot,
But being too happy in thine happiness,—
That thou, light-winged Dryad of the trees,
In some melodious plot
Of beechen green, and shadows numberless,
Singest of summer in full-throated ease.

.   .   .   .   .

"Darkling I listen; and for many a time
I have been half in love with easeful Death,
Call'd him soft names in many a mused rhyme,
To take into the air my quiet breath;
Now more than ever seems it rich to die,
To cease upon the midnight with no pain,
While thou art pouring forth thy soul abroad
In such an ecstasy!
Still wouldst thou sing, and I have ears in vain—
To thy high requiem become a sod

"Thou wast not born for death, immortal Bird!
No hungry generations tread thee down;
The voice I hear this passing night was heard
In ancient days by emperor and clown·
Perhaps the selfsame song that found a path
Through the sad heart of Ruth, when, sick for home,
She stood in tears amid the alien corn;
The same that oft times hath
Charm'd magic casements, opening on the foam
Of perilous seas, in faery lands forlorn.

"Forlorn! the very word is like a bell
To toll me back from thee to my sole self!
Adieu! the fancy cannot cheat so well
As she is famed to do, deceiving elf.
Adieu! Adieu! thy plaintive anthem fades
Past the near meadows, over the still stream,
Up the hill-side, and now 'tis buried deep
In the next valley glades;
Was it a vision, or a waking dream?
Fled is the music·—Do I wake or sleep?'"

As another poet[1] has said, speaking of Keats's odes,
"Greater lyrical poetry the world may have seen than

[1] Swinburne

any that is in these; lovelier it surely has never seen, nor ever can it possibly see."

Hyperion, which also ranks among Keats's great poems, is an unfinished epic. In a far-off way the subject of the poem reminds us of *Paradise Lost*. For here Keats sings of the overthrow of the Titans, or earlier Greek gods, by the Olympians, or later Greek gods, and in the majestic flow of the blank verse we sometimes seem to hear an echo of Milton.

Hyperion, who gives his name to the poem, was the Sun-god who was dethroned by Apollo. When the poem opens we see the old god Saturn already fallen—

> "Old Saturn lifted up
> His faded eyes, and saw his kingdom gone,
> And all the gloom and sorrow of the place,
> And that fair kneeling goddess, and then spake,
> As with a palsied tongue, and while his beard
> Shook horrid with such aspen-malady:
> 'O tender spouse of gold Hyperion,
> Thea, I feel thee ere I see thy face,
> Look up, and let me see our doom in it;
> Look up, and tell me if this feeble shape
> Is Saturn's, if thou hear'st the voice
> Of Saturn; tell me, if this wrinkled brow,
> Naked and bare of its great diadem,
> Peers like the front of Saturn   Who had power
> To make me desolate? whence came the strength?
> How was it nurtur'd to such bursting forth,
> While Fate seem'd strangled in my nervous grasp?
> But it is so '"

Saturn is king no more. Fate willed it so. But suddenly he rises and in helpless passion cries out against Fate—

> "Saturn must be King
> Yes, there must be a golden victory;
> There must be gods thrown down, and trumpets blown
> Of triumph calm, and hymns of festival

Upon the gold clouds metropolitan,
Voices of soft proclaim, and silver stir
Of strings in hollow shells; and there shall be
Beautiful things made new, for the surprise
Of the sky-children; I will give command:
Thea! Thea! Thea! where is Saturn?"

The volume containing these and other poems was published in 1820, little more than three years after Keats's first volume, and never, perhaps, has poet made such strides in so short a time. And this last book was kindly received. Success had come to Keats, but young though he still was, the success was too late. For soon it was seen that his health had gone and that his life's work was done. As a last hope his friends advised him to spend the winter in Italy. So with a friend he set out. He never returned, but died in Rome in the arms of his friend on the 23rd February 1821. He was only twenty-six. Before he died he asked that on his grave should be placed the words, "Here lies one whose name was writ in water." He had his wish: but we, to whom he left his poetry, know that his name is written in the stars.

How Shelley mourned for him you have read. How the friends who knew and loved him mourned we learn from what they say of him. "I cannot afford to lose him," wrote one. "If I know what it is to love, I truly love John Keats." Another says,[1] "He was the most unselfish of human creatures," and still another,[2] "a sweeter tempered man I never knew."

In a letter which reached Rome too late was this message for Keats, "Tell that great poet and noble-hearted man that we shall all bear his memory in the most precious part of our hearts, and that the world shall bow their heads to it, as our loves do."

[1] Haydon.   [2] Bailey.

We bow our heads to his memory and say farewell to him in these words of his own fairy song—

"Shed no tear! oh shed no tear!
The flower will bloom another year.
Weep no more! oh weep no more!
Young buds sleep in the roots' white core.
Dry your eyes! oh dry your eyes!
For I was taught in Paradise
To ease my heart of melodies—
                    Shed no tear

"Overhead! look overhead!
'Mong the blossoms white and red—
Look up, look up   I flutter now
On this flush pomegranate bough.
See me! 'tis this silvery bill
Ever cures the good man's ill
Shed no tear! oh shed no tear!
The flower will bloom another year
Adieu! Adieu!—I fly, adieu!
I vanish in the heaven's blue—
                    Adieu! Adieu!"

CHAPTER LXXXII

CARLYLE—THE SAGE OF CHELSEA

JOHN KEATS was little more than a month old, when far away across the Border another little baby boy was born. His parents, too, were simple folk, and he, too, was born to be great.

This boy's name was Thomas Carlyle. His father was a stone-mason and had built with his own hands the house in which his son Thomas was born. The little village of Ecclefechan was about six miles from the Solway Firth, among the pasture lands of the vale of Annan. Here Thomas grew to be a boy running about barefooted and sturdy with his many brothers and sisters, for he had eight younger brothers and sisters, and one step-brother older than himself.

But he did not run about quite wild, for by the time he was five his mother had taught him to read and his father had taught him to do sums, and then he was sent to the village school.

James Carlyle was a good and steady workman. Long afterwards his famous son said of him, "Nothing that he undertook to do but he did it faithfully and like a true man. I shall look on the houses he built with a certain proud interest. They stand firm and sound to the heart all over his little district. No one that comes after him will ever say, 'Here was the finger of a hollow eye-servant.' They are little texts to me of the gospel of man's free will." But there were meanwhile many little folks to clothe, many hungry little mouths to fill, so their clothes were of the plainest, and porridge and milk, and potatoes forming their only fare. "It was not a joyful life," says Thomas—"what life is?—yet a safe, quiet one; above most others, or any others I have witnessed, a wholesome one."

Between the earnest and frugal father and mother and their children there was a great and reverent though quiet love, and poor though they were, the parents determined that their children should be well taught, so when Thomas was ten he was sent to a school at Annan some five miles away, where he could learn more than in the little village school.

On a bright May morning Thomas set out trotting gayly by his father's side. This was his first venture into the world, and his heart was full of hopes just dashed with sadness at leaving his mother. But the wonderful new world of school proved a bitter disappointment to the little fellow. He had a violent temper, and his mother, fearing into what he might be led when far from her, made him promise never to return a blow. Thomas kept his promise, with the result that his fellows, finding they might torment him with safety, tormented him without mercy.

In a book called *Sartor Resartus* which Carlyle wrote later, and which here and there was called forth by a memory of his own life, he says:

"My schoolfellows were boys, mostly rude boys, and obeyed the impulse of rude nature which bids the deer herd fall upon any stricken hart, the duck flock put to death any broken-winged brother or sister, and on all hands the strong tyrannise over the weak."

So Thomas at school was unhappy and lonely and tormented. But one day, unable to bear the torment longer, he flew at one of the biggest bullies in the school.

The result was a fight in which Thomas got the worst, but, he had shown his fellows what he could do, he was tormented no longer. Yet ever afterwards he bore an unhappy remembrance of those days at school.

After three years his school-days came to an end. He was not yet fourteen, but he had proved himself so eager a scholar that his father decided to send him to college and let him become a minister.

So early one November morning he set out in the cold and dark upon his long tramp of more than eighty miles to Edinburgh. It was dark when he left the house, and his father and mother went with him a little way, and then they turned back and left Tom to trudge along in the growing light, with another boy a year or two older who was returning to college.

Little is known of Carlyle's college days. After five years' study, at nineteen he became a schoolmaster, still with the intention of later becoming a minister as his father wished. But for teaching Carlyle had no love, and after some years of it, first in schools and then as a private tutor, he gave it up. He gave up, too, the idea of becoming a minister, for he found he had lost the simple faith of his fathers and could not with good conscience teach to others what he did not thoroughly believe himself. He gave up, too, the thought of becoming a barrister, for after a little study he found he had no bent for law.

Already he had begun to write. Besides other things he had translated and published *Wilhelm Meister*, a story by the great German poet, Goethe. It was well received. The great Goethe himself wrote a kind letter to his translator. It came to him, said Carlyle, "like a message from fairyland." And thus encouraged, after drifting here and there, trying first one thing and then another, Carlyle gave himself up to literature.

Meanwhile he had met and loved a beautiful and clever lady named Jane Welsh. She was above him in station, witty, and sought after. Admiring the genius of Carlyle she yet had no mind she said to marry a poor genius. But she did, and so began a long mistake of forty years.

The newly married couple took a cottage on the outskirts of Edinburgh, and there Carlyle settled down to his writing. But money coming in slowly, Carlyle found he could no longer afford to live in Edinburgh. So after a year and a half of cheerful, social life, surrounded by many cultured friends, he and his wife moved to Craigenputtock, a lonely house fourteen miles from Dumfries, which belonged to Mrs Carlyle. Here was solitude indeed. The air was so quiet that the very sheep could be heard nibbling. For miles around there was no house, the post came only once a week, and months at a time would go past without a visitor crossing the doorstep.

To Carlyle, who hated noises, who all his life long waged war against howling dogs and "demon" fowls, the silence and loneliness were delightful. His work took all his thoughts, filled all his life. He did not remember that what to him was simply peaceful quiet was for his witty, social wife a dreary desert of loneliness. Carlyle was not only, as his mother said, "gey ill to deal wi'," but also "gey ill to live wi'." For he was a genius and a sick genius. He was nervous and bilious and suffered tortures from indigestion which made him often gloomy and miserable.

It was not a happy fortune which cast Jane and Thomas Carlyle together into this loneliness. Still the days passed not all in gloom, Thomas writing a wonderful book, *Sartor Resartus,* and Jane using all her cleverness to make the home beautiful and comfortable. For they were very poor, and Jane, who before her marriage had no knowledge of housekeeping, found herself obliged to cook and do much of the housework herself.

Nearly all Carlyle's first books had to do with German literature. He translated stories from great German writers and wrote about the authors. And just as Byron had taught people on the Continent to read English literature, so Carlyle taught English people to read German literature. He steeped himself so thoroughly in German that he himself came to write English, if I may so express it, with a German accent. Carlyle's style is harsh and rugged. It has a vividness and picturesqueness all his own, but when Carlyle began to write people cared neither for his style nor for his subjects. He found publishers hard to persuade, and life was by no means easy.

When *Sartor* was finished Carlyle took it to London, but could find no one willing to publish it. So it was cut up into articles and published in a magazine "and was then mostly laughed at," says Carlyle, and many declared they would stop taking the magazine unless these ridiculous papers ceased. Not until years had passed was it published in book form.

I do not think I can make you understand the charm of *Sartor*. It is a prose poem and a book you must leave for the years to come. *Sartor Resartus* means "The tailor patched again." And under the guise of a philosophy of clothes Carlyle teaches that man and everything belonging to him is only the expression of the one great real thing— God. "Thus in this one pregnant subject of Clothes, rightly understood, is included all that men have thought, dreamed, done, and been."

The book is full of humor and wisdom, of stray lightenings, and deep growlings. There are glimpses of "a story" to be caught too. It is perhaps the most Carlylean book Carlyle ever wrote. But let it lie yet awhile on your bookshelf unread.

At the end of six years or so Carlyle decided that Craigenputtock was of no use to him. He wanted to get the ear of the world, to make the world listen to him. It would not listen to him when he spoke from a far-off wilderness. So he made the great plunge, and saying good-by to the quiet of barren rock and moorland he came to live in London. He took a house in Cheyne Row in Chelsea, and this for the rest of his life was his home. But at first London was hardly less lonely than Craigenputtock. It seemed impossible to make people want either Carlyle or his books. "He had created no 'public' of his own," says a friend who wrote his life,[1] "the public which existed could not understand his writings and would not buy them, nor could he be induced so much as to attempt to please it; and thus it was that in Cheyne Row he was more neglected than he had been in Scotland."

Still in spite of neglect Carlyle worked on, now writing his great *French Revolution*. He labored for months at this book, and at length having finished the first volume of it he lent it to a friend to read. This friend left it lying about, and a servant thinking it waste paper destroyed it. In great distress he came to tell Carlyle what had happened. It was a terrible blow, for Carlyle had earned nothing for months, and money was growing scarce. But he bravely hid his consternation and comforted his friend. "We must try to hide from him how very serious this business is to us," were the first words he said to his wife when they were alone together. Long afterwards when asked how he felt when he heard the news, "Well, I just felt like a man swimming without water," he replied.[2]

So once more he set to work rewriting all that had been lost. In 1837 the book was published, and from that time Carlyle took his place in the world as a man of genius. But money was still scarce, so as a means of making some,

<hr />

[1] Froude. [2] *Life of Tennyson.*

he gave several courses of lectures. But he hated it.
"O heaven!" he cries, "I cannot speak. I can only gasp
and writhe and stutter, a spectacle to gods and fashion-
ables,—being forced to it by want of money." One course
of these lectures—the last—was on *Heroes and Hero
Worship*. This may be one of the first of Carlyle's books
that you will care to read, and you may now like to hear
what he has to say of Samuel Johnson in *The Hero as a
Man of Letters*.

"As for Johnson, I have always considered him to be,
by nature, one of our great English souls. A strong and
noble man; so much left undeveloped in him to the last;
in a kindlier element what might he not have been,—Poet,
Priest, Sovereign Ruler! On the whole, a man must not
complain of his 'element,' or his 'time' or the like; it
is thriftless work doing so. His time is bad; well then,
he is there to make it better!—

"Johnson's youth was poor, isolated, hopeless, very
miserable. Indeed, it does not seem possible that, in any
of the favourablest outward circumstances, Johnson's
life could have been other than a painful one. The world
might have had more profitable *work* out of him, or less;
but his *effort* against the world's work could never have
been a light one. Nature, in return for his nobleness,
had said to him, 'Live in an element of diseased sorrow.'
Nay, perhaps the sorrow and the nobleness were intimately
and even inseparably connected with each other. . . .

"The largest soul that was in all England; and provision made for it of 'fourpence halfpenny a day.' Yet
a giant, invincible soul; a true man's. One remembers
always that story of the shoes at Oxford; the rough,
seamy-faced, raw-boned College Servitor stalking about,
in winter season, with his shoes worn out; how the
charitable Gentleman Commoner secretly places a new
pair at his door, and the raw-boned Servitor, lifting them,

looking at them near, with his dim eyes, with what thought, —pitches them out of window! Wet feet, mud, frost, hunger, or what you will; but not beggary: we cannot stand beggary! Rude stubborn self-help here; a whole world of squalor, rudeness, confused misery and want, yet of nobleness and manfulness withal.

"It is a type of the man's life, this pitching away of the shoes, an original man;—not a second hand, borrowing or begging man. Let us stand on our own basis, at any rate! On such shoes as we ourselves can get. On frost and mud, if you will, but honestly on that;—On the reality and substance which nature gives *us,* not on the semblance, on the thing she has given another than us!—

"And yet with all this rugged pride of manhood and self-help, was there ever soul more tenderly affectionate, loyally submissive to what was really higher than he? Great souls are always loyally submissive, reverent to what is over them; only small souls are otherwise. . . .

"It was in virtue of his *sincerity,* of his speaking still in some sort from the heart of Nature, though in the current artificial dialect, that Johnson was a Prophet. . . . Mark, too, how little Johnson boasts of his 'sincerity.' He has no suspicion of his being particularly sincere,— of his being particularly anything! A hard-struggling, weary-hearted man, or 'scholar' as he calls himself, trying hard to get some honest livelihood in the world, not to starve, but to live,—without stealing! A noble unconsciousness is in him. He does not 'engrave *Truth* on his watch-seal'; no, but he stands by truth, speaks by it, works and lives by it. Thus it ever is. . . .

"Johnson was a Prophet to his people: preached a Gospel to them,—as all like him always do. The highest Gospel he preached we may describe as a kind of moral Prudence: 'in a world where much is to be done, and little is to be known,' see how you will *do* it! A thing well worth preaching. 'A world where much is to be done, and little is to be known,' do not sink yourselves in boundless, bottomless abysses of Doubt. . . .

"Such Gospel Johnson preached and taught;—coupled with this other great Gospel. 'Clear your mind of Cant!' Have no trade with Cant: stand on the cold mud in the frosty weather, but let it be in your own *real* torn shoes: 'that will be better for you,' as Mahomet says! I call this, I call these two things *joined together,* a great Gospel, the greatest perhaps that was possible at that time."

I give this quotation from *Heroes* because there is, in some ways, a great likeness between Johnson and Carlyle. Both were sincere, and both after a time of poverty and struggle ruled the thought of their day. For Carlyle became known by degrees, and became, like Johnson before him, a great literary man. He was sought after by the other writers of his day, who came to listen to the growlings of the "Sage of Chelsea."

Carlyle, like Johnson, was a Prophet with a message. "Carlyle," says a French writer, "has taken up a mission; he is a prophet, the prophet of sincerity. This sincerity or earnestness he would have applied everywhere: he makes it the law, the healthy and holy law, of art, of morals, of politics." [1] And through all Carlyle's exaggeration and waywardness of diction we find that note ring clear again and again. Be sincere, find the highest, and worship it with all thy mind and heart and will.

And although for us of to-day the light of Carlyle as a prophet may be somewhat dimmed, we may still find, as a great man of his own day found, that the good his writings do us, is "not as philosophy to instruct, but as poetry to animate." [2]

Carlyle went steadily on with his writing. In the

[1] Scherer   [2] J. S. Mill.

summer he would have his table and tray of books brought out into the garden so that he could write in the open air, but much of his work, too, was done in a "sound proof" room which he built at the top of the house in order to escape from the horror of noise. The sound-proof room was not, however, a great success, for though it kept out some noises it let in others even worse.

When visitors came they were received either indoors or in the little garden which Carlyle found "of admirable comfort in the smoking way." In the garden they smoked and talked sitting on kitchen chairs, or on the quaint china barrels which Mrs. Carlyle named "noblemen's seats."

Among the many friends Carlyle made was the young poet Alfred Tennyson. Returning from a walk one day he found a splendidly handsome young man sitting in the garden talking to his wife. It was the poet.

Here is how Carlyle describes his new friend: "A fine, large-featured, dime-eyed, bronze-coloured, shaggy-headed man is Alfred; dusty, smoky, free and easy; who swims outwardly and inwardly with great composure in an articulate element as of tranquil chaos and tobacco smoke; great, now and then when he does emerge; a most restful, brotherly, whole-hearted man." Or again: "Smokes infinite tobacco. His voice is musical, metallic, fit for loud laughter and piercing wail, and all that may lie between. I do not meet in these late decades such company over a pipe. We shall see what he will grow to." [1]

Although Carlyle was older than Tennyson by fourteen years, this was the beginning of a friendship which strengthened with years and lasted when they were both gray-haired men. They talked and smoked and walked about together often at night through the lamp-lit streets, sometimes in the wind, and rain, Carlyle crying out as they walked along against the dirt and squalor and noise of

[1] Hallam, Lord Tennyson, *Life of Tennyson.*

London, "that healthless, profitless, mad and heavy-laden place," "that Devil's Oven."

The years passed and Carlyle added book to book. Perhaps of them all that which we should be most grateful for is his *Life and Letters of Cromwell.* For in this book he set Cromwell in a new light, a better light than he had ever been set before. Carlyle is a hero worshiper, and in Cromwell as a hero he can find no fault. He had of course his faults like other men, and he had no need of such blind championship. For in his letters and speeches, gathered together and given to the world by Carlyle, he speaks for himself. In them we find one to whom we may look up as a true hero, a man of strength to trust. We find, too, a man of such broad kindliness, a man of such a tender human heart that we may love him.

Another great book was Carlyle's *History of Frederick the Great.* It is a marvelous piece of historical work, and as volume after volume appeared Carlyle's fame steadily rose.

"No critic," says his first biographer, Froude, "no critic after the completion of *Frederick,* challenged Carlyle's right to a place beside the greatest of English authors, past and present." He was a great historian, but in the history he gives us not dead facts, but living, breathing men and women. His pages are as full of color and of life as the pages of Shakespeare.

The old days of struggle and want were long over, but the Carlyles still lived the simple life in the little Chelsea house. As another writer[1] has quaintly put it, "Tom Carlyle lives in perfect dignity in a little £40 house in Chelsea, with a snuffy Scotch maid to open the door, and the best company in England ringing at it."

Then in 1865 Carlyle was chosen Lord Rector of Edinburgh University, and although this could add little to

[1] Thackeray

his fame, he was glad that his own country had recognized his greatness.

Fifty years before, he had left the University a poor and unknown lad. Now at seventy-one, a famous man, he returned to make his speech upon entering his office as Rector.

The speech was a splendid success, his reception magnificent, "a perfect triumph," as a friend telegraphed to Mrs. Carlyle waiting anxiously for news in London. For a few days Carlyle lingered in Scotland. Then he was suddenly recalled home by the terrible news that his wife had died suddenly while out driving. It was a crushing blow. Only when it was too late did Carlyle realize all that his wife had been to him. She was, as he wrote on her tombstone, "Suddenly snatched away from him, and the light of his life as if gone out."

The light indeed had gone out. The rest of his life was a sad twilight, filled with cruel remorse. He still wrote a little, and friends were kind, but his real work in life was done, and he felt bitterly alone.

Honors were offered him, a title if he would, a pension. But he declined them all. For fifteen years life dragged along. Then at the age of eighty-five he died.

He might have lain in Westminster among the illustrious dead. But such had not been his wish, so he was buried beside his father and mother in the old churchyard at Ecclefechan.

BOOKS TO READ

Stories from Carlyle, by D M Ford   *Readings from Carlyle,* by W. Keith Leask.

CHAPTER LXXXIII

THACKERAY—THE CYNIC?

A LITTLE time after Carlyle's *French Revolution* was published he wrote to his brother, "I understand there have been many reviews of a very mixed character. I got one in the *Times* last week. The writer is one, Thackeray, a half-monstrous Cornish giant, kind of painter, Cambridge man, and Paris newspaper correspondent, who is now writing for his life in London. . . . His article is rather like him, and I suppose calculated to do the book good."

In these few sentences we have a sketch of William Makepeace Thackeray's life, from the time he finished his education up to the age of twenty-six, when Carlyle met him. He was the son of Richmond Thackeray, a collector in the service of the East India Company, and was born in Calcutta in 1811.

Little Billy-man, as his mother called him, in after years could remember very little of India. He remembered seeing crocodiles and a very tall, lean father. When Billy was quite a tiny chap, his father died. Soon after, the little boy was sent home, as Indian children always are, but his mother remained out in India, and a year or two later married Major Henry Carmichael Smyth. Major Smyth was a simple, kindly gentleman, and proved a good stepfather to his wife's little boy, who, when he grew up and became famous drew his stepfather's portrait in the character of Colonel Newcome.

Meanwhile Billy-man was separated from both father

and mother, and sailed home under the care of a black servant. His ship called at St. Helena, and there the black servant took the little boy a long walk over rocks and hills until they came to a garden. In the garden a man was walking. "That is he." said the black man, "that is Bonaparte. He eats three sheep every day, and all the little children he can lay hands on." Ugh! We think that the little boy did not want to stay there long.

William reached home safely and was very happy with kind aunts and grandmother until he went to school. And school he did not like at all. Long afterwards in one of his books he wrote, "It was governed by a horrible little tyrant, who made our young lives so miserable, that I remember kneeling by my little bed of a night and saying, Pray God, I may dream of my mother.' " [1]

But he left this school and when he was about eleven went to Charterhouse. Here Thackeray was not much happier. He was a pretty, gentle boy, and not particularly clever, either at games or at lessons. The boys were rough and even brutal to each other, and Thackeray had to take his share of the blows, and got a broken nose which disfigured his good-looking face ever after. And when he left school he took away with him a painful remembrance of all he had had to suffer. But by degrees the suffering faded out of his memory and he looked upon his old school with kindly eyes, and called it no longer Slaughterhouse, but Grey Friars, in his books.

Before Thackeray went to Charterhouse his mother and stepfather had come home to England and made a home for the little boy where he spent happy holidays. Thackeray was not very diligent, but in his last term at school he writes to his mother, "I really think I am becoming terribly industrious, though I can't get Dr. Russell (the headmaster) to think so. . . . There are but

[1] *Roundabout Papers*

three hundred and seventy in the school. I wish there
were only three hundred and sixty-nine."

Soon he had his wish, and leaving Charterhouse he
went to Trinity College, Cambridge. He liked Cambridge
better than Charterhouse, but did not learn much more.
In little more than a year he left because he felt that he
was wasting his time, and went abroad to finish his
education. After spending a happy year in Germany
he came home to study at the bar, but soon finding he had
no taste for law, he gave that up.

Thackeray was now of age and had come into a little
fortune of about £500 a year, left to him by his father.
So he decided to try his hand at literature, and bought
a paper called the *National Standard,* and became editor
of it. He could not, however, make his paper pay, and
in that and other ways he had soon lost all his money.

It was now necessary that he should do something to
earn a living, and he determined to be an artist, and went
to Paris to study. But although he was fond of drawing,
and was able afterwards to illustrate some of his own
books, he never became a real artist.

Meanwhile in Paris he met a young Irish lady with
whom he fell in love, and being offered the post of Paris
correspondent on another paper, he married. But very
soon after he married the paper failed and Thackeray and
his young wife returned to London, very poor indeed, and
there he remained, as Carlyle said, "writing for his life."

It was a struggle, doubtless, but not a bitter one, and
Thackeray was happy in his home with his wife and two
little daughters. Long afterwards one of these daughters
wrote, "Almost the first time I can remember my parents
was at home in Great Coram Street on one occasion,
when my mother took me upon her back, as she had a way
of doing, and after hesitating for a moment at the door,
carried me into a little ground floor room where some one

sat bending over a desk. This some one lifted up his head and looked round at the people leaning over his chair. He seemed pleased, smiled at us, but remonstrated. Nowadays I know by experience that authors don't get on best, as a rule, when they are interrupted in their work —not even by their own particular families—but at that time it was all wondering, as I looked over my mother's shoulder."

But these happy days did not last long. The young mother became ill; gradually she became worse, until at last the light of reason died out of her brain, and although she lived on for many years, it was a living death, for she knew no one and took no notice of anything that went on around her.

The happy home was broken up. The children went to live with their great-grandmother, who found them "inconveniently young," while Thackeray remained alone in London. But though he was heart-broken and lonely, he kept a loving memory of the happy days gone by Long after he wrote to a friend who was going to be married, "Although my own marriage was a wreck, as you know, I would do it over again, for behold, Love is the crown and completion of all earthly good. The man who is afraid of his future never deserved one."

Thackeray was already making a way with his pen, and now he found a new opening. Most of you know *Punch*. He and his dog Toby are old friends. And Mr. Punch with his humped back and big nose "comes out" every week to make us laugh. He makes us laugh, too, with kindly laughter, for, as Thackeray himself said, "there never were before published in this world so many volumes that contained so much cause for laughing, so little for blushing. It is so easy to be witty and wicked, so hard to be witty and wise!" But once upon a time there was no *Punch*, strange though it may seem. It was just at this time, indeed, that *Punch* was published and Thackeray became one of the earliest contributors, and continued for ten years both to draw pictures and write papers for it. It was in *Punch* that his famous *"Snob Papers"* appeared. What is a Snob? Thackeray says, "He who meanly admires mean things."

It has been said that by reason of writing so much about snobs that Thackeray came to see snobbishness where there was none. But certain it is he laid a smart but kindly finger on many a small-minded prejudice. Several times in this book you have heard of sizars and commoners, stupid distinctions which are happily now done away with. Perhaps you would like to know how Thackeray thought of them. For although it is not a very good illustration of real snobbishness, it is interesting to read in connection with the lives of many great writers.

"If you consider, dear reader, what profound snobbishness the University System produced, you will allow that it is time to attack some of those feudal Middle-age superstitions. If you go down for five shillings to look at the 'College Youths,' you may see one sneaking down the court without a tassel to his cap: another with a gold or silver fringe to his velvet trencher; a third lad with a master's gown and hat, walking at ease over the sacred College grass-plats, which common men must not tread on.

"He may do it because he is a nobleman. Because a lad is a lord, the University gives him a degree at the end of two years which another is seven in acquiring. Because he is a lord, he has no call to go through an examination. . . .

"The lads with gold and silver lace are sons of rich gentlemen, and called Fellow Commoners; they are privileged to feed better than the pensioners, and to have wine with their victuals, which the latter can only get in their rooms.

"The unlucky boys who have no tassels to their caps,

are called sizars—*servitors* at Oxford—(a very pretty and gentlemanlike title). A distinction is made in their clothes because they are poor; for which reason they wear a badge of poverty, and are not allowed to take their meals with their fellow students."

But the same pen that wrote sharply and satirically about snobs, wrote loving letters in big round hand to his dear daughters, who were living far away in Paris. For either child he used a different hand, so that each might know at once to whom the letter was addressed. Here is part of one to his "dearest Nanny." "How glad I am that it is a black *puss* and not a black *nuss* you have got! I thought you did not know how to spell nurse, and had spelt it en-you-double-ess; but I see the spelling gets better as the letters grow longer: they cannot be too long for me. Laura must be a very good-natured girl. I hope my dear Nanny is so too, not merely to her school mistress and friends, but to everybody—to her servants and her nurses. I would sooner have you gentle and humble-minded than ever so clever. Who was born on Christmas Day? Somebody Who was so great, that all the world worships Him; and so good that all the world loves Him; and so gentle and humble that He never spoke an unkind word. And there is a little sermon and a great deal of love and affection from papa." [1]

The Book of Snobs brought Thackeray into notice, and now that he was becoming well known and making more money, he once more made a home for his daughters, and they came to London to live with their father. Everything was new and strange to the little girls. There was a feeling of London they thought, in the new house, and "London smelt of tobacco." Thus once more, says his daughter, "after his first happy married years, my father had a home and a family—if a house, two young children,

[1] Mrs. Ritchie's introduction to *Contributions to Punch*

three servants, and a little black cat can be called a family."

Thackeray was a very big man, being six feet three or four. He must have seemed a very big papa to the little girls of six and eight, who were, no doubt, very glad to be again beside their great big kind father, and he, on his side, was very glad to have his little girls to love, and he took them about a great deal to the theater and concerts. They helped him in many little ways and thought it joy to leave lessons in the schoolroom upstairs and come downstairs to help father, and be posed as models for his drawings.

It was now that Thackeray wrote his first great novel, his greatest some people think, *Vanity Fair*. I cannot tell you about it now, but when you are a very little older you will like to read of clever and disagreeable Becky Sharp, of dear Dobbin, and foolish Amelia, and all the rest of the interesting people Thackeray creates for us. Thackeray has been called a cynic, that is one who does not believe in the goodness of human nature, and who sneers at and finds fault with everything. And reading *Vanity Fair* when we are very young we are apt to think that is so, but later we come to see the heart of goodness there is in him, and when we have read his books we say to ourselves, "What a truly good man Thackeray must have been." "He could not have painted *Vanity Fair* as he has," says another writer,[1] "unless Eden had been shining brightly in his inner eyes."

Though Thackeray is no cynic he is a satirist as much as Pope or Dryden, but the most kindly satirist who ever wrote. His thrusts are keen and yet there is always a humorous laugh behind, and never a spark of malice or uncharitableness. Thackeray bore no hatred in his heart towards any man. He could not bear to give pain, and

[1] George Brimley

as he grew older his satire became more gentle even than at first, and he regretted some of his earlier and too sharp sayings.

After *Vanity Fair* other novels followed, the best of all being *Esmond*. *Esmond* is perhaps the finest historical novel in our language. It is a story of the time of Queen Anne, and when we read it we feel as if the days of Addison and Steele lived again. But with Thackeray the historical novel is very diff'erent from the historical novel of Scott. With Thackeray his imaginary people hold the chief place, the real people only form a background, while in many of Scott's novels the real people claim our attention most.

Before *Esmond* was written Thackeray had added the profession of lecturer to that of author. He was a very loving father and was always anxious not only that his daughters should be happy when they were young, but that when he died he should leave them well off. Again and again in his letters we find him turning to this thought: "If I can't leave them a fortune, why, we must try to leave them the memory of having had a good time," he says. But he wanted to leave them a fortune, and so he took to lecturing. His lectures were a great success, and he delivered them in many places in England, Scotland, Ireland and America.

It was while he was lecturing in Scotland that he heard a little boy read one of his ballads. It was a satirical ballad, and somehow Thackeray did not like to hear it from the little boy's lips. Turning away he said to himself, "Pray God I may be able some day to write something good for children. That will be better than glory or Parliament."

But already he had written something good for children in the fairy tale of *The Rose and the Ring*. One year he spent the winter with his children in Rome, and wrote the fairy tale for them and their friends, and drew the pictures too.

I have no room in this book to tell you the story, but there is a great deal of fun in it, and I hope you will read it for yourselves. Here, for instance, is what happened to a porter for being rude to the fairy Blackstick. After saying many other rude things, he asked if she thought he was going to stay at the door all day.

" 'You *are* going to stay at that door all day and all night, and for many a long year,' the fairy said, very majestically; and Gruffenuff, coming out of the door, straddling before it with his great calves, burst out laughing, and cried 'Ha, ha, ha! this *is* a good un! Ha—ah —what's this? Let me down—O-o-H'm!' and then he was dumb.

"For as the fairy waved her wand over him, he felt himself rising off the ground, and fluttering up against the door, and then, as if a screw ran into his stomach, he felt a dreadful pain there, and was pinned to the door; and then his arms flew up over his head; and his legs, after writhing about wildly, twisted under his body; and he felt cold, cold, growing over him, as if he was turning into metal; and he said, 'O-o-H'm!' and could say no more, because he was dumb.

"He *was* turned into metal! He was from being *brazen, brass!* He was neither more nor less than a knocker! And there he was, nailed to the door in the blazing summer day, till he burned almost red-hot; and there he was, nailed to the door all the bitter winter nights, till his brass nose was dropping with icicles. And the postman came and rapped at him, and the vulgarist boy with a letter came and hit him up against the door. And the King and Queen coming home from a walk that evening, the King said, 'Hallo, my dear! you have had a new knocker put on the door. Why, it's rather like our porter in the face. What has become of that old vagabond?' And the housemaid came and scrubbed his nose with sand-paper; and once when the Princess Angelica's little sister was born, he was tied up in an old kid glove; and another night, some *larking* young men tried to wrench him off, and put him to the most excruciating agony with a turnscrew. And then the Queen had a fancy to have the colour of the door altered, and the painters dabbed him over the mouth and eyes, and nearly choked him, as they painted him pea-green. I warrant he had leisure to repent of having been rude to the Fairy Blackstick."

As the years went on, Thackeray became ever more and more famous, his company more and more sought after. "The kind, tall, amusing, grey-haired man"[1] was welcome in many a drawing-room. Yet with all his success he never forgot his little girls. They were his fast friends and companions, and very often they wrote while he dictated his story to them. He worked with a lazy kind of diligence. He could not, like Scott, sit down and write a certain number of pages every morning. He was by nature indolent, yet he got through a great deal of work.

Death found him still working steadily. He had not been feeling well, and one evening he went to bed early. Next morning, Christmas Eve of 1863, he was found dead in bed.

Deep and widespread was the grief at Thackeray's death. The news "saddened England's Christmas." His friends mourned not only the loss of a great writer but "the cheerful companionship, the large heart, and open hand, the simple courteousness, and the endearing frankness of a brave, true, honest gentleman."[2]

Although he was buried in a private cemetery, a bust

[1] Lord Houghton.   [2] In *Punch*.

was almost at once placed in Westminster by his sorrowing friends.

The following verses were written by the editor of *Punch* [1] in his memory:—

"He was a cynic! By his life all wrought
Of generous acts, mild words, and gentle ways;
His heart wide open to all kindly thought,
His hand so great to give, his tongue to praise.

"He was a cynic! You might read it writ
In that broad brow, crowned with its silver hair,
In those blue eyes, with childlike candour lit,
In the sweet smile his lips were wont to wear.

"He was a cynic! By the love that clung
About him from his children, friends, and kin,
By the sharp pain, light pen and gossip tongue
Wrought in him chafing the soft heart within.

   .   .   .   .   .

"He was a cynic? Yes—if 'tis the cynic's part
To track the serpent's trail with saddened eye,
To mark how good and ill divide the heart,
How lives in chequered shade and sunshine he:

"How e'en the best unto the worst is knit
By brotherhood of weakness, sin and care;
How even in the worst, sparks may be lit
To show all is not utter darkness there"

BOOK TO READ

The Rose and the Ring
NOTE—*The Rose and the Ring* can be found in any complete edition of Thackeray's works

[1] Shirley Brooks

CHAPTER LXXXIV

DICKENS—SMILES AND TEARS

CHARLES DICKENS was a novelist who lived and wrote at the same time as Thackeray. He was indeed only six months younger, but he began to make a name much earlier and was known to fame while Thackeray was still a struggling artist. When they both became famous these two great writers were to some extent rivals, and those who read their books were divided into two camps. For though both are men of genius, they are men of widely differing genius.

John Dickens, the father, was a clerk with a small salary in the Navy Pay Office, and his son Charles was born in 1812 at Portsea. When Charles was about four his father was moved to Chatham, and here the little boy Charles lived until he was nine. He was a very puny little boy, and not able to join in the games of the other boys of his own age. So he spent most of his time in a small room where there were some books and where no one else besides himself cared to go. He not only read the books, but lived them, and for weeks together he would make believe to himself that he was his favorite character in whatever book he might be reading. All his life he loved acting a part and being somebody else, and at one time thought of becoming an actor.

Then when Charles was seven he went to a school taught by a young Baptist minister. It was not an un‑

happy life for the "Very queer small boy" as he calls himself. There were fields in which he could play his pretending games, and there was a beautiful house called Gad's Hill near, at which he could go to look and dream that if he were very good and very clever he might some day be a fine gentleman and own that house.

When the very queer small boy was nine he and all his family moved to London. Here they lived in a mean little house in a mean little street. There were now six children, and the father had grown very poor, so instead of being sent to school Charles used to black the boots and make himself useful about the house. But he still had his books to read, and could still make believe to himself. Things grew worse and worse however, and John Dickens, who was kind and careless, got into debt deeper and deeper. Everything in the house that could be done without was sold, and one by one the precious books went. At length one day men came and took the father away to prison because he could not pay his debts.

Then began for Charles the most miserable time of his life. The poor, sickly little chap was set to work in a blacking factory. His work was to cover the pots of paste-blacking, tie them down neatly and paste on labels. Along with two or three other boys he worked all day long for six or seven shillings a week. Oh, how the little boy hated it! He felt degraded and ashamed. He felt that he was forgotten and neglected by every one, and that never never more would he be able to read books and play pretending games, or do anything that he loved. All week he worked hard, ill clad and only half fed, and Sunday he spent with his father at the prison. It was a miserable, sordid, and pitiful beginning to life.

How long this unhappy time lasted we do not know. Dickens himself could not remember. He seldom spoke of this time, but he never forgot the misery of it. Long afterwards in one of his books called *David Copperfield,* when he tells of the unhappy childhood of his hero, it is of his own he speaks.

But presently John Dickens got out of prison, Charles left the blacking factory, and once more went to school. And although in after years he could never bear to think of these miserable days, at the time his spirits were not crushed, and at school he was known as a bright and jolly boy. He was always ready for any mischief, and took delight in getting up theatricals.

At fifteen Dickens left school and went into a lawyer's office, but he knew that he had learned very little at school, and now set himself to learn more. He went to the British Museum Reading-room, and studied there, and he also with a great deal of labor taught himself shorthand.

He worked hard, determined to get on, and at nineteen he found himself in the Gallery of the House of Commons as reporter for a daily paper. Since the days when Samuel Johnson reported speeches without having heard them things had changed. People were no longer content with such make-believe reporting, and Dickens proved himself one of the smartest reporters there had ever been. He not only reported the speeches, but told of everything that took place in the House. He had such a keen eye for seeing, and such a vivid way of describing what he saw, that he was able to make people realize the scenes inside the House as none had done before.

Besides reporting in the Houses of Parliament Dickens dashed about the country in post-chaises gathering news for his paper, writing by flickering candle-light while his carriage rushed along, at what seemed then the tremendous speed of fifteen miles an hour. For those were not the days of railways and motors, and traveling was much slower than it is now.

But even while Dickens was leading this hurried, busy

life he found time to write other things besides newspaper reports, and little tales and sketches began to appear signed by Boz. Boz was a pet name for Dickens's youngest brother. His real name was Augustus, but he had been nicknamed Moses after Moses in the *Vicar of Wakefield.* Pronounced through the nose it became Boses and then Boz. That is the history of the name under which Dickens at first wrote and won his earliest fame.

The sketches by Boz were well received, but real fame came to Dickens with the *Pickwick Papers* which he now began to write. This story came out in monthly parts. The first few numbers were not very successful, only about four hundred copies being sold, but by the fifteenth number London was ringing with the fame of it, and forty thousand copies were quickly sold. "Judges on the bench and boys in the street, gravity and folly, the young and the old"[1] all alike read it and laughed over it. Dickens above everything is a humorist, and one of the chief features in his humor is caricature, that is exaggerating and distorting one feature or habit or characteristic of a man out of all likeness to nature. This often makes very good fun, but it takes away from the truth and realness of his characters. And yet no story-teller perhaps is remembered so little for his stories and so much for his characters. In *Pickwick* there is hardly any story, the papers ramble on in unconnected incidents. No one could tell the story of *Pickwick* for there is really none to tell; it is a series of scenes which hang together anyhow. "*Pickwick* cannot be classed as a novel," it has been said; "it is merely a great book."[2]

So in spite of the fact that they are all caricatures it is the persons of the Pickwick club that we remember and not their doings. Like Jonson long before him, Dickens sees every man in his humor. By his genius he enables

[1] Forster.   Gissing

us to see these humors too, though at times one quality in a man is shown so strongly that we fail to see any other in him, and so a caricature is produced.

Dickens himself was full of fun and jollity. His was a florid personality. He loved light and color, and sunshine. He almost covered his walls with looking-glasses and crowded his garden with blazing geraniums. He loved movement and life, overflowed with it himself and poured it into his creations, making them live in spite of rather than because of their absurdities.

Winkle, one of the Pickwickians, is a mild and foolish boaster, who pretends that he can do things he cannot. He pretends to be able to shoot and succeeds only in hitting one of his friends. He pretends to skate, and this is how he succeeds:—

" 'Now,' said Wardle, after a substantial lunch had been done ample justice to, 'what say you to an hour on the ice? We shall have plenty of time.'

" 'Capital!' said Mr. Benjamin Allen.

" 'Prime!' ejaculated Mr. Bob Sawyer.

" 'You skate of course, Winkle?' said Wardle.

" 'Ye-yes; oh, yes,' replied Mr. Winkle. 'I—I am *rather* out of practice.'

" 'Oh, *do* skate, Mr. Winkle,' said Arabella. 'I like to see it so much.'

" 'Oh, it is *so* graceful,' said another young lady. A third young lady said it was elegant, and a fourth expressed her opinion that it was 'swanlike.'

" 'I should be very happy, I'm sure,' said Mr. Winkle, reddening, 'but I have no skates.'

"This objection was at once overruled. Trundle had a couple of pair, and the fat boy announced that there were half-a-dozen more, downstairs: whereat Mr. Winkle expressed exquisite delight, and looked exquisitely uncomfortable.

"Old Wardle led the way to a pretty large sheet of ice, and the fat boy and Mr. Weller, having shovelled and swept away the snow which had fallen on it during the night, Mr. Bob Sawyer adjusted his skates with a dexterity which to Mr. Winkle was perfectly marvellous, and described circles with his left leg, and cut figures of eight, and inscribed upon the ice, without once stopping for breath, a great many other pleasant and astonishing devices, to the excessive satisfaction of Mr. Pickwick, Mr. Tupman, and the ladies: which reached a pitch of positive enthusiasm, when old Wardle and Benjamin Allen, assisted by the aforesaid Bob Sawyer, performed some mystic evolutions, which they called a reel.

"All this time Mr. Winkle, with his face and hands blue with the cold, had been forcing a gimlet into the soles of his boots, and putting his skates on, with the points behind, and getting the straps into a very complicated and entangled state, with the assistance of Mr. Snodgrass, who knew rather less about skates than a Hindoo. At length, however, with the assistance of Mr. Weller, the unfortunate skates were firmly screwed and buckled on, and Mr. Winkle was raised to his feet.

" 'Now, then, Sir,' said Sam, in an encouraging tone; 'off with you, and show 'em how to do it.'

" 'Stop, Sam, stop!' said Mr. Winkle, trembling violently and clutching hold of Sam's arms with the grasp of a drowning man. 'How slippery it is, Sam!'

" 'Not a uncommon thing upon ice, Sir,' replied Mr. Weller. 'Hold up, Sir!'

"This last observation of Mr. Weller's bore reference to a demonstration Mr. Winkle made at the instant, of a frantic desire to throw his feet in the air, and dash the back of his head on the ice.

" 'These—these—are very awkward skates; ain't they, Sam?' inquired Mr. Winkle, staggering.

" 'I'm afeerd there's an orkard gen'l'm'n in 'em, Sir,' replied Sam.

" 'Now, Winkle,' cried Mr. Pickwick, quite unconscious that there was anything the matter. 'Come, the ladies are all anxiety.'

" 'Yes, yes,' replied Mr. Winkle, with a ghastly smile. 'I'm coming.'

" 'Just a-goin' to begin,' said Sam, endeavouring to disengage himself. 'Now, Sir, start off!'

" 'Stop an instant, Sam,' gasped Mr. Winkle, clinging most affectionately to Mr. Weller. 'I find I've got a couple of coats at home, that I don't want, Sam. You may have them, Sam.'

" 'Thank'ee, Sir,' replied Mr. Weller.

" 'Never mind touching your hat, Sam,' said Mr. Winkle, hastily. 'You needn't take your hand away to do that. I meant to have given you five shillings this morning for a Christmas-box, Sam. I'll give it you this afternoon, Sam.'

" 'You're wery good, Sir,' replied Mr. Weller.

" 'Just hold me at first, Sam; will you?' said Mr. Winkle. 'There—that's right. I shall soon get in the way of it, Sam. Not too fast, Sam; not too fast.'

"Mr. Winkle, stooping forward with his body half doubled up, was being assisted over the ice by Mr. Weller, in a very singular and un-swanlike manner, when Mr. Pickwick most innocently shouted from the opposite bank,—

" 'Sam!'

" 'Sir?' said Mr. Weller.

" 'Here, I want you.'

" 'Let go, Sir,' said Sam. 'Don't you hear the governor a-callin'? Let go, Sir.'

"With a violent effort Mr. Weller disengaged himself from the grasp of the agonised Pickwickian; and, in so doing, administered a considerable impetus to the unhappy Mr. Winkle. With an accuracy which no degree of dexterity or practice could have insured, that unfortunate gentleman bore swiftly down into the centre of the reel, at the very moment when Mr. Bob Sawyer was performing a flourish of unparalleled beauty. Mr. Winkle struck wildly against him, and with a loud crash they both fell heavily down.

"Mr. Pickwick ran to the spot. Bob Sawyer had risen to his feet, but Mr. Winkle was far too wise to do anything of the kind, in skates. He was seated on the ice, making spasmodic efforts to smile, but anguish was depicted on every lineament of his countenance.

"'Are you hurt?' inquired Mr. Benjamin Allen, with great anxiety.

"'Not much,' said Mr. Winkle, rubbing his back very hard.

"'I wish you'd let me bleed you,' said Mr. Benjamin, with great eagerness.

"'No, thank you,' replied Mr. Winkle, hurriedly.

"'What do you think, Mr. Pickwick?' enquired Bob Sawyer.

"Mr. Pickwick was excited and indignant. He beckoned to Mr. Weller, and said in a stern voice, 'Take his skates off.'

"'No; but really I had scarcely begun,' remonstrated Mr. Winkle.

"'Take his skates off,' repeated Mr. Pickwick firmly.

"The command was not to be resisted. Mr. Winkle allowed Sam to obey it, in silence.

"'Lift him up,' said Mr. Pickwick. Sam assisted him to rise.

"Mr. Pickwick retired a few paces apart from the bystanders; and beckoning his friend to approach, fixed a searching look upon him, and uttered in a low, but distinct and emphatic tone, these remarkable words,—

" 'You're a humbug, Sir.'

" 'A what!' said Mr. Winkle starting.

" 'A humbug, Sir. I will speak plainer, if you wish it. An impostor, Sir.'

"With these words Mr. Pickwick turned slowly on his heel, and rejoined his friends."

There is much life and fun and jollity and some vulgarity in *Pickwick*. There is a good deal of eating and far too much drinking. But when the fun is rather rough, we must remember that Dickens wrote of the England of seventy years ago and more, when life was rougher than it is now, and when people did not see that drinking was the sordid sin we know it to be now.

To many people *Pickwick* remains Dickens's best book. "The glory of Charles Dickens," it has been said, "will always be in his *Pickwick,* his first, his best, his inimitable triumph." [1]

Just when Dickens began to write *Pickwick* he married, and soon we find him comfortably settled in a London house, while the other great writers of his day gathered round him as his friends.

Although not born in London, Dickens was a true Londoner, and when his work was done he loved nothing better than to roam the streets. He was a great walker, and thought nothing of going twenty or thirty miles a day, for though he was small and slight he had quite recovered from his childish sickliness and was full of wiry energy. The crowded streets of London were his books. As he wandered through them his clear blue eyes took note of everything, and when he was far away, among the lovely sights of Italy or Switzerland, he was homesick for the grimy streets and hurrying crowds of London.

[1] Fred Harrison

After *Pickwick* many other stories followed; in them Dickens showed his power not only of making people laugh, but of making them cry. For the source of laughter and the source of tears are not very far apart. There is scarcely another writer whose pathetic scenes are so famous as those of Dickens.

In life there is a great deal that is sad, and one of the things which touched Dickens most deeply was the misery of children. The children of to-day are happy in knowing nothing of the miseries of childhood as it was in the days when Dickens wrote. In those days tiny children had to work ten or twelve hours a day in factories, many schools were places of terror and misery, and few people card. But Dickens saw and cared and wrote about these things. And now they are of a bygone day. So children may remember Dickens with thankful hearts. He is one of their great champions.

Dickens loved children and they loved him, for he had a most winning way with them and he understood their little joys and sorrows. "There are so many people," says his daughter writing about her father, "There are so many people good, kind, and affectionate, but who can *not* remember that they once were children themselves, and looked out upon the world with a child's eyes *only*." This Dickens did always remember, and it made him a tender and delightful father to whom his children looked up with something of adoration. "Ever since I can remember anything," says his daughter, "I remember him as the good genius of the house, or as its happy, bright and funny genius." As Thackeray had a special handwriting for each daughter, Dickens had a special voice for each child, so that without being named each knew when he or she was spoken to. He sang funny songs to them and told funny stories, did conjuring tricks and got up theatricals, shared their fun and comforted their sorrows. And this same power of understanding which made him enter into the joys and sorrows of his children, made him enter into the joys and sorrows of the big world around him. So that the people of that big world loved him as a friend, and adored him as a hero.

As the years went on Dickens wrote more and more books. He started a magazine too, first called *Household Words* and later *All the Year Round*. In this, some of his own works came out as well as the works of other writers. It added greatly to his popularity and not a little to his wealth. And as he became rich and famous, his boyish dream came true. He bought the house of Gad's Hill which had seemed so splendid and so far off in his childish eyes, and went to live there with his big family of growing boys and girls.

It was about this time, too, that Dickens found a new way of entertaining the world. He not only wrote books but he himself read them to great audiences. All his life Dickens had loved acting. Indeed he very nearly became an actor before he found out his great powers of writing. He many times took part in private theatricals, one of his favorite parts, you will like to know, being Captain Bobadil, in Jonson's *Every Man in his Humour*. And now all the actor in him delighted in the reading of his own works, so although many of his friends were very much against these readings, he went on with them. And wherever he read in England, Scotland, Ireland, and America, crowds flocked to hear him. Dickens swayed his audiences at will. He made them laugh, and cry, and whether they laughed or whether they cried they cheered and applauded him. It was a triumph and an evidence of his power in which Dickens delighted and which he could not forego, although his friends thought it was beneath his dignity as an author.

But the strain and excitement were too much. These

readings broke down Dickens's health and wore him out. He was at last forced to give them up, but it was already too late. A few months later he died suddenly one evening in June 1870 in his house at Gad's Hill. He was buried in Westminster, and although the funeral was very quiet and simple as he himself had wished, for two days after a constant stream of mourners came to place flowers upon his grave.

I have not given you a list of Dickens's books because they are to be found in nearly every household. You will soon be able to read them and learn to know the characters whose names have become household words.

Dickens was the novelist of the poor, the shabby genteel, and the lower middle class. It has been said many times that in all his novels he never drew for us a single gentleman, and that is very nearly true. But we need little regret that, for he has left us a rich array of characters we might never otherwise have known, such as perhaps no other man could have pictured for us.

BOOKS TO READ

Stories from Dickens, by J. W. M'Spadden. *The Children's Dickens.*

CHAPTER LXXXV

TENNYSON—THE POET OF FRIENDSHIP

KEATS had lain beneath the Roman violets six years, and Shelley somewhat less than five, when a little volume of poems was published in England. It was called *Poems by two Brothers*. No one took any notice of it, and yet in it was the first little twitter of one of our sweetest singing birds. For the two brothers were Alfred and Charles Tennyson, boys then of sixteen and seventeen. It is of Alfred that I mean to tell you in this last chapter. You have heard of him already in one of the chapters on the Arthur story, and also you have heard of him as a friend of Carlyle. And now I will tell you a little more about him.

Alfred Tennyson was born in 1809 in the Lincolnshire village of Somersby. His father was the rector there, and had, besides Alfred, eleven other children. And here about the Rectory garden, orchard and fields, the Tennyson children played at knights and warriors. Beyond the field flowed a brook—

> "That loves
> To purl o'er matted cress and ribbed sand,
> Or dimple in the dark of rushy coves,
> Drawing into his narrow earthen urn,
> In every elbow and turn,
> The filter'd tribute of the rough woodland." [1]

Of the garden and the fields and of the brook especially, Alfred kept a memory all through his long life. But at

[1] *Ode to Memory.*

seven he was sent to live with his grandmother and go to school at Louth, about ten miles away. "How I did hate that school!" he said, long afterwards, so we may suppose the years he spent there were not altogether happy. But when he was eleven he went home again to be taught by his father, until he went to Cambridge.

At home Alfred read a great deal, especially poetry. He wrote, too, romances like Sir Walter Scott's, full of battles, epics in the manner of Pope, plays, and blank verse. He wrote so much that his father said, "If Alfred die, one of our greatest poets will have gone." And besides writing poems, Alfred, who was one of the big children, used to tell stories to the little ones,—stories these of knights and ladies, giants and dragons and all manner of wonderful things. So the years passed, and one day the two boys, Charles and Alfred, resolved to print their poems, and took them to a bookseller in Louth. He gave them £20 for the manuscript, but more than half was paid in books out of his shop. So the grand beginning was made. But the little book caused no stir in the great world. No one knew that a poet had broken silence.

The next year Charles and Alfred went to Cambridge. Alfred soon made many friends among the clever young men of his day, chief among them being Arthur Hallam, whose father was a famous historian.

At college Tennyson won the Chancellor's prize for a poem on Timbuctoo, and the following year he published a second little volume of poems. This, though kindly received by some great writers, made hardly more stir than the little volume by "Two Brothers."

Tennyson did not take a degree at Cambridge, for, owing to his father's failing health, he was called home. He left college, perhaps with no very keen regret, for his heart was not in sympathy with the teaching. In his undergraduate days he wrote some scathing lines about it. You "teach us nothing," he said, "feeding not the heart." But he did remember with tenderness that Cambridge had been the spot where his first and warmest friendships had been formed.

Soon after Alfred left college, his father died very suddenly. Although the father was now gone the Tennysons did not need to leave their home, for the new rector did not want the house. So life in the Rectory went quietly on; friends came and went, the dearest friend of all, Arthur Hallam, came often, for he loved the poet's young sister, and one day they were to be married. It was a peaceful happy time—

> "And all we met was fair and good,
>   And all was good that Time could bring,
>   And all the secret of the Spring,
> Moved in the chambers of the blood."

Long days were spent reading poetry and talking of many things—

> "Or in the all-golden afternoon
>   A guest, or happy sister, sung,
>   Or here she brought the harp and flung
> A ballad to the brightening moon.

> "Nor less it pleased the livelier moods,
>   Beyond the bounding hill to stray,
>   And break the live long summer day
> With banquet in the distant woods."

And amid this pleasant country life the poet worked on, and presently another little book of poems appeared. Still fame did not come, and one severe and blundering review kept Tennyson, it is said, from publishing anything more for ten years.

But now there fell upon him what was perhaps the darkest sorrow of his life. Arthur Hallam, who was traveling on the Continent, died suddenly at Vienna.

When the news came to Tennyson that his friend was
gone—

> "That in Vienna's fatal walls
> God's finger touch'd him, and he slept,"

for a time all joy seemed blotted out of life, and only that
he might help to comfort his sister did he wish to live, for—

> "That remorseless iron hour
> Made cypress of her orange flower,
> Despair of Hope"

As an outcome of this grief we have one of Tennyson's
finest poems, *In Memoriam.* It is an elegy which we
place beside *Lycidas* and *Adonais.* But *In Memoriam*
strikes a yet sadder note. For in *Lycidas* and *Adonais*
Milton and Shelley mourned kindred souls rather than
dear loved friends. To Tennyson, Arthur Hallam was
"The brother of my love"—

> "Dear as the mother to the son
> More than my brothers are to me"

In Memoriam is a group of poems rather than one
long poem—

> "Short swallow-flights of song, that dip
> Their wings in tears, and skim away"

It is written in a meter which Tennyson believed he had
invented, but which Ben Jonson and others had used
before him. Two hundred years before Jonson had
written a little elegy beginning—

> "Though Beautie be the Marke of praise,
> And yours of whom I sing be such
> As not the world can praise too much,
> Yet is't your vertue now I raise"

Here again we see that our literature of to-day is no
new born thing, but rooted in the past. Jonson's poem,

however, is a mere trifle, Tennyson's one of the great things of our literature. The first notes of *In Memoriam* were written when sorrow was fresh, but it was not till seventeen years later that it was given to the world. It is perhaps the most perfect monument ever raised to friendship. For in mourning his own loss Tennyson mourned the loss of all the world. " 'I' is not always the author speaking of himself, but the voice of the human race speaking thro' him," he says.

After the prologue, the poem tells of the first bitter hopeless grief, of how friends try to comfort the mourners.

"One writes, that 'Other friends remain,'
That 'Loss is common to the race'—
And common is the common-place,
And vacant chaff well meant for grain

"That loss is common would not make
My own less bitter, rather more
Too common! Never morning wore
To evening, but some heart did break."

And yet even now he can say—

"I hold it true, whate'er befall;
I feel it, when I sorrow most;
'Tis better to have loved and lost
Than never to have loved at all."

And so the months glide by, and the first Christmas comes, "The time draws near the birth of Christ," the bells ring—

"Peace and goodwill, goodwill and peace,
Peace and goodwill, to all mankind.

"This year I slept and woke with pain,
I almost wish'd no more to wake,
And that my hold on life would break
Before I heard those bells again."

But when Christmas comes again the year has brought calm if not forgetfulness—

"Again at Christmas did we weave
    The holly round the Christmas hearth;
    The silent snow possess'd the earth,
And calmly fell our Christmas-eve:

"The yule-log sparkled keen with frost,
    No wing of wind the region swept,
    But over all things brooding slept
The quiet sense of something lost.

"As in the winters left behind,
    Again our ancient games had place,
    The mimic picture's breathing grace,
And dance and song and hoodman-blind "

The years pass on, the brothers and sisters grow up and scatter, and at last the old home has to be left. Sadly the poet takes leave of all the loved spots in house and garden. Strangers will soon come there, people who will neither care for nor love the dear familiar scene—

"We leave the well-beloved place
    Where first we gazed upon the sky,
    The roofs, that heard our earliest cry,
Will shelter one of stranger race

"We go, but ere we go from home,
    As down the garden-walks I move,
    Two spirits of a diverse love
Contend for loving masterdom.

"One whispers, 'Here thy boyhood sung
    Long since its matin song, and heard
    The low love-language of the bird
In native hazels tassel-hung.'

"The other answers, 'Yea, but here
    Thy feet have stray'd in after hours
    With thy lost friend among the bowers,
And this hath made them trebly dear.' "

The poem moves on, and once again in the new home Christmas comes round. Here everything is strange, the very bells seem like strangers' voices. But with this new life new strength has come, and sorrow has henceforth lost its sting. And with the ringing of the New Year bells a new tone comes into the poem, a tone no more of despair, but of hope.

> "Ring out, wild bells, to the wild sky,
>   The flying cloud, the frosty light:
>   The year is dying in the night;
> Ring out, wild bells, and let him die.
>
> "Ring out the old, ring in the new,
>   Ring, happy bells, across the snow:
>   The year is going, let him go;
> Ring out the false, ring in the true
>
> "Ring out the grief that saps the mind,
>   For those that here we see no more;
>   Ring out the feud of rich and poor,
> Ring in redress to all mankind
>
> .   .   .   .   .   .
>
> "Ring in the valiant man and free,
>   The larger heart, the kindlier hand;
>   Ring out the darkness of the land,
> Ring in the Christ that is to be "

After this the tone of the poem changes and the poet says—

> "I will not shut me from my kind,
>   And, lest I stiffen into stone,
>   I will not eat my heart alone,
> Nor feed with sighs a passing wind:
>
> .   .   .   .   .
>
> "Regret is dead, but love is more
>   Than in the summers that are flown,
>   For I myself with these have grown
> To something greater than before "

One more event is recorded, the wedding of the poet's youngest sister, nine years after the death of his friend.

And with this note of gladness and hope in the future the poem ends.

Time heals all things, and time healed Tennyson's grief. But there was another reason, of which we hardly catch a glimpse in the poem, for his return to peace and hope. Another love had come into his life, the love of the lady who one day was to be his wife. At first, however, it seemed a hopeless love, for in spite of his growing reputation as a poet, Tennyson was still poor, too poor to marry. And so for fourteen years he worked and waited, at times wellnigh losing hope. But at length the waiting was over and the wedding took place. Tennyson amused the guests by saying that it was the nicest wedding he had ever been at. And long afterwards with solemn thankfulness he said, speaking of his wife, "The peace of God came into my life before the altar when I wedded her."

A few months before the wedding Wordsworth had died. One night a few months after it Tennyson dreamt that the Prince Consort came and kissed him on the cheek. "Very kind but very German," he said in his dream. Next morning a letter arrived offering him the Laureateship.

One of the first poems Tennyson wrote as laureate was his *Ode on the Death of Wellington*. Few people liked it at the time, but now it has taken its place among our fine poems, and many of its lines are familiar household words.

Of Tennyson's many beautiful short poems there is no room here to tell. He wrote several plays too, but they are among the least read and the least remembered of his works. For Tennyson was a lyrical rather than a dramatic poet. His long poems besides *In Memoriam* are *The Princess, Maud,* and the *Idylls of the King. The Princess* is perhaps the first of Tennyson's long poems that you will like to read. It is full of gayety, young life, and color. It is a mock heroic tale of a princess who does not wish to marry and who founds a college for women, within the walls of which no man may enter. But the Prince to whom the Princess has been betrothed since childhood and who loves her from having seen her portrait only, enters with his friends disguised as women students. The result is confusion, war, and finally peace. The story must not be taken too seriously; it is a poem, not a treatise, but it is interesting, especially at this time. For even you who read this book must know that the question has not yet been settled as to how far a woman ought to be educated and take her share in the world's work. But forget that and read it only for its light-hearted poetry. *The Princess* is in blank verse, but throughout there are scattered beautiful songs which add to the charm. Here is one of the most musical—

"Sweet and low, sweet and low,
    Wind of the western sea,
Low, low, breathe and blow,
    Wind of the western sea!
Over the rolling waters go,
Come from the dying moon, and blow,
    Blow him again to me,
While my little one, while my pretty one, sleeps.

"Sleep and rest, sleep and rest,
    Father will come to thee soon,
Rest, rest, on mother's breast,
    Father will come to thee soon;
Father will come to his babe in the nest,
Silver sails all out of the west
    Under the silver moon
Sleep, my little one, sleep, my pretty one, sleep."

In the *Idylls of the King,* Tennyson, as you have already heard in Chapter IX., used the old story of Arthur. He used the old story, but he wove into it something new, for we are meant to see in his twelve tales of the round table an allegory. We are meant to see the struggle between what is base and what is noble in human nature. But this inner meaning is not always easy to follow, and we may cast the allegory aside, and still have left to us beautiful dream-like tales which carry us away into a strange wonderland. Like *The Faery Queen,* the *Idylls of the King* is full of pictures. Here we find a fairy city, towered and turreted, dark woods, wild wastes and swamps, slow gliding rivers all in a misty dreamland. And this dreamland is peopled by knights and ladies who move through it clad in radiant robes and glittering armor. Jewels and rich coloring gleam and glow to the eye, songs fall upon the ear. And over all rules the blameless King.

> "And Arthur and his knighthood for a space
> Were all one will, and thro' that strength the King
> Drew in the petty princedoms under him,
> Fought, and in twelve great battles overcame
> The heathen hordes, and made a realm and reign'd."

One story of the *Idylls* I have already told you. Some day you will read the others, and learn for yourselves—

> "This old imperfect tale,
> New-old, and shadowing Sense at war with Soul
> Rather than that gray King, whose name, a ghost,
> Streams like a cloud, man-shaped, from mountain peak,
> And cleaves to cairn and cromlech still; or him
> Of Geoffrey's book, or him of Malleor's."

Tennyson led a peaceful, simple life. He made his home for the most part in the Isle of Wight. Here he lived quietly, surrounded by his family, but sought after by all the great people of his day. He refused a baronetcy, but at length in 1883 accepted a peerage and became Lord Tennyson, the first baron of his name. He was the first peer to receive a title purely because of his literary work. And so with gathering honors and gathering years the poet lived and worked, a splendid old man. Then at the goodly age of eighty-four he died in the autumn of 1892.

He was buried in Westminster, not far from Chaucer, and as he was laid among the mighty dead the choir sang *Crossing the Bar,* one of his latest and most beautiful poems.

> "Sunset and evening star,
>   And one clear call for me!
> And may there be no moaning of the bar,
>   When I put out to sea,
>
> "But such a tide as moving seems asleep,
>   Too full for sound and foam,
> When that which drew from out the boundless deep
>   Turns again home
>
> "Twilight and evening bell,
>   And after that the dark!
> And may there be no sadness of farewell,
>   When I embark,
>
> "For tho' from out our bourne of Time and Place
>   The flood may bear me far,
> I hope to see my Pilot face to face
>   When I have crost the bar."

With Tennyson I end my book, because my design was not to give you a history of our literature as it is now, so much as to show you how it grew to be what it is. In the beginning of this book I took the Arthur story as a pattern or type of how a story grew, showing how it passed through many stages, in each stage gaining something of beauty and of breadth. In the same way I have tried to show how from a rough foundation of minstrel tales and monkish legends the great palace of our literature has slowly risen to be a glorious house of song. It is only an outline that I have given you. There are some great names that demand our reverence, many that call for our love, for whom no room has been found in this book. For our literature is so great a thing that no one book can compass it, no young brain comprehend it. But if I have awakened in you a desire to know more of our literature, a desire to fill in and color for yourselves this outline picture, I shall be well repaid, and have succeeded in what I aimed at doing. If I have helped you to see that Literature need be no dreary lesson I shall be more than repaid.

"They use me as a lesson-book at schools," said Tennyson, "and they will call me 'that horrible Tennyson.'" I should like to think that the time is coming when schoolgirls and schoolboys will say, "We have Tennyson for a school-book. How nice." I should like to think that they will say this not only of Tennyson, but of many other of our great writers whose very names come as rest and refreshment to those of us who have learned to love them.

BOOK TO READ

Tennyson for the Young, Alfred Ainger.

CHRONOLOGICAL LIST OF WRITERS
NOTICED IN THIS VOLUME

Writers prior to Fourteenth Century.

Caedmon fl 670, Bede 673-735, Alfred 849-901, Geoffrey of Monmouth, Wace (1170), Layamon fl. 1200, Map fl. 1200.

1301-1400—EDWARD I, EDWARD II, EDWARD III., RICHARD II

Langland, Barbour, Chaucer, Wyclif, all belonging to the second half of the century

1401-1450—HENRY IV, HENRY V, HENRY VI.

James I

1451-1500—HENRY VI, EDWARD IV. & V, RICHARD III, HENRY VII.

Malory, Caxton.

1501-1550—HENRY VII, HENRY VIII, EDWARD VI.

Skelton, Dunbar, Wyatt, Surrey, Tyndale, Coverdale, Udall

1551-1600—EDWARD VI, MARY, ELIZABETH

Sackville, Sidney, Spenser, Raleigh, Shakespeare

1601-1650—JAMES I, CHARLES I.

Raleigh, Shakespeare, Jonson, Bacon, Herbert, Cowley, Davenant, Milton, Lovelace, Montrose

1651-1700—COMMONWEALTH, CHARLES II., JAMES II., WILLIAM III.

Cowley, Davenant, Milton, Lovelace, Marvel, Herrick, Dryden, Bunyan

1701-1750—ANNE, GEORGE I., GEORGE II

Swift, Defoe, Steele, Addison, Pope, Richardson, Johnson

1751-1800—GEORGE II., GEORGE III.

Richardson, Johnson, Goldsmith, Macpherson (Ossian), Percy, Boswell, Cowper, Burns, Coleridge, Southey.

1801-1850—GEORGE III., GEORGE IV, WILLIAM IV, VICTORIA

Coleridge, Southey, Wordsworth, Scott, Byron, Shelley, Keats, Carlyle, Tennyson, Dickens, Thackeray

1851-1900—VICTORIA.

Carlyle, Tennyson, Dickens, Thackeray.

INDEX

681

CPSIA information can be obtained
at www.ICGtesting.com
Printed in the USA
*1921140717
1BV00009B/111/P